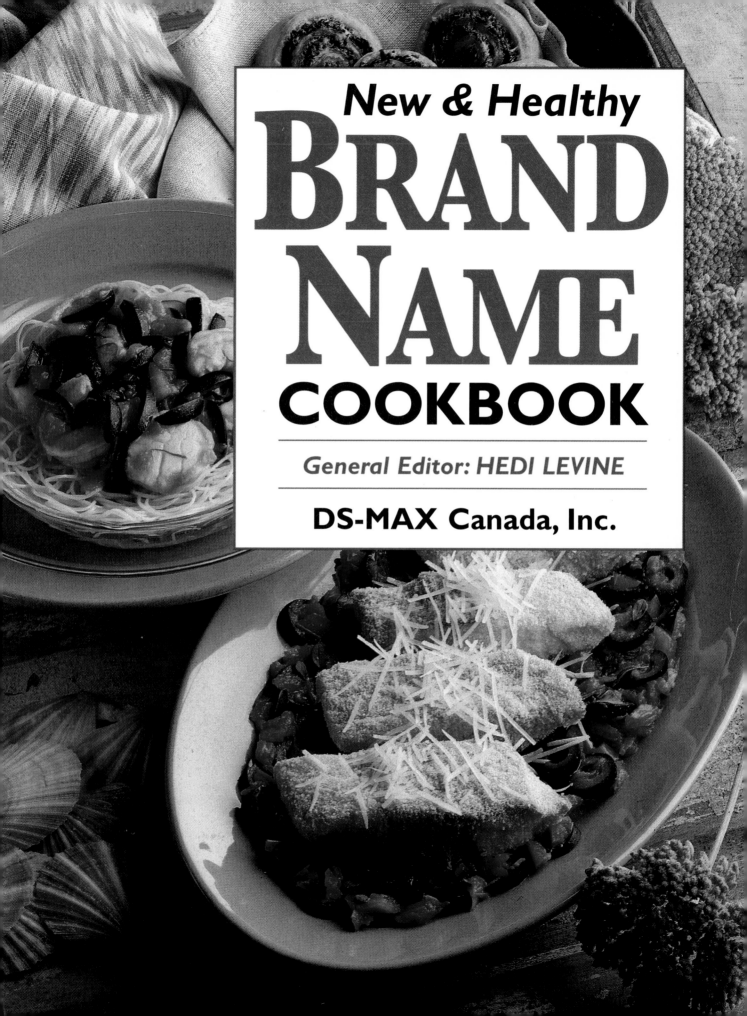

New & Healthy
BRAND NAME
COOKBOOK

General Editor: HEDI LEVINE

DS-MAX Canada, Inc.

Published by DS-MAX Canada, Inc.
250 Granton Drive
Richmond Hill, Ontario L4B 1H7, Canada

Copyright © 1995 The Triangle Group, Ltd.

Produced by The Triangle Group, Ltd.
227 Park Avenue
Hoboken, NJ 07030

Editorial Director: Hedi Levine
Creative Director: Tony Meisel
Composition: Diane Specioso
Origination: Creative Edge Graphic Design

Manufactured in the United States of America

ISBN 1-896353-41-X

The editors would like to thank the following for their cooperation and contributions of recipes and photographs: Kraft Foods, Hershey Foods, Libby's , Land O' Lakes, Lipton, McCormick/Schilling, Nestle, Nabisco Foods, Chiquita, Chef Paul Prudhomme's Magic Seasoning Blends, Dannon, The Pillsbury Company, Quaker Oats Company, Smucker's, General Mills, Tabasco, Heinz, American Egg Board, American Dry Bean Board, Bertolli Olive Oil, Bell's Seasonings, Bumble Bee Tuna, Blue Diamond, Bacardi Rum, California Kiwifruit, Contadina, Comstock, California Olive Industry, California Prune Board, California Strawberry Advisory Board, California Raisin Advisory Board, Cape Cod Cranberry Growers' Association, Driscoll's Strawberries, De Cecco Pasta, Empire Kosher Poultry, Florida Tomato Commission, Florida's Natural, Farm Fresh Catfish, Yoplait, Bisquick, Betty Crocker, Total, Goya, Ghirardelli Chocolate, Healthy Choice, Hormel, Idaho Apples, Idaho-Oregon Onions, Imperial Sugar, London Fruit Company, Louisiana Yams, Mattus, National Potato Board, National Livestock Board, National Pork Council, Norbest, National Watermelon Board, Northwest Cherry Growers, Oregon-Washington-California Pear Bureau, Hazelnut Marketing Board, Papaya Committee, Pineapple Growers of Hawaii, Pecan Marketing Board, Pompeian Olive Oil, Ronzoni, Sonoma Dried Tomatoes, Table Grape Commission, Traverse Bay Fruit, United Soybean Board, Vidalia Onion Committee, Young n' Tender Chicken. We would like to thank George G. Wieser for additional photography; and PhotoDisc™ Images © 1994 PhotoDisc, Inc. for photos on pages 10, 12, 31, 61, 63, 65, 71, 72, 85, 183, 280, 282, 346, 426, 430, 459 and 463.

CONTENTS

INTRODUCTION

Welcome to the *New & Healthy Brand Name Cookbook*. This cookbook delivers to your kitchen a collection of fresh contemporary recipes culled from the test kitchens of some of the largest and most forward-thinking food manufacturers and advisory boards. Our contributors include Quaker, Kraft, Pillsbury and Nabisco as well as The California Raisin Advisory Board (those dancing raisins can cook, too).

Although you see your favorite brand name ingredients in the supermarket when you shop, figuring out how to use them in a variety of tasty yet quick, simple yet satisfying ways is the daily dilemma of the committed home cook. And cooking at home is the single best way to control calories and fat.

If "What's for dinner?" is the persistent question, then here's the answer. Or answers. The over 1500 recipes herein range from appetizers to desserts, and include everything in-between. You will find a recipe to please everyone, including the cook. Quickly prepared versions of favorite dishes answer your needs for weeknight dinners that happen as fast as you can race down the supermarket aisle and unpack your grocery bags at home. A few whirs of the food processor and you'll be slipping your shoes off under the kitchen table. Slow cooking, savory recipes satisfy your needs on special occasions when time is what you have to spend.

In all cases, because this is the *New & Healthy Brand Name Cookbook*, the ingredients are readily available. In your pantry. In your supermarket.

Where does the new and healthy come in? Is this one of those books that will tell you what to eat, what not to eat and how much to eat? Absolutely not. We know you want to eat healthfully but you don't want to drive yourself crazy doing it.

Information can help you make healthful decisions. At the end of each recipe in the *New & Healthy Brand Name Cookbook* is a nutritional analysis with a per serving breakdown of calories, fat, protein, carbohydrates, cholesterol and sodium. (If a recipe offers a choice of ingredients, say a choice between butter or margarine, the nutritional analysis reflects the first choice listed. Optional ingredients are not included.)

Compare recipes. Anticipate what ingredients make a recipe higher or lower in calories, fat, cholesterol. Are higher calorie recipes bad and lower calorie versions good? No dietician will say so. But by knowing the caloric and other values per serving you can decide if this is a day to indulge in moderation or to simply indulge!

Opposite: Grilled Chicken with Three-Bean Salsa

As you read and cook through these recipes you will learn techniques to lower calories and fat:

- Sauté in a nonstick pan to reduce cooking fats and oils
- Remove skin from poultry
- Trim all visible fat from meat before cooking
- Substitute reduced-fat or nonfat dairy products for whole milk and whole milk products (with care when baking)
- Prepare soups and stews one day ahead so you can remove fat that has solidified on the surface
- Cook meat (on the broiler or grill) so fat drips away during cooking

The information in the nutritional analyses will also help you gain perspective about serving sizes. The National Livestock and Meat Board and The National Pork Producers Council base their nutritional analyses on a per-serving size of three ounces of cooked meat which is approximately four ounces raw, trimmed of all visible fat. By those standards, one pound of lean boneless meat should yield four servings.

Reduce serving sizes for high-calorie foods and increase serving sizes for lowfat foods.

To experienced cooks recipes are often the source of an idea but not the blueprint for its final execution. In the *New & Healthy Brand Name Cookbook*, you will often find a number of interpretations of a single dish. By comparing several ways of preparing a dish, you can come up with your own variations, depending upon your goals. Is it speed, spice or fat content you're after? The range of recipes will help you customize. Whatever your goals, we hope that the *New & Healthy Brand Name Cookbook* will guide you through the shopping, inspire you to do the cooking and leave you at peace to enjoy the eating.

BON APPETIT!

NOTE: In different countries, basic ingredients vary enormously. All-purpose flour in the United States is harder than all-purpose flour in the United Kingdom or France. Oils and butter are of different consistencies. Vegetables and fruits may be smaller or larger in different countries. The weights and measures given in the recipes should clear up some of the national discrepancies; others may demand a certain spirit of adventure and experimentation. Some of the combinations of ingredients may also be unusual in certain countries. However, all these recipes have been tested, and all produce tasty and nourishing food.

BREAKFAST

The breakfast rut is the easiest to get into. What's fast? What's available? A few minutes' thought and preparation the night before can open up new options — sweet and savory — for the first meal. Who knows? Maybe your family will actually sit down.

OLD-FASHIONED BUTTERMILK PANCAKES

1¼ cups (295 ml) all purpose flour
1 tbs (15 ml) IMPERIAL Granulated Sugar
2 tsp (10 ml) baking powder
½ tsp (3 ml) salt
½ tsp (3 ml) baking soda
1 egg, beaten
1¼ cups (295 ml) buttermilk
    or 1¼ cups (295 ml) milk plus 4 tsp (20 ml)
        lemon juice
2 tbs (30 ml) margarine, melted

Combine flour, IMPERIAL Granulated Sugar, baking powder, salt, baking soda in a mixing bowl. In another bowl, combine beaten egg, milk, margarine; add to dry ingredients. Stir until barely mixed. Heat lightly greased griddle or skillet. Using quarter cupfuls of batter for each pancake, drop onto hot, greased griddle, baking until top of pancake is covered with tiny bubbles. Turn and bake until lightly browned on underside. Yields 12 pancakes.

Approximate nutritional analysis per pancake:
Calories 82, Protein 3 g, Carbohydrates 12 g, Fat 3 g,
Cholesterol 19 mg, Sodium 229 mg

GOLDEN GRIDDLE CAKES

2½ cups (590 ml) sifted flour
1½ tsp (8 ml) baking powder
½ tsp (3 ml) salt
¼ cup (60 ml) sugar
½ cup (120 ml) raw LOUISIANA Golden Yams,
    grated
1½ cups (355 ml) milk
2 tbs (30 ml) shortening, melted
2 eggs, well beaten

Sift dry ingredients together; add grated yams and mix well. Add milk and melted shortening to beaten eggs; combine with the dry ingredients, mixing only enough to moisten the flour. Drop by spoonfuls on a hot lightly greased griddle and brown slowly on both sides. Serves 6.

Approximate nutritional analysis per serving:
Calories 329, Protein 10 g, Carbohydrates 53 g, Fat 9 g,
Cholesterol 79 mg, Sodium 327 mg

Courtesy of Louisiana Sweet Potatoes.

ALMOND BREAKFAST PANCAKES

2 cups (480 ml) milk
2 eggs
¼ cup (60 ml) butter, melted
½ tsp (3 ml) almond extract
2 cups (480 ml) flour
1 tbs (15 ml) baking powder
¼ cup (60 ml) sugar
½ tsp (3 ml) salt
1 cup (240 ml) BLUE DIAMOND
    Chopped Natural Almonds, toasted

Lightly beat together milk, eggs, butter, and almond extract; reserve. Combine flour, baking powder, sugar, and salt; add all at once to the milk mixture, stirring just enough to blend. Do not overmix. Thin with additional milk, if necessary. Fold in almonds. Pour by quarter cup amounts onto a hot, greased griddle or frying pan. Cook until underside is golden. Turn and cook second side. Serves 6.

Approximate nutritional analysis per serving:
Calories 431, Protein 12 g, Carbohydrates 49 g, Fat 22 g,
Cholesterol 32 mg, Sodium 386 mg

SHORTCUT CALICO FLAPJACKS

2 cups (480 ml) buckwheat pancake mix
2 cups (480 ml) milk
2 eggs, beaten
2 tbs (30 ml) cooking oil
¾ cup (180 ml) raisins
1 medium banana, thinly sliced

Mix together pancake mix, milk, eggs and oil to blend. Stir in banana and raisins just enough to distribute evenly. Drop by scant quarter cupfuls onto lightly oiled griddle, and cook, turning once, until done. Leftover pancakes may be frozen to be reheated later. Yields 24 pancakes.

Approximate nutritional analysis per pancake:
Calories 308, Protein 8 g, Carbohydrates 51 g, Fat 9 g,
Cholesterol 82 mg, Sodium 296 mg

Courtesy of California Raisin Advisory Board.

DUTCH BABY WITH BLUEBERRY SAUCE

SAUCE:
1 pint (480 ml) fresh or frozen blueberries
2 cups (480 ml) water
¼ cup (60 ml) sugar
2 tbs (30 ml) cornstarch
¼ tsp (1 ml) salt
2 tbs (30 ml) lemon juice
6 tbs (90 ml) butter or margarine

DUTCH BABY BATTER:
6 eggs
1½ cups (355 ml) lowfat milk
1½ cups (355 ml) flour

Rinse and drain blueberries; add water and heat until warm. Combine sugar, cornstarch and salt; add to blueberries. Cook and stir until thickened and clear. Add lemon juice. Cool if desired.

Dutch Baby Batter: Process 6 eggs in blender or food processor at HIGH 1 minute. With motor running, gradually add remaining ingredients, one at a time; blend 30 seconds longer.

Melt 3 tbs butter in 10-inch oven-safe skillet (wrap handle in foil) or shallow baking dish in preheated 425°F (220°C) oven. Pour half of batter into hot butter. Bake at 425°F (220°C) for 20 minutes or until puffy and golden. Spoon blueberry sauce into center of Dutch Baby. Sprinkle with powdered sugar. Repeat with remaining batter. Serves 6.

Approximate nutritional analysis per serving including sauce:Calories 386, Protein 12 g, Carbohydrates 45 g, Fat 18 g, Cholesterol 245 mg, Sodium 188 mg

Courtesy of North American Blueberry Council.

Dutch Baby with Blueberry Sauce

APPLE CRISP OVEN PANCAKE

¼ cup (60 ml) BISQUICK Reduced Fat Baking Mix
¼ cup (60 ml) packed brown sugar
2 tbs (30 ml) margarine softened
¾ tsp (4 ml) ground cinnamon
2 cups (480 ml) BISQUICK Reduced Fat Baking Mix
¾ cup (180 ml) skim milk
¾ cup (180 ml) chunky applesauce
¼ tsp (1 ml) vanilla
½ cup (120 ml) regular or quick-cooking oats
2 egg whites
      or **¼ cup (60 ml) cholesterol-free egg product**

Heat oven 425°F (220°C). Grease jelly roll pan, 15½x10½x1 inch. Mix baking mix, brown sugar, margarine and cinnamon; reserve. Beat remaining ingredients thoroughly with spoon. Spread batter in pan. Sprinkle with reserved brown sugar mixture. Bake 14 -16 minutes or until light golden brown. Cut into 6 pieces; serve immediately. Serves 6.

High Altitude (3500 - 6500 ft): Heat oven to 450°F (230°C).

Approximate nutritional analysis per serving:
Calories 280, Protein 7 g, Carbohydrates 46 g, Fat 7 g, Cholesterol 0 mg, Sodium 580 mg

PRUNE HOTCAKES WITH YOGURT TOPPING

1 cup (240 ml) all purpose flour
½ cup (120 ml) *each* whole wheat flour
    and unprocessed bran
2 tsp (10 ml) baking soda
2 tsp (10 ml) sugar
1 tsp (5 ml) salt
2 cups (480 ml) buttermilk
2 eggs, lightly beaten
2 tbs (30 ml) melted butter or margarine
1 cup (240 ml) prunes, chopped and pitted

PRUNE YOGURT TOPPING:

1 - 8 oz (240 g) carton unflavored lowfat yogurt
⅓ cup (80 ml) prunes, pitted
2 tsp (10 ml) honey

In bowl combine flours, bran, soda, sugar, and salt. Stir in buttermilk, eggs, butter and prunes; mix with fork just to blend. Drop by spoonfuls into hot, nonstick skillet that has been sprayed with vegetable cooking spray. Cook over medium heat until golden brown on both sides, turning once. Serve hot, with Prune Yogurt Topping. Yields 12 pancakes.

    Prune Yogurt Topping: In container of electric blender or food processor combine yogurt and prunes. Blend to coarsely chop prunes. Sweeten with honey, if desired.

    Note: Cooked, cooled pancakes can be individually wrapped and frozen for a quick breakfast when there is no time to cook. Simply wrap and pop into your toaster to thaw and reheat.

Approximate nutritional analysis per pancake including topping:
Calories 168, Protein 6 g, Carbohydrates 30 g, Fat 4 g, Cholesterol 40 mg, Sodium 423 mg

Courtesy of The California Prune Board.

CRANBERRY NEWTON PANCAKES

reduced calorie complete pancake mix
8 Fat Free Cranberry NEWTONS
    Fruit Chewy Cookies, chopped

Prepare pancake batter according to package directions for 12 pancakes; stir in chopped cookies.

    On lightly greased preheated griddle or skillet, pour quarter cup batter for each pancake. Cook over medium heat until surface is bubbly and bottom is lightly browned. Turn carefully and cook until done. Remove and keep warm. Serves 4.

Approximate nutritional analysis per serving:
Calories 285, Fat 4 g, Cholesterol 10 mg, Sodium 720 mg

FRUITED WHOLE-WHEAT PANCAKES

1 - 16 oz can (480 g) LIBBY'S LITE Fruit Cocktail
2 tsp (10 ml) cornstarch
¼ cup (60 ml) butter
½ cup (120 ml) honey
1½ tsp (8 ml) grated orange peel
2 cups (480 ml) whole wheat flour
¾ tsp (4 ml) baking powder
¾ tsp (4 ml) baking soda
½ tsp (3 ml) cinnamon
3 eggs, separated
1½ cups (355 ml) plain yogurt
2 tbs (30 ml) orange juice

Drain fruit cocktail reserving all juice. Combine reserved fruit cocktail juice with cornstarch in small saucepan. Bring to boil; cook until thickened, about one minute. Stir in half of fruit cocktail, butter, ¼ cup honey and ½ tsp orange peel; keep warm. In large bowl combine flour, baking powder, baking soda and cinnamon. Beat egg yolks. Stir in remaining ¼ cup honey, yogurt, remaining 1 tsp orange peel and orange juice; mix well. Stir in remaining fruit cocktail. Add to dry ingredients, stirring just until all of flour is moistened. Beat egg whites stiff, but not dry; fold into batter. Bake over medium to low heat on hot oiled griddle using ½ cup batter. Cook on each side until brown, turning once. Serve with warm syrup. Yields 8 pancakes.

Approximate nutritional analysis per pancake:
Calories 602, Protein 17 g, Carbohydrates 98 g, Fat 19 g, Cholesterol 201 mg, Sodium 252 mg

Opposite: Prune Hotcakes

Pancake and Waffle Accompaniments

ALMOND-LEMON PUFFED PANCAKE

3 eggs
½ cup (120 ml) milk
½ cup (120 ml) flour
1 tsp (5 ml) grated lemon peel
1 tsp (5 ml) vanilla extract
⅛ tsp (.5 ml) almond extract
pinch nutmeg
6 tbs (90 ml) butter, divided
3 tbs (45 ml) powdered sugar
½ cup (120 ml) BLUE DIAMOND
    Sliced Natural Almonds, toasted
2 tbs (30 ml) lemon juice

Preheat oven to 425°F (220°C). Lightly beat eggs and combine with next 6 ingredients. Leave batter slightly lumpy. Melt 4 tbs butter in a medium skillet with a heat-proof handle. When butter is very hot, pour in batter. Bake for 15 minutes or until puffed and golden brown. Sprinkle with powdered sugar; return to oven for 1 minute. Remove from oven. Sprinkle almonds over pancake. Melt the remaining 2 tbs butter. Drizzle butter and lemon juice over pancake. Serve immediately. Serves 4.

Approximate nutritional analysis per serving:
Calories 373, Protein 10 g, Carbohydrates 22 g, Fat 28 g, Cholesterol 210 mg, Sodium 66 mg

FRUITY YOGURT PANCAKES

2 cups (480 ml) BISQUICK Reduced Fat Baking Mix
1 tbs (15 ml) sugar
½ cup (120 ml) skim milk
1 - 6 oz container (180 g) YOPLAIT
    Original Fruit Flavor Yogurt
4 egg whites *or*
    ½ cup (120 ml) cholesterol-free egg product
2 cups (480 ml) BISQUICK Reduced Fat Baking Mix
1 tbs (15 ml) sugar
½ cup (120 ml) skim milk
1 - 6 oz container (180 g) YOPLAIT
    Original Fruit Flavor Yogurt

Beat all ingredients with wire whisk or hand beater until well blended (batter will be thick). Pour by scant quarter cupfuls onto hot griddle. (Grease griddle if necessary.) Spread batter lightly. Cook until edges are dry. Turn; cook until golden brown. Yields 12 pancakes.

Approximate nutritional analysis per pancake:
Calories 100, Protein 4 g, Carbohydrates 17 g, Fat 2 g, Cholesterol 0 mg, Sodium 260 mg

APPLE PANCAKES

1 cup (240 ml) all-purpose flour
3 tbs (45 ml) sugar
½ tsp (3 ml) cinnamon
¼ tsp (1 ml) nutmeg
⅛ tsp (.5 ml) salt
2 tsp (10 ml) baking powder
¾ cup (180 ml) soy milk
1 tbs (15 ml) soy flour
1 tsp (5 ml) vanilla extract
2 tbs (30 ml) margarine, melted and cooled
1 tart apple, peeled, cored and grated

Mix the sugar with the cinnamon, nutmeg and salt. Blend sugar mixture with flour, soy flour and baking soda. In a separate bowl, whisk together the soy milk, vanilla extract and margarine. Pour liquid ingredients over the dry mixture and blend together. Fold in the apples. Pour quarter cupfuls of batter onto hot teflon griddle or pan. Cook for about two minutes on first side or until bubbles appear on surface. Flip and cook for another minute or until heated through. Serve topped with applesauce and maple syrup. Yields 12 pancakes.

Approximate nutritional analysis per pancake:
Calories 241, Protein 5 g, Carbohydrates 40 g, Fat 7 g,
Cholesterol 0 mg, Sodium 313 mg

Courtesy of Soyfoods Association of America.

BANANA PANCAKES

1 cup (240 ml) all-purpose flour
½ cup (120 ml) soy flour
1 tsp (10 ml) salt
1¾ tsp (9 ml) baking powder
3 tbs (44 ml) soy oil
1¼ cups (295 ml) plain soy milk
2 bananas, thinly sliced

Sift together the all purpose flour, the soy flour, salt and baking powder. In a separate bowl, mix the soy oil and soy milk together. Mix the wet ingredients quickly into the dry ingredients. Stir just to blend. Add the bananas and stir into the batter with just a few strokes. Cook pancakes on a lightly oiled griddle for 2-3 minutes until bubbles begin to form on the surface. Then flip and cook on the other side for 1-2 minutes. Serve with fresh fruit or maple syrup. Serves 4.

Approximate nutritional analysis per serving:
Calories 328, Protein 10 g, Carbohydrates 42 g, Fat 14 g,
Cholesterol 0 mg, Sodium 688 mg

Courtesy of United Soybean Board.

RAISIN RICE GRIDDLE CAKES

1 cup (240 ml) milk
1 cup (240 ml) cooked rice, cooled
2 eggs, separated
1 tbs (15 ml) melted butter or margarine
½ tsp (3 ml) *each* vanilla, salt and cinnamon
1 cup, less 2 tbs (120 ml) all purpose flour
⅓ cup (80 ml) raisins

ORANGE MARMALADE SAUCE:
½ cup (120 ml) orange marmalade
¼ cup (60 ml) butter or margarine
½ cup (120 ml) orange juice

In large bowl mix milk, rice, egg yolks, butter, vanilla, salt and cinnamon to blend thoroughly. Sprinkle flour over rice mixture; mix to blend thoroughly. In another bowl beat the egg whites to form stiff peaks; fold into the rice mixture. Gently mix in the raisins. On a hot, greased griddle or skillet over medium heat, bake quarter cupfuls until browned, turning once. Grease griddle and repeat as necessary. Serve hot with Orange Marmalade Sauce. Yields 12 griddle cakes.

Orange Marmalade Sauce: In small saucepan over low heat stir orange marmalade until melted. Add butter and orange juice. Stir until butter is melted. Serve slightly warm. Yields 1 cup.

Approximate nutritional analysis per griddle cake including sauce:
Calories 636, Protein 11 g, Carbohydrates 81 g, Fat 31 g,
Cholesterol 184 mg, Sodium 343 mg

Courtesy of Raisin Advisory Board.

WAFFLES

2¼ cups (530 ml) all-purpose flour
4 tsp (20 ml) baking powder
¾ tsp (4 ml) salt
1½ tbs (20 ml) IMPERIAL Granulated Sugar
2 eggs, beaten
2¼ cups (530 ml) milk
¾ cup (180 ml) salad oil

Combine all dry ingredients. Combine remaining ingredients and add just before baking, beating only until moistened. (Batter should be thin.) Bake in preheated waffle iron. Yields 12 waffles.

Note: Buttermilk variation: Substitute buttermilk for sweet. Add ½ tsp baking soda and reduce baking powder to 2 tsp.

Approximate nutritional analysis per waffle:
Calories 246, Protein 5 g, Carbohydrates 21 g, Fat 16 g,
Cholesterol 42 mg, Sodium 263 mg

GOLDEN WAFFLES

1 cup (240 ml) sifted flour
½ tsp (3 ml) salt
2 tsp (10 ml) baking powder
2 tbs (30 ml) sugar
½ cup (120 ml) LOUISIANA Golden Yams,
    boiled and mashed
2 eggs, well beaten
1 cup (240 ml) milk
¼ cup (60 ml) shortening, melted

Sift dry ingredients together. Combine mashed yams, eggs, milk and shortening; add to first mixture, stirring only enough to moisten. Bake mixture on hot waffle iron and serve hot with butter or margarine and honey, or with hard sauce for dessert. Serves 2.

Approximate nutritional analysis per serving:
Calories 360, Protein 9 g, Carbohydrates 41 g, Fat 18 g,
Cholesterol 114 mg, Sodium 516 mg

Courtesy of Louisiana Sweet Potatoes.

IDAHO APPLE WAFFLES

2 cups (480 ml) milk
2 eggs
2 cups (480 ml) pancake mix
⅓ cup (80 ml) butter or margarine, melted
1 cup (240 ml) IDAHO Jonathan or Rome apples,
finely chopped

Place milk, eggs, pancake mix and melted butter in bowl. Beat with rotary beater until batter is fairly smooth. Stir in apples. Bake in hot waffle baker until steaming stops. Serve with butter and cinnamon sugar. Serves 6.

Approximate nutritional analysis per serving:
Calories 330, Protein 9 g, Carbohydrates 40 g, Fat 15 g,
Cholesterol 109 mg, Sodium 323 mg

VERY BERRY BUTTERMILK WAFFLES

1 cup (240 ml) all purpose flour
½ cup (120 ml) Regular, Quick or Instant
    CREAM OF WHEAT Cereal
2 tbs (30 ml) sugar
1 tsp (5 ml) baking soda
½ tsp (3 ml) baking powder
1½ cups (355 ml) buttermilk
¼ cup (60 ml) FLEISCHMANN'S Margarine, melted
2 eggs
1 tsp (5 ml) vanilla extract
¾ cup (180 ml) fresh or frozen blueberries

BERRY SYRUP:
¾ cup (180 ml) maple syrup
1 cup (240 ml) strawberries, sliced
¼ cup (60 ml) *each* raspberries and blueberries

In large bowl, mix flour, cereal, sugar, baking soda and baking powder. In small bowl, whisk buttermilk, margarine, eggs and vanilla; stir into flour mixture just until moistened. Stir in blueberries.

For waffles, pour half the batter onto hot greased 9-inch square waffle iron. (Adjust batter amount to waffle iron size.) Cook until golden brown; repeat with remaining batter. For pancakes, pour about ¼ cup batter onto preheated greased griddle. Cook until bubbly; turn and cook until done. Serve topped with Berry Syrup. Yields 8 waffles or 10 pancakes.

Berry Syrup: In medium saucepan, warm maple syrup, sliced strawberries, blueberries and raspberries.

Approximate nutritional analysis per waffle including syrup:
Calories 259, Protein 5 g , Carbohydrates 43 g, Fat 8 g,
Cholesterol 55 mg, Sodium 277 mg
Per pancake including syrup: Calories 207, Protein 4 g,
Carbohydrates 34 g, Fat 6 g, Cholesterol 44 mg, Sodium 222 mg

ORANGE FRENCH TOAST

2 large eggs, beaten
1 tsp (5 ml) cinnamon
½ cup (120 ml) FLORIDA'S NATURAL BRAND
    Orange Juice
10 English muffin halves
1 cup (240 ml) graham crackers, crushed
butter or margarine

Combine beaten eggs, FLORIDA'S NATURAL BRAND Orange Juice and cinnamon. Dip muffin halves into mixture and then into crumbs. Fry on both sides in margarine until brown. Serve with butter and warm maple syrup. Serves 5.

Approximate nutritional analysis per serving:
Calories 361, Protein 10 g, Carbohydrates 43 g, Fat 16 g,
Cholesterol 137 mg, Sodium 564 mg

Opposite: Orange French Toast

FRENCH TOAST STICKS

½ cup (120 ml) Regular, Quick or Instant
　　CREAM OF WHEAT Cereal
¼ cup (60 ml) pecans, finely chopped
3 tbs (45 ml) sugar
¾ tsp (4 ml) ground cinnamon
2 eggs
⅓ cup (80 ml) skim milk
6 (¾ inch thick) slices whole wheat bread
2 tbs (30 ml) FLEISCHMANN'S Margarine
maple syrup, for dipping

In medium bowl, combine cereal, pecans, sugar and cinnamon. In small bowl, combine eggs and milk. Cut each bread slice into 3 lengthwise sticks for a total of 18 sticks. Dip bread sticks into egg mixture and roll in cereal mixture. In large nonstick skillet or griddle, melt 1 tbs margarine. Add half the breadsticks; cook until golden on both sides, about 5-7 minutes. Repeat using remaining margarine and bread sticks. Serve warm with syrup for dipping. Serves 6.

Approximate nutritional analysis per serving:
Calories 199, Protein 6 g, Carbohydrates 23 g, Fat 10 g,
Cholesterol 71 mg, Sodium 271 mg

YOGURT ORANGE FRENCH TOAST

1 cup (240 ml) fresh orange juice
2 tbs (30 ml) grated orange peel
1 tbs (15 ml) frozen orange juice concentrate, thawed
5 eggs
2 tbs (30 ml) granulated sugar
½ cup (120 ml) DANNON Plain Nonfat
　　or Lowfat Yogurt
1 loaf brioche bread
1 tbs (15 ml) butter or margarine
confectioner's sugar
orange slices

In large bowl combine orange juice, orange peel, orange juice concentrate, eggs and granulated sugar. Beat until well blended. Stir in yogurt. Cut bread into 1- to 1½-inch-thick slices (about 16 slices). Dip bread slices into egg mixture, turning to coat. Place single layer in a shallow pan. Pour any remaining egg mixture over slices. Cover; chill up to 2 hours.

　　Heat griddle or large skillet over medium-high heat. Melt butter in pan. Lightly brown French toast on both sides. Keep French toast warm in oven until ready to serve. Dust with confectioner's sugar and garnish with orange slices before serving. Serves 8.

Approximate nutritional analysis per serving:
Calories 500, Protein 10 g, Carbohydrates 37 g, Fat 6 g,
Cholesterol 137 mg, Sodium 341 mg

APPLE RAISIN QUICHE

pastry for a 9-inch one-crust pie
3¾ cup (890 ml) Granny Smith apples, peeled,
　　cored and thinly sliced (about 3 medium)
½ cup (120 ml) raisins
¼ cup (60 ml) packed light brown sugar
2 tsp (10 ml) cinnamon
3 cups (12 oz) (360 g) Monterey Jack cheese, shredded
3 eggs
1 cup (240 ml) whipping cream

Preheat oven to 400°F (205°C). Line 9-inch pie plate with pastry. Crimp edge and prick bottom and sides with fork at ½ inch intervals. To prevent shrinkage, set 8-inch round cake pan into pie shell (or line snugly with aluminum foil); bake 6 minutes. Remove cake pan or foil and continue to bake shell until lightly browned, about 10 minutes. Remove from oven. Layer half the apples, raisins, sugar and cinnamon in pie shell; repeat layers. Cover completely with cheese. Beat eggs with cream. Make a small hole in cheese; pour egg mixture into hole. Cover hole with cheese. Bake about 1 hour until top is brown and apples are tender when tested with pick. Cool 10-15 minutes before cutting into wedges. Serves 6.

Approximate nutritional analysis per serving:
Calories 568, Protein 20 g, Carbohydrates 44 g, Fat 36 g,
Cholesterol 184 mg, Sodium 591 mg

Courtesy of The California Raisin Advisory Board.

EGGS DANNON

4 eggs
4 thin slices Canadian bacon
1 cup (240 ml) DANNON Plain Nonfat
　　or Lowfat Yogurt
½ tsp (3 ml) dry mustard
dash ground red pepper
2 English muffins, split and toasted

Spray large skillet with vegetable cooking spray. Fill half with water. Bring to a boil; reduce heat until water simmers. Break egg into a small dish and slide into the water. Repeat with remaining eggs. Simmer 3-5 minutes or until yolks are firm.

　　In a large skillet over medium-high heat cook bacon 3-4 minutes or until heated through, turning once; set aside. In a small saucepan whisk together yogurt, mustard and red pepper. Cook and stir over low heat just until warm. *Do not boil.* Top each English muffin half with bacon slice, egg and ¼ cup sauce. Serve immediately. Serves 4.

Approximate nutritional analysis per serving:
Calories 224, Protein 17 g, Carbohydrates 18 g, Fat 8 g,
Cholesterol 229 mg, Sodium 655 mg

CRAB NEWBERG MUFFINS

½ cup (120 ml) halved CALIFORNIA
  ripe olives
½ cup (120 ml) crab meat , rinsed,
  drained and picked
2 tbs (30 ml) dry white wine
1 tbs (15 ml) dry sherry
1 tbs (15 ml) lemon juice
½ tsp (3 ml) garlic salt
½ tsp (3 ml) dried mustard
3 tbs (45 ml) margarine, melted
3 tbs (45 ml) flour
1½ cups (355 ml) half and half
3 egg yolks from large eggs
6 English muffins, split
1 tsp (5 ml) paprika

Combine first seven ingredients. Combine margarine and flour in a 1 ½ quart bowl and cook on HIGH for 1 minute. Whip in half and half. Cook on HIGH for 2 minutes. Stir well. Cook on HIGH for 2-4 more minutes, until thick and smooth. Beat egg yolks in small bowl. Stir in small amount of cream sauce. Pour egg mixture back into cream sauce. Mix well. Cook on HIGH for 1 ½ minutes, stirring every 30 seconds. Add reserved olive-crab mixture. Cook on HIGH for 1-2 minutes, or until well heated. Toast split English muffins. Pour crab mixture over each half. Sprinkle with paprika. Serves 6.

Approximate nutritional analysis per serving:
Calories 336, Protein 11 g, Carbohydrates 32 g,
Fat 17 g, Cholesterol 138 mg, Sodium 688 mg

Canadian-Style Bacon Breakfast Sandwich

CANADIAN-STYLE BACON BREAKFAST SANDWICH

8 slices Canadian-style bacon
4 slices cinnamon raisin bread
3 tbs (45 ml) soft cream cheese
2 tsp (10 ml) light brown sugar, packed
16 thin apple slices*
2 tbs (30 ml) apple jelly
assorted fresh fruit and berries

Toast bread until crisp; cool. Spread each toast slice with equal amount of cream cheese; sprinkle with equal amount brown sugar. Top each toast slice with 4 apple slices and 2 slices Canadian-style bacon. Place open-faced sandwiches on 12-inch microwave-safe plate. Microwave, uncovered, at HIGH 3-4 minutes or until Canadian-style bacon is hot, rotating plate ¼ turn after 1 ½ minutes. Garnish with fresh fruit and berries. Serve immediately. Serves 4.

  *Thin banana slices may be substituted for apple slices. Follow procedure as directed above, omitting apple slices. Microwave at HIGH 2-3 minutes. Garnish open-faced sandwiches with banana slices after heating.

  Note: Recipe was tested in 650-watt microwave oven. If your oven has a different wattage adjust times accordingly.

Approximate nutritional analysis per serving:
Calories 213, Protein 10 g, Carbohydrates 28 g, Fat 7 g,
Cholesterol 30 mg, Sodium 632 mg

SWISS MUESLI

1½ cup (355 ml) rolled oats
1½ cup (355 ml) water
2 cups (480 ml) apples, shredded and unpeeled
1½ cups (9 oz) (270 g) prunes, pitted, whole
     or halved
2 tbs (30 ml) honey
2 tbs (30 ml) lemon juice
½ tsp (3 ml) cinnamon
fresh fruits (sliced banana, apple, pineapple,
orange segments)
chopped almonds or pecans

Combine first seven ingredients. Cover and refrigerate over-night. In the morning, spoon some of the muesli into a cereal bowl. Top with your choice of fresh fruit and nuts. Serve with a dollop of plain lowfat yogurt, or milk, if desired. Muesli can be stored in covered container in refrigerator for several days. Serves 6.

Approximate nutritional analysis per serving:
Calories 179, Protein 4 g, Carbohydrates 40 g, Fat 2 g,
Cholesterol 0 mg, Sodium 3 mg

SUNNYSIDE-UP CURRY

⅓ cup (80 ml) butter or margarine
2 tsp (10 ml) curry powder
½ tsp (3 ml) garlic salt
¼ cup (60 ml) onion, finely chopped
⅔ cup (160 ml) flour
2 cups (473 ml) chicken broth
1½ cups (355 ml) milk
1 cup (240 ml) raisins
1 tart apple, peeled and diced
1 tbs (15 ml) lemon juice
10 hard-cooked eggs, peeled
4 slices ham, halved
4 English muffins
4 tbs (60 ml) butter

In large saucepan, heat butter, curry powder and garlic salt until bubbly. Add onion; cook until wilted. Blend in flour and cook, stirring constantly, one minute. Gradually stir in broth and milk; cook and stir until mixture thickens. Stir in raisins, apple and lemon juice. Pour into serving dish. Cut a slice from the wide end of each of 8 eggs; place upright in sauce. Cut an "X" on the narrow ends (pointing up) of the eggs. Chop remaining 2 eggs and sprinkle around outer edge. To serve, place half slice of ham on toasted buttered English muffin half. Spoon egg and sauce over all. Serves 8.

Approximate nutritional analysis per serving:
Calories 448, Protein 17 g, Carbohydrates 42 g, Fat 24 g,
Cholesterol 295 mg, Sodium 956 mg

DRIED FRUIT GRANOLA

1½ cups (355 ml) old-fashioned oats, cooked
¼ cup (60 ml) wheat germ
¼ cup (60 ml) sunflower seeds
¼ cup (60 ml) walnuts, chopped
¼ cup (60 ml) flaked coconut
¼ tsp (1 ml) ground cinnamon
¼ cup (60 ml) honey
2 tbs (30 ml) vegetable oil
¼ cup (60 ml) dried cherries
¼ cup (60 ml) dried blueberries
¼ cup (60 ml) dried cranberries

In medium bowl, combine oats, wheat germ, sunflower seeds, walnuts, coconut and cinnamon. Stir in honey and oil to coat. Spread out mixture into a lightly greased 9-inch square baking pan. Bake at 300°F (150°C) for 20 minutes, stirring after 10 minutes. Remove from oven and stir in dried fruit. Cool. Yields 3 ¼ cup (770 ml). Serves 13.

Nutritional analysis per serving:
Calories 122, Protein 3 g, Carbohydrates 15 g, Fat 6 g,
Cholesterol 0 mg, Sodium 5 mg

Courtesy of Traverse Bay Fruit Company.

DRIED STRAWBERRY-APPLE SPREAD

1 - 8 oz package (240 g) cream cheese, softened
⅓ cup (80 ml) dried strawberries
⅓ cup (80 ml) apple, peeled and chopped
1 tbs (15 ml) powdered sugar
1 tbs (15 ml) milk
¼ tsp (1 ml) ground cinnamon

Combine all ingredients in bowl or food processor. Process until mixed and Dried Strawberries are chopped, scraping down sides as necessary. Chill overnight before serving. Yields 1 ½ cups (355 ml) (24 tbs).
      Serve on bagels, toast, quick breads.

Approximate nutritional analysis per tbs:
Calories 57, Protein 1 g, Carbohydrates 1 g, Fat 5 g,
Cholesterol 7 mg, Sodium 45 mg

Courtesy of Traverse Bay Fruit Company.

Opposite: Swiss Muesli

BROWN SUGAR SYRUP

1 pound (2½ cups) (480 g) IMPERIAL Brown Sugar
dash salt
1 cup (240 ml) water

Add IMPERIAL Brown Sugar and dash salt to water. Slowly bring ingredients to boil. Reduce heat, simmer 10 minutes. Thickens upon cooling. Yields 24 - 1 oz servings.

Note: For pancake or waffle syrup, add imitation maple flavoring to taste.

Approximate nutritional analysis per serving:
Calories 70, Protein 0 g, Carbohydrates 18 g, Fat 0 g,
Cholesterol 0 mg, Sodium 6 mg

FRESH VEGETABLE AND EGG BURRITOS

1 cup (240 ml) red, green or yellow bell pepper strips
1 cup (240 ml) fresh mushrooms, sliced
½ cup (120 ml) yellow squash, sliced
½ cup (120 ml) zucchini, sliced
½ cup (120 ml) red onion, sliced
1 tsp (5 ml) fresh garlic, minced
2 tbs (30 ml) olive oil
6 eggs
1 - 10 oz can (300 g) CHI-CHI'S Diced Tomatoes
**　　and Green Chilies, drained**
¼ tsp (1 ml) pepper
6 large flour tortillas, warmed
1½ cups (355 ml) hot pepper Monterey Jack
cheese, shredded
guacamole
sour cream

Heat oven to 350°F (180°C). In 10-inch non-stick skillet, cook and stir pepper strips, mushrooms, yellow squash, zucchini, red onion and garlic in oil until crisply tender. Remove from skillet; set aside. In skillet, combine eggs, tomatoes and green chilies and pepper. Cook over medium heat, stirring occasionally, until eggs are firm but still moist. Stir in cooked vegetables. In center of each tortilla, spoon about ½ cup vegetable-egg mixture; roll up. Place filled tortillas seam-side down in 13x9-inch baking dish. sprinkle with shredded cheese. Bake 6-8 minutes or until cheese is melted. Serve immediately with guacamole and sour cream. Serves 4.

Approximate nutritional analysis per serving:
Calories 420, Protein 19 g, Carbohydrates 39 g, Fat 22 g,
Cholesterol 240 mg, Sodium 690 mg

SCRAMBLED EGG BURRITOS

1 cup (240 ml) broccoli pieces
1 cup (240 ml) tomato, chopped
2 tbs (30 ml) minced onion
2 tsp (10 ml) FLEISCHMANN'S Margarine
½ tsp (3 ml) dried oregano leaves
1 - 8 oz (240 ml) carton EGG BEATERS
**　　Real Egg Product**
4 medium flour tortillas, warmed
⅓ cup (80 ml) reduced fat cheddar cheese, shredded

In medium skillet, over medium heat, cook broccoli and ½ cup tomato in margarine until tender. Stir in oregano and EGG BEATERS; cook, stirring occasionally until mixture is set.

Divide egg mixture evenly among tortillas. Top with cheese. Fold up tortillas over filling like an envelope. Serve immediately with remaining tomato. Serves 4.

Approximate nutritional analysis per serving:
Calories 191, Protein 11 g, Carbohydrates 25 g, Fat 5 g,
Cholesterol 2 mg, Sodium 272 mg

BREAKFAST BURRITO WITH TURKEY SAUSAGE

¼ lb (120 g) turkey sausage
½ cup (120 ml) onion, chopped
½ cup (120 ml) green pepper, chopped
⅛ tsp (.5 ml) chili pepper, optional
1 - 8 oz (240 ml) carton HEALTHY CHOICE
**　　Cholesterol Free Egg Product**
4 large flour tortillas
½ cup (120 ml) salsa, hot, medium or mild

In medium skillet, cook sausage, onion and green pepper until sausage is done; drain. Mix chili powder with egg product, add to sausage mixture. Cook over medium heat, stirring occasionally, until egg product is set. Warm tortillas according to package directions. Assemble burritos by placing ½ cup egg product mixture on each tortilla, top with salsa. Roll up tortillas, place seam side down. Serves 4.

Approximate nutritional analysis per serving:
Calories 303, Protein 18 g, Carbohydrates 35 g, Fat 11 g,
Cholesterol 24 mg, Sodium 536 mg

Opposite:Scrambled Egg Burritos

BRUNCH SANDWICHES

1 - 8 oz (240 ml) carton HEALTHY CHOICE
    Cholesterol Free Egg Product
¼ cup (60 ml) nonfat mayonnaise dressing
½ tsp (3 ml) Dijon-style mustard
dash pepper
4 slices tomato
4 lettuce leaves
4 wheat English muffins, toasted

In 8-inch skillet sprayed with vegetable oil spray, cook egg product, covered, over very low heat 10 minutes or until just set. Cut egg product into 4 pieces.

    In small bowl, combine mayonnaise, mustard and pepper. To make sandwiches, spread muffin halves with mayonnaise mixture. Layer egg product, tomato and lettuce between muffin halves. Serves 4.

Approximate nutritional analysis per serving:
Calories 190, Protein 12 g, Carbohydrates 28 g, Fat 2 g,
Cholesterol 0 mg, Sodium 560 mg

SPINACH-POTATO OMELET

1 tbs (15 ml) olive oil
1 large baking potato, diced
½ cup (120 ml) onion, chopped
1 - 10 oz package (300 g) frozen chopped
    spinach, thawed and squeezed dry
4 slices bacon, cut crosswise into ¼-inch pieces,
    cooked crisp
1 - 10 oz can (300 g) CHI-CHI'S Diced Tomatoes
    and Green Chilies, drained
9 eggs
1 tsp (5 ml) garlic salt
CHI-CHI'S Salsa

In 10-inch ovenproof skillet, heat oil over medium-high heat until hot. Cook and stir potatoes and onion 15-20 minutes or until potatoes are golden brown (add a little water to skillet if mixture begins to stick). Stir in spinach and bacon. In large bowl, whisk tomatoes and chilies, eggs and garlic salt together. Pour egg mixture into skillet. Reduce heat to low; stir so ingredients are well distributed. Cover; cook 15 minutes or until egg is set on top but still looks moist. Heat broiler. Place skillet in oven 6 inches from heat source. Broil 1-2 minutes or until top of omelet is lightly browned. Sprinkle with cheese, if desired. Cut into wedges. Serve with salsa. Serves 6.

Approximate nutritional analysis per serving:
Calories 210, Protein 13 g, Carbohydrates 12 g, Fat 12 g,
Cholesterol 325 mg, Sodium 710 mg

SUNNY EGGS ON SPAGHETTI SQUASH

3 tbs (45 ml) butter
½ cup (120 ml) fresh mushrooms, sliced
6 cloves garlic, minced
⅓ cup (80 ml) green onions with tops, chopped
1 tbs (15 ml) basil leaves, crushed
½ tsp (3 ml) salt
3 cups (720 ml) cooked spaghetti squashstrands*
8 eggs, poached or steam-basted**
¼ cup (60 ml) dairy sour cream
romaine leaves, optional

In large saucepan over medium heat, cook mushrooms and garlic in butter until mushrooms are tender but not brown, about 3 minutes. Stir in onions, basil and salt. Add squash and heat through. Cover and keep warm while preparing eggs. To serve, stir in sour cream. For each serving, top about ⅛ cup of the squash mixture with 2 cooked eggs. Garnish with romaine leaves, if desired. Serves 4.

    * To cook squash, cook whole in steamer or in boiling water to cover until fork tender, about 20-30 minutes *or* pierce with fork and cook in microwave oven at full power, turning occasionally, allowing 4-5 minutes per pound.

    Cool until comfortable to handle. Cut in half crosswise. Scoop out seeds and discard. With a fork, pull across squash to loosen the strands.

    ** To poach eggs, in 3-quart saucepan or 10-12-inch omelette pan or skillet, heat 2-3 inches of water to boiling. Reduce heat to keep water simmering. Break eggs into large bowl. Then, slip eggs into water, holding bowl close to water's surface, letting the eggs slide one by one into the water. Cook 3-5 minutes, depending on desired doneness. With slotted spoon, lift out eggs. Drain in spoon or on paper towels and trim any rough edges, if desired.

    To steam-baste eggs, use just enough butter to grease skillet. In large skillet over medium-high heat, heat butter until just hot enough to sizzle a drop of water. Break and slip eggs into skillet. Reduce heat to low immediately. Cook until edges turn white, about 1 minute. Add about 3 tsp water. Cover skillet tightly to hold in steam. Cook to desired doneness.

Approximate nutritional analysis per serving:
Calories 304, Protein 15 g, Carbohydrates 13 g, Fat 22 g,
Cholesterol 454 mg, Sodium 425 mg

Courtesy of the American Egg Board.

EGGS IN A POCKET

12 eggs
½ cup (120 ml) milk
½ tsp (3 ml) salt
½ tsp (3 ml) tarragon
¼ cup (60 ml) butter
6 pita breads
2 cups (480 ml) fresh spinach or lettuce,
    shredded
12 slices onion
12 slices tomato

Beat together eggs, milk, salt and tarragon with fork, mixing thoroughly for uniform yellow or slightly for white and yellow streaks. Heat butter in 10-inch fry pan over medium heat until just hot enough to sizzle a drop of water. Pour in egg mixture. As mixture begins to set, gently draw spatula completely across the bottom, forming large soft curds. Continue until eggs are thickened throughout but still moist*, but do not stir constantly. Cut each pita in half crosswise and gently pull open. Arrange spinach, onion and tomato slice and about ¼ cup scrambled eggs in each pocket. Serve hot. Serves 6.

Approximate nutritional analysis per serving:
Calories 422, Protein 21 g, Carbohydrates 41 g, Fat 20 g,
Cholesterol 447 mg, Sodium 673 mg

Courtesy of the American Egg Board.

BAYOU EGGS BENEDICT

SAUCE:
1 - 16 oz can (480 g) Italian tomatoes, chopped
1 small clove garlic, minced
½ cup (120 ml) fresh mushrooms, sliced
¼ cup (60 ml) onions, finely chopped
½ green pepper, chopped
1 stalk celery, sliced
¼ cup (60 ml) wine or chicken broth
1 bay leaf
2 tbs (30 ml) fresh parsley, chopped
1 tbs (15 ml) Worcestershire sauce
½ tsp (3 ml) *each* dried thyme, oregano and salt
½ cup (120 ml) raisins, coarsely chopped

8 eggs, poached
4 English muffins, halved and toasted
8 thin slices ham

In 1-quart bowl, mix tomatoes and their liquid, plus all remaining sauce ingredients except raisins. Microwave, uncovered on HIGH for 6 minutes, stirring every 2 minutes. Add raisins and microwave on HIGH 4 minutes longer. Remove bay leaf; set aside while cooking eggs. Break eggs into buttered custard cups; pierce yolk with fork tines. Cover egg

Eggs in a Pocket

cups with plastic wrap and microwave on medium low until nearly done to desired doneness (eggs will continue to cook while covered in dish). Toast English muffins. Place 2 muffin halves on each plate; top with ham slices and then eggs. Pour about ¼ cup sauce over each egg and serve. Serves 4.

Approximate nutritional analysis per serving:
Calories 490, Protein 30 g, Carbohydrates 53 g, Fat 18 g,
Cholesterol 456 mg, Sodium 416   mg

PIPERADA

6 eggs
1 medium onion, chopped
2 cloves garlic, minced
1 green pepper, chopped
1 GOYA Chorizo, sliced
3 tbs (45 ml) GOYA Olive Oil
4 slices prosciutto, chopped
2 small tomatoes, chopped
1 whole GOYA Pimiento, chopped
½ tsp (3 ml) GOYA Adobo with Pepper

In a mixing bowl, beat eggs with a whisk until smooth. In a skillet, sauté onion, garlic, green pepper and chorizo in olive oil until green peppers are tender. Add prosciutto, tomatoes and pimiento, and sauté over medium heat for 1 minute. Pour beaten eggs into same skillet, add adobo and stir over low-medium heat until eggs are set.
Serves 4.

Approximate nutritional analysis per serving:
Calories 338, Protein 20 g, Carbohydrates 9 g, Fat 25 g,
Cholesterol 343 mg, Sodium 765 mg

Fresh Pea Fritatta

FRESH PEA FRITTATA

1 cup (1 lb in shell) (240 ml) fresh peas, shelled
½ cup (120 ml) water
1 tbs (15 ml) butter
1 cup (4 oz) (120 g) fresh mushrooms, sliced
½ cup (120 ml) onion, chopped
4 eggs
¼ cup (60 ml) water
½ cup (2 oz) (60 g) cheddar cheese, shredded

In small saucepan, bring peas and water to boiling. Reduce heat, cover and simmer until crisp-tender, 8-15 minutes. Drain. Set aside.

In 6-8-inch omelet pan or skillet over medium heat, cook mushrooms and onion in butter until tender but not brown, 3-4 minutes. Stir in reserved peas. Beat together eggs and water. Pour over vegetables. Cook over low to medium heat until eggs are almost set and cheese is melted, 7-10 minutes. Slide from pan onto serving platter. Cut in half to serve. Serves 2.

Approximate nutritional analysis per serving:
Calories 281, Protein 19 g, Carbohydrates 17 g, Fat 16 g, Cholesterol 45 mg, Sodium 292 mg

Courtesy of the American Egg Board.

ASPARAGUS AND PARMESAN FRITTATA

1 - 12 oz bunch (360 g) slender asparagus, rinsed and trimmed
1 tbs (15 ml) BERTOLLI Olive Oil
½ cup (120 ml) scallions, sliced
¼ cup (60 ml) red bell pepper, sliced
1 tsp (5 ml) fresh thyme leaves, stripped from stems *or* pinch of dried thyme
1 cup (240 ml) long grain white rice, cooked
salt and freshly ground pepper, to taste
3 large eggs
5 egg whites
2 tsp (10 ml) Parmesan cheese, grated

Steam asparagus until crisp-tender, about 4 minutes. Cool. Cut 1½ cups into ½-inch diagonal slices. Reserve remaining whole asparagus for garnish.

Approximate nutritional analysis per serving:
Calories 202, Protein 14 g, Carbohydrates 20 g, Fat 8 g, Cholesterol 160 mg, Sodium 140 mg

CHICKEN FRITTATA

2 - 16 oz cartons (960 ml) HEALTHY CHOICE Cholesterol Free Egg Product
¼ cup (60 ml) skim milk
2 tbs (30 ml) Dijon-style mustard
¾ tsp (4 ml) salt
½ tsp (3 ml) pepper
2 cups (480 ml) chicken breast, cooked and chopped
1 - 10 oz package (300 g) frozen whole kernel corn, thawed
1½ cups (355 ml) potatoes, cooked, peeled and cubed
½ cup (120 ml) mushrooms, sliced
¼ cup (60 ml) red pepper, diced
2 tbs (30 ml) green onion, sliced

In medium bowl, combine egg product, milk, mustard, salt and pepper. In 12-inch, oven-proof skillet, sprayed with vegetable oil spray, cook remaining ingredients until vegetables are tender, stirring occasionally. Pour egg product mixture over chicken mixture. Cook over medium-low heat 10-12 minutes or until egg product mixture is almost set. Broil 6-inches from heat 3-5 minutes or until egg product mixture is completely set. Serves 8.

Approximate nutritional analysis per serving:
Calories 160, Fat 2 g, Cholesterol 30 mg, Sodium 440 mg

POTATO AND CHEESE OMELET

1 tsp (5 ml) olive oil
1 small potato, thinly sliced
1 small onion, thinly sliced
1 - 8 oz (240 ml) carton HEALTHY CHOICE
    Cholesterol Free Egg Product
½ tsp (3 ml) pepper
1½ cup (6 oz) (180 g) HEALTHY CHOICE
    Fat Free Natural Shredded Cheddar Cheese

In 10-inch non-stick skillet, cook potato and onion in olive oil over medium heat until potato is tender. Remove from pan and set aside. In same skillet add egg product and pepper. As egg begins to set, run spatula under edge of omelet, lifting cooked portion and allowing uncooked portion to spread to bottom of pan tilting pan as necessary. When eggs are almost set, sprinkle with 1 cup cheese. Continue cooking until cheese just begins to melt. Spoon potato-onion mixture into half of the omelet. Lift unfilled side of omelet over filling. Sprinkle with ½ cup cheese. To remove from pan, tilt pan slightly, turn omelet onto plate. Serves 3.

Approximate nutritional analysis per serving:
Calories 202, Protein 26 g, Carbohydrates 16 g, Fat 4 g,
Cholesterol 10 mg, Sodium 532 mg

Potato and Cheese Omelet

PUFFY SPINACH OMELET

4 eggs, separated
¼ cup (60 ml) water
½ tsp (3 ml) salt
¼ tsp (1 ml) cream of tartar
¼ tsp (1 ml) dry mustard
¼ tsp (1 ml) marjoram
1 tbs (15 ml) butter
2 slices bacon
1 small onion, sliced
½ cup (120 ml) spinach, cooked, chopped and
    drained (5 oz (150 g) frozen spinach)
½ cup (2 oz) (60 g) Swiss cheese, shredded

Beat egg whites with water, salt and cream of tartar at high speed until stiff but not dry, or just until whites no longer slip when bowl is tilted. Beat egg yolks, dry mustard and marjoram at high speed until thick and lemon-colored. Fold yolks into whites.

Heat butter in 10-inch omelet or fry pan with oven-proof handle* over medium-high heat until just hot enough to sizzle a drop of water. Pour in omelet mixture and gently smooth surface. Reduce heat to medium. Cook slowly until puffy and lightly browned on bottom, about 5 minutes. Lift omelet at edge to judge color. Bake in preheated 350°F (180°C) oven until knife inserted halfway between center and outside edge comes out clean, 10-12 minutes.

Meanwhile fry bacon until crisp. Remove from pan and drain on paper towel. Cook onion in bacon drippings just until tender, about 3-4 minutes.

To serve, loosen omelet edges with spatula. With a sharp knife cut upper surface down center of omelet but do not cut through to bottom of omelet. Arrange spinach over half of omelet. Crumble bacon and sprinkle over spinach. Top with onion and cheese. Tip pan. With pancake turner, fold omelet in half and gently slide into serving plate. Serve immediately. Serves 2.

Approximate nutritional analysis per serving:
Calories 360, Protein 24 g, Carbohydrates 6 g, Fat 27 g,
Cholesterol 471 mg, Sodium 866 mg

Courtesy of the American Egg Board.

Fluffy Spinach Omelet

Bacon and Apple Scramble

BACON AND APPLE SCRAMBLE

4 slices bacon
1 cup (240 ml) apple, chopped (1 medium)
¼ cup (60 ml) onion, chopped
¼ cup (60 ml) celery, chopped
8 eggs
¼ cup (60 ml) milk
½ tsp (3 ml) salt

In 10-inch omelette pan or skillet, over medium heat, cook bacon until crisp. Drain. Reserve 2 tbs drippings. Crumble bacon and set aside. Over medium heat cook apple, onion and celery in reserved drippings 2 minutes.

Mix eggs, milk and salt until blended. Stir in reserved bacon. Pour egg mixture over apple mixture in pan. As mixture begins to set, gently draw spatula completely across the bottom and sides of pan, forming large soft curds. Continue until eggs are thickened, but still moist. Do not stir constantly. Serves 4.

Approximate nutritional analysis per serving:
Calories 212, Protein 15 g, Carbohydrates 6 g, Fat 14 g,
Cholesterol 431 mg, Sodium 507 mg

Courtesy of American Egg Board.

BREADS & MUFFINS

Homemade breads and muffins can transform a meal from everyday to special in minutes. When you have the ingredients assembled you can make muffins between wake-up and shower in the morning. If mixed together first thing, a savory bread hot from the oven can cool between spritzers and pasta. Because quick breads tend to be moist, they keep nicely if well wrapped and make a great leftover or prepared-ahead accompaniment.

RANCHEROS CHEESE-OLIVE MUFFIN

2 cups (480 ml) flour
1 tbs (15 ml) baking powder
¾ tsp (4 ml) baking soda
¾ tsp (4 ml) salt
1½ tsp (8 ml) oregano
½ cup (120 ml) packaged dry Parmesan cheese
2-3 tsp (10 - 15 ml) crushed red pepper (dried flakes)
⅓ cup (80 ml) vegetable oil
2 eggs
¾ cup (180 ml) milk
½ cup (120 ml) CALIFORNIA ripe olives,chopped

Combine flour with baking powder, baking soda, salt, oregano, cheese and red pepper in large bowl. In another bowl, mix oil, eggs and milk. Pour into flour mixture and stir just until moistened but a bit lumpy. Stir in olives. Spoon into well-greased muffin cups. Bake at 375°F (190°C) for 15 minutes or until golden and baked in center. Serves 12.

Approximate nutritional analysis per serving:
Calories 173, Protein 5 g, Carbohydrates 17 g, Fat 9 g,
Cholesterol 41 mg, Sodium 379 mg

SWISS CHEESE-SPINACH SPOON BREAD

1 cup (280 ml) boiling water
½ cup (120 ml) Regular, Quick or Instant
CREAM OF WHEAT Cereal
1 tbs (15 ml) margarine
1 tsp (5 ml) salt
1 clove garlic, crushed
3 eggs, separated
2 tsp (10 ml) baking powder
½ cup (120 ml) milk
1 - 10 oz package (300 g) frozen chopped spinach,
thawed and well drained
½ cup (120 ml) Swiss cheese, shredded
1 tsp (5 ml) dried basil leaves

In large bowl, stir boiling water into cereal until thickened; let stand 5 minutes for Regular or Quick; 1-2 minutes for Instant. Stir in margarine, salt, garlic and egg yolks. Gradually add baking powder and milk until blended. Stir in spinach, cheese and basil.

In medium bowl, with electric mixer at high speed, beat egg whites until stiff; gently fold into cereal mixture. Pour into 2-quart round casserole which has been greased and sprinkled with additional cereal. Bake 375°F (190°C) for 35-40 minutes or until knife inserted in center comes out clean. Serve warm. Serves 6.

Approximate nutritional analysis per serving:
Calories 169, Protein 8 g, Carbohydrates 7 g, Fat 8 g,
Cholesterol 118 mg, Sodium 648 mg

SOUTH-OF-THE-BORDER TRIPLE CORN MUFFINS

6-8 dried cornhusks (6-8 inches long)
1 cup (240 ml) yellow or blue cornmeal
1 cup (240 ml) all-purpose flour
1 tbs (15 ml) baking powder
¼ tsp (1 ml) salt
¾ cup (180 ml) milk
½ cup (120 ml) CHI-CHI'S Salsa Verde
¼ cup (60 ml) vegetable oil
2 tbs (30 ml) honey
1 egg
½ cup (120 ml) fresh or frozen whole kernel corn

Heat oven to 375°F (190°C). Grease 12 - 2½ inch muffin cups. Separate cornhusks. In large bowl, pour boiling water over cornhusks to cover. Soak about 10 minutes or until soft and pliable. Drain; pat dry. Tear cornhusks lengthwise into 2-inch strips. Set aside.

In large bowl, combine cornmeal, flour, baking powder and salt. In medium mixing bowl, beat milk, salsa verde, oil, honey and egg until well blended. Stir liquid ingredients into flour mixture; mix just enough to moisten dry ingredients. Stir in corn. Place 2-3 cornhusk strips in each muffin cup, crossing centers in bottom of cups so husk ends fan out around sides. As each cup is lined, fill with batter. Bake 20-25 minutes or until tops are golden brown. Remove muffin from cornhusks before eating. Serves 10.

Approximate nutritional analysis per serving:
Calories 180, Protein 4 g, Carbohydrates 26 g, Fat 7 g,
Cholesterol 25 mg, Sodium 220 mg

SOUTHERN SPOON BREAD

2 cups (480 ml) milk
4 tsp (20 ml) butter, margarine or oil
1 cup (280 ml) cornmeal
½ tsp (3 ml) salt
½ tsp (3 ml) IMPERIAL Granulated Sugar
2 eggs, separated

Heat milk and butter, margarine or oil to boiling point. Slowly stir in cornmeal, salt and IMPERIAL Granulated Sugar. Cook about 1 minute, stirring. Separate eggs; beat whites to stiff peak stage and reserve. Beat egg yolks and fold into cornmeal mixture; then fold in stiffly beaten egg whites. Pour into buttered 8-inch square pan or casserole. Bake in preheated 350°F (180°C) oven about 45 minutes. Serve while hot. Serves 9.

Note: This is not a traditional bread. It is an old- fashioned recipe and makes almost a custard-type soufflé-type bread.

Approximate nutritional analysis per serving:
Calories 115, Protein 4 g, Carbohydrates 13 g, Fat 5 g,
Cholesterol 55 mg, Sodium 186 mg

OLD-FASHIONED JOHNNY CAKE

1 cup (240 ml) all-purpose flour
1 cup (240 ml) cornmeal
¼ cup (60 ml) IMPERIAL Granulated
   Sugar
1 tsp (5 ml) salt
2 tsp (10 ml) baking powder
1 egg, beaten
1 cup (240 ml) milk
1 tbs (15 ml) melted butter,
   margarine or oil

Combine dry ingredients and set aside. Beat egg and combine with milk and melted butter, margarine or oil. Lightly stir together the two mixtures and pour into greased 8-inch square pan. Bake in preheated 350°F (180°C) oven about 25 minutes, or until done. Serve warm with butter. Serves 9.

Approximate nutritional analysis per serving:
Calories 165, Protein 4 g, Carbohydrates 29 g,
Fat 3 g, Cholesterol 31 mg, Sodium 335 mg

Spicy Cornbread

SPICY CORNBREAD

¾ cup (180 ml) yellow cornmeal
1¼ cups (295 ml) all-purpose flour
¼ cup (60 ml) IMPERIAL Granulated Sugar
½ tsp (3 ml) salt
1 tbs (15 ml) baking powder
½ tsp (3 ml) red pepper (cayenne)
dash garlic powder
1 egg, beaten or egg substitute
¾ cup (180 ml) milk
¼ cup (60 ml) cooking oil
1 tbs (15 ml) minced onion
2 tbs (30 ml) green pepper, minced
2 tbs (30 ml) pimiento, minced

Combine dry ingredients in large bowl and mix well with slotted spoon. Combine remaining ingredients and stir lightly into first mixture. Bake in 8-inch, heavy, preheated dish (cast iron or thick pottery) containing 2 tbs cooking oil or shortening. Bake in preheated 425°F (220°C) oven 20-25 minutes. Preheating dish or pan produces brown, crusty bread. Serves 9.

Approximate nutritional analysis per serving:
Calories 224, Protein 4 g, Carbohydrates 28 g, Fat 11 g,
Cholesterol 26 mg, Sodium 233 mg

SPICY PECAN COUNTRY CORNBREAD

2 eggs
1 cup (280 ml) cornmeal
1 cup (280 ml) all-purpose flour
2 tsp (10 ml) baking powder
½ tsp (3 ml) baking soda
½ tsp (3 ml) salt
1 cup (280 ml) buttermilk
4 tbs (60 ml) oil (1 for pan)
1 - 7 oz can (210 g) chopped green chili
4 oz (120 g) cheddar cheese, shredded
½ cup (120 ml) pecan pieces
1 jalapeño pepper, seeds and membrane removed
½ red bell pepper, quartered
1 - 11 oz can (330 g) whole kernel corn, drained

Preheat oven to 375 °F (190°C). Use 1 tbs oil to coat a 10-inch cast iron or other oven-proof baking pan. Place oiled pan in oven while preheating takes place.

Mix cornmeal, flour, baking powder, baking soda and salt in large bowl. Set aside.

In processor combine remaining ingredients and pulse in short bursts until vegetables are cut into small pieces. Mix with dry ingredients until well combined, about 1 minute. Pour into hot pan and bake for 25-30 minutes or until crust is golden brown. Serves 12.

Approximate nutritional analysis per serving:
Calories 235, Protein 7 g, Carbohydrates 24 g, Fat 13 g,
Cholesterol 46 mg, Sodium 550 mg

Courtesy of The Pecan Marketing Board.

SKILLET WHITE CORN BREAD

1¼ cups (295 ml) white cornmeal
¾ cups (180 ml) all-purpose unbleached flour
2½ tsp (13 ml) baking powder
1 tbs (15 ml) sugar
½ tsp (3 ml) salt
2 large eggs
3 tbs (45 ml) vegetable oil
1 cup (240 ml) apple juice
1 cup (240 ml) fresh "white" corn, cut off cob
    or frozen kernels
1 tbs (15 ml) vegetable oil for greasing pan

Preheat oven to 425°F (220°C). Place 9-inch round cast iron skillet in the oven and let heat while making batter. In large bowl, combine cornmeal, flour, baking powder, sugar and salt. In a small bowl, beat eggs with oil and juice, until well blended. Add egg mixture to the dry mix. Stir in corn. Pour 1 tbs oil into the preheated skillet, swirl it around to cover, spoon batter and bake 25 minutes, until golden on top. To serve, cut into wedges. Serves 6.

Approximate nutritional analysis per serving:
Calories 305, Protein 7 g, Carbohydrates 45 g, Fat 12 g,
Cholesterol 71 mg, Sodium 347 mg

Courtesy of Empire Kosher Poultry Test Kitchens.

CHILI CORN SPOON BREAD

2 cups (480 ml) water
1½ cups (355 ml) skim milk
2 cups (480 ml) yellow cornmeal
¼ cup (60 ml) sugar
2 tsp (10 ml) baking powder
1 tsp (5 ml) garlic powder
½ tsp (3 ml) ground black pepper
1 - 8 oz carton (240 ml) EGG BEATERS
    Real Egg Product
1 cup (240 ml) canned or frozen corn
1 - 4 oz can (120 g) diced green chilies, drained
1 cup (240 ml) reduced fat cheddar cheese, shredded

In large saucepan, over medium-high heat, heat water and milk almost to a boil; remove from heat. Using a whisk, slowly stir in cornmeal, sugar, baking powder, garlic powder and black pepper until smooth. Blend in remaining ingredients. Spoon into lightly greased 2-quart soufflé or baking dish. Bake at 375°F (190°C) for 35-40 minutes or until puffed and golden brown. Let stand for 10 minutes before serving. Serves 12.

Approximate nutritional analysis per serving:
Calories 172, Protein 8 g, Carbohydrates 25 g, Fat 2 g,
Cholesterol 7 mg, Sodium 223 mg

BARBARA'S VIDALIA MUFFINS

¾ cup (180 ml) milk
1 egg
1 cup (240 ml) oatmeal
½ cup (120 ml) vidalia onions, chopped
¾ cup (180 ml) extra sharp cheese, grated
⅓ cup (80 ml) vegetable oil
1 cup (240 ml) self-rising flour
¼ cup (60 ml) sugar
⅓ cup (80 ml) broken pecans

Preheat oven to 400°F (205 °C). Spray muffin pans with cooking spray. Beat milk, oil and egg and stir in flour, oatmeal and sugar just until moistened. Fold in vidalia onions, cheese and pecans. Divide batter among the muffin cups, filling the cups ¾ full. Bake until brown. Remove from pans and keep warm until served. Serves 12.

Approximate nutritional analysis per serving:
Calories 179, Protein 5 g, Carbohydrates 15 g, Fat 11 g,
Cholesterol 26 mg, Sodium 195 mg.

Opposite: Vidalia Onions

JUST SAVORY BAYOU YAM MUFFINS

1 cup (240 ml) flour
1 cup (240 ml) cornmeal
¼ cup (60 ml) sugar
1 tbs (15 ml) baking powder
1¼ tsp (6 ml) ground cinnamon
½ tsp (3 ml) salt
2 eggs
½ cup (120 ml) cold strong coffee
¼ cup (60 ml) butter or margarine, melted
1 cup (240 ml) yams or sweet potatoes, mashed
½ tsp (3 ml) TABASCO pepper sauce

Preheat oven to 425°F (220°C). Grease twelve 3x1½-inch muffin cups. In large bowl combine flour, cornmeal, sugar baking powder, cinnamon and salt. In medium bowl beat eggs; stir in coffee, butter, yams and TABASCO sauce. Make well in center of dry ingredients; add yam mixture and stir just to combine. Spoon batter into prepared muffin cups. Bake 20-25 minutes or until a cake tester inserted in center comes out clean. Cool 5 minutes on wire rack. Remove from pans. Serve warm or at room temperature. Serves 12.

    Microwave directions: Prepare muffin batter as directed above. Spoon approximately ⅓ cup batter into each of 6 paper baking cup-lined 6-oz custard cups or microwave-safe muffin pan cups. Cook uncovered on HIGH 4-5½ minutes or until cake tester inserted in center comes out clean; turn and rearrange cups or turn muffin pan ½ turn once during cooking. With small spatula, remove muffins. Cool 5 minutes on wire rack. Remove from pans. Repeat procedure with remaining batter. Serve warm or at room temperature.

Approximate nutritional analysis per serving:
Calories 165, Protein 3 g, Carbohydrates 25 g, Fat 5 g,
Cholesterol 55 mg, Sodium 215 mg

HERBED TOMATO FLAT BREAD

1 - 28 oz can (840 g) LIBBY'S Whole Peeled
    Tomatoes in Juice

TOPPING:
½ cup (120 ml) green onions, chopped
¾ cup (180 ml) sour cream
⅓ cup (80 ml) mayonnaise
1 cup (240 ml) cheddar cheese, grated
¾ tsp (4 ml) salt
¼ tsp (1 ml) pepper
¼ tsp (1 ml) garlic powder
¼ tsp (1 ml) sweet basil

BREAD:
⅔ cup (160 ml) milk
2 cups (480 ml) biscuit mix
paprika

Drain tomatoes well and cut in half. Blend together topping ingredients. Stir milk into biscuit mix to make soft dough. Turn dough onto well-floured board and knead lightly 10-12 strokes. Pat evenly into bottom of greased 13x9x2 -inch baking dish and form shallow rim around outer edge. Arrange drained tomatoes over dough. Spread sour cream topping over tomatoes and sprinkle with paprika. Bake in 400°F (205°C) oven 20-25 minutes. Serve 12.

Approximate nutritional analysis per serving:
Calories 201, Protein 6 g, Carbohydrates 20 g, Fat 11 g,
Cholesterol 18 mg, Sodium 530 mg

SPICY ONION BREAD

2 tbs (30 ml) minced onion
⅓ cup (80 ml) water
1½ cups (355 ml) biscuit mix
1 egg, slightly beaten
½ cup (120 ml) milk
½ tsp (3 ml) TABASCO pepper sauce
½ tsp (3 ml) caraway seeds, optional
2 tbs (30 ml) butter, melted

Preheat oven to 400°F (205°C). Soak instant minced onion in water 5 minutes. Combine biscuit mix, egg, milk and TABASCO sauce and stir until blended. Stir in onion. turn into greased 8-inch pie plate. Sprinkle with caraway seeds. Brush melted butter over all. Bake 20-25 minutes or until bread is golden brown. Serves 8.

Approximate nutritional analysis per serving:
Calories 144, Protein 3 g, Carbohydrates 16 g, Fat 7 g,
Cholesterol 36 mg, Sodium 340 mg

ITALIAN TOMATO BREAD

2 - 14½ oz cans (870 g) CONTADINA Pasta
    Ready Chunky Tomatoes with Three Cheeses
¼ cup (60 ml) green onions, sliced
1 loaf (1 lb) (480 g) Italian or French bread
1½ cups (355 ml) mozzarella cheese, shredded

In medium bowl, combine tomatoes and green onions. Cut bread in half lengthwise; scoop out ½-inch layer of bread to within 1 inch of crust. Spoon tomato mixture onto bread; top with cheese. Place on baking sheet; bake in preheated 450°F (230°C) oven for 5-8 minutes or until hot and cheese is melted. Serves 24.

Approximate nutritional analysis per serving:
Calories 70, Protein 3 g, Carbohydrates 10 g, Fat 2 g,
Cholesterol 5 mg, Sodium 200 mg

CRUNCHY BREAD STICKS

4 hot dog buns
¼ cup (½ stick) (60 ml) butter or margarine, melted
dash garlic powder
¼ tsp (1 ml) Worcestershire sauce
dash salt
dash white pepper or red pepper (cayenne)
dash IMPERIAL Granulated Sugar
1 tsp (5 ml) chives, finely minced

Split hot dog buns in half, then cut each half vertically to make 4 bread sticks from each bun. Combine all other ingredients and brush onto edges of bread sticks. Place on baking sheet and brown in preheated 325°F (165°C) oven, about 10 minutes. Let remain in oven a few minutes after heat is turned off to make sticks very crisp. Serves 16.

Approximate nutritional analysis per serving:
Calories 54, Protein 1 g, Carbohydrates 5 g, Fat 3 g,
Cholesterol 8 mg, Sodium 90 mg

SWEET MUFFINS

1¾ cups (415 ml) BISQUICK Reduced Fat Baking Mix
¾ cup (180 ml) skim milk
⅓ cup (80 ml) sugar
1 tbs (15 ml) margarine, melted
2 egg whites
    or **¼ cup (60 ml) cholesterol free egg product**

OATMEAL-RAISIN VARIATION:
¾ cup (180 ml) quick-cooking oats
½ cup (120 ml) raisins
1 tsp (5 ml) ground cinnamon

Heat oven to 400°F (205°C). Grease bottoms of 12 medium muffin cups, 2½x1¼ inches, or line with paper baking cups. Mix all ingredients just until moistened. Divide batter evenly among muffin cups. Bake 13-18 minutes or until golden brown. Cool slightly; remove from pan. Yields 12 muffins.

    Oatmeal Raisin Muffins: Add quick-cooking oats, raisins and ground cinnamon with the baking mix.

    High Altitude: 3500-6500 feet: Heat oven to 425°F (220°C).

Approximate nutritional analysis per serving Sweet Muffin:
Calories 100, Protein 3 g, Carbohydrates 17 g, Fat 2 g,
Cholesterol 0 mg, Sodium 220 mg

Approximate nutritional analysis per serving Oatmeal-Raisin Muffin:
Calories 130, Protein 3 g, Carbohydrate 24 g, Fat 2 g,
Cholesterol 0 mg, Sodium 230 mg

HOT CHEESE, OLIVE AND HERB BREAD

1 loaf French bread
½ cup (120 ml) butter or margarine, melted
1 - 6 oz package (180 g) sliced Monterey Jack cheese
⅓ cup (80 ml) dried Parmesan or Romano cheese
1 cup (240 ml) CALIFORNIA ripe olives, chopped
1 tsp (5 ml) thyme

Vertically slice bread thickly but not quite all the way through so that the loaf holds together. Brush in between slices with melted butter. Insert cheese, olives and thyme between slices. Wrap loaf in foil and bake at 400°F (205°C) for 25 minutes or until hot in center. Serves 6.

Approximate nutritional analysis per serving:
Calories 493, Protein 16 g, Carbohydrates 43 g, Fat 29 g,
Cholesterol 73 mg, Sodium 914 mg

Sweet Muffins

SPIRAL OLIVE ROLLS

1 loaf (1 lb) (480 g) frozen bread dough, thawed
¼ cup (60 ml) butter or margarine, melted
½ cup (120 ml) packaged Parmesan cheese, grated
1¼ cups (295 ml) CALIFORNIA ripe olives, chopped

Roll out dough on floured surface to 14x10-inch rectangle. Brush with butter then sprinkle with cheese and olives. Roll up, starting from long side and pinch seam down at end so it will stay rolled. Slice into 10 spirals. Lay spirals on baking sheet. Place pan over large bowl of hot water (or other warm place) for 30 minutes or until rolls are puffy. Bake at 375°F (190°C) for 25-30 minutes or until baked and golden. Serves 10.

Approximate nutritional analysis per serving:
Calories 78, Protein 2 g, Carbohydrates 2 g, Fat 7 g,
Cholesterol 16 mg, Sodium 205 mg

CHEESY GARLIC BREAD

½ cup (120 ml) butter or margarine, melted
2 tbs (30 ml) fresh grated Parmesan cheese
1 tsp (5 ml) GILROY FARMS Crushed Garlic
1½ tsp (8 ml) fresh oregano leaves, chopped
    ***or* ½ tsp (3 ml) McCORMICK or SCHILLING**
    Oregano Leaves
1 loaf fresh Italian bread, sliced

Beat butter, cheese, garlic and oregano together until well blended. Spread on bread slices and broil 2-3 minutes or until lightly browned. Serves 8.

Approximate nutritional analysis per serving:
Calories 266, Protein 6 g, Carbohydrates 32 g, Fat 12 g,
Cholesterol 33 mg, Sodium 477 mg

SAVORY FLATBREAD

1 tbs (15 ml) plus 2 tsp (10 ml) dried rosemary
    leaves, crushed
1 tbs (15 ml) plus 2 tsp (10 ml) olive oil
1 lb (480 g) white or wheat frozen bread dough,
    thawed
½ cup (120 ml) CHI-CHI'S Pico de Gallo

TOPPINGS:
¼ cup (60 ml) dry roasted unsalted sunflower nuts
¼ cup (60 ml) ripe olives, chopped
½ cup (120 ml) shredded asiago or
    grated Parmesan cheese
½ cup (120 ml) fresh cilantro, chopped
coarse salt

Heat oven to 475°F (250°C). Grease 2 rimmed 15x10x1-inch baking pans. In small bowl, combine rosemary and oil; set aside. Divide dough in to 4 equal pieces. On a lightly floured board, roll each piece into 7-8-inch round. Place two rounds on each baking sheet. Brush dough with oil mixture. Spoon 2 tbs pico de gallo on each. Sprinkle with one or more suggested toppings. Cover breads loosely with plastic wrap. Let rise in warm place about 20 minutes or until puffy. Bake 8-10 minutes or until deep golden brown. Cut into wedges; serve warm. Serves 4.

Tip: Flat breads can be frozen up to 5 days. Wrap tightly before freezing. Thaw wrapped. Unwrap and reheat at 350°F (180°C) for 3-5 minutes or until crisp.

Approximate nutritional analysis per serving:
Calories 420, Protein 14 g, Carbohydrates 60 g, Fat 15 g,
Cholesterol 0 mg, Sodium 740 mg

ALMOND BEER BREAD

2 cups (480 ml) BLUE DIAMOND Chopped
    Natural Almonds
6 tbs (90 ml) butter, divided
1½ cups (360 ml) dark beer at room temperature
½ cup (120 ml) brown sugar, firmly packed
1 package (¼ oz) (7 g) active dry yeast
4-5 cups (960-1200 ml) flour, divided
2 tsp (10 ml) powdered ginger
2 eggs, divided
1½ tsp (8 ml) salt
½ tsp (3 ml) almond extract
1 tbs (15 ml) water

Sauté almonds in 2 tbs butter until crisp; reserve. Melt remaining 4 tbs butter; reserve. Mix beer and brown sugar. Stir in yeast and let stand until yeast is dissolved, about 10 minutes. Beat in 2 cups flour, ginger, 1 egg, salt and almond extract. Add melted butter and another cup flour. Stir in almonds. Continue to add flour as needed to make a firm dough that cleans the bowl. Turn out onto a floured board and knead until dough is smooth and elastic, about 10 minutes. Place in an oiled bowl and turn to coat with oil. Cover and let rise until double in volume, about 1-1½ hours. Punch dough down and let rest for 10 minutes. Divide dough in half and form 2 round loaves. Place on baking sheet, cover, and let rise until double in volume, about 1-1½ hours. Beat remaining egg with 1 tbs water and brush loaves. Bake at 350°F (180°C) for 30-35 minutes or until golden brown and loaves sound hollow when tapped on the bottom. Yields 2 loaves or 24 servings.

Approximate nutritional analysis per serving:
Calories 215, Protein 6 g, Carbohydrates 27 g, Fat 9 g ,
Cholesterol 25 mg, Sodium 172 mg

PARKERHOUSE ROLLS

1 package dry yeast
1½ cup (355 ml) milk, scalded and cooled
⅓ cup (80 ml) IMPERIAL Granulated Sugar
2 eggs, beaten
1¼ tsp (6 ml) salt
4 cups (960 ml) all-purpose flour; divided use
⅓ cup (80 ml) shortening, melted

Dissolve yeast in lukewarm milk and stir well; add IMPERIAL Granulated Sugar, beaten eggs, salt and half the flour. Combine well and add melted shortening. Beat and add balance of flour or enough to make a stiff dough. Turn dough out onto a floured surface, knead into a smooth dough, about 8 minutes. Transfer to large greased bowl and cover with plastic wrap or cloth; let rise in warm place until doubled in bulk, about 1 hour. Turn dough out onto floured surface, roll out ¼-inch thick and brush lightly with melted butter. Cut with biscuit cutter, dip handle of knife in flour and make a deep crease in center of each roll. Place close together on greased pan and let rise about 15 minutes. Bake in preheated 425°F (220°C) oven for 15-20 minutes. Yields 3 dozen.

Note: These can be shaped into larger rolls such as hot dog or hamburger rolls. Shape them in 5-inch rounds or 5x2 inches, both about ½-inch thick. Bake as above.

Approximate nutritional analysis per serving:
Calories 85, Protein 2 g, Carbohydrates 13 g, Fat 3 g,
Cholesterol 13 mg, Sodium 83 mg

DANNON MUFFINS

1½ cups (355 ml) all-purpose flour
¾ cups (180 ml) sugar
2 tsp (10 ml) baking powder
1 tsp (5 ml) baking soda
½ tsp (3 ml) salt
⅔ cup (160 ml) DANNON Plain Nonfat or
    Lowfat Yogurt
⅔ cup (160 ml) skim milk
½ cup (120 ml) blueberries or grated apple, optional

Preheat oven to 400°F (205°C). Grease muffin cups or line with paper baking cups. In large bowl combine flour, sugar, baking powder, baking soda and salt. Gently add yogurt, milk and blueberries; stir just until dry ingredients are moistened.

Fill prepared muffin cups ⅔ full. Bake 18 minutes or until lightly brown and toothpick inserted in center comes out clean. Serve warm. Yields 12 muffins.

Approximate nutritional analysis per serving:
Calories 122, Protein 3 g, Carbohydrates 1 g, Fat .4 g,
Cholesterol 1 mg, Sodium 140 mg

MARVELOUS MUFFINS

¼ cup (60 ml) IMPERIAL Granulated Sugar
1½ cups (355 ml) all-purpose flour
2 tsp (10 ml) baking powder
1 tsp (5 ml) salt
1 cup (240 ml) quick-cooking oatmeal
1 egg, well beaten
¾ cup (180 ml) milk
¼ cup (½ stick) (60 ml) butter or margarine, melted
¼ cup (60 ml) molasses

VARIATION:
1 tsp (5 ml) chopped nuts, chocolate morsels
    or raisins

Combine IMPERIAL Granulated Sugar, flour, baking powder, salt in medium-sized bowl; stir in quick-cooking oatmeal. Combine egg, milk, melted butter or margarine, molasses in small bowl and add all at once to flour mixture, stirring only enough to combine liquid with dry ingredients. Do not overmix. Spoon batter into 12 medium-size, greased muffin cups, about ⅓ batter in each. Bake in preheated 400°F (205°C) oven 20 minutes, or until richly browned. Remove from pan at once. Yields 12 muffins.

Variation: After spooning batter into muffin cups, add 1 tsp of any of the following to top of batter, then press gently into batter: chopped nuts, chocolate morsels, raisins.

Approximate nutritional analysis per serving:
Calories 163, Protein 4 g, Carbohydrates 25 g, Fat 5 g,
Cholesterol 20 mg, Sodium 291 mg

APRICOT-ORANGE HAZELNUT MUFFINS

MUFFINS:
1½ cup (355 ml) all-purpose white flour
1 tsp (5 ml) baking soda
½ cup (120 ml) OREGON Hazelnut Meal
    (finely ground roasted hazelnuts)
⅔ cup (160 ml) buttermilk
¼ cup (60 ml) orange juice
1 tsp (5 ml) grated orange rind
¾ cup (180 ml) granulated sugar
6 tbs (90 ml) butter or margarine, room temperature
1 large egg
½ cup (120 ml) OREGON Hazelnuts,
    roasted and coarsely chopped
½ cup (120 ml) dried apricots, coarsely chopped

ORANGE GLAZE:
¾ cup (180- ml) powdered sugar
1½ tbs (25 ml) milk
1 tsp (5 ml) grated orange rind
¼ cup (60 ml) OREGON Hazelnuts,
   roasted and finely chopped

In 2-quart bowl, sift together flour and baking soda. Whisk in OREGON Hazelnut Meal. Reserve. In 2-cup glass measuring cup, combine buttermilk, orange juice and rind. Reserve. In 4-quart bowl, with electric mixer, cream butter and sugar together. Add egg and beat until smooth. With mixer on low speed, mix in dry and liquid ingredients, alternately, in several additions, starting and ending with dry ingredients. Stir in chopped hazelnuts and apricots.Divide batter among 12 - 2½-inch muffin cups. Bake in 375°F (190°C) oven for 18-20 minutes, or until muffins are golden and spring back when lightly touched with fingertips. Remove from pan and cool on rack. To make glaze, in a small bowl, whisk powdered sugar, milk and orange rind until smooth. Drizzle over cooled muffins and sprinkle with hazelnuts. Yields 12 muffins.

Approximate nutritional analysis per serving:
Calories 284 , Protein 5 g, Carbohydrates 37 g, Fat 14 g,
Cholesterol 34 mg, Sodium 149 mg

BANANA MUFFINS

2 egg whites
   or ¼ cup (60 ml) cholesterol free egg product
1¾ cup (415 ml) BISQUICK Reduced Fat Baking Mix
1¼ cups (295 ml) ripe bananas, mashed
⅓ cup (80 ml) sugar
2 tbs (30 ml) water
1 tbs (15 ml) vegetable oil

Heat oven to 400°F (205°C). Grease bottoms of 12 muffin cups, 2½x1¼ inches, or line with paper baking cups. Beat egg whites slightly; stir in remaining ingredients just until moistened. Divide batter evenly among cups. Bake about 15 minutes or until golden brown. Serve warm. Yields 12 muffins.

   High altitude: 3500-6500 feet: Heat oven to 425°F (220°C). Decrease sugar to ¼ cup.

Approximate nutritional analysis per serving:
Calories 130, Protein 2 g, Carbohydrates 23 g, Fat 3 g,
Cholesterol 0 mg, Sodium 200 mg

GOLDEN BANANA-OAT BRAN MUFFINS

1¼ cups (295 ml) whole wheat flour
¾ cup (180 ml) oat bran
½ cup (120 ml) brown sugar, firmly packed
2 tsp (10 ml) baking powder
½ tsp (3 ml) salt
½ tsp (3 ml) cinnamon
¼ tsp (1 ml) nutmeg
½ cup (120 ml) raisins
¾ cup (180 ml) skim milk
2 egg whites, slightly beaten
2 tbs (30 ml) vegetable oil
1 tsp (5 ml) vanilla
1 medium CHIQUITA Banana, mashed

Preheat oven to 425°F (220°C). Prepare 12 muffin cups with nonstick baking spray or baking cups. Combine all dry ingredients well. Add all remaining ingredients and mix just until dry ingredients are moistened. Fill muffin cups ¾ full. Bake 20-25 minutes or until golden brown. Yields 12 muffins.

Approximate nutritional analysis per serving:
Calories 140, Protein 4 g, Carbohydrates 24 g, Fat 3 g,
Cholesterol 0 mg, Sodium 20 mg

Golden Banana-Oat Bran Muffins

BANANA WHEAT MUFFINS

⅔ cup (160 ml) flour
⅔ cup (160 ml) whole wheat flour
⅓ cup (80 ml) sugar
2 tsp (10 ml) baking powder
¾ cup (180 ml) nonfat buttermilk
¼ cup (60 ml) HEALTHY CHOICE
    Cholesterol Free Egg Product
2 tbs (30 ml) vegetable oil
½ tsp (3 ml) grated lemon peel
¾ cup (180 ml) ripe bananas, mashed (about 2)

In large bowl, combine flour, whole wheat flour, sugar and baking powder. In small bowl, combine buttermilk, egg product, oil and lemon peel. Stir buttermilk mixture into flour mixture just until moistened. Fold in bananas. Spoon into 12 muffin cup pan sprayed with vegetable oil spray, filling each cup ¾ full. Bake in 400°F (205°C) oven for 20 minutes or until light brown. Yields 12 muffins.

Approximate nutritional analysis per serving:
Calories 113, Protein 3 g, Carbohydrates 20 g, Fat 3 g,
Cholesterol 1 mg, Sodium 81 mg

BUTTERFLAKE BISCUITS

2 cups (480 ml) all-purpose flour
1 tbs (15 ml) baking powder
¾ tsp (4 ml) salt
1 tbs (15 ml) IMPERIAL Granulated Sugar
½ cup plus 2 tbs (150 ml) butter or margarine
2 eggs, well beaten
⅓ cup (80 ml) cold milk

Combine dry ingredients; cut butter or margarine into mixture with pastry blender. Mix well beaten eggs and milk, add to mixture and mix lightly with fork. Shape dough into ball and turn out on lightly floured surface. With rolling pin, lightly roll dough into a rectangle about ½ inch thick. Fold dough into thirds and roll into oblong two more times. With dough ½ inch thick, cut into 2-inch diameter biscuits. Bake on ungreased baking sheet in preheated 475°F (250°C) oven until biscuits are puffed and golden brown. Yields 16 biscuits.

Approximate nutritional analysis per serving:
Calories 124, Protein 3 g, Carbohydrates 13 g, Fat 7 g,
Cholesterol 27 mg, Sodium 241 mg

BLUEBERRY-OATMEAL MUFFINS

2 egg whites
1 cup (240 ml) YOPLAIT Fat Free Plain
    or Vanilla Yogurt
¼ cup (60 ml) butter or margarine, softened
1¼ cups (295 ml) GOLD MEDAL All-Purpose Flour
1 cup (280- ml) quick cooking oats
½ cup (120 ml) brown sugar, packed
2 tsp (10 ml) baking powder
1 tsp (5 ml) ground cinnamon
½ tsp (3 ml) baking soda
¼ tsp (1 ml) ground nutmeg
¼ tsp (1 ml) salt, if desired
1 cup 9240 ml) fresh or frozen
    (thawed and drained) blueberries

Heat oven to 400°F (205°C). Line 12 medium muffin cups, 2½x1¼ inches, with paper baking cups, or grease bottoms only of muffin cups. Mix all ingredients except blueberries just until flour is moistened (batter will be lumpy). Fold in blueberries. Divide batter evenly among muffin cups. Bake 20-25 minutes or until golden brown. Immediately remove from pan. Yields 12 muffins.

   High altitude: 3500-6500 feet: Heat oven to 425°F (220°C). Decrease brown sugar to ⅓ cup. Bake about 20 minutes.

Approximate nutritional analysis per serving:
Calories 140, Protein 3 g, Carbohydrates 24 g, Fat 4 g,
Cholesterol 0 mg, Sodium 190 mg

QUICK LEMONY BLUEBERRY MUFFINS

¾ tsp (4 ml) McCORMICK or SCHILLING
    Pure Lemon Extract
13 oz package (390 g) blueberry muffin mix

Add lemon extract to blueberry muffin mix and prepare according to package directions. Yields 12 muffins.

Approximate nutritional analysis per serving:
Calories 96, Protein 2 g, Carbohydrates 15 g, Fat 3 g,
Cholesterol 31 mg, Sodium 154 mg

Opposite: Banana Wheat Muffins

BLUEBERRY-LEMON MUFFINS

1 ¾ cups (415 ml) all-purpose flour
⅓ cup (80 ml) sugar
2 ½ tsp (15 ml) baking powder
¾ tsp (4 ml) salt
1 egg, beaten
1 cup (240 ml) DANNON Plain or Lemon
    Lowfat Yogurt
⅓ cup (80 ml) vegetable oil
2 tbs (30 ml) milk
½-1 tsp (3-5 ml) grated lemon peel
¾ cup (180 ml) fresh or frozen blueberries

Preheat oven to 400°F (205°C). Grease muffin cups or line with paper baking cups. In a large bowl combine flour, sugar, baking powder and salt. In a medium bowl combine egg, yogurt, oil, milk and lemon peel; stir well. Add egg mixture all at once to flour mixture. Stir just until dry ingredients are moistened (batter should be lumpy). Gently fold blueberries into batter. Fill prepared muffin cups ⅔ full. Bake 20-25 minutes or until golden and toothpick inserted into center comes out clean. Serve warm. Yields 12 muffins.

Approximate nutritional analysis per serving:
Calories 166, Protein 4 g, Carbohydrates 22 g, Fat 7 g,
Cholesterol 19 mg, Sodium 222 mg

EVER-FRESH BRAN MUFFINS

3 cups (720 ml) whole bran cereal
2 cups (960 ml) buttermilk
1 cup (240 ml) water
½ cup (120 ml) cooking oil
2 eggs, beaten
1 cup (240 ml) brown sugar, packed
1 ½ cups (355 ml) all-purpose flour
2 tsp (10 ml) baking powder
1 tsp (5 ml) baking soda
1 tsp (5 ml) salt
1 ½ cups (355 ml) CALIFORNIA raisins

Place bran cereal in large mixing bowl. Pour in buttermilk, water, oil; stir well. Mix in eggs and brown sugar. Add dry ingredients all at once; stir just enough to combine. Fold in raisins. Store batter in tightly-covered container in refrigerator up to 6 weeks.

To bake muffins, fill greased or paper-lined muffin tins ⅔ full. Bake at 375°F (190°C) for 20-25 minutes. Yields 30 muffins.

Approximate nutritional analysis per serving:
Calories 137, Protein 3 g, Carbohydrates 25 g, Fat 4 g ,
Cholesterol 15 mg, Sodium 242 mg

Above: Blueberry-Lemon Muffins

BLUEBERRY-STREUSEL MUFFINS

MUFFINS:
1½ cups (355 ml) QUAKER Toasted Oatmeal
Cereal, any flavor
1 - 8 oz carton (240 g) plain nonfat yogurt
1 tsp (5 ml) grated lemon peel
2 egg whites *or* 1 egg, slightly beaten
2 tbs (30 ml) vegetable oil
1¼ cups (295 ml) all-purpose flour
⅓ cup (80 ml) sugar
1 tbs (15 ml) baking powder
¼ tsp (1 ml) salt, optional
½ cup (120 ml) fresh or frozen blueberries

STREUSEL TOPPING:
¼ cup (60 ml) QUAKER Toasted Oatmeal
    Cereal, any flavor
¼ cup (60 ml) all-purpose flour
¼ cup 960 ml) sugar
2 tbs (30 ml) margarine, chilled

Heat oven to 400°F (205°C). Line 12 muffin cups with paper baking cups or spray bottoms only with non-stick cooking spray. For muffins, combine cereal, yogurt and lemon peel; let stand 5 minutes or until cereal has softened. Add egg whites and oil; mix well. Add combined remaining ingredients, mixing just until dry ingredients are moistened. Fill prepared muffin cups almost full. For streusel topping, combine dry ingredients; cut in margarine until mixture is crumbly. Sprinkle evenly over batter, patting gently. Bake 20-25 minutes or until golden brown. Yields 12 muffins.

Note: To freeze, wrap muffins securely in foil or place in freezer bag. Seal, label and freeze. To reheat frozen muffins, unwrap; microwave at HIGH about 30 seconds for each muffin.

Approximate nutritional analysis per serving:
Calories 170, Protein 4 g, Carbohydrates 30 g, Fat 5 g,
Cholesterol 0 mg, Sodium 200 mg

MICHIGAN DRIED-BLUEBERRY MUFFINS WITH STREUSEL TOPPING

STREUSEL TOPPING:
½ cup (120 ml) sugar
1 tsp (5 ml) grated lemon peel
¼ cup (60 ml) flour
2 tbs (30 ml) butter or margarine, cold

MUFFINS:
¼ cup (60 ml) butter or margarine
¼ cup (60 ml) vegetable oil
¾ cup (180 ml) milk
⅔ cup (160 ml) MICHIGAN Dried Blueberries
2 cups (480 ml) flour
¾ cup (180 ml) milk
⅔ cup (180 ml) sugar
1 tbs (15 ml) baking powder

For streusel topping, vigorously mix grated lemon peel with sugar to release lemon oils. Add flour and mix well. Add butter or margarine and blend with pastry blender or two knives until mixture resembles coarse meal. Set aside.

For muffins, place butter or margarine, oil, milk and MICHIGAN Dried Blueberries in a microwave safe bowl. Heat 1½ minutes in microwave on HIGH; butter or margarine should be melted and the mixture warm. Set aside.

Prepare muffin tins by greasing or lining with cupcake papers. Mix together flour, sugar and baking powder in a large mixing bowl; add warm butter and milk mixture. Mix all ingredients just until blended. Spoon batter into prepared muffin tins.

Sprinkle with 1 tsp streusel topping on each muffin and bake in preheated 400°F (205°C) oven for 20 minutes. Remove from pan and cool on rack. Yields 12 muffins.

Approximate nutritional analysis per serving:
Calories 271, Protein 3 g, Carbohydrates 41 g, Fat 11 g,
Cholesterol 18 mg, Sodium 149 mg

Courtesy of Traverse Bay Fruit Co.

HAZELNUT, ORANGE & YOGURT MUFFINS

TOPPING:
2 tbs (30 ml) granulated sugar
2 tbs (30 ml) OREGON Hazelnuts,
    roasted and finely chopped
¼ tsp (1 ml) ground cinnamon
¼ tsp (1 ml) ground nutmeg

MUFFINS:
1 ¾ cup (415 ml) all-purpose white flour
½ cup (120 ml) granulated sugar
1 ¼ tsp (6 ml) baking powder
½ tsp (3 ml) baking soda
½ tsp (3 ml) salt
⅛ tsp (.5 ml) ground nutmeg
½ cup (120 ml) OREGON Hazelnuts,
    roasted and chopped
1 large egg
½ cup (120 ml) vegetable oil
½ cup (120 ml) plain yogurt
⅓ cup (80 ml) orange juice concentrate
½ cup (120 ml) raisins

In small bowl, mix topping ingredients until well blended. Set aside. In small mixing bowl, whisk together flour, sugar, baking powder, baking soda, salt and nutmeg. Stir in hazelnut and set aside. In large mixing bowl, whisk egg until blended. Add vegetable oil, yogurt and orange juice concentrate. Whisk until smooth. Add dry ingredients, all at once, stirring just until flour is evenly moistened. Mix in raisins.

    Prepare 1 standard-size muffin tin or 3 miniature muffin tins by generously spraying with non-stick spray, or by placing liners in cups. Divide batter evenly among prepared pans, filling each cup a generous ¾ full. Sprinkle each muffin lightly with topping mixture. Bake in 400°F (205°C) oven for about 18 minutes for the standard-sized muffins, or about 12 minutes for the miniature muffins, or until golden brown. Remove from oven and cool 5 minutes before removing from tins. Cool on racks. Yields 12 standard-sized or 36 miniature muffins.

Approximate nutritional analysis per standard sized muffin:
Calories 268, Protein 4 g, Carbohydrates 34 g, Fat 14 g,
Cholesterol 18 mg, Sodium 82 mg

MULTIGRAIN CHEESE MUFFINS

⅓ cup (800 ml) cooking oil
2 eggs
3 tbs (45 ml) sugar
1 cup (240 ml) milk
1 ½ cups (355 ml) all-purpose flour
½ cup (120 ml) rye flour or cornmeal
2 tsp (10 ml) baking powder
½ tsp (3 ml) baking soda
½ tsp (3 ml) salt
¾ cup (180 ml) NATURAL Raisins
6 oz (180 g) sharp cheddar or Provolone cheese,
    coarsely shredded

In mixing bowl whisk together cooking oil, eggs, sugar; whisk in milk. In another bowl, stir together dry ingredients; stir into liquid mixture until almost blended. Stir in raisins and cheese, just to distribute and finish mixing the batter. Fill paper-lined custard cups or microwave cupcaker about ⅔ full. If using custard cups, arrange 6 in microwave in a circle. Microwave for 2 minutes on Medium - High (70%); rotate a quarter turn and microwave 2-3 minutes longer at Medium High. Muffins are baked when tops and edges are moist, but dry beneath when touched with fingertips. Tops will dry within seconds. Yields 18 muffins.

Approximate nutritional analysis per serving:
Calories 158, Protein 5 g, Carbohydrates 18 g, Fat 8 g,
Cholesterol 33 mg, Sodium 186 mg

CHEDDAR BISCUITS

2 ¼ cups (540 ml) buttermilk baking mix
1 ½ tsp (8 ml) McCORMICK or SCHILLING
    Butter Flavor
½ cup (120 ml) cheddar cheese, grated
1 ½ tsp (8 ml) McCORMICK or SCHILLING
    Parsley Flakes

Prepare biscuits according to package directions adding butter flavor, cheese and parsley. Bake according to package directions. Yields 12 biscuits.

Approximate nutritional analysis per serving:
Calories 80, Protein 3 g, Carbohydrates 10 g, Fat 3 g,
Cholesterol 5 mg, Sodium 213 mg

NEWTON GINGERBREAD MUFFIN

2½ cups (590 ml) all-purpose flour
1 cup (240 ml) light molasses
¾ cup (180 ml) buttermilk
½ cup (120 ml) FLEISCHMANN'S margarine,
    softened
⅓ cup (80 ml) sugar
¼ cup (960 ml) EGG BEATERS real egg product
2 tsp (10 ml) baking soda
1 tsp (5 ml) ground cinnamon
½ tsp (3 ml) ground ginger
¼ tsp (1 ml) ground cloves
12 Fat Free FIG NEWTONS Fruit Chewy Cookies
confectioner's sugar, optional

In large bowl, with electric mixer at low speed, blend first 10 ingredients until moistened; scrape down bottom and side of bowl. Beat at medium speed for 3 minutes. Stir in cookie pieces. Spoon N cup batter into each of 24 paper lined 2½-inch muffin pan cups. Bake at 400°F (205°C) for 18-20 minutes or until toothpick comes out clean. Cool in pan on wire rack for 10 minutes. Remove from pan to cool completely on wire rack. To serve, dust with confectioner's sugar if desired. Yields 24 muffins.

Approximate nutritional analysis per serving:
Calories 169, Protein 2 g, Carbohydrates 26 g, Fat 4 g,
Cholesterol 0 mg, Sodium 202 mg

PUMPKIN SPICE MUFFINS

2 cups (480 ml) sugar
½ cup (120 ml) vegetable oil
3 eggs
1½ cups (355 ml) canned pumpkin
½ cup (120 ml) water
3 cups (720 ml) bread flour
1½ tsp (8 ml) baking powder
1 tsp (5 ml) *each*, baking soda and salt
¾ tsp (4 ml) cinnamon
½ tsp (3 ml) each nutmeg and ground cloves
1½ cups (355 ml) raisins
1 cup (240 ml) walnuts, coarsely chopped

In large bowl, mix sugar, oil, eggs, pumpkin and water to blend thoroughly. In another bowl combine flour, baking powder, baking soda, salt and spices; sift into pumpkin mixture. Mix to blend thoroughly. Fold in raisins and walnuts. Let stand 1 hour at room temperature. With ⅓ cup measure, portion into greased 2¾-inch muffin tin cups. Bake in preheated 400°F (205°C) oven 15-20 minutes until springy to the touch. Cool slightly on racks. Serve warm. Completely cooled muffins can be wrapped and frozen. Reheat, loosely wrapped, in aluminum foil in moderate oven. Yields 24 muffins.

Approximate nutritional analysis per serving:
Calories 235, Protein 4 g, Carbohydrates 38 g, Fat 9 g,
Cholesterol 27 mg, Sodium 154 mg

Above: Pumpkin Spice Muffins

ORANGEY SUNSHINE MUFFINS

4 tbs (60 ml) butter or margarine, softened
¼ cup (60 ml) sugar
1 large egg, completely beaten
1 tsp (5 ml) grated orange peel
½ cup (120 ml) FLORIDA'S NATURAL BRAND
    Orange Juice
1 cup (240 ml) all-purpose flour
1 tsp (5 ml) baking powder
½ tsp (3 ml) salt
¼ tsp (1 ml) baking soda
½ tsp (3 ml) ground ginger
½ cup (120 ml) oat bran

In small bowl, blend butter and sugar. Add egg, grated orange peel and FLORIDA'S NATURAL BRAND Orange Juice; blend thoroughly. In a separate bowl, stir together flour, baking powder, salt, baking soda, ginger and oat bran. Make a well in center of flour mixture; add liquid ingredients all at once, stir just to moisten. Spoon into well-greased 2½-inch muffin cups, filling each ⅔ full.

Bake in a 375°F (190°C) oven for about 20 minutes or until browned and top springs back when lightly touched. Yields 12 muffins.

Approximate nutritional analysis per serving:
Calories 109, Protein 2 g, Carbohydrates 16 g, Fat 5 g,
Cholesterol 28 mg, Sodium 178 mg

BROWN BAG PEACH MUFFINS

1½ cups (355 ml) all-purpose flour
¾ tsp (4 ml) slat
½ tsp (3 ml) baking soda
1 cup (240 ml) IMPERIAL Granulated Sugar
2 eggs, well beaten
½ cup (120 ml) salad oil
½ tsp (3 ml) vanilla
⅛ tsp (.5 ml) almond extract
1¼ cups (295 ml) fresh or drained canned peaches,
    coarsely chopped
½ cup (120 ml) almonds, chopped

Combine flour, salt, baking soda, and IMPERIAL Granulated Sugar. Make well in center of dry ingredients. Add eggs, oil, vanilla and almond extract. Stir only until dry ingredients are moistened. Stir in peaches and nuts. Measure ⅓ cup batter into each cavity of greased muffin tin. Bake in preheated oven at 350°F (180°C) for 20-25 minutes, or until muffins test done. Yields 12 muffins.

Approximate nutritional analysis per serving:
Calories 253, Protein 4 g, Carbohydrates 32 g, Fat 13 g,
Cholesterol 35 mg, Sodium 179 mg

SWEET POTATO MUFFINS

¾ cup (180 ml) oat bran
¾ cup (180 ml) whole wheat flour
⅔ cup (160 ml) granulated sugar
1½ tsp (8 ml) ground cinnamon
1 tsp (5 ml) baking powder
1 tsp (5 ml) baking soda
⅛ tsp (.5 ml) salt
½ cup (120 ml) apples, skinless and finely chopped
1 cup (240 ml) sweet potatoes, baked and
    mashed or canned
1 egg, large
2 egg whites, large
3 tbs (45 ml) canola oil
⅔ cup (160 ml) lowfat plain yogurt
1 cup (240 ml) raisins, optional

Preheat oven to 350°F (180°C). In bowl, combine bran, flour, sugar, cinnamon, baking powder, baking soda, salt and apples. Add sweet potatoes, egg, egg whites, oil and yogurt. Stir all ingredients thoroughly. Spray muffin tins with vegetable cooking spray. Spoon ¼ cup or batter per muffin. Yields 20 muffins.

Approximate nutritional analysis per serving:
Calories 92, Protein 3 g, Carbohydrates 16 g, Fat 3 g,
Cholesterol 11 mg, Sodium 94 mg

Courtesy of Louisiana Sweet Potatoes.

GOLDEN YAM BISCUITS

2 cups (480 ml) sifted flour
3 tsp (15 ml) baking powder
1 tsp (5 ml) salt
4 tbs (60 ml) shortening
½ cup (120 ml) raw LOUISIANA Yams, grated
¾ cup (180 ml) milk

Sift flour, baking powder and salt together. Using two knives or pastry blender, cut in shortening until it is the size of small peas. Stir in grated yams. Add milk to make a soft dough, stirring only enough to moisten dry ingredients. Turn out on a lightly floured board and knead lightly for 30 seconds. Roll or pat out to 1 inch thickness; cut with a cookie cutter or cut in squares with a knife. Bake on baking sheet in hot oven, 450°F (230°C), for 10-12 minutes. Serve hot. Yields 12 biscuits.

Approximate nutritional analysis per serving:
Calories 131, Protein 3 g, Carbohydrates 19 g, Fat 5 g,
Cholesterol 2 mg, Sodium 268 mg

Tea-Time Raisin Scones

GOLDEN DOOR YOGURT-BRAN MUFFINS

1 ½ cups (355 ml) wheat bran
½ cup (120 ml) boiling water
1 ⅓ cups (320 ml) whole wheat flour
1 ¼ tsp (6 ml) baking soda
½ tsp (3 ml) ground cinnamon
¼ tsp (1 ml) salt
¼ tsp (1 ml) ground cloves
¼ tsp (1 ml) ground nutmeg
1 egg
⅓ cup (80 ml) honey
½ cup (120 ml) DANNON Plain Nonfat or
    Lowfat Yogurt
3 tbs (45 ml) vegetable oil
¾ cup (180 ml) fresh or frozen blueberries

Preheat oven to 350°F (180°C). Line muffin cups with paper
baking cups. In a medium bowl combine wheat bran and
boiling water; let stand 10 minutes to soften.

In a large bowl combine flour, baking soda, cinnamon,
salt, cloves and nutmeg. In a small bowl combine egg, honey,
yogurt and oil; stir well. Add to bran mixture.

Add egg mixture all at once to flour mixture; stir just until
dry ingredients are moistened. Batter will be stiff. Fold in
blueberries.

Fill prepared muffin cups ⅔ full. Bake 20-25 minutes or
until toothpick inserted into center comes out clean. Serve
warm. Yields 12.

Approximate nutritional analysis per serving:
Calories 137, Protein 4 g, Carbohydrates 24 g, Fat 5 g,
Cholesterol 18 mg, Sodium 144 mg

TEA-TIME RAISIN SCONES

2 cups (480 ml) flour
2 tbs (30 ml) sugar
2 tsp (10 ml) baking powder
½ tsp (3 ml) baking soda
½ tsp (3 ml) salt
finely grated peel of 1 lemon
½ cup (120 ml) butter, cut into chunks
1 cup (240 ml) walnuts, chopped
½ cup (120 ml) CALIFORNIA raisins
¾ cup (180 ml) buttermilk
additional buttermilk and sugar

In large bowl combine flour, sugar, baking powder, baking
soda, salt and lemon peel. With pastry blender or 2 knives, cut
in butter until mixture resembles coarse meal. Mix in nuts and
raisins, then stir in buttermilk with fork. Gather into ball and
knead for about 2 minutes on lightly floured board. Roll or pat
out ¾ inch thick. Cut into 3-inch triangles. Place, spaced
1 inch apart, on greased baking sheet. Brush tops with buttermilk; sprinkle with sugar. Bake in center of 425°F (220°C) oven
about 15 minutes until lightly browned. Serve warm.
Yields 16 scones.

Approximate nutritional analysis per serving:
Calories 181, Protein 3 g, Carbohydrates 19 g, Fat 11 g,
Cholesterol 16 mg, Sodium 139 mg

Courtesy of The California Raisin Advisory Board.

DRIED BLUEBERRY-ORANGE SCONES

½ cup (120 ml) dried blueberries
½ cup (120 ml) boiling water
2 cups (480 ml) all-purpose flour
2 tsp (10 ml) baking powder
¼ tsp (1 ml) salt
¼ cup (60 ml) sugar
¼ cup (½ stick) (60 ml) butter, chilled
1 egg
¼ cup (60 ml) buttermilk
¼ cup (60 ml) orange juice
1 tsp (5 ml) grated orange peel , optional
1 egg white, slightly beaten
1 tbs (15 ml) sugar

Preheat oven to 425°F (220°C). In small bowl pour the boiling water over the dried blueberries; let stand 5 minutes. Drain. In a large mixing bowl combine the flour, baking powder, salt and ¼ cup sugar. Using a pastry blender or two knives work in the butter until it resembles coarse meal. Mix together the egg, buttermilk and orange juice. Add to the flour mixture with the orange peel and the dried blueberries, stirring just until moistened. Turn the dough onto a floured surface and knead until smooth, about 2 minutes. Roll out the dough until it is ½ inch thick. Cut out the scones using a 3-inch round cookie cutter. Place them on a greased baking sheet. Brush with the egg white and sprinkle with the 1 tbs sugar. Bake in the center of the oven until lightly golden, 12-15 minutes. Serve warm with butter and honey. Yield 12 scones.

Approximate nutritional analysis per serving:
Calories 146, Protein 3 g, Carbohydrates 23 g, Fat 5 g,
Cholesterol 28 mg, Sodium 154 mg

Courtesy of the Traverse Bay Fruit Co.

Golden Cream Biscuits

HAZELNUT POTATO BISCUITS

½ lb (120 g) butter
2 cups (480 ml) flour
3 tsp (15 ml) baking powder
¼ tsp (1 ml) garlic powder
½ tsp (3 ml) salt
1 tsp (5 ml) pepper, coarsely ground
1 cup (240 ml) mashed potatoes
¾ cup (180 ml) hazelnuts, chopped
1 egg yolk mixed with 1 tsp (5 ml) water

Blend butter, flour, baking powder, garlic, salt and pepper to form crumbly mixture. Add potatoes and mix quickly. Mix in hazelnuts. After a few minutes, roll dough onto a floured board, fold once and chill for 20 minutes. Knead, roll and chill 3 more times. Heat oven to 375°F (190°C). Roll out dough to 1 inch thick. Cut into 1½-inch rounds. Criss-cross top of biscuits with knife blade, then brush with egg yolk and water mixture. Place on greased baking sheet and bake for 20-25 minutes. Biscuits are done when they are shiny gold. Serve with red wine, cocktails or a hearty soup. Serves 12.

Approximate nutritional analysis per serving:
Calories 272, Protein 4 g, Carbohydrates 20 g, Fat 21 g,
Cholesterol 59 mg, Sodium 329 mg

GOLDEN CREAM BISCUITS

2 cups (480 ml) flour
½ cup (120 ml) golden raisins
1 tbs (15 ml) baking powder
2 tsp (10 ml) sugar
1 tsp (5 ml) salt
1 cup (240 ml) whipping cream
butter or margarine, melted, as needed

In mixing bowl combine flour, raisins, baking powder, sugar and salt. Stir in cream with a fork, mixing just until moistened. Knead dough 8-10 times on floured surface. Roll out to ½ inch thickness; cut into rounds with 1½-inch biscuit cutter. Dip biscuits in melted butter to coat; place on baking sheet. Bake in 425°F (220°C) oven about 10 minutes, until golden brown. Serve warm. Yields 2 dozen biscuits.

Approximate nutritional analysis per serving:
Calories 91, Protein 1 g, Carbohydrates 11 g, Fat 5 g,
Cholesterol 15 mg, Sodium 148 mg

ROLLED HERB BISCUITS

2 cups (480 ml) BISQUICK Reduced Fat Baking Mix
¾ cup (180 ml) milk
1 tbs (15 ml) Parmesan cheese, grated
2 tsp (10 ml) parsley flakes
1 tsp (5 ml) instant minced onion
¼ tsp (1 ml) dried dill weed
    or ½ tsp (3 ml) Italian seasoning

Heat oven to 450°F (230°C). Mix all ingredients just until soft dough forms. If dough is too sticky, gradually mix in enough baking mix - up to 2 tbs - to make dough easier to handle. Turn dough onto surface well dusted with baking mix; gently roll in baking mix to coat. Shape into ball; knead gently 10 times. Roll ½ inch thick. Cut with 2-inch biscuit cutter dipped in baking mix. Place on ungreased cookie sheet. Bake 7-9 minutes or until golden brown. Yields 10 biscuits.

Approximate nutritional analysis per serving:
Calories 140, Protein 4 g, Carbohydrates 23 g, Fat 3 g,
Cholesterol 0 mg, Sodium 410 mg

APPLESAUCE-RAISIN BREAD

1 cup (240 ml) applesauce
1 egg
¼ cup (60 ml) butter or margarine, melted
¼ cup (60 ml) granulated sugar
¼ cup (60 ml) brown sugar, packed
2 cups (480 ml) all-purpose flour
2 tsp (10 ml) baking powder
½ tsp (3 ml) *each* salt, baking soda, cinnamon
    and nutmeg
1 cup (240 ml) raisins
¾ cup (180 ml) walnuts, chopped

Preheat oven to 350°F (180°C). In large bowl mix applesauce and egg. Mix in butter and sugars; set aside. In another bowl combine remaining ingredients except raisins and walnuts. Add flour mixture to applesauce mixture. Mix just until blended. Fold in raisins and walnuts. Turn into greased 9x5-inch loaf pan. Bake about 1 hour until pick inserted into center comes out clean. Cool in pan 6 minutes. Remove to rack to cool completely. Slice to serve. Serves 16.

Approximate nutritional analysis per serving:
Calories 182, Protein 3 g, Carbohydrates 28 g, Fat 7 g,
Cholesterol 21 mg, Sodium 170 mg

Courtesy of The California Raisin Advisory Board.

BANANA BREAD

1¼ cups (295 ml) sugar
¼ cup (60 ml) butter or margarine, softened
3 egg whites
1¼ cups (295 ml) ripe bananas, mashed
    (3-4 medium)
¾ cup (180 ml) YOPLAIT Fat Free Plain or Vanilla
    Yogurt
1 tsp (5 ml) vanilla
2¾ cups (660 ml) GOLD MEDAL All-Purpose Flour
1¼ tsp (6 ml) baking soda
1 tsp (5 ml) salt
1 tsp (5 ml) ground cinnamon
¾ cup (180 ml) pecans or walnuts, chopped

Place oven rack in lowest position. Heat oven to 350°F (180°C). Grease bottom only of 2 loaf pans, 8½x4½x2½ inches or 1 loaf pan 9x5x3 inches. Mix sugar and margarine with spoon in large bowl. Stir in egg whites until well blended. Add bananas, yogurt and vanilla. Beat until smooth. Stir in remaining ingredients except pecans just until moistened. Stir in pecans. Pour into pans.

Bake 8-inch loaves about 1 hour, 9-inch loaf about 1¼ hours or until tooth pick inserted in center comes out clean. Cool 5 minutes Loosen sides of loaves from pans. Cool completely before slicing. Makes 2 loaves.

High altitude: 3500-6500 feet: Heat oven to 375°F (190°C). Decrease sugar to 1 cup and baking soda to 1 tsp. Increase egg whites to 4. Bake 8-inch loaves about 45 minutes, 9-inch loaf 55-60 minutes.

Approximate nutritional analysis per serving:
Calories 70, Protein 1 g, Carbohydrates 12 g, Fat 2 g,
Cholesterol 0 mg, Sodium 90 mg

Banana Bread

BANANA-ORANGE-RAISIN BREAD

BREAD:
2½ cups (590 ml) all purpose flour
¾ cup (180 ml) KRETSCHMER Wheat Germ,
    any flavor
½ cup (120 ml) sugar
2 tsp (10 ml) baking powder
½ tsp (3 ml) baking soda
½ tsp (3 ml) salt, optional
¾ cup (180 ml) raisins or chopped dried figs
1 egg
2 egg whites
⅓ cup (80 ml) vegetable oil
1 cup (240 ml) ripe bananas, mashed (about 2 large)
¾ cup (180 ml) orange juice
2 tsp (10 ml) grated orange peel
1 tsp (5 ml) vanilla

GLAZE:
½ cup (120 ml) powdered sugar
3-4 tsp (15-20 ml) orange juice
½ tsp (3 ml) grated orange peel

Heat oven to 350°F (180 °C). For bread, spray 9x5-inch loaf
pan with non-stick cooking spray. In large bowl combine dry
ingredients and raisins; mix well. In separate bowl, combine
remaining ingredients, mixing well; add to dry ingredients.
Mix just until moistened. Pour into prepared pan. Bake 60-70
minutes or until wooden toothpick inserted in center comes out
clean. Cool 10 minutes; remove from pan. Cool completely on
wire rack.

For glaze, combine powdered sugar, orange juice and
orange peel. Drizzle evenly over loaf. Serves 16.

Approximate nutritional analysis per serving:
Calories 200, Protein 5 g, Carbohydrates 34 g, Fat 6 g,
Cholesterol 15 mg, Sodium 110 mg

ALMOND-BANANA BREAD

2 cups (480 ml) ripe banana purée (4 large bananas)
½ cup (120 ml) vegetable oil
½ cup (120 ml) granulated sugar
½ cup (120 ml) light brown sugar, firmly packed
3 eggs
1 tsp (5 ml) vanilla extract
2 cups (480 ml) flour
1 tsp (5 ml) baking soda
½ tsp (3 ml) baking powder
½ tsp (3 ml) salt
1¼ cups (295 ml) BLUE DIAMOND Chopped
    Natural Almonds, toasted and divided

Beat together first 6 ingredients; reserve. Combine next
4 ingredients; stir into banana mixture. Reserving 2 tbs
almonds for top, stir remaining almonds into batter. Pour
batter into one greased and floured 9x5x3-inch loaf pan or two
8½x4½x2½-inch loaf pans; sprinkle each loaf with remaining
almonds. Bake at 350°F (180°C) for 50 minutes or until
toothpick inserted in center comes out clean. If browning too
quickly, cover tops loosely with foil. Cool in pans 10 minutes;
turn out onto wire rack and cool completely.
Serves 16 per large loaf.

Approximate nutritional analysis per serving:
Calories 248, Protein 5 g, Carbohydrates 33 g, Fat 12 g,
Cholesterol 40 mg, Sodium 143 mg

APRICOT NUT BREAD

1 cup (240 ml) dried apricots, chopped
1 cup (240 ml) IMPERIAL Granulated Sugar
2 tbs (30 ml) shortening
1 egg, well beaten
½ cup (120 ml) orange juice
¼ cup (60 ml) IMPERIAL Granulated Sugar
2 cups (480 ml) all purpose flour
2 tsp (10 ml) baking powder
½ tsp (3 ml) baking soda
1 tsp (5 ml) salt
1 cup (240 ml) chopped nuts

Soak chopped apricots 20 minutes in water to cover. Cream
1 cup IMPERIAL Granulated Sugar, shortening and egg. Stir
in orange juice and ½ cup IMPERIAL Granulated Sugar.
Combine dry ingredients; add to creamed mixture and blend
well. Drain apricots and stir into batter, adding nuts at same
time. Pour into greased and floured 8x4x3-inch loaf pan, Bake
in preheated 350°F (180°C) oven 65 minutes, or until done.
Cool on rack. Serves 12.

Approximate nutritional analysis per serving:
Calories 270, Protein 4 g, Carbohydrates 45 g, Fat 9 g,
Cholesterol 18 mg, Sodium 268 mg

BARBADOS COCONUT BREAD

2½ cups (590 ml) flour
¾ cup (180 ml) sugar
2 tsp (10 ml) baking powder
½ tsp (3 ml) salt
½ tsp (3 ml) McCORMICK or SCHILLING
    Cinnamon
2⅓ cups (560 ml) coconut, shredded
1¼ cups (295 ml) buttermilk
6 tbs (90 ml) butter, melted
1 tsp (5 ml) McCORMICK or SCHILLING
    Pure Vanilla Extract
2 tsp (10 ml) McCORMICK or SCHILLING
    Coconut Extract

Preheat oven to 350°F (180°C). Grease 9x5x3-inch loaf pan.
Sift dry ingredients and put in medium bowl. Toss with 2 cups
of the coconut. Add remaining ingredients, stirring until dry
ingredients are wet. Put in prepared pan and top with remaining ⅓ cup coconut. Press lightly into batter. Bake 55-60
minutes or until tester comes out clean. Serves 16.

Approximate nutritional analysis per serving:
Calories 221, Protein 3 g, Carbohydrates 32 g, Fat 9 g,
Cholesterol 12 mg, Sodium 208 mg

CRANBERRY FRUIT-NUT BREAD

2 cups (480 ml) flour
1 cup (240 ml) sugar
1¼ tsp (6 ml) baking powder
¼ cup (60 ml) shortening
1 tsp (5 ml) grated orange peel
1 egg, beaten
¾ cup (180 ml) orange juice
1 cup (240) cranberries, chopped
½ cup (120 ml) nuts, chopped
½ tsp (3 ml) nutmeg
½ tsp (3 ml) cinnamon

Sift together dry ingredients. Cut in shortening. Combine peel,
juice and egg. Add to dry ingredients, mixing just enough to
moisten. Fold in cranberries and nuts. Turn into greased
9x5x3-inch loaf pan. Bake at 350°F (180°C) for 60 minutes.
Cool, wrap and store overnight before slicing. Serves 16.

Approximate nutritional analysis per serving:
Calories 169, Protein 3 g, Carbohydrates 26 g, Fat 6 g,
Cholesterol 13 mg, Sodium 25 mg

Courtesy of Cape Cod Cranberry Growers' Association.

GRANDMOTHER ADA'S GINGERBREAD

½ cup (120 ml) butter or margarine
½ cup (120 ml) IMPERIAL Granulated Sugar
1 egg, well beaten
1 cup (240 ml) molasses
2½ cups (590 ml) all-purpose flour
½ tsp (3 ml) salt
1 tsp (5 ml) ground cloves
1 tsp (5 ml) ground ginger
1 tsp (5 ml) ground cinnamon
1½ tsp (8 ml) baking soda
1 cup (240 ml) hot water

Cream butter and IMPERIAL Granulated Sugar; add egg and molasses, mixing well. Combine dry ingredients and add to first mixture; add hot water and stir until smooth. Pour into lightly greased and floured 9-inch square pan. Bake in preheated oven at 350°F (180°C) for 35-40 minutes. Serves 9.

Approximate nutritional analysis per serving:
Calories 336, Protein 4 g, Carbohydrates 56 g, Fat 11 g,
Cholesterol 24 mg, Sodium 405 mg

Above: Grandmother Ada's Gingerbread

CRANBERRY ORANGE BREAD

1 cup (240 ml) sugar
4 tbs (60 ml) shortening
1 cup (240 ml) milk
1 egg
1 tsp (5 ml) McCORMICK or SCHILLING
   Pure Vanilla Extract
1 tsp (5 ml) McCORMICK or SCHILLING
   Pure Orange Extract
2 cups (480 ml) flour
3 tsp (15 ml) baking powder
1 tsp (5 ml) salt
1 tsp (5 ml) McCORMICK or SCHILLING Cinnamon
1½ cups (355 ml) cranberries, chopped

Cream sugar and shortening. Add milk, egg and extracts. Beat well. Sift together flour, baking powder, salt and cinnamon. Gradually add to sugar mixture. Pour into greased and floured 9x5x3-inch loaf pan. Bake in 350°F (180°C) oven for 50-60 minutes, or until bread tests done. Serves 16.

Approximate nutritional analysis per serving:
Calories 152, Protein 3 g, Carbohydrates 26 g, Fat 4 g,
Cholesterol 15 mg, Sodium 207 mg

DATED-UP WALNUT LOAF

1 - 8 oz pkg (240 g) pitted dates
1¼ cups (295 ml) boiling water
6 tbs (90 ml) butter or margarine
1½ cups (355 ml) IMPERIAL Brown Sugar
1 egg, beaten
1 cup (240 ml) walnuts, chopped
2¼ cups (540 ml) all-purpose flour
1½ tsp (8 ml) baking soda
1½ tsp (8 ml) salt

Cut dates in fine pieces into medium bowl; add boiling water and stir in butter or margarine and IMPERIAL Brown Sugar. Let cool to room temperature. Stir in egg and nuts. Combine dry ingredients; then stir quickly into date mixture just until blended. Empty into greased, waxed-paper-lined 9x5x3-inch loaf pan; let rest 15 minutes. Bake in preheated 350°F (180°C) oven 70 minutes, or until it tests done. Cool in pan 5 minutes, then turn out on wire rack. Cool before attempting to slice. Keeps for several days. Serves 16.

   Note: Baker's parchment, available in kitchen specialty shops, is even better than waxed paper and can also be used on cookie sheets, muffin tins, etc.

Approximate nutritional analysis per serving:
Calories 266, Protein 3 g, Carbohydrates 44 g, Fat 9 g,
Cholesterol 13 mg, Sodium 346 mg

PRALINE PECAN LOAF

PAN PREPARATION:

2 tbs (30 ml) butter or margarine
¾ cup (180 ml) IMPERIAL Brown Sugar
1 tsp (5 ml) cinnamon
1 cup (240 ml) pecan halves
2 tbs (30 ml) honey
2 tbs (30 ml) water

STREUSEL:

½ cup (120 ml) pecans, chopped
3 tbs (45 ml) butter or margarine, melted
½ cup (120 ml) all-purpose flour
½ cup (120 ml) IMPERIAL Brown Sugar
½ tsp (3 ml) cinnamon

LOAF:

1 pkg dry yeast
¼ cup (60 ml) warm water
2¼ cups (540 ml) all-purpose flour
2 tbs (30 ml) IMPERIAL Granulated Sugar
1¼ tsp (6 ml) cinnamon
2 tsp (10 ml) baking powder
½ tsp (3 ml) salt
⅓ cup (80 ml) butter or margarine
⅓ cup (80 ml) milk, scalded, cooled
1 egg

Pan preparation: Melt butter or margarine, spread on bottom of 9x5x3-inch loaf pan. Sprinkle with IMPERIAL Brown Sugar and cinnamon. Toast pecans in oven and spread over mixture. Combine honey with water and drizzle over pecans. Set pan aside.

   Streusel: Mix all ingredients in bowl. Mixture should be very crumbly. Set aside.

   Dissolve yeast in warm water; set aside. Combine flour, IMPERIAL Granulated Sugar, cinnamon, baking powder and salt in mixing bowl; cut in butter or margarine until mixture resembles fine crumbs. Combine dissolved yeast with milk, beaten egg and stir into crumb mixture and beat well. Knead about 5 minutes on floured surface until dough is no longer sticky. Roll out to 15x10-inch rectangle. Sprinkle with streusel mixture and roll up from short side (like a jelly roll). Cut into three equal pieces and place in loaf pan, cut sides up; press lightly. Cover with oiled plastic wrap and let rise in warm place 1½-2 hours, or until even with top of pan. Bake in preheated 350°F (180°C) oven on middle rack about 30 minutes. Remove from pan on to rack to cool. Serves 8.

Approximate nutritional analysis per serving:
Calories 479, Protein 6 g, Carbohydrates 61 g, Fat 25 g,
Cholesterol 22 mg, Sodium 342 mg

Praline Pecan Loaf

HAZELNUT-LACED CHOCOLATE APRICOT BREAD

1 cup (240 ml) boiling water
1 cup (240 ml) dried apricots
½ tsp (3 ml) baking soda
½ cup (120 ml) sugar
½ cup (120 ml) brown sugar
2 eggs
1¼ cups (295 ml) all-purpose flour
¾ cup (180 ml) whole wheat flour
¾ cup (180 ml) unsweetened cocoa
3 tsp (15 ml) double-acting baking powder
1 cup (240 ml) hazelnuts, chopped

Pour boiling water over apricots and let stand until tender - don't oversoak. Drain off water and reserve (if you don't have 1 cup, add more water to it.) Roughly chop the apricots. Pour liquid into a large mixing bowl. Add baking soda, sugars and eggs. Mix well with a wooden spoon. Add the apricots, all purpose and whole wheat flours, unsweetneed cocoa, baking powder and hazelnuts, then mix again.

Butter and flour two 9x5x3-inch loaf tins. Divide the batter into two equal parts and pour into the tins. Bake in a preheated 350°F (180°C) oven for about 45 minutes - or until breads have risen, are dark in color, and a toothpick or knife pulls out clean when inserted in the center. Cool on racks and serve.
Yields 2 loaves, 16 servings each.

Approximate nutritional analysis per serving:
Calories 92, Protein 2 g, Carbohydrates 16 g, Fat 3 g,
Cholesterol 13 mg, Sodium 64 mg

APRICOT COFFEE CAKE

2 cups (480 ml) BISQUICK Reduced Fat Baking Mix
½ cup (120 ml) sugar
4 egg whites *or*
    ½ cup (120 ml) cholesterol free egg product
¼ cup (60 ml) skim milk
2 tbs (30 ml) margarine, melted
½ tsp (3 ml) ground nutmeg
1 - 8¾ oz can (265 g) apricot halves,
    well-drained and cut into fourths
1 - 15¼ oz can (460 g) crushed pineapple,
    well drained
⅔ cup (160 ml) apricot preserves

Heat oven to 375°F (190°C). Grease 2 round pans, 9x1½ inches. Mix all ingredients except preserves thoroughly. Divide batter between pans. Bake 20-22 minutes or until golden brown; cool completely. Place one layer with top side down on serving plate; spread with ⅓ cup preserves. Top with second layer; spread with remaining preserves. Serves 8.

Approximate nutritional analysis per serving:
Calories 310, Protein 5 g, Carbohydrates 64 g, Fat 5 g,
Cholesterol 0 mg, Sodium 400 mg

HAZELNUT MAPLE BREAD

2 cups (480 ml) all-purpose white flour
2 tsp (10 ml) baking powder
½ tsp (3 ml) salt
½ cup (120 ml) granulated sugar
¼ cup (60 ml) butter or margarine, softened
¼ cup (60 ml) OREGON Hazelnut Butter
2 eggs
¼ cup (60 ml) maple syrup
1 tsp (5 ml) vanilla extract
½ tsp (3 ml) maple extract
½ cup (120 ml) bananas, mashed
¼ cup (60 ml) milk
½ cup (120 ml) OREGON Hazelnuts,
    roasted and coarsely chopped

Sift together flour, baking powder and salt. Reserve. In a 2-quart bowl, cream sugar and butter until smooth. Beat in hazelnut butter, eggs, maple syrup, vanilla and maple extract. Mix in mashed bananas in three additions; alternately mix in the dry ingredients and milk. Fold in chopped hazelnuts. Divide the batter betweeen two greased 7x4x3-inch loaf pans. Bake in a 350°F (180°C) oven for 30-35 minutes, or until golden and toothpick inserted into the center comes out clean. Cool on rack. Yields 2 loaves, 12 servings per loaf.

Approximate nutritional analysis per serving:
Calories 121, Protein 3 g, Carbohydrates 16 g, Fat 5 g,
Cholesterol 23 mg, Sodium 111 mg

LEMON-YOGURT-RAISIN TEA BREAD

1¼ cups (295 ml) all-purpose flour
¾ cup (180 ml) whole wheat flour
4 tbs (60 ml) sugar, divided
2 tsp (10 ml) baking powder
½ tsp (3 ml) baking soda
¼ tsp (1 ml) salt
1½ cups (355 ml) DANNON Lemon Lowfat Yogurt
¼ cup (60 ml) unsalted butter or
    margarine, melted and cooled slightly
1 egg
¾ cup (180 ml) raisins

Preheat oven to 350 °F (180°C). Grease an 8½x4½-inch loaf pan. In a large bowl combine flours, 3 tbs sugar, baking powder, baking soda and salt. In a medium bowl combine yogurt, butter and egg; stir until well blended. Pour yogurt mixture into floured mixture. Add raisins: stir just until dry ingredients are moistened. Pour into prepared pan and smooth top. Sprinkle surface with remaining 1 tbs sugar.

    Bake 40-45 minutes or until lightly brown and toothpick inserted just off center comes out clean. Cool in pan on wire rack 30 minutes. Remove from pan; cool completely, sugared side up. Serves 12.

Approximate nutritional analysis per serving:
Calories 190, Protein 5 g, Carbohydrates 32 g, Fat 5 g,
Cholesterol 35 mg, Sodium 208 mg

PEAR BRAN BREAD

2 - 8 oz cans (480 g) LIBBY'S LITE Pears
2½ cups (590 ml) wheat bran flakes cereal
½ cup (120 ml) oil
½ cup (120 ml) sugar
2 eggs
1 cup (240 ml) *each* whole wheat and
    all-purpose flour
2 tsp (10 ml) baking powder
½ tsp (3 ml) salt
½ cup (120 ml) raisins

Drain pears; finely chop. Combine with bran flakes; let stand 2 minutes. Combine oil and sugar; beat in eggs and pear mixture. Combine flours, baking powder, salt and raisins. Add pear mixture; stir just until moistened. Place in greased 9¼x5x3-inch loaf pan. Bake at 350°F (180°C) about 1 hour or until wooden pick inserted near center comes out clean. Cool on rack 10 minutes; remove from pan and cool completely. Serves 18.

Approximate nutritional analysis per serving:
Calories 179, Protein 4 g, Carbohydrates 30 g, Fat 7 g,
Cholesterol 24 mg, Sodium 240 mg

Opposite: Apricot Coffee Cake

Pear Brunch Cake

PRUNE-ORANGE NUT BREAD

1½ cups (355 ml) prune juice
½ cup (120 ml) orange juice
⅓ cup (80 ml) butter or margarine, softenend
1½ cups (9 oz) (270 g) pitted prunes,
    coarsely chopped
1½ tbs (25 ml) grated orange peel
3 cups (720 ml) flour
¾ cups (180 ml) brown sugar, packed
2 tsp (10 ml) baking soda
dash salt
1 cup (240 ml) walnuts, coarsely chopped
2 eggs, beaten

Preheat oven to 350 °F (180°C). In small saucepan bring prune juice and orange juice to boiling. Pour into large bowl. Stir in butter to melt. Stir in prunes and orange peel; cool to luke-warm. Meanwhile combine flour, sugar, baking soda, salt and nuts in another large bowl. Stir eggs into prune mixture, then add to dry ingredients; mix just to blend thoroughly. Pour into greased 2½-quart soufflé dish or other baking dish. Smooth top. Bake in center of oven about 1 hour, 30 minutes until pick inserted into center comes out clean. Cool in dish 10 minutes. Remove from dish; cool on rack. Slice to serve. Serves 16.

Wrap remainder securely in plastic wrap or foil. This bread is good toasted. Wrap and freeze a portion for later use, if you wish.

Approximate nutritional analysis per serving:
Calories 274, Protein 5 g, Carbohydrates 44 g, Fat 10 g,
Cholesterol 32 mg, Sodium 180 mg

Courtesy of The California Prune Board.

PUMPKIN BREAD

3 cups (720 ml) flour
2 cups (480 ml) sugar
2 tsp (10 ml) baking soda
1½ tsp (8 ml) ground cinnamon
1 tsp (5 ml) ground nutmeg
½ tsp (3 ml) baking powder
½ tsp (3 ml) salt, optional
¼ tsp (1 ml) ground cloves
2 eggs
1 - 16 oz can (480 g) COMSTOCK Pumpkin
⅔ cup (160 ml) oil

Stir together flour, sugar, baking soda, cinnamon, nutmeg, baking powder, salt and cloves in large mixing bowl. Lightly beat eggs. Beat in pumpkin and oil. Add to flour mixture, stirring just to combine. Spoon into two greased 8½x4½x2¾-inch loaf pans. Batter will be stiff. Bake at 350°F (180°C) for 55-60 minutes, or until wooden pick inserted near center comes out clean. Cool 5 minutes; remove from pans. Cool completely and wrap. Freezes well. Yields 2 loaves, 16 servings each.

Approximate nutritional analysis per serving:
Calories 140, Protein 2 g, Carbohydrates 23 g, Fat 5 g,
Cholesterol 13 mg, Sodium 61 mg

HEALTHY PUMPKIN BREAD

⅔ cup (160 ml) sifted soy flour
1 cup (240 ml) sifted all-purpose flour
¼ tsp (1 ml) baking powder
¾ tsp (4 ml) baking soda
1½ tsp (8 ml) cinnamon
½ tsp (3 ml) ground cloves
¼ tsp (1 ml) nutmeg
¾ tsp (4 ml) salt
¼ cup (60 ml) soy oil
1¼ cups (295 ml) sugar
4 egg whites, well beaten
¾ cup (180 ml) pumpkin, canned
2 tbs (30 ml) water

Sift and measure soy flour and all purpose flour. Measure other dry ingredients except sugar, and sift together with flour. Set aside. Cream soy oil and sugar together. Add egg whites and beat until light. Blend in pumpkin and water. Add dry ingredients in two portions, blending well after each addition. Pour batter into greased 9x5x3-inch loaf pan. Bake at 350°F (180°C) for 65-70 minutes. Remove loaf from pan immediately and cool on wire rack. Serves 16.

Approximate nutritional analysis per serving:
Calories 139, Protein 4 g, Carbohydrates 24 g, Fat 4 g,
Cholesterol 0 mg, Sodium 159 mg

GOLDEN-GRAINED TEA BREAD

2 cups (480 ml) graham cracker crumbs
2 cups (480 ml) granola (crush large lumps)
1 cup (240 ml) flour
½ cup (120 ml) whole wheat flour
⅓ cup (80 ml) wheat germ
2 tsp (10 ml) baking soda
½ tsp (3 ml) salt
1 cup (240 ml) raisins *or* Zante currants
2 eggs
1¼ cups (295 ml) buttermilk
⅔ cup (160 ml) cooking oil
½ cup (120 ml) molasses
⅓ cup (80 ml) brown sugar, firmly packed
2 tbs (30 ml) sesame seeds

Mix dry ingredients in a large bowl; stir in raisins. In another bowl, beat together eggs, buttermilk, molasses and brown sugar. Stir into dry ingredients just to blend. Pour into 9x5-inch loaf pan, greased on bottom only. Sprinkle sesame seeds over top of batter. Bake at 325°F (165°C) for 60-70 minutes, or until a pick inserted in the center comes out clean. If loaf browns too quickly while baking, lay a sheet of foil, shiny side up, on top. Cool in pan 10 minutes; remove and cool completely. Wrap and store. Serves 16.

Approximate nutritional analysis per serving:
Calories 357, Protein 7 g, Carbohydrates 48 g, Fat 17 g,
Cholesterol 27 mg, Sodium 295 mg

Courtesy of The California Raisin Advisory Board.

Pumpkin Bread

SWEET POTATO BREAD

3 cups (720 ml) sugar
1 cup (240 ml) cooking oil
4 eggs
3½ cups (840 ml) sifted flour
2 tsp (10 ml) baking soda
½ tsp (3 ml) salt
1 tsp (5 ml) cinnamon
1 tsp (5 ml) nutmeg
⅔ cup (160 ml) water
2 cups (480 ml) cooked sweet potatoes, mashed
1 cup (240 ml) chopped nuts, optional

Combine sugar and oil; beat well. Add eggs and beat. Combine dry ingredients and add to egg mixutre alternately with water. Stir in sweet potatoes and chopped nuts. Pour batter into three greased loaf pans. Bake at 350°F (180°C) for 1 hour.
Yields 3 loaves, 16 servings each.

Approximate nutritional analysis per serving:
Calories 138, Protein 2 g, Carbohydrates 22 g, Fat 5 g,
Cholesterol 18 mg, Sodium 70 mg

Sweet Potato Bread

BANANA-CHIP STREUSEL LOAF

½ cup (120 ml) light brown sugar, firmly packed
⅓ cup (80 ml) FLEISCHMANN'S Margarine,
    softened
1 tsp (5 ml) vanilla extract
2 eggs
2 ripe medium-sized bananas, mashed
1½ cups (355 ml) all-purpose flour
½ cup (120 ml) regular, quick or instant
    CREAM OF WHEAT Cereal
1 tbs (15 ml) baking powder

STREUSEL TOPPING:
1 tbs (15 ml) CREAM OF WHEAT Cereal
1 tbs (15 ml) sugar
1 tbs (15 ml) flour
1 tbs (15 ml) FLEISCHMANN'S Margarine
½ tsp (3 ml) ground cinnamon
¼ cup (60 ml) miniature semisweet chocolate chips

In large bowl, with electric mixer at medium speed, beat sugar and margarine until creamy. Mix in vanilla and eggs. Beat in banana until almost smooth. Combine flour, cereal and baking powder; stir in banana mixture just until moistened. Spread batter into greased and floured 8½x4½x2½-inch loaf pan; sprinkle with streusel topping. Bake at 350°F (180°C) for 50 -60 minutes or until toothpick inserted in center comes out clean. Cool in pan 10 minutes. Cool completely on wire rack. Drizzle with confectioner's sugar glaze if desired. Serves 12.

Streusel topping: combine CREAM OF WHEAT Cereal, sugar and flour; cut in FLEISCHMANN'S Margarine until crumbly. Stir in ground cinnamon and chocolate chips.

Approximate nutritional analysis per serving:
Calories 233, Protein 3 g, Carbohydrates 30 g, Fat 8 g,
Cholesterol 35 mg, Sodium 173 mg

LUNCH

It's a treat to enjoy a sit-down lunch at home. A meal that should be easy-to-prepare and fun-to-eat is a great opportunity to include a few servings of those fruits and vegetables we keep hearing about. Now, to come up with the occasion . . .

SONOMA PITA PIZZAS

1 cup (1½ oz) (45 g) Sonoma Dried Tomatoes
3 tbs (45 ml) olive oil
1 large clove garlic, pressed
4 small pita breads
2 cups (480 ml) mozzarella cheese, shredded
1 - 2 oz can (60 g) anchovy fillets, drained, optional
2-3 tbs (30-45 ml) fresh herbs, chopped (basil,
    rosemary, oregano, parsley, savory)
    or 2-3 tsp (10-15 ml) dried herbs

Preheat oven and baking sheet to 450°F (230°C). In bowl cover tomatoes with boiling water. Let stand 5 minutes; drain. In small bowl combine oil; and garlic. Brush onto sides of breads, reserving about 1 tbs. Cover breads with half the cheese. Arrange the tomatoes, anchovies and herbs over cheese, dividing equally. Top with the remaining cheese; drizzle with the reserved oil. Place in preheated baking sheet. Bake 8-10 minutes just until breads are crisp. Serve immediately. Seves 4.

Approximate nutritional analysis per serving:
Calories 483, Protein 23 g, Carbohydrates 43 g, Fat 25 g,
Cholesterol 57 mg, Sodium 1 g

Courtesy of Timber Crest Farms.

BEST BARBECUE

2 tbs (30 ml) butter
¼ cup (60 ml) onion, chopped
1 cup (240 ml) tomato catsup
¼ cup (60 ml) white vinegar
½ cup (120 ml) dark brown sugar
1 tbs (15 ml) OLD BAY Seasoning
¾ lb (340 g) cooked roast beef, thinly sliced
8 toasted sliced hamburger buns

In a large skillet, melt butter and brown onions. Stir in catsup, vinegar, brown sugar and OLD BAY Seasoning. Cook at low-medium heat until hot. Place roast beef on buns, cover with sauce and serve. Serves 8.

Approximate nutritional analysis per serving:
Calories 357, Protein 17 g, Carbohydrates 45 g, Fat 13 g,
Cholesterol 49 mg, Sodium 689 mg

TURKEY BARBECUE

3 cups (720 ml) NORBEST Cooked Turkey, shredded
1 cup (240 ml) bottled barbecue sauce
½ cup (120 ml) reduced sodium chicken bouillon
1 - 11 oz can (330 ml) corn with red and
    green peppers, drained
4 slices Texas-style bread, toasted

In medium saucepan, over medium-high heat, combine turkey, barbecue sauce, bouillon and corn. Cook 5 minutes or until mixture is heated throughout. To serve, spoon barbecue evenly over each slice of toast. Serves 4.

Approximate nutritional analysis per serving:
Calories 415, Protein 42 g, Carbohydrates 51 g, Fat 4 g,
Cholesterol 94 mg, Sodium 1,250 mg

MEXICAN TURKEY CHILI MAC

1 lb (455 g) NORBEST Ground Turkey
1 - 1¼ oz pkg (4 g) taco seasoning mix
1 - 14½ oz can (435 g) stewed tomatoes
1 - 11 oz can (330 g) corn with red and green
    peppers, undrained
1½ cup (355 ml) cooked elbow macaroni,
    without salt, drained
1 oz (30 g) low-salt corn chips, crushed
½ cup (120 ml) low-fat cheddar, shredded

In large skillet, over medium-high heat, sauté turkey 5-6 minutes or until no longer pink; drain. Stir in taco seasoning, tomatoes, corn and macaroni. Reduce heat to medium and cook 4-5 minutes until heated throughout. Sprinkle corn chips over meat mixture and top with cheese. Cover and heat 1-2 minutes or until cheese is melted. Serves 6.

Approximate nutritional analysis per serving:
Calories 286, Protein 20 g, Carbohydrates 31 g, Fat 10 g,
Cholesterol 62 mg, Sodium 671 mg

Mexican Turkey Chili Mac

MEXICAN BARBECUE BEEF SANDWICHES

3 lbs (1365 g) boneless beef chuck roast
½ cup (120 ml) onion, chopped
2 tsp (10 ml) fresh garlic, minced
1 - 16 oz jar (480 ml) CHI-CHI'S Picante Sauce
4 tsp (20 ml) chili powder
1 tsp (5 ml) sugar
¼ tsp (1 ml) ground red pepper (cayenne)
12 hamburger buns

Heat oven to 325°F (165°C). In Dutch oven, place chuck roast. Sprinkle with onions and garlic. Cover; bake 2½-3 hours or until meat is tender and shreds easily with fork. Remove roast from pan; cool slightly. Set pan and drippings aside. Shred roast with fork, removing any fat. In pan with drippings, place shredded roast and remaining ingredients *except* hamburger buns. Cook over medium heat, stirring occasionally, until beef mixture is heated through.Serve on buns. Serves 12.

Approximate nutritional analysis per serving:
Calories 300, Protein 29 g, Carbohydrates 25 g, Fat 9 g,
Cholesterol 80 mg, Sodium 520 mg

OLD BAY TURKEY CAKES

1 egg, slightly beaten
1 heaping tbs (15 ml) mayonnaise
2 tsp (10 ml) cracked black pepper
2 tsp (10 ml) OLD BAY Seasoning
⅓ cup (80 ml) Italian seasoned bread crumbs
2 green onions, finely chopped
1 lb (455 g) cooked turkey meat (white works best), chopped
3-4 tbs (45-60 ml) butter

In a small mixing bowl, combine all ingredients except turkey and butter. After ingredients are thoroughly combined, gently stir in turkey. Form into 4-5 turkey cakes. Sauté in butter over medium heat until browned on both sides. Serves 2.

Note: The turkey cakes can be made ahead and frozen. There's no need to defrost them before cooking.

Approximate nutritional analysis per serving:
Calories 632, Protein 74 g, Carbohydrates 16 g, Fat 29 g,
Cholesterol 357 mg, Sodium 540 mg

POTACOS

9 baking potatoes
Chef Paul Prudhomme's MEAT MAGIC
1 - 12 oz container (360 g) cottage cheese
1 tbs (15 ml) apple cider vinegar

SEASONING MIX:
1½ tsp (8 ml) ground cumin
¾ tsp (4 ml) dried leaf oregano
1½ tsp (8 ml) dried leaf cilantro
¾ tsp (4 ml) ground cinnamon
¼ tsp (1 ml) nutmeg
1 tsp (5 ml) salt

FILLING:
1½ cups (355 ml) onions, chopped
1 cup (240 ml) celery, chopped
1½ cups (355 ml) green bell peppers, chopped
2 tbs (30 ml) Chef Paul Prudhomme's
    POULTRY MAGIC
1 tbs (15 ml) fresh garlic, minced
3 cups (720 ml) chicken stock, defatted, in all
1 lb (455 g) very lean ground turkey
1 tbs (15 ml) ground roasted Ultimo chili peppers*
1 tbs (15 ml) ground roasted CALIFORNIA
    beauty chili peppers*
4 tbs (60 ml) yellow cornmeal
½ cup (120 ml) canned green chilies,
    chopped shredded lettuce
1 cup plus 2 tbs (270 ml) tomatoes, finely chopped
9 tbs (135 ml) onions, finely chopped
6 tbs (90 ml) low-moisture part-skim
    mozzarella cheese

*These are the chili powders we used; you can use whatever is available in your area. If you can't find roasted chili peppers, substitute 2 tbs (30 ml) commercial chili powder.

Preheat oven to 375°F (190°C). Rinse and cut potatoes in half lengthwise, then cut a small slice off the bottom of each half. Place the potatoes on a baking sheet in oven for 1 hour, or until brown, and the potato comes easily out of the skin. Let cool at least ½ hour. Using a sharp knife, cut the insides of the potato away from the skin (save for another use), leaving as thin a shell as you can without leaving holes. (This may take a little practice.) Sprinkle potato shells with a little MEAT MAGIC and put back in the oven for about 15-20 minutes, or until skins are brown and crisp.

Combine seasoning mix ingredients thoroughly in a small bowl.

To make mock sour cream, place cottage cheese in blender and process until smooth. Add vinegar and process again until completely blended.

To make the filling, preheat a large heavy skillet over high heat. Add 1½ cups chopped onions, the chopped celery and green bell peppers, and cook 2 minutes. Add POULTRY MAGIC and the seasoning mix and cook 4 minutes, stirring once to distribute the seasoning evenly. Add the minced garlic and ½ cup stock. Scrape the bottom and cook 9 minutes, stirring occasionally. Push the cooked vegetables to the edges of the skillet, making a clearing in the center. Add the chopped turkey to the center of the skillet and cook 9 minutes, breaking the meat up with a wooden spoon, turning occasionally to brown it evenly and eventually incorporating it into the vegetable mixture. Add the chili powders and the cornmeal and cook 2 minutes, scraping the bottom of the pan, because the cornmeal will stick and form a brown crust. Add ½ cup stock, scrape the bottom well and spread the turkey mixture over the bottom of the skillet. Stir occasionally and cook 3 minutes, or until the mixture is sticking hard. Add 1 cup stock, scrape the bottom well and cook 3 minutes. Stir in the chopped chilies and cook 2 minutes. Add ½ cup stock, stir well and cook 5 minutes. Add the remaining ½ cup stock and cook 8 minutes, stirring and scraping the bottom well as the mixture sticks. Remove from heat.

Place crisp potato shells on a baking sheet. Line the bottom of each with a little shredded lettuce. Add 1 tsp chopped tomatoes and ½ tbs finely chopped onions. Fill 2 tbs meat mixture and top with ⅓ tbs shredded mozzarella. Place baking sheet under preheated broiler about 1 minute or until cheese is brown and bubbly. Garnish with 1½ tbs mock sour cream. Serves 18.

Approximate nutritional analysis per serving:
Calories 226, Protein 14 g, Carbohydrates 32 g, Fat 5 g,
Cholesterol 21 mg, Sodium 439 mg

BAKED POTATO LUNCH

Top a baked potato with LIGHT & LEAN 97 ham or turkey cuts, a little low fat cheese, your favorite vegetables and a dollop of light sour cream for a healthy satisfying meal. Add chives or parsley for some extra color and zest.

BAKED HAM AND CHEESE SANDWICHES

16 slices whole wheat bread
8 slices HEALTHY CHOICE Deli Thin-Sliced
   Smoked Ham
8 slices HEALTHY CHOICE Fat Free Pasteurized
   Process Cheese Singles Product
¾ cup (180 ml) HEALTHY CHOICE Cholesterol
   Free Egg Product
2½ cup (590 ml) skim milk
2 tbs (30 ml) Dijon mustard
¼ tsp (1 ml) cracked black pepper

Heat oven to 350°F (180°C). Arrange bread slices in 13x9-inch baking pan sprayed with non-stick cooking spray. Cover each bread slice with one ham slice, one cheese slice and second slice of bread. Combine egg product, milk, mustard and pepper; mix well. Pour over bread. Bake 35 minutes or until knife inserted in center comes out clean. Serves 8.

Approximate nutritional analysis per serving:
Calories 223, Protein 17 g, Carbohydrates 32 g, Fat 4 g,
Cholesterol 10 mg, Sodium 833 mg

Baked Ham and Cheese Sandwiches

ARIZONA MONTE CARLO SANDWICHES

3 tbs (60 ml) butter or margarine
3 large eggs
1 cup (240 ml) low fat milk
8 slices whole wheat bread
1 - 4¼ oz can CHI-CHI'S Whole Green Chilies,
   each cut in half lengthwise
4 thin slices smoked ham
1 small avocado, sliced
1½ cup (355 ml) Colby cheese, shredded
CHI-CHI'S Salsa, if desired

Heat oven to 400°F (205°C). Place butter in rimmed 15x10x1-inch baking pan. Heat in oven until butter is melted. In shallow dish, beat eggs and milk. Dip 4 slices of bread in egg mixture, coating both sides. Arrange slices on top of butter in baking pan. Top bread evenly with chilies, ham, avocado and cheese. Dip remaining 4 slices bread into egg mixture, coating both sides. Place on top of sandwiches. Bake 8-15 minutes or until sandwiches begin to brown. Turn sandwiches over using wide spatula. Bake 10 more minutes or until puffed and browned. Cut and serve with salsa, if desired. Serves 4.

Approximate nutritional analysis per serving:
Calories 560, Protein 27 g, Carbohydrates 34 g, Fat 37 g,
Cholesterol 235 mg, Sodium 860 mg

SOUTHWEST PICNIC LOAF

GREEN CHILI SPREAD:
1 - 4¼ oz can (130 g) CHI-CHI'S Whole Green Chilies
½ cup (120 ml) Parmesan cheese, grated
⅓ cup (80 ml) walnuts
⅓ cup (80 ml) parsley, tightly packed
2 cloves garlic
1 tbs (15 ml) chicken broth or water
salt

SANDWICH:
½ cup (120 ml) mayonnaise
⅓ cup (80 ml) CHI-CHI'S Salsa
1 - 1 lb oblong loaf (455 g) sourdough French bread
½ small cucumber, sliced
6 oz (180 g) mesquite-smoked turkey, thinly sliced
2 small tomatoes, sliced
1¼ cups (295 ml) Muenster cheese, shredded
4 slices red onion
¼ cup (60 ml) green chili spread (above)

Prepare green chili spread in food processor bowl fitted with metal blade. Process all ingredients *except* salt until smooth. Add salt to taste. Reserve ¼ cup; refrigerate remaining spread to be used later on hot pasta or rice or spread on other sandwiches.

Heat oven to 350°F (180°C). In small bowl, combine mayonnaise and salsa; set aside. Slice off top third of bread loaf to create lid. Remove bread from top and bottom of loaf leaving a ½-inch shell.* Spread ½ cup salsa - mayonnaise mixture inside of loaf on the bottom. Layer cucumbers, turkey, tomatoes, cheese and red onion inside loaf. Spread reserved ¼ cup green chili spread on underside of bread lid; place on top of loaf. Wrap in aluminum foil; place on ungreased baking sheet. Bake 20-25 minutes or until heated through and cheese is melted. Let stand 5 minutes. Cut into thick slices. Serve with remaining salsa - mayonnaise. Serves 6.

* Freeze bread removed from loaf to use for stuffings or bread crumbs.

Approximate nutritional analysis per serving:
Calories 370, Protein 18 g, Carbohydrates 16 g, Fat 26 g, Cholesterol 60 mg, Sodium 580 mg

PICNIC PERFECT PITA

2 cups (480 ml) spinach leaves, sliced
1 cup (240 ml) sweet red pepper, thinly sliced
1 cup (240 ml) carrots, grated
¼ cup (60 ml) green onion with top, thinly sliced
3 tbs (45 ml) plain nonfat yogurt
3 tbs (45 ml) commercial 91% fat-free ranch-style salad dressing
¼ tsp (1 ml) dried dill weed
¼ cup (2 oz) (60 g) reduced fat mozzarella cheese shredded
3 small whole wheat pita bread rounds, in half
1 - 6 oz pkg (180 g) HEALTHY CHOICE Deli Thin Sliced Turkey, Ham or Bologna

Combine first 7 ingredients; mix well. Cover and chill. Just before serving, stir in cheese. Line pita halves evenly with meat slices. Spoon salad mixture evenly in pita halves, serve immediately. Serves 6.

Approximate nutritional analysis per serving: Calories 136, Protein 6 g, Fat 3 g, Cholesterol 19 mg, Sodium 544 mg

HEARTY TUNA MELTS

1 - 6⅛ oz can (185 g) water-packed tuna, flaked
⅓ cup (80 ml) fat-free mayonnaise
½ cup (120 ml) celery
⅓ cup (80 ml) green pepper, chopped
2 tbs (30 ml) ripe olives, chopped
¼ tsp (1 ml) crushed dried thyme
6 slice dark rye bread
6 slices HEALTHY CHOICE Fat Free Pasteurized Process Cheese Singles Product

Heat oven to 350°F (180°C). Combine tuna, mayonnaise, celery, green pepper, olives and thyme; mix lightly. For each sandwich, top bread slice with ¼ cup tuna mixture; cover with slice of cheese. Bake 10 minutes or broil until cheese melts. Serves 6.

Approximate nutritional analysis per serving:
Calories 139, Protein 13 g, Carbohydrates 18 g, Fat 2 g, Cholesterol 17 mg, Sodium 637 mg

Opposite: Picnic Perfect Pita

TURKEY PASTRAMI SANDWICH ON IRISH SODA BREAD

IRISH SODA BREAD:
2 cups (480 ml) unsifted flour
1½ tsp (8 ml) baking powder
¾ tsp (4 ml) salt
¼ tsp (1 ml) baking soda
1 cup (240 ml) nonfat buttermilk
vegetable cooking spray

SANDWICH:
1 - 8-inch loaf Irish soda bread
8 oz (240 g) nonfat Thousand Island dressing
4 cups (960 ml) packaged coleslaw mix, divided
½ lb (230 g) NORBEST Turkey Pastrami, thinly sliced

In medium bowl combine flour, baking powder, salt and baking soda. Add buttermilk and mix to form soft dough. In 8-inch cake pan, sprayed with vegetable cooking spray, pat dough into 8-inch circle. With sharp knife, cut a cross on top of dough. Bake at 350°F (180°C), 40 minutes or until bread sounds hollow when tapped with knuckles. Remove bread from pan and cool on rack.

Sandwich: Cut Irish soda bread in half. On each half of bread, spread ⅓ cup dressing. Layer bottom of loaf with ⅓ of coleslaw and ½ of the pastrami. Repeat layering with ⅓ coleslaw, ⅓ cup dressing, remaining pastrami and remaining ⅓ cup coleslaw. Cover with top half of loaf. Wrap sandwich tightly in plastic wrap. Refrigerate overnight. To serve, cut sandwich into 4 wedges. Serves 4.

Approximate nutritional analysis per serving:
Calories 435, Protein 20 g, Carbohydrates 77 g,
Fat 5 g, Cholesterol 33 mg, Sodium 1,891 mg

GOOEY CHEESE LOAF

1 - 1 lb loaf (455 g) Italian bread
1 - 12 oz pkg (360 g) HEALTHY CHOICE Fat Free Natural Shredded Mozzarella Cheese
½ cup (120 ml) red onion, finely chopped
¼ cup (60 ml) fat free mayonnaise
1 tsp (5 ml) crushed dried marjoram or basil

Heat oven to 350°F (180°C). Slice loaf into 16 equal parts cutting through to within ½ inch of bottom of loaf. Combine remaining ingredients; mix to blend. Spread cheese mixture on cut surfaces of bread. Loosely wrap loaf in foil. Bake 25 minutes or until heated through. Serves 16.

Approximate nutritional analysis per serving:
Calories 118, Protein 10 g, Carbohydrates 19 g, Fat .5 g,
Cholesterol 4 mg, Sodium 359 mg

GOLDEN GATE OPEN-FACE SANDWICH

4 oz (120 g) crab-style surimi seafood blend
¼ cup (60 ml) sweet red pepper, chopped
2 tbs (30 ml) green onion slices
1 tsp (5 ml) lemon juice
1 - 8 oz pkg (240 g) HEALTHY CHOICE Fat Free Natural Fancy Shredded Mozzarella Cheese
¼ cup (60 ml) plus 12 tsp (60 ml) fat free mayonnaise
6 sour dough bread slices, toasted
1 cup (240 ml) alfalfa sprouts

Combine seafood, pepper, onion, lemon juice and half of cheese with ¼ cup mayonnaise; mix lightly. For each sandwich, spread slice of bread with 2 tsp mayonnaise; top with 2 tbs sprouts, ⅓ cup seafood mixture and ½ oz of remaining cheese. Bake at 350°F (180°C), for 10 minutes. Serves 6.

Approximate nutritional analysis per serving: .
Calories 157, Protein 17 g, Carbohydrates 20 g, Fat 1.5 g,
Cholesterol 10 mg, Sodium 624 mg

GRILLED CHICKEN & TOMATO SANDWICH

2 large (1 lb) (455 g) fresh FLORIDA tomatoes
½ cup (120 ml) plain lowfat yogurt
2 tbs (30 ml) reduced calorie mayonnaise
1 tbs (15 ml) chili powder
¼ tsp (1 ml) salt
4 - 6-inch long hero or French rolls, toasted
4 lettuce leaves
1 lb (455 g) chicken breasts, boned and skinned, cut in halves horizontally

Prepare outdoor barbecue grill or preheat broiler. Use tomatoes held at room temperature until fully ripe. Core tomatoes; slice tomatoes vertically ½ inch thick; set aside. In a bowl combine yogurt, mayonnaise, chili powder and salt. Spread about half of yogurt mixture on one side of each roll; top with lettuce leaf. Place chicken on grill or on a rack of a broiler pan; brush with half of the remaining yogurt mixture; grill about 3 inches from heat until chicken is partially cooked, 2-3 minutes; turn, brush chicken with remaining yogurt mixture; grill until chicken is tender, 2-3 minutes longer. Remove chicken to platter; set aside. Place tomatoes on grill or broiler pan; grill until tomatoes are slightly softened, about 2 minutes per side; remove to platter. Arrange grilled chicken and tomatoes on prepared rolls. Serve warm or at room temperature. Serves 4.

Approximate nutritional analysis per serving:
Calories 335, Protein 29 g, Carbohydrates 46 g, Fat 6 g,
Cholesterol 56 mg, Sodium 671 mg

GARDEN GLORY EGG SALAD

3 oz (90 g) spinach leaves
2 hard cooked eggs, wedged
6 cherry tomatoes, halved
½ cup (120 ml) celery, sliced
½ cup (120 ml) fresh mushrooms, sliced
½ green pepper, cut in julienne strips
1 tbs (15 ml) green onions with tops, minced

TARRAGON DRESSING:
½ cup (120 ml) water
¼ cup (60 ml) lemon juice
1 egg
¾ tsp (8 ml) dry mustard
¼ tsp (1 ml) salt
¼ tsp (1 ml) tarragon leaves, crushed
artificial sweetener to equal 1 tbs (15 ml) sugar

Line plate or salad bowl with spinach leaves. Arrange egg wedges at sides of plate. Lightly toss together remaining ingredients except dressing and place in center of plate. Serve with tarragon dressing. Serves 1.

Tarragon dressing: In small saucepan combine ingredients. Cook over medium heat, stirring constantly, until mixture thickens and just starts to boil. Remove from heat. Cover and chill. Yields I cup.

Approximate nutritional analysis per serving:
Calories 325, Protein 24 g, Carbohydrates 24 g, Fat 17 g, Cholesterol 636 mg, Sodium 854 mg

Courtesy of the American Egg Board.

APPLE CHEESE GRILLS

whole wheat bread slices
thin apple slices
HEALTHY CHOICE Fat Free Pasteurized
**   Process Cheese Singles Product**

For each sandwich, cover 1 slice of bread with 3 apple slices, 2 cheese slices and second slice of bread. Spray pan and both sides of sandwich with non-sticking cooking spray; grill sandwich on each side until golden brown.

Approximate nutritional analysis per serving:
Calories 219, Protein 14 g, Carbohydrates 34 g, Fat 4 g, Cholesterol 7 mg, Sodium 873 mg

Garden Glory Egg Salad

SUMMER GARDEN PITAS

1 cup (240 ml) tomatoes, chopped
½ cup (120 ml) yellow squash, chopped
½ cup (120 ml) zucchini, chopped
¼ cup (60 ml) parsley, chopped
2 tbs (30 ml) chives, chopped
1 tbs (15 ml) olive oil
1 tbs (15 ml) wine vinegar
cracked black pepper
4 small pita pocket breads, halved
8 red lettuce leaves
8 slices HEALTHY CHOICE Fat Free Pasteurized
    Process Cheese Singles Product

Combine tomatoes, squash, zucchini, parsley and chives; mix
lightly with oil and vinegar. Season to taste with pepper. For
each sandwich, fill pita half with lettuce leaf, cheese slice and
¼ cup vegetable mixture. Serves 8.

Approximate nutritional analysis per serving:
Calories 149, Protein 10 g, Carbohydrates 22 g, Fat 3 g,
Cholesterol 5 mg, Sodium 569 mg

WEST COAST TUNA PITA

½ cup (120 ml) HEALTHY CHOICE Cholesterol
    Free Egg Product
1 - 6⅛ oz can (185 g) tuna in water, drained
¼ cup (60 ml) nonfat mayonnaise dressing
¼ cup (60 ml) reduced-calorie cream cheese spread
¼ cup (60 ml) water chestnuts, chopped
1 tbs (15 ml) green onion, sliced
1 tsp (5 ml) lemon juice
1 tsp (5 ml) Dijon-style mustard
¼ tsp (1 ml) dill weed
4 pita rounds, cut in half
1 cucumber, thinly sliced
1 tomato, thinly sliced
Alfalfa sprouts

In 8-inch skillet sprayed with vegetable oil spray, cook
egg product, covered, over very low heat 5 minutes or just until
set. Cool egg product and dice. In medium bowl, combine egg
product, tuna, dressing, creamed cheese spread, chestnuts,
onion, lemon juice, mustard and dill weed; chill. To serve, fill
pita halves with cucumber and tomato slices, sprouts and
¼ cup tuna spread. Serves 8.

Approximate nutritional analysis per serving:
Calories 156, Protein 12 g, Carbohydrates 19 g, Fat 3 g,
Cholesterol 12 mg, Sodium 302 mg

ZESTY FAJITAS

½ lb (230 g) boneless skinless chicken breast
    halves, cut into strips
1 cup (240 ml) green or red pepper, sliced
½ cup (120 ml) onion, sliced
⅔ cup (160 ml) KRAFT FREE Italian Fat Free
    Dressing or KRAFT Italian Reduced Calorie
    Dressing
4 medium flour tortillas
½ cup (120 ml) salsa

Reserve ⅓ cup dressing. Pour remaining dressing over chicken
strips, peppers and onion; cover. Refrigerate 2 hours to
marinate; drain. Cook and stir chicken and vegetables in
reserved dressing in skillet on medium-high. Heat 8-10 minutes
or until chicken is cooked through. Serve in warmed tortillas;
top with salsa. Serves 2.

Approximate nutritional analysis per serving:
Calories 440, Protein 40 g, Carbohydrates 37 g, Fat 16 g,
Cholesterol 100 mg, Sodium 814 mg

CHUNKY SALSA CHICKEN SANDWICHES

2½ cups (590 ml) cooked chicken, diced
1 cup (240 ml) DANNON Plain Nonfat or
    Lowfat Yogurt
¼ cup (60 ml) chunky salsa
½ tsp (3 ml) ground cumin
½ cup (120 ml) red or green bell pepper,
    finely chopped
⅓ cup (80 ml) fresh cilantro or parsley,
    finely chopped
⅓ cup (80 ml) green onions, finely chopped
3 small pita bread rounds, cut in half

TOPPINGS:
shredded lettuce
sliced ripe olives
chopped tomatoes
shredded cheddar cheese

In a large bowl, combine chicken, yogurt, salsa and cumin; stir
gently. Stir in bell pepper, cilantro and green onions. Line each
pita half with lettuce. Spoon chicken salad mixture evenly into
pockets; sprinkle remaining toppings over chicken salad
mixture. Serve immediately. Serves 6.

Approximate nutritional analysis per serving:
Calories 300, Protein 22 g, Carbohydrates 21 g, Fat 7 g,
Cholesterol 90 mg, Sodium 256 mg

CHICKEN-MUSHROOM CRÊPES

CRÊPES:

5 egg whites
3 tbs (45 ml) rolled oats
1 tbs (15 ml) onion, finely chopped
1 tbs (15 ml) green onion, chopped
½ tsp (3 ml) salt
1 tbs (15 ml) spinach, finely chopped
2 packets EQUAL
½ tsp (3 ml) vanilla, optional

CHICKEN FILLING:

1 - 12 oz pkg (360 g) lowfat cottage cheese
8 oz (240 g) chicken breasts, boneless, skinless,
**   cut in short strips**
1 tbs (15 ml) Chef Paul Prudhomme's
**   POULTRY MAGIC**
½ cup (120 ml) onion, chopped
¼ cup (60 ml) green bell pepper, chopped
1 cup (240 ml) plus 2 tbs (30 ml)
**   defatted chicken stock**
½ cup (120 ml) yellow squash, diced
½ cup (120 ml) zucchini, diced
½ tsp (3 ml) fresh garlic, minced
3 cups (720 ml) mushrooms, thinly sliced
2 tsp (10 ml) arrowroot

In small skillet over high heat, lightly toast the oats, shaking the pan almost constantly until they're light brown. Place all ingredients except the EQUAL in blender. Process well, add EQUAL and blend again. Heat a 10-inch Teflon skillet until very hot. Pour ¼ crêpe batter into pan, tip the pan quickly to coat bottom with batter and cook about 1 minute, or until edges begin to curl away from pan. Turn crêpe out onto dish and repeat process 3 more times, blending batter until frothy each time. Set aside.

Filling: Make a mock cream by placing cottage cheese in blender and processing until very creamy, about 4 minutes. Add 3 tbs chicken stock and blend again until very smooth and creamy. Set aside.

Combine arrowroot with 1 tbs stock and set aside.

Mix 1 tsp POULTRY MAGIC into chicken, blending well with your hands until all chicken is evenly coated.

Place a 10-inch skillet over high heat. When pan is very hot, add seasoned chicken and quickly bronze, cooking approximately 2 minutes on each side. Remove from skillet. Let skillet get very hot again; add onion, bell peppers and 1 tsp POULTRY MAGIC and cook 3 minutes, stirring once just to brown evenly and distribute the seasoning throughout the vegetables. Stir in 3 tbs stock and scrape up pan bottom. Cook 3 minutes and add 3 tbs stock around sides of pan and scrape. Cook 1½ minutes, and add minced garlic and mushrooms. Stir well and add squash and zucchini. Stir gently and continue cooking 1 minute. Add ½ tsp POULTRY MAGIC and stir to coat vegetables with seasoning. If sides of pan are browning

fast, move vegetables to edges and use their moisture to scrape up brown on sides. Cook 4 minutes, add chicken back to pan and the remaining ½ cup stock. Scrape up pan bottom and cook 4 minutes. Add the arrowroot mixture to pan. Cook 1 minute and add 1 cup of the mock cream. Bring to a simmer and turn off heat. Add ½ tsp POULTRY MAGIC. Mix well. Makes 3 cups. Place ½ cup chicken mixture in each crêpe, roll up and top with another ¼ cup. Serves 4.

Approximate nutritional analysis per serving:
Calories 230, Protein 35 g, Carbohydrates 12 g, Fat 4 g,
Cholesterol 54 mg, Sodium 961 mg

MULTI-VEGGIE CRÊPES WITH LO-CAL HOLLANDAISE

4 slices bacon, diced
1 tsp (5 ml) ground cumin
1 tsp (5 ml) dry oregano, crumbled
1 medium zucchini
1 medium carrot
1 medium yellow bell pepper
1 medium red bell pepper
½ cup (120 ml) onion, chopped
1½ cups (355 ml) mozzarella or jack cheese,
**   shredded**
½ cup (120 ml) NATURAL Raisins
¼ cup (60 ml) toasted almonds, chopped
8 crêpes *or* 8 small flour tortillas

LO-CAL HOLLANDAISE:

1 - 8 oz carton (240 g) unflavored yogurt
4 egg yolks, beaten
1 tsp (5 ml) dry chicken bouillon powder
1 tsp (5 ml) sugar
dash hot pepper sauce

Place bacon in a shallow dish, cover with paper towel and microwave on HIGH 1 minute. Stir in cumin and oregano, microwave on HIGH 45 seconds. Julienne all vegetables and stir in with onion. Microwave on HIGH 4 minutes, stirring after 2 and 3 minutes. Vegetables should be crisp-tender. Stir in cheese, raisins and almonds. Place ⅛ of mixture in a strip down center of crêpe; fold over sides and repeat with remaining crêpes. Place crêpes wheel spoke-fashion on serving plate. Cover loosely with paper towels and microwave on MEDIUM-HIGH (70%) about 3 minutes, until heated through and cheese is melted. Serves 4.

Lo-Cal Hollandaise: In 2-cup measure, stir all ingredients together. Microwave on MEDIUM (50%) for 10-12 minutes, stirring every 60 seconds, until thickened to Hollandaise consistency.

Approximate nutritional analysis per serving:
Calories 574, Protein 23 g, Carbohydrates 71 g, Fat 25 g,
Cholesterol 249 mg, Sodium 1,288 mg

Opposite: Chicken-Mushroom Crêpes

TURKEY PASTRAMI BAKE

4 tbs (60 ml) olive oil
2 lbs (910 g) potatoes
1 lb (455 g) onions
2 green peppers
2 hot peppers, if desired
8 oz (240 g) EMPIRE Kosher Turkey Pastrami

Peel and slice raw potatoes, slice onions and peppers. In heavy frying pan, fry potatoes, onions and peppers until done, about 45 minutes. Add pastrami, toss, heat through and serve. Serves 4.

Approximate nutritional analysis per serving:
Calories 437, Protein 16 g, Carbohydrates 56 g, Fat 17 g,
Cholesterol 31 mg, Sodium 607 mg

Empanadillas de Atún

EMPANADILLAS DE ATÚN

2 - 4 oz cans (240 g) GOYA White Tuna,
    drained and chopped
¾ cup (180 ml) GOYA Large Pimiento-Stuffed
    Olives, chopped
2 hard-boiled eggs, peeled and chopped
2 tbs (30 ml) GOYA Tomato Sauce
1 packet Sazón GOYA Sin Achiote
2 tbs (3 ml) parsley, chopped
GOYA Discos or any prepared pie crust dough,
    cut into 5-inch diameter pieces
1½ cups (355 ml) GOYA Olive Oil

In a large bowl, combine chopped tuna, olives, eggs, tomato sauce, sazón and parsley. Place disco or pie dough flat on a plate and spoon a heaping tbs of tuna mixture onto the dough, just off-center. Wet edge of disco with water and fold over tuna mixture, crimping edges closed with fork. In a skillet, heat olive oil to 350°F (180°C). Fry empanadilla in hot olive oil until brown. Turn and brown the other side. Remove with slotted spoon and drain on paper towel. Serves 12.

Approximate nutritional analysis per serving:
Calories 367, Protein 9 g, Carbohydrates 7 g, Fat 34 g,
Cholesterol 5 mg, Sodium 708 mg

TOFU SOUTH OF THE BORDER ENCHILADAS

½ cup (120 ml) onion, chopped
¾ cup (180 ml) sweet green pepper, chopped
1 - 4 oz can (120 g) chopped green, mild chilies
1 clove garlic, minced
½ tsp (3 ml) cumin seed
1 tsp (5 ml) dried cilantro
12 oz (360 g) silken firm tofu, drained and mashed
2 cups (460 ml) tomato, diced and drained
8 medium whole wheat tortillas
2 cups (460 ml) thick tomato salsa
½ cup (120 ml) lowfat cheddar cheese, shredded

Preheat oven to 350°F (180°C). Lightly spray a 9x13-inch baking pan with no stick vegetable (soy) spray. In bowl, combine all ingredients except tortillas, tomato salsa and cheese. Place ½ cup of the mixture in center of each tortilla and roll. Place in baking dish, seam side down. Pour salsa over enchiladas. Sprinkle with shredded cheese. Cover pan with aluminum foil and bake for 25-30 minutes. Serves 8.

Approximate nutritional analysis per serving:
Calories 199, Protein 9 g, Carbohydrates 28 g, Fat 7 g,
Cholesterol 4 mg, Sodium 409 mg

CHEESE-STUFFED ENCHILADA WITH RED SAUCE

SAUCE:
1 tbs (15 ml) vegetable oil
1 cup (240 ml) green onions, chopped
2 tsp (10 ml) fresh garlic, minced
8 cups (1.9 L) ripe tomatoes, chopped (6 medium)
1 tbs (15 ml) chili powder
1 tsp (5 ml) ground cumin
1 tsp (5 ml) dried oregano
¼ tsp (1 ml) pepper

ENCHILADA:
12 medium whole wheat tortillas
1 10 oz pkg (360 g) HEALTHY CHOICE Fat Free
Natural Shredded Cheddar Cheese

Heat oven to 350°F (180°C). In large saucepan, cook green onions and garlic in oil until tender. Add tomatoes, chili powder, cumin, oregano and pepper. Continue cooking until sauce boils; reduce heat to low and continue cooking about 30 minutes, stirring occasionally. Remove from heat.

Dip each tortilla into sauce. Spoon about 2 tbs cheese onto each tortilla. Roll tortilla around filling. Place seam side down in 13x9-inch baking dish sprayed with non-stick cooking spray. Pour remaining sauce over tortillas; sprinkle with remaining cheese. Bake at 350°F (180°C) for 20 minutes or until cheese is melted. Serves 12.

Approximate nutritional analysis per serving:
Calories 170, Protein 13 g, Carbohydrates 27 g, Fat 3 g,
Cholesterol 5 mg, Sodium 355 mg

TOMATO, BRIE AND BACON SANDWICH

1 lb (455 g) fresh FLORIDA tomatoes
8 slices bacon
8 slices sourdough bread
¼ cup (60 ml) mustard
4 lettuce leaves
8 oz (240 g) Brie, sliced ¼ inch thick

Use tomatoes held at room temperature until fully ripe. Core; slice off ends (reserve for soups and sauces). Slice ¼ inch thick; set aside. Cook bacon until crisp; drain, keep warm or refrigerate and heat when ready to use.

For each sandwich spread one slice of bread with 1 tbs mustard. Top with lettuce, Brie, 2-3 tomato slices and 2 strips bacon. Serve with second bread slice. Serves 4.

Approximate nutritional analysis per serving:
Calories 629, Protein 28 g, Carbohydrates 69 g, Fat 27 g,
Cholesterol 70 mg, Sodium 1,457 mg

Courtesy of the Florida Tomato Committee.

SPICY CHICKEN AND HAZELNUT ENCHILADAS

1 lb (455 g) fresh tomatillos
or 1 - 12 oz can (360 ml) tomatillos
2 cloves garlic, peeled
2 jalapeño peppers, seeded
2 tbs (30 ml) cilantro leaves
2 tbs (30 ml) onion
⅓ cup (80 ml) sour cream
⅓ cup (80 ml) plain yogurt
1 tbs (15 ml) honey
¼ tsp (1 ml) salt
⅓ cup (80 ml) canned diced green chilies
6 corn tortillas
2 cups (480 ml) cooked shredded chicken
1 cup (240 ml) OREGON Hazelnuts,
roasted and chopped

If using fresh tomatillos, prepare by washing and removing husks. Place in saucepan, cover with water and simmer until tender, about 5-7 minutes; drain. If using canned tomatillos, drain and discard liquid. For sauce, mince garlic, jalapenos, cilantro and onions in food processor or blender. Add drained tomatillos, sour cream, yogurt, honey and salt; puree. Mix in green chilies and set aside. Soften tortillas either by frying on both sides in a small amount of vegetable oil, by wrapping in foil and placing in hot oven until hot, or by placing in microwave oven until heated. In the center of each tortilla, place about 2 tbs each of chicken, sauce and cheese. Add about 2 tsp chopped hazelnuts. Pour ¼ of the sauce in the bottom of a greased 9x12-inch baking dish. Place filled enchiladas in dish and pour remaining sauce over top. Sprinkle with remaining cheese and then with hazelnuts. Bake in a 350°F (180°C) oven until heated through, about 20 minutes. Serves 6.

Approximate nutritional analysis per serving:
Calories 492, Protein 30 g, Carbohydrates 28 g, Fat 31 g,
Cholesterol 81 mg, Sodium 269 mg

Tomato, Brie and Bacon Sandwiches

SMOKED TURKEY TORTILLAS

8 oz (240 g) fat-free cream cheese
1 - 4 oz can (120 g) chopped green chilies, undrained
¼ cup (60 ml) red onion, finely chopped
1 tbs (15 ml) Dijon mustard
8 medium flour tortillas
3 cups (720 ml) lettuce, shredded
1½ lbs (685 g) NORBEST Smoked Turkey
    Breast, shredded
½ cup (120 ml) reduced fat cheddar cheese,
grated, divided
8 red onion slices

In small bowl combine cream cheese, chilies, onions and mustard. Spread 3 tbs cream cheese mixture over each tortilla. In center of each tortilla top with ⅓ cup lettuce, 3 oz turkey, 1 tbs cheese and 2 onion slices. Fold up lower edge of tortilla over filling and fold in left and right sides. Serves 8.

Note: Roll-ups may be made several hours before serving. Wrap tightly in plastic wrap and refrigerate.

Approximate nutritional analysis per serving:
Calories 265, Protein 30 g, Carbohydrates 25 g, Fat 5 g,
Cholesterol 47 mg, Sodium 1,419 mg

TASTY TOMATO RAREBIT

1 - 28 oz can (840 g) LIBBY'S Concentrated
    Crushed Tomatoes
1 cup (240 ml) green onion, chopped
½ lb (230 g) cheddar cheese, thinly sliced
2 eggs, separated
1 tsp (5 ml) Worcestershire sauce
1 tsp (5 ml) prepared mustard
1 tsp (5 ml) salt
¼ tsp (1 ml) paprika
⅛ tsp (.5 ml) white pepper
English muffins or toast

In saucepan combine tomatoes, green onions and cheddar cheese. Heat and stir until cheese is melted. Remove from heat. In separate bowl mix together egg yolks, Worcestershire sauce, mustard, salt, paprika and white pepper. Stir in tomato mixture. Beat egg whites until stiff peaks form and fold into tomato mixture. Top toasted English muffins with tomato mixture. Garnish with additional shredded cheddar cheese and chopped green onion, if desired. Serves 8.

Approximate nutritional analysis per serving:
Calories 301, Protein 14 g, Carbohydrates 33 g, Fat 12 g,
Cholesterol 83 mg, Sodium 1,014mg

EASY BEEF AND SALSA BURRITOS

1 lb (455 g) lean ground beef
1 tbs (15 ml) chili powder
¼ tsp (1 ml) ground cumin
¼ tsp (1 ml) salt
¼ tsp (1 ml) pepper
1 - 10 oz pkg (300 g) frozen chopped spinach,
    defrosted, well drained
1 cup (240 ml) prepared chunky salsa
¾ cup (180 ml) co-jack cheese, shredded
8 medium flour tortillas, warmed

In large nonstick skillet, brown ground beef over medium heat 8-10 minutes or until no longer pink, stirring occasionally. Pour off drippings. Season beef with chili powder, cumin, salt and pepper. Stir in spinach and salsa; heat through. Remove from heat; stir in cheese. To serve, spoon ½ cup beef mixture in center of each tortilla. Fold bottom edge up over filling; fold sides to center, overlapping edges. Serves 8.

Approximate nutritional analysis per serving:
Calories 281, Protein 18 g, Carbohydrates 30 g, Fat 11 g,
Cholesterol 45 mg, Sodium 587 mg

Courtesy of the National Livestock and Meat Board.

SAUTÉED VEGGIE SUB

1 cup (240 ml) red onion wedges
1 medium green pepper, cut into strips
2 cloves garlic, minced
2 tbs (30 ml) FLEISCHMANN'S Margarine
2 cups (480 ml) eggplant, thinly sliced
1 cup (240 ml) zucchini, thinly sliced
1 cup (240 ml) yellow squash, thinly sliced
1 - 8 oz can (240 ml) tomato sauce
1 tsp (5 ml) dried basil leaves
6 - 2 oz (60 g) soft sub or hero rolls

In large skillet, over medium-high heat, cook onion, peppers and garlic in margarine for 3 minutes or until tender-crisp. Add eggplant, zucchini and squash; cover. Cook 5 minutes more or until heated through. Spoon vegetable mixture onto roll bottoms; replace roll tops. Serve immediately. Serves 6.

Approximate nutritional analysis per serving:
Calories 234, Protein 8 g, Carbohydrates 22 g, Fat 6 g,
Cholesterol 0 mg, Sodium 377 mg

MEXICAN CHICKEN SKEWERS WITH SPICY YOGURT SAUCE

1 - 1¼ oz pkg (38 g) taco seasoning mix,
    divided 6 boneless skinless chicken breast
    halves, cut into 1-inch cubes
1 large clove garlic
¼ tsp (1 ml) salt
2 tbs (30 ml) olive oil
1 cup (240 ml) DANNON Nonfat or Lowfat Yogurt
1 red bell pepper, cut into chunks
1 green bell pepper, cut into chunks
1 yellow bell pepper, cut into chunks

In a large bowl combine 3 tbs taco seasononng mix and chicken; toss to coat well. Cover; chill 2 hours.

To make spicy yogurt sauce, in a mortar and pestle or with a large knife press garlic and salt together until a smooth paste forms. Place in a small bowl with olive oil; mix well. Stir in yogurt and remaining taco seasoning mix. Cover; chill 30 minutes before serving.

Thread chicken onto skewers alternately with peppers; grill over hot coals 10-12 minutes, turning occasionally. Serve with spicy yogurt sauce. Serves 12.

Note: If using wooden skewers, soak them in water 30 minutes before serving. This will prevent skewers from charring and crumbling.

Approximate nutritional analysis per serving:
Calories 140, Protein 15 g, Carbohydrates 4 g, Fat 5 g,
Cholesterol 50 mg, Sodium 179 mg

FALAFEL

3 -16 oz cans (1.4 kg) garbanzo beans
1 cup (240 ml) onion, chopped
1 tsp (5 ml) garlic, minced
½ cup (120 ml) fresh parsley, chopped
1 tsp (5 ml) jalapeño pepper, minced, or to taste
1 tsp (5 ml) ground cumin
1 tsp (5 ml) baking powder
salt to taste
pepper to taste
Approximately 4 cups (960 ml) vegetable oil
6 whole wheat pita breads, warm
2 cups (480 ml) iceberg lettuce, shredded

TAHINI SAUCE:
1 cup (240 ml) tahini (sesame seed paste)
juice of 2 lemons
2 cloves garlic, crushed
salt to taste
approximately ½ cup (120 ml) cool water

Combine garbanzo beans, onion, garlic, parsley, cilantro, jalapeño pepper, cumin, baking powder, salt and pepper in food processor fitted with the metal blade, using quick on-and-off turns. Do not puree. Cover and refrigerate for 30 minutes. When chilled, form garbanzo mixture into patties 2 inches round and about ¾ inch thick. Set aside.

Heat oil in deep-sided frying pan over high heat. When hot, carefully lower patties into hot oil a few at a time using a slotted spoon. Fry about 3 minutes, turning frequently, until patties are golden. Drain on paper towel.

Cut pitas in half. Place 2 falafel in each pocket and sprinkle with lettuce and drizzle with tahini sauce. Serves 6.

Tahini sauce: Place tahini, lemon juice, garlic and salt in food processor fitted with the metal blade. Process until smooth, adding enough water to make a thin sauce. Cover and refrigerate until ready to use. Yields 1½ cups.

Approximate nutritional analysis per serving with tahini:
Calories 854, Protein 34 g, Carbohydrates 104 g, Fat 37 g,
Cholesterol 0 mg, Sodium 579 mg

APPETIZERS

*From savory nibbles that wet your whistle to casual
dips and salsas that make the first dent in hearty
appetites to more formal first courses, appetizers are
about enthusiastic anticipation of the food to come.
Look here for cocktail party food; a fanciful collection
of appetizers can make a lovely light supper or form
the basis for a buffet.*

FRESH TOMATO SALSA

4½ lbs (2 kg) fresh FLORIDA tomatoes
½ cup (120 ml) red onion finely chopped
½ cup (120 ml) ancho chili powder
⅓ cup (80 ml) lime juice, fresh
¼ cup (60 ml) jalapeño pepper, seeded
    and finely chopped
2 tbs (30 ml) salt
1 tsp (5 ml) ground white pepper

Use tomatoes held at room temperature until fully ripe. Core and cut into ½-inch dice (makes about 2 qts). Place in a large bowl with onion, chili powder, cilantro, lime juice, jalapeño, salt and white pepper; stir until combined. Serve with tortilla chips. Yields 2 quarts.

Approximate nutritional analysis per ½ cup serving:
Calories 18, Protein 1 g, Carbohydrates 0 g
Cholesterol 0 mg, Sodium 388 mg

WATERMELON PICO DE GALLO

4 cups (960 ml) watermelon, diced and seeded
1½ cups (355 ml) jicama, diced
½ cup (120 ml) green pepper, diced
¼ cup (60 ml) fresh cilantro, chopped
1 tbs (15 ml) jalapeño pepper, chopped
2 tbs (30 ml) fresh lemon juice
1 tbs (15 ml) honey
1 tsp (5 ml) salt
1 tsp (5 ml) garlic pepper
¼ tsp (1 ml) hot pepper sauce

In large bowl, combine all ingredients; mix well. Refrigerate, covered, at least 1 hour to blend all flavors. Stir before serving. Serves 12.

Approximate nutritional analysis per serving:
Calories 32, Protein .7 g, Carbohydrates 7 g, Fat .3 g,
Cholesterol 0 mg, Sodium 182 mg

Previous page: Cheesy Tortilla Trap

CARIBBEAN WATERMELON SALSA

2 cups (480 ml) watermelon, seeded and chopped
1 cup (240 ml) fresh pineapple, chopped
1 cup (240 ml) onion, chopped
¼ cup (60 ml) fresh cilantro, chopped
¼ cup (60 ml) orange juice
1-2 tbs (15-30 ml) jerk seasoning,* or to taste

In large bowl, combine all ingredients; mix well. Refrigerate, covered, at least 1 hour to blend flavors. Stir before serving. Serves 8.

    * Jerk spices differ in hotness so start with 1 tbs seasoning for more tender palates.

Approximate nutritional analysis per serving:
Calories 34, Protein .7 g, Carbohydrates 8 g, Fat .3 g,
Cholesterol 0 mg, Sodium 3 mg

WATERMELON BITES

1 cup (240 ml) fresh lime juice
½ tsp (3 ml) salt
¼ tsp (1 ml) hot pepper sauce, or to taste
6 cups (1.4 L) watermelon, seeded and cubed

In small bowl suitable for dipping, stir together lime juice, salt and hot pepper sauce; adjust seasonings to taste. Place bowl in center of large platter; arrange watermelon around bowl. Serve with wooden picks. Serves 6.

Approximate nutritional analysis per serving:
Calories 60, Protein 1 g, Carbohydrates 14 g, Fat .8 g,
Cholesterol 0 mg, Sodium 191 mg

WATERMELON FIRE AND ICE SALSA

3 cups (720 ml) watermelon, seeded and chopped
½ cup (120 ml) green pepper
2 tbs (30 ml) lime juice
1 tbs (15 ml) cilantro, chopped
1 tbs (15 ml) green onion, chopped
1-2 tbs (15-30 ml) jalapeño pepper (2-3 medium)
½ tsp (3 ml) garlic salt

Combine all ingredients; mix well. Cover and refrigerate at least 1 hour. Yields 3 cups.

    Serving tips: Serve on sliced oranges or cheese-filled manicotti or with corn or potato chips. Or, top 1 cup dairy sour cream with 1 cup salsa and serve with chips.

Approximate nutritional analysis per ½ cup serving:
Calories 30, Protein < 1 g, Carbohydrates 7 g, Fat < 1 g,
Cholesterol 0 mg, Sodium 91 mg

Courtesy of the National Watermelon Promotion Board.

Watermelon Fire & Ice Salsa

OREGON HAZELNUT TORTILLA DIP

2 ripe avocados, peeled, pitted and diced
1 - 8 oz pkg (240 g) cream cheese, softened
2 green onions, finely sliced
1½ tsp (8 ml) lemon juice
1 clove garlic, minced
½ tsp (3 ml) chili powder
¼ tsp (1 ml) salt
1 tomato, seeded and diced
chopped parsley
⅓ cup (80 ml) OREGON Hazelnuts,
**   roasted and chopped**

Combine softened cream cheese, avocado, onion, lemon juice, garlic, chili powder and salt. Blend well. Add half the nuts and tomato; blend. Mold into ball. Top with remaining nuts and parsley. Chill to improve flavor. Serve with tortilla chips. Yields approximately 4 cups.

Approximate nutritional analysis per ½ cup serving:
Calories 219, Protein 4 g, Carbohydrates 7 g, Fat 21 g,
Cholesterol 31 mg, Sodium 159 mg

EGGPLANT CAVIAR

1 large eggplant, unpeeled
¼ cup (60 ml) onion, chopped
2 tbs (30 ml) lemon juice
1 tbs (15 ml) olive or vegetable oil
1 small clove garlic
½ tsp (3 ml) salt
¼ tsp (1 ml) Tabasco pepper sauce
sieved egg white, optional

Preheat oven to 350°F (180°C). Place eggplant in shallow baking dish. Bake 1 hour or until soft, turning once. Trim off ends; slice eggplant in half lengthwise. Place cut side down in colander and let drain 10 minutes. Scoop out pulp; reserve pulp and peel. In blender or food processor combine eggplant peel, onion, lemon juice, garlic, salt and Tabasco sauce. Cover; process until peel is finely chopped. Add eggplant pulp. Cover; process just until chopped. Place in serving dish. Garnish with egg white, if desired. Serve with toast points. Yields 1½ cups.

Approximate nutritional analysis per ¼ cup serving:
Calories 39, Protein 1 g, Carbohydrates 5 g, Fat 2 g,
Cholesterol 0 mg, Sodium 180 mg

CRAB DIP

½ cup (120 ml) nonfat yogurt or sour cream
2 tbs (30 ml) nonfat mayonnaise
1 - 8 oz pkg (240 g) HEALTHY CHOICE Fat Free
   Pasteurized Process Cream Cheese Product,
   softened
1 tsp (5 ml) prepared horseradish
½ tsp (3 ml) dry mustard
½ tsp (3 ml) Worcestershire sauce
¼ tsp (1 ml) hot pepper sauce
1 cup (4 oz) (120 g) HEALTHY CHOICE fat free
   natural fancy shredded cheddar cheese
½ lb (230 g) imitation crab, flaked
paprika

Combine yogurt or sour cream, mayonnaise, cream cheese and
seasonings. Mix well. Then, stir in cheddar cheese and crab.
Cover and chill 2 hours. Sprinkle with paprika. Serve with
crackers, breadsticks or vegetables. Serves 20.

Approximate nutritional analysis per serving:
Calories 44, Protein 9 g, Carbohydrates 2 g, Fat 1 g,
Cholesterol 10 mg, Sodium 194 mg

SICILIAN EGGPLANT APPETIZER

1 - 1 lb (455 g) eggplant, peeled and cut into
   ¼-inch cubes
1 tsp (5 ml) salt
¾ cup (180 ml) onion, chopped
½ cup (120 ml) green pepper, chopped
2 cloves garlic, minced
2 tbs (30 ml) vegetable oil
2 medium tomatoes, peeled and chopped
¼ cup (60 ml) HEINZ Chili Sauce
2 tbs (30 ml) HEINZ Vinegar
1 tbs (15 ml) capers
½ tsp (3 ml) dried basil leaves
½ tsp (3 ml) dried oregano leaves
¼ tsp (1 ml) pepper
⅓ cup (80 ml) ripe olives, sliced
toasted pita bread or crackers

Place eggplant in sieve or colander; sprinkle with salt. Let stand
30 minutes. Rinse eggplant; drain on paper towels. In a large
skillet, sauté onions, green pepper and garlic in oil; add
eggplant and sauté until tender, adding more oil if necessary.
Add tomatoes and next 6 ingredients; simmer, uncovered,
10 minutes. Stir in olives. Cover; chill overnight to blend
flavors. Serve at room temperature with pita bread or crackers.
Yields about 3½ cups.

Approximate nutritional analysis per ¼ cup serving:
Calories 49, Protein 1 g, Carbohydrates 7 g, Fat 3 g,
Cholesterol 0 mg, Sodium 258 mg

VELVEETA® SALSA DIP

1 lb (455 g) VELVEETA LIGHT Pasteurized Process
   Cheese Product or VELVEETA
   Pasteurized Process Cheese Spread, cubed
1 - 14½ oz can (435 g) tomatoes, chopped and drained
2 tbs (30 ml) cilantro, chopped, optional

Microwave process cheese product and tomatoes in 1½-qt
microwavable bowl on HIGH 5 minutes or until process cheese
product is melted, stirring after 3 minutes. Stir in cilantro.
Serve hot with tortilla chips or vegetable dippers. Serves 20.

   Top of stove: Heat process cheese product and tomatoes in
saucepan on low heat until process cheese product is melted.
Stir in cilantro. Serve as directed.

Approximate nutritional analysis per serving:
Calories 70, Protein 4 g, Carbohydrates 3 g, Fat 5 g,
Cholesterol 13 mg, Sodium 338 mg

Velveeta Salsa Dip

ALMOND CHEDDAR PINECONES

16 oz (480 g) cream cheese, softened
½ lb (230 g) cheddar cheese, grated
6 tbs (90 ml) port
⅛ tsp (.5 ml) cayenne
¼ cup (60 ml) green onion, finely sliced
2 cups (480 ml) BLUE DIAMOND Whole Natural
or Blanched Whole Almonds, toasted crackers

Combine first 4 ingredients; beat until smooth. Stir in green onions. Cover and refrigerate 1 hour. Form cheese mixture into the shape of a large pinecone. Place on serving plate. Beginning at narrow end of cone, carefully press almonds about ¼ inch deep into cheese mixture in rows, making sure that pointed end of each almond extends at a slight angle. Continue pressing almonds into cheese mixture in rows, with rows slightly overlapping, until all cheese is covered. Garnish pinecone with pine sprigs, if desired. Serve with crackers. Serves 25.

Approximate nutritional analysis per serving:
Calories 174, Protein 9 g, Carbohydrates 3 g, Fat 14 g,
Cholesterol 32 mg, Sodium 154 mg

ALMOND BLUE CHEESE PINECONE

16 oz (480 g) cream cheese, softened
¼ lb (115 g) blue cheese, crumbled
¼ lb (115 g) Swiss cheese, grated
¼ cup (60 ml) brandy
1 clove garlic, chopped finely
¼ tsp (1 ml) white pepper
2 cups (480 ml) BLUE DIAMOND Whole Natural
or Blanched Whole Almonds, toasted

Combine first 6 ingredients; beat until smooth. Cover and refrigerate 1 hour. Form cheese mixture into the shape of a large pinecone. Place on serving plate. Beginning at narrow end of cone, carefully press almonds about ¼ inch deep into cheese mixture in rows, making sure that pointed end of each almond extends at a slight angle. Continue pressing almonds into cheese mixture in rows, with rows slightly overlapping, until all cheese is covered. Garnish pinecone with pine sprigs, if desired. Serve with crackers. Serves 25.

Approximate nutritional analysis per serving:
Calories 170, Protein 6 g, Carbohydrates 4 g, Fat 15 g,
Cholesterol 28 mg, Sodium 130 mg

SWISS 'N' CHEDDAR CHEESEBALL

1 - 8 oz pkg (240 g) cream cheese, softened
½ cup (120 ml) DANNON Plain Nonfat or
Lowfat Yogurt
2 cups (8 oz) (240 g) Swiss cheese, shredded
2 cups (8 oz) (240 g) cheddar cheese, shredded
½ cup (120 ml) onion, finely chopped
1 - 2 oz jar (60 g) diced pimiento, undrained
2 tbs (30 ml) sweet pickle relish
10 slices bacon, crisp-cooked, drained,
crumbled and divided
½ cup (120 ml) pecans, finely chopped and divided
¼ cup (60 ml) fresh parsley, snipped
1 tbs (15 ml) poppy seeds
assorted crackers

In a large bowl beat cream cheese and yogurt until fluffy. Beat in Swiss cheese, cheddar cheese, onion, undrained pimiento, pickle relish, half the bacon and ¼ cup pecans. If desired, season with salt and pepper. Cover; chill until firm. Shape into 1 large or 2 small balls on waxed paper; set aside.

In a small bowl combine remaining bacon, remaining ¼ cup pecans, parsley and poppy seeds, turn out onto clean sheet of waxed paper. Roll ball in bacon mixture to coat. Cover in plastic wrap; chill. Serve with crackers. Serves 24.

Approximate nutritional analysis per serving:
Calories 143, Protein 7 g, Carbohydrates 2 g, Fat 12 g,
Cholesterol 32 mg, Sodium 166 mg

Swiss 'n' Cheddar Cheeseball

SPLENDID SPINACH DIP

**2 cups (480 ml) DANNON Plain Nonfat or
  Lowfat Yogurt
1 - 10 oz pkg (300 g) frozen chopped spinach,
  thawed and squeezed dry
⅓ cup (80 ml) fresh onion, finely chopped
2 tbs (30 ml) reduced calorie mayonnaise
1 - 1.4 oz pkg (42 g) instant vegetable soup mix
assorted fresh vegetable dippers**

In a medium bowl combine yogurt, spinach, onion, mayonnaise and vegetable soup mix; mix well. Serve immediately or cover and chill up to 3 hours. Serve with vegetable dippers. Serves 24.

Approximate nutritional analysis per serving:
Calories 22, Protein 2 g, Carbohydrates 3 g, Fat < 1 g,
Cholesterol 2 mg, Sodium 108 mg

CHUNKY CHILI DIP

**⅔ cup (160 ml) DANNON Plain Nonfat or
  Lowfat Yogurt
⅓ cup (80 ml) mayonnaise or salad dressing
¼ cup (60 ml) green bell pepper, finely chopped
¼ cup (60 ml) chili sauce
2 tbs (30 ml) green onion, finely chopped
1 tbs (15 ml) prepared horseradish
assorted fresh vegetable dippers**

In medium bowl combine yogurt, mayonnaise, bell pepper, chili sauce, green onion and horseradish; mix well. Cover; chill before serving. Serve with vegetable dippers. Serves 12.

Approximate nutritional analysis per serving:
Calories 40, Protein 1 g, Carbohydrates 4 g, Fat 2 g,
Cholesterol 3 mg, Sodium 131 mg

CREAMY TARRAGON DIP

**1 cup (240 ml) DANNON Plain Nonfat or
  Lowfat Yogurt
1 cup (240 ml) mayonnaise or salad dressing
1 tbs (15 ml) green onion, chopped
1 tbs (15 ml) fresh parsley, snipped
2 tsp (10 ml) lemon juice
½ tsp (3 ml) dried tarragon, crushed
dash freshly ground pepper
assorted vegetable dippers**

In medium bowl combine yogurt, mayonnaise, green onion, parsley, lemon juice, tarragon and pepper; mix well. Cover; chill up to 24 hours before serving. Serve with vegetable dippers. Serves 16.

Approximate nutritional analysis per serving:
Calories 66, Protein 1 g, Carbohydrates 5 g, Fat 5 g,
Cholesterol 5 mg, Sodium 114 mg

CALIFORNIA HOT ARTICHOKE AND CHILI DIP

**1 - 14 oz can (420 g) artichoke hearts,
  drained and chopped
1 - 4¼ oz can (128 g) CHI-CHI'S Diced Green
  Chilies, drained
¾ cup (180 ml) cheddar cheese,
  shredded and divided
½ cup (120 ml) Parmesan cheese, grated
½ cup (120 ml) mayonnaise
¼ cup (60 ml) green onions, sliced and divided
1 tbs (15 ml) CHI-CHI'S Whole Red Jalapeño
  Peppers, diced
CHI-CHI'S Salsa
toasted french bread slices**

Heat oven to 350°F (180°C). In medium bowl, combine artichoke hearts, chilies, ½ cup shredded cheddar cheese (reserve ¼ cup for topping), Parmesan cheese, mayonnaise, 3 tbs sliced green onions (reserve 1 tbs for topping) and jalapeño peppers. Spoon into 9-inch glass pie plate or similar baking dish. Sprinkle with reserved ¼ cup cheddar cheese and 1 tbs green onions. Bake 25-30 minutes or until light golden brown and bubbling. Serve with salsa and toasted french bread slices. Yields 2½ cups.

Approximate nutritional analysis per 1 tbs serving:
Calories 40, Protein 1 g, Carbohydrates 1 g, Fat 3 g,
Cholesterol 5 mg, Sodium 60 mg

HERBED SPINACH DIP

**1 - 8 oz container spreadable HEALTHY CHOICE Fat
  Free Pasteurized Process Herb
  and Garlic Cream Cheese Product
1 - 10 oz pkg (300 g) frozen chopped spinach, thawed
  and well drained
¼ cup (60 ml) radish, chopped
2 tbs (30 ml) green onion slices
2 tbs (30 ml) white wine
cracked black pepper
carrot sticks, cucumber slices, zucchini slices**

Combine ingredients; mix well. Chill to blend flavors. Serve as dip with carrot sticks and cucumber or zucchini slices. Serves 28.

Approximate nutritional analysis per serving:
Calories 25, Protein 4 g, Carbohydrates 2 g, Fat .5 g,
Cholesterol 1 mg, Sodium 134 mg

Opposite: Assorted Dips

LAYERED CATFISH DIP

3 cups (720 ml) water
1 lb (455 g) Mississippi farm-raised catfish fillets
12 oz (360 g) cream cheese, softened
2 tbs (30 ml) mayonnaise
2 tbs (30 ml) Worcestershire sauce
1 tbs (15 ml) lemon juice
dash garlic salt
1 small onion, chopped
1 - 12 oz bottle (360 g) chili sauce
parsley, optional

In a large skillet bring water to a boil. Add catfish. Return to boil; reduce heat. Cover and simmer gently for 5-7 minutes until fish flakes easily. Remove from water. Cool slightly. Flake catfish; set aside. In a mixing bowl stir together cream cheese, mayonnaise, Worcestershire sauce, lemon juice and garlic salt. Stir in chopped onion.

To assemble, spread cheese mixture over bottom of a 12-inch plate or shallow serving bowl. Spread chili sauce over cheese layer. Top with cooked catfish. Garnish with parsley, if desired. Serve with sturdy crackers. Serves 12.

Approximate nutritional analysis per serving:
Calories 256, Protein 23 g, Carbohydrates 9 g, Fat 14 g,
Cholesterol 92 mg, Sodium 538 mg

Courtesy of the Catfish Institute.

OLIVE CAVIAR

1 cup (240 ml) CALIFORNIA ripe olives
2-3 tbs (30-45 ml) garlic, bottled or freshly
    chopped (fresh is more potent)
½ tsp (3 ml) black pepper
1 tsp (5 ml) lemon peel, finely grated
2 tbs (30 ml) fresh lemon juice
1-2 tbs (15-30 ml) olive oil
1 tbs (15 ml) Worcestershire sauce
1 tbs (15 ml) onion, grated

Mix all ingredients. If finer texture is desired, turn ingredients into food processor and process a few seconds just until fine. Chill and serve with sliced fresh baguettes or crackers. Serves 6.

Approximate nutritional analysis per serving:
Calories 79, Protein < 1 g, Carbohydrates 4 g, Fat 7 g,
Cholesterol 0 mg, Sodium 374 mg

Courtesy of the California Olive Industry.

MEXICALI DIP

1 lb (455 g) ground beef
½ cup (120 ml) onion, chopped
1 clove garlic, minced
1 - 14 oz can (420 g) green chili salsa
1 - 17 oz can (510 g) spicy refried beans
¼ tsp (1 ml) ground cumin
½-1 tsp (3-5 ml) seasoned salt
¼ tsp (1 ml) chili powder
1 cup (240 ml) raisins
½ cup (120 ml) cheddar or jack cheese, shredded

Brown beef with onion and garlic; crumble beef. Stir in all remaining ingredients except raisins. Stirring occasionally, bring mixture to boil. Remove from heat and stir in raisins. Serve warm, with cheese sprinkled on top, as a dip for tortilla chips and/or raw vegetable dippers. Serves 40.

Approximate nutritional analysis per serving:
Calories 67, Protein 4 g, Carbohydrates 6 g, Fat 3 g,
Cholesterol 11 mg, Sodium 117 mg

Courtesy of the California Raisin Advisory Board.

FRESH GUACAMOLE

1 small yellow onion, quartered
2 tsp (10 ml) GILROY FARMS Chopped Jalapeño
    Peppers, drained
2 medium ripe avocados, peeled, pitted
    and quartered
2 tsp (10 ml) fresh lime or lemon juice
1 tsp (5 ml) GILROY FARMS Crushed Garlic

In food processor fitted with metal blade, finely chop onion and jalapeño peppers. Add avocados and process until smooth. Add lime or lemon juice and garlic; process 5 seconds. Serve with nachos, fajitas, taco salad, hamburgers and turkey sandwiches. Yields 1½ cups.

Approximate nutritional analysis per ¼ cup serving:
Calories 120, Protein 2 g, Carbohydrates 8 g, Fat 10 g,
Cholesterol 0 mg, Sodium 8 mg

Courtesy of McCormick/Schilling Spices.

CANNELLINI BEAN DIP

1 - 19 oz can (570 g) white kidney (cannellini)
    beans, drained and rinsed
3 tbs (45 ml) fresh lemon juice
3 tsp (15 ml) BERTOLLI Extra Virgin Olive Oil
1 tsp (5 ml) garlic, finely chopped
1 tsp (5 ml) fresh oregano leaves, chopped
    or ¼ tsp (1 ml) dried oregano
pinch of salt
4 cups (960 ml) assorted raw vegetables: carrots,
    yellow squash, bell peppers, celery sticks,
    broccoli and/or cauliflower florets

Combine the beans, lemon juice, 2 tsp of the olive oil, garlic, half of the oregano and the pinch of salt in food processor. Process until smooth. Spread in small shallow bowl and drizzle the remaining olive oil on top. Sprinkle with the remaining oregano and serve spread on crostini (toasted Italian bread) or as a dip with vegetables. Serves 12.

Approximate nutritional analysis per serving:
Calories 53, Protein 3 g, Carbohydrates 1 g, Fat 8 g,
Cholesterol 0 mg, Sodium 79 mg

REFRIED BEAN DIP

1 cup (240 ml) GOYA Refried Beans
1 cup (240 ml) sour cream
½ tbs (8 ml) prepared mustard
½ tsp (3 ml) salt

Combine ingredients and mix well. Chill before serving.

Nutritional analysis not available.

CHICK PEA & TAHINI DIP

1 can GOYA Chick Peas
½ cup (120 ml) tahini (from can)
¼ cup (60 ml) onion, chopped
4 cloves garlic
¼ cup (60 ml) GOYA Extra Virgin Olive Oil
1 tsp (5 ml) dill, chopped
1 tsp (5 ml) lemon juice
salt and pepper to taste

Mash peas in blender or by hand. Combine with remaining ingredients. Chill before serving. Yields 2½ cups.

Approximate nutritional analysis per ¼ cup serving, unsalted:
Calories 152, Protein 5 g, Carbohydrates 14 g, Fat 9 g,
Cholesterol 0 mg, Sodium 1 mg

MIDDLE EASTERN ALMOND DIP

1½ cups (355 ml) BLUE DIAMOND Blanched
    Whole Almonds, toasted
7 tbs (105 ml) olive oil, divided
1 - 15 oz can (450 g) garbanzo beans, drained
¾ cup (180 ml) water
6 tbs (90 ml) lemon juice
2 cloves garlic, chopped finely
1 tsp (5 ml) salt
½ tsp (3 ml) cumin
¼ tsp (1 ml) white pepper
1 tbs (15 ml) fresh parsley, chopped
½ tsp (3 ml) paprika
fresh vegetables for dipping
pita bread for dipping

Finely grind almonds with 6 tbs oil in food processor or blender. Add beans, water, lemon juice, garlic, salt, cumin and pepper, continuing to process until smooth. Spread about 1 inch thick onto a serving dish. Chill. Just before serving, drizzle remaining 1 tbs oil over top and sprinkle with parsley and paprika. Serve with fresh vegetables and pita bread. Serves 6.

Approximate nutritional analysis per serving:
Calories 457, Protein 14 g, Carbohydrates 27 g, Fat 35 g,
Cholesterol 0 mg, Sodium 360 mg

BLACK BEAN 'N SALSA DIP

1 - 16 oz can (480 g) black beans, drained
½ cup (120 ml) ORTEGA Mild, Medium or Hot
    Thick and Chunky Salsa
1 tbs (15 ml) lemon juice
1 large clove garlic, crushed
¼ cup (60 ml) scallions, sliced
scallions, for garnish
Fat Free MR. PHIPPS Pretzel Chips

Reserve ½ cup beans. In electric blender or food processor, blend remaining beans, salsa, lemon juice and garlic until smooth. Stir in scallions and reserved beans. Chill for 1 hour to blend flavors. Garnish with scallions if desired. Serve as a dip with pretzel chips. Yields 1¾ cups.

Approximate nutritional analysis per 1 tbs serving plus 4 pretzel chips:
Calories 36, Fat 0 g, Cholesterol 0 mg, Sodium 207 mg

Spicy Stuffed Mushrooms

LAYERED BLACK BEAN DIP

1 - 16 oz can (480 g) black beans, drained
⅓ cup (80 ml) ORTEGA Mild, Medium or Hot
    Thick and Chunky Salsa
1 clove garlic, minced
¼ cup (60 ml) light sour cream
2 tbs (30 ml) tomatoes, chopped
1 tbs (15 ml) scallions, chopped
ripe olives, sliced, optional
WHEAT THINS Snack Crackers

In electric blender or food processor container, blend black
beans, salsa and garlic just until combined (mixture will be
chunky). Spread bean mixture on large serving plate; top with
light sour cream, tomatoes, scallions and olives, if desired.
Serve as a dip with snack crackers. Yields 1½ cups.

Approximate nutritional analysis per 2 tbs serving, without olives,
plus 8 crackers: Calories 114, Fat 4 g, Cholesterol 2 mg, Sodium 307 mg

SPICY STUFFED MUSHROOMS

1 lb (455 g) small to medium mushrooms
    (about 30)
½ lb (230 g) bulk hot or regular sausage
¼ cup (60 ml) onion, chopped
⅓ cup (80 ml) HEINZ Tomato Ketchup
2 tbs (30 ml) dry bread crumbs
1 tsp (5 ml) dried parsley flakes

Remove stems from mushrooms; finely chop enough stems to
measure ½ cup. Crumble sausage in large skillet; add chopped
mushroom stems and onion and cook until sausage is browned,
stirring frequently. Drain excess fat; stir in ketchup, bread
crumbs and parsley. Fill each mushroom cap with sausage
mixture; place in 3-qt baking dish. Bake in preheated 350°F
(180°C) oven 12-15 minutes. Yields 30 mushrooms.

Approximate nutritional analysis per mushroom:
Calories 40, Protein 1 g, Carbohydrates 2 g, Fat 3 g,
Cholesterol 5 mg, Sodium 86 mg

COCKTAILS AT TIFFANY'S

1 cup (240 ml) cooked wild rice
1 cup (240 ml) raw potato, shredded
⅓ cup (80 ml) golden raisins
1 egg, beaten
2 tbs (30 ml) chives, snipped
2 tbs (30 ml) half and half
1 tbs (15 ml) butter or margarine, melted
3 tbs (45 ml) flour
¼ tsp (1 ml) salt
¼ tsp (1 ml) pepper
sour cream
golden and black caviars, optional

In bowl combine rice, potato, raisins, egg, chives, half and half, and butter. Stir in flour, salt and pepper; mix to blend. Spoon into hot, oiled skillet, a few at at time, to make 2-3-inch pancakes. Fry until golden on both sides. Serve hot with sour cream and caviars. Serves 4.

Approximate nutritional analysis per serving, without sour cream and caviar: Calories 153, Protein 5 g, Carbohydrates 23 g, Fat 5 g, Cholesterol 64 mg, Sodium 185 mg

Approximate nutritional analysis per serving, with 1 tbs sour cream and 1 tsp caviar: Calories 198, Protein 6 g, Carbohydrates 24 g, Fat 9 g, Cholesterol 101 mg, Sodium 272 mg

QUESADILLAS WITH CRABMEAT

4 oz (120 g) light Monterey Jack cheese, shredded
¾ cup (180 ml) nonfat salad dressing or
    nonfat mayonnaise
⅓ cup (80 ml) LAND O LAKES No-Fat,
    Light or Regular Sour Cream
6 oz (180 g) cooked crabmeat, drained, flaked*
2 tbs (30 ml) green onions, sliced
2 tbs (30 ml) chopped mild green chilies, drained
10 medium flour tortillas
1 large ripe tomato, chopped
cilantro leaves, if desired

Heat oven to 425°F (220 °C). In large bowl stir together all ingredients except tortillas, tomato and cilantro. Spread 2-3 tbs filling on each tortilla; fold in half. Place on cookie sheets. Bake 8-10 minutes or until heated through. Cut each quesadilla into 3 wedges. Top with tomato; garnish with cilantro.
Yields 30 appetizers.
    * 6 oz imitation crabmeat (surimi), drained, flaked, can be substituted for 6 oz crabmeat, drained, flaked.

Approximate nutritional analysis per serving:
Calories 70, Protein 4 g, Carbohydrates 10 g, Fat 2 g, Cholesterol 5 mg, Sodium 210 mg

MOCK CRAB CAKES

1 large eggplant
1 tbs (15 ml) minced dried onion
1 tbs (15 ml) minced parsley
1 tbs (15 ml) Worcestershire sauce
4 tbs (60 ml) diced bread crumbs
2 tbs (30 ml) OLD BAY Seasoning
1 egg, separated, with white beaten stiff
2 tbs (30 ml) oil

Prick eggplant with a fork several times and put on a plate in the microwave. Microwave on HIGH for 7 minutes, or until the eggplant is soft and cooked through. Remove the skin and put the inside of the eggplant (the "meat") in a blender or food processor. Process on high for about 20 seconds.

In a large bowl, put eggplant and all remaining ingredients (except oil), folding in the beaten egg white last.

In a nonstick skillet, heat about 1 tbs of the oil. When hot, drop about ¼ cup of the eggplant mixture into the skillet and fry the "crab" cakes for about 2-3 minutes on each side, until crispy. You should be able to fry about three at a time. Repeat with the remainder of the mixture, adding additional oil as needed. Serves 3.

Approximate nutritional analysis per serving:
Calories 158, Protein 4 g, Carbohydrates 12 g, Fat 11 g, Cholesterol 71 mg, Sodium 427 mg

Courtesy of McCormick/Schilling Spices.

HAZELNUT, BRIE & APPLE APPETIZER

4 oz (120 g) cream cheese, room temperature
8 oz (240 g) Brie cheese, rind trimmed,
    room temperature
1 cup (240 ml) OREGON Hazelnuts,
    roasted and chopped
1 tart apple, grated

Blend well the cream cheese with the Brie cheese. Add the hazelnuts and apple; blend. Spread on melba toast or crackers. Serves 24.

Approximate nutritional analysis per serving:
Calories 81 , Protein 3 g, Carbohydrates 2 g, Fat 7 g, Cholesterol 15 mg, Sodium 73 mg

---

Opposite: Cocktails at Tiffany's

Spanish Sweet Onion Bowls with Artichoke Dip

SPANISH SWEET ONION BOWLS WITH ARTICHOKE DIP

1 large (about 1 lb) (455 g) Idaho-Oregon
    Spanish sweet onion, peeled
2 tbs (30 ml) water
½ cup (120 ml) prepared marinated artichoke
    hearts, drained and coarsely chopped
¼ cup (60 ml) mayonnaise
1 tsp (5 ml) fresh lemon juice
dash cayenne pepper
2 tbs (30 ml) Parmesan cheese, grated
assorted fresh vegetables
sliced French bread

Cut off top inch and bottom root of onion. Cut and scoop out center, leaving about ½ inch along sides and bottom of onion. Chop scooped out center to equal 2 tbs. Microwave chopped onion and water in microwave-safe bowl at HIGH (100%) 30-45 seconds. Microwave onion "bowl" with cut side down in microwave-safe dish at HIGH for 1½ minutes. Turn onion over and microwave 1½ minutes longer or until tender but still holding shape. Thoroughly mix artichokes, mayonnaise, cooked chopped onion, lemon juice and cayenne. Spoon into onion center, mounding slightly. Sprinkle with Parmesan cheese, covering dip. Bake at 400°F (205°C) 15 minutes or until cheese browns. Serve hot with vegetables and bread. Serves 4.

Approximate nutritional analysis per serving without vegetables and bread: Calories 124, Protein 3 g, Carbohydrates 16 g, Fat 6 g, Cholesterol 6 mg, Sodium 177 mg

PROSCIUTTO FRUIT BUNDLES IN ENDIVE

3 oz (90 ml) domestic prosciutto ham, thinly sliced
2 tbs (30 ml) rice or white wine vinegar
1 tbs (15 ml) vegetable oil
1 tbs (15 ml) light soy sauce
1 green onion, cut up
1 rib (4-inch) celery, cut up
½ tsp (3 ml) sugar
½ tsp (3 ml) grated lime peel
¼ tsp (1 ml) ground ginger
4 slices (3x½-inch) *each* cantaloupe, honeydew
**   melon and pineapple**
8 julienne strips (2x¼-inch) *each* celery, green
**   and red bell pepper**
24 Belgian endive leaves

Combine vinegar, oil, soy sauce, onion, celery, sugar, lime peel and ginger in food processor bowl fitted with steel blade or blender container; cover and process until fairly smooth, scraping side of bowl, as necessary. Place fruits and vegetables in plastic bag; add dressing, turning to coat. Close bag securely and marinate in refrigerator 30 minutes. Remove fruits and vegetables from dressing. Meanwhile trim and discard excess fat from ham; cut ham into ½-inch wide strips. Wrap ham strips around following combinations: cantaloupe/celery; honeydew melon/red bell pepper and pineapple/green bell pepper. Place each bundle on endive leaf. Cover with plastic wrap and refrigerate until ready to serve. Yields 24 appetizers.

Approximate nutritional analysis per appetizer:
Calories 18, Protein < 1 g, Carbohydrates 2 g, Fat 1 g,
Cholesterol 2 mg, Sodium 99 mg

Prosciutto Fruit Bundles in Endive

PESTO DEVILED EGGS

6 hard-cooked eggs
3 tbs (45 ml) Parmesan cheese, grated
2 tbs (30 ml) plain lowfat yogurt
1 tsp (5 ml) basil leaves, crushed
½ tsp (3 ml) garlic powder

Cut eggs in half lengthwise. Remove yolks and set whites aside. Mash yolks with fork. Stir in remaining ingredients until well blended. Refill whites, using about 1 tbs yolk mixture for each egg half. Chill to blend flavors.

　　Quick and Easy Method: Cut eggs in half lengthwise. Place yolks in 1-qt plastic food storage bag and set whites aside. Add remaining ingredients to bag. Press out air. Seal bag and knead until ingredients are well blended. Push kneaded mixture toward corner of bag and snip off about ½ inch from corner of bag. Squeezing bag gently, refill whites with yolk mixture. Chill to blend flavors.

Approximate nutritional analysis per serving:
Calories 106, Protein 9 g, Carbohydrates 1 g, Fat 7 g,
Cholesterol 217 mg, Sodium 183 mg

Courtesy of the American Egg Board.

PEPPER CHEESE STRIPS

1 small green bell pepper, cut into 1-inch strips,
**　　then cut in half crosswise**
1 small red bell pepper, cut into 1-inch strips,
**　　then cut in half crosswise**
1 small yellow bell pepper, cut into 1-inch strips,
**　　then cut in half crosswise**
2 tbs (30 ml) ripe olives, sliced
2 tbs (30 ml) CHI-CHI'S Diced Green Chilies
2 tbs (30 ml) green onions, sliced
1 cup (240 ml) medium cheddar cheese, shredded
sour cream
CHI-CHI'S Salsa

Heat oven to 400°F (205°C). In 9-inch glass pie plate, arrange pepper strips. Sprinkle with olives, chilies, green onions and cheese. Bake 8-10 minutes or until cheese is melted. Serve with sour cream and salsa. Serves 8.

Approximate nutritional analysis per serving:
Calories 70, Protein 4 g, Carbohydrates 2 g, Fat 5 g,
Cholesterol 15 mg, Sodium 105 mg

STUFFED JALAPEÑO PEPPERS

12 CHI-CHI'S Whole Green or Red Jalapeño Peppers
1 - 3 oz pkg (90 g) cream cheese, softened
½ cup (120 ml) cheddar cheese, shredded
¼ cup (60 ml) green onions, sliced
dash garlic powder
12 pimiento strips, if desired

Heat oven to 375°F (190°C). Rinse and drain jalapeño peppers. Slit lengthwise on one side up to stem, leaving stem attached. Remove seeds and veins. In small mixer bowl, beat cream cheese until fluffy. Beat in cheddar cheese, onions and garlic powder. Fill each pepper with cheese mixture. Arrange stuffed peppers on baking sheet or in heatproof serving dish. Bake about 10 minutes or until cheese is melted. Top each pepper with pimiento strip, if desired. Serves 12.

Approximate nutritional analysis per serving:
Calories 60, Protein 3 g, Carbohydrates 5 g, Fat 4 g,
Cholesterol 15 mg, Sodium 55 mg

ORIENTAL CRAB APPETIZERS

½ cup (120 ml) Swiss cheese, shredded
¼ cup (60 ml) toasted almonds, finely chopped
3 tbs (45 ml) green onions, minced
2 tbs (30 ml) mayonnaise or salad dressing
1½ tsp (8 ml) HEINZ Worcestershire Sauce
½ tsp (3 ml) seasoned salt
1 - 6 oz can (180 g) lump crabmeat,
**　　rinsed and drained**
25-30 wonton skins
vegetable oil
Chinese hot mustard or sweet-sour sauce

In medium bowl, combine first 6 ingredients; gently stir in crabmeat. Place about 1 tbs of crab mixture in center of each wonton skin. Moisten wonton edges with water; roll into a log, pressing ends to seal. Pour oil into saucepan or skillet to a depth of 1 inch; heat oil to 375°F (190°C). Fry wontons, a few at a time, until golden brown. Serve with Chinese hot mustard or sweet-sour sauce, if desired. Yields 25 appetizers.

Approximate nutritional analysis per appetizer:
Calories 14, Protein 1 g, Carbohydrates < 1 g, Fat < 1 g,
Cholesterol 4 mg, Sodium 37 mg

Opposite: Stuffed Jalapeño Peppers

BEAN-STUFFED GREEN CHILES

1 cup (240 ml) DANNON Plain Nonfat or
    Lowfat Yogurt
½ tsp (3 ml) ground cumin
¼ tsp (1 ml) salt
2 cloves garlic, minced
1 tbs (15 ml) corn oil
½ cup (120 ml) green onions, minced
1 - 16 oz can (480 g) pinto beans, drained
½ cup (120 ml) fresh cilantro, minced
8 whole fresh mild green chiles, roasted and peeled*

RED PEPPER SAUCE:
3 large red bell peppers, coarsely chopped
2 cloves garlic, minced
2 tbs (30 ml) olive oil
1 tbs (15 ml) balsamic vinegar
½ tsp (3 ml) freshly ground pepper
1 cup (240 ml) DANNON Plain Nonfat or
    Lowfat Yogurt

In small bowl combine yogurt, cumin and salt. Cover; chill until ready to serve.

    In a medium skillet over medium-high heat cook and stir garlic in oil 1 minute. Add green onions; cook and stir 2 minutes. Add pinto beans; reduce heat to low. Mash beans with a potato masher or wooden spoon until chunky. Stir in cilantro.

    Preheat oven to 325°F (165°C). Beginning at stem end, make a lengthwise cut down each chile; open chile flat. Divide bean mixture evenly among the chiles. Gently shape bean mixture to fit chiles. Arrange chiles in 11x7-inch baking dish. Bake 15-20 minutes or until thoroughly heated. Spoon Red Pepper Sauce onto 4 serving plates; arrange 2 stuffed chiles on each plate. Top with yogurt mixture. Serves 4.

    * To roast and peel fresh chiles, place on foil-lined broiler rack; roast 2-3 inches from heat until evenly blistered and charred, turning as needed. Immediately place chiles in plastic bag; close bag. Let stand in bag 20 minutes. Peel each chile under cold running water, rubbing and pulling off charred skin. Slit chile open lengthwise using scissors or knife. Carefully pull out and discard seeds and veins. Rinse chiles well; pat dry with paper towels.

    RED PEPPER SAUCE: In a large skillet over medium-high heat cook and stir bell peppers and garlic in oil 15 minutes or until tender. Cool. In food processor or blender combine bell pepper mixture, vinegar and ground pepper. Process until smooth; set aside. Spoon yogurt into strainer lined with double thickness of cheese cloth or a coffee filter. Place bowl beneath, but not touching strainer to catch liquid. Let stand at room temperature 15 minutes. Scrape yogurt into a small bowl. Discard liquid. Add pepper mixture to yogurt; stir.

Approximate nutritional analysis per serving:
Calories 391, Protein 18 g, Carbohydrates 55 g, Fat 13 g,
Cholesterol 7 mg, Sodium 226 mg

CURRIED TUNA ALMONDINE

2 - ¼ oz envelopes (15 g) unflavored gelatin
½ cup (120 ml) cold milk
1 cup (240 ml) milk, heated to boiling
16 oz (480 g) cream cheese, softened
1 tbs (15 ml) lemon juice
1 tbs (15 ml) curry powder
2 cloves garlic, chopped finely
1 tsp (5 ml) salt
½ tsp (3 ml) white pepper
½ cup (120 ml) green onion, finely sliced
1 - 2 oz jar (60 g) diced pimiento
2 - 7 oz cans (420 g) water-packed, white tuna,
    drained and flaked
1 cup (240 ml) BLUE DIAMOND Sliced Natural
    Almonds, toasted, divided
green olive slices
crackers

In large bowl, sprinkle gelatin over cold milk; let stand 1 minute. Gradually add heated milk, stirring until gelatin is dissolved. Blend in cheese, a little at a time, until smooth. Add lemon juice and next 4 ingredients; blend well. Fold in onion, pimiento, tuna and ½ cup almonds. Turn into a 5 or 6 cup mold or bowl. Chill until firm, about 2-3 hours. Unmold onto platter and garnish with remaining almonds and green olives. Serve with crackers. Serves 6.

    Note: Put this savory mixture in a fish-shaped mold and decorate with overlapping sliced almonds to create fish scales. Green olive slices make the eyes.

Approximate nutritional analysis per serving:
Calories 378, Protein 24 g, Carbohydrates 6 g, Fat 30 g,
Cholesterol 72 mg, Sodium 624 mg

HEARTY CHILE CON QUESO

1 -12 oz pkg (360 g) pork sausage
1 -15 oz can (450 g) CHI-CHI'S San Antonio Chile
1 cup (240 ml) cheddar cheese, shredded
½ cup (120 ml) CHI-CHI'S Salsa
½ cup (120 ml) green onion, sliced
CHI-CHI'S Tortilla Chips, pita bread, crackers

In medium saucepan, crumble and brown sausage. Drain, if necessary. Stir in chili, cheese, salsa and onion. Cook and stir over medium-low heat just until cheese is melted. Serve warm with tortilla chips, pita bread wedges or crackers. Serves 4.

Approximate nutritional analysis per serving:
Calories 420, Protein 24 g, Carbohydrates 13 g, Fat 30 g,
Cholesterol 85 mg, Sodium 1210 mg

DILLY DEVILED EGGS

½ cup (120 ml) cucumber, shredded (1 medium)
1 tsp (5 ml) salt
6 hard-cooked eggs*
¼ cup (60 ml) dairy sour cream
¼ tsp (60 ml) dill weed
carrot, radish and celery garnishes, optional

Thoroughly combine cucumber and salt. Let stand 15 minutes. Drain well, pressing out excess liquid. Set aside. Cut eggs in half lengthwise. Remove yolk and set whites aside. Mash yolks with fork. Blend in sour cream and dill weed. Stir in drained cucumber. Refill whites, using 1 heaping tbs yolk mixture for each egg half. Garnish platter with vegetable garnishes, if desired. Serves 6.

   * To hard-cook eggs, put eggs in single layer in saucepan. Add enough tap water to come at least 1 inch above eggs. Cover and quickly bring just to boiling. Turn off heat. If necessary, remove pan from burner to prevent further boiling. Let eggs stand covered in the hot water 15-17 minutes for large eggs. (Adjust time up or down by about 3 minutes for each size larger or smaller.) Immediately run cold water over eggs or put them in ice water until completely cooled. To remove shell, crackle it by tapping gently all over. Roll egg between hands to loosen shell, then peel, starting at large end. Hold egg under running cold water or dip in bowl of water to help ease off shell.

Approximate nutritional analysis per serving:
Calories 102, Protein 7 g, Carbohydrates 2 g, Fat 7 g,
Cholesterol 216 mg, Sodium 424 mg

FISH EN ESCABECHE

1 lb (455 g) firm white fish fillets (orange roughy,
    mackerel or haddock), cut into ¾-inch cubes
1 - 11½ oz jar (345 ml) CHI-CHI'S Pico de Gallo
2 tbs (30 ml) vegetable oil
2 tbs (30 ml) fresh lemon juice
2 tbs (30 ml) fresh lime juice
1 garlic clove, minced
½ tsp (3 ml) salt
¼ tsp (1 ml) dried oregano leaves
⅛ tsp (.5 ml) pepper
1 CHI-CHI'S Whole Green Jalapeño Pepper,
    finely chopped
16 small pimiento-stuffed green olives
1 avocado, peeled and chopped
crackers, snack breads or CHI-CHI'S
    Tortilla Chips, if desired

In 10-inch skillet, bring ¾-inch water to a boil. Carefully add fish. Bring to a boil; cook 15 seconds or just until fish is opaque (do not overcook). Drain carefully. In large glass or plastic bowl, combine remaining ingredients except olives and avocado. Mix well. Carefully stir in fish and olives. Cover; refrigerate at least 4 hours or up to 2 days, stirring occasionally. Just before serving, gently stir in avocado. Serve with crackers, snack breads or tortilla chips, if desired. Serves 12.

Approximate nutritional analysis per serving:
Calories 110, Protein 7 g, Carbohydrates 4 g, Fat 8 g,
Cholesterol 10 mg, Sodium 350 mg

Dilly Deviled Eggs

MEXICAN SHRIMP COCKTAIL

24 large raw fresh shrimp
1½ cups (355 ml) water
½ cup (120 ml) lime juice
2 tsp (10 ml) fresh garlic, minced
1 CHI-CHI'S Whole Green or Red Jalapeño
Pepper, minced
2 tsp (10 ml) salt
1 tsp (5 ml) chili powder

COCKTAIL SAUCE:
1 cup (240 ml) CHI-CHI'S Picante Sauce
¼ cup (60 ml) ketchup
2 tsp (10 ml) fresh cilantro, chopped

Peel, devein and rinse shrimp, leaving tails attached, if desired. Set aside. In medium saucepan, combine water, lime juice, garlic, jalapeño pepper, salt and chili powder. Bring to a boil; boil until reduced to 1 cup. Add shrimp. Bring to a boil; cook 1-2 minutes or until shrimp turn pink. Drain. Cover and refrigerate until chilled. In small bowl, combine all Cocktail Sauce ingredients. Mix well. Serve shrimp with Cocktail Sauce. Serves 6.

Approximate nutritional analysis per serving:
Calories 50, Protein 6 g, Carbohydrates 6 g, Fat 1 g,
Cholesterol 45 mg, Sodium 430 mg

LEMONY ASPARAGUS SOUFFLÉ

butter
Parmesan cheese, grated
¼ cup (60 ml) butter
¼ cup (60 ml) flour
½ tsp (3 ml) salt
¾ cup (180 ml) milk
1 cup (4 oz) (120 g) Monterey Jack cheese, shredded
4 eggs, separated
1 tsp (5 ml) grated lemon peel
2 tbs (30 ml) lemon juice, divided
1 lb (455 g) fresh asparagus, cleaned, trimmed,
cooked, drained and cut into ½-inch lengths
***or* 1 - 10 oz pkg frozen asparagus spears;**
cooked, drained and cut in ½-inch lengths

Butter a 1-qt soufflé dish or straight sided casserole and dust with Parmesan cheese. Wrap band around dish and overlap 2 inches. Butter band and dust lightly with Parmesan cheese. Wrap band around dish with dusted side in and fasten with straight pins, paper clips or string. Collar should stand at least 2 inches above rim of dish. Set aside.

In medium saucepan over medium-high heat, melt ¼ cup butter. Blend in flour and salt. Cook, stirring constantly, until mixture is smooth and bubbly. Stir in milk all at once. Cook and stir until mixture boils and is smooth and thickened. Remove from heat and stir in cheese until melted. Set aside.

In large mixing bowl, beat egg whites with 1 tsp of the lemon juice at high speed until stiff but not dry, just until whites no longer slip when bowl is tilted. Thoroughly blend egg yolks, asparagus, lemon peel and remaining lemon juice into reserved sauce. Gently, but thoroughly, fold yolk mixture into whites. Carefully pour into prepared soufflé dish

For a "top hat", hold spoon upright and circle mixture to make ring about 1 inch from side of dish and 1 inch deep. Bake in preheated 350°F (180°C) oven until puffy, delicately browned and soufflé shakes slightly when oven rack is moved gently back and forth, about 35-40 minutes. Quickly, but gently, remove collar. Serve immediately. Serves 4.

Approximate nutritional analysis per serving:
Calories 369, Protein 19 g, Carbohydrates 15 g, Fat 27 g,
Cholesterol 274 mg, Sodium 626 mg

Courtesy of the American Egg Board.

Mexican Shrimp Cocktail

MOLDED CRABMEAT MOUSSE

1 cup (240 ml) water
1 envelope unflavored gelatin
3 hard-cooked eggs*, chunked
4 oz (120 g) fresh crabmeat, flaked and cooked
    or flaked refrigerated flake-style imitation
    crabmeat blend or sliced thawed frozen
    imitation crabmeat blend
3 large stalks celery, quartered
½ cup (120 ml) bottled seafood sauce
4 green onions with tops, quartered
green onion fans, optional

In small saucepan, sprinkle gelatin with water. Cook over medium heat, stirring occasionally, until gelatin is dissolved. Pour into blender container. Add remaining ingredients except onion fans. Cover and blend at medium speed until smooth. Pour into 3-cup mold. Cover and chill until firm, several hours or overnight. Garnish with onion fans, if desired. Serves 3.

To prepare without blender: In medium bowl, stir sauce into dissolved gelatin mixture until well blended. Chill until mixture mounds slightly when dropped from spoon. Chop eggs. Fold into chilled gelatin mixture along with chopped crabmeat, celery and onions. Mold as above.

* If you've ever had trouble peeling hard-cooked eggs, it's likely your eggs were very fresh. Eggs that have been refrigerated for a week to ten days are more likely to peel easily after hard cooking than very fresh eggs.

Approximate nutritional analysis per serving, using fresh crabmeat: Calories 177, Protein 19 g, Carbohydrates 13 g, Fat 6 g, Cholesterol 252 mg, Sodium 800 mg

Courtesy of the American Egg Board.

GREEN CHILI AND MUSHROOM PHYLLO TARTS

1 - 3 oz pkg (90 g) cream cheese, softened
¾ cup (180 ml) sour cream
¼ cup (60 ml) fine dry bread crumbs
1 - 4¼ oz can (128 g) CHI-CHI'S Diced Green
    Chilies, drained
1 - 4½ oz jar (135 g) sliced mushrooms, drained
1 tbs (15 ml) fresh lime juice
2 tsp (10 ml) dried dill weed
½ tsp (3 ml) salt
1 clove garlic, slightly mashed
½ cup (120 ml) butter or margarine
8 - 17x12-inch frozen phyllo (filo) pastry sheets,
    thawed
12 red or green CHI-CHI'S Jalapeño Wheels
CHI-CHI'S Salsa Picante Sauce

Heat oven to 350°F (180°C). In small bowl, combine cream cheese and sour cream. Mix well. Stir in bread crumbs, chilies, mushrooms, lime juice, dill weed and salt. In small skillet or saucepan, cook garlic in butter until tender. Coat 12 - 2½-inch muffin cups with garlic butter. Set aside. Brush large cookie sheet with garlic butter. On work surface, unroll phyllo sheets; cover with plastic wrap or dampened towel. Place one phyllo sheet on greased cookie sheet; brush with butter. Top with second phyllo sheet. Repeat with remaining phyllo sheets. With sharp knife, cut layers of phyllo sheets to make 12 - 4¼x4-inch rectangles. Place one rectangle in each buttered muffin cup. Spoon cream cheese mixture into phyllo-lined cups. Bake 15-22 minutes or until phyllo is golden brown. Garnish with jalapeño wheels, if desired. Serve with salsa or picante sauce. Yields 12 large servings.

Mini-Tart Variation: Coat 24 mini-muffin cups with garlic butter. Cut layered phyllo sheets into 24 - 3x2H-inch rectangles. Continue as directed above. Yields 24 mini servings.

Approximate nutritional analysis per serving, 1 large or 2 mini: Calories 150, Protein 2 g, Carbohydrates 7 g, Fat 13 g, Cholesterol 35 mg, Sodium 390 mg

CHICKEN CROSTINI

3 eggs, lightly beaten
2 tsp (10 ml) milk
1 - 9 oz pkg (270 g) CONTADINA Refrigerated
    Chicken and Rosemary Ravioli, cooked,
    drained and kept warm
¾ cup (180 ml) all purpose flour
2 cups (480 ml) Parmesan cheese, grated
¼ cup (60 ml) butter, divided
4 cloves garlic, divided
⅔ cup (7 oz) (210 g) CONTADINA Refrigerated
    Pesto with Sun Dried Tomatoes
    or ⅔ cup (7 oz) (210 g) CONTADINA
    Refrigerated Pesto with Basil
    and 1 cup (10 oz) (300 g) CONTADINA
    Refrigerated Alfredo Sauce

In small bowl, combine eggs and milk; set aside. Dip each ravioli in flour, egg mixture then cheese. In medium skillet, heat 2 tbs butter; sauté lightly 2 whole cloves garlic. Add ravioli; sauté for 1-2 minutes on each side or until golden brown. Remove from pan; keep warm. Repeat process with remaining ravioli adding butter and garlic to skillet as needed. Serve immediately with sauces for dipping. Yields 40 appetizers.

Approximate nutritional analysis per appetizer, without sauces: Calories 53, Protein 3 g, Carbohydrates 3 g, Fat 3 g, Cholesterol 23 mg, Sodium 129 mg

CHINESE CHICKEN TOASTS

1 ½ lbs (685 g) **EMPIRE KOSHER ground chicken**
1 cup (240 ml) onion, coarsely chopped
2 eggs, beaten
¼ cup (60 ml) cornstarch
1 tsp (5 ml) sesame oil
1 small can water chestnuts, drained and chopped
16 slices firm white bread, crusts trimmed
vegetable oil for frying

Mix ground chicken with onion, egg, cornstarch and sesame oil. Stir in chopped water chestnuts. Spread the mixture over the slices of bread, cover and refrigerate until ready to cook. Add ¾ inch vegetable oil to a large frying pan, or use a deep fryer. Heat over medium heat. Add the bread, chicken side down, and fry until golden brown, about 1-2 minutes. Drain and cut triangles and serve hot. Yields 64 appetizers.

Approximate nutritional analysis per appetizer:
Calories 56, Protein 4 g, Carbohydrates 3 g, Fat 3 g,
Cholesterol 16 mg, Sodium 37 mg

ROLLED JALAPEÑO PINWHEELS

FILLING:
1 - 8 oz pkg (240 g) cream cheese, softened
1 cup (240 ml) medium cheddar cheese, shredded
½ cup (120 ml) ripe olives, sliced
2 tbs (30 ml) fresh cilantro, chopped
2 tbs (30 ml) green onions, sliced
½ tsp (3 ml) garlic powder

4 medium flour tortillas
3 ½ oz (105 g) **CHI-CHI'S Whole Red Jalapeno Peppers, each pepper split in half and seeded**

In medium mixing bowl, combine all filling ingredients. Mix well. On each flour tortilla, spread about ½ cup filling mixture. In center of each tortilla, place 6 jalapeño pepper halves lengthwise across tortilla. Roll tortilla up tightly jelly-roll fashion. Wrap in plastic wrap. Refrigerate at least 2 hours or until chilled. To serve, cut each tortilla roll in to 12 slices. Yields 48 appetizers.

Approximate nutritional analysis per appetizer:
Calories 45 , Protein 1 g, Carbohydrates 3 g, Fat 3 g,
Cholesterol 10 mg, Sodium 65 mg

Rolled Jalapeño Pinwheels and Southwest Wonton Bundles

SPICY CHICKEN WINGS

2 lbs (910 g) **EMPIRE KOSHER Chicken Wings**
vegetable oil
1 stick parve margarine
¼ cup (60 ml) hot sauce
2 tbs (30 ml) honey

Trim off the wing tip. Add about ½ inch of vegetable oil in a heavy skillet, and fry wings in batches without crowding, about 10-15 minutes. Drain wings on paper towels. Melt margarine with hot sauce and honey. Brush each wing generously with sauce, place in a dish; pour remainder of sauce over the top layer. Serves 6-8.

Approximate nutritional analysis per serving:
Calories 528, Protein 35 g, Carbohydrates 10 g, Fat 38 g,
Cholesterol 109 mg, Sodium 282 mg

POLENTA TOASTS WITH ROASTED PEPPERS

TOASTS:
¼ cup (60 ml) onion, finely chopped
1 tsp (5 ml) BERTOLLI Classico or
    Extra Virgin Olive Oil
1½ cup (355 ml) reduced-sodium chicken broth
1 cup (240 ml) water
⅔ cup (160 ml) yellow cornmeal
1 tbs (15 ml) Parmesan cheese, grated
salt, to taste

ROASTED PEPPERS WITH HERBS:
1 - 7 oz jar (210 g) roasted red peppers,
    rinsed and drained
1 tbs (15 ml) fresh basil or parsley, chopped
1 tsp (5 ml) BERTOLLI Extra Virgin Olive Oil
freshly ground black pepper

Polenta toasts: Combine the onion and olive oil in a 4 qt saucepan; cook stirring over low heat until tender, about 5 minutes. Stir in the broth. In a separate bowl combine the water and cornmeal; stir into the broth and cook stirring constantly, until the mixture boils and is very thick, about 10 minutes. Add cheese and salt to taste.

Line a 13x9-inch baking pan with foil; spray foil lightly with olive oil cooking spray. Add the polenta and spread in a smooth layer with a spatula. Refrigerate until very cold and firm, about 2 hours. Turn polenta out of pan and peel off the foil. Cut into 12 squares. Preheat oven to 425°F (220°C). Spray a nonstick coated baking sheet with olive oil cooking spray. Arrange the polenta squares on the pan without touching.

Bake on bottom oven rack until browned on bottom, about 15 minutes. Turn and bake until browned and crisp, about 10 minutes more.

Meanwhile cut peppers into 12 even portions and arrange on a platter. Drizzle with olive oil and sprinkle with herbs and a grinding of black pepper. Arrange on top of each polenta square. Serve warm or at room temperature. Serves 12.

Approximate nutritional analysis per serving:
Calories 69, Protein 2 g, Carbohydrates 11 g, Fat 2 g,
Cholesterol 1 mg, Sodium 136 mg

TUSCAN BRUSCHETTA

1 cup (240 ml) dried tomato halves,
    halved with kitchen shears
2½ tbs (38 ml) olive oil
1 large garlic clove, pressed
1 - 15 oz can (450 g) any white beans
    (great northern or navy), rinsed and drained
    or 1½ cups (355 ml) cooked white beans
2 tbs (30 ml) red onion, finely chopped
2 tbs (30 ml) water
1-2 tbs (15-30 ml) lemon juice
salt and pepper to taste
16 slices Italian or French bread (¾-inch thick,
    about 3½ inches in diameter)
1 cup (4 oz) (120 g) part skim mozzarella or
    provolone cheese, shredded

In bowl, cover tomatoes with boiling water; let stand 10-15 minutes. Preheat oven to 450°F (230°C). Meanwhile, in small bowl, mix olive oil and garlic. On large plate, mash beans with fork. Mix in 2 tsp olive oil mixture, onion, water and lemon juice. Season with salt and pepper. Brush top of each bread slice with olive oil mixture, then spread with about 2 tsp bean mixture. Place, spaced apart, on large baking sheet. Thoroughly drain tomatoes; place pieces, equally divided, on bread slices; top each with 1 tbs cheese. Bake 5-6 minutes until bread is crisp and cheese is melted. Serve immediately. Serves 8.

Approximate nutritional analysis per serving:
Calories 140, Protein 8 g, Carbohydrates 17 g, Fat 5 g,
Cholesterol 10 mg, Sodium 160 mg

Courtesy of the American Dry Bean Board.

CHICKEN BITES

2 whole chicken breasts, boned and cut into
    bite-sized pieces
paprika, salt and pepper
1 tsp (5 ml) POMPEIAN Red Wine Vinegar
⅓ cup (80 ml) POMPEIAN 100% Pure Olive Oil

Sprinkle chicken pieces with paprika, salt and pepper to taste. Add vinegar. Stir well to coat the pieces. Marinate for 1 hour. Heat olive oil in a skillet to 320°F (160°C). Add chicken and sauté in both sides until golden brown. Serve immediately on wooden picks. Serves 12.

Approximate nutritional analysis per serving:
Calories 100, Protein 9 g, Carbohydrates < 1 g, Fat 7 g,
Cholesterol 24 mg, Sodium 21 mg

CHICKEN BAYOU PETITES

**4 PREMIUM YOUNG 'N TENDER Brand split
chicken breasts, skinned, boned and cut into
½-inch chunks**
1 tsp (5 ml) salt
2 tbs (30 ml) butter
1 large clove garlic, minced
½ cup (120 ml) onion, chopped
1 - 8 oz can (240 g) stewed tomatoes,
chopped, liquid reserved
1 tbs (15 ml) dried sweet pepper flakes
¼ tsp (1 ml) hot pepper sauce
2 - 11 oz cans (660 g) refrigerated cornbread twists
⅔ cup (160 ml) dairy sour cream
1 tbs (15 ml) honey
½ tsp (3 ml) paprika

Season chicken chunks with salt. Melt butter in a large skillet; add chicken, garlic and onion. Cook, stirring until chicken is done, about 3 minutes. Stir in tomatoes and liquid, pepper flakes and hot sauce. Set aside to cool while preparing cornbread cups.

Lightly grease muffin tins. Preheat oven to 350°F (180°C). Unroll cornbread twists dough keeping strips together in twos. You should have 8 strips of 2 cornbread twists. Cut each strip of two in half, crosswise. Place pieces together to make a square and press to seal along perforations. Press into muffin cup; repeat for each strip of 2 and repeat for second can of cornbread twists dough. This will fill 16 muffin cups.

Add sour cream and honey to cooled chicken mixture, stirring to blend. Spoon into cornbread muffin cups, filling almost to top. Sprinkle filling with paprika. Bake for 20 minutes or until done and cornbread cups are lightly browned. Yields 16 appetizers.

Approximate nutritional analysis per appetizer:
Calories 75, Protein 7 g, Carbohydrates 2 g, Fat 4 g,
Cholesterol 26 mg, Sodium 192 mg

EMPANADITAS

**2 - 9 oz pkgs (540 g) refrigerated pie crust circles
(4 crusts total)**
½ lb (230 g) lean ground beef
1¼ cups (295 ml) CHI-CHI'S Salsa, divided
½ cup (120 ml) onion, finely chopped
3 tbs (45 ml) raisins
3 tbs (45 ml) pimiento-stuffed green olives, chopped
1 tbs (15 ml) firmly packed brown sugar
1 tbs (15 ml) cider vinegar
¼ tsp (1 ml) salt
⅛ tsp (.5 ml) pepper
⅛ tsp (.5 ml) ground cinnamon
1 egg, beaten
1 - 8 oz pkg (240 g) cream cheese, softened

Let wrapped pie crusts stand at room temperature 20-30 minutes. Heat oven to 400°F (205°C). In large skillet, brown ground beef. Drain, if necessary. Stir in ½ cup salsa, onion, raisins, olives, brown sugar, vinegar, salt, pepper and cinnamon. Bring to boil. Reduce heat to low; simmer 10 minutes, stirring occasionally, until liquid is absorbed. Using ¾-inch round cutter, cut each piecrust into 8 circles. Spoon scant tbs beef mixture onto half of each circle. Brush edge of dough with beaten egg. Fold dough in half; seal edges with fingers, fork or pastry crimper. Place on ungreased baking sheet. Brush with beaten egg. Bake 12-18 minutes or until golden brown. Mix cream cheese and remaining ¾ cup salsa until smooth. Serve empanaditas warm with cream cheese and salsa mixture. Yields 32 appetizers.

Approximate nutritional analysis per appetizer:
Calories 120, Protein 3 g, Carbohydrates 9 g, Fat 8 g,
Cholesterol 25 mg, Sodium 180 mg

Chicken Bayou Petites

SMOKED TURKEY AND SPINACH QUESADILLAS

vegetable oil
8 medium flour tortillas
2 cups (480 ml) Monterey Jack cheese, shredded
¼ cup (60 ml) CHI-CHI'S Diced Green Chilies
pepper
1 lime
16-24 fresh spinach leaves or cilantro leaves
CHI-CHI'S Salsa, Picante Sauce or CHI-CHI'S
    Pico de Gallo, if desired
guacamole , if desired
sour cream, if desired

Brush oil on one side of each tortilla.On one half of un-oiled side, sprinkle ¼ cup cheese, ¼ cup diced turkey and 2 tsp chilies. Season with pepper; drizzle with lime juice. Top with 2 or 3 spinach leaves. Fold tortilla in half. In large skillet, cook both sides over low heat until golden brown. Cut into 3 wedges; keep warm while cooking remaining tortillas. Serve with salsa, picante sauce or Pico de Gallo, guacamole and sour cream, if desired. Yields 24 appetizers.

Approximate nutritional analysis per serving:
Calories 100, Protein 6 g, Carbohydrates 7 g, Fat 6 g,
Cholesterol 15 mg, Sodium 115 mg

SWEET AND SPICY MEATBALLS

1 egg
1⅓ cup (320 ml) CHI-CHI'S Picante Sauce, divided
½ cup (120 ml) CHI-CHI'S Tortilla Chips,
    finely crushed
⅓ cup (80 ml) green onions, sliced
¾ tsp (4 ml) salt
½ tsp (3 ml) ground cumin
¼ tsp (1 ml) garlic powder
1 lb (455 g) lean ground beef
vegetable oil
½ cup (120 ml) apricot preserves
¼ tsp (1 ml) chili powder

In large mixing bowl, lightly beat egg. Stir in ⅓ cup picante sauce. Stir in tortilla chips, green onions, salt, cumin and garlic powder. Mix well. Stir in ground beef. Shape into 1-inch meatballs. Lightly coat large skillet with oil. Over medium heat, brown meatballs half at a time. Drain, if necessary. Remove all meatballs from skillet. Combine remaining 1 cup picante sauce, apricot preserves and chili powder in skillet. Cook and stir until well blended. Stir in meatballs. Bring to a boil. Reduce heat to low; simmer 10 minutes, stirring occasionally. Serve with toothpicks. Yields 32 meatballs.

Approximate nutritional analysis per meatball:
Calories 50, Protein 3 g, Carbohydrates 4 g, Fat 2 g,
Cholesterol 15 mg, Sodium 115 mg

SOUTHWEST WONTON BUNDLES

vegetable oil
¼ lb (115 g) Italian sausage
1 cup (240 ml) Monterey Jack cheese, shredded
¼ cup (60 ml) green onions, sliced
8 whole water chestnuts
2 tbs (30 ml) CHI-CHI'S Diced Green Chilies
1 CHI-CHI'S Whole Green or Red Jalapeno
    Pepper, halved and seeded
1 tbs (15 ml) fresh cilantro, chopped
1 - 1 lb pkg (455 g) wonton wrappers
1-2 eggs, beaten
chives or green onion strips, if desired
CHI-CHI'S Salsa or Picante Sauce

Heat 2 inches of oil to 350°F (180°C). In food processor bowl fitted with metal blade, combine sausage, cheese, green onions, water chestnuts, chilies, jalapeño pepper and cilantro. Process until a somewhat smooth paste forms. Place 1 tsp sausage filling in center of each wonton wrapper. Brush wonton wrapper from edge almost to filling with beaten egg. Gather points of wrapper; twist and pinch to form bundle. Deep fry in hot oil until golden brown; drain on paper towels. Tie each bundle with chive or green onion strip. Serve with salsa or picante sauce. Yields 60 appetizers.

Approximate nutritional analysis per appetizer:
Calories 60, Protein 2 g, Carbohydrates 4 g, Fat 4 g,
Cholesterol 5 mg, Sodium 25 mg

PINCHOS DE CHORIZO/ CHORIZO KABOBS

3 tbs (45 ml) GOYA Olive Oil
pinch of thyme
1 sprig parsley
½ tsp (3 ml) paprika
1 bay leaf
4 GOYA Chorizos, cut into ½-inch slices
1 jar GOYA large Pimiento-Stuffed Olives

In a skillet, heat olive oil with thyme, parsley, paprika and bay leaf. Add chorizo slices and sauté until well browned. Remove bay leaf and parsley. Serve on skewers, alternating chorizo slices with olives. Serves 6.

Nutritional analysis not available.

SANTA FE CHICKEN WINGS

2½ lbs (1138 g) chicken wings
1⅓ cup (320 ml) CHI-CHI'S Picante Sauce
⅔ cup (160 ml) ketchup
⅓ cup (80 ml) honey
½ tsp (3 ml) ground cumin
½ tsp (3 ml) chili powder
1 tsp (5 ml) fresh garlic, minced
⅔ cup (160 ml) sour cream

Cut wings at joints; discard wing tips. In large reclosable plastic food bag, combine ⅔ cup picante sauce, ketchup, honey, cumin, chili powder and garlic. Mix well. Add chicken wings to marinade; seal bag and turn several times to coat. Place bag in 13x9-inch pan. Refrigerate, turning occasionally, at least 2 hours. Heat oven to 400°F (205°C). Remove chicken from marinade; reserve marinade. Place chicken in nonstick or foil-lined rimmed 15x10x1-inch baking pan. Bake 30 minutes, basting once with reserved marinade. Turn wings over; baste with marinade. Bake 20-30 minutes or until well glazed and browned, basting once with marinade. Spoon sour cream into small shallow glass bowl; top with remaining ⅔ cup picante sauce. Serve as dip for chicken wings. Yields 24 appetizers.

Approximate nutritional analysis per appetizer:
Calories 70, Protein 4 g, Carbohydrates 4 g, Fat 4 g,
Cholesterol 15 mg, Sodium 125 mg

CHICKEN FLAUTAS

vegetable oil
2 cups (480 ml) cooked chicken, shredded
    or finely chopped
⅔ cup (160 ml) CHI-CHI'S Salsa
⅓ cup (80 ml) green onions, sliced
½ tsp (3 ml) ground cumin
¼ tsp (1 ml) salt
32 corn tortillas
2 cups (480 ml) cheddar or Monterey Jack
    cheese, shredded
guacamole, if desired
additional salsa, if desired

Heat about 1 inch of oil to 350°F (180°C). In medium bowl, combine chicken, salsa, green onions, cumin and salt. Mix well. Briefly dip each tortilla in hot oil just to soften. Drain on paper towels. Spoon 1 tbs chicken mixture and 1 tbs shredded cheese down center of each tortilla. Roll up tightly; secure with wooden pick. Cook tortilla in hot oil about 2 minutes or until golden brown, turning once. Drain. remove wooden picks. Serve with guacamole and salsa, if desired. Yields 32 flautas.

Approximate nutritional analysis per flauta:
Calories 220, Protein 7 g, Carbohydrates 17 g, Fat 15 g,
Cholesterol 15 mg, Sodium 230 m

CHICKEN BROCCOLI TRIANGLES

1½ lbs (685 g) (8-10 pieces) PREMIUM YOUNG
    'N TENDER Brand boneless, skinless
    chicken thighs
2 tbs (30 ml) oil
¼ tsp (1 ml) crushed red pepper
1 clove garlic, minced
1 - 10 oz pkg (300 g) frozen chopped broccoli, thawed
1 - 10¾ oz can (320 ml) condensed cream of
    chicken mushroom soup
¾ cup (180 ml) Parmesan cheese, grated
½ cup (120 ml) fresh cilantro, chopped
12 sheets phyllo pastry, thawed
1¼ cups (295 ml) butter or margarine, melted

Chop chicken thighs into very small pieces or grind in food processor. Heat oil in large skillet and sauté chicken, red pepper and garlic over medium heat until done. Drain; set aside to cool. When cool, add broccoli, soup, cheese and cilantro. Refrigerate until thoroughly chilled.

Work with 1 sheet of phyllo dough at a time, keeping others covered with plastic wrap to prevent drying out. Place 1 sheet on dry work surface with short edge toward you. Brush with melted butter. Fold bottom up about 3 inches. Cut dough vertically into 6 even strips. Place 1 full tsp of chicken filling at the bottom of each strip. Fold into a triangle folding alternately to the right and to the left until entire strip of dough is used. Repeat with remaining dough and filling. Brush tops of each triangle with butter and place on 15x10x1-inch ungreased baking sheet. Bake in preheated 375°F (190°C) oven for 15-20 minutes or until golden brown. Can be served hot or cold. Yields 72 triangles.

Note: May be prepared ahead and frozen, up to 1 month. To cook, remove from freezer. Let stand 10 minutes to thaw and bake as above. May also be cooked under oven broiler.

Approximate nutritional analysis per triangle
Calories 61, Protein 3 g, Carbohydrates 1 g, Fat 5 ,
Cholesterol 19 mg, Sodium 94 mg

GOLDEN YULETIDE CANAPÉS

½ **cup (120 ml) mayonnaise**
1 **tbs (15 ml) freeze-dried chopped chives**
½ **tsp (3 ml) prepared mustard**
¼ **tsp (1 ml) salt**
⅛-¼ **tsp (.5-1 ml) liquid red pepper seasoning**
6 **hard-cooked eggs*, chopped**
½ **cup (2 oz) (60 g) cheddar cheese, shredded**
¼ **cup (60 ml) pecans, chopped**
16 **slices cocktail-size rye bread**

Above: Golden Yuletide Canapés

Blend together mayonnaise, chives, mustard, salt and seasoning. Stir in eggs, cheese and pecans. Top each bread slice with 1 rounded tbs of the egg mixture. Broil about 6 inches from heat until lightly browned and bubbly, about 1-2 minutes. Yields 16 canapes, 2 per serving.

＊ To hard-cook, put eggs in single layer in saucepan. Add enough tap water to come at least 1 inch above eggs. Cover and quickly bring just to boiling. Turn off heat. If necessary, remove pan from burner to prevent further boiling. Let eggs stand, covered, in the hot water 15-17 minutes for large eggs. (Adjust time up or down by 3 minutes for each size larger or smaller.) Immediately run cold water over eggs or put them in ice water until completely cooled. To remove shell, crackle it by tapping gently all over. Roll egg between hand to loosen shell, then peel, starting at large end. Hold egg under running cold water or dip in bowl of water to help ease off shell.

Approximate nutritional analysis per canape:
Calories 83, Protein 3 g, Carbohydrates 6 g, Fat 6 g,
Cholesterol 82 mg, Sodium 146 mg

Courtesy of the American Egg Board.

CHEESY TURKEY SAUSAGE BITES

1 lb (455 g) bulk turkey sausage
3 cups (720 ml) **BISQUICK** Reduced Fat baking mix
2 cups (8 oz) (240 g) reduced fat cheddar
　　cheese, shredded
½ cup (120 ml) green onions, chopped
1 tsp (5 ml) dry mustard
½ tsp (3 ml) ground red pepper (cayenne)
¾ cup (180 ml) skim milk

HONEY MUSTARD SAUCE:
1 cup (240 ml) Dijon mustard
¼ cup (60 ml) honey

Heat oven to 350°F (180°C). Cook and stir sausage in 10-inch skillet until brown, crumbling sausage into small bits; drain on paper towel. Mix sausage, baking mix, cheese, onions, mustard and red pepper thoroughly in large bowl. Stir in milk. Drop dough by rounded teaspoonfuls about 2 inches apart onto ungreased cookie sheet. Bake about 15 minutes or until golden brown. Serve hot with Honey-Mustard Sauce. Yields 6 dozen appetizers.

　　Honey-Mustard Sauce: Stir mustard and honey in small bowl until blended. Yields 1¼ cups sauce.

Approximate nutritional analysis per serving:
Calories 50, Protein 2 g, Carbohydrates 5 g, Fat 2 g,
Cholesterol 5 mg, Sodium 150 mg

PORTUGUESE CHICKEN AND KIELBASA KEBABS

1½ lbs (685 g) **EMPIRE KOSHER** Turkey Kielbasa
2 lbs (910 g) **EMPIRE KOSHER** boneless,
　　skinless Chicken Breast Cutlets
bay leaves
2 tbs (30 ml) olive oil
1 garlic clove, crushed
½ tsp (3 ml) paprika

Use small bamboo skewers and pre-soak them in water to prevent burning. Cut the chicken breasts into 1-inch cubes, slice the kielbasa into ½ -inch rounds. Alternate chicken, a small piece of bay leaf, and a piece of kielbasa. Place kebabs in a shallow pan. Combine the oil, garlic and paprika, brush over kebabs and marinate in the refrigerator for about 2 hours. Broil, turning frequently, until the chicken is cooked through but still moist, about 5 minutes. To grill, cook over moderately hot coals, turning every 5 minutes, about 12-15 minutes. Yields 12-16 kebabs.

Nutritional analysis not available.

SHRIMP AND PESTO ROUNDS

½ cup (120 ml) **GILROY FARMS** Pesto Sauce
2 tbs (30 ml) fresh Parmesan cheese, grated
1 French bread baguette, sliced
1 lb (455 g) medium shrimp, cooked,
　　peeled and deveined

Combine pesto sauce and cheese. Spread on one side of each bread slice. Top each with a shrimp. Broil 2-3 minutes or until lightly toasted. Arrange on serving plate and serve immediately. Yields 30 appetizers.

Approximate nutritional analysis per appetizer, without pesto:
Calories 52, Protein 4 g, Carbohydrates 7 g, Fat < 1 g,
Cholesterol 24 mg, Sodium 98 mg

Courtesy of McCormick/Schilling Spices.

SAVORY VEGETABLE CANAPÉS

1 - 14 oz can (420 g) artichoke hearts,
　　drained and rinsed
1 - 8 oz container (240 g) spreadable **HEALTHY
　　CHOICE** Fat Free Pasteurized Process Herb
　　and Garlic Cream Cheese Product
¼ cup (60 ml) ripe olives, chopped
¼ cup (60 ml) green onions, sliced
cracked black pepper
24 cherry tomatoes
24 mushroom caps
24 - 1-inch pieces celery

Process artichoke hearts in food processor until finely chopped. Add to combined cream cheese, olives and onions; mix well. Season to taste. Cut tops from tomatoes, remove seeds and fill each with 1 tsp cheese mixture. Fill mushrooms and celery stalks with 1 tsp cheese mixture also. Serves 24.

Approximate nutritional analysis per serving:
Calories 31, Protein 3 g, Carbohydrates 4 g, Fat 1 g,
Cholesterol 2 mg, Sodium 184 mg

FRESH VEGETABLE PIZZA

**2 - 8 oz cans (480 g) PILLSBURY Refrigerated
    Crescent Dinner Rolls
1 - 8 oz carton (240 g) dairy sour cream
1-2 tbs (15-30 ml) prepared horseradish
¼ tsp (1 ml) salt
⅛ tsp (.5 ml) pepper
2 cups (480 ml) fresh mushrooms, chopped
1 cup (240 ml) seeded tomatoes, chopped
1 cup (240 ml) small broccoli florets
½ cup (120 ml) green bell pepper, chopped
½ cup (120 ml) green onions, chopped**

Heat oven to 375°F (190°C). Separate dough into 4 long rectangles. Place rectangles crosswise in ungreased 15x10x1-inch baking pan; press over bottom and 1 inch up sides to form crust. Seal perforations. Bake for 14-19 minutes or until golden brown. Cool completely.

    In small bowl, combine sour cream, horseradish, salt and pepper; blend until smooth. Spread evenly over cooled crust. Top with remaining ingredients. Cut into appetizer-sized pieces. Store in refrigerator. Yields 60 appetizers.

Approximate nutritional analysis per appetizer:
Calories 35, Protein 1 g, Carbohydrates 4 g, Fat 2 g,
Cholesterol 2 mg, Sodium 75 mg

CHEESY STUFFED MUSHROOMS

**1 lb (455 g) medium-sized fresh mushrooms
½ cup (120 ml) onion, chopped
1 - 8 oz pkg (240 g) HEALTHY CHOICE
    Fat Free Natural Shredded Cheddar cheese
2 tbs (30 ml) parsley, chopped
cracked black pepper
1 tbs (15 ml) vegetable oil**

Remove stems from mushrooms; chop enough stems to make ½ cup. Sauté stems with onions in oil until tender. Combine cheese, parsley and mushroom mixture in bowl or food processor. Process mixture until finely chopped and blended. Fill each mushroom cap with heaping spoonful of mixture. Bake at 350°F (180°C), 15 minutes. Serves 8.

Approximate nutritional analysis per serving:
Calories 74, Protein 10 g, Carbohydrates 5 g, Fat 2 g,
Cholesterol 5 mg, Sodium 205 mg

TOMATO, BASIL AND MOZZARELLA CHEESE SALAD

**3 large tomatoes, sliced ¼ inch thick
8 oz (240 g) mozzarella cheese, sliced ⅛ inch thick
1 small red onion, sliced ⅛ inch thick
¼ cup (60 ml) whole fresh basil leaves
1 cup (240 ml) CHI-CHI'S Pico de Gallo
¼ cup (60 ml) olive oil
2 tbs (30 ml) balsamic vinegar
1 tsp (5 ml) fresh garlic, minced**

On large serving platter with 1-inch rim, alternately arrange tomatoes, cheese, onion and basil. Top with Pico de Gallo. In small bowl, combine olive oil, vinegar and garlic. Mix well. Pour over salad. Cover; refrigerate 1 hour to blend flavors. Remove from refrigerator ½ hour before serving. Serves 6.

Approximate nutritional analysis per serving:
Calories 220, Protein 12 g, Carbohydrates 10 g, Fat 16 g,
Cholesterol 20 mg, Sodium 360 mg

BROILED CHEESE TRIANGLES

**4 small pocket pita breads
butter or margarine, melted
1½ cups (355 ml) process American cheese, shredded
¼ cup (60 ml) HEINZ Tomato Ketchup
2 tbs (30 ml) green pepper, finely chopped
2 tbs (30 ml) ripe olives, finely chopped
2 tbs (30 ml) mayonnaise or salad dressing**

Split each pita in half horizontally; brush split side with butter. Cut each pita half into 6 triangles. Place on baking sheet; bake in preheated 350°F (180°C) oven, 6-8 minutes or until they are crisp and golden brown. Meanwhile, combine cheese and remaining ingredients. Spread cheese mixture on pita triangles; place on baking sheet. Broil, 5-6 inches from heat source, 2-3 minutes or until cheese is melted. Yields 4 dozen appetizers.

    Note: Pita toast may be prepared in advance. Cool and store in an airtight container for up to 7 days.

Approximate nutritional analysis per appetizer:
Calories 42, Protein 1 g, Carbohydrates 3 g, Fat 3 g,
Cholesterol 6 mg, Sodium 90 mg

ULTIMATE NACHOS

1 lb (455 g) ground beef or chorizo sausage
1 cup (240 ml) onion, chopped
salt and pepper
2 - 15 oz cans (900 g) CHI-CHI'S Refried Beans
1 - 4¼ oz can (130 g) CHI-CHI'S Diced Green Chilies
1 cup (240 ml) CHI-CHI'S Salsa or
      CHI-CHI'S Pico de Gallo
1½ cups (355 ml) cheddar cheese, shredded
1½ cups (355 ml) Monterey Jack cheese, shredded
1 - 16 oz carton (480 g) sour cream
2 - 6 oz containers (360 g) frozen avocado dip or
      guacamole, thawed
½ cup (120 ml) green onions, sliced
1 - 2¼ oz can (68 g) sliced ripe olives, drained
CHI-CHI'S Tortilla Chips, if desired

Heat oven to 400°F (205°C). Lightly grease 13x9 -inch baking
dish. Brown ground beef and onions; drain. Season with salt
and pepper. Spread refried beans over bottom of greased
baking dish. Sprinkle with beef mixture and chilies. Spoon on
salsa. Sprinkle with cheeses. Cover and bake 35-45 minutes or
until heated through. Top with sour cream, avocado dip, onions
and olives. Serve with tortilla chips, if desired. Yields 3 dozen
appetizer servings.

Approximate nutritional analysis per serving:
Calories 140, Protein 6 g, Carbohydrates 6 g, Fat 11 g,
Cholesterol 25 mg, Sodium 250 mg

DRIED TOMATO PARTY POCKETS

¼ cup (60 ml) SONOMA Dried Tomato Bits
2 tbs (30 ml) boiling water
1 cup (4 oz) (120 g) sharp cheddar cheese, shredded
3 tbs (45 ml) green onions, sliced
1 - 10 oz pkg (300 g) prepared refrigerated biscuits
1 egg, beaten
2 tsp (10 ml) sesame seeds

Preheat oven to 400°F (205°C). In medium bowl mix tomato
bits and water; set aside 5 minutes. Add cheese and onions; toss
to blend evenly. On lightly floured surface, roll out each biscuit
to a 4-5 -inch circle. For each pocket, place about 2 tbs tomato
mixture onto center of circle. Brush edge with egg. Fold over
and press to seal completely. Place, spaced apart, on baking
sheet. Brush with egg and sprinkle with sesame seeds. Bake
8-10 minutes until golden brown. Serve warm or at room
temperature. Yields 10 pockets.

Approximate nutritional analysis per serving:
Calories 128, Protein 5 g, Carbohydrates 9 g, Fat 8 g,
Cholesterol 35 mg, Sodium 224 mg

TINY TACO TRIANGLES

½ cup (120 ml) dry textured vegetable protein,
      small granules
1 tsp (5 ml) apple cider vinegar
½ cup (120 ml) salsa, mild or medium
4 small flour tortillas
1¼ cups (5 oz) (150 g) mild reduced-fat cheddar
      cheese, shredded, divided
¼ cup (60 ml) red pepper, chopped
⅓ cup (80 ml) frozen corn, thawed
1 tbs (15 ml) cilantro, optional

Heat oven to 350°F (180°C). Pour ½ cup boiling water over
½ cup dry textured soy protein in microwavable bowl. Add
cider vinegar. Stir and let stand for 5 minutes. Add salsa to the
rehydrated soy protein. Cover tightly with plastic wrap and
microwave on HIGH for 5-6 minutes; check after 2 minutes
and add a little water if needed. Place tortillas on cookie sheet.
Bake 5-7 minutes or until lightly browned. Sprinkle 2 tbs of
cheese on each tortilla. Spoon soy protein mixture evenly over
cheese. Top with corn, red pepper, and remaining cheese. Bake
7-10 minutes or until cheese has melted. Sprinkle with cilantro.
Cut into quarters. Yields 8 triangles, 2 per serving.

Approximate nutritional analysis per serving:
Calories 127, Protein 8 g, Carbohydrates 13 g, Fat 5 g,
Cholesterol 9 mg, Sodium 215 mg

Dried Tomato Party Pockets

SPICY TOMATO GOAT CHEESE APPETIZER

½ cup (120 ml) onion, chopped
1 tbs (15 ml) butter or margarine
1 - 10 oz can (300 g) CHI-CHI'S Diced Tomatoes
    and Green Chilies
1 - 14½ oz can (435 g) whole tomatoes, cut up
1 tsp (5 ml) sugar
½ tsp (3 ml) salt
¼ tsp (1 ml) dried thyme leaves
6-7 oz (180-210 g) goat cheese*
coarsely ground pepper
fresh cilantro, chopped, if desired
toasted French bread slices, crackers or
    CHI-CHI'S Tortilla Chips, if desired

Heat oven to 350°F (180°C). In medium saucepan, sauté onion in butter until golden brown. Stir in tomatoes and chilies, whole cut up tomatoes, sugar, salt and thyme. Bring to a boil; boil at medium-high heat 10-15 minutes, stirring occasionally, until thickened and liquid is greatly reduced. Spoon tomato mixture into 9-inch glass pie plate or other 1-qt oven-proof serving dish. Cut goat cheese into ¼-inch slices. Arrange on top of tomato mixture. Sprinkle with pepper. Bake 12-18 minutes until cheese is heated through. Sprinkle with cilantro, if desired. Serve with toasted French bread slices, crackers or tortilla chips, if desired. Serves 7.

* 2 - 4 oz pkgs (240 g) garlic and herb flavored soft spreadable cheese can be substituted for the goat cheese. Drop by large tablespoonfuls on top of tomato mixture, forming about 8 dollops. Sprinkle with pepper.
Bake 8-12 minutes.

Approximate nutritional analysis per serving:
Calories 100, Protein 4 g, Carbohydrates 7 g, Fat 7 g,
Cholesterol 25 mg, Sodium 710 mg

INDONESIAN CHICKEN ON A STICK

CHICKEN:
1¼ lbs (570 g) EMPIRE KOSHER Chicken Breast
    Cutlets (or Turkey Tenders)
2 tbs (30 ml) sesame oil
2 tbs (30 ml) vegetable oil
¼ cup (60 ml) dry kosher sherry
¼ cup (60 ml) reduced sodium soy sauce
2 tbs (30 ml) lemon juice
1½ tsp (8 ml) fresh garlic, minced
1½ tsp (8 ml) fresh ginger, minced
¼ tsp (1 ml) pepper
dash of hot sauce

SAUCE:
2 tbs (30 ml) vegetable oil
1 tbs (15 ml) sesame oil
½ cup (120 ml) red onion, minced
2 tbs (30 ml) garlic, minced
1 tsp (5 ml) fresh ginger, minced
1 tbs (15 ml) kosher red wine vinegar
1 tbs (15 ml) brown sugar
⅓ cup (80 ml) peanut butter (smooth or chunky)
½ tsp (3 ml) ground coriander
3 tbs (45 ml) ketchup
3 tbs (45 ml) soy sauce
1 tbs (15 ml) lemon juice
pepper
dash hot sauce
½ cup (120 ml) hot water

Chicken: Cut the chicken into strips ½ inch wide and about 3 inches long. Combine with remaining ingredients and marinate in the refrigerator up to 12 hours. Preheat oven to 375°F (190°C). Thread each piece ribbon style on a wooden toothpick or small skewer and arrange on baking sheet. Bake for 5-10 minutes or until just cooked. Serve hot with bowl of sauce for dipping. Serves 8.

Sauce: Heat the two oils in a small saucepan, add the onion, garlic and ginger and cook over medium heat until soft. Add vinegar and sugar, continue to cook and stir to dissolve sugar. Remove from heat, add remaining ingredients and mix well. Use a food processor for a smoother sauce. May be made in advance, serve at room temperature.

Approximate nutritional analysis per serving:
Calories 222, Protein 21 g, Carbohydrates 6 g, Fat 13 g,
Cholesterol 48 mg, Sodium 652 mg

LITTLE BEAN CAKES

1 can GOYA White Kidney Beans, drained
1 onion, chopped
2 egg yolks
2 tbs (30 ml) milk
¼ tsp (1 ml) salt
½ tsp (3 ml) pepper
¼ cup (60 ml) flour
GOYA Corn Oil for frying
flour for rolling bean balls

Mash beans; combine with remaining ingredients. Shape into balls, about the size of a walnut, and roll in flour. Chill 1 hour or more. Sauté in oil until brown and crisp.
Yields 20 bean cakes.

Approximate nutritional analysis per bean cake before frying:
Calories 29, Protein 2 g, Carbohydrates 4 g, Fat < 1 g,
Cholesterol 21 mg, Sodium 29 mg

Opposite: Spicy Tomato Goat Cheese Appetizer

ALMONDS ITALIANO

1½ tbs (25 ml) butter
1 tsp (5 ml) salt
1 tsp (5 ml) oregano
1 tsp (5 ml) basil
2 cloves garlic, crushed
2 cups (480 ml) BLUE DIAMOND
    Whole Natural Almonds

Melt butter in 8-inch square baking dish in 375°F (190°C) oven. Stir in salt, oregano, basil and garlic. Add almonds, stirring until coated. Bake 15-20 minutes, stirring occasionally, until almonds are crisp. Yields 2 cups.

Approximate nutritional analysis per ¼ cup serving:
Calories 232, Protein 7 g, Carbohydrates 7 g, Fat 21 g,
Cholesterol 6 mg, Sodium 292 mg

GARBANZO FRITTERS

2 cans GOYA Chick Peas, drained
1 egg, slightly beaten
½ tsp GOYA Adobo Seasoning
2 tbs (30 ml) parsley, chopped
¼ cup (60 ml) flour
1 tsp (5 ml) salt
½ tsp (3 ml) baking powder
1 tsp (5 ml) Parmesan cheese, grated
1 tbs (15 ml) onion, minced
GOYA Corn Oil for frying

Mash beans; combine with remaining ingredients. Drop by tablespoonfuls into hot oil (360°F (182°C) and fry until golden brown. Drain on absorbent paper. Serve hot. Yields 2 dozen fritters.

Approximate nutritional analysis per fritter before frying:
Calories 29, Protein 2 g, Carbohydrates 5 g, Fat < 1 g,
Cholesterol 9 mg, Sodium 181 mg

SPICED ALMONDS

1 large egg white
3 cups (720 ml) whole almonds
⅓ cup (80 ml) sugar
2 tsp (10 ml) ground cinnamon
½ tsp (3 ml) ground allspice
½ tsp (3 ml) SEASON-ALL Seasoned Salt
¼ tsp (1 ml) ground nutmeg

Beat egg white until foamy. Add almonds, tossing to coat. In a small bowl, combine sugar, cinnamon, allspice, SEASON-ALL Seasoned Salt and nutmeg; toss with almonds to coat. Spread almonds on greased baking sheet in single layer. Bake in 250°F (121°C) oven 1 hour. Cool slightly and break apart. Cool completely and store in airtight container. Yields approximately 3 cups.

Approximate nutritional analysis per ¼ cup serving:
Calories 278, Protein 8 g, Carbohydrates 23 g, Fat 19 g,
Cholesterol 0 mg, Sodium 97 mg

Courtesy of McCormick/Schilling.

SOUPS

Comforting or elegant, light or hearty, hot or cold, soups make an enticing beginning to a meal or a whole meal by themselves — add bread and salad. Try doubling recipes and storing half in the freezer for a rainy day.

CHILLED WATERMELON MINT SOUP

4 cups (960 ml) watermelon, seeded, cubed,
    divided
⅓ cup (80 ml) frozen apple juice concentrate, thawed
1 tbs (15 ml) fresh mint leaves
½ tsp (3 ml) ground ginger
⅓ cup (80 ml) plain nonfat yogurt
freshly ground pepper
mint sprigs

Dice enough watermelon to measure ⅓ cup; reserve for garnish. In blender or food processor, process remaining watermelon, apple juice concentrate, mint leaves and ginger until smooth. Refrigerate, covered, for 1 hour to blend flavors. Serve in small chilled bowls; garnish with reserved diced watermelon, dollop of yogurt, pepper and mint sprig. Serves 6.

Approximate nutritional analysis per serving:
Calories 62, Protein 1 g, Carbohydrates 14 g, Fat < 1 g,
Cholesterol < 1 mg, Sodium 14 mg

Courtesy of the National Watermelon Promotion Board.

GAZPACHO

1½ cups (355 ml) toasted bread cubes
4 cups (960 ml) mixed vegetable juice,
    regular or low sodium
1 green pepper, seeded, diced
1 cucumber, peeled, diced
1 small onion, finely minced
1 clove garlic, chopped
1 tbs (15 ml) salad oil
2 tbs (30 ml) vinegar
2 tomatoes, fresh or whole, canned, peeled, diced
3 drops hot pepper sauce
¼ tsp (1 ml) IMPERIAL Granulated Sugar
salt to taste

Combine 1 cup bread cubes and 2 cups vegetable juice; reserve. In blender, combine half the green pepper, cucumber, onion with garlic, oil, vinegar; blend until smooth. Pour into 2-qt container. Put crouton-juice mixture into blender with remaining vegetable juice, 1 tomato, pepper sauce, IMPERIAL Granulated Sugar, salt. Blend a few seconds until smooth and add to first mixture. Serve chilled and pass remaining green pepper, cucumber, onion, tomato, croutons in individual bowls. Serves 8.

Approximate nutritional analysis per serving:
Calories 66, Protein 2 g, Carbohydrates 12 g, Fat 2 g,
Cholesterol 0 mg, Sodium 489 mg

GAZPACHO WITH ALMONDS AND SHERRY

¾ cup (180 ml) almonds, roasted, blanched
2 lbs (910 g) tomatoes, cut up
1 cup (240 ml) tomato juice
1 medium green pepper, sliced
1 large red pepper, sliced
2 cucumbers, peeled and sliced
3 cloves garlic, chopped
½ cup (120 ml) GOYA Red Wine Vinegar
1 cup (240 ml) GOYA Olive Oil
1½ cups (355 ml) ice water
1½ tsp (8 ml) paprika
2 slices bread, toasted, broken up
2 oz (60 g) sweet dark Spanish sherry
salt to taste

Combine all ingredients in blender or food processor and puree thoroughly. Correct seasonings to taste. Chill overnight or serve over ice, garnished with croutons, chopped peppers, eggs or onions. Serves 8. For a thinner soup, strain before serving.

Approximate nutritional analysis per serving:
Calories 384, Protein 5 g, Carbohydrates 2 g, Fat 34 g,
Cholesterol < 1 mg, Sodium 150 mg

Gazpacho with Almonds and Sherry

PAPAYA COLD FRUIT SOUP

1 qt (960 ml) water
12 oz (360 g) sugar
8 oz (240 g) papaya
8 oz (240 g) sweet pitted cherries
8 oz (240 g) peaches
11 oz (330 g) Mandarin oranges
3 oz (90 g) raisins
1½ qts (1.4 L) orange juice
1½ oz (45 g) cornstarch
8 oz (240 ml) water

Bring 1 qt of water to boil. Stir in sugar until dissolved. Add fruits and lower heat. In a separate pot, heat orange juice. Thicken with cornstarch and 8 oz water. Add fruit to thickened juice. Cool to room temperature. Refrigerate. Serve chilled. Yields 1½ gallons.

Approximate nutritional analysis per 2 cup serving:
Calories 119, Protein < 1 g, Carbohydrates 30 g, Fat < 1 g,
Cholesterol 0 mg, Sodium 2 mg

Courtesy of The Papaya Administrative Committee and Pineapple Growers Association of Hawaii

CHILLED CARROT SOUP

2 tbs (30 ml) vegetable oil
1 cup (240 ml) onion, chopped
1½ tsp (8 ml) curry powder
3½ cups (840 ml) low sodium chicken broth
1 lb (455 g) carrots, sliced
2 stalks celery, sliced
1 bay leaf
½ tsp (3 ml) ground cumin
½ tsp (3 ml) Tabasco pepper sauce
1 tbs (15 ml) cornstarch
2 cups (480 ml) yogurt

In large saucepan over medium-high heat, heat oil; sauté onion and curry over medium heat 3-5 minutes or until onion is translucent. Reduce heat to low. Add chicken broth, carrots, celery, bay leaf, cumin and Tabasco pepper sauce; mix well. Bring to a boil; reduce heat, simmer 25 minutes or until vegetables are tender. Remove bay leaf. Spoon mixture, in several batches, into container of electric blender or food processor; process until smooth. Add cornstarch to yogurt and stir until well blended. Gradually stir yogurt into soup mixture, stirring after each addition. Chill before serving. Serve with additional Tabasco pepper sauce, if desired. Serves 7.

Approximate nutritional analysis per serving:
Calories 139, Protein 6 g, Fat 6 g, Cholesterol 4 mg, Sodium 80 mg

COLD PAPAYA SOUP

3 large ripe papayas
1 small Maui onion, chopped
2 medium limes, juice only
2 cups (480 ml) vegetable stock (below)
1 cup (240 ml) heavy cream

VEGETABLE STOCK:
1 medium onion, finely chopped
1 large zucchini, finely chopped
1 small leek, trimmed, washed and finely chopped
½ fennel bulb, finely chopped
1 clove garlic, finely chopped
1 tbs (15 ml) unsalted butter
1 qt (960 ml) cold water
3 sprigs tarragon, chopped
small bunch of chives and chervil, chopped
freshly ground white pepper

Cut the papayas in half. Remove all seeds and then scoop out the flesh. Combine the papaya flesh with chopped onion and half of the lime juice in a food processor or blender and puree. Strain into a large bowl. Stir the vegetable stock into the puree and mix well. Add the cream. Season with salt and freshly ground white pepper and rest of lime juice. Refrigerate. When cold, fill in individual bowls and serve. Serves 6.

Vegetable stock: In a medium saucepan, sweat all the vegetables in butter for 2 minutes, without coloring. Cover with 1 qt of cold water. Bring to a boil and simmer 10 minutes. Add the chopped herbs and simmer for another 5 minutes. Season with white pepper. No salt. Force through a fine strainer into a bowl. Serves 6.

Courtesy of The Papaya Administrative Committee and Pineapple Growers Association of Hawaii.

MISO SOUP

¼ cup (60 ml) miso
1 qt (960 ml) water
1 cup (240 ml) ramen noodles, cooked
8 oz (240 g) tofu, cut into chunks
2 green onions, chopped, including an inch
   of the green part

Dissolve the miso in water. Add the tofu chunks and the cooked ramen noodles. Simmer until heated through. Garnish with chopped green onions. Serves 6.

Approximate nutritional analysis per serving:
Calories 89, Protein 6 g, Carbohydrates 10 g, Fat 4 g,
Cholesterol 0 mg, Sodium 561 mg

Chilled Zucchini Soup

CHILLED ZUCCHINI SOUP

3½ cups (840 ml) low sodium chicken broth
5 medium zucchini, sliced
1 large onion, chopped
1 clove garlic, chopped
½ tsp (3 ml) salt
½ tsp (3 ml) TABASCO pepper sauce
½ tbs (8 ml) cornstarch
1 cup (240 ml) lowfat plain yogurt

In large saucepan, combine chicken broth, zucchini, onion, garlic, basil, salt and TABASCOsauce. Bring to a boil, reduce heat, simmer 15 minutes or until vegetables are tender. Pour mixture, in several batches, into container of electric blender or food processor; process until smooth. Add cornstarch to yogurt and stir until well blended. Gradually add yogurt to soup mixture; stirring after each addition. Chill before serving. Serves 7.

Approximate nutritional analysis per serving: Calories 71, Protein 5 g, Fat 2 g, Cholesterol 2 mg, Sodium 184 mg

BLUEBERRY-ORANGE SOUP

1 pt (480 ml) fresh or frozen North American blueberries
5 cups (1.2 L) fresh orange juice
3 tbs (45 ml) honey
¼ tsp (1 ml) ground cinnamon
2 tbs (30 ml) cornstarch
2 tbs (30 ml) water
1 tsp (5 ml) grated orange peel
½ cup (120 ml) buttermilk
6 mint sprigs

Rinse and drain blueberries; reserve 12-18 berries. Bring blueberries, orange juice, honey and cinnamon to a boil. Dissolve cornstarch in water; gradually add to blueberry mixture while stirring mixture. Bring mixture to a boil. Add orange peel and refrigerate overnight. For each serving, pour 1 cup into soup bowl and garnish with a swirl of buttermilk, 2-3 blueberries and a mint sprig. Serves 6.

Approximate nutritional analysis per serving:
Calories 169, Protein 2 g, Carbohydrates 40 g, Fat < 1 g,
Cholesterol 1 mg, Sodium 27 mg

Opposite: Blueberry Orange Soup

CHILLED MINT-CUCUMBER-YOGURT SOUP

2 cucumbers
½ small onion, cut into chunks
1 clove garlic
2 cups (480 ml) DANNON Plain Nonfat or
    Lowfat Yogurt, divided
3 tbs (45 ml) fresh mint leaves, thinly sliced
½ tsp (3 ml) salt
⅛ tsp (.5 ml) freshly ground pepper
pinch ground red pepper
4 thin cucumber slices, optional

Peel cucumbers and halve lengthwise. Scoop out seeds with spoon and discard. Cut cucumbers into chunks. Place cucumbers, onion and garlic in food processor. Process until smooth. Add 1 cup yogurt and process until smooth. Scrape into a medium bowl or soup tureen. Stir in remaining 1 cup yogurt, mint, salt, pepper and ground red pepper. Cover; chill at least 2 hours before serving. To serve, ladle into 4 soup bowls and garnish each with a cucumber slice. Serves 4.

Approximate nutritional analysis per serving:
Calories 99, Protein 7 g, Carbohydrates 14 g, Fat 2 g,
Cholesterol 7 mg, Sodium 350 mg

ARTICHOKE SOUP

1 bunch green onions, mostly white part, chopped
4 medium cloves garlic, crushed
2 tbs (30 ml) butter, margarine or oil, melted
2 tbs (30 ml) all purpose flour
1 - 15½ oz can (465 ml) chicken broth
1 - 14 oz can (420 g) artichoke hearts with juice
salt and pepper to taste
sprinkle of crushed, dried thyme
2 bay leaves
1 tsp (5 ml) IMPERIAL Granulated Sugar
1 cup (240 ml) milk
1 cup (240 ml) light cream
parsley

In soup kettle, sauté onions and garlic in butter, margarine or oil until tender. Stir in flour. Pour in chicken broth and blend well. Bring to a low boil and cook, stirring, 1 minute. Cut artichokes into small pieces and add to soup mixture along with salt, pepper, thyme, bay leaves, IMPERIAL Granulated Sugar. Simmer, covered, 10-15 minutes. Add milk and cream; heat just to boiling. Remove bay leaves and add parsley before serving. Serves 6. Garnish with green onion tops and one piece of artichoke heart for each bowl.

Approximate nutritional analysis per serving:
Calories 224, Protein 6 g, Carbohydrates 11 g, Fat 18 g,
Cholesterol 50 mg, Sodium 366 mg

ROOTS AND TUBERS SOUP

8 cups (1.9 L) chicken broth or bouillon
1 - 14½ oz can (435 g) stewed tomatoes
1 - 6 oz can (180 g) tomato paste
1 medium onion, chopped
1 carrot, sliced
1 small turnip, peeled and cubed
1 small rutabaga, peeled and cubed
1 parsnip, peeled and cubed
2 stalks celery, sliced
2 medium potatoes, cubed
1½ cups (355 ml) green cabbage, chopped
2 bay leaves
1½ tsp (8 ml) ground sage
½ tsp (3 ml) black pepper

In 6-qt pot combine all ingredients; bring to a boil. Cover, reduce heat and simmer about 25-30 minutes or until vegetables are tender. Serve hot. Soup can be stored, covered, in refrigerator up to 1 week. Serves 10.

Approximate nutritional analysis per serving:
Calories 141, Protein 6 g, Carbohydrates 25 g, Fat 3 g,
Cholesterol 8 mg, Sodium 872 mg

ZUCCHINI SOUP MILANO

2 tbs (30 ml) margarine
1 large onion, diced
2 medium zucchini, diced
1 cup (240 ml) heavy cream
1 cup (240 ml) chicken broth
½ tsp (3 ml) McCORMICK or SCHILLING
    Pure Anise Extract
¼ tsp (1 ml) McCORMICK or SCHILLING
    Black Walnut Extract
1 tsp (5 ml) salt
toasted walnut halves for garnish

In a 2-qt pan melt margarine. Add onion and zucchini and cook over medium-high heat 15 minutes, stirring occasionally. Put in blender and puree. Add cream, chicken broth, extracts and salt. Blend well. Serve warm or chilled garnished with walnut halves. Serves 4.

Approximate nutritional analysis per serving:
Calories 329, Protein 5 g, Carbohydrates 16 g, Fat 29 g,
Cholesterol 84 mg, Sodium 342 mg

Opposite: Roots and Tubers Soup

THREE-PEPPER HAZELNUT SOUP

1 qt (960 ml) chicken stock
1 cup (240 ml) lentils
½ cup (120 ml) onions, chopped
½ cup (120 ml) carrots, chopped
¼ cup (60 ml) celery, chopped
2 cloves garlic
½ tsp (3 ml) coriander
½ tsp (3 ml) fenugreek
¼ tsp (1 ml) cumin
2 cups (480 ml) water
1½ cups (355 ml) hazelnuts, toasted and chopped
1 tsp (5 ml) mixed peppercorns, pink,
    green and black, cracked
2 tbs (30 ml) roux (equal parts butter and all-
purpose flour worked into a smooth paste)

GARNISH:
sour cream
chopped onion or chives
shredded carrots or hazelnuts

Combine stock, lentils, onions, carrots, celery, garlic, coriander, fenugreek and cumin in a heavy 3-qt soup pot. Bring to a boil, reduce heat and simmer 1 hour. Remove from heat and put through a sieve or puree and return to pot. Add water, hazelnuts and 3 peppers and simmer 15 minutes. Beat in roux to thicken and cook an additional 15 minutes. Salt to taste, then garnish. Serves 6 as main dish.

Approximate nutritional analysis per serving:
Calories 322, Protein 13 g, Carbohydrates 26 g, Fat 20 g,
Cholesterol 5 mg, Sodium 32 mg

CURRIED CARROT SOUP

6 medium carrots, thinly sliced
2 cups (480 ml) vegetable stock
1 small onion, chopped
½ cup (120 ml) plain soymilk
2 tsp (10 ml) curry powder

Combine all ingredients except soymilk and cook over medium heat until carrots are tender. Pour into a blender and puree until smooth. Stir in the soymilk. Cook over low heat until hot. Serves 4.

Approximate nutritional analysis per serving:
Calories 66, Protein 2 g, Carbohydrates 14 g, Fat 1 g,
Cholesterol 0 mg, Sodium 33 mg

Courtesy of the United Soybean Board.

BUTTERNUT SQUASH SOUP

1 medium yellow onion, peeled and chopped
1 medium leek (white end), washed and sliced
1 large carrot, peeled and sliced thin
4 tbs (60 ml) butter, margarine or oil
1 tsp (5 ml) coriander
1 tsp (5 ml) ground cumin
pinch IMPERIAL Granulated Sugar
1 medium-large butternut squash, peeled,
seeded and cut into 1-2-inch chunks
4 cups (960 ml) chicken broth, regular or low-sodium
½ cup (120 ml) Fume Blanc wine, if desired
salt and white pepper to taste
sour cream and minced fresh parsley
    for garnish, if desired

In soup kettle, sauté onion, leek, carrot in butter, margarine or oil over medium heat until limp. Stir in coriander, cumin, IMPERIAL Granulated Sugar and continue to sauté, stirring occasionally, about 5 minutes. Add chopped squash and chicken stock. Cook until squash is tender, about 20 minutes. In food processor or blender, puree mixture until smooth. Add more chicken stock and wine (if used) for desired consistency. Return pureed mixture to pot, taste for seasonings, and add more coriander and cumin, if desired. Stir well and simmer 10 minutes. Add salt and white pepper to taste. Garnish with spoonful of light sour cream sprinkled with parsley. Serves 4.

Note: Squash will be easier to peel, if, after seeding and cutting into large pieces, it is processed on high in microwave with 2 tbs water, covered. If necessary, cool heated squash in cold water and proceed to peel.

Approximate nutritional analysis per serving:
Calories 212, Protein 7 g, Carbohydrates 19 g, Fat 13 g,
Cholesterol 0 mg, Sodium 941 mg

Mexican Minestrone

MEXICAN MINESTRONE

2 tbs (30 ml) olive oil
¾ cup (180 ml) green onions, sliced
1 tsp (5 ml) fresh garlic, minced
1 - 16 oz can (480 g) CHI-CHI'S Salsa
1 - 14½ oz can (435 ml) low sodium chicken broth
2 cups (480 ml) water
2 cups (480 ml) cooked chicken, shredded
¾ lb (340 g) small red new potatoes,
   cooked and quartered
1 cup (240 ml) carrots, sliced
1 cup (240 ml) red, green, yellow and/or
   orange bell pepper, 1-inch cubes
1 cup (240 ml) zucchini, ⅛ -inch slices
1 - 19 oz can (570 g) white kidney beans, drained
2 bay leaves
1 tsp (5 ml) dried basil leaves
1 tsp (5 ml) dried oregano leaves
2 tbs (30 ml) lime juice
1 tsp (5 ml) grated lime peel, if desired

In Dutch oven, sauté green onions and garlic in oil until onions are soft. Add remaining ingredients except lime juice and lime peel. Bring to a boil, stirring occasionally. Reduce heat to medium-low. Cover; cook 30-40 minutes or until potatoes are just tender, stirring occasionally. Stir in lime juice and lime peel, if desired. Remove bay leaves. Serves 9.

Approximate nutritional analysis per serving:
Calories 190, Protein 15 g, Carbohydrates 22 g, Fat 6 g,
Cholesterol 30 mg, Sodium 290 mg

QUICK BLACK BEAN SOUP

½ lb (230 g) bacon, cut into 1-inch pieces
1 cup (240 ml) celery, sliced
1 cup (240 ml) onion, chopped
2 tsp (10 ml) fresh garlic, minced
2 - 15 oz cans (900 g) black beans, drained
1 - 16 oz jar (480 ml) CHI-CHI'S Picante Sauce
1 - 10½ oz can (315 ml) chicken broth
1 tsp (5 ml) crushed red pepper flakes
½ tsp (3 ml) pepper
2 tbs (30 ml) fresh cilantro, chopped

In large saucepan, combine bacon, celery, onion and garlic. Cook over medium heat, stirring occasionally, until bacon is crisp and vegetables are tender. Drain. Add remaining ingredients **except** cilantro. Bring to a boil; reduce heat to low. Simmer, stirring occasionally, 25-30 minutes. Stir in cilantro. Serves 6.

Approximate nutritional analysis per serving:
Calories 220, Protein 13 g, Carbohydrates 29 g, Fat 6 g,
Cholesterol 10 mg, Sodium 920 mg

CALDO GALLEGA

White Bean soup

1 - 16 oz can (480 g) GOYA Small White Beans
8 cups (1.9 L) water
4 packets GOYA Chicken Bouillon
2 GOYA Chorizos, sliced
3 potatoes, peeled and cubed
3 turnips, peeled and sliced
½ lb (230 g) smoked ham, diced
½ lb (230 g) fresh kale, broccoli rabe or
   turnip greens, chopped
1 onion, sliced
½ tsp (3 ml) GOYA Adobo with Pepper
1 packet Sazón GOYA sin Achiote

In a large saucepan, combine chicken bouillon, water, chorizo, potatoes, turnips, ham, kale and onion. Bring to a boil, reduce heat, and simmer, covered, for 50 minutes. Add beans, Adobo, and Sazón. Simmer, covered, for 10 more minutes, or until potatoes are tender. Serves 6.

Nutritional analysis not available.

DAD'S THICK VEGETABLE SOUP

1 lb (455 g) stew meat
2 tbs (30 ml) oil
3 cloves garlic, minced
1 tsp (5 ml) oregano
½ tsp (3 ml) cumin
2 - 10 oz cans (600 g) beef consommé
1 large onion, finely chopped
4 potatoes, shredded
6 carrots, shredded
5 stalks and leaves celery, chopped
1½ tsp (8 ml) salt
¼ tsp (1 ml) pepper
1 - 28 oz can (840 g) LIBBY'S Whole
     Peeled Tomatoes in Puree
½ cup (120 ml) dry vermouth, optional

Brown stew meat in 2 tbs hot oil in pressure cooker with garlic. Add 1 cup water, oregano and cumin. Cook about 12 minutes in pressure cooker, following manufacturer's instructions for pressure cooker use.* Transfer meat mixture to soup kettle. Add consommé. Fill each can with water and stir in along with remaining ingredients except vermouth. Cook about 1 hour, then add vermouth. Refrigerate until serving time. Heat to serve and garnish with sprinkle of grated Parmesan cheese, if desired. Yields 1 gallon.

     * May be cooked by the conventional method by adding one of the cans of beef consommé plus 1 cup water and simmering 40 minutes.

Approximate nutritional analysis per 1 cup serving:
Calories 179, Protein 12 g, Carbohydrates 19 g, Fat 6 g, Cholesterol 31 mg, Sodium 297 mg

FROM SCRATCH BLACK BEAN SOUP

1 lb (2½ cups) (455 g) dried black beans, soaked
½ lb (230 g) spicy Italian sausage, sliced ½ inch thick
2 tbs (30 ml) garlic
2 medium onions, chopped
2 large carrots, chopped
2 tbs (30 ml) ground cumin
½ tsp (3 ml) cinnamon
½ tsp (3 ml) IMPERIAL Granulated Sugar
2 bay leaves
6 cups (1.4 L) water
2 tsp (10 ml) salt, or to taste
1 tsp (5 m) black pepper
¼ tsp (1 ml) red pepper sauce

Soak beans overnight in enough water to cover 2-3 inches above beans. Drain and discard water. In soup kettle, sauté sausage drippings 5 minutes, or until onion is translucent. Add cumin, cinnamon, IMPERIAL Granulated Sugar; sauté for 30 seconds. Add bay leaves, water beans; cover and bring to a boil over high heat. Lower heat and simmer 1½ hours, or until beans are soft. Stir occasionally to prevent beans from sticking; add more water if necessary. If desired, remove half the mixture and puree in blender or food processor or mash with potato masher. Stir back into soup. Add salt, black pepper, and red pepper sauce. Serves 8.

     Note: To reduce fat, discard sausage drippings and substitute small amount of vegetable oil to sauté.

     To soak beans the quick method, bring beans and water to boil about 2 minutes. Cover and let set about one hour. Then proceed with the recipe.

Approximate nutritional analysis per serving:
Calories 313, Protein 17 g, Carbohydrates 40 g, Fat 10 g, Cholesterol 22 mg, Sodium 756 mg

TUSCAN PASTA AND BEAN SOUP

2 tbs (30 ml) extra virgin olive oil
5 tsp (25 ml) minced garlic
1 - 12 oz can (360 g) CONTADINA Tomato Paste
2 - 15 oz cans (900 g) Great Northern, kidney
     or pinto beans, undrained
2 tbs (30 ml) fresh basil, chopped
2 tbs (30 ml) fresh parsley, chopped
2 - 14½ oz cans (870 ml) chicken broth
3 cups (720 ml) hot water
½ cup (120 ml) dry red wine
½ cup (120 ml) small shells or macaroni
½ tsp (3 ml) ground black pepper
Parmesan cheese, grated, optional
basil strips, optional

In large saucepan, heat oil; sauté garlic until light golden. Stir in tomato paste, beans and liquid, basil and parsley; cook for 2 minutes. Stir in broth, water, wine; bring to a boil. Add pasta and pepper; cook for 8 minutes, stirring occasionally or until pasta is tender. Serve with Parmesan cheese and basil. Serves 10.

Approximate nutritional analysis per serving:
Calories 220, Protein 10 g, Carbohydrates 36 g, Fat 4 g, Cholesterol 0 mg, Sodium 395 mg

Opposite: Tuscan Pasta and Bean Soup

NAOMI'S CHICKEN SOUP

2 EMPIRE KOSHER chicken quarters
4 large carrots, sliced into 2-inch sticks
2 stalks celery, diced
1 large onion, whole
2 tbs (30 ml) kosher parve onion soup mix
salt, pepper, onion and garlic powder to taste
2 tsp (10 ml) sugar
¼ tsp (1 ml) dried dill

Bring chicken and vegetables to a boil in a 4-qt pot full of water. Skim. Lower heat and add seasonings, simmer covered for 1½ hours. If more liquid is needed, add water. Serves 4.

Approximate nutritional analysis per serving:
Calories 91, Protein 12 g, Carbohydrates 4 g, Fat 3 g,
Cholesterol 35 mg, Sodium 78 mg

TRIBECA GRILL'S WHITE BEAN & CHORIZO SOUP

1 lb (455 g) Great Northern or Navy beans
2 medium onions, chopped fine
5 cloves garlic, chopped
½ lb (230 g) bacon, cooked and chopped fine
½ bunch celery, chopped fine
¼ cup (60 ml) olive oil
1 lb (455 g) chorizo sausage, cooked and diced
1 sprig thyme
1 tbs (15 ml) cracked black pepper
salt to taste

Soak the beans overnight. Drain, rinse and reserve the beans.

Put the onions, garlic, bacon, celery, olive oil and chorizo into a soup pot. Slowly bring up the heat and cook over a medium fire for about 5 minutes or until onions and vegetables are translucent. Do not brown. In a cheesecloth, wrap the black pepper and half the sprig of thyme and add to the pot. Add the beans and cover with a gallon of water. Cook until the beans are tender. Garnish with diced tomato, chopped spinach and the rest of the thyme (chopped). Serves 5.

Cooking tips: To eliminate lengthy soaking and cooking time, substitute canned beans for dry beans: 3 - 15 oz cans Great Northern or Navy beans, drained and rinsed. When using canned beans, first simmer ingredients in 1 qt of water and 1 qt chicken broth for about 10 minutes. Then add the beans and simmer for another 10 minutes.

Several carrots, extra celery and onions may be substituted for the chorizo and bacon.

Approximate nutritional analysis per serving:
Calories 885, Protein 44 g, Carbohydrates 37 g, Fat 63 g,
Cholesterol 100 mg, Sodium 200 mg

Courtesy of the American Dry Bean Board.

YELLOWEYE BEAN SOUP

8 oz (240 g) dry Yelloweye Beans
1 ham shank
2 carrots, diced
2 onions, thinly sliced
2 potatoes, sliced
1 tsp (5 ml) salt
black pepper, freshly ground
lemon slices for garnish

Soak washed beans overnight in 2 qts water. Do not drain liquid after soaking. Combine all ingredients and cook slowly until the beans are tender, adding more liquid if necessary. Serve with beans whole, mashed or rub mixture through a sieve and season. Add hot water if too thick. Serve topped with lemon slices. Serves 8.

Approximate nutritional analysis per serving:
Calories 186, Protein 10 g, Carbohydrates 35 g, Fat 1 g,
Cholesterol 4 mg, Sodium 389 mg

Courtesy of the American Dry Bean Board.

TOMATO RICE AND BEAN SOUP

1 tbs (15 ml) butter or margarine
1 cup (240 ml) onions, diced
1 cup (240 ml) carrots, diced
1 cup (240 ml) celery, diced
6 - 8 oz cans (1.4 ml) GOYA Tomato Sauce
2 packets GOYA Beef Bouillon
1 tsp (5 ml) GOYA Adobo
1 packet Sazón GOYA sin Achiote
1 cup (240 ml) white rice, cooked
1 - 16 oz can (480 g) GOYA Black Beans,
    rinsed and drained
pinch sugar
1 cup (240 ml) half and half or lowfat milk
salt and pepper to taste

In stockpot, sauté diced vegetables in butter on low heat until golden. Add tomato sauce, bouillon, Adobo, Sazón and bring to a boil. Cover pot and simmer 10 minutes. In blender puree soup in batches and return to pot. Add rice, beans, sugar and simmer 5 minutes more. Add half and half and simmer another 5 minutes. Do not boil. Serves 6-8.

Nutritional analysis not available.

CREAMY CHICK PEA SOUP

1 cup (240 ml) water
2 packets GOYA Chicken Bouillon
3 - 16 oz cans (1.4 kg) GOYA Chick Peas with liquid
1 tsp (5 ml) GOYA Adobo
1 packet Sazón GOYA sin Achiote
1 tbs (15 ml) dried rosemary, finely crushed
1 - 28 oz can (840 g) plum tomatoes, chopped
1 cup (240 ml) small macaroni (elbows, small shells)
salt and pepper to taste

In stockpot, dissolve bouillon in water. Add 1 can chick peas, Adobo, Sazón, rosemary and plum tomatoes. Bring to a boil, lower heat, and simmer for 10 minutes. In blender puree 2 cans chick peas with liquid, add to pot, and simmer an additional 5 minutes. Add macaroni and cook 8 minutes more, stirring frequently. Serves 4-6.

Nutritional analysis not available.

OLD-FASHIONED SPLIT PEA SOUP

1 cup (240 ml) split peas
1 ham bone
   or **½ cup ham, cubed, with excess fat removed**
1 carrot, grated
2 medium onions, minced
1 potato, grated
¼ cup (60 ml) celery, diced
¼ cup (60 ml) green pepper, finely chopped
1 tsp (5 ml) IMPERIAL Granulated Sugar
salt and pepper to taste
additional pieces of ham, diced

Cover split peas with 6 cups boiling water; let soak for 1 hour. Add ham bone, carrot, onion, potato, celery, green pepper, IMPERIAL Granulated Sugar. Simmer 30-40 minutes or until peas are tender. Season with salt and pepper. Add water if needed; simmer 5-10 minutes longer. Pour into soup bowls; garnish with diced ham. Serves 4.

Approximate nutritional analysis per serving:
Calories 260, Protein 17 g, Carbohydrates 41 g, Fat 4 g,
Cholesterol 11 mg, Sodium 230 mg

Navy Bean Soup

NAVY BEAN SOUP

¼ cup (60 ml) onion, chopped
2 tbs (30 ml) olive oil
1 - 1 lb can (455 g) navy beans
   with bacon
1 cup (240 ml) water
1 small potato, peeled and diced
2 small carrots, sliced or diced
1 clove garlic, finely minced
¼ tsp (60 ml) IMPERIAL
   Granulated Sugar
½ tsp (3 ml) salt
chopped parsley
thin lemon slices

In medium saucepan, sauté onions in olive oil over moderate heat. Add beans, water, potato, carrots, garlic, IMPE-RIAL Granulated Sugar, salt. When about to boil, turn heat down and simmer about 20 minutes. Garnish with parsley and thin lemon slices. Serves 4.

Approximate nutritional analysis per serving:
Calories 238, Protein 10 g, Sodium 791 mg,
Carbohydrates 35 g, Fat 8 g, Cholesterol 9 mg

BLACK-EYED PEA SOUP

5-6 slices bacon, cut in small pieces and fried
1 cup (240 ml) onion, chopped
2 tbs (30 ml) jalapeños, seeds removed,
  finely chopped
2 cups (480 ml) Italian-style tomatoes, chopped
1 garlic clove, minced and mashed
1 tsp (5 ml) IMPERIAL Granulated Sugar
pinch salt and pepper
2 - 15½ oz cans (930 ml) beef broth
4 - 15½ oz cans (1.9 kg) black-eyed peas, drained
3 cups (720 ml) cheddar or Swiss cheese, grated

Fry bacon in soup kettle until lightly browned; add onions, jalapeños, tomatoes, garlic, IMPERIAL Granulated Sugar, salt, pepper, and sauté in bacon drippings over medium-high heat, about 5 minutes. Add beef broth and black-eyed peas; stir and simmer about 15 minutes. At serving time, add cheese and simmer gently until cheese is melted. Sprinkle each serving with additional cheese. Serves 10.

Approximate nutritional analysis per serving:
Calories 355, Protein 15 g, Carbohydrates 31 g, Fat 19 g,
Cholesterol 44 mg, Sodium 648 mg

SOPA DE POLLO FRIJOLES

Chicken and Bean Soup

4 PREMIUM YOUNG 'N TENDER Brand
  boneless, skinless split chicken breasts
3 - 10 oz cans (900 ml) chicken broth
2 tbs (30 ml) vegetable oil
1 large onion, chopped
2 cloves garlic, minced
4 medium, fresh jalapeño peppers, seeded, chopped
1 tbs (15 ml) chili powder
1 - 16 oz can (480 g) tomatoes, chopped
2 - 15 oz cans (900 g) pinto beans, drained
salt and pepper
¼ cup (60 ml) vegetable oil
6 corn tortillas, cut into ¼-½-inch strips
3 oz (90 g) sharp cheddar cheese, shredded
⅓ cup (80 ml) sour cream
3 tbs (45 ml) fresh cilantro, finely chopped

Place chicken and chicken broth in a Dutch oven or kettle and cook about 20 minutes or until done. Remove chicken from broth to cool; reserve broth. Heat 2 tbs oil in a medium skillet. Sauté onion, garlic and jalapeño peppers until tender, stirring occasionally; add chili powder. To the reserved broth, add sauteed vegetables, tomatoes with juice, beans, salt and pepper. Bring to a boil, then reduce to simmer. Shred or chop cooked chicken and add to soup, simmer 20 minutes. Remove from heat; cool, cover and refrigerate 3-4 hours or overnight to blend flavors.

Just before serving, heat ¼ cup vegetable oil in a skillet until hot, but not smoking. Fry tortilla strips until crisp; drain on paper towels and salt, if desired. Reheat soup. To serve, divide cheddar cheese and tortillas strips among the soup bowls. Ladle soup over them. Garnish each serving with a dollop of sour cream and sprinkle with cilantro. If desired, serve soup and allow guests to add condiments of their choice. Serves 6.

Approximate nutritional analysis per serving:
Calories 603, Protein 38 g, Carbohydrates 57 g, Fat 27 g,
Cholesterol 77 mg, Sodium 903 mg

WILD AND CREAMY CHICKEN RICE SOUP

4 PREMIUM YOUNG 'N TENDER Brand
  boneless, skinless split chicken breasts
8 slices bacon
3 - 14½ oz cans (1.3 L) chicken broth
1 - 6 oz pkg (180 g) long grain and wild rice
  with seasoning packet
½ cup (120 ml) carrots cut in julienne strips
½ cup (120 ml) green onions, thinly sliced
¾ cup (180 ml) broccoli florets
½ cup (120 ml) butter or margarine
½ cup (120 ml) all purpose flour
⅛ tsp (.5 ml) pepper
2 cups (480 ml) milk or half and half cream
1 tbs (15 ml) pimiento, chopped
¼ cup (60 ml) dry sherry, dry white wine
1 tbs (15 ml) fresh chives, chopped

Simmer chicken in a covered saucepan in ½ cup water until done. Drain, cut into chunks; set aside. Combine chicken broth, rice, seasoning packet, carrots and onions in a large kettle or stockpot. Bring to a boil, reduce heat, cover and simmer 30 minutes. Add broccoli and simmer 10 minutes more.

Melt butter in a medium saucepan. Gradually stir in flour and pepper; cook 1 minute or until smooth, stirring constantly. Gradually add milk or cream and cook, stirring continually until thickened. Add milk mixture to broth mixture, stirring. Add chicken, crumbled bacon, pimiento and wine. Heat gently, stirring often. Do not boil. If thicker than desired, thin with small amount of broth or cream. Garnish each serving with fresh chives. Serve with crusty bread or muffins. Serves 6.

Approximate nutritional analysis per serving:
Calories 541, Protein 30 g, Carbohydrates 40 g, Fat 27 g,
Cholesterol 118 mg, Sodium 1416 mg

GREEK LEMON CHICKEN SOUP

8 cups (1.9 L) chicken broth
½ cup (120 ml) fresh lemon juice
freshly ground pepper
½ cup (120 ml) long grain white rice
1 medium carrot, shredded
4 raw egg yolks
1 cup (240 ml) EMPIRE KOSHER chicken,
cooked and chopped
1 lemon, thinly sliced for garnish

Combine chicken broth, lemon juice and pepper. Bring to a boil, add rice and carrot. Reduce heat, cover and simmer 25 minutes or until rice and carrots are tender. Remove ½ cup soup and gradually whisk into raw egg yolks. Whisk back into the soup, add the chicken and heat long enough for the chicken to become heated through. Make sure soup does not boil, or eggs will curdle. Serve with lemon slices as garnish. Serves 8 for a first course.

Approximate nutritional analysis per serving:
Calories 187, Protein 11 g, Carbohydrates 20 g, Fat 7 g,
Cholesterol 131 mg, Sodium 966 mg

Greek Lemon Chicken Soup

CHICKEN VEGETABLE SOUP

1 lb (455 g) boneless chicken breast,
    cut into 1-inch pieces
1 cup (240 ml) onion, chopped
2 cloves garlic, minced
2 tbs (30 ml) FLEISCHMANN'S Margarine
1 - 10 oz pkg (300 g) frozen sliced carrots
4 cups (960 ml) low sodium
    vegetable juice cocktail
4 cups (960 ml) water
1½ cups (355 ml) large bowtie macaroni
1 tbs (15 ml) Italian seasoning
1 - 10 oz pkg (300 g) frozen chopped spinach
60 HARVEST CRISPS 5-Grain Crackers

In large saucepan, over medium-high heat, cook chicken, onion and garlic in margarine until onion is tender. Add carrots, vegetable juice, water, macaroni and Italian seasoning. Heat to a boil. Cover; reduce heat to low. Simmer for 20 minutes. Stir in spinach; cook 5 minutes more. Serve 1 cup soup with 6 crackers. Serves 10.

Approximate nutritional analysis per serving:
Calories 241, Protein 24 g, Carbohydrates 14 g, Fat 5 g,
Cholesterol 27 mg, Sodium 255 mg

HEARTY POTATO SOUP

1 cup (240 ml) green onions, white part, thinly sliced
2 tbs (30 ml) butter, margarine or oil
1 large potato, peeled and diced
2 cups (480 ml) chicken stock
    or 2 chicken bouillon cubes and 2 cups
    (480 ml) water
dash white pepper
dash nutmeg
salt to taste
⅛ tsp (.5 ml) IMPERIAL Granulated Sugar
1 - 5 oz can (150 ml) evaporated milk

Sauté green onions in butter, margarine or oil. Add diced potato, chicken stock, white pepper, nutmeg, salt, IMPERIAL Granulated Sugar. Bring to a boil, turn down heat and simmer until potatoes are soft; about 10 minutes. Blend in blender until smooth. Add evaporated milk and heat. Can be served cold. Yields 1 qt.

Approximate nutritional analysis per 1 cup serving:
Calories 157, Protein 6 g, Carbohydrates 13 g, Fat 9 g,
Cholesterol 10 mg, Sodium 507 mg

CHICKEN TORTILLA SOUP

½ cup (120 ml) onion,
    chopped
1 tsp (5 ml) fresh garlic,
    minced
2 tbs (30 ml) butter or
    margarine
3 - 10½ oz cans (945 ml)
    low sodium
    chicken broth
1 - 16 oz jar (480 ml)
    CHI-CHI'S Picante Sauce
2 cups (480 ml) chicken
    breasts, cooked and
    shredded
½ cup (120 ml) red bell
    pepper, chopped
¼ tsp (1 ml) coarsely ground
    pepper
2 bay leaves
½ cup (120 ml) vegetable oil
6 small corn tortillas, cut into
    ½-inch strips
2 avocados, peeled and cut
    into ½-inch pieces
1 cup (240 ml) cheddar
    cheese, shredded
sour cream

Chicken Tortilla Soup

In Dutch oven, cook onion and
garlic in butter over medium heat,
stirring occasionally, until onion is tender. Add chicken broth,
picante sauce, shredded chicken, bell pepper, pepper and bay
leaves. Bring to a boil. Cover; reduce heat to low. Simmer,
stirring occasionally, 20 minutes. Remove bay leaves. In large
skillet, heat oil over medium heat until hot. Fry tortillas strips in
oil until light golden brown. Drain. Divide tortilla strips among
6 serving bowls; ladle soup over strips. Top with avocado,
shredded cheese and sour cream. Serves 8.

Approximate nutritional analysis per serving:
Calories 550, Protein 26 g, Carbohydrates 22 g, Fat 40 g,
Cholesterol 70 mg, Sodium 990 mg

PURRUSALDA

Leek and Potato Soup

½ lb (230 g) leeks, chopped,
    including some green tops
¼ cup (60 ml) GOYA Olive Oil
½ lb (230 g) potatoes, peeled and cubed
2 cloves garlic, chopped
4 cups (960 ml) water
2 packets GOYA Chicken bouillon
pepper to taste

In a large saucepan or soup pot, sauté leeks in olive oil over low
heat, stirring continuously, until leeks are soft. Add potato
cubes and garlic and sauté lightly, 1-2 minutes. Add water and
bouillon. Bring to a boil, reduce heat, and simmer gently for
approximately 20 minutes or until potatoes are tender. Add
pepper to taste. Serves 4.

Approximate nutritional analysis per serving:
Calories 213, Protein 2 g, Carbohydrates 20 g, Fat 14 g,
Cholesterol < 1 mg, Sodium 572 mg

CREAMY POTATO SOUP

3 medium potatoes, cubed
2 - 13¾ oz cans (825 ml) COLLEGE INN
    Lower Salt Chicken Broth
½ cup (120 ml) onion, chopped
½ cup (120 ml) green pepper, chopped
1 tbs (15 ml) FLEISCHMANN'S Margarine
¼ cup (60 ml) all purpose flour
2 cups (480 ml) skim milk
parsley, for garnish
48 HARVEST CRISPS 5-Grain Crackers

In large saucepan, over medium-high heat, heat potatoes and chicken broth to a boil; reduce heat. Cover; simmer 15 minutes or until potatoes are tender. Meanwhile, in medium skillet, over medium heat, sauté onion and green pepper in margarine until tender but not browned; stir in flour. Gradually whisk in milk; cook and stir until thickened. Stir into potato mixture; cool slightly. Remove 1 cup potatoes and ½ cup liquid to food processor or blender container; blend until smooth. Stir potato puree into soup; cook and stir until heated through. Garnish each serving with parsley if desired. Serve hot with crackers. Serves 8.

Approximate nutritional analysis per serving soup plus 6 crackers: Calories 166, Fat 1 g, Cholesterol 4 mg, Sodium 457 mg

VIDALIA ONION SOUP

3 medium Vidalia Onions, thinly sliced
2 tbs (30 ml) butter or margarine, melted
4 cups (960 ml) beef broth *or* 2 cans beef consommé
½ cup (120 ml) water
salt and pepper to taste
½ cup (120 ml) Madeira wine, optional
Parmesan croutons
½ cup (120 ml) Swiss cheese, shredded

In a large covered skillet, cook Vidalias in butter, until tender, about 5 minutes. Uncover skillet and continue cooking until well browned; stir occasionally. Stir in water and beef broth, cover and simmer 30 minutes. Add salt and pepper, stir in wine, if desired. Ladle soup into individual, ovenproof dishes. Place Parmesan croutons on each serving and sprinkle with cheese. Bake at 400°F (205°C) for 15 minutes, until cheese is melted and golden brown. Serves 6.

Approximate nutritional analysis per serving: Calories 176, Protein 5 g, Carbohydrates 19 g, Fat 7 g, Cholesterol 19 mg, Sodium 410 mg

FRESH TOMATO AND BOUILLABAISSE

4 medium fresh FLORIDA tomatoes
2 tbs (30 ml) olive oil
2 cups (480 ml) yellow or red sweet
    bell pepper chunks
1 cup (240 ml) red onion chunks
1 tbs (15 ml) garlic, minced
1 tsp (5 ml) fennel seeds, crushed
½ tsp (3 ml) thyme leaves, crushed
1 cup (240 ml) zucchini, sliced
1 cup (240 ml) chicken broth
¼ cup (60 ml) dry white wine
2 - 4x1-inch pieces orange peel
1 - 19 oz can (570 g) white kidney (cannellini)
    beans, rinsed and drained
½ tsp (3 ml) salt

Use tomatoes held at room temperature until fully ripe. Core tomatoes; cut in halves, then cut in wedges; set aside. In a large skillet heat oil until hot. Add peppers, onions, garlic, fennel seeds and thyme; cook and stir for 5 minutes. Add zucchini; cook and stir for 5 minutes longer. Add broth, wine and orange peel; bring to a boil; reduce heat and simmer, covered, for 5 minutes. Stir in beans, salt and reserved tomatoes; simmer until tomatoes are tender, about 5 minutes. Serve with toasted French bread, if desired. Serves 4.

Approximate nutritional analysis per serving: Calories 235, Protein 10 g, Carbohydrates 30 g, Fat 8 g, Cholesterol 0 mg, Sodium 769 mg

Vidalia Onion Soup

PROVENÇALE TOMATO AND POTATO SOUP

1½ lbs (685 g) fresh FLORIDA tomatoes
1 tbs (15 ml) olive or vegetable oil
½ cup (120 ml) onion, chopped
1 tsp (5 ml) fresh garlic, minced
3 cups (720 ml) chicken broth
2 tsp (10 ml) paprika
½ tsp (3 ml) thyme leaves, crushed
½ tsp (3 ml) fennel seed
¼ tsp (1 ml) grated orange peel
1½ cups (355 ml) potatoes, diced and peeled

Use tomatoes held at room temperature until fully ripe. Dice tomatoes (makes about 3 cups); set aside. In a medium saucepan heat oil until hot. Add onion and garlic; sauté until onion is transparent, about 5 minutes. Add chicken broth, paprika, thyme, fennel and orange peel. Bring to a boil. Add potatoes and 1½ cups of the reserved tomatoes. Bring to a boil. Reduce heat and simmer, covered, until vegetables are tender, about 10 minutes. Place half of vegetables and liquid in the container of an electric blender; whirl until smooth. Repeat with remaining mixture. Return all soup to saucepan. Bring to a boil. Add remaining 1½ cups tomatoes. Simmer, covered, until tomatoes are soft, about 5 minutes. Add additional liquid if necessary. Serves 4.

Approximate nutritional analysis per serving:
Calories 144, Protein 5 g, Carbohydrates 22 g, Fat 6 g,
Cholesterol 0 mg, Sodium 771 mg

CORN SOUP

¾ lb (340 g) chicken pieces
1 qt (960 ml) water
1 cup (240 ml) whole kernel corn, fresh or canned
1 tbs (15 ml) green pepper, finely chopped
1 tbs (15 ml) onion, finely chopped
1 tbs (15 ml) celery, finely chopped
1 tsp (5 ml) butter or margarine
1½ tsp (8 ml) salt
½ tsp (3 ml) IMPERIAL Granulated Sugar
dash red pepper (cayenne)
egg noodles or rice, if desired

Simmer chicken in water until tender. Remove chicken from broth and set aside to cool. Add corn to chicken broth and bring to simmer. Meanwhile, sauté green pepper, onion and celery in butter or margarine until tender; add to broth. Remove chicken from bone, chop, and add back to broth along with salt, IMPERIAL Granulated Sugar and red pepper. Add ½ cup uncooked egg noodles or 3 tbs uncooked rice, if desired, and cook 10-15 minutes or until tender. Serves 8.

Approximate nutritional analysis per serving:
Calories 44, Protein 4 g, Carbohydrates 4 g, Fat 1 g,
Cholesterol 9 mg, Sodium 485 mg

HAM BONE SOUP

1 ham bone with meat *or* ½ lb (230 g) ham steak,
     cut in narrow 2-inch strips
2 qts (1.4 L) water
1 cup (240 ml) onion, diced
1 cup (240 ml) celery, diced
1 cup (240 ml) turnip, diced
1½ cups (355 ml) green beans, ends removed,
     cut in 2-inch lengths
1 cup (240 ml) black-eyed peas, fresh,
     canned or frozen
1 cup (240 ml) corn, fresh, canned or frozen
2 cups (480 ml) potato, peeled and diced
1½ cups (355 ml) tomato, fresh or canned,
     peeled and diced
½ cup (120 ml) green peas, fresh or frozen
1 tsp (5 ml) IMPERIAL Granulated Sugar
1 tsp (5 ml) salt
½ tsp (3 ml) black pepper

Add ham bone or ham strips to water and bring to boil. Simmer 15 minutes. Add vegetables and simmer until barely tender. Add remaining ingredients. Simmer 5 minutes. Adjust seasonings to taste. Serve with hot cornbread. Serves 10.

Approximate nutritional analysis per serving:
Calories 134, Protein 8 g, Carbohydrates 19 g, Fat 3 g,
Cholesterol 12 mg, Sodium 617 mg

VEAL AND VEGETABLE SOUP

1½ lbs (685 g) veal for stew, cut into 1-inch pieces
2 cloves garlic, crushed
1 tbs (15 ml) olive oil, divided
½ tsp (3 ml) salt
3½ cups (840 ml) water
1 - 13¾ oz can (410 ml) ready -to-serve beef broth
1 tbs (15 ml) fresh marjoram leaves, crushed
    ***or* 1½ tsp (8 ml) dried marjoram leaves, crushed**
¼ tsp (1 ml) coarse grind black pepper
½ lb (230 g) red potatoes, cut into ½-inch cubes
1½ cups (355 ml) fresh corn kernels or
    frozen whole kernel corn
1 small zucchini

Combine veal stew and minced garlic; reserve. Heat 2 tsp oil in Dutch oven or large deep saucepan over medium heat. Brown veal, ½ lb at a time, using remaining oil as needed. Pour off drippings, if necessary. Sprinkle veal with salt. Return veal to pan; add water, beef broth, marjoram and pepper. Bring to a boil; reduce heat to low. Cover and simmer 45 minutes. Add potatoes and corn; continue simmering, covered 15 minutes or until veal and vegetables are tender. Meanwhile cut zucchini in half lengthwise; cut crosswise into ¼-inch slices. Add zucchini to pan; continue cooking, covered, 5 minutes or until zucchini is crisp-tender. Serves 6.

Approximate nutritional analysis per serving:
Calories 234, Protein 25 g, Carbohydrates 16 g, Fat 8 g,
Cholesterol 93 mg, Sodium 477 mg

Courtesy of the National Livestock and Meat Board.

VEAL AND BARLEY SOUP

1 lb (455 g) veal for stew, cut into 1-inch pieces
5 tsp (25 ml) vegetable oil, divided
1 tsp (5 ml) salt
¼ tsp (1 ml) coarse grind black pepper
1 medium onion, coarsely chopped
5 cups (1.2 L) water
⅓ cup (80 ml) medium pearled barley
¾ cup (180 ml) carrot, chopped (2 medium)
1 tsp (5 ml) Italian seasoning, crushed
1 cup (240 ml) short, thin fresh asparagus strips,
    lightly packed or Swiss chard

Heat 2 tsp oil in Dutch oven or large heavy deep saucepan over medium heat. Brown veal for stew, ½ lb at a time, using additional 2 tsp oil as needed. Remove veal from pan; season with salt and pepper. Reserve. Heat remaining 1 tsp oil in same pan over medium heat. Add onion; cook 5 minutes or until tender, stirring occasionally. Return reserved veal to pan. Stir in water, barley, carrots and Italian seasoning. Bring to a boil; reduce heat to low. Cover and simmer 45 minutes or until veal and barley are tender. Stir in spinach; heat through. Serves 4.

Approximate nutritional analysis per serving:
Calories 274, Protein 25 g, Carbohydrates 19 g, Fat 11 g,
Cholesterol 93 mg, Sodium 653 mg

Courtesy of the National Livestock and Meat Board.

CHICKEN VEGETABLE DUMPLING SOUP

1 cup (240 ml) onion, chopped
½ cup (120 ml) celery, chopped
½ cup (120 ml) red pepper, chopped
2 cloves garlic, minced
1 tbs (15 ml) FLEISCHMANN'S Margarine
2 - 13¾ oz cans (825 ml) COLLEGE INN
    Lower Salt Chicken Broth
½ lb (230 g) cooked chicken, shredded
1 cup (240 ml) fresh green beans, cut
1 cup (240 ml) carrots, sliced
1 - 14½ oz can (435 g) low salt stewed tomatoes
1¼ cups (295 ml) water
½ cup (120 ml) Regular, Quick or Instant
    CREAM OF WHEAT Cereal
¼ cup (60 ml) parsley, chopped
2 eggs, slightly beaten

In 4-qt saucepan, over medium heat, cook ¾ cup onion, celery, pepper and half the garlic in margarine until tender. Stir in chicken broth, chicken, beans, carrots and stewed tomatoes; cover and simmer for 20 minutes.

In medium saucepan, over high heat, heat water, ¼ cup onion and remaining garlic to a boil; slowly stir in cereal. Cook and stir in parsley and eggs. Drop mixture by tablespoonfuls into simmering soup; cover. Cook over low heat for 10 minutes or until dumplings are cooked. Serves 8.

Approximate nutritional analysis per serving:
Calories 176, Protein 12 g, Carbohydrates 12 g, Fat 6 g,
Cholesterol 81 mg, Sodium 382 mg

Opposite: Veal and Barley Soup

Oriental-Style Hot and Sour Soup

ORIENTAL-STYLE HOT AND SOUR SOUP

1 ¾ lbs (795 g) boneless beef chuck arm pot roast
¼ cup (60 ml) reduced-sodium soy sauce
5 cups (1.2 L) water, divided
1 tbs (15 ml) instant beef bouillon granules
4 oz (120 g) fresh mushrooms, sliced
    or ½ oz dried shitake mushrooms*
1 - 8 oz can (240 g) sliced bamboo shoots,
    drained and cut into thin strips
3 tbs (45 ml) red wine vinegar
¼ tsp (1 ml) crushed red pepper pods
2 tbs (30 ml) cornstarch
1 egg, well beaten
4 oz (120 g) firm tofu (bean curd), cut into
    thin strips, if desired
2 tsp (10 ml) Oriental dark-roasted sesame oil
2 green onions, thinly sliced

Trim excess fat from beef chuck arm pot roast; cut across the grain into 2x⅛x⅛-inch strips. Pour soy sauce over beef strips, stirring to coat. Combine 4½ cups water and bouillon granules in Dutch oven; bring to a boil. Add beef mixture. Reduce heat; cover tightly and simmer 1 hour or until beef is tender. Stir in mushrooms, bamboo shoots, wine vinegar and pepper pods. Simmer, uncovered, 10 minutes. Dissolve cornstarch in remaining ½ cup water; gradually stir into soup and continue cooking until slightly thickened. Slowly pour egg, in a thin stream, into soup, stirring constantly to form fine shreds. Add tofu; cook until heated through. Remove from heat. Stir in sesame oil. Garnish with green onions. Serves 6.

    *To prepare shitake mushrooms, soak in warm water to cover approximately 30 minutes. Remove and discard stems; slice tops into strips.

Approximate nutritional analysis per serving:
Calories 267, Protein 32 g, Carbohydrates 6 g, Fat 12 g,
Cholesterol 131 mg, Sodium 897 mg

Ground Beef Borscht

GROUND BEEF BORSCHT

1 lb (455 g) ground beef, 80% lean
1 tsp (5 ml) dill weed, divided
½ tsp (5 ml) salt
¼ tsp (1 ml) pepper, divided
2½ cups (590 ml) ready-to serve beef broth
1 - 16 oz can (480 g) whole beets,
    undrained, quartered
2 cups (480 ml) cabbage, finely shredded
1 medium onion, chopped
2 tbs (30 ml) fresh lemon juice
¼ cup (60 ml) plain yogurt

Combine ground beef, ½ tsp dill weed, salt and ⅛ tsp pepper, mixing lightly but thoroughly. Pinch of 1½-inch pieces of beef mixture to make approximately 20 free-form meatballs; place tightly around sides of 11¾x7½-inch microwave-safe baking dish. Cover with waxed paper and microwave on HIGH 2½-3 minutes (meatballs may appear undercooked); reserve. Combine beef broth, beets with liquid, cabbage, onion, remaining ½ tsp dill weed and ⅛ tsp pepper in 3-qt microwave-safe casserole. Cover and microwave on HIGH 15-17 minutes, stirring halfway through cooking. Add reserved meatballs and any accumulated liquid; cover and microwave at HIGH 2-2½ minutes. Stir in lemon juice. Serve with yogurt. Serves 4.

Approximate nutritional analysis per serving:
Calories 373, Protein 24 g, Carbohydrates 14 g, Fat 25 g,
Cholesterol 86 mg, Sodium 1183 mg

Courtesy of the National Livestock and Meat Board.

CREOLE-FLAVORED BEEF SOUP

3-4 lbs (1.4-1.8 kg) beef shank cross cuts, 1-inch thick
4 cups (960 ml) water
1 - 28 oz can (840 g) crushed tomatoes, undrained
1 cup (240 ml) celery , sliced
1 large onion, chopped
2 cloves garlic, crushed
2 beef bouillon cubes
½ tsp (3 ml) salt
¼ tsp (1 ml) black pepper
¼ tsp (1 ml) ground red pepper
2 cups (480 ml) cabbage, chopped
1 green bell pepper, chopped
¼ cup (60 ml) fresh lemon juice
2 cups (480 ml) hot cooked rice, if desired

Combine beef shank cross cuts, water, tomatoes, celery, onion, garlic, bouillon cubes, salt, black pepper and red pepper in Dutch oven. Bring to a boil; reduce heat. Cover tightly and simmer 2 hours, stirring occasionally. Remove shanks. Cut beef from bone; cut beef into small pieces. Skim and discard fat from broth, if desired. Return beef to broth; add cabbage and bell pepper. Cover and continue to simmer 30 minutes or until beef and vegetables are tender. Stir in lemon juice. Spoon ¼ cup rice into each serving of soup, if desired. Serves 8.

Approximate nutritional analysis per serving:
Calories 241, Protein 27 g, Carbohydrates 21 g, Fat 5 g, Cholesterol 44 mg, Sodium 525 mg

Courtesy of the National Livestock and Meat Board.

CHEESE CHOWDER

3 cups (720 ml) potatoes, cubed
2 cups (480 ml) carrots, cut into chunks
1 cup (240 ml) celery, cut into chunks
1 cup (240 ml) water
1 - 10 oz can (300 ml) low sodium chicken broth
1 lb (455 g) HEALTHY CHOICE Fat Free
    Pasteurized Process Cheese Product, cubed
¼ cup (60 ml) parsley, chopped
cracked black pepper

Cook potatoes, carrots and celery in chicken broth and water until vegetables are tender. Combine cheese and ½ cup of broth from cooked vegetables in microwave-proof bowl. Microwave on HIGH 6 minutes or until cheese melts, stirring every 2 minutes. Add melted cheese to vegetables and broth; stir in parsley. Add more water for thinner chowder. Season with pepper. Serves 8.

Approximate nutritional analysis per serving:
Calories 136, Protein 14 g, Carbohydrates 20 g, Fat .5 g, Cholesterol 10 mg, Sodium 884 mg

CHICKEN CORN CHOWDER

1 - 3 lb (1.4 kg) EMPIRE KOSHER chicken
    with neck and giblets
1 medium onion, chopped
1 stalk celery, chopped
2 large carrots, chopped
1 can corn kernels with liquid
1 can whole tomatoes, drained and cut up
1 tsp (5 ml) lemon juice
salt and pepper

Bring chicken to a boil in 4 cups water. Skim. Simmer with onion, celery and carrots until tender, about 45 minutes. Remove chicken, let cool. Discard skin and bones, cut meat in bite size pieces, along with giblets if desired. Skim fat from chicken broth. Combine chicken meat, broth, corn, tomatoes and lemon juice. Season with salt and pepper, simmer for 30-45 minutes. Serves 4.

Approximate nutritional analysis per serving:
Calories 781, Protein 103 g, Carbohydrates 32 g, Fat 26 g, Cholesterol 301 mg, Sodium 787 mg

CHICKEN CHOWDER WITH POTATO DUMPLINGS

2 cups (480 ml) cooked chicken, cut up
1 cup (240 ml) frozen or canned whole kernel corn
2 cups (480 ml) skim milk
½ tsp (3 ml) salt
1 - 16 oz can (480 g) cream style corn
1 - 2 oz jar (60 g) sliced pimientos, drained
1 cup (240 ml) BISQUICK Reduced Fat Baking Mix
⅓ cup (80 ml) BETTY CROCKER Potato Buds
    Mashed Potatoes, dry
2 tbs (30 ml) skim milk
1 tbs (15 ml) fresh parsley, chopped
    or 1 tsp (5 ml) dried parsley flakes
2 egg whites
    or ¼ cup (60 ml) cholesterol free egg product

Mix chicken, whole kernel corn, 2 cups milk, the salt, creamed corn and pimientos in 4-qt Dutch oven. Heat to boiling over medium heat, stirring occasionally. Beat baking mix, potatoes, 2 tbs milk, the parsley and egg whites until dough forms (dough will be very stiff). Turn dough onto surface well dusted with baking mix; roll in baking mix to coat. Knead about 30 times or until no longer sticky. Pat dough into ½-inch squares. Drop squares into gently boiling chowder. Cook uncovered 6-8 minutes or until dumplings are slightly puffy and dry inside. Sprinkle with parsley if desired. Serves 6.

Approximate nutritional analysis per serving:
Calories 290, Protein 22 g, Carbohydrates 39 g, Fat 5 g, Cholesterol 45 mg, Sodium 730 mg

TURKEY HAM AND CORM CHOWDER

1 cup (240 ml) onion, chopped
1 tbs (15 ml) vegetable oil
3 tbs (45 ml) flour
½ tsp (3 ml) black pepper
1 qt (960 ml) skim milk
2 cups (480 ml) frozen hash brown potatoes
2 - 11 oz cans (660 g) corn with red and
    green peppers, drained
¾ lb (340 g) NORBEST Turkey Ham,
    cut into ½-inch cubes

In 3-qt saucepan, over medium-high heat, sauté onions in oil 3 minutes or until translucent. Blend in flour and pepper. Remove pan from heat; slowly add milk stirring constantly. Return pan to heat. Add potatoes; bring mixture to boil, stirring constantly. Add corn and turkey ham; return mixture to boil. Reduce heat to low and simmer soup 15 minutes or until potatoes are tender and mixture has thickened. Serves 8.

Approximate nutritional analysis per serving:
Calories 233, Protein 16 g, Carbohydrates 34 g, Fat 5 g,
Cholesterol 29 mg, Sodium 770 mg

SATIN SALMON CHOWDER

1 tbs (15 ml) margarine or butter
½ cup (120 ml) onion, chopped
1 clove garlic, minced
2 cups (480 ml) water
1 cup (240 ml) potatoes, peeled and diced
1 - 3½ g envelope low sodium instant
    chicken bouillon
1 - 8 oz can (240 g) corn kernels, drained
1 - 7½ oz can (225 g) salmon, drained and flaked
¼ cup (60 ml) green or red bell pepper, diced
¼ tsp (1 ml) freshly ground pepper
2 cups (480 ml) DANNON Plain Nonfat or
    Lowfat Yogurt
¼ cup (60 ml) all purpose flour

In large saucepan melt margarine over medium heat. Add onion and garlic; cook and stir 2-3 minutes or just until tender. Stir in water, potatoes and chicken bouillon. Bring to a boil and simmer, stirring occasionally, 4-5 minutes or until potatoes are tender. Reduce heat to low. Add corn, salmon, bell pepper and ground pepper. *Do not boil.* In a medium bowl, combine yogurt and flour; blend well. Gradually add to soup, stirring constantly, until smooth and slightly thickened. Serves 4.

Approximate nutritional analysis per serving:
Calories 316, Protein 21 g, Carbohydrates 39 g, Fat 10 g,
Cholesterol 38 mg, Sodium 940 mg

VEGETABLE GUMBO

3 tbs (45 ml) butter or margarine
2 cups (480 ml) onions, chopped, in all
1¼ oz (40 g) tasso or lean ham, minced, optional
1½ cups (355 ml) celery, chopped, in all
1¼ cups (295 ml) green bell peppers, chopped, in all
4 cups (960 ml) okra, sliced, in all
2 cups (480 ml) tomatoes, peeled and chopped
1 tbs (15 ml) CHEF PAUL PRUDHOMME'S
    Seafood Magic*
¾ tsp (4 ml) dried leaf thyme, in all
3 bay leaves
6 cups (1.4 L) vegetable or chicken stock, in all**
1¾ tsp (9 ml) fresh garlic, minced, in all
2 tsp (10 ml) salt
2 cups (480 ml) eggplant, unpeeled, in chunks
1½ cups (355 ml) zucchini squash, in chunks
1½ cups (355 ml) yellow squash, in chunks
1 cup (240 ml) sugar snap pea pods, trimmed
1 cup (240 ml) baby green beans, ends trimmed
¼ cup (60 ml) green onions, minced, tops only
6 cups (1.4 L) hot cooked rice

* For hotter, spicier flavor, add 1 more tsp Seafood Magic with the second tsp salt.
** Feel free to substitute your favorite fresh vegetables - almost any vegetable will work well in this recipe. To make this a vegetarian dish, eliminate the tasso and use vegetable stock.

Melt the butter in a large, heavy pot over high heat. Add 1 cup chopped onions and the tasso or ham, if desired. Cook over high heat about 3½ minutes, occasionally stirring and scraping the bottom of the pot with a wooden spoon. Add 1 cup celery and ¾ cup bell peppers; lower heat to medium, cover and cook about 2 minutes. Stir in 3 cups okra and all of the tomatoes. Add Seafood Magic, ½ tsp thyme and bay leaves and stir, scraping up all the browned bits on the bottom of the pot. Raise heat to high, re-cover the pot and cook, stirring and scraping occasionally, about 8 minutes. Stir in 1 cup stock, scrape the bottom of the pot, cover and cook 12 minutes. Add another cup cup of stock and ¾ tsp garlic. Stir, scrape, cover and cook 11 minutes. Add 4 cups stock, the remaining 1 cup onions, ½ cup celery, 1 cup okra, ½ cup bell peppers and 1 tsp garlic. Cook, stirring, 2 minutes. Add the salt and the remaining thyme. Stir in the eggplant, zucchini and yellow squash, cover and cook 6 minutes over high heat. Add the pea pods, cover and cook 2 minutes. Add the green beans, cover and cook 2 more minutes. Turn off heat, stir in green onions and let stand, covered, 5-10 minutes to allow the flavors to develop. Serve over hot rice. Serves 12.

Approximate nutritional analysis per serving:
Calories 211, Protein 6 g, Carbohydrates 39 g, Fat 4 g,
Cholesterol 9 mg, Sodium 640 mg

BEEF BARLEY SOUP

3 lbs (1.4 kg) beef shank cross cuts, cut 1-inch thick
1 tbs (15 ml) vegetable oil
1 medium onion, chopped
½ cup (120 ml) carrot, chopped
½ cup (120 ml) celery with leaves, chopped
3 cloves garlic, crushed
5 cups (1.2 L) water
1½ tsp (8 ml) salt
1½ tsp (8 ml) dried thyme leaves, crushed
1 bay leaf
½ tsp (3 ml) pepper
⅓ cup (80 ml) medium pearled barley
   or ½ cup (120 ml) quick cooking barley*
1 - 9 oz pkg frozen French-cut green beans

Heat oil in Dutch oven over medium heat. Add onion, carrot, celery and garlic; cook 5 minutes or until tender, stirring occasionally. Add beef shank cross cuts, water, salt, thyme, bay leaf and pepper. Bring to a boil; reduce heat. Cover tightly and simmer 1 hour. Remove shanks. Cut beef from bone; cut beef into I-inch pieces. Skim and discard fat from broth. Return beef to broth; add barley. Cover and simmer 50-60 minutes or until beef and barley are tender. Add green beans; return to a boil. Reduce heat; simmer 2-3 minutes or until green beans are tender. Remove bay leaf. Serves 6.

   * If using quick cooking barley, add to soup after cooking 1 hour 40 minutes.

Approximate nutritional analysis per serving:
Calories 235, Protein 27 g, Carbohydrates 15 g, Fat 7 g,
Cholesterol 44 mg, Sodium 637 mg

Courtesy of the National Live Stock and Meat Board.

QUICK CATFISH GUMBO

1 cup (240 ml) celery, chopped
1 cup (240 ml) onion, chopped
1 cup (240 ml) green pepper, chopped
2 cloves garlic, minced
3 tbs (45 ml) cooking oil
4 cups (960 ml) beef broth
1 - 16 oz can (480 g) whole tomatoes, cut up
1 bay leaf
1 tsp (5 ml) salt
½ tsp (3 ml) dried thyme
½ tsp (3 ml) ground red pepper
½ tsp (3 ml) dried oregano, crushed
2 lbs (910 g) Mississippi farm-raised catfish
   fillets, cut into bite-size pieces
1 - 10 oz pkg (300 g) frozen sliced okra
4 cups (960 ml) hot cooked rice

In a large kettle or Dutch oven cook celery, onion, green pepper and garlic in hot oil until tender. Stir in beef broth, tomatoes, bay leaf, salt, thyme, red pepper and oregano. Bring to a boil; reduce heat. Cover and simmer for 15 minutes.

   Add catfish and okra to kettle. Return to boiling. cover and simmer for 15 minutes or until fish flakes easily. Remove and discard bay leaf. Serve in bowl over hot cooked rice. Serves 8.

Approximate nutritional analysis per serving:
Calories 350, Protein 25 g, Carbohydrates 37 g, Fat 11 g,
Cholesterol 66 mg, Sodium 708 mg

Courtesy of the Catfish Institute.

SEAFOOD CHOWDER

1 lb (455 g) frozen haddock
2 tbs (30 ml) butter
1 large onion, chopped
3 stalks celery, chopped
3 carrots, chopped
3 potatoes, sliced
½ cup (120 ml) flour
½ tsp (3 ml) salt
2 tbs (30 ml) OLD BAY Seasoning
2 - 10¾ oz cans (645 ml) undiluted chicken broth
3 cups (720 ml) milk
1 - 8 oz pkg (240 g) small shrimp
1½ lbs (685 g) sea legs, chopped
   (imitation crab meat)
1 cup (240 ml) cheddar cheese, grated

Thaw fish enough to cut into cubes. In large saucepan, melt butter and add vegetables; cook until onions are transparent. Blend in flour, salt, OLD BAY Seasoning. Cook for 1 minute, stirring constantly. Add chicken broth and milk and cook over medium heat for 25 minutes. Add haddock, shrimp, sea legs and cook for an additional 10 minutes. Add the cheese and cook until cheese is melted. Serve hot. Serves 8.

Approximate nutritional analysis per serving:
Calories 388, Protein 39 g, Carbohydrates 24 g, Fat 15 g,
Cholesterol 151 mg, Sodium 816 mg

OYSTER STEW

1 - 12 oz pkg (360 g) lowfat cottage cheese
2 tbs (30 ml) arrowroot
1¾ cup (415 ml) oyster liquid*
1 qt (960 ml) skim milk
¾ cup (180 ml) onion, chopped, in all
½ cup (120 ml) celery, chopped, in all
2 tbs (30 ml) diet margarine, in all
2 tsp (10 ml) CHEF PAUL PRUDHOMME'S
    Seafood Magic
¼ cup (60 ml) parsley, finely chopped
36 oysters

* Drain off the liquid for your oysters. If there is less than 1¾ cups, add the missing amount in water to the oysters, wait 10 minutes and drain into the oyster liquid.

Place cottage cheese in blender or food processor and blend about 5 minutes, or until thick and creamy and all lumps are gone. Measure out ½ cup of this mock cream, and reserve the rest to use in cream sauces or as a dip. (Or add 2 tsp cider vinegar to remainder and use as a sour cream substitute.) Mix arrowroot with 4 tbs oyster liquid and set aside. In a saucepan over high heat, bring skim milk to steaming. Turn off heat.

Place a 10-inch skillet over high heat. When skillet is very hot, add ½ cup chopped onion and ¼ cup chopped celery and cook another 2 minutes. Add 1 tbs diet margarine and cook another 2 minutes. Add Seafood Magic, and cook 1 minute. Add remaining ¼ cup each chopped onion and celery, and all of the parsley. When vegetables begin to stick hard to the bottom of the skillet, about 6 minutes, add 1 cup oyster liquid and cook 4 minutes. Add remaining ½ cup oyster liquid, stir and cook 1 minute. Add the arrowroot mixture and stir well. Transfer this mixture to a large pot placed over high heat and bring to a simmer. Add the oysters and cook 2 minutes. Add remaining 1 tbs diet margarine, and, when it begins to melt, add the skim milk. Cook 4 minutes and turn off heat. Add the ½ cup mock cream, stirring until thoroughly blended into mixture. Serve immediately. Serves 6.

Approximate nutritional analysis per serving:
Calories 166, Protein 19 g, Carbohydrates 13 g, Fat 6 g,
Cholesterol 51 mg, Sodium 464 mg

CAJUN SHRIMP CHOWDER

3 tbs (45 ml) olive oil
1 medium green pepper, chopped
1 medium red pepper, chopped
3 stalks celery, chopped
1 large red onion, chopped
3 cloves garlic, chopped
1 - 16 oz can (480 g) crushed tomatoes
½ cup (120 ml) red cooking wine
½ cup (120 ml) water
1½ tbs (25 ml) OLD BAY Seasoning
¼ tsp (1 ml) cayenne pepper
½ tsp (3 ml) salt
1 tsp (5 ml) black pepper
1½ lbs (685 g) medium shrimp, peeled and deveined
chopped green onions for garnish

In a large pot, heat olive oil. Add peppers, celery, onion and garlic and sauté until tender, about 5 minutes. Mix in crushed tomatoes, wine and water. Bring to a boil, add OLD BAY Seasoning, cayenne, salt and black pepper. Cover and simmer for 35 minutes, stirring occasionally. Add shrimp, cover and simmer for 5 minutes, then remove from heat. Garnish with chopped green onions. Serves 6.

Approximate nutritional analysis per serving:
Calories 243, Protein 25 g, Carbohydrates 13 g, Fat 9 g,
Cholesterol 172 mg, Sodium 496 mg

SALADS

The salad has appropriately risen to take its rightful place in meal planning. Salads can be as refined and elegant as any food preparation, and when designed as main courses can satisfy with a variety of bright and sassy flavors. Even salads that seem elaborate are usually imaginative combinations of simple ingredients. Don't be intimidated! Well-dressed leafy salads can tempt the diner at the opening of a meal, or in the French tradition, refresh the palate after.

ORIENTAL TURKEY SLAW

DRESSING:
¼ cup (60 ml) canola oil
2 tbs (30 ml) lime juice
2 tbs (30 ml) reduced sodium soy sauce
2 tsp (10 ml) sugar
2 tsp (10 ml) peanut butter
1 tsp (5 ml) garlic, minced
¼-½ tsp (1-3 ml) red pepper flakes

SALAD:
¾ lb (340 g) **NORBEST Oven Roasted Turkey Breast,**
    fully cooked, cut into ⅛-inch julienne strips
2 cups (480 ml) packaged cole slaw mix
¼ cup (60 ml) fresh cilantro, chopped
¼ cup (60 ml) green onions, chopped

In small bowl whisk oil, lime juice, soy sauce, sugar, peanut butter, garlic and red pepper flakes; set aside. In large bowl combine turkey, cole slaw, cilantro and onions. Fold dressing into turkey slaw mixture. Serve immediately. Serves 8.

Approximate nutritional analysis per serving:
Calories 122, Protein 9 g, Carbohydrates 4 g, Fat 8 g,
Cholesterol 18 mg, Sodium 647 mg

CRUNCHY LAYERED DELI SALAD

8 oz (240 g) **EMPIRE KOSHER Pastrami,**
    Salami or Smoked Turkey Breast,
    julienned into ¼-inch strips
½ cup (120 ml) reduced calorie mayonnaise
¼ cup (60 ml) low calorie Italian dressing
2 cups (480 ml) frozen peas, thawed and drained
1 cup (240 ml) celery, chopped
1 cup (240 ml) peanuts
1 cup 9240 ml) red onion, thinly sliced
2 cups (480 ml) shredded lettuce

Spread the lettuce in a layer on a serving platter. Mix peas, celery and onion and spoon over the lettuce layer. Top with meat. Stir together the mayonnaise and the salad dressing. Spoon on top, add peanuts. Serves 8.

Approximate nutritional analysis per serving:
Calories 218, Protein 13 g, Carbohydrates 14 g, Fat 13 g,
Cholesterol 23 mg, Sodium 467 mg

TURKEY SALAD WITH POPPY SEED-BALSAMIC VINAIGRETTE

SALAD:
¾ lb (340 g) **NORBEST Oven Roasted**
    Turkey Breast , cut into ½-¾-inch cubes
2 cups (480 ml) broccoli florets
2 cups (480 ml) spinach, torn
2 cups (480 ml) leaf lettuce pieces
1 small green pepper, cut into ⅛-inch strips
½ cup (120 ml) red onion, thinly sliced
1 - 8 oz can (240 g) pineapple chunks,
    juice drained and reserved

POPPY SEED BALSAMIC VINAIGRETTE:
¼ cup (60 ml) olive oil
2 tbs (30 ml) balsamic vinegar
2 tbs (30 ml) reserved pineapple juice
1 tbs (15 ml) poppy seeds
2 tsp (10 ml) sugar
2 tsp (10 ml) Dijon mustard

In large bowl combine turkey, broccoli, spinach, lettuce, pepper, onion and pineapple; set aside. In small bowl whisk oil, vinegar, juice, poppy seeds and mustard. Fold vinaigrette into salad just before serving. Serves 8.

Approximate nutritional analysis per serving:
Calories 149, Protein 10 g, Carbohydrates 11 g, Fat 8 g,
Cholesterol 18 mg, Sodium 544 mg

AVOCADO, CHICKEN AND EGG SALAD

1 cup (240 ml) **EMPIRE KOSHER Chicken**
    or Turkey, cooked, diced
2 avocados, cubed finely
1 tbs (15 ml) lemon juice
2 tbs (30 ml) minced onion
2 hard-boiled eggs, peeled and chopped coarsely
¼ cup (60 ml) reduced calorie mayonnaise
salt and pepper to taste

Mix all ingredients. Season to taste with salt and pepper. Stuff in pita pockets, on pumpernickel bread or serve on lettuce leaves. Yields 3 sandwiches.

Approximate nutritional analysis per serving:
Calories 385, Protein 21 g, Carbohydrates 12 g, Fat 30 g,
Cholesterol 193 mg, Sodium 149 mg

Curried Turkey and Peanut Salad

POPPY SEED PINEAPPLE CHICKEN SALAD

**10½ oz (315 g) COMSTOCK Pineapple Filling
    or Topping**
2 tbs (30 ml) white wine vinegar
2 tbs (30 ml) lemon juice
1 tbs (15 ml) honey
1 tbs (15 ml) corn syrup
1 tbs (15 ml) poppy seeds
1 tsp (5 ml) dry mustard
1 tsp (5 ml) onion, grated
**1 lb (455 g) pre-cooked chicken (or turkey)
    cut into ½-inch cubes**
1 cup (240 ml) celery, sliced
⅔ cup (160 ml) sliced almonds
½ cup (120 ml) carrots, thinly sliced
lettuce leaves

Dressing: Combine pineapple filling, vinegar, lemon juice, honey, corn syrup, poppy seeds, dry mustard and grated onion.

In a serving bowl mix together chicken, celery, almonds and carrots. Fold in dressing. Line 6 plates with lettuce leaves. Mound salad on lettuce to serve. Serves 6.

Approximate nutritional analysis per serving:
Calories 273, Protein 25 g, Carbohydrates 15 g, Fat 13 g,
Cholesterol 67 mg, Sodium 90 mg

CURRIED TURKEY AND PEANUT SALAD

**½ cup (120 ml) DANNON Plain Nonfat
    or Lowfat Yogurt**
¼ cup (60 ml) mayonnaise or salad dressing
1-1½ tsp (5-8 ml) curry powder
¼ tsp (1 ml) salt
⅛ tsp (.5 ml) pepper
3 cups (720 ml) cooked turkey or chicken, chopped
1 cup (240 ml) seedless grapes, halved
½ cup (120 ml) water chestnuts, chopped
½ cup (120 ml) red or green bell pepper, chopped
lettuce leaves
⅓ cup (80 ml) chopped peanuts

In a large bowl combine yogurt, mayonnaise, curry powder, salt and pepper; mix well. Fold in turkey, grapes, water chestnuts and bell pepper. Cover; chill thoroughly before serving. To serve, line 6 plates with lettuce leaves. Spoon turkey salad over lettuce leaves. Top with chopped peanuts. Serves 6.

Approximate nutritional analysis per serving:
Calories 234, Protein 23 g, Carbohydrates 10 g, Fat 11 g,
Cholesterol 57 mg, Sodium 255 mg

CHICKEN GUACAMOLE SALAD

5 cups (1.2 L) PREMIUM YOUNG 'N TENDER
    Brand cooked chicken, boned and cut into chunks
1 cup (240 ml) celery, chopped
1¼ cups (295 ml) onion, chopped
1 cup (240 ml) red or green bell pepper, chopped
1 cup (240 ml) fresh cilantro, chopped
1 cup (240 ml) mayonnaise
4 ripe avocados
½ fresh lime, juiced
1¼ tsp (6 ml) pepper
2 tsp (10 ml) ground cumin
¾ tsp (4 ml) garlic powder
3-4 jalapeño peppers, minced, optional

Combine chicken chunks, celery, onion, bell pepper, cilantro and mayonnaise in a large bowl. In a separate bowl, mash avocados with the lime juice, leaving some chunks. Add to the chicken mixture, mixing well. Add pepper, cumin, garlic powder and jalapeños. Serve immediately or cover with plastic wrap and refrigerate until ready to serve.

    Serving suggestions: Serve as is; over a tossed salad; as a dip; as a sandwich in a pita pocket with chopped tomatoes and alfalfa sprouts; or roll into a hot flour tortilla with your favorite toppings. Serves 10.

Approximate nutritional analysis per serving:
Calories 372, Protein 23 g, Carbohydrates 16 g, Fat 26 g,
Cholesterol 68 mg, Sodium 247 mg

HEALTHY HEARTS CHICKEN SALAD

6 PREMIUM YOUNG 'N TENDER Brand
    chicken breasts, cut into bite-size pieces
1 cup (240 ml) white wine
½ cup (120 ml) chicken broth or water
2 cloves garlic, minced
¼ tsp (1 ml) dried basil
Healthy Hearts Salad Dressing (below)
6 cups (1.4 L) mixed salad greens, torn
1 - 14 oz can (420 g) hearts of palm, drained,
    cut into bite-size pieces
1 medium tomato, seeded, chopped
1 red onion, cut into thin rings

HEALTHY HEARTS SALAD DRESSING:

¼ cup (60 ml) balsamic vinegar
¼ tsp (1 ml) dried tarragon
¼ tsp (1 ml) thyme
¼ tsp (1 ml) basil
⅓ cup (80 ml) olive oil
2 tbs (30 ml) Dijon mustard
1 clove garlic, minced
¼ tsp (1 ml) salt
½ tsp (3 ml) crushed red pepper

Combine chicken, wine, broth, garlic, tarragon and basil in a 2-qt saucepan. Cover and simmer about 15-20 minutes, or until done. Set aside to cool in liquid. Drain chicken and cut into 1-inch strips.

    To make dressing, combine vinegar, herbs, olive oil, mustard, garlic, salt and red pepper in a cruet or a screw top jar. Shake well to blend; refrigerate and let stand 15 minutes. Can be made ahead.

    Combine salad greens, hearts of palm, tomato, onion and chicken. Toss with chilled dressing, mixing thoroughly. Serve on lettuce lined platter or individual serving plates. Garnish with additional tomato wedges or hearts of palm, if desired. Serves 6.

Approximate nutritional analysis per serving:
Calories 305, Protein 29 g, Carbohydrates 7 g, Fat 15 g,
Cholesterol 73 mg, Sodium 13 mg

ORIENTAL TOMATO SALAD AND DRESSING

SALAD:
1 lb (455 g) fresh FLORIDA tomatoes, diced
1 lb (455 g) cooked chicken breasts, sliced
1 cup (240 ml) celery, sliced
½ cup (120 ml) roasted cashew nuts

DRESSING:
⅓ cup (80 ml) peanut oil
2 tbs (30 ml) rice wine vinegar
1½ tbs (25 ml) soy sauce
1 tsp (5 ml) sugar
¾ tsp (4 ml) ground ginger
½ tsp (3 ml) garlic powder

Use tomatoes held at room temperature until fully ripe. Arrange chicken slices on a serving platter. In a bowl combine tomatoes, celery and cashews. Toss with Oriental Dressing until evenly coated. Arrange vegetable combination with chicken on a serving plate. Serves 4.

    Oriental Dressing: Place oil, vinegar, soy sauce, sugar, ginger and garlic in electric blender. Blend until smooth. Yields ½ cup, 1 tbs per serving.

Approximate nutritional analysis per serving salad:
Calories 310, Protein 39 g, Carbohydrates 11 g, Fat 12 g,
Cholesterol 96 mg, Sodium 121 mg

Approximate nutritional analysis per serving dressing:
Calories 84, Protein < 1 g, Carbohydrates 1 g, Fat 9 g,
Cholesterol 0 mg, Sodium 194 mg

Opposite: Oriental Tomato Salad and Dressing

CHICKEN SALAD WITH CAJUN DRESSING

2 cups (480 ml) PREMIUM YOUNG 'N TENDER
　　Brand cooked chicken, cut into bite- size pieces
1 cup (240 ml) cooked black beans
　　or 1 - 15 oz can (450 g) black beans,
　　rinsed and drained
1 cup (240 ml) cooked white rice
1 cup (240 ml) whole kernel corn
　　or 1 - 11 oz can (330 g) whole kernel corn, drained
1 avocado, peeled, cut into chunks
12 cherry tomatoes, halved
8 spinach leaves, optional

CAJUN DRESSING:
¾ cup (80 ml) olive oil
¼ cup (60 ml) balsamic vinegar
½ cup (120 ml) tomato ketchup
2 cloves garlic, crushed
2 tbs (30 ml) fresh parsley, minced
1 tbs (15 ml) brown mustard
½ tsp (3 ml) cayenne pepper

Combine chicken, black beans, rice, corn, avocado and cherry tomatoes. Arrange spinach leaves on salad plate and top with chicken salad. Mixture may be divided among four individual salad plates with 2 spinach leaves per plate.

　　To make dressing, combine olive oil, vinegar, ketchup, garlic, parsley, mustard and cayenne in a pint jar. Cover and shake well. Pour desired amount over salad. Serves 4.

Approximate nutritional analysis per serving:
Calories 784, Protein 29 g, Carbohydrates 50 g, Fat 55 g,
Cholesterol 62 mg, Sodium 616 mg

CHICKEN SALAD SUPREME

⅓ cup (80 ml) mayonnaise
1 tsp (5 ml) lemon juice
½ tsp (3 ml) onion powder
2 whole chicken breasts, cooks and cubed
4 hard-cooked eggs, chopped
1 cup (240 ml) fresh spinach leaves
½ cup (120 ml) celery, finely chopped
2 tbs (30 ml) bottled capers, well drained

In medium bowl, stir together mayonnaise, lemon juice and onion powder until well blended. Stir in remaining ingredients until evenly coated with dressing. Cover and chill to blend flavors. Serve as a salad on spinach leaves or as a sandwich between slices of whole wheat bread lined with spinach leaves. Serves 4.

Approximate nutritional analysis per serving:
Calories 191, Protein 14 g, Carbohydrates 6 g, Fat 12 g,
Cholesterol 235 mg, Sodium 241 mg

TOMATO AND CHICKEN SALAD FLORIDIAN

1½ lbs (680 g) fresh FLORIDA tomatoes,
　　diced (3 large)
12 oz (360 g) cooked chicken cut in ½-inch cubes
¼ cup (60 ml) scallions, thinly sliced
⅓ cup (80 ml) orange juice
2 tbs (30 ml) lemon juice
2 tbs (30 ml) vegetable oil
1 egg yolk
2 tsp (10 ml) grated orange peel
¾ tsp (4 ml) ground ginger
½ tsp (3 ml) salt
¼ tsp (1 ml) garlic powder
⅛ tsp (.5 ml) ground black pepper

Use tomatoes held at room temperature until fully ripe. Remove cores; reserve 1 tomato for later use. Slice 2 of the tomatoes ½ inch from the top. Squeeze out seeds and juice (use in soups, stews, etc.). Cut juiced tomatoes into ½-inch dice; place in a bowl along with chicken and scallions; set aside.

　　To prepare dressing, place in the container of an electric blender: orange and lemon juices, oil ,egg yolk, orange peel, ginger, salt, garlic and black pepper. Blend until smooth. Pour over tomato and chicken mixture; toss gently to coat. Spoon into the center of a serving platter. Cut remaining tomato in ¼ inch thick slices; cut slices in halves; garnish salad with tomato slices or lettuce leaves. Serves 4.

Approximate nutritional analysis per serving:
Calories 282, Protein 27 g, Carbohydrates 11 g, Fat 15 g,
Cholesterol 129 mg, Sodium 363 mg

CHICKEN SALAD CHIQUITA™

2 cups (480 ml) cooked chicken, diced
⅓ cup (80 ml) plain yogurt
⅓ cup (80 ml) mayonnaise
½ CHIQUITA Banana, diced
2 tbs (30 ml) strawberries, diced
2 tbs (30 ml) pineapple, diced
2 tbs (30 ml) grapes, diced
2 tbs (30 ml) scallions or green onions, sliced
½ tsp (3 ml) celery salt
¼ tsp (1 ml) paprika
¼ tsp (1 ml) chili powder
2 tbs (30 ml) pecans, toasted and chopped, to garnish

Combine all ingredients except pecans in bowl; toss gently to mix well. Serve on a bed of lettuce or with whole grain bread for sandwiches. Garnish with pecans, if desired. Serves 4.

Approximate nutritional analysis per serving:
Calories 310, Protein 15 g, Carbohydrates 14 g, Fat 20 g,
Cholesterol 45 mg, Sodium 165 mg

Opposite: Tomato and Chicken Salad Floridian

HOT CHICKEN SALAD

3 - 4 oz chicken breasts (360 g), skinless,
    boneless, cut crosswise in strips
2 tsp (10 ml) CHEF PAUL PRUDHOMME'S
    Poultry Magic
1 tsp (5 ml) diet margarine, softened
6 cups (1.4 L) spinach, rinsed, stems removed
½ medium potato, peeled, cut into sticks
½ medium sweet potato, peeled, cut into sticks
4-5 ribs celery, cut in diagonal slices
½ medium onion, julienned
1 fennel bulb, cut in strips, optional
2 carrots, cut in short sticks
¼ red bell pepper, cut in strips
¼ green bell pepper, cut in strips
¼ yellow bell pepper, cut in strips

DRESSING:

1 cup (240 ml) vegetable stock, from vegetables
1 tbs (15 ml) soy sauce
1 tbs (15 ml) tamari*
1 tbs (15 ml) cider vinegar
1 tbs (15 ml) Worcestershire sauce
3 packets EQUAL

Salad: Combine the chicken strips with the Poultry Magic and margarine. Mix well and set aside.

Fill a large pot with water (about 5 qts), place a strainer over the pot so the bowl of the strainer is submerged, and bring water to a rolling boil. Place the spinach in the strainer and cook 2-3 minutes. Drain and place spinach in a small container. Repeat the same procedure with each vegetable separately, cooking the onions, celery, fennel and carrots each 2 minutes; the peppers and sweet potatoes each 1½ minutes; and the white potato about 3 minutes. Keep each vegetable warm in its own separate container, preferably covered.

Heat a large skillet to about 350°F (180°C). Bronze the chicken over high heat, turning it as it browns. When the chicken is all a rich, bronze color, remove from the skillet.

Dressing: Keeping the same skillet over the high heat, add 1 cup of the vegetable stock (the water in which the vegetables cooked) to the pan, scraping up all the browned bits off the bottom. Stir in the soy sauce, tamari, vinegar and Worcestershire. Cook 2 minutes, remove from the heat and add the EQUAL.

To serve, arrange a thin bed of spinach on four 10-inch plates. Artfully arrange small groupings of the vegetables around the edges of the plates. Mound ¼ cup of the chicken in the center of each plate. Sprinkle about ¼ cup of the dressing over each salad, and serve. Serves 4.

Approximate nutritional analysis per serving:
Calories 245, Protein 31 g, Carbohydrates 21 g, Fat 4 g,
Cholesterol 72 mg, Sodium 712 mg

MEXICAN CHICKEN SALAD

1 lb (455 g) chicken breasts, boneless,
    skinless, cooked and shredded
1 cup (240 ml) CHI-CHI'S Salsa, drained
2 hard-cooked eggs, finely chopped
½ cup (120 ml) sour cream
¼ cup (60 ml) mayonnaise
2 tbs (30 ml) onion, finely chopped
1 tsp (5 ml) grated lime peel
½ tsp (3 ml) chili powder
¼ tsp (1 ml) ground cumin
lettuce leaves

In large bowl, combine all ingredients except lettuce leaves. Mix well. Serve on lettuce leaves. Serves 6.

Approximate nutritional analysis per serving:
Calories 240, Protein 20 g, Carbohydrates 4 g, Fat 15 g,
Cholesterol 130 mg, Sodium 300 mg

CHICKEN SALAD QUEEN LILIUOKALANI

2 lbs (910 g) boneless chicken meat
    or 1 - 4½ lb (2.0 kg) whole roaster
1 small can papaya nectar
2 oz (60 g) ginger, shredded
salt and white pepper to taste
8 oz (240 g) ripe-soft papaya meat
8 oz (240 g) mayonnaise or lowfat yogurt
1 lemon, squeezed for juice
honey, to taste
2 lbs (910 g) firm papaya, diced

FOR GARNISH:

1 lime or lemon, 1 papaya, 8 strawberries
macadamia nuts, sliced parsley

Boil the chicken, debone and cut in ¾-inch diagonal pieces. Marinate with papaya nectar, ginger, salt, white pepper overnight.

Dressing: puree the soft papaya in kitchen blender, with the mayonnaise and add to taste the following: ginger, salt, white pepper, lemon juice and honey.

Drain the papaya nectar from the chicken meat. Add the diced papaya to the chicken, then add the papaya dressing. Mix together and check flavor. Serve on cold glass plate, place chicken salad, 8-10 oz serving, in center of plate and garnish with sliced papaya, sliced lemons or limes, chopped macadamia nuts, strawberries, parsley. Serve with Melba toast. Serves 8.

Approximate nutritional analysis per serving, without garnish:
Calories 363, Protein 36 g, Carbohydrates 23 g, Fat 14 g,
Cholesterol 104 mg, Sodium 297 mg

Hot Turkey Salad with Sage Biscuits

HOT TURKEY SALAD WITH SAGE BISCUITS

¼ cup (60 ml) reduced-calorie mayonnaise
2 tbs (30 ml) BISQUICK Reduced Fat Baking Mix
2 cups (480 ml) cooked turkey, cut up
1 cup (240 ml) celery, sliced
2 green onions, sliced
2 cups (480 ml) BISQUICK Reduced Fat Baking Mix
⅔ cup (160 ml) skim milk
½ tsp (3 ml) dried sage leaves
¼ cup (60 ml) reduced-fat cheddar cheese, shredded

Heat oven to 425°F (220°C). Mix mayonnaise and 2 tbs baking mix in medium bowl until well blended. Stir in turkey, celery and onions; reserve.

Mix 2 cups baking mix, the milk, and sage just until soft dough forms. Turn onto surface well dusted with baking mix; gently roll in baking mix to coat. Shape into ball; knead gently 10 times. Roll ½ inch thick. Cut with 1½ -inch biscuit cutter dipped in baking mix. Place close together around edges of ungreased square pan, 9x9x2 inches.

Spoon reserved turkey mixture in mound in center of biscuits; sprinkle turkey mixture with cheese. Bake 18-20 minutes or until biscuits are golden brown and salad is hot. Serves 4.

Approximate nutritional analysis per serving:
Calories 430, Protein 30 g, Carbohydrates 46 g, Fat 14 g,
Cholesterol 60 mg, Sodium 950 mg

CURRIED CHICKEN SALAD

¾ cup (180 ml) YOPLAIT Fat Free Plain Yogurt
¼ cup (60 ml) cholesterol-free reduced-calorie
   mayonnaise or salad dressing
1 tsp (5 ml) curry powder
½ tsp (3 ml) salt
⅛ tsp (.5 ml) pepper
2 cups (480 ml) cooked chicken or turkey, cubed
1 cup (240 ml) seedless red grapes, halved
½ cup (120 ml) water chestnuts, chopped
½ cup (120 ml) celery, chopped

Mix yogurt, mayonnaise, curry powder, salt and pepper in medium bowl. Mix in remaining ingredients. Cover and refrigerate at least 1 hour or until chilled. Serve on lettuce leaves if desired. Serves 4.

Approximate nutritional analysis per serving:
Calories 270, Protein 24 g, Carbohydrates 22 g, Fat 3 g,
Cholesterol 65 mg, Sodium 490 mg

HONEY OF A CHICKEN SALAD

4 cups (960 ml) cooked chicken, cubed
1½ cups (355 ml) papaya, cubed
    or seedless green grapes
1 cup (240 ml) pecan pieces, toasted
½ cup (120 ml) mayonnaise
¼ cup (60 ml) DANNON Vanilla Lowfat Yogurt
2 tbs (30 ml) honey
1 tsp (5 ml) poppy seeds
¼ tsp (1 ml) white pepper
1 tbs (15 ml) fresh lime juice
lettuce leaves
papaya slices and pecan pieces, optional

In a large bowl combine chicken, papaya and pecan pieces. In a small bowl combine mayonnaise, yogurt, honey, poppy seeds, white pepper and lime juice. Add to chicken mixture. Gently toss to coat. To serve, line 6 plates with lettuce leaves. If desired, fan papaya slices on each plate. Top with chicken salad mixture. If desired, garnish with pecan pieces. Serves 6.

Approximate nutritional analysis per serving:
Calories 415, Protein 29 g, Carbohydrates 18 g, Fat 26 g,
Cholesterol 88 mg, Sodium 227

MUSTARD SWEET CHICKEN SALAD

1 - 2½-3 lb broiler-fryer chicken, cut up
¾ cup (180 ml) peach jam or apricot-pineapple jam
1 small can sliced water chestnuts, drained
½ cup (120 ml) Golden raisins
3 tbs (45 ml) Dijon mustard
2 tbs (30 ml) brandy or bourbon
½ tsp (3 ml) salt
1 small head iceberg lettuce, shredded
raw salad vegetables, julienned

Skin chicken. In 12x8x2-inch dish, arrange chicken with larger pieces to outside of dish. In mixing bowl stir together remaining ingredients except lettuce. Spread over chicken, evenly coating each piece. Cover with waxed paper and microwave at Medium-High (70%) for 20-25 minutes, rotating dish a half turn after 10 minutes. Allow chicken to cool only until it can be handled. Remove meat from bones and shred with 2 forks; toss with the cooking sauce in the dish. Cover and set aside to cool or keep warm if desired. Cover serving platter with lettuce. Mound chicken on top of lettuce. Surround with julienned vegetables using a few to garnish the top. Serves 4.

Approximate nutritional analysis per serving:
Calories 845, Protein 92 g, Carbohydrates 63 g, Fat 23 g,
Cholesterol 276 mg, Sodium 550 mg

Courtesy of The California Raisin Advisory Board.

CHICKEN PEAR SALAD ORIENTALE

1¾ oz (55 g) uncooked rice sticks (Maifun)
¼ cup (60 ml) vegetable oil
1 qt (960 ml) iceberg lettuce, shredded
1 fresh USA Pear, cored and sliced
1 cup (240 ml) cooked chicken, shredded
½ cup (120 ml) green onion, diagonally sliced
½ cup (120 ml) green pepper, diagonally sliced
1 tbs (15 ml) toasted sesame seeds

SESAME OIL DRESSING:
¼ cup (60 ml) vinegar
¼ cup (60 ml) sesame oil
1 tbs (15 ml) soy sauce
1 tsp (5 ml) salt
1 tsp (5 ml) sugar

HOISIN DRESSING:
2 tbs (30 ml) catsup
1 tbs (15 ml) Hoisin sauce
1 tbs (15 ml) salad oil
1 tbs (15 ml) sugar
1 tbs (15 ml) vinegar
½ tsp (3 ml) salt

Break rice sticks into 3-4-inch lengths. Heat oil to 375-400°F (190-205°C); fry rice sticks until white and fluffy. Turn once to fry pieces evenly. (Entire process takes less than ½ minute.) Drain on paper towels. Toss rice sticks with remaining ingredients. Serve with choice of dressing. Serves 4.
    Sesame Oil Dressing: Combine all ingredients; mix well. Yields ½ cup, serves 6.
    Hoisin Dressing: Combine all ingredients; mix well. Yields ⅓ cup, serves 6.

Approximate nutritional analysis per serving salad:
Calories 181, Protein 8 g, Carbohydrates 13 g, Fat 11 g,
Cholesterol 21 mg, Sodium 25 mg

Approximate nutritional analysis per serving sesame oil dressing:
Calories 86, Protein < 1 g, Carbohydrates 2 g, Fat 9 g,
Cholesterol 0 mg, Sodium 527 mg

Approximate nutritional analysis per serving Hoisin dressing:
Calories 39 , Protein < 1 g, Carbohydrates 5 g, Fat 3 g,
Cholesterol 0 mg, Sodium 250 mg

Mustard Sweet Chicken Salad

TUNA-SPINACH SALAD WITH DILL DRESSING

2 - 6½ oz cans (390 g) tuna in water, drained
   or 1 - 15½ oz can (465 g) salmon,
   drained and flaked
8-10 cups (1.9-.24 L) spinach,
   torn into bite-size pieces
1 cup (240 ml) lowfat cheddar cheese, cubed
1 medium tomato, seeded and chopped
1 - 8 oz can (240 g) sliced water chestnuts, drained
¾ cup (180 ml) seasoned croutons
1-1½ cups (240-355 ml) Dill Dressing

DILL DRESSING:
2 cups (480 ml) YOPLAIT Fat Free Plain Yogurt
1 cup (240 ml) cholesterol-free reduced-calorie
   mayonnaise or salad dressing
¼ cup (60 ml) skim milk
¼ cup (60 ml) green onions with tops, chopped
1 tbs (15 ml) parsley flakes
1½ tsp (8 ml) dried dill weed
½ tsp (3 ml) celery salt
¼ tsp (1 ml) onion powder

Toss all salad ingredients. Serve with dressing. Serves 4.
   Dill Dressing: Mix yogurt, mayonnaise and milk until blended. Stir in remaining ingredients. Refrigerate remaining dressing. Yields 3 cups. (Dressing will be adequate for more than 1 salad recipe.)

Approximate nutritional analysis per serving:
Calories 420, Protein 42 g, Carbohydrates 29 g, Fat 15 g,
Cholesterol 70 mg, Sodium 900 mg

CURRIED TURKEY AND PEANUT SALAD

½ cup (120 ml) DANNON Plain Nonfat
   or Lowfat Yogurt
¼ cup (60 ml) mayonnaise or salad dressing
1-1½ tsp (5-8 ml) curry powder
¼ tsp (1 ml) salt
⅛ tsp (.5 ml) pepper
3 cups (720 ml) cooked turkey or chicken, chopped
1 cup (240 ml) seedless grapes, halved
½ cup (120 ml) water chestnuts, chopped
½ cup (120 ml) red or green bell pepper, chopped
lettuce leaves
⅓ cup (80 ml) chopped peanuts

In a large bowl combine yogurt, mayonnaise, curry powder, salt and pepper; mix well. Fold in turkey, grapes, water chestnuts and bell pepper. Cover; chill thoroughly before serving. To serve, line 6 plates with lettuce leaves. Spoon turkey salad over lettuce leaves. Top with chopped peanuts. Serves 6.

Approximate nutritional analysis per serving:
Calories 198, Protein 24 g, Carbohydrates 8 g, Fat 8 g,
Cholesterol 54 mg, Sodium 275 mg

CARIBBEAN RUMORS CHICKEN SALAD

1 medium onion, minced
¼ cup (60 ml) fresh lemon juice
¼ cup (60 ml) fresh lime juice
⅓ cup (80 ml) olive oil
½ tsp (3 ml) McCORMICK or SCHILLING
   Ground Cumin
½ tsp (3 ml) McCORMICK or SCHILLING
   Thyme Leaves
1 tsp (5 ml) McCORMICK or SCHILLING
   Garlic Powder
½ tsp (3 ml) salt
12 oz (360 g) chicken breasts, boneless, skinless,
   cut into 1-inch strips
1½ tsp (8 ml) McCORMICK or SCHILLING
   Rum Extract
¼ lb (115 g) small fresh mushrooms
1½ cups (355 ml) yellow crookneck squash,
   thinly sliced
6 oz (180 g) linguine, cooked

In a non-aluminum saucepan, combine onion, lemon and lime juices, olive oil, seasonings and salt. Bring to a gentle boil and cook 5 minutes. Add chicken strips and extract and cook 10 minutes more, stirring occasionally. Remove from heat. Put mushrooms and squash in a flat glass dish. Add warm chicken and marinade; toss. Cover and marinate in refrigerator 4 hours or overnight. Drain chicken and toss marinade with linguine. Put on lettuce and top with chicken mixture. Serves 4.

Approximate nutritional analysis per serving:
Calories 365, Protein 29 g, Carbohydrates 17 g, Fat 21 g,
Cholesterol 72 mg, Sodium 335 mg

Pasta Salad Piccata with Red Peppers

PASTA SALAD PICCATA WITH RED PEPPERS

6¾ cups (16 oz) (480 g) **RONZONI**
    Medium Shells, uncooked
1 lb (455 g) **boneless, skinless chicken breasts**
½ cup (120 ml) **dry white wine**
½ cup (120 ml) **water**
⅓ cup (80 ml) **olive or vegetable oil**
2 tbs (30 ml) **white wine vinegar**
2 tbs (30 ml) **lemon juice**
2 cloves **garlic, minced**
½ tsp (3 ml) **salt**
¼ tsp (1 ml) **coarsely ground black pepper**
1½ cups (355 ml) **thinly sliced sweet red pepper,**
    cut in 2-inch lengths
½ cup (120 ml) **chopped fresh parsley**
½ cup (120 ml) **sliced green onion**
2 tbs (30 ml) **capers**

Cook pasta according to package directions; drain.
Rinse with cold water to cool quickly; drain well. In small
saucepan, place chicken breasts; cover with wine and water.
Simmer, uncovered about 20 minutes or until cooked through;
discard liquid. Set chicken aside to cool; cut thin strips. In small
bowl, whisk together oil, vinegar, lemon juice, garlic, salt and
pepper. In large bowl combine pasta, chicken and oil mixture.
Add red pepper, parsley, onion and capers; mix thoroughly.
Cover; refrigerate. Serves 8.

Approximate nutritional analysis per serving:
Calories 400, Protein 25 g, Carbohydrates 46 g, Fat 12 g,
Cholesterol 50 mg, Sodium 300 mg

SALAD WITH STRAWBERRIES, SMOKED TURKEY, ENOKI MUSHROOMS AND STRAWBERRY VINAIGRETTE

1 large head bibb or Boston lettuce
8 oz (240 g) thinly sliced smoked turkey or chicken
2 cups (480 ml) stemmed and halved Driscoll's strawberries
1 - 3½ oz pkg (105 g) Enoki mushrooms, stems trimmed
8 whole Driscoll's strawberries
4 sprigs edible flowers or watercress, optional

STRAWBERRY VINAIGRETTE:
½ cup (120 ml) strawberry or balsamic vinegar
2 tbs (30 ml) honey
1 tsp (5 ml) minced chives
½ tsp (3 ml) salt
⅛ tsp (.5 ml) coarsely ground pepper
3 tbs (45 ml) olive oil

Arrange turkey, halved strawberries and mushrooms on lettuce on 4 individual salad plates. Garnish with whole strawberries and flower or watercress, if desired. Serve or drizzle with Strawberry Vinaigrette. Serves 4.

Strawberry Vinaigrette: Combine vinegar, honey, chives, salt and pepper; mix well. Slowly whisk in olive oil into vinegar mixture. Yields ¾ cup.

Approximate nutritional analysis per serving:
Calories 331, Protein 13 g, Carbohydrates 39 g, Fat 17 g, Cholesterol 0 mg, Sodium 271 mg

Courtesy of Driscoll Strawberry Associates, Inc.

MY FAVORITE TURKEY SALAD

2 cans GOYA Black Eye Peas, drained and rinsed
1 cup (240 ml) celery, sliced
1 cup (240 ml) onion, chopped
2 cups (480 ml) cooked turkey, cubed
½ cup (120 ml) dark raisins
1 can crushed pineapple, drained
1 cup (240 ml) GOYA Vegetable Oil
2 tbs (30 ml) GOYA Cider Vinegar
½ tsp (3 ml) granulated sugar
¼ tsp (1 ml) dry mustard
½ tsp (3 ml) salt
¼ tsp (1 ml) pepper

DRESSING:
½ cup (120 ml) mayonnaise
½ cup (120 ml) sour cream
⅛ tsp (.5 ml) prepared mustard
½ tsp (3 ml) lemon juice

Combine beans, celery, onion, turkey, raisins and pineapple in large bowl. Blend together vegetable oil, vinegar, sugar, mustard, salt and pepper. Pour over bean mixture and toss well. Cover and chill. Combine dressing ingredients, mix until smooth. Serve dressing on the side in a separate bowl. Serves 6.

Approximate nutritional analysis per serving salad:
Calories 589, Protein 22 g, Carbohydrates 40 g, Fat 39 g, Cholesterol 35 mg, Sodium 55 mg

Approximate nutritional analysis per serving dressing:
Calories 118, Protein < 1 g, Carbohydrates 6 g, Fat 11 g, Cholesterol 14 mg, Sodium 155 mg

CHINESE CHICKEN SALAD

¼ cup (60 ml) soy sauce
1 tbs (15 ml) sesame oil
1 tbs (15 ml) honey
1 tbs (15 ml) dry sherry
2 tsp (10 ml) GILROY FARMS Stir-Fry Seasoning
1 lb (455 g) chicken breast halves, boneless and skinless
1 head leaf lettuce
1 - 11 oz can (330 g) Mandarin oranges, drained
1 red bell pepper, cut into strips
sliced almonds or chopped cashews, optional

ORIENTAL DRESSING:
3 tbs (45 ml) vegetable oil
2 tbs (30 ml) rice vinegar
1 tbs (15 ml) honey
1 tbs (15 ml) soy sauce
1 tsp (5 ml) GILROY FARMS Stir-Fry Seasoning

Combine first 5 ingredients in large self-closing plastic bag. Add chicken and marinate in refrigerator at least 30 minutes. Grill or broil until no longer pink in center. Place cooked chicken on bed of lettuce and arrange oranges and pepper around chicken. Spoon Oriental Dressing over top and sprinkle with nuts, if desired. Serves 4.

Oriental Dressing: Whisk together all ingredients in small bowl. Serves 4.

Approximate nutritional analysis per serving salad:
Calories 286, Protein 37 g, Carbohydrates 16 g, Fat 8 g, Cholesterol 96 mg, Sodium 331 mg

Approximate nutritional analysis per serving dressing:
Calories 110, Protein < 1 g, Carbohydrates 5 g, Fat 10 g, Cholesterol 0 mg, Sodium 257 mg

CALIFORNIA GRILLED CHICKEN SALAD

2 tbs (30 ml) balsamic vinegar
¼ cup (60 ml) olive oil
1 - 16 oz can (480 g) THANK YOU Tart Red
    Pitted Cherries in water, drained
12 cups (3.0 L) mixed greens
3 chicken boneless breast halves, grilled and
    sliced diagonally into thin strips
¾ cup (180 ml) feta cheese, crumbled
6 tbs (90 ml) red onion, thinly sliced
6 tbs (90 ml) walnuts, chopped and toasted

Combine vinegar, oil and ½ cup reserved juice. Set dressing aside. Arrange 2 cups greens on each plate. Top each salad with chicken, cherries, cheese, onion and walnut. Sprinkle evenly with dressing. Serves 6.

Approximate nutritional analysis per serving:
Calories 310, Protein 23 g, Carbohydrates 13 g, Fat 19 g,
Cholesterol 61 mg, Sodium 215 mg

SALAD GREENS WITH TURKEY AND ORANGES

ORANGE VINAIGRETTE DRESSING:
1 cup (240 ml) rice vinegar or other mild vinegar
1-2 cloves garlic, minced or crushed
2 tbs (30 ml) frozen orange juice
2 tbs (30 ml) olive oil
½ tsp (3 ml) freshly ground black pepper

SALAD:
2 heads red leaf lettuce torn into bite-size pieces
5 oz (60 g) LIGHT & LEAN 97 Turkey Cuts
3 oranges, peeled and sectioned
1 small red onion, thinly sliced into rings

Combine the dressing ingredients and mix well. Combine the lettuce, turkey, oranges and red onion. Toss all ingredients with ½ of the dressing. Serve remaining dressing on the side. Serves 6.

Approximate nutritional analysis per serving salad:
Calories 80, Protein 9 g, Carbohydrates 11 g, Fat < 1 g,
Cholesterol 20 mg, Sodium 17 mg

Approximate nutritional analysis per serving dressing:
Calories 28, Protein < 1 g, Carbohydrates 2 g, Fat 2 g,
Cholesterol 0 mg, Sodium < 1 mg

FIESTA TACO SALAD PLATTER

1 lb (455 g) ground beef, browned and drained
1 - 15 oz can (450 g) kidney beans, drained
1 - 15 oz can (450 ml) tomato sauce
1 - 8 oz jar (240 g) CHI-CHI'S Thick and
    Chunky Taco Sauce
1 - 10½ oz bag (315 g) CHI-CHI'S Tortilla chips,
    crumbled
3 cups (720 ml) shredded lettuce
1 cup (240 ml) shredded cheddar cheese
1 cup (240 ml) chopped tomato
additional taco sauce, if desired

In large saucepan, combine ground beef, kidney beans, tomato sauce and taco sauce. Bring to a boil; reduce heat to low. Simmer, stirring occasionally, 15 minutes. Spread crumbled tortilla chips on large serving platter. Spoon hot meat mixture over chips. Top with lettuce, cheese and tomato. Serve with additional taco sauce, if desired. Serve immediately. Serves 6.

Approximate nutritional analysis per serving:
Calories 570, Protein 26 g, Carbohydrates 50 g, Fat 31 g,
Cholesterol 65 mg, Sodium 1090 mg

WHITE BEAN & SMOKED TURKEY SALAD

½ lb (230 g) smoked turkey breast, julienned
1 cup (240 ml) pitted CALIFORNIA ripe olives,
    wedged
½ cup (120 ml) chopped red onion
2 tbs (30 ml) chopped parsley
¼ cup (60 ml) salad oil
2 tbs (30 ml) white wine vinegar
1 tbs (15 ml) Dijon mustard
2 tsp (10 ml) sugar
1 tsp (5 ml) minced garlic
1 - 14½-15 oz can (435-450 g) white beans, drained
lettuce

Combine turkey, olives, onion and parsley in bowl; toss to mix. Measure oil, vinegar, mustard, sugar and garlic into jar, shake well and pour over salad. Add beans and toss gently to coat. Spoon onto lettuce-lined plates. Serves 4.

Approximate nutritional analysis per serving:
Calories 379, Protein 27 g, Carbohydrates 31 g, Fat 17 g,
Cholesterol 49 mg, Sodium 208 mg

Grilled Turkey and Vegetable Salad

GRILLED TURKEY AND VEGETABLE SALAD

BALSAMIC MARINADE AND DRESSING:
½ cup (120 ml) balsamic vinegar
¼ cup (60 ml) olive oil
1½ tsp (8 ml) chopped garlic
¾ tsp (4 ml) dried basil
½ tsp (3 ml) red pepper flakes
¼ tsp (1 ml) salt

SALAD:
1 lb (455 g) NORBEST Turkey Tenderloins, butterflied
2 Japanese eggplants
2 medium zucchini cut into ½-inch diagonal slices
1 red pepper, seeded
1 yellow pepper, seeded
1 small red onion, cut into 8 equal wedges
vegetable cooking spray

Dressing: In small bowl whisk together vinegar, oil, garlic, basil, pepper flakes and salt.

Salad: In large self-closing plastic bag, place tenderloins with ¼ cup dressing; seal bag. Refrigerate 4 hours, turning bag several times.

Pierce eggplants with fork. Place on paper towel and cook in microwave oven at HIGH (100% power) 1½-2 minutes or until eggplants are soft; allow to cool. Make 4 lengthwise slices in each eggplant, leaving stem end in tact to fan slices out. In large bowl combine eggplant, zucchini, red and yellow pepper and onion with ¼ cup dressing. Cover and refrigerate remaining dressing.

Spray charcoal grill rack with vegetable cooking spray. Preheat grill for direct-heat cooking. Remove tenderloins from plastic bag, discarding remaining marinade, and place on grill rack. Fan eggplants and place with other vegetable around turkey. Grill over hot coals 5 minutes, turn and continue cooking 4-5 minutes or until turkey is no longer pink in center. Watch vegetables closely to prevent burning.

To serve, slice tenderloins and peppers into ½-inch slices. Arrange turkey on 4 plates, surround with grilled vegetables and drizzle with 1 tbs dressing each. Serves 4.

* Tested in 700 watt microwave oven.

Approximate nutritional analysis per serving:
Calories 281, Protein 30 g, Carbohydrates 12 g, Fat 13 g, Cholesterol 70 mg, Sodium 180 mg

CHICKEN CAESAR SALAD

Parmesan Cracker Croutons (below)
1 lb (455 g) boneless chicken breasts
¼ cup (60 ml) EGG BEATERS Real Egg Product
16 PREMIUM Crackers (any variety), crushed
2 tbs (30 ml) margarine
6 cups (1.4 L) torn Romaine lettuce leaves
2 small red or yellow peppers, cut into strips
¾ cup (180 ml) bottled Caesar salad dressing
    or other favorite dressing

PARMESAN CRACKER CROUTONS:
24 PREMIUM Crackers
2 tbs (30 ml) melted margarine
2 tbs (30 ml) grated Parmesan cheese

Prepare Parmesan Cracker Croutons: Brush tops of crackers with melted margarine; sprinkle with Parmesan cheese. Place on baking sheet. Bake at 325°F (165°C) for 5-7 minutes or until lightly golden. Cool. Set aside.

Dip chicken in egg product; coat with cracker crumbs. In large nonstick skillet over medium heat, cook chicken in margarine for 5 minutes on each side or until done. Cut chicken crosswise into slices. To serve, arrange lettuce, pepper strips, sliced chicken and 4 cracker croutons on each of 6 individual plates; serve with dressing. Serves 6.

Approximate nutritional analysis per serving:
Calories 396, Protein 31 g, Carbohydrates 18 g, Fat 26 g,
Cholesterol 45 mg, Sodium 762 mg

"RATTLESNAKE" SALAD PLATE

½ lb (230 g) deli roast turkey or leftover
    cooked turkey or chicken meat
½ lb (230 g) jicama, pared, cut into julienne strips
½ cup (120 ml) whole pitted CALIFORNIA ripe olives
salad greens
½ cup (120 ml) bottled roasted bell pepper, drained,
    cut into strips

SNAKEBITE CUMIN-HOT PEPPER VINAIGRETTE:
⅓ cup (80 ml) salad oil
¼ cup (60 ml) red wine vinegar
2 tbs (30 ml) freshly squeezed lime juice
1 tbs (15 ml) sugar
2½ tsp (13 ml) ground cumin
1-1½ tsp (5-8 ml) bottled red pepper flakes

Shred turkey, toss with jicama and ripe olives; spoon onto greens on two plates. Curve roasted pepper "snakes" over top. Drizzle with Vinaigrette before serving. Serves 2.

Snakebite Cumin-Hot Pepper Vinaigrette: Combine all ingredients in jar. Shake well before pouring. Refrigerate any dressing left for use another time. Serves 2.

Approximate nutritional analysis per serving:
Calories 405, Protein 23 g, Carbohydrates 18 g, Fat 27 g,
Cholesterol 48 mg, Sodium 879 mg

GRILLED TURKEY SALAD WITH RASPBERRY VINAIGRETTE

RASPBERRY VINAIGRETTE:
2 tbs (30 ml) olive oil
2 tbs (30 ml) raspberry vinegar
1 tsp (5 ml) honey
½ tsp (3 ml) minced garlic
¼ tsp (1 ml) salt
¼ tsp (1 ml) pepper

SALAD:
vegetable cooking spray
1 lb (455 g) NORBEST Turkey Tenderloins,
    butterflied
1 tbs (15 ml) plus 2 tsp (10 ml) Chinese five-spice
8 cups (1.9 L) spinach leaves
1 cup (240 ml) fresh raspberries
¼ cup (60 ml) thinly sliced green onion
1 - 8 oz can (240 g) sliced water chestnuts, drained
    and cut into ⅛-inch slices
Enoki mushrooms, optional

Raspberry Vinaigrette: In small bowl whisk together oil, vinegar, honey, garlic, mustard, salt and pepper; cover and refrigerate several hours.

Salad: Spray charcoal grill rack with vegetable cooking spray. Preheat grill for direct heat cooking. Sprinkle both sides of tenderloins with Chinese Five-spice. Place tenderloins on grill rack and grill over hot coals 5 minutes, turn and continue cooking 4-5 minutes or until turkey is no longer pink in center. To serve, on each of 4 plates arrange 2 cups spinach. Slice turkey into thin slices and place over spinach. Top each with ¼ cup raspberries, 1 tbs green onions, 2 tbs water chestnuts, 1 tbs vinaigrette and garnish with mushrooms, if desired. Serves 4.

Approximate nutritional analysis per serving:
Calories 279 , Protein 32 g, Carbohydrates 19 g, Fat 9 g,
Cholesterol 70 mg, Sodium 231 mg

Opposite: Chicken Caesar Salad

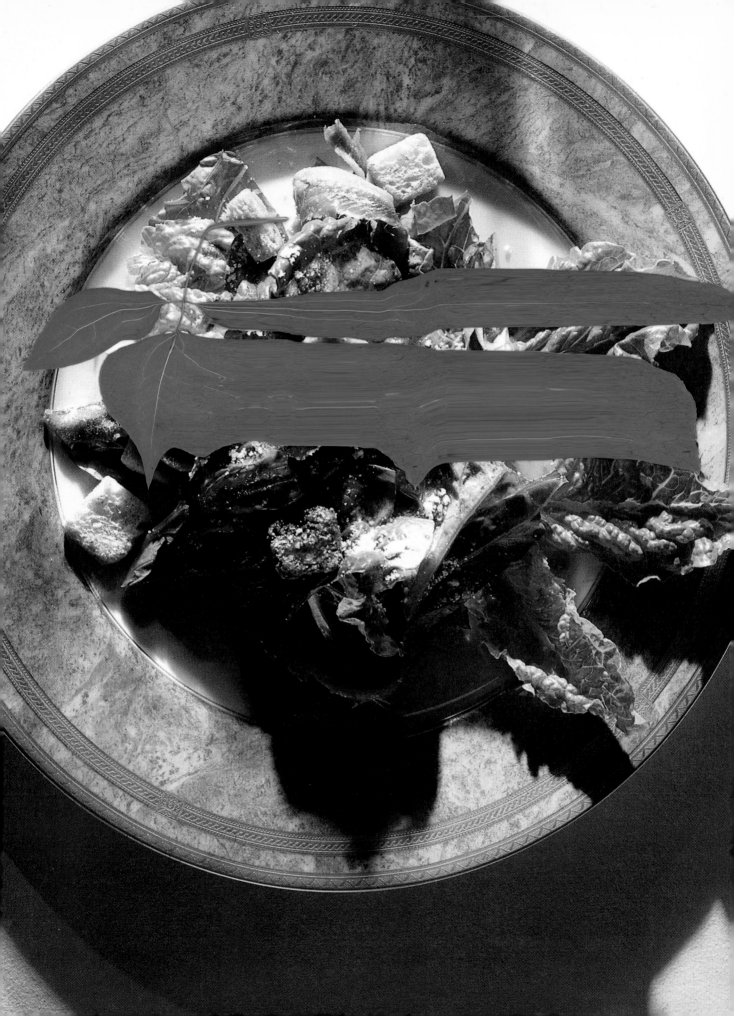

SMUCKER'S WALDORF SALAD WITH TURKEY AND APRICOT

⅓ cup (80 ml) SMUCKER'S Apricot Preserves
½ cup (120 ml) nonfat plain yogurt
1 tbs (15 ml) *each* chopped dried tarragon, chives,
　parsley *or* 1 tsp (5 ml) curry powder
1 tsp (5 ml) Dijon-style prepared mustard
2 tbs (30 ml) lemon juice
½ tsp (3 ml) lemon zest
½ tsp (3 ml) salt
⅛ tsp (.5 ml) fresh ground black pepper
1 lb (455 g) cooked boneless, skinless turkey
　or chicken, cubed
1 red apple with skin on, cut into ½-inch pieces
2 celery stalks, cut into ¼-inch pieces
¼ cup (60 ml) raisins
6 lettuce leaves
1 tbs (15 ml) fresh chopped parsley or chives

Combine SMUCKER'S Apricot Preserves, yogurt, chopped herbs or curry powder, mustard, lemon juice, lemon zest, salt and pepper in a large mixing bowl. Stir with spatula until well blended. Add cubes of turkey or chicken, diced apples, celery and raisins. Stir to coat salad ingredients. Correct seasoning with more salt and pepper as needed. Place lettuce cup on each of 6 serving plates. Spoon mound of the salad on each plate. Garnish each salad with fresh chopped parsley or chives. Serves 6 for lunch.

This also makes an excellent sandwich filling for a pita bread pocket.

Approximate nutritional analysis per serving:
Calories 239, Protein 25 g, Carbohydrates 28 g, Fat 3 g,
Cholesterol 64 mg, Sodium 318 mg

SOUTHWESTERN TURKEY SALAD

SPICY SOUTHWESTERN DRESSING:
¼ cup (60 ml) plus 2 tbs (30 ml) prepared salsa
2 tbs (30 ml) no-fat sour cream
1 tbs (30 ml) chopped fresh cilantro

SALAD:
vegetable cooking spray
1 - 1¼ oz pkg (40 g) reduced-sodium
　taco seasoning mix
1 lb (455 g) NORBEST Turkey Tenderloins,
　butterflied
1 large head romaine lettuce,
　cut in quarters lengthwise

In small bowl, combine salsa, sour cream and cilantro; cover and refrigerate.

Spray charcoal grill rack with vegetable cooking spray. Preheat grill for direct-heat cooking. Sprinkle seasoning mix evenly over each side of tenderloins. Place turkey on grill rack and grill over hot coals 5 minutes and turn. Place lettuce on grill and cook turkey and lettuce 4-5 minutes or until turkey is no longer pink in center and lettuce is slightly wilted. To serve, on each of 4 oblong plates arrange 1 lettuce quarter. Slice tenderloins into thin strips and place over lettuce. Drizzle with dressing. Serves 4.

Approximate nutritional analysis per serving:
Calories 191, Protein 31 g, Carbohydrates 12 g, Fat 1 g,
Cholesterol 70 mg, Sodium 720 mg

CHICKEN SALAD WITH GARLIC-GINGER MAYONNAISE

¾ cup (180 ml) BLUE DIAMOND Blanched
　Slivered Almonds
1 tsp (5 ml) vegetable oil
⅓ cup plus 2 tbs (110 ml) mayonnaise
2½ tsp (13 ml) lime juice
2 large cloves garlic, chopped finely
1¾ tsp (9 ml) grated, fresh ginger
　or ½ tsp (3 ml) powdered ginger
½ tsp (3 ml) salt
3 cups (720 ml) cooked, cubed chicken
6 green onions, sliced
2 stalks celery, sliced
1 small carrot, quartered and sliced thinly
1 medium zucchini, quartered and sliced thinly
2 tbs (30 ml) chopped, fresh parsley

Sauté almonds in oil until golden; reserve. In large bowl, combine mayonnaise, lime juice, garlic, ginger and salt. Add chicken, green onions, celery, carrots and zucchini. Fold in parsley and almonds. Serves 6.

Approximate nutritional analysis per serving:
Calories 322, Protein 25 g, Carbohydrates 12 g, Fat 21 g,
Cholesterol 67 mg, Sodium 398 mg

*Opposite: Smucker's Waldorf Salad
with Turkey and Apricot*

Salade Niçoise

SALADE NIÇOISE

2 large FLORIDA tomatoes
1 can oil-packed tuna, undrained
½ cup (120 ml) bottled Italian salad dressing
2 anchovy fillets
1 tbs (15 ml) capers
½ tsp (3 ml) paprika
Boston or bibb lettuce leaves
4 hard-cooked eggs, cut into halves
2 cups (480 ml) sliced cooked potatoes
1½ cups (355 ml) cooked whole green beans
8 large ripe olives

Use tomatoes held at room temperature until fully ripe. Core and cut tomatoes into wedges (makes about 2⅔ cups); set aside. Remove ½ cup tuna; set aside. To prepare dressing, place in the container of an electric blender salad dressing, anchovies, capers, paprika and remaining tuna and its oil; whirl until smooth and set aside. Line a platter with lettuce leaves. Arrange eggs, potatoes, green beans, olives and reserved tomatoes and tuna on lettuce. Spoon dressing over salad and serve immediately. Serves 4.

Approximate nutritional analysis per serving:
Calories 468, Protein 21 g, Carbohydrates 28 g, Fat 31 g,
Cholesterol 239 mg, Sodium 882 mg

ALMOND CHICKEN SALAD SHANGHAI

1 cup (240 ml) BLUE DIAMOND
    Blanched Slivered Almonds
1 tbs (15 ml) butter
2 whole chicken breasts, skinned, boned, and cubed
¼ cup (60 ml) plus 1 tbs (15 ml) olive oil, divided
1½ tbs (25 ml) soy sauce
1 clove garlic, chopped finely
1 tbs (15 ml) white wine vinegar
½ tsp (3 ml) lemon juice
1½ tsp (8 ml) sugar
¾ tsp (4 ml) grated fresh ginger
    or ¼ tsp (1 ml) powdered ginger
½ tsp (3 ml) salt
¼ tsp (1 ml) white pepper
2 cups (480 ml) sliced celery
6 green onions, thinly sliced
1 large green bell pepper, diced
2 tbs (30 ml) chopped, fresh cilantro
lettuce

Sauté almonds in butter until golden; reserve. Sauté chicken in 1 tbs oil over high heat for 2-3 minutes or until chicken is cooked and moisture is evaporated. Add soy sauce and garlic. Cook 1-2 minutes. Cool. Combine vinegar, lemon juice, sugar, ginger, salt and pepper. Beat in remaining ¼ cup oil. Toss dressing with chicken, celery, onions, green pepper and cilantro. Chill. Just before serving, fold in almonds. divide among individual lettuce-lined plates. Serves 4.

Approximate nutritional analysis per serving:
Calories 316, Protein 14 g, Carbohydrates 10 g, Fat 26 g,
Cholesterol 30 mg, Sodium 516 mg

GRILLED CHICKEN DIJON SALAD

¼ cup (60 ml) Dijon mustard
2 tsp (10 ml) crushed dried tarragon leaves
¼ tsp (1 ml) cracked black pepper
3 tbs (45 ml) tarragon vinegar
1 tbs (15 ml) sugar
⅓ cup (80 ml) water
2 tbs plus 2 tsp (40 ml) olive oil
2 whole chicken breasts, skinned, boned,
    fat removed
½ lb (230 g) fresh mushrooms, cleaned, cut in half
2 cups (480 ml) broccoli flowerettes
5 cups (1.2 L) Boston lettuce, torn
5 cups (1.2 L) red leaf lettuce, torn
1 - 8 oz pkg (240 g) HEALTHY CHOICE Fat Free
    Natural Fancy Shredded Mozzarella Cheese
½ cup (120 ml) red onion rings

Mix together mustard, tarragon and pepper; stir in vinegar and water. Gradually add oil, beating until well blended. Pour ⅓ cup of dressing mixture over chicken. Marinate mushrooms and broccoli in remaining dressing.

Drain chicken reserving marinade. Grill chicken over medium coals, 4 minutes on each side or to desired doneness, brushing with reserved marinade mixture. Cut chicken into 8 strips.

Combine mushrooms, broccoli and marinade with torn greens and cheese in serving bowl; toss lightly. Arrange lettuce mixture on large platter; top with chicken and onion rings. Serves 8.

Approximate nutritional analysis per serving:
Calories 170, Protein 22 g, Carbohydrates 9 g, Fat 6 g,
Cholesterol 30 mg, Sodium 343 mg

GRILLED CHICKEN SALAD

1 cup (240 ml) WISH-BONE Italian Dressing,
    (or Robusto Italian or Lite Italian Dressing)
4 tsp (20 ml) honey
4 tsp (20 ml) prepared mustard
4 boneless, skinless chicken breast halves
    (about 1¼ lbs (570 g))
2 small zucchini, halved lengthwise
2 small red bell peppers, quartered
6 cups (1.4 L) assorted salad greens

Combine Italian dressing, honey and mustard. Reserve ½ cup marinade for salad greens.

In large shallow baking dish or plastic bag, pour remaining marinade over chicken and vegetables. Cover, or close bag, and marinate in refrigerator, turning occasionally, up to 3 hours. Remove chicken and vegetables, reserving marinade. Grill or broil chicken and vegetables, turning and basting frequently with reserved marinade, until chicken is done. Do not brush with marinade last 5 minutes of cooking.

Meanwhile, toss salad greens with reserved ½ cup marinade. Evenly divide salad greens on 4 plates. Slice and arrange 1 chicken breast on top of each salad. Cut vegetables and equally divide onto greens. Serves 4.

Approximate nutritional analysis per serving:
Calories 384, Protein 29 g, Carbohydrates 17 g, Fat 22 g,
Cholesterol 73 mg, Sodium 1328 mg

Courtesy of The Lipton Kitchens.

DRIED BLUEBERRY CHICKEN SALAD

3 cups (720 ml) diced cooked chicken
½ cup (120 ml) Dried Blueberries
⅓ cup (80 ml) slivered, almonds, toasted
½ cup (120 ml) mayonnaise
½ cup (120 ml) dairy sour cream
2 tbs (30 ml) orange marmalade
½ tsp (3 ml) salt
dash pepper
lettuce leaves
orange slices

Combine chicken, Dried Blueberries and almonds. Combine mayonnaise, sour cream, orange marmalade, salt and pepper; add to chicken mixture and toss well. Cover and chill. Serve on lettuce leaves and garnish with orange slices, if desired.
 Serves 4.

Approximate nutritional analysis per serving:
Calories 496, Protein 34 g, Carbohydrates 25 g, Fat 30 g,
Cholesterol 113 mg, Sodium 586 mg

SAUTÉED CHICKEN-SPINACH SALAD WITH RASPBERRY SAUCE

8 cups (1.9 L) torn, fresh spinach
4 boneless, skinless chicken breast halves, sauteed
    (1¼ lbs (570 g))
1 tbs (15 ml) mirin (sweet rice cooking wine)
1 tbs (15 ml) reduced sodium soy sauce
1 - 8 oz can (240 g) sliced water chestnuts, drained

RASPBERRY SAUCE:
½ cup (120 ml) frozen unsweetened raspberries,
    thawed or fresh
8 oz (240 g) silken/soft tofu
3 tbs (45 ml) white wine vinegar
3 tbs (45 ml) sugar

Blend all sauce ingredients in blender or food processor until well blended. Sauté chicken in the mirin and reduced sodium soy sauce until cooked through. Remove from heat and slice. Arrange spinach on individual serving plates. Top with chicken; evenly distribute water chestnuts over each serving. Serve with tofu raspberry sauce. Serves 4.

Approximate nutritional analysis per serving:
Calories 486, Protein 61 g, Carbohydrates 47 g, Fat 9 g,
Cholesterol 47 mg, Sodium 626 mg

CRUNCHY CURRIED SALAD WITH SHRIMP

½ cup (120 ml) bottled Russian salad dressing
2 tbs (30 ml) plain yogurt
1 tsp (5 ml) curry powder
1 lb (455 g) small to medium shrimp, cleaned,
    cooked and shelled
¾ cup (180 ml) raisins
½ cup (120 ml) sliced celery
½ cup (120 ml) green pepper, chopped
lettuce, torn into bite-size pieces

In a large bowl blend dressing, yogurt and curry powder. Add shrimp, raisins, celery and green pepper; toss to coat well. Chill. Serve on lettuce-lined plates, or stuffed into avocado halves or cored tomatoes that have been cut and fanned. Serves 4.

Approximate nutritional analysis per serving:
Calories 363, Protein 25 g, Carbohydrates 27 g, Fat 18 g,
Cholesterol 179 mg, Sodium 453 mg

PASTA SALAD WITH SHRIMP

½ lb ((240 ml) twist pasta
1 red bell pepper, finely julienned
1 cup (240 ml) sliced CALIFORNIA ripe olives
½ cup (120 ml) green onion, chopped
1 lb (455 g) tiny cooked shrimp

CREAMY MUSTARD VINAIGRETTE:
¼ cup (60 ml) white wine vinegar
1 tbs (15 ml) Dijon mustard
1½ tsp (8 ml) dried tarragon
4 tsp (20 ml) sugar
½ tsp (3 ml) pepper
1 cup (240 ml) salad or olive oil

Boil pasta as directed, drain. Mix pasta, bell pepper, olives, onion and shrimp. Mix in ½ cup Mustard Vinaigrette to coat everything well. Chill. Turn salad onto salad greens and serve with extra dressing. Serves 4.
    Creamy Mustard Vinaigrette: Combine white wine vinegar with Dijon mustard, dried tarragon, sugar and pepper in electric blender. Whir to blend then gradually blend in oil. Salt to taste. Chill. Yields 1⅓ cups.

Approximate nutritional analysis per serving salad:
Calories 221, Protein 25 g, Carbohydrates 16 g, Fat 6 g,
Cholesterol 172 mg, Sodium 479 mg

Approximate nutritional analysis per ¼ cup serving dressing:
Calories 276, Protein < 1 g, Carbohydrates < 1 g, Fat 31 g,
Cholesterol 0 mg, Sodium 28 mg

CONFETTI SHRIMP SALAD

2½ lbs (1.1 kg) medium shrimp, cooked and cleaned
½ cup (120 ml) red peppers, diced
½ cup (120 ml) green peppers, diced
½ cup (120 ml) yellow peppers, diced
½ cup (120 ml) celery, diced
½ cup (120 ml) red onions, diced
½ cup (120 ml) GOYA Capers, drained
1 - 16 oz. can (480 g) GOYA Black Beans,
    drained and rinsed
½ cup (120 ml) GOYA Olive Oil
3 tbs (45 ml) Dijon-style mustard
salt and pepper to taste

In large bowl, combine shrimp, diced vegetables, capers and beans. Toss well. Combine oil and mustard in small cup and stir well. Pour over shrimp and let flavors meld for 1 hour before serving. Serves 8.

Approximate nutritional analysis per serving minus capers:
Calories 336, Protein 33 g, Carbohydrates 13 g, Fat 17 g,
Cholesterol 215 mg, Sodium 291 mg

SHRIMP SALAD WITH GRAPES

2 tbs (30 ml) salt
3 bay leaves
2 lbs (910 g) small or medium shrimp,
    shelled, uncooked
¾ cup (180 ml) celery, finely chopped
8 scallions, chopped
1½ tsp (8 ml) celery seed
1 tbs (15 ml) OLD BAY Seasoning, or more to taste
salt and freshly ground pepper, to taste
2 cups (480 ml) mayonnaise
1 cup (240 ml) seedless green grapes
1 tbs (15 ml) capers, optional

Bring 4 quarts of water to a boil. Add salt and bay leaves. Add shrimp, cook for 1 minute, then pour into a colander. Cool. Chop shrimp to desired size, place into a large bowl and rub and toss with celery seed, OLD BAY Seasoning, salt and pepper. Add mayonnaise, grapes and capers (if using). Cool salad in refrigerator for several hours. Adjust seasonings before serving. Serves 8.

Approximate nutritional analysis per serving:
Calories 365, Protein 24 g, Carbohydrates 19 g , Fat 22 g,
Cholesterol 188 mg, Sodium 596 mg

PEAR AND RICE VINAIGRETTE SALAD

⅔ cup (160 ml) rice
1 - 6 oz jar (180 g) marinated artichoke hearts, halved
12 oz (360 g) small cooked shrimp
Lime Vinaigrette Dressing (below)
2 USA Pears, cored and diced
¼ cup (60 ml) Monterey Jack cheese, cubed
3 tbs (45 ml) green onions, sliced
2 tsp (10 ml) lime juice
radish roses and slices for garnish
USA Pear wedges for garnish

LIME VINAIGRETTE DRESSING:
vegetable oil
1 tbs (15 ml) lime juice
1 tbs (15 ml) vinegar
1 dash crushed dill weed

Cook rice according to package directions until just tender. Drain artichoke hearts; reserve liquid for Lime Vinaigrette Dressing. Reserve 8 to 10 attractive whole shrimp for garnish. Combine hot rice, shrimp and ¼ cup Lime Vinaigrette Dressing; let stand until cool. Combine pears, artichokes, cheese, green onions and lime juice with rice mixture; toss gently. Place rice mixture in deep 1½-qt mold or bowl such as small mixer bowl, or in 6 small custard cups. Refrigerate several hours or until thoroughly chilled. Unmold onto serving platter. Garnish top with reserved shrimp and radish slices. Garnish platter with pear wedges and radish roses. Serves 6.

Lime Vinaigrette Dressing: Add vegetable oil to reserved artichoke liquid to equal 3 tbs. Stir in lime juice, vinegar and dill weed.

Approximate nutritional analysis per serving:
Calories 234, Protein 14 g, Carbohydrates 19 g, Fat 11 g,
Cholesterol 90 mg, Sodium 260 mg

Opposite: Fresh Salad Vegetables

PEAR AND SALMON SALAD

4 fresh ripe USA Pears of any variety salad greens
1 - 7¾ oz can (235 g) salmon
¼ cup (60 ml) green pepper, chopped
¼ cup (60 ml) green onions, sliced
⅓ cup (80 ml) water chestnuts, sliced
¼ cup (60 ml) toasted slivered almonds

LEMON FRENCH DRESSING:
6 tbs (90 ml) oil
3 tbs (45 ml) lemon juice
½ tsp (3 ml) dry mustard
¼ tsp (1 ml) salt
1 tsp (5 ml) sugar
⅛ tsp (.5 ml) pepper

Halve and core pears. A measuring teaspoon or melon ball cutter is handy for coring pears neatly. Arrange 2 pear halves on each of 4 salad plates lined with greens. Drain salmon and break into chunks. Toss with green pepper, green onions, water chestnuts and toasted almonds. Spoon between pear halves. Serve with Lemon French Dressing. Serves 4.

Lemon French Dressing: Combine all ingredients in a small jar and shake well. Serves 4.

Approximate nutritional analysis per serving salad:
Calories 248, Protein 14 g, Carbohydrates 31 g, Fat 9 g,
Cholesterol 24 mg, Sodium 300 mg

Approximate nutritional analysis per serving dressing:
Calories 188, Protein < 1 g, Carbohydrates 2 g, Fat 20 g,
Cholesterol 0 mg, Sodium 267 mg

WATERCRESS SALAD WITH SCALLOPS AND PEARS

1 cup (240 ml) CHI-CHI'S Salsa Verde
½ cup (120 ml) dry white wine
1 tsp (5 ml) fresh garlic, minced
1 lb (455 g) bay scallops
2 bunches watercress, washed,
**   dried and stems removed**
2 Bosc pears, sliced ¼ inch thick
⅓ cup (80 ml) Gorgonzola cheese, crumbled
⅓ cup (80 ml) toasted pecans, chopped

In medium saucepan, combine salsa verde, wine and garlic. Bring to a boil. Cook 5 minutes, stirring occasionally. Add scallops. Cook 4 to 5 minutes or until scallops start to turn opaque. Drain, cool. Place watercress on large serving platter. Arrange pears around edge; place scallops in center. Sprinkle with Gorgonzola cheese and pecans. Serves 6.

Approximate nutritional analysis per serving:
Calories 180, Protein 15 g, Carbohydrates 13 g, Fat 7 g,
Cholesterol 30 mg, Sodium 280 mg.

CREAMY CATFISH SALAD

2 cups (480 ml) water
2 tbs (30 ml) lemon juice
1 lb (455 g) Mississippi farm-raised catfish fillets
3 hard-cooked eggs, chopped
½ cup (120 ml) celery, chopped
⅓ cup (80 ml) ripe olives, chopped
¼ cup (60 ml) dill pickle, chopped
2 tbs (30 ml) pimiento, chopped
⅓ cup (80 ml) mayonnaise
2 tbs (30 ml) horseradish
1 tsp (5 ml) lemon juice
½ tsp (3 ml) salt
¼ tsp (1 ml) pepper

In a skillet bring water and 2 tbs lemon juice to boiling. Add catfish. Return to boiling, reduce heat. Cover and simmer gently for 5 to 7 minutes or until fish flakes easily. Remove from water. Cool slightly. Finely chop cooked fish.

In a bowl combine cooked catfish, eggs, celery, ripe olives, dill pickle and pimiento. Stir together mayonnaise, horseradish, 1 tsp lemon juice, salt and pepper. Add catfish mixture, stirring until well combined. Chill. Serves 6.

Approximate nutritional analysis per serving:
Calories 195, Protein 17 g, Carbohydrates 6, Fat 11 g,
Cholesterol 153 mg, Sodium 730 mg.

SHRIMP AND POTATO SALAD

1½ lbs (685 g) red new potatoes,
**   cooked and cut into eighths**
1 cup (240 ml) fresh green beans,
**   cooked and cut into 3-inch pieces**
1 cup (240 ml) fresh mushrooms, sliced
⅓ cup (80 ml) celery, sliced
¼ cup (60 ml) green onions, sliced
¾ lb (340 g) fresh or frozen cooked shrimp,
**   shelled and deveined (30-40)**
1 - 16 oz jar (480 g) CHI-CHI'S Salsa, drained
⅓ cup (80 ml) vegetable oil
¼ cup (60 ml) lemon juice
1 tbs (15 ml) Dijon mustard
½ tsp (3 ml) coarsely ground pepper

In a shallow baking dish, combine potatoes, green beans, mushrooms, celery, onions and shrimp. In 1-pint jar with tight fitting lid, combine remaining ingredients. Shake well. Toss with shrimp mixture. Cover, refrigerate 3 to 4 hours, stirring occasionally. Serves 8.

Approximate nutritional analysis per serving:
Calories 220, Protein 12 g, Carbohydrate 21 g, Fat 10 g,
Cholesterol 85 mg, Sodium 400 mg

GREEK SALAD WITH CATFISH

2 cups (480 ml) water
2 tbs (30 ml) lemon juice
8 oz (240 g) Mississippi farm-
    raised catfish fillets
1 lb (455 g) fresh spinach, torn
1 cup (240 ml) Calamata ripe
    olives, pitted and halved
¼ cup (60 ml) green onion, sliced
2 medium tomatoes, chopped
8 oz (240 g) feta cheese, cubed
½ cup (120 ml) olive oil
¼ cup (60 ml) lemon juice
¼ cup (60 ml) white wine vinegar
2 cloves garlic, minced
1 tbs (15 ml) chopped fresh oregano
    or ½ tsp (3 ml) dried oregano

In a skillet bring water and 2 tbs lemon juice to
boil. Add catfish. Return to boil; reduce heat.
Cover and simmer gently for 5 to 7 minutes,
until fish flakes easily. Remove from water.
Cool slightly. Cut into bite-size pieces. Chill.

In a large bowl combine spinach, olives,
green onion and tomatoes. Add feta cheese and
catfish. In a screw top jar combine olive oil,
lemon juice, vinegar, garlic and oregano. Cover
and shake until well combined. Pour dressing over spinach
mixture, tossing to coat. Serves 6.

Approximate nutritional information per serving:
Calories 299, Protein 16 g, Carbohydrates 13 g, Fat 22 g,
Cholesterol 56 mg, Sodium 760 mg

Courtesy of the Catfish Institute.

SALADE PROVENÇALE

1¼ cups (295 ml) dried tomato halves,
    cut into strips with kitchen shears
1 - 15 oz can (450 g) red kidney beans,
    rinsed and drained
    or 1½ cups (355 ml) cooked red kidney beans
1 - 15 oz can (450 g) great northern beans,
    rinsed and drained
    or 1½ cups (355 ml) cooked beans
1 - 2¼ oz can (70 g) sliced ripe olives, drained
½ cup (120 ml) green onions, sliced
2 - 6⅛ oz cans (370 g) white tuna in water, drained
3 tbs (45 ml) chopped fresh basil leaves
    or 1 tbs (15 ml) dried basil
Dijon Dressing (below)
Salt to taste
3 cups (720 ml) spinach leaves
Basil sprigs (optional)

Salade Provençale

DIJON DRESSING:
¼ cup (60 ml) balsamic vinegar
    or ¼ cup (60 ml) red wine vinegar
    plus 1½ tsp (8 ml) sugar
3 tbs (45 ml) olive oil
2 tsp (10 ml) Dijon-style mustard
½ tsp (3 ml) pepper
1 large garlic clove, pressed

In bowl, cover tomatoes with boiling water, let stand 10 to 15
minutes. Meanwhile, in large bowl, lightly toss beans with
remaining ingredients **except** salt, spinach and tomatoes.
Thoroughly drain tomatoes and add to salad; toss. Season with
salt. Line platter with spinach. Spoon salad onto spinach.
Garnish with basil, if desired. Serves 4.

Dijon Dressing: In bowl, whisk balsamic vinegar, olive oil,
mustard, pepper and garlic.

Approximate nutritional analysis per serving:
Calories 470, Protein 38 g, Carbohydrates 49 g, Fat 15 g,
Cholesterol 35 mg, Sodium 1250 mg

Courtesy of the American Dry Bean Board.

NEPTUNE SALAD

½ lb (230 g) bay scallops
½ lb (230 g) little bay shrimp
1 lb (455 g) sea legs (imitation crab meat)
¾-1 cup (180-240 ml) mayonnaise
juice of 1 lemon
2-3 scallions, chopped
1 tbs (15 ml) OLD BAY Seasoning
1 tsp (5 ml) dill
salt to taste

Cook scallops and shrimp until tender (don't overcook). Drain all seafood and pat dry with paper towels. In a large bowl, mix seafood with mayonnaise and lemon juice. Mix in chopped scallions. Add OLD BAY Seasoning, dill and salt to taste. Chill 45-60 minutes before serving. Serves 8.

Approximate nutritional analysis per serving:
Calories 228, Protein 23 g, Carbohydrates 9 g, Fat 11 g,
Cholesterol 110 mg, Sodium 552 mg

WEST INDIES SEAFOOD SALAD

SALAD:
8 oz (240 g) large shrimp, cooked and peeled
8 oz (240 g) grouper or white fish filet,
    cubed and sautéed
½ medium purple onion, very thinly sliced
2 tsp (10 ml) capers, optional
2 tbs (30 ml) pineapple juice
1 tbs (15 ml) fresh lime juice
1 tbs (15 ml) olive oil
1 tsp (5 ml) McCORMICK or SCHILLING
    Chili Powder
½ ripe papaya, peeled and sliced
fresh pineapple slices, optional

TROPICAL DRESSING:
½ cup (120 ml) mayonnaise
¼ cup (60 ml) sour cream
¼ cup (60 ml) pineapple juice
2 tbs (30 ml) fresh lime juice
1 medium banana
1 tsp (5 ml) McCORMICK or SCHILLING
    Banana Extract

Salad: Combine all ingredients except fruit and toss. Marinate in refrigerator at least 2 hours. Serve mounded around fruit slices. Top with dressing. Serves 4.

    Tropical Dressing: Process in a blender or mash banana and whip with other ingredients until creamy. Serves 8.

Approximate nutritional analysis per serving salad:
Calories 180, Protein 24 g, Carbohydrates 7 g, Fat 6 g,
Cholesterol 104 mg, Sodium 116 mg

Approximate nutritional analysis per serving dressing:
Calories 95, Protein < 1 g, Carbohydrates 10 g, Fat 7 g,
Cholesterol 7 mg, Sodium 108 mg

CRAB AND SHRIMP SALAD

1 lb (455 g) small or medium shrimp,
    cooked (reserve a few for garnish)
1 lb (455 g) crab meat, cooked
½ cup (120 ml) chopped celery
1 tbs (15 ml) OLD BAY Seasoning
1 tbs (15 ml) pimiento
salt and pepper to taste
1 medium onion, chopped
1 tsp (5 ml) paprika
½ cup (120 ml) mayonnaise or salad dressing
lettuce and capers to garnish

In a large bowl, mix all ingredients together and garnish with shrimp. Put salad on a bed of lettuce. Chill in refrigerator until ready to serve. Serves 8.

Approximate nutritional analysis per serving:
Calories 188, Protein 24 g, Carbohydrates 7 g, Fat 7 g,
Cholesterol 14 mg, Sodium 354 mg

SPICY SHRIMP SALAD

1 lb (455 g) medium shrimp, cooked,
    peeled and deveined
2 tsp (10 ml) OLD BAY Seasoning
2 tsp (10 ml) lemon juice
½ cup (120 ml) mayonnaise
⅓ cup (80 ml) celery
¼ cup (60 ml) green onion, chopped
¼ tsp (1 ml) Worcestershire sauce
⅛ tsp (.5 ml) cayenne pepper, optional
1-2 dashes hot sauce

Chop shrimp into ½-inch pieces. Add OLD BAY Seasoning and mix to coat. Set aside. In a large bowl, add lemon juice and mayonnaise and mix well. Add celery, green onion, Worcestershire sauce, cayenne (if using), and pepper sauce to mixture and blend well. Fold in shrimp. Place in refrigerator for at least 30 minutes to allow the flavors to blend. Serve over lettuce or on sandwich rolls. Serves 6.

Approximate nutritional analysis per serving:
Calories 159, Protein 16 g, Carbohydrates 6 g, Fat 8 g,
Cholesterol 120 mg, Sodium 257 mg

Opposite: Crab and Shrimp Salad

OLD BAY SEAFOOD PASTA SALAD

2 cups (480 ml) dry macaroni twists
1 lb (455 g) imitation crab meat chunks,
    sliced lengthwise
2 stalks celery, chopped
½ cup (120 ml) chopped red onion
¾ tsp (4 ml) OLD BAY Seasoning
4 tbs (60 ml) Salad Supreme Seasoning
2 tbs (30 ml) dry parsley flakes
2 tbs (30 ml) red wine vinegar
1 tsp (5 ml) sugar
1 cup (240 ml) light mayonnaise
    (or just enough to bind salad)

Cook macaroni twists in salted boiling water until just tender.
Drain and rinse well in cold water. In a large bowl, add
macaroni and all other ingredients and mix well. Chill several
hours before serving. Serves 6.

Approximate nutritional analysis per serving:
Calories 272, Protein 21 g, Carbohydrates 31 g, Fat 7 g,
Cholesterol 87 mg, Sodium 416 mg

SPRING SHRIMP AND ASPARAGUS SALAD

¾ cup (180 ml) tomato juice
⅓ cup (80 ml) HEINZ 57 Sauce
1 tbs (15 ml) lemon juice
1 tbs (15 ml) vegetable oil
1 tsp (5 ml) Dijon-style mustard
1 tsp (5 ml) granulated sugar
¼ tsp (1 ml) dried thyme leaves, crushed
¼ tsp (1 ml) salt
¼ tsp (1 ml) pepper
1 lb (455 g) fresh asparagus spears
assorted salad greens
1 lb (455 g) medium-size raw shrimp,
    cooked, shelled, deveined
1 cup (240 ml) fresh Enoki or button mushrooms
2 tomatoes, cut into wedges
2 tsp (10 ml) grated lemon peel

In jar with tight-fitting lid, combine first 9 ingredients; shake
well and set aside. Cook asparagus in small amount of boiling
water 3 to 5 minutes or until tender-crisp. Drain, cool slightly.
On individual serving plates lined with salad greens, arrange
asparagus spears, shrimp, mushrooms and tomatoes. Drizzle
salad with dressing. Sprinkle with grated lemon peel. Serves 6.

Approximate nutritional analysis per serving:
Calories 116, Protein 11 g, Carbohydrates 12 g, Fat 4 g,
Cholesterol 58 mg, Sodium 274 mg

CARIBBEAN SHRIMP SALAD

1 large head leaf lettuce or any other
    curly-edged lettuce
1½ cups (355 ml) medium shrimp,
    cooked, cleaned and deveined
1 - 16 oz can (480 g) bean of your choice:
    Black-Eyed Beans, Great Northern Beans
    or Navy Beans, drained
2 cups (480 ml) cooked rice
½ cup (120 ml) diced green bell pepper
½ cup (120 ml) diced red onion
⅓ cup (80 ml) peanut oil
½ cup (120 ml) fresh lime juice
¼ cup (60 ml) chopped fresh parsley or cilantro
1 tsp (5 ml) hot pepper sauce
salt and pepper to taste
2 ripe avocados, peeled, pitted and sliced
2 ripe papayas, peeled, seeded and sliced
1 cup (240 ml) chopped, roasted, unsalted peanuts

Pull lettuce apart. Wash and dry leaves well. Generously line a
serving platter with leaves. Refrigerate.

Combine shrimp, beans, rice, bell pepper, red onion, oil,
¼ cup fresh lime juice, parsley or cilantro, hot pepper sauce,
and salt and pepper. Stir until well combined. Cover and
refrigerate for about 1 hour.

Remove lettuce lined platter and shrimp salad from
refrigerator. Using a slotted spoon, carefully place shrimp salad
in the center of lettuce. Place alternate slices of avocado and
papaya around the edge of the shrimp salad. Sprinkle on any
remaining dressing and the remaining lime juice. Garnish with
chopped peanuts and serve immediately. Serves 6.

Approximate nutritional analysis per serving.
Calories 638, Protein 28 g, Carbohydrates 58 g, Fat 36 g,
Cholesterol 86 mg, Sodium 497 mg

SPICY MACARONI SHRIMP SALAD

8 oz (240 g) macaroni, cooked and drained
1 - 8 oz can (240 g) shrimp, drained
1 medium tomato, diced
1 small onion, diced, optional
2 hard-cooked eggs, diced
1 tbs (15 ml) OLD BAY Seasoning
¼ tsp (1 ml) garlic salt
¾ cup (180 ml) mayonnaise
salt and pepper to taste

In a large bowl, toss all ingredients together. Cover and chill
before serving. Serves 3.

Approximate nutritional analysis per serving:
Calories 682, Protein 33 g, Carbohydrates 79 g, Fat 26 g,
Cholesterol 287 mg, Sodium 688 mg

Oriental Papaya Salad

ORIENTAL PAPAYA SALAD

1 medium-size green papaya, julienned
1 lb (455 g) cold, cooked shrimp or cooked,
   julienned calamari
1 tbs (15 ml) lemon juice
1 tbs (15 ml) fish sauce
1 tbs (15 ml) white vinegar
pinch of ground black pepper
1½ tbs (25 ml) sugar
2 tbs (30 ml) finely chopped garlic
2 oz (60 g) onion, julienned
1 oz (30 g) peanut or vegetable oil
6 fresh basil leaves, julienned
½ small cucumber
⅓ cup (80 ml) chopped macadamia nuts or peanuts
2 oz (60 g) cooked Thai shrimp chips
   (available in Asian markets)

Peel, halve and seed papaya. Cut the flesh into thin strips. Place in a large bowl. Mix papaya, cooked shrimp and chopped nuts together and chill. Mix peanut oil, lemon juice, vinegar, fish sauce, garlic and onion. Salt to taste. Pour dressing over the salad just before serving. Serves 6.

Approximate nutritional analysis per serving minus shrimp chips:
Calories 203, Protein 18 g, Carbohydrates 11 g, Fat 10 g,
Cholesterol 115 mg, Sodium 320 mg

Courtesy of the Papaya Administrative Committee and Pineapple Growers Association of Hawaii.

THAI SALAD WITH USA PEARS

2 USA Pears, sliced, unpeeled
lemon juice
12 medium sized cooked shrimp,
    shelled and deveined
1 medium cucumber, seeded and julienned
1 medium carrot, peeled and julienned
1 tbs (15 ml) chopped parsley or cilantro
2 cups (480 ml) various greens, torn to bite-size
    pieces (Romaine, butter lettuce, endive, etc.)
¾ cup (180 ml) Hot Peanut Dressing

HOT PEANUT DRESSING:
¼ cup (60 ml) peanut butter
2 tbs (30 ml) soy sauce
1 tbs (15 ml) sesame oil
1 tbs (15 ml) vinegar
1 tbs (15 ml) honey
1 clove minced garlic
¾ tsp (4 ml) bottled hot pepper sauce
¼ tsp (1 ml) cayenne pepper, optional

Dip pear slices in diluted lemon juice to prevent browning. Toss together shrimp, cucumber, carrot and cilantro or parsley. On individual salad plates, mound shrimp mixture on bed of greens. Arrange pear slices at edge of plates. Serve with Hot Peanut Dressing. Serves 4.

Hot Peanut Dressing: Combine ingredients and mix well. Cayenne may be omitted, to taste. Yields ¾ cup, serves 4.

Approximate nutritional analysis per serving salad:
Calories 94, Protein 6 g, Carbohydrates 18 g, Fat < 1 g,
Cholesterol 33 mg, Sodium 42 mg

Approximate nutritional analysis per serving dressing:
Calories 147, Protein 4 g, Carbohydrates 9 g, Fat 11 g,
Cholesterol 0 mg, Sodium 591 mg

Courtesy the Oregon Washington California Pear Bureau.

MUSHROOM AND SNOW PEA SALAD

¼ lb (115 g) fresh snow peas, strings removed
1 cup (240 ml) DANNON Plain Nonfat or
    Lowfat Yogurt
1 tbs (15 ml) red wine vinegar
1 tsp (5 ml) minced garlic
½ tsp (3 ml) salt
¼ tsp (1 ml) pepper
¼ tsp (1 ml) dried oregano leaves, crushed
1 lb (455 g) raw mushrooms, peeled and sliced
6 cherry tomatoes, halved
½ cup (120 ml) red bell pepper strips
¼ cup (60 ml) sliced green onions
large lettuce leaves

In a large saucepan bring water to a boil. Add snow peas and boil 1-2 minutes or until tender-crisp. Remove from saucepan with slotted spoon; place in ice water to cool quickly. Drain. In a large bowl combine yogurt, vinegar, garlic, salt, pepper and oregano; stir well. Add mushrooms, snow peas, cherry tomatoes, bell pepper and green onions. Toss gently. To serve, line large platter with lettuce leaves; spoon salad over lettuce. Serves 4.

Approximate nutritional analysis per serving:
Calories 376, Protein 34 g, Carbohydrates 50 g, Fat 4 g,
Cholesterol 176 mg, Sodium 483 mg

SEAFOOD SALAD SANDWICH

1 - 14¾ oz can (440 g) BUMBLE BEE
    Pink or Red Salmon
1 - 12¼ oz can (370 g) BUMBLE BEE
    White or Light Tuna
7½ oz (225 g) shrimp
8 slices sour dough bread
8 leaves curly green leaf lettuce
8 slices tomato
8 slices avocado
8 slices melon

SEAFOOD SALAD DRESSING:
2 tbs (30 ml) light cream cheese
2 tbs (30 ml) plain yogurt or light mayonnaise
1 tbs (15 ml) minced celery
1 tbs (15 ml) green onion
1 tsp (5 ml) lemon juice
1 tbs (15 ml) fresh dill weed
1 tbs (15 ml) fresh minced parsley, optional

GARNISH:
½ basket fresh berries of your choice
lemon wedges or wheels
Romaine
sprigs of dill.

Seafood Salad Dressing: Cream first 2 ingredients completely. Fold in remaining ingredients.

Top open faced sandwiches with a lettuce leaf. Divide seafood salad topped with dressing evenly among four slices. Top each of the remaining four slices with 2 tomato slices and then with 2 avocado slices. Arrange 2 melon slices, berries and lemon wheels on plate. Garnish seafood salad sandwich tops with sprig of dill. Serves 4.

Approximate nutritional analysis per serving salad with dressing:
Calories 827, Protein 84 g, Carbohydrates 57 g, Fat 29 g,
Cholesterol 191 mg, Sodium 1850 mg

Opposite: Mushroom and Snow Pea Salad

Italian Bean and Tuna Salad

ITALIAN BEAN AND TUNA SALAD

1 - 17 oz can (510 g) baby lima beans, rinsed, drained
1 - 16 oz can (480 g) dark red kidney beans,
    rinsed, drained
1 - 15 oz can (450 g) great northern beans,
    rinsed, drained
8 cherry tomatoes, cut in fourths
½ small cucumber, cut lengthwise into halves,
    seeded, sliced
⅓ cup (80 ml) chopped green or red pepper
¼ cup (60 ml) thinly sliced red onion
Basil Vinaigrette (below)
2 - 8 oz (480 g) tuna steaks, broiled or grilled
    or 1 - 12¼ oz can (370 g) white tuna in water,
    drained, flaked into 1-inch pieces
lettuce leaves
basil or parsley sprigs

BASIL VINAIGRETTE:

3 tbs (45 ml) olive oil
¼ cup (60 ml) tarragon wine vinegar
3-4 tbs (45-60 ml) finely chopped fresh basil leaves
    or 1-1½ tsp (5-8 ml) dried basil leaves
3 tbs (45 ml) fat free plain yogurt
1-1½ tbs (15-25 ml) lemon juice
¾ tsp (4 ml) sugar
1½ tbs (25 ml) water
1-2 cloves garlic

Combine beans, tomatoes, cucumber, pepper and onion in large bowl; add Basil Vinaigrette and toss. Refrigerate mixture at least 4 hours for flavors to blend, stirring mixture occasionally. Add tuna to mixture 1-2 hours before serving time. Spoon salad onto lettuce-lined plate; garnish with basil. Serves 6.

    Basil Vinaigrette: Mix all ingredients; refrigerate until serving time. Mix before using.

    Note: Bean salad can be made and refrigerated 1 day in advance; add tuna as directed above.

Approximate nutritional analysis per serving:
Calories 460, Protein 34 g, Carbohydrates 48 g, Fat 12 g,
Cholesterol 28 mg, Sodium 457 mg

SALADS

BARLEY SEAFOOD SALAD WITH CREAMY DILLED DRESSING

2 cups (480 ml) barley cooked in 4 cups
   (960 ml) chicken broth
1 cup (240 ml) red and green pepper, julienned
1 cup (240 ml) crookneck squash and zucchini,
   quartered and sliced
1 cup (240 ml) broccoli, steamed or
   microwaved for 4 minutes
1 cup (240 ml) cauliflower, steamed or
   microwaved for 4 minutes
1 - 14¾ oz can (445 g) BUMBLE BEE
   Red or Pink Salmon
1 - 12¼ oz can (370 g) BUMBLE BEE
   White or Light Tuna in Water

DRESSING:
½ cup (120 ml) plain yogurt
½ cup (120 ml) kefir or sour half and half
¼ cup (60 ml) lemon juice
2 tbs (30 ml) minced celery
2 tbs (30 ml) green onion
2 tbs (30 ml) minced fresh dill
2 tbs (30 ml) parsley

Bring rinsed barley to boiling point in chicken broth. Reduce heat and simmer. Cover and cook for 20 minutes. Combine dressing ingredients and set aside in refrigerator. Prepare all vegetables and toss in large bowl with seafood. Combine with barley and fold in dressing. Serve main dish salad garnished with lemon wedges and parsley sprigs. Serves 4.
Dressing serves 6.

Approximate nutritional analysis per serving salad:
Calories 392, Protein 53 g, Carbohydrates 27 g, Fat 8 g, Cholesterol 57 mg, Sodium 847 mg

Approximate nutritional analysis per serving dressing:
Calories 26, Protein 2 g, Carbohydrates 3 g, Fat 1 g, Cholesterol 3 mg, Sodium 16 mg

ISLAND SHRIMP SALAD

1 large pineapple
1 lb (455 g) medium shrimp, cleaned and cooked
1 cup (240 ml) snow peas
1 medium red pepper, cut into ¾-inch pieces
⅓ cup (80 ml) GREY POUPON
   Specialty Mustard: Honey
1 tbs (15 ml) teriyaki sauce
1 tbs (15 ml) sesame seed, toasted

Slice pineapple in half lengthwise, slicing through top. Scoop out pineapple; reserve shells. Cut pineapple into ¾-inch pieces. Combine pineapple, shrimp, snow peas and red pepper. Blend mustard and teriyaki sauce; gently stir into shrimp mixture. Chill at least 1 hour. Just before serving, spoon shrimp mixture into pineapple shells. Sprinkle with sesame seed. Serves 4.

Approximate nutritional analysis per serving:
Calories 255, Protein 27 g, Carbohydrates 27 g, Fat 4 g, Cholesterol 140 mg, Sodium 312 mg

GRILLED GOAT CHEESE AND SEAFOOD SALAD WITH MANGO LIME DRESSING

SALAD:
1 - 8½ oz can (255 g) artichokes in water
1 - 6½ oz can (195 g) BUMBLE BEE
   Skinless Boneless Salmon, Red or Pink
1 - 12¼ oz can (370 g) BUMBLE BEE
   Albacore Chunk Tuna
1 - 2 oz can (60 g) sliced ripe black olives
1 head Romaine lettuce, cut
1 tsp (5 ml) grated lime rind
¼ cup (60 ml) lime juice
2 tbs (30 ml) walnut oil
sprig of parsley, minced
½ cup (120 ml) walnuts, toasted
4 thick slices goat cheese, broiled but briefly

MANGO DRESSING:
2 tbs (30 ml) mango chutney
2 tbs (30 ml) yogurt
2 tbs (30 ml) kefir
2 tbs (30 ml) red wine vinegar or Balsamic vinegar
1 mango, peeled and sliced or bottled mango spears

Drain artichokes and olives. Combine artichokes, seafood, olives and lime rind. Stir in juice and oil. Chill for 1 or more hours. Arrange mixture on Romaine. Drizzle Mango Dressing over all and serve remainder in a separate bowl. Garnish with goat cheese and minced parsley. Serves 4.
   Mango Dressing: Puree all ingredients and refrigerate. Yields 1 cup.

Approximate nutritional analysis per serving salad:
Calories 486, Protein 51 g, Carbohydrates 10 g, Fat 27 g, Cholesterol 64 mg, Sodium 970 mg

Approximate nutritional analysis per ¼ cup serving dressing:
Calories 64, Protein 1 g, Carbohydrates 1 g, Fat < 1 g, Cholesterol < 1 mg, Sodium 17 mg

HONEY DIJON SALAD WITH SHRIMP

8 cups (1.9 L) torn Romaine lettuce
1 lb (455 g) cooked cleaned shrimp
3 cups (720 ml) sliced mushrooms
2 cups (480 ml) sliced carrots
½ cup (120 ml) EGG BEATERS Real Egg Product
¼ cup (60 ml) corn oil
¼ cup (60 ml) white wine vinegar
¼ cup (60 ml) GREY POUPON Dijon Mustard
¼ cup (60 ml) honey
2 cups (480 ml) plain croutons

In large bowl, combine lettuce, shrimp, mushrooms and carrots; cover and chill until serving time.

In a small bowl, whisk EGG BEATERS, oil, vinegar, mustard and honey until well blended. To serve, pour dressing over salad and croutons, tossing until well coated. Serves 8.

Approximate nutritional information per serving:
Calories 252, Protein 17 g, Carbohydrates 21 g, Fat 9 g,
Cholesterol 111 mg, Sodium 538 mg

KAHUKU SHRIMP AND PAPAYA SALAD WITH FRESH FRUITS

2 lbs (455 g) fresh Kahuku shrimp
2 tsp (10 ml) pickling spice
½ gallon (1.9 L) water
salt
1 medium tomato, peeled, seeded, finely diced
¼ cup (60 ml) Maui onion, finely diced
1 tbs (15 ml) green onion, sliced
1 tbs (15 ml) fresh basil, minced
1 tsp (5 ml) fresh marjoram, minced
Hawaiian salt to taste
fresh ground pepper to taste
3-4 Island papayas
6-8 slices honeydew melon
6-8 slices cantaloupe
6-8 slices pineapple
18 fresh strawberries
24 leaves Manoa lettuce

Poach KAHUKU Shrimp in water with pickling spice and salt. Remove shells and chill shrimp until ready to use. Combine the next seven ingredients and add chilled shrimp. Line a plate or rim soup bowl with Manoa lettuce. Arrange the fruits and place a half papaya in the middle. Fill papaya with Kahuku shrimp mixture and garnish with an orchid. Serves 6.

Approximate nutritional analysis per serving:
Calories 317, Protein 34 g, Carbohydrates 40 g, Fat 4 g,
Cholesterol 230 mg, Sodium 245 mg

CRUNCHY TUNA WALDORF SALAD

1 - 9¼ oz can (280 g) tuna packed in water,
    drained and flaked
1 large apple, cored and chopped
⅓ cup (80 ml) chopped celery
⅓ cup (80 ml) chopped walnuts
⅓ cup (80 ml) raisins, currants or
    chopped pitted dates
½ cup (120 ml) DANNON Plain Nonfat or
    Lowfat Yogurt
¼ cup (60 ml) mayonnaise or salad dressing
leaf lettuce
½ cup (2 oz) (60 g) shredded cheddar or Monterey
    Jack cheese

In a medium bowl combine tuna, apple, celery, walnuts and raisins; set aside. In a small bowl combine yogurt and mayonnaise. Add to tuna-fruit mixture; toss gently. Cover; chill before serving. To serve, line 4 salad plates with lettuce leaves. Sprinkle cheese over lettuce. Spoon tuna-fruit mixture on top of cheese. Serves 4.

Approximate nutritional analysis per serving:
Calories 339, Protein 27 g, Carbohydrates 23 g, Fat 17 g,
Cholesterol 32 mg, Sodium 456 mg

CURRIED TUNA AND FRUIT SALAD

2 tbs (30 ml) light mayonnaise
2 tbs (30 ml) plain yogurt or kefir
2 tbs (30 ml) fresh lemon juice
1-2 tsp (5-10 ml) curry powder
1 tbs (15 ml) mango chutney
1 - 12¼ oz can (370 g) BUMBLE BEE White
    or Light, Solid or Chunk, Tuna, drained
½ cup (120 ml) celery, thinly sliced
½ cup (120 ml) thinly sliced green onion
1 cup (240 ml) red apple, cored and diced
1 cup (240 ml) green tart apple, cored and diced
1 cup (240 ml) seedless grapes, halved
2 small cantaloupe or honeydew melons
sliced almonds toasted for garnish
red or green grapes to garnish

Combine mayonnaise, yogurt (or kefir), lemon juice, curry powder and mango chutney. Gently fold in remaining ingredients. Season to taste and chill. Flute and seed melons. Refrigerate until ready to fill. Fill hollows with mixture and garnish with almonds and grapes. Serves 4.

Approximate nutritional analysis per serving salad with cantaloupe:
Calories 299, Protein 28 g, Carbohydrates 44 g, Fat 3 g,
Cholesterol 19 mg, Sodium 348 mg

Fruits for Salad

TUNA CORN SALAD

2 - 7 oz cans (420 g) tuna packed in water
2 - 10 oz pkgs (600 g) frozen whole kernel corn,
    cooked according to package directions
    and drained
½ cup (120 ml) vegetable oil
¼ cup (60 ml) cider vinegar
1½ tsp (8 ml) lemon juice
3 tbs (45 ml) chopped parsley
½ tsp (3 ml) salt
¾ tsp (4 ml) dried basil leaf
½ tsp (3 ml) Tabasco pepper sauce
2 large tomatoes, peeled and chopped
1 medium zucchini, peeled and shredded
½ cup (120 ml) green onions

In large bowl mix all ingredients. Cover and chill several hours.
Serve in a bowl lined with salad greens. Serves 6.

Approximate nutritional analysis per serving:
Calories 254, Protein 15 g, Carbohydrates 22 g, Fat 15 g,
Cholesterol 7 mg, Sodium 292 mg

TUNA SALAD WITH APPLES AND ALMONDS

½ cup (120 ml) **BLUE DIAMOND**
    Blanched Slivered Almonds
1 tsp (5 ml) vegetable oil
1 tbs (15 ml) firmly packed brown sugar
1 tbs (15 ml) lemon juice
1 tsp (5 ml) grated fresh ginger
    or ¼ tsp (1 ml) powdered ginger
1 clove garlic, chopped finely
½ cup (120 ml) mayonnaise
1 - 7 oz can (210 g) water-packed, white tuna,
    drained and flaked
1 medium, tart green apple, unpeeled,
    cored and diced
½ cup (120 ml) sliced green onion
⅓ cup (80 ml) diced celery
¼ cup (60 ml) sliced pimiento-stuffed olives

Sauté almonds in oil until golden; reserve. Combine brown
sugar, lemon juice, ginger and garlic. Gently mix mayonnaise
with tuna. Fold in apple, green onion, celery and olives. Chill.
Just before serving, fold in almonds. Serves 2.

Approximate nutritional analysis per serving:
Calories 454, Protein 32 g, Carbohydrates 31 g, Fat 25 g,
Cholesterol 15 mg, Sodium 671 mg

SOUTHWEST BEAN SALAD

1 - 15 oz can (450 g) pinto beans, drained and rinsed
1 - 15 oz can (450 g) red kidney beans,
    drained and rinsed
1 ½ cups (355 ml) pitted **CALIFORNIA**
    ripe olives, cut into wedges
¾ cup (180 ml) diced celery
½ cup (120 ml) chopped green onion
2 cups (480 ml) seeded and chopped tomatoes
¼ cup (60 ml) finely chopped cilantro or parsley
lettuce

PIQUANT VINAIGRETTE:
½ cup (120 ml) olive or vegetable oil
3 tbs (45 ml) red wine vinegar
1 ½ tsp (8 ml) ground cumin
1 ½ tsp (8 ml) Tabasco sauce
¼ tsp (1 ml) salt

CILANTRO CREAM:
1 cup (240 ml) sour cream
¼ cup (60 ml) finely chopped cilantro

Combine beans, olives, celery, green onion, tomatoes, cilantro and Piquant Vinaigrette in large bowl. Toss gently to mix. Serve in lettuce-lined bowl and dollop with Cilantro Cream or plain sour cream. Serves 4.
    Piquant Vinaigrette: Combine all ingredients in a jar. Shake to blend.
    Cilantro Cream: Mix sour cream and cilantro.

Approximate nutritional analysis per serving:
Calories 673, Protein 18 g, Carbohydrates 53 g, Fat 46 g,
Cholesterol 26 mg, Sodium 633 mg

SNAPPY WALDORF SALAD

3 red apples, cored and coarsely chopped
¾ cup (180 ml) chopped celery
⅓ cup (80 ml) raisins
¼ cup (60 ml) chopped walnuts
⅓ cup (80 ml) reduced-calorie mayonnaise
¼ tsp (60 ml) ground cinnamon
⅛ tsp (.5 ml) ground nutmeg

Combine apples, celery, raisins and walnuts in a large bowl. In a small bowl, combine remaining ingredients. Mix into apple mixture. Cover and chill. Stir before serving. Serves 6.

Approximate nutritional analysis per serving:
Calories 117, Protein 1 g, Carbohydrates 19 g, Fat 5 g,
Cholesterol 6 mg, Sodium 30 mg

CAULIFLOWER SALAD

1 cup (240 ml) vegetable oil
½ cup (120 ml) **HEINZ** Tarragon or
    Apple Cider Vinegar
2 tsp (10 ml) granulated sugar
1 tsp (5 ml) salt
½ tsp (3 ml) paprika
1 small head cauliflower, separated into flowerets
½ large mild onion, thinly sliced,
    separated into rings
⅓ cup (80 ml) sliced stuffed olives
½ cup (120 ml) crumbled blue or Roquefort cheese
1 small head lettuce, shredded

Combine first 5 ingredients in jar; cover and shake vigorously. In large bowl, combine cauliflower, onion rings and olives. Pour dressing over vegetables. Cover; marinate several hours in refrigerator turning occasionally. Just before serving, add cheese and lettuce; toss to coat. Serves 10.

Approximate nutritional analysis per serving:
Calories 251, Protein 3 g, Carbohydrates 7 g, Fat 24 g,
Cholesterol 4 mg, Sodium 353 mg

TAOS TACO SALAD

8 medium corn tortillas
vegetable oil cooking spray
1 - 15 oz can (450 g) black beans, drained and rinsed
1 - 10 oz pkg (300 g) frozen corn, cooked and drained
¼ cup (60 ml) sliced green onion
2 tbs (30 ml) chopped cilantro
4 cup (960 ml) shredded lettuce
2 cup (480 ml) chopped tomato
½ cup (120 ml) commercially prepared tomato
1 - 8 oz pkg (240 g) **HEALTHY CHOICE**
    Fat Free Natural Shredded Mexican Cheese

Heat oven to 400°F (205°C). Lightly spray both sides of each tortilla with non-stick cooking spray. Place on baking sheet and bake 3 minutes on each side or until crisp. Combine beans, corn, onion and cilantro; mix lightly. For each salad, top tortilla with ½ cup lettuce, ¼ cup tomato, ¼ cup bean mixture, 1 tbs salsa and 1 oz cheese. Serves 8.

Approximate nutritional analysis per serving:
Calories 218, Protein 17 g, Carbohydrates 36 g, Fat 2 g,
Cholesterol 5 mg, Sodium 225 mg

FOUR STAR HAM SALAD

8 oz (240 g) baked ham, cut into match sticks
4 oz (120 g) Swiss cheese, cut into match sticks
2 cups rigatoni or ziti pasta, cooked,
    drained and kept warm
3 scallions, chopped
1 cup (240 ml) sour cream
¼ cup (60 ml) orange juice
2 tbs (30 ml) fruity chutney
2 tsp (10 ml) Dijon-style mustard
2 tsp (10 ml) horseradish
1 tsp (5 ml) McCORMICK or SCHILLING
    Brandy Extract
lettuce leaves
1 orange, peeled and sectioned for garnish

Combine all ingredients except lettuce and orange. Toss well. Line plates with lettuce leaves. Add salad and garnish with orange sections. Serves 4.

Approximate nutritional analysis per serving:
Calories 582, Protein 27 g, Carbohydrates 58 g, Fat 27 g,
Cholesterol 84 mg, Sodium 890 mg

SUNSHINE RAISIN-FRUIT SALAD

¼ cup (60 ml) orange juice
1 tbs (15 ml) honey
1 cup (240 ml) strawberry halves
1 cup (240 ml) red or green seedless grapes
1 cup (240 ml) orange segments
1 banana, sliced
¾ cup (180 ml) CALIFORNIA raisins
1 cup (240 ml) granola cereal
1 cup (240 ml) vanilla yogurt

Into large bowl measure orange juice and honey; mix. Add strawberries, grapes, oranges, banana and raisins; toss gently. Spoon fruit mixture into 4 bowls, dividing equally. Top each bowl, with ¼ cup granola and ¼ cup yogurt. Garnish with whole strawberries, if desired. Serves 4.

Approximate nutritional analysis per serving:
Calories 383, Protein 8 g, Carbohydrates 71 g, Fat 11 g,
Cholesterol 7 mg, Sodium 35 mg

Courtesy of The California Raisin Advisory Board.

WARM PORK AND PEAR SALAD

2 large firm pears
2 tbs (30 ml) vegetable oil, divided
12 oz (360 g) boneless pork, cut into strips
½ cup (120 ml) HEINZ Apple Cider Vinegar
3 tbs (45 ml) granulated sugar
1 tsp (5 ml) salt
⅛ tsp (.5 ml) pepper
½ cup (120 ml) halved red seedless grapes
10 cups (2.4 L) torn mixed salad greens
¼ cup (60 ml) chopped toasted walnuts

Peel and core pears; cut each pear into 12 slices. In skillet, sauté pears in 1 tbs oil until tender but still firm, remove. In same skillet, quickly sauté pork over high heat in remaining tbs oil until no longer pink, about 3 minutes. Remove, reserving pan juices. Add vinegar, sugar, salt and pepper to pan juices; simmer until sugar dissolves. Add pears, pork and grapes; heat. Divide salad greens among 4 individual salad bowls; spoon pork mixture over greens. Sprinkle with nuts, serve immediately. Serves 4.

Approximate nutritional analysis per serving:
Calories 538, Protein 27 g, Carbohydrates 34 g, Fat 34 g,
Cholesterol 93 mg, Sodium 621 mg

WATERMELON GINGER SALAD

3 cups (720 ml) cubed seeded watermelon
1 cup (240 ml) julienne strips jicama
¼ cup (60 ml) finely chopped green onion
1 tbs (15 ml) finely chopped fresh ginger
2 tbs (30 ml) rice or white wine vinegar
¼ tsp (60 ml) salt
3-4 drops hot-pepper sauce
lettuce leaves

In large bowl, gently toss all ingredients except lettuce. Serve on individual lettuce-lined plates. Serves 4.

Approximate nutritional analysis per serving:
Calories 56, Protein 1 g, Carbohydrates 13 g, Fat < 1 g,
Cholesterol 0 mg, Sodium 140 mg

SOUTH OF THE BORDER SUN BOWL

1 lb (455 g) ground beef
1 - 1¼ oz pkg (40 g) taco seasoning mix
1 cup (240 ml) raisins
1 head iceberg lettuce
1 cup (240 ml) cooked kidney beans
1 tomato, diced
½ cup (120 ml) shredded cheddar cheese
corn chips

Prepare beef with seasoning mix according to package directions. Stir ½ cup of the raisins into meat mixture; cool. Line serving bowl with lettuce leaves. Tear remaining lettuce into bite-size pieces; place ⅓ into bowl. Top with meat mixture, another ⅓ of the lettuce, the beans, final ⅓ of the lettuce; then tomato, cheese and remaining ½ cup raisins. Sprinkle with corn chips as desired around outer edge of salad. Serves 6.

Approximate nutritional analysis per serving:
Calories 375, Protein 24 g, Carbohydrates 28 g, Fat 19 g,
Cholesterol 78 mg, Sodium 291 mg

Courtesy of The California Raisin Advisory Board.

CRANBERRY FRUIT SALAD

1 - 6 oz pkg (180 g) raspberry gelatin
2 cups (480 ml) boiling water
1 - 16 oz can (480 g) jellied cranberry sauce
1 - 8¾ oz can (265 g) crushed pineapple
¾ cup (180 ml) fresh orange juice
1 tbs (15 ml) fresh lemon juice
½ cup (120 ml) chopped walnuts

Dissolve gelatin in boiling water. Break up and stir in cranberry sauce, undrained pineapple, orange juice, lemon juice and nuts. Pour into a shallow casserole dish. Chill until firm. Cut into squares or slices and serve as salad or side dish. Serves 10.

Approximate nutritional analysis per serving:
Calories 148, Protein 1 g, Carbohydrates 29 g, Fat 4 g,
Cholesterol 0 mg, Sodium 26 mg

Courtesy of the Cape Cod Cranberry Growers' Association.

South of the Border Sun Bowl

QUICK AND EASY RAISIN-RICE SALAD

3 cups (720 ml) cooked rice, cooled
2 cups (480 ml) shredded green cabbage
1 cup (240 ml) CALIFORNIA raisins
¾ cup (180 ml) sliced red radishes
3 green onions, sliced

LEMON VINAIGRETTE:
⅓ cup (80 ml) olive oil
¼ cup (60 ml) fresh lemon juice
1 small garlic clove, minced
1 tsp (5 ml) dried basil
1 tsp (5 ml) salt
⅛ tsp (.5 ml) hot pepper sauce

Combine all ingredients except vinaigrette in medium bowl; toss well. Add vinaigrette; toss to coat. If desired, serve salad in hollowed-out cabbage. Serves 4.
    Lemon Vinaigrette: In small bowl whisk together all ingredients.

Approximate nutritional analysis per serving salad:
Calories 491, Protein 8 g, Carbohydrates 127 g, Fat 1 g, Cholesterol 0 mg, Sodium 58 mg

Approximate nutritional analysis per serving dressing:
Calories 162, Protein <1 g, Carbohydrates 2 g, Fat 18 g, Cholesterol 0 mg, Sodium 533 mg

Courtesy of The California Raisin Advisory Board.

CHICKEN SUPPER SALAD

½ cup (120 ml) mayonnaise
½ cup (120 ml) dairy sour cream or yogurt
1 tbs (15 ml) lemon juice
1 tsp (5 ml) grated lemon rind
½ tsp (3 ml) ginger, optional
½ tsp (3 ml) salt
2 cups (480 ml) cubed cooked chicken
2 cups (480 ml) cold cooked macaroni
1 cup (240 ml) raisins
1 cup (240 ml) sliced celery
1 small red onion, chopped
1 cup (240 ml) halved cherry tomatoes
lettuce

Mix together first 6 ingredients for dressing; set aside. Toss together all remaining ingredients except lettuce. Stir dressing into chicken mixture, cooling well. Store in refrigerator until serving time. To serve, spoon salad atop lettuce bed. Serves 6.

Approximate nutritional analysis per serving:
Calories 354, Protein 18 g, Carbohydrates 40 g, Fat 15 g, Cholesterol 55 mg, Sodium 390 mg

IMPERIAL WALDORF SALAD

2 red apples, cored and diced
½ cup (120 ml) raisins
½ avocado, diced
⅓ cup (80 ml) sliced celery
¼ cup (60 ml) broken walnuts
⅓-½ cup (80-120 ml) mayonnaise
1 tbs (15 ml) lemon juice
lettuce

In mixing bowl combine all ingredients except lettuce; toss lightly to coat. Spoon into individual lettuce cups or a large lettuce-lined bowl. Serves 6.

Approximate nutritional analysis per serving:
Calories 124, Protein 2 g, Carbohydrates 19 g, Fat 6 g, Cholesterol 0 mg, Sodium 9 mg

SUNBURST SALAD

2 USA Pears, sliced and unpeeled
1 cup (240 ml) strawberries
2 oranges, sliced, peels left on
2 kiwifruit, peeled, sliced
selected greens (include colorful kale and radicchio, or Romaine and butter lettuce)
¼ cup (60 ml) coconut, toasted if desired
1½ cups (355 ml) Yogurt Honey Dressing

YOGURT HONEY DRESSING:
1½ cups (355 ml) plain yogurt
2 tbs (30 ml) mayonnaise
2 tbs (30 ml) honey

Cut orange slices into wedges. On 4 individual salad plates, arrange greens and all fruits to make a composed salad. Top with coconut. Serve Honey Yogurt Dressing by the side. Serves 4.
    Honey Yogurt Dressing: Mix all ingredients. Garnish dressing with orange zest or a sprig of mint.

Approximate nutritional analysis per serving salad:
Calories 132, Protein 2 g, Carbohydrates 30 g, Fat 2 g, Cholesterol 0 mg, Sodium 3 mg

Approximate nutritional analysis per serving dressing:
Calories 113, Protein 3 g, Carbohydrates 14 g, Fat 5 g, Cholesterol 13 mg, Sodium 92 mg

GREEN PAPAYA SALAD #1

1 lb (455 g) green papaya
2 cloves garlic
2-3 red chili peppers, seeded
1 tomato, sliced in strips
2 tbs (30 ml) fish sauce*
3 tbs (45 ml) fresh lime juice
lettuce leaves or cabbage squares
1 lime, cut into wedges
red chili peppers for garnish

* The amount of fish sauce used in this recipe depends on the brand selected and personal taste.

Peel and seed papaya; shred. Grind together garlic and red chili peppers in a food processor or mortar. Mix together papaya, tomato, fish sauce and lime juice; add garlic mixture and toss lightly. To eat place a portion of papaya mixture onto a leaf lettuce or cabbage square and form into a packet. Serve with wedges of lime. Garnish with red chili peppers. Serves 4.

Note: There are many variations of papaya salad in southeast Asia. Thais like theirs with ground peanuts, sugar and salted shrimp powder. The Laotian version usually calls for pickled fresh water crabs and long string beans. Vietnamese like theirs with beef jerky and mint leaves.

Approximate nutritional analysis per serving:
Calories 61, Protein 1 g, Carbohydrates 15 g, Fat <1 g,
Cholesterol 0 mg, Sodium 265 mg

Courtesy of The Papaya Administrative Committee.

GREEN PAPAYA SALAD #2

4 lbs (1.8 kg) green papayas, skinned and seeded
1 carrot
¼ cup (60 ml) raisins
½ cup (120 ml) rice vinegar
½ cup (120 ml) fresh lemon or lime juice
1 cup (240 ml) sugar
¼ cup (60 ml) water
1 tbs (15 ml) black pepper
2 tbs (30 ml) patis (fish sauce)

Grate papayas and carrot into a large mixing bowl. Add raisins and set aside. In a separate bowl, mix the marinade ingredients. Add marinade to papaya salad and refrigerate for 4 hours. Garnish with pineapple spear, papaya spear and mint leaf. Serves 14.

Approximate nutritional analysis per serving:
Calories 124, Protein 1 g, Carbohydrates 32 g, Fat <1 g,
Cholesterol 0 mg, Sodium 80 mg

Courtesy of The Papaya Administrative Committe.

GREEN PAPAYA SALAD #3

½ lb (230 g) green papaya
2-3 red chili peppers, seeded
1 clove garlic
1 tomato, sliced in strips
3 tbs (45 ml) lime juice
2 tbs (30 ml) fish sauce
½ cup (120 ml) ground peanut
salted shrimp powder
dash sugar
1 lime cut into wedges
lettuce leaves or cabbage, squared

Peel and seed papaya; shred. Grind together garlic and red chili peppers in food processor or mortar. Mix together the papaya, tomato, fish sauce and lime juice; add garlic mixture and toss lightly. Place a portion of papaya mixture onto a lettuce or cabbage square, sprinkle with ground peanuts, salted shrimp powder, dash of sugar and form into a packet to eat. Serve with wedges of lime. Garnish with red chili peppers and crushed peanuts (optional). Serves 4.

Approximate nutritional analysis per serving:
Calories 141, Protein 6 g, Carbohydrates 12 g, Fat 9 g,
Cholesterol 0 mg, Sodium 341 mg

Courtesy of The Papaya Administrative Committee.

Papaya

COOL FRUIT AND VEGETABLE SALAD WITH HOT TOMATO DIPPING SAUCE

2 medium tomatoes
¼ cup (60 ml) olive oil
2 tbs (30 ml) red wine vinegar
¾ tsp (4 ml) Tabasco pepper sauce
3 sprigs cilantro
¼ tsp (1 ml) salt
1 small head green leaf lettuce
4 large honeydew melon slices
1 large naval orange, peeled and sliced
1 medium cucumber, thinly sliced
1 red bell pepper, cut into thin strips
3 green onions

In food processor or blender combine tomatoes, olive oil, vinegar, Tabasco pepper sauce, cilantro and salt. Process until mixture is smooth. Refrigerate until ready to serve. On large platter arrange lettuce leaves; top with melon slices, orange slices, cucumber slices, red pepper strips and green onions. Serve salad with dipping sauce. Serves 6.

Approximate nutritional analysis per serving:
Calories 168, Protein 3 g, Carbohydrates 22 g, Fat 10 g,
Cholesterol 0 mg, Sodium 113 mg

MANDARIN HAZELNUT SALAD

7-8 cups (1.7-1.9 kg) mixed greens,
**   torn into bite-size pieces**
2 green onions, chopped
¼ cup (60 ml) celery, chopped
1 cup (240 ml) drained Mandarin oranges

PARSLEY DRESSING:
½ cup (120 ml) salad oil
¼ cup (60 ml) parsley, chopped
2 tbs (30 ml) sugar
2 tbs (30 ml) cider vinegar
salt and pepper to taste
dash of Tabasco sauce
CARAMELIZED HAZELNUTS:
2 tbs (30 ml) sugar
1 cup (240 ml) OREGON Hazelnuts

Toss greens, onions, celery and oranges with dressing. Sprinkle with hazelnuts. Serves 6.
    Parsley Dressing: Mix all ingredients and allow flavors to blend.
    Caramelized Hazelnuts: Slowly melt sugar in heavy skillet. Mix nuts, covering well with sugar. Cook until light amber color. Allow to cool on wax paper before use.

Approximate nutritional analysis per serving salad:
Calories 167, Protein 4 g, Carbohydrates 14 g, Fat 12 g,
Cholesterol 0 mg, Sodium 14 mg

Approximate nutritional analysis per serving dressing:
Calories 178, Protein < 1 g, Carbohydrates 5 g, Fat 18 g,
Cholesterol 0 mg, Sodium 1 mg

FRUIT SALAD WITH DRIED CHERRIES

DRESSING:
¼ cup (60 ml) mayonnaise or salad dressing
1 tbs (15 ml) sugar
½ tsp (3 ml) lemon juice
dash salt
½ cup (120 ml) whipping cream or plain yogurt

SALAD:
1 large red apple, chopped
1 large yellow apple, chopped
1 large banana, sliced
½ cup (120 ml) chopped toasted almonds
½ cup (120 ml) plus 2 tbs (30 ml)
**   toasted flaked coconut**
½ cup (120 ml) plus 2 tbs (30 ml) Dried Cherries
lettuce leaves

In a mixing bowl, combine mayonnaise, sugar, lemon juice and salt. With electric mixer whip the cream until soft peaks form; fold into the mayonnaise mixture. If using yogurt, stir in with the mayonnaise. Gently fold in the apples, banana, almonds, ½ cup coconut and ½ cup Dried Cherries. Cover and chill.
    Line a salad bowl with lettuce leaves; spoon in the chilled fruit mixture. Garnish with the 2 tbs coconut and Dried Cherries. Serves 6.

Approximate nutritional analysis per serving:
Calories 290, Protein 4 g, Carbohydrates 30 g, Fat 19 g,
Cholesterol 37 mg, Sodium 34 mg

Courtesy of the Traverse Bay Fruit Co.

Opposite: Cool Fruit and Vegetable Salad with Hot Tomato Dipping Sauce

CHERRY FRUIT SALAD WITH YOGURT DRESSING

2 cups (480 ml) Northwest fresh sweet cherries,
   pitted
1 small fresh pineapple, pared and cut into segments
1 orange, peeled and cut into segments
½ small honeydew melon, pared and cut into spears
¼ cup (60 ml) toasted sliced almonds

ORANGE YOGURT DRESSING:
½ cup (120 ml) plain nonfat yogurt
3 tbs (45 ml) orange juice
2 tbs (30 ml) mayonnaise
1 tbs (15 ml) lemon juice
1 tbs (15 ml) sugar
1 tsp (5 ml) orange peel

Arrange cherries, pineapple, grapefruit, orange and melon on serving dish; sprinkle with almonds. Serve with Orange Yogurt Dressing. Serves 4.

Orange Yogurt Dressing: Combine first 5 ingredients; blend until smooth. Sprinkle with orange peel. Yields ¾ cup, 4 servings.

Approximate nutritional analysis per serving salad:
Calories 248, Protein 4 g, Carbohydrates 52 g, Fat 6 g,
Cholesterol 0 mg, Sodium 17 mg

Approximate nutritional analysis per serving dressing:
Calories 36, Protein 2 g, Carbohydrates 7 g, Fat <1 g,
Cholesterol 2 mg, Sodium 20 mg

DRIED STRAWBERRY SALAD

2 tbs (30 ml) olive oil
2 tbs (30 ml) red wine vinegar
1 tsp (5 ml) sugar
¼ tsp (1 ml) dry mustard
¼ tsp (1 ml) poppy seeds
2 cups (480 ml) torn salad greens
¼ cup (60 ml) Dried Strawberries
¼ cup (60 ml) sliced mushrooms
2 tbs (30 ml) sliced red onion

Dressing: In small bowl combine oil, vinegar, sugar, mustard and poppy seeds. Whisk to combine. Stir in Dried Strawberries. Refrigerate for 2 hours. Stir dressing before serving.

On 2 serving plates arrange salad greens, mushrooms, onion and strawberries from dressing mixture. Drizzle with dressing. Serves 2.

Approximate nutritional analysis per serving:
Calories 167, Protein 2 g, Carbohydrates 11 g, Fat 14 g,
Cholesterol 0 mg, Sodium 6 mg

Courtesy of the Traverse Bay Fruit Co.

FRUIT SALAD WITH MICHIGAN DRIED CHERRY VINAIGRETTE

3 tbs (45 ml) MICHIGAN Dried Cherry Vinegar
   (below) (or vinegar of your choice)
4 tbs (60 ml) vegetable oil
¼ tsp (1 ml) salt
¼ tsp (1 ml) ground black pepper
1 cup (240 ml) MICHIGAN Dried Cherries
1 small apple, thinly sliced
1 small orange, peeled and cut into sections
¼ cup (60 ml) whole salted cashews
1½ cups (355 ml) Belgian endive
1½ cups (355 ml) spinach
1½ cups (355 ml) Boston lettuce salad greens

MICHIGAN DRIED CHERRY VINEGAR:
1 cup (240 ml) MICHIGAN Dried Cherries
2 cups (480 ml) white wine vinegar

For dressing, whisk together MICHIGAN Dried Cherry Vinegar, oil, salt and pepper. Arrange greens on serving plate, add MICHIGAN Dried Cherries, fruits and cashews. Serve with vinaigrette. Serves 4.

MICHIGAN Dried Cherry Vinaigrette: Combine MICHIGAN Dried Cherries and vinegar in a glass container. Cover and allow to steep for 2 days at room temperature. Heat just to boiling point, strain through cheesecloth; discard cherries. Cool and store in tightly sealed container.

Approximate nutritional analysis per serving salad minus vinaigrette:
Calories 218, Protein 3 g, Carbohydrates 14 g,
Fat 18 g, Cholesterol 0 mg, Sodium 157 mg

Courtesy of the Traverse Bay Fruit Co.

GINGERED FRUIT SALAD

2 oranges, peeled and sectioned
2 tart apples, cored and chopped
2 peaches, sliced
1 cup (240 ml) strawberry halves
1 cup (240 ml) DANNON Plain Nonfat or
   Lowfat Yogurt
2 tbs (30 ml) packed brown sugar
½ tsp (3 ml) ginger

In a large bowl, toss oranges, apples, peaches and strawberries. In a small bowl combine yogurt, brown sugar and ginger. Blend well with wire whisk or fork. Toss with fruit. Serves 8.

Approximate nutritional analysis per serving:
Calories 81, Protein 2 g, Carbohydrates 18 g, Fat < 1 g,
Cholesterol 2 mg, Sodium 21 mg

Opposite: Cherry Fruit Salad with Yogurt Dressing

WATERCRESS ORANGE SALAD

3 bunches watercress, washed
3 oranges, peeled and cut into wedges; save juice
½ small onion, halved and thinly sliced
¼ cup (60 ml) olive oil
2 tbs (30 ml) kosher red wine vinegar or
    kosher balsamic vinegar
2 tsp (10 ml) Dijon mustard
¼ tsp (1 ml) cumin
salt and pepper to taste

Toss together watercress, orange pieces and onion slices in a large bowl. In a small bowl whisk together oil, vinegar, mustard, cumin, salt, pepper and orange juice. Toss salad with dressing and serve. Serves 6.

Approximate nutritional analysis per serving:
Calories 122, Protein 1 g, Carbohydrates 10 g, Fat 9 g, Cholesterol 0 mg, Sodium 73 mg

Courtesy of the Empire Kosher Poultry Test Kitchens.

WHITE BEAN, OLIVE AND TOMATO SALAD

1 - 15 oz can (450 g) white beans, drained and rinsed
1 cup (240 ml) pitted CALIFORNIA ripe olives, halved
½ cup (120 ml) chopped red onion
1 cup (½ lb) (230 g) tomatoes, seeded and diced
⅓ cup (80 ml) minced parsley
2 tbs (30 ml) lemon juice
½ tsp (3 ml) basil
½ tsp (3 ml) thyme
½ tsp (3 ml) oregano
¼ tsp (1 ml) pepper
2 tbs (30 ml) olive oil

Combine all ingredients; toss gently to mix. Taste and add lemon juice if desired. Chill until ready to serve. Serves 4.

Approximate nutritional analysis per serving:
Calories 284, Protein 11 g, Carbohydrates 36 g, Fat 12 g, Cholesterol 0 mg, Sodium 381 mg

GRILLED CHICKEN SALAD BERTOLLI

MARINADE:
1 tsp (5 ml) BERTOLLI Extra Virgin Olive Oil
½ garlic clove, crushed through a press
pinch of crushed hot red pepper, to taste
4 boneless and skinless chicken cutlets, pounded thin
salt and pepper to taste

SALSA:
1 cup (240 ml) red and/or yellow plum
    tomatoes, ¼-inch diced
¼ cup (60 ml) sweet yellow onion, ¼-inch diced
2 tbs (30 ml) fresh basil, chopped
2 tsp (10 ml) BERTOLLI Extra Virgin Olive Oil
1 brine cured black olive (Kalamata),
    pitted and chopped
1 tsp (5 ml) red wine vinegar
salt and freshly ground black pepper, to taste

SALAD:
6 cups (1.4 L) packed mixed salad greens
1 tsp (5 ml) BERTOLLI Extra Virgin Olive Oil
2 tsp (10 ml) red wine vinegar
fresh basil leaves

Marinade: Combine the olive oil, garlic and crushed pepper on a large plate. Add the chicken cutlets and turn to coat. Cover and let stand for 30 minutes.

Salsa: Combine the tomatoes, onion, basil, olive oil, olives and red wine vinegar; add salt and pepper. Cover and let stand until ready to serve.

Salad: Combine the salad greens in a large bowl; sprinkle with the olive oil and vinegar; toss to coat.

Heat a large 12-inch non-stick skillet or grill over high heat until very hot. Add the cutlets and sear on both sides until lightly browned and cooked through, about 2 minutes per side. Sprinkle with salt and pepper; cut into ½-inch wide strips.

Divide the salad evenly among 4 large plates. Place chicken on salad, dividing evenly. Top with a spoonful of the salsa. Garnish with fresh basil leaves. Serves 4.

Approximate nutritional analysis per serving:
Calories 198, Protein 28 g, Carbohydrates 6 g, Fat 7 g, Cholesterol 66 mg, Sodium 95 mg

Ceci Pea Salad

CECI PEA SALAD

1 cup (240 ml) canned ceci beans (chick peas),
    rinsed and drained
1 cup (240 ml) seedless cucumber or Kirby,
    ¹/₂-inch cubed
2 cups (480 ml) tomatoes, ¹/₂-inch cubed
1 cup (240 ml) sweet yellow onion, ¹/₂-inch cubed
2 tbs (30 ml) red wine vinegar
1 tbs (15 ml) BERTOLLI Extra Virgin Olive Oil
2 tbs (30 ml) basil or mint, finely chopped
1 tbs (15 ml) Italian parsley, finely chopped
salt and freshly ground black pepper to taste

In a large bowl, combine the ceci beans, cucumber, tomatoes, onion, basil or mint and parsley. Add the vinegar, olive oil and salt and pepper to taste. Toss to blend. Let stand 1 hour before serving. Serves 6.

Approximate nutritional analysis per serving:
Calories 80, Protein 3 g, Carbohydrates 11 g, Fat 3 g,
Cholesterol 0 mg, Sodium 63 mg

PANZANELLA

4 thick ¹/₂-inch slices Italian bread (preferably whole
    wheat), toasted, cut into ¹/₂-inch chunks.
1 lb (455 g) ripe juicy tomatoes, cored,
    cut into ¹/₂-inch chunks
¹/₄ cup (60 ml) red onion, finely chopped
¹/₄ cup (60 ml) fresh basil, finely chopped
¹/₂ clove garlic, crushed through press
5 tsp (25 ml) BERTOLLI Extra Virgin Olive Oil
salt and freshly ground black pepper, to taste

In a large bowl combine the bread, tomatoes, red onion, basil, garlic, olive oil, salt and pepper; toss to blend. Season to taste. Serve at room temperature. Serves 8.

Approximate nutritional analysis per serving:
Calories 78, Protein 2 g, Carbohydrates 11 g, Fat 3 g,
Cholesterol 0 mg, Sodium 88 mg

LENTIL, RED PEPPER AND POTATO SALAD

2 cups (480 ml) cooked lentils
1 cup (240 ml) cooked potatoes, diced ¼ inch
½ cup (120 ml) cooked fresh or thawed
    frozen green peas
½ cup (120 ml) red bell pepper, finely chopped
¼ cup (60 ml) red onion, chopped
¼ cup (60 ml) celery, chopped
1 tbs (15 ml) Italian, flat leaf, parsley, finely chopped
1 tbs (15 ml) basil, finely chopped
2 tbs (30 ml) red wine vinegar
2 tbs (30 ml) BERTOLLI Extra Virgin Olive Oil
salt and freshly ground black pepper

Combine the lentils, potatoes, peas, red peppers, red onion, celery, parsley and basil in a large bowl. Whisk the vinegar, oil, salt and pepper in a separate bowl; add to the lentil mixture; toss and serve. Serves 6.

Approximate nutritional analysis per serving:
Calories 157, Protein 7 g, Carbohydrates 22 g, Fat 5 g,
Cholesterol 0 mg, Sodium 9 mg

ROUGE ET NOIR SALAD

1 cup (240 ml) whole pitted CALIFORNIA ripe olives
2 cups (480 ml) cherry tomatoes, halved
½ lb (230 g) small fresh mushrooms, sliced
½ cup (120 ml) vegetable or olive oil
¼ cup (60 ml) vinegar
3 tbs (45 ml) chopped fresh basil leaves
2 tbs (30 ml) grated Parmesan cheese
1 tsp (5 ml) minced garlic
2 bunches watercress or assorted torn lettuces

Combine olives, tomatoes and mushrooms in bowl. Combine oil, vinegar, basil, cheese and garlic in jar, shake and pour over salad. Toss well and spoon onto watercress-lined salad plates. Serves 6.

Approximate nutritional analysis per serving:
Calories 230, Protein 3 g, Carbohydrates 8 g, Fat 22 g,
Cholesterol 2 mg, Sodium 300 mg

SWEET CORN SALAD WITH OLIVES

2 - 11 oz cans (660 g) Mexicorn kernels, drained
1 cup (240 ml) CALIFORNIA ripe olive wedges
¼ cup (60 ml) green onion, chopped
½ cup (120 ml) vegetable oil
⅓ cup (80 ml) white wine vinegar
2 tbs (30 ml) sugar
1 tsp (5 ml) ground cumin
¼ tsp (1 ml) black pepper
lettuce
2 medium tomatoes, sliced
blue corn tortilla chips

Combine corn, olives and green onion. Combine oil, vinegar, sugar, cumin, and black pepper in jar, shake well, pour over salad and toss to coat. Line platter with lettuce, top with overlapping tomato slices and spoon corn salad into center. Just before serving, poke in tortilla chips at edge. Serve with grilled chicken or turkey breast. Serves 4.

Approximate nutritional analysis per serving:
Calories 437, Protein 5 g, Carbohydrates 38 g, Fat 33 g,
Cholesterol 0 mg, Sodium 776 mg

SECKEL SALAD VERDE

4 tbs (60 ml) pine nuts
12 assorted leaves of salad greens (butter
    lettuce, endive, arugula, red leaf lettuce)
2 ripe Seckel pears
2 stalks broccoli, separated into florets
12 green beans
8 large fresh basil leaves
3 tbs (45 ml) olive oil
3 tbs (45 ml) balsamic vinegar
salt and pepper, to taste, optional

Toast pine nuts under broiler until barely tanned. Watch carefully, as they toast quickly. Set aside to cool. Steam the broccoli and beans until crisp tender. Toss vegetables with olive oil and vinegar and chill, an hour or overnight. Slice pears into 8 to 12 slices each, eliminating core. Do not peel. Arrange greens on two salad plates, followed by broccoli and beans. Arrange Seckel pear slices in fan, and add basil leaves. Divide pine nuts between two salads, and garnish each salad. Pour any remaining oil and vinegar sparingly on the salads. Serves 2.

Approximate nutritional analysis per serving:
Calories 476, Protein 17 g, Carbohydrates 35 g, Fat 36 g,
Cholesterol 0 mg, Sodium 66 mg

ENSALADA DE LENTEJAS
Lentil Salad

½ lb (230 g) GOYA Lentils
1 stalk celery
1 carrot
fresh thyme, optional
1 onion, peeled
1 clove garlic, peeled
1 bay leaf
1 whole clove
2 packets SAZÓN GOYA SIN ACHIOTE
salt and pepper to taste
White cheese to garnish

DRESSING:
½ cup (120 ml) GOYA Olive Oil
3 tbs (45 ml) GOYA Red Wine Vinegar
2 tbs (30 ml) red onion, minced
1 clove garlic, crushed
1 whole GOYA Pimiento, minced
1 tsp (5 ml) GOYA Adobo with Pepper

Combine all dressing ingredients in a mixing bowl. Set aside. Rinse and drain lentils (do not soak). In a medium saucepan or soup pot, cover lentils with water. Add celery, carrot, thyme, peeled onion, peeled garlic, bay leaf, clove, SAZÓN, salt and pepper. Bring to a boil; reduce heat and simmer, covered, about 30 minutes, or until lentils are tender but firm. Drain and transfer lentil mixture into a large bowl. Discard onion, garlic and bay leaf. Remove carrot and celery, slice, and mix back into lentils. Add dressing and mix thoroughly. Serve warm over lettuce, garnished with sliced pimiento and white cheese. Serves 6.

Approximate nutritional analysis per serving:
Calories 309, Protein 11 g, Carbohydrates 27 g, Fat 19 g,
Cholesterol 0 mg, Sodium 190 mg

Ensalada de Lentejas

CUCUMBER RIBBON SALAD

1 seedless cucumber
1 cup (240 ml) plain lowfat yogurt
1 cup (240 ml) golden raisins
¼ cup (60 ml) toasted slivered almonds
¼ cup (60 ml) thinly sliced green onions
1½ tbs (25 ml) chopped fresh mint leaves
    or 1 tsp (5 ml) dried mint
1 garlic clove, pressed
¼ tsp (1 ml) pepper
salt to taste

Using a vegetable peeler, cut cucumber lengthwise into paper-thin slices; place in bowl of ice water 30 minutes until curled. Meanwhile, prepare yogurt dressing. In medium bowl combine remaining ingredients except salt to blend thoroughly. Season with salt. Drain cucumber; pat dry. Place cucumber on 4 plates, dividing equally. Drizzle with dressing, dividing equally.

Note: Cucumber can be thinly sliced instead of cut into ribbons, if desired. Serves 4.

Approximate nutritional analysis per serving:
Calories 205, Protein 6 g, Carbohydrates 37 g, Fat 5 g,
Cholesterol 3 mg, Sodium 48 mg

Courtesy of The California Raisin Advisory Board.

ORANGE-HONEY-SPINACH SALAD

2 cups (480 ml) orange segments
1 cup (240 ml) cucumber, thinly sliced
10 cups (2.4 L) fresh spinach, torn
2 tbs (30 ml) fresh mint, chopped
1 - 8 oz ball (240 g) HEALTHY CHOICE
    Fat Free Natural Mozzarella Cheese, cubed.

ORANGE-HONEY DRESSING:
¼ cup (60 ml) orange juice
2 tbs (30 ml) water
1 tbs (15 ml) cider vinegar
1 tbs (15 ml) honey
2 tbs (30 ml) vegetable oil
dash of pepper

Combine dressing ingredients; mix well. Marinate oranges and cucumbers in dressing at least 30 minutes. Add spinach, mint and cheese; toss lightly. Serves 10.

Approximate nutritional information per serving:
Calories 117, Protein 11 g, Carbohydrates 10 g, Fat 4 g,
Cholesterol 5 mg, Sodium 238 mg.

PEAR WALDORF SALAD MOLD

2 fresh USA Pears
1 - 3 oz package (90 g) lemon flavor gelatin
½ tsp (3 ml) salt
1 cup (240 ml) boiling water
¾ cup (180 ml) cold water
½ cup (120 ml) red grapes, halved and seeded
¼ cup (60 ml) celery, chopped
¼ cup (60 ml) walnuts, chopped
Creamy Waldorf Dressing (below)
pear slices and grapes for garnish

CREAMY WALDORF DRESSING:
¾ cup (180 ml) mayonnaise
½ tsp (3 ml) lemon peel, grated
1 tbs (15 ml) sugar
¼ cup (60 ml) heavy cream, whipped
chopped walnuts for garnish

Core and dice pears, but do not peel. Dissolve lemon gelatin and salt in boiling water. Add cold water. Chill until partially set. Add pears, grapes, celery and walnuts. Pour into 4 - cup mold and chill until firm. Unmold and serve with Creamy Waldorf Dressing. Garnish with pear slices and grapes. Serves 6.

Creamy Waldorf Dressing: Combine mayonnaise, lemon peel and sugar. Fold in whipped cream. Serve, garnished with chopped nuts. Yields 1¼ cups.

Approximate nutritional analysis per serving:
Calories 83, Protein 1 g, Carbohydrates 14 g, Fat 3 g,
Cholesterol 0 mg, Sodium 190 mg

CRANBERRY BEAUTY SALAD

1 lb (455 g) fresh cranberries
2 cups (480 ml) IMPERIAL Granulated Sugar
2 cups (480 ml) Thompson seedless
    or other white grapes
1 cup (240 ml) chopped pecans
2 cups (480 ml) miniature marshmallows
1 cup (240 ml) heavy cream, whipped

Wash and drain cranberries. Grind cranberries coarsely in blender or food processor. Add IMPERIAL Granulated Sugar and refrigerate for 4 hours or overnight. Add grapes, pecans, marshmallows. Fold in whipped cream. Store in refrigerator until serving time. Serves 15.

Approximate nutritional analysis per serving:
Calories 248, Protein 1 g, Carbohydrates 39 g, Fat 11 g,
Cholesterol 22 mg, Sodium 9 mg

Heidelberg Potato Salad

HEIDELBERG POTATO SALAD

4 slices bacon
1 tbs (15 ml) flour
1 tbs (15 ml) sugar
½ tsp (3 ml) salt
½ tsp (3 ml) dry mustard
¼-½ tsp (1-3 ml) celery seed
½ cup (120 ml) water
¼ cup (60 ml) vinegar
6 hard-cooked eggs, sliced
3 medium potatoes, cooked, peeled and chopped
¼ cup (60 ml) chopped green onions with tops
celery leaves, optional

In 10-inch skillet over medium heat, cook bacon until crisp. Remove from pan, drain, crumble and set aside. Pour off all but 1 tbs bacon drippings. Blend in flour, sugar, salt, mustard and celery seed. Cook, stirring constantly, until mixture is smooth and bubbly. Combine water and vinegar. Stir into flour mixture all at once. Cook until mixture boils and is smooth and thickened.

Reserve 2 center egg slices for garnish. Chop remaining eggs. Add chopped eggs, potatoes, onions and reserved bacon to sauce. Gently stir to mix. Heat to serving temperature. Garnish with reserved egg slices and celery leaves, if desired. Serves 4.

Approximate nutritional analysis per serving:
Calories 258, Protein 13 g, Carbohydrates 27 g, Fat 11 g,
Cholesterol 323 mg, Sodium 468 mg

DOUBLE ARTICHOKE SALAD

8 cups (1.9 L) romaine leaves, torn
2 cups (480 ml) sweet red pepper strips
1 - 14 oz can (420 g) artichoke hearts, drained
2½ cups (590 ml) HEALTHY CHOICE Fat Free
Natural Fancy Shredded Cheddar Cheese

ARTICHOKE DRESSING:
1 - 14 oz can (420 g) artichoke hearts, drained
3 tbs (45 ml) olive oil
1 tbs (15 ml) tarragon vinegar
1 tbs (15 ml) chopped onion
2 tsp (10 ml) Dijon mustard
1 clove garlic, chopped
½ cup (120 ml) water
cracked black pepper

Cover serving platter with romaine. Arrange artichokes, red pepper and cheese shreds on romaine. For salad dressing, combine artichoke hearts, oil, vinegar, onion, mustard and garlic in food processor; process until smooth. Continue to process, gradually adding water. Season to taste with pepper. Chill. Serve over salad. Serves 8.

Approximate informational analysis per serving:
Calories 147, Protein 14 g, Carbohydrates 12 g, Fat 5 g,
Cholesterol 6 mg, Sodium 390 mg

CHOICE POTATO SALAD

3 medium potatoes
1 small onion, minced
1 tbs (15 ml) fresh parsley, minced
2 tbs (30 ml) celery, minced
1 tbs (15 ml) green pepper, minced
1 hard-cooked egg, chopped
1 clove garlic, minced
1 tsp (5 ml) Creole or regular mustard
¼ cup (60 ml) mayonnaise, regular or light
1 tbs (15 ml) cider or wine vinegar
1 tbs (15 ml) salad oil
1 tsp (5 ml) celery seed or caraway seed
1 tsp (5 ml) salt
1 tsp (5 ml) IMPERIAL Granulated Sugar
¼ tsp (1 ml) pepper

Boil potatoes in jackets until done in centers; peel, dice, place in mixing bowl. Add remaining ingredients and mix well. Serve while warm or chill first. If desired, decorate with extra sliced hard-cooked egg and parsley sprigs. Serves 4.

Approximate nutritional analysis per serving:
Calories 245, Protein 4 g, Carbohydrates 23 g, Fat 16 g,
Cholesterol 61 mg, Sodium 635 mg

LOW-CAL SUMMER SALAD

2 cucumbers
1 large tomato
1 small onion
2 tbs (30 ml) vinegar
1 tbs (15 ml) oil
1 tbs (15 ml) OLD BAY Seasoning

Slice cucumbers into very thin rounds. Chop tomato into small cubes. Slice onion and separate the circular pieces. Set all vegetables aside in bowl. Mix vinegar, oil and OLD BAY Seasoning and toss with salad. Cover and chill for 2 hours before serving. Serves 4.

Approximate nutritional analysis per serving:
Calories 75, Protein 2 g, Carbohydrates 10 g, Fat 4 g,
Cholesterol 0 mg, Sodium 8 mg

CHILLED POTATOES IN CREAMY HERB SAUCE

4 red new potatoes, unpeeled and scrubbed
1 cup (240 ml) frozen peas, thawed
½ cup (120 ml) green bell pepper, chopped
1½ cups (355 ml) DANNON Plain Nonfat
or Lowfat Yogurt
2 tbs (30 ml) fresh parsley, snipped
2 tbs (30 ml) green onion, sliced
1 tsp (5 ml) dried basil leaves, crushed
¼ tsp (1 ml) salt
dash white pepper

In a medium saucepan bring small amount of water to a boil. Add potatoes; cook, covered, 25 to 30 minutes or until tender. Drain and cool. Slice and place in a large bowl. Toss with peas and bell pepper. Add yogurt, parsley, green onion, basil, salt and white pepper. Toss gently to coat. Cover; chill until ready to serve. Serves 8.

Approximate nutritional analysis per serving:
Calories 104, Protein 5 g, Carbohydrates 20 g, Fat < 1 g,
Cholesterol 3 mg, Sodium 101 mg

Spanish Sweet Onion, Citrus and Tomato Vinaigrette Salad

SWEET AND SAUERKRAUT SALAD

¾ cup (180 ml) IMPERIAL Granulated Sugar
¾ tsp (4 ml) salt
½ cup (120 ml) cider vinegar
¼ cup (60 ml) vegetable oil
½ cup (120 ml) onion, chopped
½ cup (120 ml) green pepper, chopped
½ cup (120 ml) celery, chopped
1 - 4 oz jar (120 g) diced pimiento
1 cup (240 ml) unpeeled apple, diced
1 - 1 lb can (2 cups) (455 g) sauerkraut,
    rinsed, drained

Combine IMPERIAL Granulated Sugar, salt, vinegar, oil to make dressing. Combine remaining ingredients and toss well with dressing. Chill thoroughly and drain before serving. Dressing may be saved and used again. Serves 8.

Approximate nutritional analysis per serving:
Calories 163, Protein 1 g, Carbohydrates 26 g, Fat 7 g,
Cholesterol 0 mg, Sodium 584

SPANISH SWEET ONION, CITRUS AND TOMATO VINAIGRETTE SALAD

⅓ cup (80 ml) Balsamic vinegar
⅓ cup (80 ml) orange juice
2 tbs (30 ml) olive oil
½ tsp (3 ml) dried basil, crushed
⅛ tsp (.5 ml) salt
dash pepper
2 large Idaho-Oregon Spanish Sweet onions,
    peeled and thinly sliced
2 navel oranges or grapefruit, peeled and
    cut into ½-inch slices
2 large tomatoes, cut into ½-inch slices
6 lettuce leaves
Chives

Blend vinegar, orange juice, oil, basil, salt and pepper; mix well. Arrange 2 slices each of onion, orange and tomato on lettuce lined salad plates. Drizzle dressing over salads and garnish with chives. Serves 6.

Approximate nutritional analysis per serving:
Calories 141, Protein 3 g, Carbohydrates 24 g, Fat 5 g,
Cholesterol 0 mg, Sodium 56 mg

CALIFORNIA CELEBRATION SLAW

1 small head cabbage, chopped or shredded
1 medium apple, cored and diced
1 medium orange, peeled and cubed
1 medium carrot, pared and thinly sliced
1 small green pepper, chopped
½ cup (120 ml) golden raisins
½ cup (120 ml) natural raisins
2 to 4 tbs (30-60 ml) chopped nuts
1 cup (240 ml) mayonnaise*
½ cup (120 ml) bottled chili sauce
1 tbs (15 ml) lemon juice
salt to taste

* Plain yogurt may be substituted for half of the mayonnaise.

In large bowl, toss together cabbage, apple, orange, carrot, green pepper, raisins and nuts. Combine mayonnaise with chili sauce, lemon juice and salt. Pour dressing over slaw mixture; toss lightly to coat. Serves 6.

Approximate nutritional analysis per serving:
Calories 359, Protein 4 g, Carbohydrates 48 g, Fat 19 g,
Cholesterol 10 mg, Sodium 603 mg

CARROTS AND RAISINS REVISITED

2 cups (480 ml) DANNON Plain Nonfat or
    Lowfat Yogurt
1 tbs (15 ml) packed brown sugar
¼ tsp (1 ml) grated orange peel
2 tbs (30 ml) orange juice
¼ tsp (1 ml) cardamom or nutmeg
pinch salt
6-7 medium carrots, peeled and coarsely shredded
¼ cup (60 ml) raisins
3 tbs (45 ml) chopped cashews, almonds or pecans

Spoon yogurt into large strainer lined with double thickness of cheesecloth or a coffee filter. Place bowl beneath, but not touching strainer to catch liquid. Chill 1½ hours. Scrape yogurt into a medium bowl. Discard liquid. Add brown sugar, orange peel and juice, nutmeg and salt; stir until smooth. Add carrots and raisins; toss to coat. Cover; chill 20-30 minutes before serving. Just before serving, sprinkle with cashews. Serves 6.

Approximate nutritional analysis per serving:
Calories 103, Protein 5 g, Carbohydrates 14 g, Fat 4 g,
Cholesterol 5 mg, Sodium 58 mg

BEAN AND TOMATO SALAD

¼ cup (60 ml) olive oil
1½ tsp (8 ml) GILROY FARMS Minced Garlic
1 tsp (5 ml) Dijon mustard
1 tsp (5 ml) McCORMICK/SCHILLING
    Italian Seasoning
½ tsp (3 ml) McCORMICK/SCHILLING
    Ground Black Pepper
½ tsp (3 ml) salt
3 large tomatoes, each cut into eight wedges
1 small red onion, sliced
1 cup (240 ml) garbanzo beans (chick peas)

Combine first 6 ingredients in large bowl. Add remaining ingredients; toss to coat. Cover and refrigerate at least 1 hour to allow flavors to blend. Serve on a bed of lettuce. Serves 4.

Approximate nutritional analysis per serving:
Calories 235, Protein 6 g, Carbohydrates 24 g, Fat 14 g,
Cholesterol 0 mg, Sodium 301 mg

CHUNKY NEW POTATO SALAD WITH TOMATOES

2 medium FLORIDA tomatoes
2 lbs (910 g) small new potatoes,
    cut in 1½-inch pieces
1 cup (240 ml) unpeeled cucumber, thinly sliced
¾ cup (180 ml) chopped green bell pepper
¾ cup (180 ml) thinly sliced celery
⅓ cup (80 ml) sliced scallions (green onions)
⅓ cup (80 ml) mayonnaise
⅓ cup (80 ml) dairy sour cream
1¼ tsp (6 ml) tarragon leaves, crushed
¾ tsp (4 ml) salt
½ tsp (3 ml) ground black pepper

In a medium saucepan bring potatoes and enough water to cover to a boil; reduce heat and simmer, covered, until potatoes are tender, 10-12 minutes, drain. In a large bowl place potatoes, cucumber, green pepper, celery and scallions. Make dressing by combining mayonnaise, sour cream, tarragon, salt and black pepper. Cut each tomato into 8 wedges; cut wedges in halves (makes about 2 cups). Just before serving gently stir in tomatoes. Line a salad bowl with tomatoes or lettuce as garnish. Serves 6.

Approximate nutritional analysis per serving:
Calories 258, Protein 4 g, Carbohydrates 33 g, Fat 13 g,
Cholesterol 13 mg, Sodium 382 mg

BLACK BEAN AND CORN SALAD

1 - 15 oz can (450 g) black beans, drained
1 - 11 oz can (330 g) whole kernel corn, drained
½ cup (120 ml) green bell pepper, cubed 1 inch
½ cup (120 ml) red bell pepper, cubed 1 inch
½ cup (120 ml) red onion, cut into ⅛-inch slices,
    then cut in half
¼ cup (60 ml) CHI-CHI'S Green Jalapeño Wheels

DRESSING:
¼ cup (60 ml) vegetable oil
2 tbs (30 ml) red wine vinegar
½ tsp (3 ml) salt
¼ tsp (1 ml) ground cumin
¼ tsp (1 ml) coarsely ground pepper

In large bowl, combine all Salad ingredients. Mix well; set aside. In small bowl, combine all Dressing ingredients. Mix well. Toss with Salad. Refrigerate 1 hour to blend flavors. Serves 6.

Approximate nutritional analysis per serving:
Calories 180, Protein 5 g, Carbohydrates 20 g, Fat 10 g,
Cholesterol 0 mg, Sodium 290 mg

WESTERN BEAN SALAD

SALAD:
1 - 15 oz can (450 g) CHI-CHI'S
    Ranchero Beans, drained
1 - 15 oz can (450 g) garbanzo beans, drained
2 cups (480 ml) cherry tomato halves
1 cup (240 ml) CHI-CHI'S Salsa
½ lb (230 g) bacon, cooked and crumbled
1 small red onion, sliced ⅛ inch
lettuce leaves

DRESSING:
¼ cup (60 ml) vegetable oil
2 tbs (30 ml) white wine vinegar
1 tsp (5 ml) sugar
¾ tsp (4 ml) chili powder
¼ tsp (1 ml) coarsely ground pepper
¼ tsp (1 ml) salt

In large bowl, combine all Salad ingredients except lettuce leaves. Mix well; set aside. In small bowl, combine all Dressing ingredients. Mix well. Toss with Salad. Cover; refrigerate 1 hour to blend flavors. Serve on lettuce leaves. Serves 8.

Approximate nutritional analysis per serving:
Calories 240, Protein 9 g, Carbohydrates 20 g, Fat 15 g,
Cholesterol 15 mg, Sodium 610 mg

ROASTED PEPPER SALAD

1 green pepper, halved and seeded
1 red pepper, halved and seeded
1 yellow pepper, halved and seeded
8 oz (240 g) mozzarella cheese, ½-inch cubed
1 cup (240 ml) CHI-CHI'S Picante Sauce
¼ cup (60 ml) olive oil
2 tbs (30 ml) balsamic vinegar
½ tsp (3 ml) salt
¼ tsp (1 ml) coarsely ground pepper

Heat broiler. Place pepper halves cut-side-down, on broiler pan. Broil 6-7 inches from heat source 10-12 minutes or until uniformly blistered and charred. Cool; remove skins. cut peppers into ⅛-inch strips. In medium bowl, combine pepper strips and remaining ingredients. Mix well. Refrigerate 1 hour to blend flavors. Serves 4.

Approximate nutritional analysis per serving:
Calories 310, Protein 17 g, Carbohydrates 9 g, Fat 23 g,
Cholesterol 30 mg, Sodium 950 mg

MOROCCAN VEGETABLE SALAD

½ lb (230 g) small whole mushrooms
1½ cups (355 ml) cooked garbanzo beans (chick peas)
1 cup (240 ml) pitted large black olives
12 cherry tomatoes, halved
¾ cup (180 ml) coarsely chopped green onions
2 green bell peppers, chopped
2 red bell peppers, chopped
1 cup (240 ml) DANNON Plain Nonfat or
    Lowfat Yogurt
½ cup (120 ml) reduced-calorie mayonnaise
2 garlic cloves, crushed
2 tbs (30 ml) olive oil
1 tbs (15 ml) lemon juice
1 tsp (5 ml) ground cumin
⅛ tsp (.5 ml) ground turmeric
salt and pepper
lettuce leaves

Steam mushrooms over boiling water 5 minutes; cool. In a large bowl, combine mushrooms, garbanzo beans, olives, tomatoes, green onions and bell peppers. Cover; chill 2 hours. In a small bowl combine yogurt, mayonnaise, garlic, olive oil, lemon juice, cumin and turmeric. Season with salt and pepper. Cover; chill 2 hours. Just before serving, lightly toss mushroom mixture with some of dressing. Serve on lettuce leaves. Serve with remaining ingredients. Serves 10.

Approximate nutritional analysis per serving:
Calories 134, Protein 5 g, Carbohydrates 15 g, Fat 7 g,
Cholesterol 7 mg, Sodium 184 mg

Opposite: Moroccan Vegetable Salad

SUNSET SALAD

1 lb (455 g) green beans
2-3 medium carrots, julienned
4 eggs
1 bunch fresh spinach
1 head red lettuce
1 cup (240 ml) whole pitted CALIFORNIA ripe olives
½ lb (230 g) Monterey Jack cheese, cut into strips

TAHINI SALAD DRESSING:
¾ cup (180 ml) tahini
1½ cups (355 ml) plain yogurt
1 tbs (15 ml) bottled or freshly minced garlic
½ cup (120 ml) fresh lemon juice
¼ cup (60 ml) olive oil
¼ cup (60 ml) minced green onion
few dashes Tabasco

Steam green beans and carrots; chill. Hard-cook eggs; chill and slice. Tear up fresh spinach and lettuce and line one large platter or 4 individual plates with greens. Arrange other ingredients on top. Serve with Tahini Salad Dressing. Serves 4.

Tahini Salad Dressing: Combine all ingredients in mixing bowl. Beat or whisk until nice and thick. Yields 2½ cups.

Approximate nutritional analysis per serving salad:
Calories 419, Protein 26 g, Carbohydrates 21 g, Fat 27 g,
Cholesterol 263 mg, Sodium 833 mg

Approximate nutritional analysis per ¼ cup serving dressing:
Calories 184, Protein 5 g, Carbohydrates 7 g, Fat 17 g,
Cholesterol 4 mg, Sodium 16 mg

FRESH BASIL AND PEPPER POTATO SALAD

3 medium potatoes
1 cup (240 ml) DANNON Plain Nonfat or
    Lowfat Yogurt
2 tbs (30 ml) snipped fresh parsley
    or ½ tsp (3 ml) dried parsley flakes
1 tbs (15 ml) snipped fresh basil
    or 1 tsp (5 ml) dried basil, crushed
1 tbs (15 ml) sliced green onion
½ tsp (3 ml) salt
several dashes pepper
½ cup (120 ml) frozen peas, thawed
½ cup (120 ml) chopped red or
    green bell pepper

In a large saucepan bring water to a boil; add potatoes. Cover and cook 25-30 minutes or until tender; drain. Cool. If desired, peel potatoes. Cut potatoes into cubes. In a large bowl combine yogurt, parsley, basil, green onion, salt and pepper. Add potatoes, peas and bell pepper; stir lightly to coat. Cover; chill several hours before serving. Serves 5.

Approximate nutritional analysis per serving:
Calories 124, Protein 5 g, Carbohydrates 25 g, Fat < 1 g,
Cholesterol 3 mg, Sodium 251 mg

SMUCKER'S THREE-BEAN SALAD WITH SWEET AND SOUR APRICOT DRESSING

½ cup (120 ml) SMUCKER'S Apricot Preserves
¼ cup (60 ml) red wine vinegar
1 tsp (5 ml) celery seeds
1 - 16 oz can (480 g) kidney beans, drained and rinsed
1 small red onion, thinly sliced
1 cup (240 ml) cooked green beans,
    fresh or frozen, cut into 2-inch pieces
¼ lb (1 cup) (115 g) cooked yellow wax beans,
fresh or frozen, cut into 2-inch pieces
salt and pepper to taste

Combine SMUCKER'S Apricot Preserves, vinegar and celery seeds in a salad bowl. Add sliced onion, kidney beans, green and yellow beans. Toss well to combine. Adjust seasonings with salt and fresh ground pepper to taste. Serves 6.

Approximate nutritional analysis per serving:
Calories 161, Protein 4 g, Carbohydrates 59 g, Fat 2 g,
Cholesterol 0 mg, Sodium 213 mg

RED SALAD

1½ lbs (685 g) Italian plum tomatoes, quartered
½ cup (120 ml) fresh herb leaves (basil,
    Italian parsley, summer savory, thyme)
salt and pepper to taste
6 cups (1.4 L) radicchio leaves, torn
2 tbs (30 ml) chopped shallots
¼ cup (60 ml) sherry wine vinegar
¼ cup (60 ml) chicken broth
1 tsp (5 ml) Dijon mustard
1 tsp (5 ml) sugar, optional
2 tsp (10 ml) good green olive oil
1 tbs (15 ml) orange juice

In a large bowl, toss tomatoes, herbs and radicchio leaves. In a small bowl, whisk together remaining ingredients, then toss on salad. Serves 6.

Approximate nutritional analysis per serving:
Calories 56, Protein 2 g, Carbohydrates 9 g, Fat 2 g,
Cholesterol 0 mg, Sodium 74 mg

Courtesy of Empire Kosher Poultry Test Kitchens.

Opposite: Smucker's Three Bean Salad with Sweet and Sour Apricot Dressing

WARM PORK AND SPINACH SALAD

1 lb (455 g) boneless pork loin,
    cut into thin strips (2x ¼ inch)
1 lb (455 g) fresh spinach leaves, coarsely shredded
3 cups (720 ml) watercress sprigs
1 cup (240 ml) thinly sliced celery
1 cup (240 ml) seedless green grapes
½ cup (120 ml) thinly sliced green onion
1 - 8 oz can (240 g) sliced water chestnuts, drained
1 large Golden Delicious apple, cored and chopped
1 cup (240 ml) low-calorie Italian salad dressing
2 tbs (30 ml) dry white wine
2 tbs (30 ml) Dijon mustard
3 tbs (45 ml) light brown sugar
2 tbs (30 ml) toasted sesame seeds

Spray non-stick skillet with vegetable cooking spray; stir-fry pork strips until cooked through, about 4 minutes. Set aside; keep warm. In large serving bowl, toss spinach, watercress, celery, grapes, green onion, water chestnuts and apples; toss to mix. In small saucepan, combine salad dressing, white wine, mustard and brown sugar; heat just until brown sugar is dissolved, stirring constantly. Stir cooked pork into hot dressing to coat well. Remove pork; pour ½ of dressing over greens mixture in bowl; toss well. Place pork strips on top of salad. Sprinkle with sesame seeds. Pass remaining dressing. Serves 6.

Approximate nutritional analysis per serving:
Calories 275, Protein 22 g, Carbohydrates 20 g, Fat 7 g,
Cholesterol 46 mg, Sodium 602 mg

BEANS AND CASHEW SALAD

1 bag spinach
1 cup (240 ml) broccoli
½ cup (120 ml) Navy or Pinto Beans, cooked
¼ cup (60 ml) toasted cashew bits
½ cup (120 ml) no-oil Italian dressing*

* Purchase in packaged (mix with water) or bottled varieties. It cuts the "fat", but leaves the flavor.

Steam broccoli until tender, or cook covered in microwave for 2 minutes, and combine with beans in dressing. Chill. Wash and dry spinach, discard stems, and tear leaves into bite size pieces. Add spinach and cashews to vegetable and bean mixture. Toss prior to serving. Serves 2.

Approximate nutritional analysis per serving:
Calories 212, Protein 13 g, Carbohydrates 26 g, Fat 9 g,
Cholesterol 0 mg, Sodium 416 mg

Courtesy of the American Dry Bean Board.

THAI HOT AND COLD SALAD

1 cup (240 ml) chunk beef-style textured
    vegetable protein
1 tbs (15 ml) catsup
2 tbs (30 ml) low-sodium soy sauce
2 tbs (30 ml) mirin (sweet cooking rice wine)
2 garlic cloves, minced
¼ (1 ml) red pepper flakes
¼ tsp (1 ml) hot red pepper sauce
1 tbs (15 ml) lemon juice
4 cups (960 ml) Chinese cabbage, shredded
1 ½ cups (355 ml) thinly sliced carrots
1 cup (240 ml) thinly sliced green onions
1 tbs (15 ml) soy oil

Combine 1 cup dry beef-style vegetable protein, with 1 cup hot water and the catsup. Let stand 5 minutes. Meanwhile, combine soy sauce, mirin, garlic, red pepper flakes, hot pepper sauce and lemon juice and set aside. Slice carrots, green onion and shred Chinese cabbage and chill. Combine soy protein mixture with the soy sauce mixture in a microwaveable dish. Cover with plastic wrap and microwave on MEDIUM-HIGH for 8 minutes until chunks are tender. Drain off any liquid. Heat soy oil in a large non-stick skillet and lightly brown soy protein about 3 minutes. Remove from heat and toss with carrots and onions and place on platter of Chinese cabbage. Serves 4.

Approximate nutritional analysis per serving:
Calories 137, Protein 13 g, Carbohydrates 16 g, Fat 4 g,
Cholesterol 0 mg, Sodium 279 mg

Courtesy of the United Soybean Board.

ROMAN BEANS WITH HEART

1 can GOYA Roman Beans, drained and rinsed
1 - 6 oz jar (180 g) GOYA Artichoke Hearts
1 cup (240 ml) celery, sliced
½ cup (120 ml) red onion rings, sliced thin
½ cup (120 ml) GOYA Vegetable Oil
¼ cup (60 ml) GOYA Red Wine Vinegar
½ tsp (3 ml) granulated sugar
¼ tsp (1 ml) dry mustard
¼ tsp (1 ml) black pepper

Combine beans, artichoke hearts, celery and onion; mix well. Blend oil, vinegar, sugar, mustard and pepper. Pour over bean mixture and toss until all ingredients are coated. Cover and chill before serving. Serves 3.

Approximate nutritional analysis per serving:
Calories 537, Protein 11 g, Carbohydrates 38 g, Fat 40 g,
Cholesterol 0 mg, Sodium 238 mg

Opposite: Warm Pork and Spinach Salad

FOUR-VEGETABLE DILL SALAD

Dressing (below)
1 cup (4 oz) (120 g) shredded part-skim
    mozzarella cheese
1 cup (240 ml) ½-inch broccoli flowerets
½ cup (120 ml) ½-inch cauliflower pieces
½ cup (120 ml) thinly sliced carrots
¼ cup (60 ml) coarsely chopped red bell pepper

DRESSING:
1 cup (240 ml) YOPLAIT Fat Free Plain Yogurt
3 tbs (45 ml) lowfat sour cream
1 tbs (15 ml) finely chopped onion
½ tsp (3 ml) seasoned salt
¼ tsp (1 ml) dried dill weed

Mix all dressing ingredients. Add remaining ingredients. Cover and refrigerate about 2 hours or until chilled. Serves 5.

Approximate nutritional analysis per serving:
Calories 110, Protein 9 g, Carbohydrates 9 g, Fat 4 g,
Cholesterol 20 mg, Sodium 320 mg

PEAR AND POTATO SALAD

1 cup (240 ml) BLUE DIAMOND
    Blanched Slivered Almonds
1 tbs (15 ml) olive oil
½ cup (120 ml) mayonnaise
2 cloves garlic, chopped finely
¼ tsp (1 ml) grated, fresh ginger
    or **⅛ tsp (.5 ml) powdered ginger**
½ tsp (3 ml) salt
¼ tsp (1 ml) pepper
½ cup (120 ml) chopped, fresh parsley
½ lb (230 g) new potatoes, peeled and diced
1 lb (455 g) slightly firm pears, peeled, cored,
    diced and tossed with:
1 tbs (15 ml) lemon juice
1 medium red bell pepper, diced
½ cup (120 ml) thinly sliced green onion,
    including part of green

Sauté almonds in oil until golden; reserve. Combine mayonnaise, garlic, ginger, salt and pepper. Fold in parsley; reserve. Cook potatoes in salted, boiling water until just tender. Take care not to overcook. Drain, and while still warm, combine with dressing. Cool to room temperature. Fold in pears, red bell pepper and green onion. Chill. Just before serving, fold in almonds. Serves 6.

Approximate nutritional analysis per serving:
Calories 264, Protein 6 g, Carbohydrates 27 g, Fat 17 g,
Cholesterol 10 mg, Sodium 209 mg

TRIBECA GRILL'S SUMMER BEAN SALAD

2 cups (480 ml) Great Northern or Navy Beans
2 cups (480 ml) dry Black Beans
2 cups (480 ml) dry Red Kidney Beans
2 cups (480 ml) dry Pinto Beans
1 large red onion, diced
2 red bell peppers, diced
1 bunch cilantro, cleaned and chopped
1 pt (480 ml) olive oil
¼ cup (60 ml) balsamic vinegar
¼ cup (60 ml) fresh lime juice
fresh black pepper, salt, cayenne pepper

Soak each variety of beans separately overnight. Drain and rinse the beans. Put each variety of beans in separate pots and cover by at least 2 inches of water. Cook each variety separately for 10-15 minutes until soft, drain, then let cool.

    Mix all the beans together, except the black beans. Add the black beans just before serving, otherwise they may bleed and make all others black. Add onions and peppers, olive oil, balsamic vinegar and lime juice. Season with pepper, salt and cayenne pepper to taste. Add the chopped cilantro and the black beans right before serving. Toss and enjoy. Serves 10.

Approximate nutritional analysis per serving:
Calories 718, Protein 20 g, Carbohydrates 64 g, Fat 44 g,
Cholesterol 0 mg, Sodium 11 mg

SUMMER TOMATO SALAD

1 large onion, thinly sliced
½ cup (120 ml) distilled white vinegar
½ cup (120 ml) olive oil
1 tbs (15 ml) CHEF PAUL PRUDHOMME'S `
    Vegetable Magic
6 medium vine-ripened tomatoes, thickly sliced
2 avocados, peeled and sliced
6 oz (180 g) grated provolone cheese

Place the onions in a small mixing bowl. In a small saucepan, bring the vinegar just to a boil. As soon as it reaches a boil, pour it over the onions. Let it sit until it cools. When cool, drain the vinegar from the onions into a food processor or blender. With the machine running, add the olive oil in a slow, steady stream, until all of the oil has been added and the mixture is pale and creamy. Add the Vegetable Magic and process a few seconds more.

    Place the tomato slices on each serving plate. Arrange the onions on top of the tomatoes and avocados and sprinkle the cheese over the onions. Drizzle 2 tbs of the vinaigrette on each just before serving. Serves 6.

Approximate nutritional analysis per serving:
Calories 310, Protein 9 g, Carbohydrates 13 g, Fat 26 g,
Cholesterol 20 mg, Sodium 354 mg

Opposite: Summer Tomato Salad

LAYERED FOUR BEAN SALAD

¼ cup (60 ml) sugar
¼ cup (60 ml) red wine vinegar
¼ cup (60 ml) salad oil
2 tbs (30 ml) fresh parsley, chopped
½ tsp (3 ml) dry mustard
2 tsp (10 ml) fresh basil *or* ¾ tsp (4 ml) dried basil
½ tsp (3 ml) oregano
salt and freshly ground pepper to taste
Romaine lettuce leaves
1 - 16 oz can (480 g) Black Beans, drained, rinsed and chilled
1 - 16 oz can (480 g) Great Northern, or Navy Beans, drained, rinsed and chilled
1 - 16 oz can (480 g) Pinto Beans, drained, rinsed and chilled
1 - 16 oz can (480 g) Lima Beans, drained, rinsed and chilled
1 medium red onion, sliced and separated into rings

In a small bowl, mix sugar, vinegar, oil, parsley, mustard, basil, oregano, salt and pepper; set aside.

Line a large glass bowl with Romaine lettuce leaves. Layer the Black Beans in the bowl and drizzle with about a quarter of the oil-vinegar dressing. Add the Navy Beans and drizzle with more dressing. Continue with the other beans until you have four layers. Garnish top with red onion rings, then chill thoroughly. Serves 12.

Approximate nutritional analysis per serving:
Calories 223, Protein 10 g, Carbohydrates 36 g, Fat 5 g, Cholesterol 0 mg, Sodium 9 mg

Courtesy of the American Dry Bean Board.

BACKYARD WAGON TRAIN BEAN SALAD

1 - 16 oz can (480 g) Dark Red Kidney Beans, drained, or any canned bean
1 cup (240 ml) cooked wagon-wheel pasta, or small elbow macaroni, drained
1 cup (240 ml) whole-kernel corn, drained
¼ cup (60 ml) fresh parsley, chopped
⅓ cup (80 ml) olive oil
¼ cup (60 ml) vinegar
2 tbs (30 ml) Dijon mustard
2 garlic cloves, minced
1 tsp (5 ml) ground cumin
1 tsp (5 ml) chili powder
1 tsp (5 ml) cayenne pepper, optional

Mix beans, pasta, corn and parsley in a medium bowl. In a smaller bowl, blend oil, vinegar, mustard, garlic, cumin, chili powder and cayenne pepper. Toss together with bean and pasta mixture. Serve at room temperature. Serves 6.

Approximate nutritional analysis per serving:
Calories 242, Protein 7 g, Carbohydrates 27 g, Fat 13 g, Cholesterol 0 mg, Sodium 156 mg

Courtesy of the American Dry Bean Board.

OLD FASHIONED BEAN SLAW

1 can GOYA Pink Beans, drained and rinsed
1 cup (240 ml) celery, chopped
1 cup (240 ml) radishes, sliced
1 cup (240 ml) cucumber, sliced
2 cups (480 ml) red cabbage, shredded
¼ cup (60 ml) onion, minced
½ cup (120 ml) GOYA Vegetable Oil
¼ cup (60 ml) GOYA Wine Vinegar
¼ tsp (1 ml) dry mustard
½ tsp (3 ml) granulated sugar
1 tsp (5 ml) salt
⅛ tsp (.5 ml) black pepper
½ cup (120 ml) mayonnaise
1 clove garlic, crushed

In a very large bowl, combine beans, celery, radishes, cucumber, cabbage and onions. Mix remaining ingredients and blend until smooth. Pour over salad ingredients and toss. Cover and chill well before serving. Serves 6.

Approximate nutritional analysis per serving:
Calories 335, Protein 6 g, Carbohydrates 24 g, Fat 25 g, Cholesterol 5 mg, Sodium 521 mg

TOMATO-BASIL PLATTER

3-4 large ripe tomatoes
4 tbs (60 ml) POMPEIAN Extra Virgin Olive Oil
1 tsp (5 ml) freshly ground pepper
12-14 large, fresh basil leaves
1 tbs (15 ml) POMPEIAN Red Wine Vinegar
sea salt or kosher salt to taste

Place slices of tomato alternately with basil leaves on a large platter. Whisk together the olive oil and red wine vinegar and pour over the tomatoes. Top fresh ground pepper and salt to taste. Cover lightly with plastic wrap and allow to stand at room temperature about 30 minutes before serving. Serves 6-8.

Approximate nutritional analysis per serving:
Calories 105, Protein 1 g, Carbohydrates 6 g, Fat 9 g, Cholesterol 0 mg, Sodium 11 mg

Opposite: Tomato-Basil Platter

GARDEN COUSCOUS SALAD

1 cup (240 ml) couscous
1⅔ cups (400 ml) boiling water
1 tbs plus ⅓ cup (95 ml) olive oil
¾ cup (180 ml) whole pitted CALIFORNIA ripe olives
½ cup (120 ml) snow peas, diagonally halved
½ cup (120 ml) red bell pepper strips
½ cup (120 ml) zucchini, thinly sliced
¼ cup (60 ml) carrots, sliced
2 tbs (30 ml) parsley, minced
1½ tsp (8 ml) grated orange peel
¼ cup (60 ml) orange juice
¼ cup (60 ml) rice wine vinegar
½ tsp (3 ml) ginger root, grated
½ tsp (3 ml) garlic, minced
⅛ tsp (.5 ml) bottled red pepper flakes

For salad, stir couscous into boiling water in saucepan. Add 1 tbs olive oil, cover and remove from heat. Let stand 5 minutes. Uncover and let cool while preparing other ingredients. Combine couscous with olives and vegetables in salad bowl. Serves 4.

For dressing combine orange peel and juice, vinegar, ginger, garlic, red pepper and remaining ⅓ cup olive oil in jar. Add ¼ tsp salt if desired. Pour dressing over couscous salad and toss to mix.

Approximate nutritional analysis per serving:
Calories 375, Protein 6 g, Carbohydrates 35 g, Fat 26 g, Cholesterol 0 mg, Sodium 323 mg

ONE-BEAN SALAD

2 cans GOYA White Kidney Beans,
    drained and rinsed
1 green pepper, diced
1 red onion, sliced
¼ cup (60 ml) parsley, chopped
⅓ cup (80 ml) GOYA Wine Vinegar
¾ cup (180 ml) GOYA Extra Virgin Olive Oil
½ tsp (3 ml) black pepper
1 clove garlic, crushed
1 tbs (15 ml) chives, chopped

Combine beans, green pepper, onion, and parsley. Blend together remaining ingredients, and pour over bean mixture. Mix thoroughly, cover and chill well. Serves 5.

Approximate nutritional analysis per serving:
Calories 487, Protein 13 g, Carbohydrates 38 g, Fat 33 g, Cholesterol 0 mg, Sodium 564 mg

ANTIPASTO IN A BOWL

1 can GOYA Chick Peas, drained and rinsed
½ cup (120 ml) salami, diced
½ cup (120 ml) celery, chopped
½ cup (120 ml) GOYA Black Olives, chopped
½ green pepper, cut into strips
2 pimientos, chopped
½ tsp (3 ml) salt
½ tsp (3 ml) black pepper
¼ tsp (1 ml) chili powder
2 tbs (30 ml) GOYA Extra Virgin Olive Oil
1 tbs (15 ml) GOYA Red Wine Vinegar

Combine all ingredients in large bowl. Toss well, cover and chill before serving. Serves 4.

Approximate nutritional analysis per serving:
Calories 279, Protein 11 g, Carbohydrates 24 g, Fat 16 g, Cholesterol 22 mg, Sodium 819 mg

BEAUTIFUL FOUR-BEAN SALAD

1 can GOYA Red Kidney Beans, drained and rinsed
1 can GOYA White Kidney Beans, drained and rinsed
1 can GOYA Chick Peas, drained and rinsed
1 can GOYA Black Beans, drained and rinsed
1 cup (240 ml) chopped scallions
2 cloves garlic, crushed
1 tsp (5 ml) dry mustard
3 tbs (45 ml) GOYA Wine Vinegar
¼ cup (60 ml) GOYA Extra Virgin Olive Oil
2 tbs (30 ml) fresh dill, chopped
sliced red onion rings, garnish

In a very large mixing bowl, combine beans with all remaining ingredients. Toss gently until all ingredients are well coated. Cover and chill. Serves 10.

Approximate nutritional analysis per serving:
Calories 235, Protein 12 g, Carbohydrates 35 g, Fat 6 g, Cholesterol 0 mg, Sodium 439 mg

Opposite: Garden Couscous Salad

Southwestern Rice Salad

SOUTHWESTERN RICE SALAD

2½ cups (590 ml) cooked long grain rice
Dressing (below)
¾ cup (180 ml) CALIFORNIA ripe olives, sliced
½ cup (120 ml) corn kernels, cooked
½ cup (120 ml) red bell pepper, diced
½ cup (120 ml) tomatoes, seeded and diced
¼ cup (60 ml) green onions, sliced
1 small avocado, peeled and cubed
2 tbs (30 ml) fresh cilantro, finely chopped
2 tsp (10 ml) jalapeño peppers, finely diced

DRESSING:
⅓ cup (80 ml) olive oil
⅓ cup (80 ml) sour cream
1 tbs (15 ml) lime juice
½ tsp (3 ml) ground cumin
½ tsp (3 ml) salt
¼ tsp (1 ml) sugar
a few dashes cayenne

Combine rice with Dressing in bowl. Add all remaining
ingredients and toss gently to mix. Add salt and pepper
to taste. Serves 4.

Dressing: Mix all ingredients. Stir or shake well just before
serving.

Approximate nutritional analysis per serving:
Calories 532, Protein 7 g, Carbohydrates 51 g, Fat 35 g,
Cholesterol 8 mg, Sodium 742 mg

RED BEANS IN A SUNSET

1 can GOYA Small Red Beans, drained
1 can mandarin oranges, drained
1 red onion, sliced thin
¼ cup (60 ml) GOYA Vegetable Oil
1½ tbs (25 ml) GOYA Wine Vinegar
¼ tsp (1 ml) granulated sugar
¼ tsp (1 ml) dry mustard

Combine beans, oranges and onion. Blend together oil, vinegar, sugar and mustard. Pour over bean mixture, coating all ingredients. Cover and chill well. Serves 3.

Approximate nutritional analysis per serving:
Calories 369, Protein 10 g, Carbohydrates 42 g, Fat 19 g, Cholesterol 0 mg, Sodium 588 mg

CHICK PEAS PIQUANT

1 can GOYA Chick Peas, drained and rinsed
1 red pepper, diced
2 scallions, chopped
2 tbs (30 ml) lemon juice
2 tbs (30 ml) GOYA Red Wine Vinegar
½ cup (120 ml) GOYA Extra Virgin Olive Oil
1 clove garlic, minced
1 tsp (5 ml) oregano
¼ tsp (1 ml) salt

Combine all ingredients. Mix well. Cover and chill. Serves 2.

Approximate nutritional analysis per serving:
Calories 669, Protein 10 g, Carbohydrates 39 g, Fat 55 g, Cholesterol 0 mg, Sodium 673 mg

THREE-BEAN SALAD

1 can GOYA Pink Beans, drained and rinsed
1 can GOYA White Beans, drained and rinsed
1 can GOYA Cut Green Beans
1 red onion, sliced thin
⅔ cup Italian-style salad dressing

Combine all ingredients. Toss well and chill. Serves 8.

Approximate nutritional analysis per serving:
Calories 217, Protein 8 g, Carbohydrates 26 g, Fat 10 g, Cholesterol 0 mg, Sodium 674 mg

ROASTY TOASTY SPINACH & CHICK PEA SALAD

2 lbs (910 g) cleaned fresh spinach
2 small red onions, sliced thin
8 oz (240 g) mushrooms, cleaned and sliced
8 oz (240 g) cooked bacon, crumbled
¼ cup (60 ml) whole walnuts
4 oz (120 g) feta cheese, crumbled
1 - 16 oz can (480 g) GOYA Chick Peas,
    drained and rinsed
2 hard boiled eggs, chopped

WALNUT DRESSING:
3 cloves garlic, minced
¼ cup (60 ml) cider vinegar
2 tbs (30 ml) wine mustard
1 cup (240 ml) GOYA Olive Oil
1 tsp (5 ml) GOYA Adobo
¾ cup (180 ml) crushed walnuts

In large salad bowl, toss all salad ingredients together. In small bowl, combine dressing ingredients and stir vigorously. Pour dressing over salad, toss and serve. Serves 8.

Approximate nutritional analysis per serving salad:
Calories 294, Protein 17 g, Carbohydrates 18 g, Fat 18 g, Cholesterol 77 mg, Sodium 660 mg

Approximate nutritional analysis per ¼ cup serving dressing:
Calories 316, Protein 2 g, Carbohydrates 3 g, Fat 34 g, Cholesterol 0 mg, Sodium 117 mg

GREEN BEANS AND TOMATOES ITALIAN

¾ lb (340 g) green beans
½ cup (120 ml) red onion rings
¼ cup (60 ml) KRAFT FREE Italian Fat Free Dressing
    or KRAFT Italian Reduced Calorie Dressing
2 plum tomatoes, cut into thin wedges
2 tbs (30 ml) chopped fresh basil

Place green beans, onion and dressing in microwaveable bowl; cover. Microwave on HIGH 8-10 minutes or until beans are tender-crisp, stirring after 2 minutes. Stir in tomatoes and basil. Serves 6.

Top of stove: Cook green beans, onion and dressing in covered saucepan on medium heat 8-10 minutes or until beans are tender-crisp, stirring occasionally. Stir in tomatoes and basil.

Approximate nutritional analysis per serving:
Calories 37, Protein 1 g, Carbohydrates 6 g, Fat 1 g, Cholesterol < 1 mg, Sodium 84 mg

BROWN RICE CURRY SALAD

1 cup (240 ml) brown rice*
¼ cup (60 ml) onion, chopped
1½ tsp (8 ml) curry powder
1 tbs (15 ml) vegetable oil
1 - 14 oz can (420 ml) chicken broth
½ cup (120 ml) water
Chutney Dressing (below)
1 cup (240 ml) CALIFORNIA seedless grapes
½ cup (120 ml) green peppers, diced
2 tbs (30 ml) green onion, minced
pepper to taste

CHUTNEY DRESSING:
½ cup (120 ml) CALIFORNIA seedless grapes
½ cup (120 ml) mango chutney, regular or spicy
2 tbs (30 ml) berry vinegar
1 tbs (115 ml) vegetable oil

* Quick-cooking brown rice may be substituted. Adjust liquid per package directions.

Sauté rice, onion and curry in oil until onions are tender. Stir in broth; bring to boil. Reduce heat and simmer, covered, 25-30 minutes or until rice is tender and liquid is absorbed. Add ¼ cup Chutney Dressing and cool mixture. Add grapes, peppers, onion and additional Chutney Dressing to taste; mix well. Serves 4.

 Chutney Dressing: Puree grapes and mango chutney in blender or food processor until smooth. Add berry vinegar and oil; mix well. Yields ¾ cup.

Approximate nutritional analysis per serving:
Calories 259, Protein 7 g, Carbohydrates 46 g, Fat 6 g,
Cholesterol 0 mg, Sodium 321 mg

SPINACH & BAC'N SALAD

¼ cup (60 ml) vegetable oil
3 tbs (45 ml) cider vinegar
2 tbs (30 ml) BAC'N Chips
1 tbs (15 ml) sugar
1 tsp (5 ml) poppy seed
¼ tsp (1 ml) dry mustard
1 bag fresh spinach
½ cup (120 ml) sliced mushrooms
½ cup (120 ml) sliced red onion

In a shaker combine first 6 ingredients. Shake well. Serve over spinach, mushrooms and onion. Serves 2-3.

Approximate nutritional analysis per serving:
Calories 334, Protein 6 g, Carbohydrates 18 g, Fat 29 g,
Cholesterol 1 mg, Sodium 162 mg

GREENS WITH PEARS AND WALNUTS

1 cup (240 ml) DANNON Plain Nonfat or
 Lowfat Yogurt
1 tbs (15 ml) walnut or peanut oil
1 tbs (15 ml) raspberry vinegar or white wine vinegar
1 tsp (5 ml) sugar
¼ tsp (1 ml) salt
¼ tsp (1 ml) ground nutmeg
1 head Boston or bibb lettuce, torn
1 bunch arugula, trimmed and torn
1 head Belgian endive, leaves separated
2 ripe pears, cored and thinly sliced
¾ cup (3 oz) (90 g) shredded Swiss cheese
½ cup (120 ml) finely chopped walnuts, toasted
pomegranate seeds, optional

In a small bowl combine yogurt, oil, vinegar, salt, salt and nutmeg. Cover; chill 1 hour. To serve, line 4 plates with greens. Arrange pears and cheese on greens; sprinkle with walnuts. Drizzle dressing over salad. If desired, garnish with pomegranate seeds. Serves 4.

Approximate nutritional analysis per serving:
Calories 242, Protein 7 g, Carbohydrates 25 g, Fat 14 g,
Cholesterol 3 mg, Sodium 184 mg

TANGERINE-OLIVE BULGUR SALAD

1 cup (5 oz) (150 g) bulgur wheat
¾ cup (180 ml) hot tangerine juice, fresh,
 canned or reconstituted
½ cup (120 ml) hot water
1 cup (240 ml) tomatoes, seeded and diced
⅓ cup (80 ml) green onions, sliced
½ cucumber, pared, halved lengthwise,
 seeded and sliced
3 tbs (45 ml) parsley, finely chopped
1 tbs (15 ml) fresh mint, finely chopped
2 tbs (30 ml) lemon juice
2 tbs (30 ml) olive oil
1 tsp (5 ml) grated orange peel
½ tsp (3 ml) salt

Cover bulgur with hot tangerine juice and water in a large bowl. Let stand 1 hour until all liquid is absorbed. Mix in olives, tomatoes, onion, cucumber, parsley and mint. Mix lemon juice, olive oil, orange peel and salt. Pour over salad, mix and chill. Serve on platter lined with salad greens. Serves 4.

Approximate nutritional analysis per serving:
Calories 286, Protein 6 g, Carbohydrates 40 g, Fat 14 g,
Cholesterol 0 mg, Sodium 775 mg

MEDITERRANEAN RICE SALAD

2 tbs (30 ml) vegetable oil, divided
1 lb (455 g) large shrimp, peeled and deveined
1 large garlic clove, minced
2 green onions, sliced
2 cups (480 ml) water
1 cup (240 ml) long grain rice
1 tsp (5 ml) salt
1 medium cucumber, diced
½ cup (120 ml) feta cheese, crumbled

SPICY VINAIGRETTE:
¼ cup (60 ml) olive oil
3 tbs (45 ml) cider vinegar
1 tbs (15 ml) Dijon mustard
1 tsp (5 ml) Tabasco pepper sauce
1 tsp (5 ml) salt

In 3-qt saucepan over medium-high heat, in 1 tbs hot vegetable oil, cook half the shrimp, until well browned and tender. With slotted spoon, remove to large bowl. Repeat this with remaining shrimp and oil. Reduce heat to medium. In drippings remaining in saucepan, cook garlic and green onion about 2 minutes, stirring frequently.

Add water, rice and salt to saucepan. Over high heat, heat to boiling. Reduce heat to low; cover and simmer 20 minutes or until rice is tender. Meanwhile, add cucumber and feta cheese to bowl containing shrimp.

Spicy Vinaigrette: In small bowl combine all vinaigrette ingredients. Add rice and vinaigrette to shrimp mixture and toss to mix well. Serves 6.

Approximate nutritional analysis per serving:
Calories 376, Protein 21 g, Carbohydrates 29 g, Fat 19 g,
Cholesterol 132 mg, Sodium 1069 mg

CURRIED PEAR RICE SALAD

water
1 - 14½ oz can (435 ml) beef broth
1 cup (240 ml) rice
2 fresh USA Anjou, Bosc, or Comice pears, diced
1 cup (240 ml) celery, thinly sliced
½ cup (120 ml) mayonnaise
3 tbs (45 ml) lemon or lime juice
½-¾ tsp (3-4 ml) curry powder
½ tsp (3 ml) crushed thyme
lettuce

Add water to broth to make 2 cups; bring to a boil. Add rice; simmer about 25 minutes or until rice is tender. Cool. Combine rice, diced pears and celery. Combine mayonnaise, lemon juice, curry powder and thyme. Stir into rice mixture. Chill thoroughly. Serve on lettuce-lined platter. Serves 6.

Approximate nutritional analysis per serving:
Calories 237, Protein 3 g, Carbohydrates 41 g, Fat 7 g,

WATERMELON AND SPINACH SALAD

6 cups (1.4 L) torn fresh spinach
3 cups (720 ml) cubed seeded watermelon
1 cup (240 ml) sliced fresh mushrooms
1 tbs (15 ml) real bacon bits
⅓ cup (80 ml) Sweet and Sour Salad Dressing

DRESSING:
⅓ cup (80 ml) balsamic or red wine vinegar
3 tbs (45 ml) vegetable oil
¼ cup (60 ml) granulated sugar
¼ cup (60 ml) chopped onion
1 tsp (5 ml) Worcestershire sauce
½ tsp (3 ml) salt

In large salad bowl, mix all ingredients except dressing. Just before serving, toss spinach mixture with dressing. Serves 6.

Sweet and Sour Salad Dressing: In blender or food processor, process all ingredients until blended. 1 cup.

Approximate nutritional analysis per serving:
Calories 82, Protein 3 g, Carbohydrates 12 g, Fat 3 g,
Cholesterol < 1 mg, Sodium 129 mgCholesterol 5 mg, Sodium 243 mg

Watermelon

CURRIED RICE SALAD

1 cup (240 ml) BLUE DIAMOND
    Chopped Natural Almonds
1 tbs (15 ml) butter
1/3 cup (80 ml) mayonnaise
1 clove garlic, chopped finely
1 tbs (15 ml) curry powder
1 tbs (15 ml) lemon juice
1/2 tsp (3 ml) cumin
1/2 tsp (3 ml) salt
1/4 tsp (1 ml) pepper
1/4 tsp (1 ml) coriander
2 drops red pepper sauce
3 cups (720 ml) hot, cooked rice
1 red bell pepper, diced
1/2 cup (120 ml) green onion, sliced
1/2 cup (120 ml) raisins, soaked in boiling water
    for 20 minutes and drained
1/4 cup (60 ml) fresh or packaged coconut, shredded

Sauté almonds in butter until crisp; drain and reserve. Combine next 9 ingredients. Stir into hot, cooked rice. Fold in pepper, green onions, raisins and coconut. Chill. Just before serving, fold in almonds. Serves 6.

Approximate nutritional analysis per serving:
Calories 287, Protein 6 g, Carbohydrates 36 g, Fat 14 g,
Cholesterol 6 mg, Sodium 223 mg

SOUTHWESTERN WILD RICE SALAD

SALAD:
2 cups (480 ml) white rice, cooked and cooled
2 - 6 oz jars (360 g) marinated artichoke hearts,
    drained and halved
1 - 8 oz can (240 g) sliced water chestnuts,
    drained and chopped
1 - 11 oz can (330 g) mandarin orange segments,
    drained
1 cup (240 ml) celery, sliced
3/4 cup (180 ml) pecans, toasted and chopped
1/2 cup (120 ml) raisins
1/3 cup (80 ml) green onions, sliced

ORANGE-SALSA DRESSING:
1 cup (240 ml) CHI-CHI'S Salsa
1/4 cup (60 ml) orange juice
1/4 cup (60 ml) vegetable oil
2 tsp (10 ml) grated orange peel

In large mixing bowl, combine all salad ingredients. Mix well; set aside. In small bowl, combine all Orange-Salsa Dressing ingredients. Mix well. Toss with salad. Refrigerate 1 hour to blend flavors. Serves 8.

Approximate nutritional analysis per serving:
Calories 350, Protein 6 g, Carbohydrates 47 g, Fat 16 g,
Cholesterol 0 mg, Sodium 210 mg

FATTOUSH

Lebanese Toasted Bread Salad

3 medium fresh FLORIDA tomatoes
3 small pita breads
4 cups (960 ml) loosely packed romaine lettuce
    leaves cut in 1-inch strips
2 cups (480 ml) cucumber halves, peeled and sliced
1 - 6 1/2 oz can (195 g) tuna in water, drained
1/2 cup (120 ml) feta cheese, crumbled
1/4 cup (60 ml) red onion, quartered and sliced
3/4 cup (180 ml) bottled vinaigrette dressing
1 tbs (15 ml) fresh parsley, chopped
2 tsp (10 ml) dried mint leaves, crushed

Preheat oven to 300°F (150°C). Use tomatoes held at room temperature until fully ripe. Core tomatoes; cut in wedges; set aside. Cut pita breads in halves; cut each half into 8 wedges. Place in shallow baking pan; bake until crisp, turning once, about 25 minutes. Remove from pan; cool. In salad bowl, place lettuce, cucumber, tuna, cheese, onion, tomatoes and pita wedges. In a measuring cup combine salad dressing, parsley and mint. Pour over salad mixture; toss until combined. Serves 6.

Approximate nutritional analysis per serving:
Calories 264, Protein 17 g, Carbohydrates 33 g, Fat 7 g,
Cholesterol 26 mg, Sodium 845 mg

SAVORY PASTA SALAD WITH VIDALIA ONIONS

1 medium VIDALIA Onion, 1/4-inch diced
1 medium red bell pepper, 1/2-inch diced
12 oz (360 g) corkscrew or spiral pasta, cooked
3 tbs (45 ml) Parmesan cheese, grated
2 tbs (30 ml) nonfat mayonnaise dressing
2 tbs (30 ml) olive oil
2 tbs (30 ml) balsamic vinegar or red wine vinegar
3 tbs (45 ml) fresh basil, chopped
salt and freshly ground pepper to taste
sliced black olives for garnish, optional

In medium bowl, combine the VIDALIA Onions and bell pepper. Mix together and set aside. In large bowl, mix the hot pasta with the Parmesan cheese, nonfat mayonnaise, oil, vinegar, basil, salt and pepper. Toss with the vegetables. Cover and chill until ready to serve. Garnish with black olives if desired. Serves 6.

Approximate nutritional analysis per serving:
Calories 159, Protein 5 g, Carbohydrates 21 g, Fat 6 g,
Cholesterol 5 mg, Sodium 66 mg

Opposite: Brown Rice Curry Salad

TABBOULEH SALAD

SALAD:
½ cup (120 ml) bulgar wheat
1 cup (240 ml) water
2 tomatoes, seeded and chopped
1 cup (240 ml) cucumber, seeded and sliced
1 cup (240 ml) parsley, chopped
½ cup (120 ml) carrot, shredded
¼ cup (60 ml) green onions, sliced
1 - 2¼ oz can (70 g) sliced ripe olives, drained
1 tbs (15 ml) fresh cilantro, chopped

DRESSING:
½ cup (120 ml) CHI-CHI'S Picante Sauce
2 tbs (30 ml) lemon juice
2 tbs (30 ml) olive oil
½ tsp (3 ml) salt
¼ tsp (1 ml) coarsely ground black pepper

In medium bowl, combine bulgar wheat and water. Let stand 30 minutes. Drain; squeeze out excess moisture. In large bowl, combine bulgar wheat and remaining salad ingredients. Mix well; set aside. In small bowl, combine all Dressing ingredients. Mix well. Toss with salad. Refrigerate 30 minutes to blend flavors. Serves 8.

Approximate nutritional analysis per serving:
Calories 80, Protein 2 g, Carbohydrates 11 g, Fat 4 g,
Cholesterol 0 mg, Sodium 270 mg

MACARONI MEDLEY SALAD

¾ cup (180 ml) buttermilk
¾ cup (180 ml) fat free mayonnaise
2 tbs (30 ml) fresh dill, chopped
    or 1 tsp (5 ml) dried dill
4 cups (960 ml) cooked rotini pasta, cooled
1 - 15 oz can (450 g) kidney beans, drained
1 - 10 oz pkg (300 g) frozen green beans,
    cooked, drained, cooled
½ lb (230 g) HEALTHY CHOICE Fat Free Pasteurized
    Process Cheese Product, cut into ½-inch cubes

Mix together buttermilk, mayonnaise and dill. Pour over combined pasta, beans and cheese; mix lightly. Chill. Serves 16.

Approximate nutritional analysis per serving:
Calories 109, Protein 8 g, Carbohydrates 21 g, Fat .5 g,
Cholesterol 3 mg, Sodium 305 mg

TURKEY HAM AND BARLEY SALAD

DRESSING:
⅓ cup (80 ml) vinegar
½ cup (120 ml) onion, chopped
2 tbs (30 ml) olive oil
1½ tsp (8 ml) reduced-sodium soy sauce
1 tbs (15 ml) lemon juice
1 tsp (5 ml) salt
1 tsp (5 ml) pepper
1 tsp (5 ml) prepared mustard
½ tsp (3 ml) sugar
1 garlic clove, minced

SALAD:
¾ cup (180 ml) barley, cooked according
    to package directions and cooled
1 lb (455 g) NORBEST Turkey Ham, in ½-inch cubes
2 cups (480 ml) frozen sugar snap peas, defrosted
1 cup (240 ml) celery, coarsely chopped
½ cup (120 ml) green or red pepper, chopped
1 - 2 oz jar (60 g) pimiento, drained

Dressing: In small bowl combine vinegar, onion, oil, soy sauce, juice, salt, pepper, mustard, sugar and garlic; set aside.

Salad: In large bowl combine barley, turkey ham, peas, celery, pepper and pimiento. Fold dressing into turkey/barley mixture. Cover and refrigerate several hours or overnight. Serves 6.

Approximate nutritional analysis per serving:
Calories 507, Protein 28 g, Carbohydrates 78 g, Fat 11 g,
Cholesterol 47 mg, Sodium 1215 mg

Tabbouleh Salad

PASTA SALAD WITH TOMATOES, MOZZARELLA AND PEPPERONI

2 medium-sized FLORIDA tomatoes, cored
4½ cups (1 L) cooked pasta spirals (rotelle), cooled
1 tbs (15 ml) olive oil
4 oz (120 g) mozzarella cheese, in small chunks
½ cup (2 oz) (60 g) pepperoni, cut in thin strips
½ cup (120 ml) frozen peas, thawed
¼ cup (60 ml) Parmesan cheese, grated
2 tbs (30 ml) green onion, sliced

TOMATO VINAIGRETTE:

¾ cup (180 ml) FLORIDA tomatoes, diced
1 tbs (15 ml) fresh basil, chopped OR
1 tsp (5 ml) dried basil
3 tbs (45 ml) olive oil
1 tbs (15 ml) red wine vinegar
½ tsp (3 ml) salt
½ tsp (3 ml) Dijon-style mustard
⅛ tsp (.5 ml) ground black pepper

Use tomatoes held at room temperature until fully ripe. Core and cut into ¾-inch cubes; set aside. In a large bowl combine pasta and olive oil; toss to coat. Add tomatoes, mozzarella, pepperoni, peas, Parmesan cheese, green onion, reserved tomatoes and Tomato Vinaigrette; toss well. Serves 16.

Tomato Vinaigrette: In the container of an electric blender combine tomatoes, basil, olive oil, red wine vinegar, salt, mustard and pepper. Whirl until slightly thickened. Yields ¾ cup.

Approximate nutritional analysis per serving:
Calories 272, Protein 10 g, Carbohydrates 26 g, Fat 14 g,
Cholesterol 19 mg, Sodium 407 mg

ITALIAN PASTA SALAD

7 oz (210 g) spiral macaroni, uncooked
2 cups (480 ml) YOPLAIT Fat Free Plain Yogurt
½ (120 ml) onion, finely chopped
⅓ cup (80 ml) Parmesan cheese, grated
1½ tsp (8 ml) Italian seasoning
¾ tsp (4 ml) garlic salt
2 medium tomatoes, cut into 1-inch pieces
1 medium zucchini, cut into ¼-inch slices
½ cup (120 ml) large ripe olives, sliced

Cook macaroni as directed on package or until tender. Rinse with cold water; drain. Mix yogurt, onion, cheese, Italian seasoning and garlic salt. Stir into macaroni; toss with remaining ingredients. Serves 6.

Approximate nutritional analysis per serving:
Calories 270, Protein 12 g, Carbohydrates 35 g, Fat 1 g,
Cholesterol 10 mg, Sodium 370 mg

Pasta Salad with Tomatoes, Mozzarella and Pepperoni

CURRIED CHICKEN AND RICE SALAD

3½ cups (840 ml) chicken broth
2 tsp (10 ml) curry powder
½ tsp (3 ml) ground ginger
½ tsp (3 ml) turmeric, optional
2 cups (480 ml) long grain rice (not instant)
¼ cup (60 ml) olive oil
¼ cup (60 ml) lemon juice
2 cups (480 ml) EMPIRE KOSHER Chicken,
    cooked and cut into bite size pieces
½ cup (120 ml) dark raisins
½ cup (120 ml) golden raisins
½ cup (120 ml) green bell pepper, chopped
½ cup (120 ml) red bell pepper, chopped
¾ cup (180 ml) reduced calorie mayonnaise
½ cup (120 ml) slivered almonds, toasted
salt and pepper

Bring chicken stock, curry, ginger, turmeric and 1 cup of water to a boil. Add rice, cover tightly, reduce heat and simmer until rice is tender and dry, about 25 minutes. Mix oil and lemon juice; add rice to bowl, toss to mix. Cover, refrigerate until cool. Add all remaining ingredients and mix well. Serve cold. Serves 8.

Approximate nutritional analysis per serving:
Calories 437, Protein 16 g, Carbohydrates 56 g, Fat 17 g,
Cholesterol 42 mg, Sodium 306 mg

WARM CHINESE CHICKEN SALAD

2 cups (480 ml) romaine lettuce, torn
    into bite-size pieces
½ lb (230 g) fresh spinach, washed,
    stems removed, in bite-size pieces
1 can mandarin oranges, drained
3 tbs (45 ml) soy sauce
1 tbs (15 ml) honey
¼ tsp (1 ml) ground ginger
2 tbs (30 ml) oil
1 lb (455 g) EMPIRE KOSHER Chicken
    Breast Cutlets, in 1-inch pieces
3 tbs (45 ml) scallions, chopped
1 clove garlic, minced
¼ cup (60 ml) cashews

Combine lettuce, spinach and oranges in
bowl. Whisk together soy sauce, honey,
ginger and 3 tbs water. Set aside. Heat oil in
wok, stir fry chicken until done but still tender, about
5 minutes. Add scallions and garlic, cook another minute. Add
sauce and cook, tossing for 30 seconds. Pour chicken and sauce
over the greens and toss. Sprinkle with cashews. Serves 4.

Approximate nutritional analysis per serving:
Calories 354, Protein 40 g, Carbohydrates 16 g, Fat 15 g,
Cholesterol 96 mg, Sodium 906 mg

PASTA SALAD WITH PARMESAN-YOGURT DRESSING

8 oz (240 g) rotini pasta
1½ cup (355 ml) DANNON Plain Nonfat
    or Lowfat Yogurt
1 cup (240 ml) cooked chicken, cubed
1 cup (240 ml) carrots, sliced
1 cup (240 ml) green bell pepper, cut into thin strips
1 cup (240 ml) broccoli flowerets
1 cup (240 ml) cherry tomatoes, halved
½ cup (120 ml) Parmesan cheese, grated
1 tbs (15 ml) fresh parsley, chopped
¼ tsp (1 ml) salt
dash pepper

Cook pasta according to package directions; drain. Rinse in
cold water and drain again. Place in a large bowl. Add yogurt,
chicken, carrots, bell pepper, broccoli, tomatoes, cheese,
parsley, salt and pepper; toss until well mixed. Serve immediately or cover and chill until ready to serve. Serves 4.

Approximate nutritional analysis per serving:
Calories 420, Protein 24 g, Carbohydrates 51 g, Fat 8 g,
Cholesterol 41 mg, Sodium 421 mg

Pasta Salad

AGNOLOTTI SALAD

½ cup (120 ml) CALIFORNIA ripe olives,
    finely chopped
olive oil
2 tsp (10 ml) garlic, finely chopped
½ cup (120 ml) Gorgonzola cheese, crumbled
3 tbs (45 ml) bread crumbs
3 tbs (45 ml) walnuts, chopped and toasted
½ cup (120 ml) bottled roasted red bell peppers,
    diced
12 oz (360 g) egg and/or spinach sheet pasta
¼ cup (60 ml) unsalted butter or margarine
Parmesan cheese, grated

Sauté olives in oiled skillet, stirring constantly, about 8 minutes
or until olives are dehydrated and liquid evaporated. When
nearly dry, add garlic and sauté 1-2 minutes. Cool. Combine
olives with crumbled Gorgonzola, bread crumbs, walnuts and
half the diced peppers.

   To make agnolotti (half moons): cut 18 ½-inch rounds of
pasta using cookie cutter or by making rounds then cutting
with shears. Spoon 2 tsp filling into center of each. Moisten
edges slightly and fold circles over to meet, like turnovers,
pressing out air. Pinch edge firmly together to seal. Drop into
boiling water, return to boil and boil about 4 minutes. Meanwhile, lightly brown butter, add remaining red bell peppers.
Toss agnolotti with butter mixture. Serve with grated
Parmesan cheese on top. Serves 4.

Approximate nutritional analysis per serving:
Calories 392, Protein 12 g, Carbohydrates 30 g, Fat 26 g,
Cholesterol 52 mg, Sodium 665 mg

SICILIAN-STYLE PASTA SALAD

1 lb (455 g) dry rotini pasta, cooked,
    drained and chilled
1 cup (240 ml) yellow bell pepper, sliced
1 cup (240 ml) zucchini, sliced
⅓ cup (2¼ oz) (70 g) ripe olives, sliced
8 oz (240 g) cooked bay shrimp
2 tbs (30 ml) balsamic vinegar
2 - 14½ oz cans (840 g) CONTADINA Pasta
    Ready Chunky Tomatoes with Crushed Red
    Pepper or Pasta Ready Chunky Tomatoes
    with Three Cheeses

In large bowl, combine all ingredients; toss well. Chill for 1 hour. Serves 12.

Approximate nutritional analysis per serving:
Calories 186, Protein 10 g, Carbohydrates 33 g, Fat 2 g,
Cholesterol 29 mg, Sodium 178 mg

ITALIAN PASTA SALAD

1 cup (240 ml) MIRACLE WHIP *or*
    MIRACLE WHIP LIGHT Dressing
1½ tsp (8 ml) Italian seasoning
½ tsp (3 ml) garlic salt
¼ tsp (1 ml) pepper
3 cups (8 oz) (240 g) rotini, cooked, drained
2 cups (480 ml) broccoli flowerets
1 cup (240 ml) carrots, sliced
1 cup (240 ml) cucumber, quartered slices
½ cup (120 ml) red pepper strips

Mix dressing and seasonings in large bowl. Add remaining ingredients; mix lightly. Refrigerate. Serves 16.

Approximate nutritional analysis per serving:
Calories 72, Protein 2 g, Carbohydrates 12 g, Fat 2 g,
Cholesterol 9 mg, Sodium 157 mg

COLORFUL GRAPE, PEPPER AND PASTA SALAD

8 oz (240 g) dry thin spaghetti, cooked, warm
Mustard Vinaigrette (below)
1 cup (240 ml) CALIFORNIA seedless grapes
½ cup (120 ml) sweet red or yellow pepper,
    thinly sliced
2 tbs (30 ml) celery, minced
2 tbs (30 ml) green onion, minced
1 tbs (15 ml) fresh tarragon, chopped
    or ½ tsp (3 ml) dried tarragon, crushed
salt and pepper to taste
¼ cup (60 ml) walnuts,* quartered
fresh tarragon sprigs, optional

MUSTARD WALNUT VINAIGRETTE:
3 tbs (45 ml) white wine vinegar
2 tbs (30 ml) olive oil
2 tbs (30 ml) Dijon-style mustard
1 clove garlic, minced
½ tsp (3 ml) sugar
⅛ tsp (.5 ml) pepper

* Walnuts may be omitted; substitute 1 tbs walnut oil for 1 tbs olive oil in vinaigrette.

Combine cooked spaghetti and 3 tbs Mustard Walnut Vinaigrette; toss to coat and cool. Add remaining ingredients including vinaigrette; mix well. Serve in lettuce-lined bowl; garnish with tarragon, if desired. Serves 4.

Mustard Walnut Vinaigrette: Combine all ingredients; mix well. Yields ⅓ cup.

Approximate nutritional analysis per serving:
Calories 367, Protein 10 g, Carbohydrates 55 g, Fat 13 g,
Cholesterol 0 mg, Sodium 188 mg

Courtesy of the California Table Grape Commission.

GRILLED VEGETABLE AND PASTA SALAD

¾ cup (180 ml) WISH - BONE Italian Dressing
6 tbs (90 ml) Parmesan cheese, grated
¼ tsp (1 ml) black pepper
2 medium red or green bell peppers, cubed
1 medium onion, cut in thick rings
1 medium zucchini, cut into ½-inch diagonal slices
8 oz (240 g) penne pasta or your favorite pasta,
    cooked and drained

In small bowl, blend Italian dressing, cheese and black pepper. In large shallow baking dish or plastic bag, combine vegetables with ½ of the dressing marinade. Reserve remaining marinade. Cover, or close bag and marinate in refrigerator, stirring occasionally, 1 hour. Remove vegetables, reserving marinade.

Grill or broil vegetables until done. To serve, toss hot pasta, both reserved marinades and hot vegetables. Serves 4 side dishes.

Approximate nutritional analysis per serving:
Calories 290, Protein 8 g, Carbohydrates 26 g, Fat 17 g,
Cholesterol 5 mg, Sodium 1060 mg

Opposite: Colorful Grape, Pepper and Pasta Salad

APPLE-NUT SALAD AND TOFU-HONEY DRESSING

5 red Delicious apples, sliced
¼ cup (60 ml) fresh lemon juice
1 cup (240 ml) water
3 stalks celery, diced
1 - 8 oz can (240 g) pineapple tidbits in
    unsweetened pineapple juice, drained
⅓ cup (80 ml) walnuts, coarsely chopped
mint sprigs for garnish

DRESSING:
1 cup (240 ml) plain lowfat yogurt
½ cup (120 ml) soft tofu
1 tbs (15 ml) honey·
1 tsp (5 ml) ground cinnamon

Place sliced apples in mixture of lemon juice and water. Add more if needed to cover apples. At serving time, drain liquid from apples. Combine apples, celery, pineapple and nuts. Combine apple mixture and dressing and toss gently. Garnish with mint sprigs. Serves 8.

    Dressing: Combine yogurt, tofu, honey and cinnamon in a food processor and blend until smooth. Chill.

Approximate nutritional analysis per ¼ cup serving:
Calories 60, Protein 2 g, Carbohydrates 10 g, Fat 2 g,
Cholesterol 1 mg, Sodium 15 mg

HERB VINAIGRETTE

¾ cup (180 ml) soy oil
¼ cup (60 ml) sherry wine vinegar
½ cup (120 ml) fresh, chopped basil
    and parsley mixed
2 tsp (10 ml) finely minced leeks
salt to taste

Combine all of the ingredients in a jar and shake well.

Approximate nutritional analysis per ¼ cup serving:
Calories 244, Protein < 1 g, Carbohydrates 1 g, Fat 27 g,
Cholesterol 0 mg, Sodium 2 mg

ORANGE POPPY SEED DRESSING

1 cup (240 ml) DANNON Plain or
    Vanilla Lowfat Yogurt
1 tbs (15 ml) honey
1 tbs (15 ml) frozen orange juice concentrate, thawed
1 tsp (5 ml) poppy seeds
1 tsp (5 ml) finely shredded orange peel

In a medium bowl combine yogurt, honey, orange juice concentrate, poppy seeds and orange peel; stir well. Cover; chill 2 hours. Yields 1 cup.

Approximate nutritional analysis per ¼ cup serving:
Calories 59, Protein 3 g, Carbohydrates 10 g, Fat < 1 g,
Cholesterol 3 mg, Sodium 40 mg

Assorted Vinaigrettes

SUNFLOWER-HERB DRESSING

¼ cup (60 ml) unsalted sunflower nuts
1 clove garlic, crushed
1 cup (240 ml) DANNON Plain Nonfat or
    Lowfat Yogurt
2 tbs (30 ml) milk
1 tsp (5 ml) dried basil, crushed
½ tsp (3 ml) dried thyme, crushed
⅛ tsp (.5 ml) dry mustard
⅛ tsp (.5 ml) pepper

In food processor or blender combine sunflower nuts and
garlic. Cover; process to a fine powder, almost a paste. Add
yogurt, milk, basil, thyme, dry mustard and pepper. Process
until smooth. Cover; chill 2 hours. Yields 1 cup.

Approximate nutritional analysis per ¼ cup serving:
Calories 93, Protein 5 g, Carbohydrates 6 g, Fat 6 g,
Cholesterol 4 mg, Sodium 44 mg

COOKED CREAMY CAESAR-STYLE DRESSING

½ cup (120 ml) cooking oil
1 clove garlic, crushed
2 egg yolks
2 tbs (30 ml) wine vinegar
2 tbs (30 ml) lemon juice
¼ tsp (60 ml) dry mustard
⅛ tsp (.5 ml) Worcestershire sauce

Combine oil and garlic in jar with tight-fitting lid. Refrigerate
several hours or overnight. Remove garlic. Set oil aside.

    In small saucepan over very low heat, cook remaining
ingredients, stirring constantly, until mixture thickens and
bubbles at edges. Remove from heat. Let stand to cool
5-20 minutes. Pour into reserved oil, cover and shake until well
blended or pour into blender container, add reserved oil, cover
and blend at high speed until smooth. Cover and chill if not
using immediately. Yields ⅔ cup.

Approximate nutritional analysis per ¼ cup serving:
Calories 275, Protein 1 g, Carbohydrates 2 g, Fat 30 g,
Cholesterol 106 mg, Sodium 4 mg

Courtesy of the American Egg Board.

GREEN GODDESS DRESSING

1-1¼ cups (240-355 ml) mayonnaise
½ cup (4 oz) (120 g) sour cream or sour half-and-half
1½ tbs (25 ml) snipped fresh parsley
¼ cup (60 ml) minced green onions with tops
2 tbs (30 ml) lemon juice or tarragon or wine vinegar
½ clove garlic, minced
½ tsp (3 ml) salt
dash ground pepper

In medium bowl, stir together all ingredients until well combined. Cover and chill if not using immediately. Yields 2 cups.

Approximate nutritional analysis per ¼ cup serving:
Calories 161, Protein < 1 g, Carbohydrates 9 g, Fat 14 g,
Cholesterol 15 mg, Sodium 375 mg

Courtesy of the American Egg Board.

SOUR CREAM DRESSING

1 cup (240 ml) sour cream
½ cup (120 ml) mayonnaise, regular or light
¼ cup (60 ml) chopped chives or young green onions
2 tbs (30 ml) wine vinegar
½ tsp (3 ml) salt
½ tsp (3 ml) IMPERIAL Granulated Sugar
dash white pepper

Combine all ingredients and mix well. Chill.
Yields 1½ cups.

Approximate nutritional analysis per 1 tbs serving:
Calories 54, Protein 0 g, Carbohydrates 1 g, Fat 6 g,
Cholesterol 7 mg, Sodium 76 mg

HONEY MUSTARD DRESSING

1 cup (240 ml) mayonnaise, regular or light
½ cup (120 ml) salad oil
½ cup (120 ml) honey
½ cup (120 ml) prepared mustard
¾ cup (180 ml) apple cider vinegar
½ tsp (3 ml) IMPERIAL Granulated Sugar
½ tsp (3 ml) red pepper, cayenne

Blend mayonnaise with oil, honey, mustard. Whisk in vinegar,
then IMPERIAL Granulated Sugar and red pepper. Mix until
smooth. Yields 3 cups.

Approximate nutritional analysis per 1 tbs serving:
Calories 57, Protein 0 g, Carbohydrates 3 g, Fat 5 g,
Cholesterol 2 mg, Sodium 51 mg

PIÑA COLADA DRESSING

FRUIT SALAD:
lettuce leaves
desired fruits, peeled and sliced
½ cup (120 ml) shredded coconut

DRESSING:
1 cup (240 ml) heavy cream
¼ cup (60 ml) banana yogurt
¼ cup (60 ml) pineapple juice
¼ cup (60 ml) BACARDI Light Rum (80 proof)
1 tbs (15 ml) coconut cream

Salad: Arrange lettuce leaves on large platter. Decoratively place fruit over lettuce. Sprinkle with coconut. Serve with dressing.

Dressing: In medium bowl, whip cream until thickened but not stiff. Fold in yogurt, pineapple juice, rum and coconut cream. Yields 1¾ cups.

Approximate nutritional analysis per ¼ cup serving dressing:
Calories 165, Protein 1 g, Carbohydrates 3 g, Fat 15 g,
Cholesterol 48 mg, Sodium 18 mg

BACON DRESSING

4 slices bacon
¼ cup (60 ml) HEINZ Apple Cider Vinegar
    or Apple Cider Flavored Distilled Vinegar
2-3 tsp (10-15 ml) granulated sugar
¼ tsp (1 ml) salt
dash pepper

In skillet, cook bacon until crisp; remove and set aside; reserving drippings. Stir vinegar and remaining ingredients into reserved drippings; heat to boiling. Pour hot dressing over salad greens; toss. Crumble bacon and use as garnish. Serve immediately. Yields ½ cup.

Approximate nutritional analysis per ¼ cup serving dressing:
Calories 97, Protein 4 g, Carbohydrates 7 g, Fat 6 g,
Cholesterol 11 mg, Sodium 469 mg

CALIFORNIA SUNSHINE SALAD DRESSING

¼ cup (60 ml) catsup
¼ cup (60 ml) vegetable oil
3 tbs (45 ml) red wine vinegar
1 tbs (15 ml) soy sauce
1 tbs (15 ml) honey
½ cup (120 ml) raisins
1 tbs (15 ml) sesame seeds

Combine all ingredients except raisins and seeds in jar with tight-fitting lid. Cover; shake to mix well. Stir in raisins and seeds. Refrigerate. Yields 1¼ cups.

Variation: For a tangy, creamy dressing combine dressing with 1 cup plain yogurt or buttermilk; stir until thoroughly blended.

Dip variation: Combine dressing with 1 cup sour cream or 8 oz cream cheese, softened. Blend briefly in food processor or blender. Serve with raw vegetables, fruits, crackers and chips.

Approximate nutritional analysis per ¼ cup serving:
Calories 180, Protein 1 g, Carbohydrates 19 g, Fat 12 g,
holesterol 0 mg, Sodium 354 mg

PAPAYA DILL DRESSING

seeds from 2 medium ripe papayas
2 cups (480 ml) red wine vinegar
1 cup (240 ml) sugar
5 sprigs fresh dill
2 oz (60 g) ginger
5 sprigs mint
1 tbs (15 ml) shallots
2 tsp (10 ml) salt
2 cups (480 ml) walnut oil

Blend all ingredients. Ladle over chilled salad. Yields 4 cups.

Approximate nutritional analysis per ¼ cup serving:
Calories 293, Protein 0 g, Carbohydrates 14 g, Fat 27 g,
Cholesterol 0 mg, Sodium 267 mg

Courtesy of The Papaya Administrative Committee and Pineapple Growers Association of Hawaii.

BLUE CHEESE DRESSING

1⅓ cups (320 ml) YOPLAIT Fat Free Plain Yogurt
½ cup (120 ml) crumbled blue cheese
2 green onions with tops, chopped
1 tsp (5 ml) salt
¼ tsp (1 ml) garlic powder

Mix all ingredients. Cover and refrigerate at least 2 hours. Store remaining dressing in refrigerator. Yields 2 cups.

Approximate nutritional analysis per 1 tbs serving:
Calories 20, Protein 1 g, Carbohydrates 1 g, Fat 1 g,
Cholesterol < 5 mg, Sodium 105 mg

PARMESAN DRESSING

1 cup (240 ml) YOPLAIT Fat Free Plain Yogurt
¼ cup (60 ml) grated Parmesan cheese
⅓ cup (80 ml) skim milk
¼ tsp (1 ml) paprika
⅛ tsp (.5 ml) salt
1 small clove garlic, finely chopped

Mix all ingredients. Yields 1½ cups.

Approximate nutritional analysis per 1 tbs serving:
Calories 10, Protein 1 g, Carbohydrates 1 g, Fat < 1 g,
Cholesterol 0 mg, Sodium 35 mg

THOUSAND ISLAND DRESSING

1⅓ cups (320 ml) YOPLAIT Fat Free Plain Yogurt
⅔ cup (160 ml) chili sauce
2 tbs (30 ml) chopped pimiento-stuffed olives
1 tbs (15 ml) instant minced onion
1 tbs (15 ml) sugar
1 tsp (5 ml) prepared mustard
½ tsp (3 ml) Worcestershire sauce
2 hard-cooked eggs, chopped

Mix all ingredients. Cover and refrigerate at least 24 hours.
Store remaining dressing in refrigerator. Yields 2⅓ cups.

Approximate nutritional analysis per 1 tbs serving:
Calories 15, Protein 1 g, Carbohydrates 2 g, Fat < 1 g,
Cholesterol 15 mg, Sodium 80 mg

BLUE CHEESE YOGURT DRESSING

1 cup (240 ml) DANNON Plain Nonfat or
    Lowfat Yogurt
4 oz (120 g) crumbled blue cheese
½ cup (120 ml) buttermilk
¼ cup (60 ml) minced fresh parsley
1 tbs (15 ml) sherry
½ tsp (3 ml) pepper

In a small bowl combine all ingredients; stir well. Cover; chill
overnight. Yields 1¾ cups.

Approximate nutritional analysis per ¼ cup serving:
Calories 103, Protein 6 g, Carbohydrates 4 g, Fat 7 g,
Cholesterol 15 mg, Sodium 268 mg

CREAMY CAESAR SALAD DRESSING

1 - 8 oz container (240 g) nonfat sour cream
¼ cup (60 ml) lowfat milk (2%)
3 tbs (45 ml) grated Parmesan cheese
2 tbs (30 ml) GREY POUPON Dijon Mustard
2 tbs (30 ml) lemon juice
1 tsp (5 ml) garlic powder
¼ tsp (1 ml) coarsely cracked black pepper
¼ tsp (1 ml) salt

In small bowl, blend sour cream, milk, cheese, mustard, lemon
juice, garlic powder, pepper and salt. Cover; store in refrigerator for up to 1 week. Serve as a dressing for salad greens.
Yields 1½ cups.

Approximate nutritional analysis per 1 tbs serving:
Calories 14, Protein 1 g, Carbohydrates 1 g, Fat 0 g,
Cholesterol 1 mg, Sodium 78 mg

ROASTED RED PEPPER DRESSING

1 - 7 oz jar (210 g) roasted red peppers,
    undrained
¼ cup (60 ml) GREY POUPON Dijon Mustard
2 tbs (30 ml) REGINA Red Wine Vinegar
1 tbs (15 ml) honey

In electric blender container, blend roasted red peppers,
mustard, vinegar and honey until smooth. Cover; store in
refrigerator for up to 1 week. Serve as a dressing for salad
greens. Yields 1⅓ cups.

Approximate nutritional analysis per 1 tbs serving:
Calories 9, Protein < 1 g, Carbohydrates 2 g, Fat 0 g,
Cholesterol 0 mg, Sodium 87 mg

PASTA, POLENTA & RISOTTO

Pasta has become everyday food for almost everybody. That's a good thing for convenience, nutritional balance and just plain enjoyment. Polenta and risotto, originating in the same cuisine (that's Italian), are still a bit exotic. But they all deliver the same homey comfort, and the infinite potential for taste variety in the kitchen.

ROASTED TOMATO SAUCE
WITH FETTUCCINE AND HERBS

4 lbs (1.8 kg) fresh FLORIDA tomatoes
¼ cup (60 ml) olive oil
¼ tsp (1 ml) black pepper, ground
½ cup (120 ml) onions, chopped
1 tbs (15 ml) garlic, minced
1 tsp (5 ml) oregano leaves, crushed
2 tbs (30 ml) white wine, or chicken broth
1 tbs (15 ml) fresh parsley, chopped
⅛ tsp (.5 ml) red pepper, crushed
1 tsp (5 ml) salt
8 oz (240 g) fettuccine, cooked and drained

Preheat oven to 500°F (260°C). Use tomatoes held at room temperature until fully ripe. Core; cut into wedges. Place in a single layer on shallow baking pans; sprinkle with 2 tbs oil and all of the black pepper. Roast until edges are well browned, about 20 minutes; set aside.

In large skillet heat remaining 2 tbs oil until hot; add onions, garlic and oregano; sauté until tender, 4-5 minutes. Add wine; stir to loosen particles in pan; stir in parsley, red pepper and salt. Stir in reserved tomatoes and pan juices; cook until hot, about 2 minutes.

Divide fettuccine among serving plates. Ladle 1 cup sauce over each portion. Serve with grated Parmesan cheese, if desired. Serves 24.

Approximate nutritional analysis per serving:
Calories 430, Protein 12 g, Carbohydrates 61 g, Fat 17 g,
Sodium 596 mg

Courtesy of the Florida Tomato Committee.

Roasted Tomato Sauce with Fettuccine and Herbs

Previous page: Pasta Verde Roll, Agnolotti, Penne alla Napolitana

Sauce Niçoise

SAUCE NIÇOISE

1½ lbs (685 g) fresh **FLORIDA** tomatoes
2 tbs (30 ml) vegetable oil
¾ cup (180 ml) sliced onion
1 tsp (5 ml) crushed garlic
1 cup (240 ml) chicken broth
1¼ tsp (6 ml) thyme leaves, crushed
½ tsp (3 ml) salt
⅛ tsp (.5 ml) ground black pepper
1 - 9 oz pkg (270 g) frozen artichoke heart
    halves and quarters, defrosted
½ cup (120 ml) sliced ripe olives
8 oz (240 g) fettuccine, cooked and drained

Use tomatoes held at room temperature until fully ripe. Core and cut tomatoes into 1-inch chunks; set aside. In a large skillet heat until hot. Add onion and garlic; cook until tender, about 4 minutes. Stir in chicken broth, thyme, salt, black pepper and reserved tomatoes; cook, uncovered, until tomatoes are slightly softened, about 4 minutes. Mix in artichokes; cook for 2 minutes. Stir in olives; heat until artichokes are tender and olives are hot, about 1 minute. Serve over hot cooked fettuccine. Serves 4.

    Note: For a smoother sauce, tomatoes and artichokes can be coarsely chopped before cooking.

Approximate nutritional analysis per serving:
Calories 386, Protein 12 g, Carbohydrates 56 g, Fat 14 g,
Cholesterol 53 mg, Sodium 697 mg

ALMOND PASTA BAJA

¾ cup (180 ml) **BLUE DIAMOND**
    Chopped Natural Almonds
2 tbs (30 ml) olive oil, divided
1 cup (240 ml) chopped onion
2 cloves garlic, chopped finely
1 - 4 oz can (120 g) diced green chilies, drained
1 tsp (5 ml) salt
1 cup (240 ml) heavy cream
6 oz (180 g) Monterey Jack cheese, grated
2 tsp (10 ml) lime juice
¼ tsp (1 ml) white pepper
8 oz (240 g) corkscrew pasta, cooked

Sauté almonds in 1 tbs oil until crisp; reserve. Sauté onion in remaining 1 tbs oil until translucent. Stir in garlic, chilies, and salt. Cook 1 minute. Add cream and reduce 2-3 minutes over high heat until slightly thickened. Add cheese and cook over low heat, stirring constantly, until cheese melts, about 1 minute. Add lime juice, pepper, and almonds. Toss with hot, cooked pasta. Serves 4.

Approximate nutritional analysis per serving:
Calories 1011, Protein 26 g, Carbohydrates 58 g, Fat 77 g,
Cholesterol 201 mg, Sodium 815 mg

ZITI WITH MOZZARELLA AND PARMESAN CHEESE

1 lb (455 g) DE CECCO Ziti cut
2 cups (480 ml) diced mozzarella
⅓ cup (80 ml) butter
1 cup (240 ml) grated Parmesan cheese
salt
freshly ground black pepper

Cook the DE CECCO Ziti cut for 9 minutes in boiling salted water and drain. Season piping hot with the butter and Parmesan cheese diluted in a little pasta cooking water. Add the diced mozzarella, sprinkle generously with freshly ground black pepper and serve. You may like to add a little more grated Parmesan cheese at the table. Serves 6.

Approximate nutritional analysis per serving:
Calories 658, Protein 31 g, Carbohydrates 59 g, Fat 33 g,
Cholesterol 100 mg, Sodium 698 mg

FRESH TOMATO SAUCE WITH PINE NUTS AND RAISINS

2½ lbs (1.1 kg) fresh FLORIDA tomatoes
2 tbs (30 ml) vegetable oil
1 cup (5 oz) (150 g) onion, chopped
1 tsp (5 ml) garlic, crushed
1¼ tsp (6 ml) salt
1 tsp (5 ml) sugar
½ tsp (3 ml) ground allspice
⅔ cup (160 ml) golden raisins
⅔ cup (160 ml) pine nuts (pignolias), toasted*

Use tomatoes held at room temperature until fully ripe. Core tomatoes; chop; set aside. In a large skillet heat oil until hot. Add onion and garlic; cook and stir until crisp-tender, 3-4 minutes. Add reserved tomatoes, salt, sugar and allspice; simmer uncovered until sauce thickens, 10-12 minutes, stirring occasionally. Stir in raisins and pine nuts; cook until hot, about 1 minute. Serve over cooked fettuccine, if desired. Serves 4.

   * To toast pine nuts, place in a small skillet; cook over low heat, stirring frequently until golden brown, about 5 minutes.

Approximate nutritional analysis per serving:
Calories 332, Protein 9 g, Carbohydrates 39 g, Fat 20 g,
Cholesterol 0 mg, Sodium 714 mg

AGNOLOTTI

½ cup (120 ml) finely chopped
   CALIFORNIA ripe olives
olive oil
2 tsp (10 ml) finely chopped garlic
½ cup (120 ml) crumbled Gorgonzola cheese
3 tbs (45 ml) bread crumbs
3 tbs (45 ml) chopped walnuts, toasted
½ cup (120 ml) bottled roasted red bell
   peppers, diced
12 oz (360 g) egg and/or spinach sheet pasta
½ cup (60 ml) unsalted butter or margarine
grated Parmesan cheese

Sauté olives in oiled skillet, stirring constantly, about 8 minutes or until olives are dehydrated and liquid evaporated. When nearly dry, add garlic and sauté 11-12 minutes. Cool. Combine olives with crumbled Gorgonzola, bread crumbs, walnuts and half the diced peppers.

   To make agnolotti: cut 18 - ½-inch rounds of pasta using cookie cutter or by making rounds then cutting with shears. Spoon 2 tsp filling into center of each. Moisten edges slightly and fold circles over to meet (like turnovers), pressing out air. Pinch edge firmly together to seal. Drop into boiling water, return to boil and boil about 4 minutes. Meanwhile, lightly brown butter, add remaining red bell peppers. Toss agnolotti with butter mixture. Serve with grated Parmesan cheese on top. Serves 4.

Approximate nutritional analysis per serving:
Calories 392, Protein 12 g, Carbohydrates 30 g, Fat 26 g,
Cholesterol 52 mg, Sodium 665 mg

CONFETTI FETTUCINE DANNON

12 oz (360 g) fettucine noodles
¼ cup (60 ml) margarine, softened
1½ cups (355 ml) DANNON Plain Nonfat
   or Lowfat Yogurt
½ cup (120 ml) grated carrots
2 tbs (30 ml) snipped fresh parsley
¼ tsp (1 ml) salt
dash pepper

In a large saucepan cook pasta according to package directions; rinse and drain well. Return pasta to saucepan. Add margarine; toss until melted. Add yogurt, cheese, carrots, parsley, salt and pepper. Toss to coat pasta. Serve immediately. Serves 6.

Approximate nutritional analysis per serving:
Calories 356, Protein 14 g, Carbohydrates 48 g, Fat 12 g,
Cholesterol 10 mg, Sodium 393 mg

PENNE ALLA NAPOLITANA

12 oz (360 g) penne or other small tubular pasta
4 tbs (60 ml) virgin olive oil, divided
2 tbs (30 ml) finely chopped garlic
1 cup (240 ml) pitted CALIFORNIA ripe olives, sliced
¼ cup (60 ml) packed fresh basil leaves,
  coarsely chopped
1 tsp (5 ml) bottled red pepper flakes
2 cups (480 ml) Homemade Fresh Tomato Sauce
½ cup (120 ml) mozzarella cheese, ¼-inch cubed
½ cup (120 ml) grated Parmesan cheese

HOMEMADE FRESH TOMATO SAUCE:
2 tbs (30 ml) olive oil
¾ cup (180 ml) chopped onion
3 lbs (1.4 kg) tomatoes, seeded and chopped
1 tbs (15 ml) minced garlic
9 fresh basil sprigs
salt and pepper

Pasta: Drop penne into kettle of boiling water, return to boil and boil gently for 8-10 minutes or until al dente (tender but still with a firm bite). Drain, toss with 1 tbs olive oil, return to pan and keep warm.

Sauce: Sauté garlic slowly in 3 tbs olive oil in skillet until softened but not browned. Add olives, basil, red pepper and tomato sauce. Heat. Stir in cheeses and heat, stirring, until chunks begin to melt. Pour over pasta. Pass additional grated Parmesan cheese to sprinkle over if desired. Serves 4.

Homemade Fresh Tomato Sauce: Heat olive oil in skillet, add onions and sauté until translucent. Add tomatoes, garlic and whole basil sprigs. Cook, covered over medium heat for 45 minutes to 1 hour or until saucy. Add salt and pepper to taste. Yields 3⅔ cups.

Approximate nutritional analysis per serving:
Calories 661, Protein 23 g, Carbohydrates 78 g, Fat 29 g,
Cholesterol 30 mg, Sodium 147 mg

SALSA PASTA

1 - 16 oz jar (480 g) CHI-CHI'S Salsa
½ cup (120 ml) part-skim ricotta cheese
½ cup (120 ml) coarsely chopped Greek or ripe olives
2 cloves garlic, minced
¼ cup (60 ml) toasted chopped walnuts
fresh cilantro leaves
freshly grated Parmesan cheese
8 oz (240 g) pasta (tortellini, rigatoni, rotini),
  cooked and drained

In large saucepan, over medium-low heat, combine salsa, ricotta, olives and garlic. Cook and stir 5-10 minutes or until heated through. Spoon sauce over hot pasta. Sprinkle with walnuts, cilantro and Parmesan cheese. Serves 4.

Approximate nutritional analysis per serving:
Calories 340, Protein 13 g, Carbohydrates 51 g, Fat 10 g,
Cholesterol 10 mg, Sodium 720 mg

TRI-COLOR PEPPER LINGUINE

1 medium green pepper, cut into thin strips
1 medium red pepper, cut into thin strips
1 medium yellow pepper, cut into thin strips
½ cup (120 ml) green onions, cut in 1-inch pieces
2 large cloves garlic, minced
2 tbs (30 ml) chopped fresh basil
  ***or* 2 tsp (10 ml) dried basil leaves**
2 tbs (30 ml) FLEISCHMANN'S Margarine
1 lb (455 g) linguine, cooked in unsalted water
  and drained
1 cup (240 ml) EGG BEATERS Real Egg Product
¼ cup (60 ml) grated Parmesan cheese

In skillet over medium-high heat, cook peppers, onions, garlic and basil in margarine until peppers are tender-crisp. In large serving bowl, toss peppers with hot linguine, egg product and cheese. Serve immediately. Serves 8.

Approximate nutritional analysis per serving:
Calories 274, Fat 6 g, Cholesterol 56 mg, Sodium 125 mg

RONZONI LINGUINE A LA LEBOW
Light Lemon Sauce

¾ cup (180 ml) half-and-half
¾ cup (180 ml) milk
1½ tsp (8 ml) grated lemon peel
1 tbs (15 ml) butter or margarine
3 cups (8 oz) (240 g) sliced and halved
  fresh mushrooms
2 tbs (30 ml) grated Parmesan cheese
8 oz (240 g) RONZONI Linguine, cooked and drained
2 tbs (30 ml) chopped fresh parsley

In small saucepan, over medium heat, add half-and-half, milk and lemon peel; heat to boiling. Reduce heat to low; simmer until reduced in half, about 25 minutes. In large skillet, melt butter; add mushrooms. Cook until lightly browned. Add reduced half-and-half mixture and Parmesan cheese; mix well. Toss hot pasta and sauce. Sprinkle with chopped parsley; serve immediately. Serves 4.

Approximate nutritional analysis per serving:
Calories 445 , Protein 12 g, Carbohydrates 48 g, Fat 23 g,
Cholesterol 78 mg, Sodium 133 mg

Opposite: Penne alla Napolitana

CREAMY PASTA PRIMAVERA

1 lb (455 g) fresh asparagus, cleaned,
   cut into 1-inch pieces
2 cups (480 ml) fresh broccoli flowerettes
½ lb (230 g) fresh mushrooms, cleaned, cut in half
½ cup (120 ml) red or orange pepper strips
2 tbs (30 ml) chopped fresh chives
coarsely ground black pepper
1 cup (240 ml) nonfat sour cream alternative
½ cup (120 ml) shredded carrot
1 - 8 oz pkg (240 g) HEALTHY CHOICE Fat Free
   Natural Fancy Shredded Cheddar Cheese
12 oz (360 g) thin spaghetti, cooked, drained

Steam asparagus, broccoli, mushrooms and pepper until crisp-tender. Toss with chives; season to taste with pepper. Combine sour cream alternative, carrot, and half of cheese. Toss with cooked spaghetti; arrange on serving platter. Top with vegetable mixture; sprinkle with remaining cheese. Serves 8.

Approximate nutritional analysis per serving:
Calories 239, Protein 10 g, Carbohydrates 38 g, Fat 1 g,
Cholesterol 5 mg, Sodium 234 mg

CHICK PEA LINGREENI

2 tbs (30 ml) GOYA Olive Oil
2 tbs (30 ml) butter
2 leeks or 1 large onion, sliced thin
2 cups (480 ml) shredded green cabbage
2 - 10 oz pkgs (600 g) frozen whole leaf spinach,
   thawed and drained
1 cup (240 ml) flour
1 cup (240 ml) water
1 packet GOYA Chicken Bouillon
1 cup (240 ml) ricotta cheese
1 - 16 oz can (480 g) GOYA Chick Peas, drained
1 lb (455 g) combined green and white noodles,
   cooked and drained
1 cup (240 ml) grated cheese

Heat oil and butter in large saucepan. Sauté vegetables one at a time over medium heat. Sprinkle flour and toss well. Add water and bouillon. As mixture thickens, add ricotta. Stir in beans and cook 10 minutes. Toss in noodles. Cook 3 minutes. Top with cheese. Serves 8.

Approximate nutritional analysis per serving:
Calories 511, Protein 23 g, Carbohydrates 71 g, Fat 16 g,
Cholesterol 33 mg, Sodium 597 mg

PASTA WITH ROASTED SQUASH, BRUSSELS SPROUTS AND FENNEL

1 - 2 lb (910 g) butternut squash, peeled, seeded,
   and cut into 1-inch cubes
1 - 10 oz container (300 g) fresh Brussels
   sprouts, cut in half
1 small bulb fennel, trimmed and thinly sliced
3 large cloves garlic, peeled and halved
¼ cup (60 ml) olive oil
¾ tsp (4 ml) salt
½ tsp (3 ml) dried oregano leaves
8 oz (240 g) penne or ziti pasta
¼ cup (60 ml) pumpkin seeds
1½ tsp (8 ml) TABASCO pepper sauce
½ cup (120 ml) grated Parmesan cheese

Preheat oven to 450°F (230°C). In a roasting pan, combine squash chunks, Brussels sprouts, fennel, garlic, olive oil, salt and oregano. Bake 20 minutes, stirring occasionally. Meanwhile prepare penne or ziti as package label directs. During last 2 minutes of roasting vegetables, add pumpkin seeds to the vegetables. Continue cooking until the seeds are lightly toasted. To serve, toss drained pasta with roasted vegetables, TABASCO pepper sauce and Parmesan cheese to mix well. Serves 4.

Approximate nutritional analysis per serving:
Calories 550, Protein 18 g, Carbohydrates 76 g, Fat 22 g,
Cholesterol 10 mg, Sodium 660 mg

FETTUCCINE WITH HOT MEXICAN BEAN SAUCE

1 - 15 oz can (450 g) any colored bean, drained
vegetable cooking spray
1 medium onion, chopped
1 clove garlic, minced
1 - 14½ oz can (435 g) "no added salt" stewed
   tomatoes, undrained and chopped
2 tbs (30 ml) chopped green chilies
1 tbs (15 ml) finely chopped fresh cilantro
1 tsp (5 ml) chili powder
½ tsp (3 ml) sugar
¼ tsp (1 ml) dried whole oregano, crushed
4 cups (910 ml) hot cooked fettuccine, without salt

Coat large skillet with cooking spray. Place over medium heat until hot. Add onion and garlic, and sauté until tender. Stir in tomatoes, green chilies, cilantro, chili powder, sugar and oregano. Cover and bring to a boil. Reduce heat and simmer 15 minutes, stirring occasionally. Mash beans slightly, and stir into tomato mixture. Serve over hot cooked fettuccine. Serves 4.

Approximate nutritional analysis per serving:
Calories 358, Protein 16 g, Carbohydrates 69 g, Fat 2 g,
Cholesterol 0 mg

Opposite: Creamy Pasta Primavera

Four-Pepper Penne

FOUR-PEPPER PENNE

1 medium onion, sliced
1 small red bell pepper, thinly sliced
1 small green bell pepper, thinly sliced
1 small yellow bell pepper, thinly sliced
1½ tsp (8 ml) minced garlic
1 tbs (15 ml) vegetable oil
1 - 26 oz jar (780 ml) HEALTHY CHOICE
    Traditional Pasta Sauce
1 tsp (5 ml) dried basil
½ tsp (3 ml) dried savory
¼ tsp (1 ml) black pepper
½ lb (230 g) penne, cooked and drained

In Dutch oven or large nonstick saucepan, cook and stir onion, bell peppers and garlic in hot oil until vegetables are tender-crisp. Add pasta sauce, basil, savory and black pepper. Heat through over medium heat. Serve over penne. Serves 6.

Approximate nutritional analysis per serving:
Calories 226, Fat 4 g, Cholesterol 0 mg, Sodium 385 mg

PASTA WITH ROASTED GARDEN VEGETABLES AND HERBS

1 each red, green and yellow bell pepper, quartered,
    seeds removed and cut into ½-inch wide strips
2 red onions, cut into ½-inch wide wedges
2 yellow squash, trimmed, in ½-inch slices
1 small eggplant trimmed, in 1-inch chunks
4 garlic cloves, peeled and halved
¼ cup (60 ml) BERTOLLI Extra Virgin Olive Oil
¼ cup (60 ml) finely chopped Italian parsley
2 tsp (10 ml) chopped fresh thyme leaves,
    stripped from stems
salt and freshly ground pepper to taste
12 oz (360 g) penne, radiatore or other pasta
1 tbs (15 ml) grated Parmesan cheese

Preheat oven to 400°F (205°C). Spread vegetables in a large roasting pan; add olive oil; toss to coat. Bake, turning often, until browned and tender, about 40 minutes. Add half of the parsley, thyme, salt and pepper.Cook pasta in large pot of boiling salted water until cooked to taste. Ladle out ½ cup of the pasta cooking liquid; reserve. Drain pasta.In serving bowl toss pasta with half the vegetables, cooking liquid and cheese. Spoon remaining vegetables and parsley on top. Serves 4.

Approximate nutritional analysis per serving:
Calories 514, Protein 14 g, Carbohydrates 80 g, Fat 16 g,
Cholesterol 1 mg, Sodium 46 mg

Opposite: Pasta with Roasted Garden Vegetables and Herbs

LINGUINE FLORENTINE

12 oz (360 g) thin linguine
4 tbs (60 ml) butter or margarine
3 shallots, minced
8 oz (240 g) fresh mushrooms, sliced
10 oz (300 g) fresh spinach, coarsely chopped
½ tsp (3 ml) McCORMICK or SCHILLING
    Pure Anise Extract
1 cup (240 ml) heavy cream
½ cup (120 ml) grated Parmesan cheese

Cook linguine, drain and return to pot. While linguine is cooking, melt butter in a large skillet over medium-high heat. Add shallots and mushrooms; sauté 2 minutes. Add spinach and sauté 2 minutes more. Add to drained linguine and toss. Combine extract and cream and toss with linguine along with the Parmesan cheese. Toss until all ingredients are warm and well blended. Serves 4.

Approximate nutritional analysis per serving:
Calories 700, Protein 20 g, Carbohydrates 69 g, Fat 39 g,
Cholesterol 122 mg, Sodium 435 mg

GARLIC PEPPER PARMESAN PASTA

1 tbs (15 ml) margarine
¼ lb (115 g) fresh mushrooms. sliced
¼ cup (60 ml) sliced green onions
1½ tsp (8 ml) Instant Minced Onion
2 tsp (10 ml) flour
1 cup (240 ml) canned evaporated skimmed milk
¾ tsp (4 ml) California Style Blend Garlic Pepper
⅓ cup (80 ml) grated Parmesan cheese
8 oz (240 g) fettuccine or other pasta, cooked

Melt margarine in a saucepan over medium heat; add mushrooms and both onions. Sauté 3 minutes; remove and set aside. Add flour to saucepan; gradually add milk, stirring with a whisk. Stir in Garlic Pepper. Cook over medium heat until mixture comes to a boil, stirring constantly. Remove from heat and stir in cheese and mushroom mixture. Toss with cooked pasta. Serve immediately. Garnish with additional cheese if desired. Serves 6 side dishes.

Approximate nutritional analysis per serving:
Calories 224, Protein 11 g, Carbohydrates 34 g, Fat 5 g,
Cholesterol 5 mg, Sodium 181 mg

PASTA E FAGIOLI

2 cans GOYA White Kidney Beans, drained
4 tbs (60 ml) GOYA Extra Virgin Olive Oil
1 large onion, chopped
1 clove garlic, minced
2 cups (480 ml) canned plum tomatoes
1 cup (240 ml) macaroni, cooked
fresh basil to taste
¼ tsp (1 ml) dry basil
½ tsp (3 ml) salt
black pepper, few grains
grated parmesan cheese

Heat oil in 2-qt saucepan; add onion and garlic and sauté until onion is tender. Add tomatoes and simmer 10 minutes. Combine beans, cooked macaroni, basil, salt and pepper. Bring to a boil. Serve hot. Garnish with Parmesan cheese. Serves 4.

Approximate nutritional analysis per serving:
Calories 433, Protein 17 g, Carbohydrates 60 g, Fat 15 g,
Cholesterol 0 mg, Sodium 133   mg

SOUTHWESTERN PASTA SAUCE

2 medium onions, sliced
1 clove garlic, minced
¼ cup (60 ml) olive oil
1 - 28 oz can (840 g) tomatoes,
    crushed or coarsely chopped
¾ tsp (4 ml) TABASCO pepper sauce
¼ tsp (1 ml) salt
2-3 tbs (30-45 ml) fresh cilantro, minced
¼ tsp (1 ml) granulated sugar
12 oz (360 g) angel hair pasta, cooked and drained
grated Parmesan cheese, optional

Heat oil over medium heat in a large, heavy non-aluminum saucepan. Stir in onions and garlic; sauté 10-12 minutes, stirring occasionally, until tender. Add tomatoes, TABASCO pepper sauce, salt, cilantro and sugar; bring to a boil. Reduce heat to low and simmer uncovered 30 minutes until slightly thickened. Place hot cooked pasta on heated serving platter; top with sauce. Sprinkle with Parmesan cheese if desired. Serves 4.

Approximate nutritional analysis per serving:
Calories 490, Protein 13 g, Carbohydrates 74 g, Fat 16 g,
Cholesterol 0 mg, Sodium 470 mg

Opposite: Southwestern Pasta Sauce

ALFREDO PASTA SAUCE

1 - 10 oz pkg (300 g) soft tofu, drained
1 medium clove garlic
3 tbs (45 ml) Parmesan cheese, grated
2 tbs (30 ml) Romano cheese, grated
2 tbs (30 ml) soy oil
¼ tsp (1 ml) white pepper
1 tsp (5 ml) onion powder
1 tsp (5 ml) basil
1 tbs (15 ml) dried parsley
12 oz (360 g) fettuccine, cooked and drained

In a blender or food processor, combine all ingredients except fettuccine. Blend until creamy, about 30 seconds on high. Heat sauce and serve over hot cooked fettuccine. Serves 4.

Approximate nutritional analysis per 4 tbs serving sauce:
Calories 101, Protein 8 g, Carbohydrates 3 g, Fat 6 g,
Cholesterol 6 mg, Sodium 133 mg

Courtesy of the United Soybean Board.

Alfredo Pasta Sauce

THAILAND PEANUT PESTO

1 cup (240 ml) unsalted roasted peanuts
½ cup (120 ml) soy sauce
1 tsp (5 ml) Tabasco pepper sauce
¼ cup (60 ml) honey
⅓ cup (80 ml) water
3 cloves garlic, minced
½ cup (120 ml) sesame oil
12 oz (360 g) bow-tie pasta, freshly cooked
chopped scallions for garnish

Place peanuts in bowl of food processor, and process until finely ground. With motor running, add remaining ingredients, one at a time, through the feed tube. Process until a thick, smooth paste has formed. Transfer the mixture to a bowl, cover, and refrigerate until ready to use. Toss with hot bow-tie pasta and garnish with chopped scallions. Serves 4.

Approximate nutritional analysis per serving:
Calories 852, Protein 22 g, Carbohydrates 92 g, Fat 46 g,
Cholesterol 0 mg, Sodium 206 mg

NOODLES THAI STYLE

¼ cup (60 ml) ketchup
2 tbs (30 ml) reduced-sodium soy sauce
1 tbs (15 ml) sugar
¼-½ tsp (1-3 ml) crushed red pepper
¼ tsp (1 ml) ground ginger
2 tsp (10 ml) FLEISCHMANN'S Margarine
1 - 8 oz carton (240 ml) EGG BEATERS
    Real Egg Product
8 scallions, cut in 1½-inch pieces
1 clove garlic, minced
¾ lb (340 g) fresh bean sprouts, rinsed and drained
8 oz (240 g) linguine, cooked and hot
¼ cup (60 ml) dry roasted unsalted peanuts, chopped

Mix first 5 ingredients; set aside. In large nonstick skillet, over medium heat, heat 1 tbs margarine until bubbly. Add egg product and gently scramble until done; remove to another small bowl. In same skillet, in remaining margarine, sauté scallions and garlic for 2 minutes. Stir in bean sprouts; cook for 2 minutes. Stir in ketchup mixture until heated through; add egg product. Add hot cooked linguine, tossing until combined. Serve immediately topped with peanuts. Serves 6.

Approximate nutritional analysis per 1 cup serving:
Calories 250, Fat 5 g, Cholesterol 0 mg, Sodium 394 mg

FETTUCCINE WITH MIXED GREENS

CREAMY MIXTURE:
12 oz (360 g) nonfat cottage cheese
1 - 5 oz can (150 ml) evaporated skim milk
3 tbs (45 ml) balsamic vinegar
3 tbs (45 ml) all-purpose flour

3 cups (720 ml) chopped onions
1 cup (240 ml) chopped celery
2 tbs (30 ml) CHEF PAUL PRUDHOMME'S
    Vegetable Magic, in all
1 cup (240 ml) apple juice
4 cups (960 ml) chopped fresh mushrooms
4 cups (960 ml) chopped mustard greens
4 cups (960 ml) chopped collard greens
4 cups (960 ml) chopped chard
3½ cups (840 ml) vegetable stock, in all
3 cups (720 ml) cooked fettuccine

Place the creamy mixture ingredients in a blender and puree until smooth and creamy; set aside.

Preheat a heavy 5-qt pot, preferably nonstick, over high heat to 350°F (180°C), about 4 minutes. Add the onions, celery, and 1 tbs of the Vegetable Magic and cook, checking the bottom of the pot occasionally for sticking, until the vegetables start to brown, about 8 minutes. Add the apple juice, clear the bottom of the pot of any brown bits, then add the mushrooms and remaining Vegetable Magic. Stir and cook until most of the liquid evaporates, about 7-8 minutes. Add all the greens and 3 cups of the stock, stir, and cook 6 minutes.

Add the puréed creamy mixture and stir well. CAUTION: Dishes using these creamy mixtures can "break" or curdle easily if they are brought to a full boil. Therefore, bring the liquid just to a gentle boil, stir immediately, then reduce the heat to low and simmer, stirring occasionally, for 10 minutes. Add the remaining ½ cup stock, stir, and add the fettuccine. Stir and cook until the pasta is heated throughout, about 5-6 minutes. Serve immediately. Serves 4.

Approximate nutritional analysis per serving:Calories 392, Protein 23 g, Carbohydrates 73 g, Fat 2 g, Sodium 726 mg

LEMON-GARLIC ANGEL HAIR

3 large heads garlic
cooking spray
3 tbs (45 ml) GREY POUPON Dijon Mustard
2 tbs (30 ml) lemon juice
⅛ tsp (.5 ml) ground black pepper
2 cups (480 ml) cut-up fresh vegetables
    (snow peas, mushrooms, broccoli, carrots)
1 tbs (15 ml) FLEISCHMANN'S Margarine
½ cup (120 ml) water
8 oz (240 g) angel hair pasta, cooked and drained

Spray each head of garlic lightly with cooking spray; wrap each separately in foil. Place in small baking pan; bake at 400°F (205°C) for 45 minutes. Cool 10 minutes. Separate cloves; squeeze cloves to extract pulp (discard skins).

In food processor or electric blender, puree garlic pulp, mustard, lemon juice and pepper; set aside. In skillet, over medium-high heat, sauté vegetables in margarine until tender-crisp; add garlic mixture and water. Reduce heat to low; cook and stir until sauce is heated through. Toss with hot cooked angel hair. Serve immediately. Serves 4.

Approximate nutritional analysis per serving:
Calories 387, Fat 6 g, Cholesterol 0 mg, Sodium 398 mg

LINGUINE WITH SPINACH PESTO

1 - 10 oz pkg (300 g) frozen chopped spinach,
    thawed and drained
1 - 8 oz carton (240 ml) EGG BEATERS
    Real Egg Product
⅓ cup (80 ml) PLANTERS Walnut Pieces
¼ cup (60 ml) grated Parmesan cheese
2 cloves garlic, crushed
1 lb (455 g) thin linguine, cooked in
    unsalted water and drained
½ cup (120 ml) diced red pepper

In electric blender or food processor, blend spinach, egg product, walnuts, cheese and garlic until smooth. Toss with hot linguine and red pepper. Serve immediately with additional cheese, if desired. Serves 8.

Approximate nutritional analysis per serving:
Calories 278, Fat 5 g, Cholesterol 2 mg, Sodium 119 mg

HEARTY MEAT SAUCE

1 cup (240 ml) onions, chopped
2 carrots, peeled and shredded
1 clove garlic, minced
¼ cup (60 ml) butter, margarine or oil
1 lb (455 g) lean ground beef
1 - 28 oz can (840 g) whole tomatoes
1 - 6 oz can (180 g) tomato paste
¼ cup (60 ml) chopped fresh basil leaves
    or 1 tbs (15 ml) dried basil leaves
½ tsp (3 ml) dried oregano
1 tsp (5 ml) salt
¾ cup (180 ml) red wine or tomato juice
hot, freshly-cooked rice or pasta

Sauté onions, carrots, garlic in butter, margarine or oil in heavy skillet until vegetables are tender. Add ground meat and brown. Add remaining ingredients, except rice or pasta. Heat to boiling; reduce heat and cook over low heat until sauce is very thick, about 1 hour. Refrigerate to cool thoroughly, then skim off fat and discard. When ready to serve, heat sauce to boiling and serve over freshly cooked rice or pasta. Sauce may be frozen. Yields 6 cups.

Approximate nutritional analysis per ½ cup serving sauce:
Calories 171, Protein 11 g, Carbohydrates 8 g, Fat 10 g,
Cholesterol 42 mg, Sodium 471 mg

BROCCOLI-TUNA PASTA TOSS

16 oz (450 g) spaghetti
1 - 10 oz pkg (300 g) frozen cut broccoli
1 - 10¾ oz can (325 ml) condensed
    cream of chicken soup
1 - 8 oz can (240 g) sliced water chestnuts, drained
½ cup (120 ml) DANNON Plain Nonfat
    or Lowfat Yogurt
½ cup (2 oz) (60 g) shredded cheddar cheese
1 tsp (5 ml) Worcestershire sauce
¼ tsp (1 ml) garlic powder
1 - 9¼ oz can (280 g) tuna packed in water, flaked

Cook pasta according to package directions, adding frozen broccoli the last 5-7 minutes of cooking; drain well. Return pasta and broccoli to saucepan; cover and keep warm.

In medium bowl combine soup, water chestnuts, yogurt, cheese. Worcestershire sauce and garlic powder. Stir soup mixture into saucepan with drained pasta and broccoli. Gently fold in tuna, being careful not to break up large pieces. Cook over medium-low heat about 5 minutes or until heated through, stirring once or twice. Serve immediately. Serves 5.

Approximate nutritional analysis per serving:
Calories 306, Protein 22 g, Carbohydrates 35 g, Fat 9 g,
Cholesterol 25 mg, Sodium 815 mg

MAMA'S PASTA

1 lb (455 g) sweet Italian sausage
1 lb (455 g) hot Italian sausage
1 cup (240 ml) chopped onion
1 tbs (15 ml) minced garlic
¼ cup (60 ml) fresh parsley, minced
¾ cup (180 ml) dry white wine
5 cups (1.2 L) canned Italian plum tomatoes
    with juice
salt to taste
pepper to taste
1 lb (455 g) pasta of your choice: rigatoni,
    bow ties, rotelle, spaghetti or linguine
1 - 16 oz can (480 g) any white bean, drained
1½ cups (355 ml) chopped bitter greens
    (such as arugula or chicory)
1 cup (240 ml) freshly grated Parmesan cheese

Crumble sausages into heavy sauté pan over medium heat. Stir in onion, garlic and parsley and sauté, stirring frequently, for about 15 minutes or until sausage is cooked. Add white wine and tomatoes and cook for about 30 minutes or until sauce is well flavored. Add salt and pepper.

Cook pasta; drain well. Return to pot and stir in sausage mixture, beans and bitter greens. Return to heat to warm through. Serve with grated Parmesan cheese. Serves 6.

Approximate nutritional analysis per serving:
Calories 1063, Protein 54 g, Carbohydrates 84 g, Fat 54 g,
Cholesterol 139 mg, Sodium 260   mg

Courtesy of the American Dry Bean Board.

QUICK HOMEMADE RED SAUCE

2 tbs (30 ml) GOYA Olive Oil
1 cup (240 ml) diced onions
1 cup (240 ml) diced carrots
1 tbs (15 ml) minced garlic
2 tbs (30 ml) GOYA Sofrito
4 - 8 oz cans (960 ml) GOYA Tomato Sauce
1 tsp (5 ml) oregano

In medium saucepan, heat oil and sauté vegetables until golden. Add remaining ingredients, cover, bring to boil and simmer 15 minutes. Yields 4 cups.

Approximate nutritional analysis per ½ cup serving:
Calories 64, Protein 1 g, Carbohydrates 8 g, Fat 4 g,
Cholesterol 0 mg, Sodium 87 mg

Opposite: Broccoli-Tuna Pasta Toss

CLASSIC SPAGHETTI SAUCE

2½ oz (75 g) dried mushrooms*
1½ cups (355 ml) water
1 lb (455 g) ground round or chuck
1 lb (455 g) Italian sausage
1 tbs (15 ml) sweet basil
1 tsp (5 ml) oregano
1 tbs (15 ml) marjoram
1-2 tbs (15-30 ml) salt
1 tsp (5 ml) fresh ground black pepper
3 chopped onions
3 chopped green peppers
2 - 6 oz cans (360 g) LIBBY'S Tomato Paste
2 - 28 oz cans (1.7 kg) LIBBY'S Whole Peeled
    Tomatoes in juice
1½ cups (355 ml) dry red wine
3 bay leaves
2 tbs (30 ml) olive oil
7 cloves garlic, sliced
1 cup (240 ml) fresh chopped parsley

* ½ lb (230 g) fresh mushrooms or 1 - 6 oz can (180 g) can
 be substituted but flavor will be altered.

Soak mushrooms in 1½ cups water at least 15 minutes.
In large skillet, brown ground round and sausage adding basil,
oregano, marjoram, 1 tbs salt and pepper. Transfer to a large
soup or sauce pan; mix in onions and green peppers. Add
tomato paste; heat and mix thoroughly. Add tomatoes,
mushrooms with liquid, 1 cup red wine and bay leaves. Simmer
for 1 hour, taste and add up to 1 tbs more of salt if needed.
Cook for another 1½ hours. In a small frying pan, heat olive oil
and brown garlic. Add this to sauce along with ½ cup red wine
and parsley. Continue cooking for another 30 minutes before
removing from heat. Taste for additional seasoning.
Yields 3½ qts.
    Note: May be made ahead and frozen.

Approximate nutritional analysis per 1 cup serving:
Calories 338, Protein 18 g, Carbohydrates 15 g, Fat 21 g,
Cholesterol 62 mg, Sodium 275 mg

REDUCED CALORIE MEAT SAUCE

3 cups (720 ml) chopped onions
2½ cup (590 ml) chopped green bell pepper
2 cups (480 ml) chopped celery
3 tbs (45 ml) CHEF PAUL PRUDHOMME'S
    Meat Magic
1 tbs (15 ml) dried sweet basil leaves
1 tsp (5 ml) dried oregano
8½ cups (2 kg) defatted chicken stock, in all
4 bay leaves
2 tbs (30 ml) fresh garlic, finely minced
10 medium-large ripe tomatoes, peeled,
    stemmed and cut up
2 lbs (910 g) ground turkey
1 cup (240 ml) chopped green onions, tops only
1 tsp (5 ml) salt
4 packets EQUAL or SWEET AND LOW
1 lb (455 g) spaghetti, cooked and drained

Heat a large, deep skillet or Dutch oven over high heat. When
very hot, add 2 cups onions, 1½ cups bell peppers, 1 cup celery
and 2 tbs Meat Magic. Let cook 2-2½ minutes, add the basil
and oregano and stir once to distribute the seasonings and
brown the vegetables evenly. Cook 1-2 minutes, or until
vegetables begin sticking hard to the bottom of the pan. Add
¼ cup stock, scrape all the brown on the bottom of the pan,
stir well and continue cooking 3 minutes, stirring occasionally.
Add the remaining 1 tbs Meat Magic, stir and cook 1 minute.
Add the bay leaves and another ¼ cup stock, scrape up the pan
bottom well and cook 3 minutes. Add ½ the tomatoes, scrape
up the pan bottom, stir well and cook 4 minutes. Add the
ground turkey, breaking it up with a wooden spoon, and add
the remaining 1 cup each chopped onions, peppers and celery,
and the green onions. Continue cooking about 20 minutes,
stirring occasionally.

    When turkey has cooked about 20 minutes, stir in the
remaining cut up tomatoes and the salt, and continue cooking
8 minutes, stirring occasionally. Stir in 3 cups stock, scrape the
pan bottom if necessary, cover the pot and cook 17 minutes.
Remove the cover, add 1 cup stock, stirring well, re-cover and
cook another 30 minutes. Remove from heat and cool slightly.
Puree the sauce in batches in a blender or food processor and
return to the skillet or Dutch oven over high heat. When the
sauce begins to bubble, add the remaining 4 cups stock and
bring to a boil. Remove from heat, add the sweetener and stir
thoroughly.

    To serve, place ½ cup of spaghetti on each plate and cover
with about 1¼ cups meat sauce. Serves 12.

Approximate nutritional analysis per serving sauce:
Calories 370, Protein 25 g, Carbohydrates 41 g, Fat 12 g,
Cholesterol 52 mg, Sodium 304 mg

ROBUST RED BEANS AND BOWTIES

2 tbs (30 ml) GOYA Olive Oil
1 lb (455 g) Italian sausage
1 cup (240 ml) LA VINA Red Cooking Wine
1 - 10 oz pkg (300 g) frozen chopped broccoli,
thawed and drained
1 recipe QUICK HOMEMADE RED SAUCE
   (previous recipe)
   or 1 - 26 oz jar (780 ml) prepared sauce
1 - 16 oz can (480 g) GOYA Red Kidney Beans
1 lb (455 g) bowties, cooked and drained.

In large hot skillet, heat 1 tsp oil. Brown sausages on all sides, breaking apart. Add wine, lower flame, cover and simmer until wine is absorbed. Set aside on plate to cool. Sauté broccoli in 1 tbs oil. Add sausage, sauce and beans. Cover and boil. Lower flame and simmer 10 minutes. Stir in bowties and heat thoroughly. Serves 8.

Approximate nutritional analysis per serving:
Calories 598, Protein 25 g, Carbohydrates 63 g, Fat 26 g,
Cholesterol 47 mg, Sodium 835 mg

PASTA WITH SAUSAGE, EGGPLANT AND OLIVES

1 lb (455 g) mild or hot Italian sausage
   (or combination) sliced ½ inch thick
1 medium to large onion, chopped
2 tsp (10 ml) minced garlic
1 - 1 lb 13 oz can (845 g) whole peeled tomatoes,
   undrained
½ cup (120 ml) dry red wine
1-1¼ lbs (455 g-1 kg) eggplant, cut into ¾-inch cubes
1½ cups (355 ml) pitted CALIFORNIA
   ripe olives, cut into wedges
½ cup (120 ml) finely chopped fresh parsley
2 tbs (30 ml) finely chopped fresh basil
2 tbs (30 ml) finely chopped fresh oregano
2 tsp (10 ml) sugar
salt and pepper
1 lb (455 g) dried shell, tubular, spiral or other
   similar-sized pasta, cooked and drained
grated fresh Parmesan cheese

Brown sausage in large skillet, remove from pan and set aside. Drain pan, leaving a film of drippings on bottom. Add onion and garlic to pan and sauté gently until onion is soft. Add undrained canned tomatoes and break them up with fork. Add wine, eggplant, olives, parsley, basil, oregano and sugar. Add browned sausages. Cover, bring to boil and boil gently, stirring occasionally, for 30 minutes. If it gets too dry, add more wine. Season with salt and pepper as desired. Toss with pasta. Serve with Parmesan cheese. Serves 4.
Approximate nutritional analysis per serving:

Calories 967, Protein 42 g, Carbohydrates 113 g, Fat 37 g,
Cholesterol 88 mg, Sodium 1820 mg

RIGATONI WITH CHEESE, BACON AND PEPPERS

8 slices bacon, cut into 1-inch pieces
1 medium red pepper, cut into strips
1 medium yellow pepper, cut into strips
½ tsp (3 ml) chopped fresh garlic
2 cups (8 oz) (240 g) LAND O LAKES
   Shredded Mozzarella Cheese
½ cup (120 ml) small pitted black olives
¼ cup (60 ml) freshly grated Parmesan cheese
⅛ tsp (.5 ml) ground red pepper
¼ cup (60 ml) chopped fresh parsley
8 oz (240 g) dried rigatoni, cooked and drained

In 10-inch skillet cook bacon over medium-high heat, stirring occasionally, until bacon is crisp, 6-8 minutes. Remove bacon from pan; set aside. Drain pan drippings, reserving 2 tbs.
In same skillet, add red pepper, yellow pepper and garlic to reserved pan drippings. Cook over medium heat, stirring occasionally, until peppers are crisply tender, 4-5 minutes. Add rigatoni, bacon and all remaining ingredients except parsley. Continue cooking, stirring occasionally, until cheese is melted 3-5 minutes. Sprinkle with parsley. Toss with pasta. Serves 6.

Approximate nutritional analysis per serving:
Calories 360, Protein 19 g, Carbohydrates 31 g, Fat 18 g,
Cholesterol 35 mg, Sodium 470 mg

QUICK AND SPICY PASTA DEL MAR

1 medium onion, diced
1 tsp (5 ml) olive oil
1 - 10 oz can (300 g) baby clams, drained
2 tsp (10 ml) minced garlic
1 - 26 oz jar (780 ml) HEALTHY CHOICE
   Traditional Pasta Sauce
1 tsp (5 ml) dried basil
½ tsp (3 ml) dried thyme
⅛ tsp (.5 ml) black pepper
⅛ tsp (.5 ml) cayenne pepper
½ lb (230 g) raw medium shrimp, peeled
½ lb (230 g) linguine, cooked and drained

In large saucepan, sauté onion in hot oil until tender. Add clams and garlic; cook and stir 1 minute longer. Stir in pasta sauce, basil, thyme, black pepper and cayenne pepper. Heat, stirring occasionally, until mixture comes to a boil. Add shrimp; reduce heat to medium; cook until shrimp are pink and cooked through. Serve sauce over linguine. Serves 6.

Approximate nutritional analysis per serving:Calories 278, Protein 28 g,
Fat 3 g, Cholesterol 105 mg, Sodium 520 mg

Opposite: Pasta with Sausage, Eggplant and Olives; Orzo, Olives and Shrimp

PASTA CARBONARA

½ cup (120 ml) sliced CALIFORNIA ripe olives
½ cup (120 ml) sliced mushrooms
½ cup (120 ml) crumbled bacon
¼ cup (60 ml) minced scallion greens
½ tsp (3 ml) black pepper, coarse
3 tbs (45 ml) margarine
¾ cup (180 ml) grated Parmesan cheese
3 large eggs, beaten
1 cup (240 ml) whipping cream
7 oz (210 g) packaged linguine, cooked and drained

Combine first 5 ingredients in small bowl. Put margarine in 2-qt casserole. Microwave on HIGH for 1 minute. Add olive mixture. Microwave on HIGH for 1 minute. Add remaining ingredients. Mix well. Microwave on HIGH for 3-5 minutes, stirring once per minute, or until sauce is thickened. Serves 6.

Approximate nutritional analysis per serving:
Calories 453, Protein 15 g, Carbohydrates 31 g, Fat 31 g,
Cholesterol 174 mg, Sodium 591 mg

PASTA CALIFORNIA

½ lb (230 g) thick-sliced smoked bacon
8-10 oz (240-300 g) fettucine
boiling water
¼ cup (60 ml) unsalted butter or margarine
¼ cup (60 ml) coarsely chopped garlic
3 cups (720 ml) seeded and chopped tomatoes
¼ cup (60 ml) packed, fresh basil leaves, chopped
1 cup (240 ml) CALIFORNIA ripe olive wedges
8 oz (240 g) goat cheese, crumbled
¼-½ tsp (1-3 ml) ground black pepper

Cut bacon crosswise into 1-inch lengths. Brown in skillet and remove from pan. Drain off all but 2 tbs fat. Drop fettucine into boiling water, return to boil and cook 6-7 minutes, or just until tender. Meanwhile, add butter to pan with bacon fat; melt over low heat. Add garlic and sauté gently 2 minutes. Add tomatoes and basil and sauté lightly. Add olives and toss lightly. Just before draining pasta, add cheese to sauce along with pepper and bacon. Heat, stirring, for 1-2 minutes to heat through. Pour sauce immediately over pasta. Serve promptly. Garnish with basil sprigs if desired. Serves 4.

Approximate nutritional analysis per serving:
Calories 887, Protein 33 g, Carbohydrates 35 g, Fat 71 g,
Cholesterol 182 mg, Sodium 205 mg

PENNE ALL' ARRABBIATA

½ cup (120 ml) diced bacon
3 tbs (45 ml) butter
¾ cup (180 ml) pureed tomatoes
½ cup (120 ml) grated Romano cheese
½ cup (120 ml) grated Parmesan cheese
2 cloves garlic
4-5 fresh basil leaves chopped
1 small hot red pepper
salt
1 lb (455 g) DE CECCO Penne

In a skillet, sauté the garlic in butter and remove. Add the diced bacon and let brown for a few minutes. Add the tomato puree and red pepper; season to taste. Cover the skillet and continue cooking about 20 minutes more, over moderate heat. A few minutes before taking the sauce off the heat, remove the red pepper and add chopped basil. Cook the DE CECCO Penne for 11 minutes in boiling salted water, drain and add the sauce. Sprinkle with Romano and Parmesan cheese, toss and serve. Serves 6.

Approximate nutritional analysis per serving:
Calories 425, Protein 17 g, Carbohydrates 58 g, Fat 13 g,
Cholesterol 33 mg, Sodium 369 mg

Pasta Carbonara

CATFISH PASTA PRIMAVERA

8 oz (240 g) fettucine
½ small red pepper, cut into thin strips
½ small yellow pepper, cut into thin strips
½ small green pepper, cut into thin strips
4 oz (120 g) pea pods, trimmed
6 green onions, cut into strips
2 tbs (30 ml) chopped shallots
¼ cup (60 ml) butter or margarine
1 cup (240 ml) dry white wine or chicken broth
½ tsp (3 ml) salt
¼ tsp (1 ml) pepper
1 lb (455 g) Mississippi farm-raised catfish
fillets, cut into bite-size pieces
4 large sun-dried tomatoes in olive oil, drained
    and coarsely chopped, optional
⅔ cup (160 ml) freshly grated Parmesan cheese
¼ cup (60 ml) chopped fresh dill
    or 1 tbs (15 ml) dried dill
freshly grated Parmesan cheese
freshly ground pepper

Cook fettucine according to package directions; drain. Meanwhile, in a large skillet cook red pepper, yellow pepper, green pepper, pea pods, onions and shallots in butter or margarine until peppers are just crisp-tender. Remove vegetables from skillet.

Add white wine, salt and pepper to skillet. Bring to boil. Add catfish. Return to boil; reduce heat. Simmer, uncovered, about 3 minutes or until catfish flakes easily, stirring occasionally. Add sun-dried tomatoes, if desired. Return vegetables to skillet, tossing gently to coat.

Place cooked fettucine in a large serving bowl. Add catfish mixture, tossing to coat. Sprinkle with Parmesan cheese and dill. Stir gently to mix. Serve with fresh Parmesan cheese and pepper. Serves 4.

Approximate nutritional analysis per serving:
Calories 603, Protein 38 g, Carbohydrates 51 g, Fat 23 g,
Cholesterol 112 mg, Sodium 551 mg

Courtesy of the Catfish Institute.

SEAFOOD ROMANO WITH MUSHROOMS AND SQUASH

2 tbs (30 ml) olive oil
4-5 cloves garlic, minced
1 large onion, coarsely chopped
½ red or green pepper, chopped
1 cup (240 ml) fresh mushrooms, sliced
1 cup (240 ml) green or yellow squash, chopped
1 - 16 oz can (480 g) stewed tomatoes, chopped
1 - 28 oz can (840 ml) tomato sauce
1 - 15 oz can (450 ml) tomato sauce
1 - 6 oz can (180 g) tomato paste
1 tbs (15 ml) Italian seasoning
1 tbs (15 ml) OLD BAY Seasoning
1 seasoning cube, fish flavor
½ tsp (3 ml) garlic salt
2 tbs (30 ml) sugar
1 cup (240 ml) grated Romano cheese
½ cup (120 ml) Burgundy wine
1½ lbs (680 g) peeled and deveined shrimp, sea legs,
    chopped lobster meat, bay scallops,
    crab meat or combination of seafood

In a large pot, heat the olive oil and sauté the garlic, onion, pepper, mushrooms and squash. Add the remaining ingredients except the seafood and simmer for 2 hours, or microwave on HIGH for 45 minutes. Add the seafood and simmer an additional 45 minutes, or microwave another 15 minutes. Serve with cooked pasta. Sauce can be refrigerated for several days or frozen. Yields 3 qts. Serves 12.

Approximate nutritional analysis per 1 cup serving:
Calories 170, Protein 16 g, Carbohydrates 14 g, Fat 6 g,
Cholesterol 93 mg, Sodium 437 mg

OLD BAY NOODLES AND CRAB

4 tbs (60 ml) butter or margarine
1 lb (455 g) lump crab meat, cooked
1 tsp (5 ml) OLD BAY Seasoning, or more to taste
¾ cup (180 ml) half and half
¼ cup (60 ml) sherry
3 egg yolks, beaten
1 lb (455 g) broad noodles, cooked and drained

In a medium saucepan, heat butter. Add cooked crab meat and OLD BAY Seasoning. Cook at medium until very hot. Pour in half and half and bring to a boil; add sherry. Pour some of the hot liquid slowly into egg yolks while beating vigorously. Return to the crab mixture. Cook until sauce is thickened; do not boil. Mix with cooked noodles. Serve hot. Serves 4.

Approximate nutritional analysis per serving:
Calories 705, Protein 40 g, Carbohydrates 87 g, Fat 19 g,
Cholesterol 303 mg, Sodium 451 mg

SALSA MARINARA ALLA SARDA
Seafood Marinara with Linguine

2 tbs (30 ml) olive oil
1 cup (240 ml) chopped onion
3 large cloves garlic, minced
1 - 14½ oz can (435 g) CONTADINA Whole Peeled
 Tomatoes or Recipe Ready Diced
 Tomatoes, undrained
1 - 12 oz can (360 g) CONTADINA Tomato Paste
½ cup (120 ml) dry red wine
1 - 14½ oz can (435 ml) chicken broth
1 tbs (15 ml) chopped fresh basil
 or 2 tsp (10 ml) dried basil leaves, crushed
2 tsp (10 ml) chopped fresh oregano
 or ½ tsp (3 ml) dried oregano leaves, crushed
1 tsp (5 ml) salt, optional
8 oz (230 g) fresh or frozen medium shrimp,
 peeled and deveined
8 oz (230 g) fresh or frozen bay scallops
1 lb (455 g) linguine, cooked and drained

In large skillet, heat 1 tbs oil; sauté onion and garlic for
2 minutes. Add tomatoes and juice, tomato paste, wine and
broth; stir to break up whole tomatoes. Add basil, oregano and
salt; bring to a boil. Simmer for 10 minutes. In small skillet,
heat remaining oil; sauté shrimp and scallops for 3-4 minutes or
until cooked. Add to sauce; simmer for 2-3 minutes. Serve over
warm linguine. Serves 6.

Approximate nutritional analysis per serving:
Calories 265, Protein 20 g, Carbohydrates 35 g, Fat 5 g,
Cholesterol 70 mg, Sodium 620 mg

FARFALLE IN SALMON SAUCE

1 clove garlic
3-4 tbs (45-60 ml) DE CECCO Extra Virgin Olive Oil
1 large can salmon, drained
1½ cup (355 ml) pureed tomatoes
1 small hot red pepper
salt
3 tbs (45 ml) chopped parsley
1 lb (455 g) DE CECCO Farfalle

In a skillet, cook the garlic in olive oil, and then remove the
clove. Add the salmon, mashed with a fork, and let simmer for
a few minutes. Add the pureed tomatoes and red pepper. Mix
well, season and continue cooking over moderate heat for
about 20 minutes. Before taking the sauce from the heat,
remove the red pepper and sprinkle sauce with chopped
parsley. Cook the DE CECCO Farfalle for 10 minutes in
briskly boiling salted water. Drain the pasta, mix it with half
the sauce you have made, pouring the remainder in a bowl to
be served at the table. Serves 4.

Approximate nutritional analysis per serving:
Calories 837, Protein 53 g, Carbohydrates 88 g, Fat 29 g,
Cholesterol 81 mg, Sodium 1007 mg

PASTA WITH SHRIMP AND SCALLOPS IN CHIVE-GINGER SAUCE

1 cup (240 ml) BLUE DIAMOND
 Blanched Slivered Almonds
3 tbs (45 ml) butter, divided
½ lb (230 g) medium, raw shrimp,
 shelled and deveined
½ lb (230 g) scallops (if large, slice into medallions)
2 cloves garlic, chopped finely
1 tsp (5 ml) grated, fresh ginger
 or ⅛ tsp (.5 ml) powdered ginger
3 cups (720 ml) heavy cream
¼ cup (60 ml) thinly sliced, fresh chives
 or 1 tbs (15 ml) dried chives
1 tbs (15 ml) lemon juice
1 tsp (5 ml) grated lemon peel
½ tsp (3 ml) salt
¼ tsp (1 ml) white pepper
1 lb (455 g) fresh fettucine, cooked and drained
 or 8 oz (240 g) dried fettucine, cooked and
 drained

Sauté almonds in 1 tbs butter until golden; reserve. Slice
shrimp in half lengthwise. Sauté scallops and shrimp in
remaining 2 tbs butter over medium-high heat, about
2 minutes or until barely tender. Reserve. Mix garlic and
ginger and cream. Cook over medium-high heat until sauce
thickens and lightly coats the back of a spoon. Stir in chives,
lemon juice, lemon peel, salt and pepper. Add seafood and heat
through. Add almonds. Toss with hot, cooked pasta. Serves 4.

Approximate nutritional analysis per serving:
Calories 1205, Protein 39 g, Carbohydrates 56 g, Fat 94 g,
Cholesterol 373 mg, Sodium 605 mg

Opposite: Pasta with Shrimps and Scallops
in Chive-Ginger Sauce

SILVERADO SEAFOOD PASTA

1 - 10 oz jar (300 g) fresh oysters, halved if large
½ lb (230 g) fresh scallops, cut up if large
½ lb (230 g) prawns, shelled and deveined
2 tbs (30 ml) bottled or fresh minced garlic
¼ cup (60 ml) butter or margarine
¼ cup (60 ml) olive oil
⅛-¼ tsp (.5-1 ml) ground saffron or saffron threads
¼ cup (60 ml) chopped fresh fennel or dill leaves
1 lb (455 g) Roma or regular tomatoes, chopped
1 cup (240 ml) CALIFORNIA ripe olive wedges
¼ cup (60 ml) dry white wine mixed with
    1 tbs (15 ml) flour
8 oz (240 g) angel hair pasta (capellini)

Gently sauté oysters, scallops, prawns and garlic in butter and olive oil for 5 minutes or just until cooked. Add saffron, fennel, tomatoes and olives and cook a few minutes to heat; add wine-flour mixture and cook, stirring until thickened and glossy. Meanwhile, drop pasta into a large pot of boiling water and boil for 3 minutes; drain and toss with olive oil to coat. To serve, divide hot pasta into wide soup bowls, ladle seafood sauce over. Serves 4.

Approximate nutritional analysis per serving:
Calories 657, Protein 35 g, Carbohydrates 55 g, Fat 32 g,
Cholesterol 178 mg, Sodium 576 mg

LINGUINE WITH OLIVE-CLAM SAUCE

1 tbs (15 ml) olive oil
1 tbs (15 ml) butter or margarine
1 tbs (15 ml) minced garlic
3 tbs (45 ml) flour
2 - 6½ oz cans (390 g) chopped clams,
    packed in their own juice
½ cup (120 ml) milk
3 tbs (45 ml) wine *or* 1 tbs (15 ml) lemon juice
½ cup (120 ml) coarsely chopped
    CALIFORNIA ripe olives
2 tbs (30 ml) minced parsley
salt and pepper
4 servings hot cooked linguine

Heat oil and butter in skillet, add garlic and gently sauté 1 minute over medium-low heat. Mix in flour until blended. Remove from heat. Drain clams, saving liquid. Add milk to liquid to get a measure of 1½ cups. Add, with clams, to butter mixture. Cook, stirring until mixture comes to a boil and is thickened. Stir in wine, olives, parsley and salt and pepper to taste. Heat through. Serve over pasta. Serves 4.

Approximate nutritional analysis per serving:
Calories 599, Protein 29 g, Carbohydrates 94 g, Fat 10 g,
Cholesterol 43 mg, Sodium 191 mg

SMOKED SALMON AND OLIVE PASTA

2 cups (480 ml) heavy cream
3 medium cloves garlic, crushed
¼ tsp (1 ml) pepper
1 tsp (5 ml) finely chopped lemon zest
    (yellow part of peel)
1 cup (240 ml) pitted CALIFORNIA ripe olives,
    chopped
½ cup (120 ml) white wine
12 oz (360 g) fusilli pasta
6 oz (180 g) smoked salmon, thinly sliced
    and cut into short strips

Heat cream with garlic and sauté in pan. Add pepper, lemon zest, olives and wine; bring to boil. Simmer for 10 minutes to blend flavors and reduce a little. At same time, drop fusille into kettle of boiling water, return to boil and boil gently for 8-10 minutes or until cooked al dente. Drain pasta. Discard garlic from sauce. Add pasta and salmon to sauce and toss well. Adjust salt if necessary. Top with freshly ground black pepper and chopped parsley if you like and serve at once. Serves 4.

Approximate nutritional analysis per serving:
Calories 857, Protein 22 g, Carbohydrates 71 g, Fat 53 g,
Cholesterol 175 mg, Sodium 818 mg

PASTA PUTTANESCA

1 - 14½ oz can (435 g) stewed tomatoes
1 cup (240 ml) pitted CALIFORNIA ripe olives,
    chopped
1 small tomato, seeded and chopped
½ cup (120 ml) packed, chopped fresh basil leaves
2 tsp (10 ml) capers
6 anchovy fillets, chopped
¼ cup (60 ml) extra virgin or virgin olive oil
2 tbs (30 ml) red wine vinegar
2 tsp (10 ml) minced garlic
½ tsp (3 ml) bottled red pepper flakes
½ lb (230 g) spaghetti
grated Parmesan cheese

Whir canned tomatoes in blender until pureed. Combine tomatoes with olives, chopped fresh tomato, basil, capers, anchovy, olive oil, vinegar, garlic and red pepper in large skillet or saucepan. Bring to a boil and gently boil for 5 minutes or until flavors are well blended. Meanwhile, drop spaghetti into kettle of boiling water and gently boil for 8 minutes or until cooked but still al dente. Serve sauce over hot pasta with grated Parmesan on top. Sprinkle with additional chopped fresh basil if desired. Serves 4.

Approximate nutritional analysis per serving:
Calories 530, Protein 15 g, Carbohydrates 68 g, Fat 23 g,
Cholesterol 9 mg, Sodium 1076 mg

ORZO, OLIVES AND SHRIMP

½ lb (230 g) uncooked orzo (rice-shaped pasta)
3 tbs (45 ml) olive oil, divided
⅓ cup (80 ml) finely chopped parsley
salt
1 cup (240 ml) chopped onion
2 tsp (10 ml) minced garlic
3 cups (720 ml) chopped tomatoes,
    drained and chopped
½ cup (120 ml) dry white wine
1½ tsp (8 ml) dry rosemary, crumbled
1½ lbs (685 g) medium shrimp, shelled and
deveined, if necessary
1 cup (240 ml) pitted CALIFORNIA ripe olive, halved
¼ cup (60 ml) finely shredded basil or parsley
salt and pepper
2 oz (60 g) feta cheese, crumbled

Drop orzo into boiling water, return to boil and boil gently for 8 minutes or until tender but still firm to bite. Drain. Toss with 1 tbs olive oil, the parsley and salt as desired. Keep warm.

Heat 2 tbs olive oil in large skillet or kettle. Add onion and garlic and sauté gently until onion is soft. Add tomatoes, wine and rosemary and cook over medium heat about 5 minutes or until hot and bubbly. Add shrimp and cook, stirring, for 5 minutes or until they firm up and turn pink. Stir in olives, basil and salt and pepper to taste. If mixture seems dry, pour in a little extra wine to give a saucy character.

To serve, spoon orzo onto plate and top with shrimp sauce. Sprinkle with feta. Serves 4.

Approximate nutritional analysis per serving:
Calories 647, Protein 47 g, Carbohydrates 61 g, Fat 22 g,
Cholesterol 271 mg, Sodium 803 mg

SEAFOOD FIESTA FETTUCINE

12 oz (360 g) fettucine
1½ cups (355 ml) part skim ricotta cheese
4 oz (120 g) feta cheese, crumbled
½ cup (120 ml) milk
6 scallions, thinly sliced
1 - 8¾ oz can (260 g) whole yellow corn, drained
2 medium tomatoes, seeded and diced
1 tsp (5 ml) McCORMICK or SCHILLING
    Garlic Powder
1 tbs (15 ml) McCORMICK or SCHILLING
    Basil Leaves
1 tsp (5 ml) McCORMICK or SCHILLING
    Butter Flavor
1 lb (455 g) combination cooked and peeled
    shrimp, scallops and crab meat

Cook pasta, drain and return to pot. While pasta is cooking, puree ricotta and feta cheese and milk in blender or food processor. Add to cooked pasta along with remaining ingredients, except seafood, and toss until all ingredients are warm. Serve on a platter topped with seafood. Serves 4.

Approximate nutritional analysis per serving:
Calories 642, Protein 48 g, Carbohydrates 85 g, Fat 12 g,
Cholesterol 205 mg, Sodium 448 mg

ANGEL HAIR AL FRESCO

1 package NOODLE RONI Angel Hair Pasta
    and Herbs
1⅓ cups (300 ml) water
¾ cup (180 ml) skim milk
1 tbs (15 ml) margarine
1 - 6 oz can (180 g) white tuna packed in water,
    drained, flaked
    or 1½ cups (355 ml) chopped cooked chicken
2 medium tomatoes, chopped
⅓ cup (80 ml) sliced green onions
¼ cup (60 ml) dry white wine or water
¼ cup (60 ml) toasted slivered almonds optional
1 tbs (15 ml) chopped fresh basil OR
1 tsp (5 ml) dried basil

In a 3-qt saucepan, combine 1⅓ cups water, ¾ cup skim milk, 1 tbs margarine. Bring just to a boil. Stir in pasta, contents of seasoning packet, tuna or chicken, tomato, green onion, wine or water, almonds and basil. Bring to a boil; reduce heat to medium. Boil, uncovered, 6-8 minutes, stirring occasionally. Sauce will be very thin, but will thicken upon standing. Let stand 3 minutes or until desired consistency. Stir before serving. Serves 4.

Approximate nutritional analysis per serving:
Calories 300, Protein 19 g, Carbohydrates 32 g, Fat 10 g,
Cholesterol 20 mg, Sodium 650 mg

SHRIMP AND PASTA POMPEIAN

¼ cup (60 ml) **POMPEIAN Extra Virgin Olive Oil**
1 clove garlic, minced
1 tbs (15 ml) dried basil
1 tbs (15 ml) dried oregano
1 green sweet bell pepper, chopped
1 tsp (5 ml) dried parsley flakes
⅛ tsp (.5 ml) fennel seeds, optional
1 lb (455 g) raw shrimp, peeled and deveined
1 - 8 oz can (240 g) tomato paste
1 medium onion, chopped
1 tsp (5 ml) sugar
¼ tsp (1 ml) freshly ground pepper
⅛ tsp (.5 ml) cayenne
1 - 14½ oz can (435 g) Italian plum tomatoes,
    chopped
1 lb (455 g) cooked linguine tossed with
2 tbs (30 ml) **POMPEIAN Extra Virgin Olive Oil**

Place the extra virgin olive oil, garlic, onion and bell pepper in a medium saucepan, cook 5 minutes, stirring occasionally. Add remaining ingredients except for the shrimp and linguine. Simmer uncovered for 15 minutes. Add the prepared shrimp, cover and simmer 5 minutes. Serve over hot cooked linguine. Serves 4.

Approximate nutritional analysis per serving:
Calories 825, Protein 42 g, Carbohydrates 110 g, Fat 25 g, Cholesterol 172 mg, Sodium 416 mg

CHICKEN AND BEANS WITH PASTA

1 tbs (15 ml) **FLEISCHMANN'S Margarine**
1 whole boneless chicken breast, cut into strips
½ cup (120 ml) chopped onion
⅓ cup (80 ml) thinly sliced celery
2 cloves garlic, finely chopped
1 - 14 oz can (420 g) whole peeled tomatoes,
    coarsely chopped
1 small carrot, chopped
½ cup (120 ml) canned cannellini beans, drained
8 oz (240 g) bow-tie pasta, cooked and drained
fresh chopped parsley
grated Parmesan cheese, optional

In large skillet, over medium high heat, melt margarine. Add chicken, onion, celery and garlic; cook until chicken is no longer pink and vegetables are tender. Add tomatoes and carrots; reduce heat and cook 15 minutes. Stir in beans; heat through. Toss with hot cooked pasta. Garnish with parsley and cheese if desired. Serves 4.

Approximate nutritional analysis per serving:
Calories 362, Protein 23 g, Carbohydrates 51 g, Fat 5 g, Cholesterol 34 mg, Sodium 285 mg

Shrimp and Pasta Pompeian

Mediterranean Seafood Pasta with Smoked Tomato Pesto

MEDITERRANEAN SEAFOOD PASTA WITH SMOKED TOMATO PESTO

2 tbs (30 ml) olive oil
1 clove garlic, minced
1 medium red or green bell pepper,
    cut into thin strips
¼ cup (60 ml) dry white wine
8 oz (240 g) seafood (shrimp, scallops,
    crabmeat or lobster)
¼ cup (60 ml) sliced ripe olives
1 - 9 oz pkg (270 g) CONTADINA Refrigerated
    Linguine, cooked, drained and kept warm
1 - 7 oz container (210 g) CONTADINA
    Refrigerated Pesto with Sun Dried Tomatoes,
slightly warmed
1 tbs (15 ml) capers
1 oz (30 g) crumbled feta cheese

In medium skillet, heat oil; sauté garlic 1-2 minutes.
Add bell pepper; sauté for 2 minutes. Add wine and shrimp;
sauté 2-3 minutes. Stir in olives. In medium bowl, toss pasta
with pesto. To serve, divide onto plates; top with shrimp and
vegetable mixture. Sprinkle with capers and feta cheese.
Serves 4.

Approximate nutritional analysis per serving:
Calories 526, Protein 22 g, Carbohydrates 42 g, Fat 30 g,
Cholesterol 95 mg, Sodium 349 mg

CREAMY CHICKEN PRIMAVERA

2 cups (480 ml) water
1 cup (240 ml) diced carrots
1 cup (240 ml) broccoli flowerets
1 cup (240 ml) tri-color rotini pasta
½ lb (230 g) cooked chicken, cut into cubes
½ cup (120 ml) DANNON Plain Nonfat
    or Lowfat Yogurt
¼ cup (60 ml) finely chopped green onions,
    green part only
2 tbs plus 2 tsp (40 ml) reduced-calorie mayonnaise
½ tsp (3 ml) dried basil, crushed
⅛ tsp (.5 ml) pepper
carrot curls, optional

In a medium saucepan combine water, carrots and broccoli.
Cook, covered, 10-15 minutes or until tender-crisp; drain.
Cook pasta according to package directions; rinse and drain.
In a large bowl combine pasta, carrots and broccoli. Toss
gently.

In a small bowl combine chicken, yogurt, green onions,
mayonnaise, cheese, basil and pepper; mix well. Add to pasta
mixture. Toss gently to combine. Cover; chill several hours. If
desired, garnish with carrot curls. Serves 4.

Approximate nutritional analysis per serving:
Calories 468, Protein 35 g, Carbohydrates 72 g, Fat 9 g,
Cholesterol 60 mg, Sodium 256 mg

GAZPACHO SHRIMP

2 - 16 oz jars (960 g) CHI-CHI'S Salsa
½ cup (120 ml) diced yellow bell pepper, ¼ inch
½ cup (120 ml) diced cucumber, ¼ inch
2 tbs (30 ml) lime juice
2 tbs (30 ml) sliced green onions
1 lb (455 g) raw shrimp, peeled and deveined
2 tbs (30 ml) chopped fresh cilantro
hot cooked rice or pasta
avocado slices, if desired

GARLIC TORTILLA CHIPS:
flour tortillas
melted butter or margarine
garlic salt

In large skillet, combine salsa, yellow pepper, cucumber, lime juice and green onion. Bring to a simmer over medium heat. Stir in shrimp. Cook and stir 3-5 minutes or just until shrimp turns pink. Stir in cilantro. Serve over hot cooked rice or pasta with Garlic Tortilla Chips. Garnish with avocado, if desired. Serves 4.

Garlic Tortilla Chips: Heat oven to 375°F. Brush tortillas with melted butter or margarine. Sprinkle with garlic salt; cut into wedges. Place on baking sheets. Bake 7-10 minutes or until golden brown.

Approximate nutritional analysis per serving:
Calories 160, Protein 20 g, Carbohydrates 16 g, Fat 2 g,
Cholesterol 130 mg, Sodium 1190 mg

SILKY SPICY CHICKEN

1 lb (455 g) PREMIUM YOUNG 'N TENDER
    Brand Boneless, Skinless Chicken Breasts
½ tbs (8 ml) salt
½ tbs (8 ml) onion powder
1 tsp (5 ml) thyme
½ tsp (3 ml) black pepper
½ tsp (3 ml) white pepper
¼ tsp (1 ml) cayenne pepper
2 tbs (30 ml) butter
3 small cloves garlic, minced
8 oz (240 g) fresh mushrooms, thickly sliced
1 medium zucchini, cut into small match stick pieces
1 medium tomato, chopped
1 tbs (15 ml) cornstarch
1 cup (240 ml) milk
1 pt (480 ml) heavy cream
1 lb (455 g) linguine, cooked
fresh scallions or green onions with tops, chopped
Parmesan cheese, grated

Cut chicken breasts into bite-size pieces; set aside. Combine salt, onion powder, thyme and peppers; set aside. Melt butter in a 12-inch skillet; sauté garlic until limp. Stir in chicken, mushrooms and spices; cook 8-10 minutes. Blend cornstarch into milk and slowly add to chicken mixture along with cream. Cook over medium heat until bubbly. Reduce heat and simmer another 5 minutes. Serve sauce over hot linguine. Sprinkle with scallions and pass the Parmesan cheese. Serves 6.

Approximate nutritional analysis per serving:
Calories 762, Protein 38 g, Carbohydrates 66 g, Fat 39 g,
Cholesterol 189 mg, Sodium 333 mg

Above: Gazpacho Shrimp

DELICIOUS CHICKEN PASTA

2 - 6 oz (360 g) skinless, boneless chicken breasts
1 cup (240 ml) chopped onions
½ cup (120 ml) chopped celery
½ cup (120 ml) chopped green bell pepper
1 tbs (15 ml) CHEF PAUL PRUDHOMME'S
**   Meat Magic, in all**
2 cups (480 ml) defatted chicken stock, in all
2 tbs (30 ml) flour
3 cups (720 ml) thinly sliced fresh mushrooms
1 tsp (5 ml) minced garlic
½ cup (120 ml) chopped green onions
6 oz (180 g) pasta (fettuccine or angel hair)

Cut chicken into thin strips, place in a small bowl and combine thoroughly with 2 tsp Meat Magic.

Cook pasta according to package directions.

Place a skillet over high heat and add the white onions, celery, bell pepper and the remaining tsp Meat Magic. Cook over high heat, shaking pan and stirring occasionally (don't scrape!) for 5 minutes. Add ½ cup chicken stock, start scraping up the browned coating on the bottom of the pan and cook another 4 minutes. Stir in the chicken mixture and cook 4 minutes. Add the flour and stir well, cooking another 2 minutes. Now add the mushrooms and garlic, folding in carefully so mushrooms don't break. Add ½ cup chicken stock and scrape up the pan bottom. Cook 4 minutes and add another ½ cup stock, stirring and scraping. Continue cooking another 5 minutes, then add the green onions and the remaining ½ cup stock. Stir and scrape well. Cook 5 more minutes and remove from heat. Serves 6.

Approximate nutritional analysis per serving:
Calories 235, Protein 23 g, Carbohydrates 29 g, Fat 3 g, Cholesterol 48 mg, Sodium 57 mg

FRESH HERB CHICKEN OVER ANGEL HAIR PASTA

2 tbs (30 ml) olive or vegetable oil, divided
1 cup (240 ml) fresh broccoli florets
½ cup (120 ml) thin yellow pepper strips,
**   cut into 2-inch lengths**
½ cup (120 ml) thinly sliced snow pea pods
1 lb (455 g) boneless, skinless chicken breasts,
**   cut into thin strips**
1 shallot, minced
1 tbs (15 ml) chopped fresh cilantro
2 cloves garlic, minced
½ tsp (3 ml) freshly ground black pepper
¼ tsp (1 ml) chopped fresh tarragon
¼ cup (60 ml) dry white wine
2 tsp (10 ml) light soy sauce
8 oz (240 g) RONZONI Angel Hair Pasta, uncooked

In large nonstick skillet, heat 1 tbs oil over medium-high heat. Add broccoli, yellow pepper and snow peas; cook 1-2 minutes or until crisp-tender. Remove from pan; set aside. Heat remaining oil in skillet. Add chicken; cook 2 minutes or just until chicken begins to turn white. Add basil, shallot, cilantro, garlic, pepper and tarragon; toss to mix well. Stir in wine and soy sauce. Return vegetables to skillet; cook until heated through. Meanwhile, cook pasta according to package directions; drain. Serve sauce over hot pasta. Serves 4.

Approximate nutritional analysis per serving:
Calories 470, Protein 44 g, Carbohydrates 46 g, Fat 12 g, Cholesterol 95 mg, Sodium 210 mg

CHICKEN AND TWO-PEPPER PASTA

¼ cup (60 ml) LAND O LAKES Sweet Cream Butter
½ cup (120 ml) chopped onion
1 tsp (5 ml) finely chopped fresh garlic
½ medium yellow pepper, cut into thin strips
½ medium red pepper, cut into thin strips
3 boneless chicken breast halves, skinned,
**   cut into 3x½-inch strips**
½ tsp (3 ml) salt
¼ tsp (1 ml) coarsely ground pepper
6 oz (180 g) dried spinach fettuccine,
**   cooked and drained**
¾ cup (180 ml) half and half
1 cup (4 oz) (120 g) shredded LAND O LAKES
**   Mozzarella Cheese**
¼ cup (60 ml) freshly grated Parmesan cheese

In 10-inch skillet melt butter until sizzling. Stir in onion, garlic and peppers. Cook over medium high heat until vegetables are crisply tender, 2-3 minutes. Spoon vegetables from pan, reserving juices in pan. Set vegetables aside; keep warm. In same skillet add chicken to reserved juices. Continue cooking, stirring occasionally, until chicken is browned and fork tender, 7-9 minutes. Reduce heat to low. Add salt and pepper. Add cooked fettuccine, vegetables and half and half; continue cooking, stirring constantly, until heated through, 3-5 minutes. Add mozzarella cheese and 2 tbs Parmesan cheese; continue cooking, stirring constantly, until Mozzarella cheese is melted, 1-2 minutes. Sprinkle with remaining Parmesan cheese; serve immediately. Serves 4.

Approximate nutritional analysis per serving:
Calories 375, Protein 28 g, Carbohydrates 24 g, Fat 18 g, Cholesterol 90 mg, Sodium 486 mg

Lasagne with White Sauce

LASAGNE WITH WHITE SAUCE

¾ cup (180 ml) 1% lowfat cottage cheese
¾ cup (180 ml) part-skim ricotta cheese
¼ cup (60 ml) EGG BEATERS Real Egg Product
1 tsp (5 ml) Italian seasoning
⅓ cup (80 ml) chopped onion
1 clove garlic, minced
1 tbs (15 ml) FLEISCHMANN'S Margarine
1 tbs (15 ml) all purpose flour
⅔ cup (160 ml) skim milk
1½ cups (355 ml) thinly sliced zucchini
½ cup (120 ml) shredded carrots
¼ cup (60 ml) shredded Parmesan cheese
6 lasagna noodles, cooked and drained
¾ cup (180 ml) shredded part-skim
 mozzarella cheese

In medium bowl, combine cottage cheese, ricotta cheese, egg product and Italian seasoning; set aside.

In large skillet, over medium heat, sauté onion and garlic in margarine until tender; stir in flour. Add milk, stirring until thickened; cook and stir 1 minute more. Stir in zucchini, carrots and 2 tbs Parmesan cheese; set aside.

Spray 10x6x2-inch baking dish with nonstick cooking spray. Arrange 2 noodles in dish; spread with ⅓ cottage cheese mixture, ⅓ zucchini mixture and sprinkle with ⅓ mozzarella cheese. Repeat layers, starting with noodles, 2 more times; sprinkle with remaining 2 tbs Parmesan cheese. Bake, uncovered, at 350°F (180°C) for 35 minutes or until heated through. Let stand 10 minutes before serving. Serves 6.

Approximate nutritional analysis per serving:
Calories 257, Protein 20 g, Carbohydrates 42 g, Fat 8 g,
Cholesterol 22 mg, Sodium 334 mg

BLACK BEAN LASAGNE

10 regular or whole wheat lasagna noodles
3 - 15 oz cans (1.4 kg) black beans,
    rinsed and drained
¼ cup (60 ml) chicken broth or water
1 tsp (5 ml) garlic salt
1 tsp (5 ml) ground cumin
1 tsp (5 ml) dried thyme leaves, crushed
½ tsp (3 ml) chili powder
2 - 15 oz cartons (900 g) part-skim ricotta cheese
4 cups (960 ml) shredded Monterey Jack cheese
2 - 16 oz jars (960 g) CHI-CHI'S Salsa

Heat oven to 375°F (190°C). Grease 13x9-inch baking dish. Cook noodles according to package directions about 8 minutes or just until tender. Place in a bowl of cold water; set aside. In large bowl, combine beans, broth, garlic salt, cumin, thyme and chili powder. Mash with potato masher or back of spoon until nearly smooth and liquid is absorbed. In large bowl, combine ricotta and 3 cups Monterey Jack cheese. Mix well.

Drain noodles; blot dry. Arrange 5 noodles in bottom of greased baking dish. Spread with half the black bean mixture, then cheese mixture, than salsa. Repeat layering. Sprinkle top layer with remaining 1 cup Monterey Jack cheese. Bake, uncovered, 35-45 minutes or until top is browned. Let stand 10 minutes before serving. Serves 8

Approximate nutritional analysis per serving:
Calories 610, Protein 40 g, Carbohydrates 55 g, Fat 27 g, Cholesterol 85 mg, Sodium   230 mg

CAMP CABIN "LASAGNE"

6 oz (180 g) elbow macaroni
1 - 8 oz can (240 ml) tomato sauce
1 - 6 oz pkg (180 g) sliced jack or cheddar cheese
1 small tomato, cubed
½ pt container (240 ml) lowfat ricotta cheese
1½ tsp (8 ml) thyme
½ cup (120 ml) CALIFORNIA ripe olive slices
½ cup (120 ml) sour cream

Drop macaroni into boiling water in pot about 8 inches in diameter and 2½-qt capacity. Cover, return to boil and simmer 7 minutes or until done. Drain and remove from pot. Pour tomato sauce into bottom of pot. Make layer of macaroni on sauce, then layer sliced cheese, tomato, ricotta, thyme, olives and sour cream, in that order. Cover and place over low heat for 20 minutes or until bubbling at edges and hot in center. Serves 4.

Approximate nutritional analysis per serving:
Calories 604, Protein 32 g, Carbohydrates 47 g, Fat 32 g, Cholesterol 95 mg, Sodium 577 mg

ELEGANT CHICKEN LASAGNE

3 lbs (1.4 kg) PREMIUM YOUNG 'N TENDER
    Brand Boneless, Skinless, Split Chicken
    Breasts, cut into bite size pieces
3 tbs (45 ml) olive oil
½ cup (120 ml) butter
⅓ cup (80 ml) all purpose flour
4 cups (960 ml) milk
1 tsp (5 ml) salt
½ tsp (3 ml) ground white pepper
½ cup (120 ml) crumbled Stilton cheese,
    or bleu cheese
2 tbs (30 ml) dry white wine
8 oz (240 g) grated Muenster cheese
8 oz (240 g) grated provolone cheese
8 oz (240 g) white cheddar cheese
1 lb (455 g) lasagna noodles, cooked al dente,
    drained well
3 large firm ripe tomatoes, peeled, seeded
    and chopped
½ cup (120 ml) chopped fresh basil leaves
    or 2 tsp (10 ml) dried basil leaves
½ lb (230 g) fresh mushrooms, thinly sliced
fresh basil leaves, optional

Preheat oven to 350°F (180°C). Lightly butter a 13x9x2-inch baking dish; set aside.

Sauté chicken in heated olive oil in a large skillet over moderately high heat until done, about 5 minutes. If necessary, cook in several batches. Remove with a slotted spoon; set aside.

Melt butter in a medium saucepan over moderately low heat. Add flour, cooking and stirring about 3 minutes. Whisk in milk. Continue cooking and stirring 8-10 minutes or until smooth and thickened. Remove sauce from heat; add salt, pepper, Stilton cheese and white wine, stirring until cheese has melted. Set aside.

Combine Muenster, provolone and cheddar cheese, mixing well. Set aside.

To assemble lasagne, spread an even layer of sauce in the prepared baking dish. Top with ⅓ of the noodles, ⅓ of the remaining sauce, and half of each of the following; tomatoes, basil, mushrooms and chicken. Top with ⅓ of the cheese mixture. Repeat layering in the same manner. End with the remaining ⅓ of the noodles, sauce and cheese mixture.

Bake in center of the preheated oven for 50-60 minutes or until hot and bubbly. Let stand 10 minutes before serving. Garnish with basil leaves if desired. Serves 12.

Note: May be prepared ahead. Cover well; refrigerate or freeze and bake later.

Approximate nutritional analysis per serving:
Calories 719, Protein 59 g, Carbohydrates 37 g, Fat 37 g, Cholesterol 183 mg, Sodium 849 mg

Opposite: Camp Cabin Lasagne, Two Cheese Risotto with Olives

VEGETABLE LASAGNA

2 cups (480 ml) lowfat cottage cheese
1 - 10 oz pkg (300 g) frozen chopped spinach,
  thawed and well drained
1 cup (240 ml) shredded carrot
½ cup (120 ml) EGG BEATERS Real Egg Product
2 tbs (30 ml) minced onion
1 tsp (5 ml) Italian seasoning
2 cups (480 ml) no salt added spaghetti sauce
9 lasagna noodles, prepared without salt
1 cup (4 oz) (120 g) shredded mozzarella
2 tbs (30 ml) grated Parmesan cheese

In medium bowl, combine cottage cheese, spinach, carrot, egg product, onion and Italian seasoning; set aside.

Spread ½ cup spaghetti sauce over bottom of greased 13x9x2-inch baking dish. Layer 3 noodles and ⅓ each of the spinach filling and remaining sauce; repeat layers twice. Sprinkle top with mozzarella cheese and Parmesan cheese; cover. Bake at 375°F (190°C) for 20 minutes. Uncover; bake 25 minutes more. Let stand 10 minutes before serving. Serves 8.

Approximate nutritional analysis per serving:
Calories 271, Protein 20 g, Carbohydrates 42 g, Fat 8 g, Cholesterol 11 mg, Sodium 392 mg

PASTA WITH HAM PRIMAVERA

3 cups (720 ml) broccoli florets
1 tbs (15 ml) olive oil
2 cloves garlic, minced
2 cups (480 ml) mushrooms, sliced
1 red bell pepper, cut into chunks
6 oz (180 g) LIGHT & LEAN 97 Ham Cuts
1 tbs (15 ml) cornstarch
½ cup (120 ml) low sodium chicken stock
1 cup (240 ml) Parmesan cheese
⅓ cup (80 ml) fresh basil *or* 2 tsp (10 ml) dried basil
1 - 10 oz pkg (300 g) fresh pasta, cooked and drained
  ***or* 1 lb (455 g) dry pasta, cooked and drained**

Steam broccoli florets. In no-stick frying pan, heat olive oil over medium heat. Sauté garlic, mushrooms, bell pepper. After 2-3 minutes, add ham. In a small saucepan over medium heat, combine cornstarch with chicken stock; mix until cornstarch dissolves. Reduce heat, stirring constantly until thickened. Toss the broccoli, pasta, vegetable and turkey mixture, Parmesan cheese and basil. Combine thoroughly. Serves 6.

Approximate nutritional analysis per serving:
Calories 447, Protein 25 g, Carbohydrates 63 g, Fat 10 g, Cholesterol 28 mg, Sodium 759 mg

BEANFUL VEGETARIAN LASAGNE

1 - 15 oz can (450 g) any colored Bean
½ lb (230 g) lasagna noodles, cooked
¾ lb (180 g) mozzarella cheese, thinly sliced
2 cups (480 ml) lowfat cottage cheese (1%)
¼ cup (60 ml) Parmesan cheese, grated
2 medium onions, chopped
2 cups (480 ml) tomato sauce, canned tomatoes
  or thinned tomato paste
½ lb (230 g) sliced fresh mushrooms, sauteed
¼ cup (60 ml) parsley, chopped, optional
4 cloves garlic, minced
1 tbs (15 ml) oil
2 tsp (10 ml) dried oregano
1 tsp (5 ml) dried basil
salt to taste

Rinse cooked noodles in cold water so they won't stick together; set aside. Sauté onions and garlic in oil until soft. Stir in tomato sauce and seasonings. Cook and stir for about 30 minutes until sauce has thickened. Stir in mushrooms and beans and salt to taste. To assemble lasagne, place a layer of noodles in a shallow baking dish, 9x9 inches. Cover with ⅓ of tomato sauce, then ⅓ of each of the cheeses. Repeat layers twice more, ending with Parmesan cheese. Bake in 375°F (190°C) oven for approximately 20 minutes. Cut in squares. Serves 8.

Approximate nutritional analysis per serving:
Calories 295, Protein 25 g, Carbohydrates 24 g, Fat 11 g, Cholesterol 38 mg, Sodium 683 mg

Courtesy of the American Dry Bean Board.

QUICK FIESTA CHICKEN

1 tbs (15 ml) oil
¾ lb (340 g) boneless skinless chicken breasts,
  cut into strips
1 - 16 oz pkg (480 g) GREEN GIANT Pasta
  Accents Garlic Seasoning (or any flavor)
  Frozen Vegetables and Pasta
¾ cup (180 ml) salsa
1 tbs (15 ml) chopped fresh cilantro

In large skillet, heat oil. Add chicken; cook until no longer pink. Add vegetables and pasta and salsa. Cover; cook over medium heat 7-9 minutes until vegetables are crisp-tender, stirring occasionally. Stir in cilantro. Serve with additional salsa and sour cream, if desired. Serves 4.

Approximate nutritional analysis per serving:
Calories 300, Protein 23 g, Carbohydrates 25 g, Fat 11 g, Cholesterol 58 mg, Sodium 960 mg

Mom's Lean and Quick Lasagne

MOM'S LEAN AND QUICK LASAGNE

1 cup (240 ml) chopped onion
1 tbs (15 ml) vegetable oil
½ lb (230 g) HEALTHY CHOICE Extra Lean
    Ground Beef or ground turkey breast
1 - 26 oz jar (780 ml) HEALTHY CHOICE
    Traditional Pasta Sauce
1 - 15 oz carton (450 g) part-skim ricotta cheese
¼ cup (60 ml) grated Parmesan cheese
½ tsp (3 ml) dried basil
½ tsp (3 ml) dried oregano
6 lasagna noodles, cooked, drained
1 ½ cups (355 ml) HEALTHY CHOICE
    Fat Free Mozzarella Shreds

In large nonstick saucepan, sauté onion in hot oil until tender. Add ground beef, and brown until cooked through. Stir in pasta sauce; heat through. In small bowl, mix together ricotta and Parmesan cheeses with basil and oregano. In 13x9x2-inch baking dish, layer 3 noodles, half of cheese mixture, half of sauce and half of mozzarella cheese. Repeat layers. Bake at 350°F (180°C) for 30 minutes. Serves 8.

Approximate nutritional analysis per serving:
Calories 270, Fat 9 g, Cholesterol 38 mg, Sodium 561 mg

SPINACH, SAUSAGE AND OLIVE ROLL

½ lb (230 g) hot or mild Italian sausage
olive oil
1½ tsp (8 ml) fennel seed
¾ cup (180 ml) chopped onion
⅓ cup (80 ml) chopped fresh basil
¾ cup (180 ml) coarsely chopped
  CALIFORNIA ripe olives
1 - 10 oz pkg frozen chopped spinach, thawed
1 cup (240 ml) ricotta cheese
2 eggs
salt and pepper to taste
2 sheets fresh egg pasta, about 12x10 inches each
1 cup (240 ml) grated mozzarella cheese
basil sprigs, optional
Homemade Fresh Tomato Sauce (see previous
  recipe)

Remove sausage from casings and crumble into oiled skillet. Sprinkle with fennel seed and cook until brown. Remove from pan and drain off most of fat. Add onions and sauté until tender. Add basil and sauté 1-2 minutes longer. Combine onions and basil, sausage and olives; cool. Squeeze spinach as dry as possible. Mix well with ricotta and eggs then add to sausage mixture. Add salt and pepper to taste.

Gently unroll pasta and, if coated with flour, brush off excess. Place one sheet of pasta in large colander in sink. Gently pour boiling water over to moisten and soften. Gently rinse with cold water then carefully slip from colander onto large sheet of oiled foil on counter. Repeat with other sheet of pasta.

Spread each sheet of pasta with half the ricotta mixture, leaving a 1-inch border at long edges. Sprinkle with mozzarella and roll up, starting from long edge. Wrap foil around and twist ends to enclose. Place wrapped rolls in wide baking pan and bake at 350°F (180°C) for 25 minutes or until center reads at least 145°F (63°C) on instant (probe-style) thermometer.* Cool rolls 10 minutes in wrap then unwrap and slice. Pour Homemade Fresh Tomato Sauce onto plates, add pasta spirals and garnish with basil sprigs. Serves 6.

* If you don't have a thermometer, unwrap roll and make a small cut in center to see if it is hot enough.

Approximate nutritional analysis per serving:
Calories 777, Protein 36 g, Carbohydrates 103 g, Fat 24 g,
Cholesterol 128 mg, Sodium   528 mg

PASTA VERDE ROLL

1 pt (480 ml) ricotta cheese
⅔ cup (160 ml) grated Parmesan cheese
2 eggs
2 tbs (30 ml) milk
⅔ cup (160 ml) bottled roasted bell peppers,
  diced and well drained
1 cup (240 ml) CALIFORNIA ripe olives, chopped
¼ cup (60 ml) chopped fresh basil
2 sheets fresh spinach pasta, about 12x10 inches each
olive or vegetable oil
¼ lb (60 ml) prosciutto, very thinly sliced
1 cup (240 ml) grated mozzarella cheese

HOMEMADE FRESH TOMATO SAUCE:
2 tbs (30 ml) olive oil
¾ cup (180 ml) chopped onion
3 lbs (1.4 kg) tomatoes, seeded and chopped
1 tbs (15 ml) minced garlic
9 fresh basil sprigs
salt and pepper

Mix ricotta, Parmesan, eggs and milk. Mix in peppers, olives and basil. Gently unroll pasta and, if coated with flour, brush off excess. Place one sheet of pasta in large colander in sink. Gently pour boiling water over to moisten and soften. Gently rinse with cold water then carefully slip from colander onto large sheet of oiled foil on counter. Repeat with other sheet of pasta.

Spread each sheet of pasta with half the ricotta mixture, leaving a 1-inch border at each long edge. Cover ricotta with prosciutto and sprinkle with mozzarella. Beginning at long edge, roll pasta over filling, jellyroll fashion. Roll foil around tightly and twist ends to enclose. Place roll in wide baking pan and bake at 350°F (180°C) for 25 minutes or until center reads at least 145°F (63°C) on instant (probe-style) thermometer.* Cool rolls 10 minutes in wrap then unwrap and slice into 12 spirals. To serve, ladle about ½ cup Homemade Fresh Tomato Sauce on each plate; top with spirals of pasta. Serves 6.

* If you don't have a thermometer, unwrap roll and make a small cut in center to see if it is hot enough.

Homemade Fresh Tomato Sauce: Heat olive oil in skillet, add onions and sauté until translucent. Add tomatoes, garlic and whole basil sprigs. Cook, covered over medium heat for 45 minutes to 1 hour or until saucy. Discard basil. Puree in electric blender. Add salt and pepper to taste. Yields 3⅔ cups.

Approximate nutritional analysis per serving pasta verde roll:
Calories 417, Protein 25 g, Carbohydrates 45 g, Fat 16 g,
Cholesterol 109 mg, Sodium   571 mg

Approximate nutritional analysis per ½ cup serving sauce:
Calories 75, Protein 2 g, Carbohydrates 10 g, Fat 4 g,
Cholesterol 0 mg, Sodium 16 mg

Opposite: Spinach, Sausage and Olive Roll, Greek Style Pasta Salad

CHEF PAUL'S MACARONI AND CHEESE

1½ cups (355 ml) chopped onions
¾ cup (180 ml) chopped celery
2 tbs plus 1 tsp (35 ml) CHEF PAUL PRUDHOMME'S
    Pork and Veal Magic
½ cup (120 ml) defatted chicken stock, in all
5 egg whites
1 - 12 oz container (360 g) low-fat cottage cheese
1 - 12 oz can (360 ml) evaporated skim milk
1-2 tsp (5-10 ml) salt, optional
10 cups (2.4 L) cooked small elbow macaroni
6 oz (180 g) low-fat cheddar cheese
    (7 g fat per oz), shredded

Preheat oven to 375°F (190°C).

Heat a 10-inch skillet over high heat. Add chopped onions, celery and Pork and Veal Magic. Cook 2 minutes, then stir to blend in seasoning. When vegetables begin to stick hard to the pan, about 2-3 minutes, add ¼ cup stock, scrape up the brown on the pan bottom, stir well and cook 1-2 minutes. Turn heat down to medium and stir. Cook until vegetables begin to stick hard again, about 4-5 minutes, and add the remaining ¼ cup stock. Scrape up pan bottom, stir well and continue cooking another 4-5 minutes. Remove from heat and let cool slightly.

Place the egg whites in food processor. Process 30-45 seconds, or until the egg whites are nice and frothy, but not until they make peaks. Add the cottage cheese and the milk and process. Don't let the mixture get too smooth; a bit of lumpiness in the cottage cheese will give the dish more texture. Add the cooled mixture from the skillet and process again, about 20 seconds. Taste and add salt if you desire. Place the cooked, drained macaroni into a bowl, pour the sauce over and mix well. Pour into an <u>un</u>buttered casserole, sprinkle the cheddar cheese on top and bake for 35-40 minutes, or until brown and bubbly. Serves 10.

Approximate nutritional analysis per serving:
Calories 303, Protein 20 g, Carbohydrates 47 g, Fat 4 g,
Cholesterol 12 mg, Sodium 596 mg

Chef Paul's Macaroni and Cheese

CHEESE STUFFED SHELLS WITH BASIL

8 oz (240 g) low fat ricotta cheese
8 oz (240 g) HEALTHY CHOICE Fat Free Natural
    Shredded Mozzarella Cheese
1 cup (240 ml) chopped fresh basil
2 tsp (10 ml) minced fresh garlic
6 oz (180 g) jumbo pasta shells, cooked (16 shells)
1 - 26 oz jar (780 ml) HEALTHY CHOICE Pasta Sauce

Heat oven to 350°F (180°C). In large bowl stir together ricotta cheese, 1 cup mozzarella cheese, basil and garlic. Fill each shell with about 2 tbs cheese filling. Place in 12x7-inch baking dish sprayed with non-stick cooking spray. Pour sauce over filled shells. Sprinkle with remaining mozzarella cheese. Cover and bake 20-25 minutes. Serves 8.

Approximate nutritional analysis per serving:
Calories 189, Protein 17 g, Carbohydrates 25 g, Fat 3 g,
Cholesterol 14 mg, Sodium 479 mg

FRIED POLENTA CAKES WITH OLIVES

1½ cups (355 ml) yellow cornmeal
1½ cups (355 ml) water
¾ cup (180 ml) milk
1 tsp (5 ml) salt
1 tsp (5 ml) marjoram
½ tsp (3 ml) rosemary, crumbled
¼ cup (60 ml) butter or margarine
¼ cup (60 ml) olive oil
1 - 32 oz jar (960 ml) marinara sauce
¼ cup (60 ml) chopped fresh basil
½ lb (230 g) fontina cheese, grated
1 cup (240 ml) CALIFORNIA ripe olive wedges

Combine cornmeal, water, milk, salt, marjoram and rosemary in large saucepan. Cook, stirring, over medium heat until mixture is almost dry, about 5 minutes. Stir in butter until melted. Mixture is ready when it is dry and no longer sticks to sides of pan. When cool enough to handle, form into 8 patties. Fry in oil in nonstick skillet over medium-high heat, until crispy on bottom; turn and fry other side. Turn marinara sauce into baking dish, mix in basil and lay corn patties in sauce. Sprinkle with grated cheese and the olives. Bake covered at 400°F (205°C) for 20 minutes or until hot. Sprinkle with additional chopped fresh basil if desired. Serves 4.

Approximate nutritional analysis per serving:
Calories 852, Protein 23 g, Carbohydrates 57 g, Fat 62 g,
Cholesterol 103 mg, Sodium   117 mg

OLIVE POLENTA TRIANGLES

3 cups (720 ml) water
¾ tsp (4 ml) salt
¾ cup (180 ml) polenta
1 tsp (5 ml) olive oil
⅛ tsp (.5 ml) cayenne
1 cup (240 ml) finely grated Parmesan cheese
¾ cup (180 ml) pitted CALIFORNIA
    ripe olives, sliced
2 tsp (10 ml) finely minced parsley

Bring water to boil in large saucepan. Add salt and gradually stir in polenta. Cook, stirring constantly over medium heat for 15 minutes, or until polenta gets very thick and pulls away from side of pan. Remove from heat; stir in olive oil, cayenne and ¾ cup of the cheese. Pour polenta into oiled 8-inch square pan. Spread with wet spatula to edge of pan. Immediately top with olives, parsley and remaining ¼ cup Parmesan cheese; press lightly into polenta. Cool. Cut into 4-inch squares then cut each square into a triangle. Just before serving, bake triangles on well-oiled baking sheet at 450°F (230°C) until very hot, about 5 minutes. Serves 4.

Approximate nutritional analysis per serving:
Calories 254, Protein 11 g, Carbohydrates 24 g, Fat 13 g,
Cholesterol 16 mg, Sodium   215 mg

TWO CHEESE RISOTTO WITH OLIVES

¼ cup (60 ml) butter or margarine
1½ cups (355 ml) Arborio rice
1 chicken bouillon cube
2 cups (480 ml) water
1 cup (240 ml) dry white wine
½ cup (120 ml) heavy cream
½ cup (120 ml) grated Parmesan cheese
1 cup (240 ml) grated Jack or Muenster cheese
½ cup (120 ml) CALIFORNIA ripe olive wedges

Melt butter in heavy pan with lid, add rice and cook, stirring over medium heat for 4 minutes or until it just begins to brown and gets a toasty smell. Crumble bouillon cube into rice, add water and wine, cover and bring to boil. Simmer very gently for 13 minutes until al dente (firm-tender bite). Gradually stir in cream, then add cheeses and olives a portion at a time, stirring all the while until melted and hot. Stir in more water at the end if needed. Risotto should be very creamy and rich and a little thicker than soup. Serve in wide bowls with crusty bread and a crisp green salad. Serves 4.

Approximate nutritional analysis per serving:
Calories 680, Protein 18 g, Carbohydrates 59 g, Fat 37 g,
Cholesterol 107 mg, Sodium 890 mg

RISOTTO MILANESE

1 small onion, thinly sliced
1 tbs (15 ml) margarine
1 cup (240 ml) uncooked Arborio rice
pinch saffron
½ cup (120 ml) dry white wine
¼ tsp (1 ml) Tabasco pepper sauce
2 cups (480 ml) low sodium chicken broth
¼ cup (60 ml) grated Parmesan cheese
salt and freshly ground white pepper, optional

In a large skillet, sauté onion in margarine over medium-high heat. Add rice and saffron; stir constantly 2-3 minutes. Add wine and Tabasco pepper sauce; stir until absorbed. Stir in 1 cup of broth. Cook, uncovered, stirring frequently until broth is absorbed. Add remaining broth and hot water, ½ cup at a time, stirring constantly from bottom and sides of pan. Wait until rice just begins to dry out before adding more liquid. Cook and stir until rice is tender but firm to bite and the risotto is the consistency of creamy rice pudding. The total amount of liquid used will vary. Watch rice carefully to ensure proper consistency. Stir in cheese, salt and pepper, if desired. Serves 6.

Approximate nutritional analysis per serving:
Calories 178, Protein 5 g, Carbohydrates 28 g, Fat 4 g,
Cholesterol 3 mg, Sodium 94 mg

Polenta

SHORT CUT RISOTTO WITH SEAFOOD

**2 tbs (30 ml) BERTOLI Classico or
    Extra Virgin Olive Oil
2 tbs (30 ml) diced red onion
1¼ cups (300 ml) imported or domestic,
    medium or long grain white rice
⅓ cup (80 ml) dry white wine, optional
4-5 cups (960-1200 ml) unsalted chicken broth,
    kept hot over low heat
12 oz (360 g) small scallops, rinsed, patted dry
    or small shrimp, shelled and deveined
1 cup (240 ml) peas or broccoli florets
1 tsp (5 ml) grated lemon zest
1 tbs (15 ml) fresh lemon juice
½ tsp (3 ml) salt, or more to taste
freshly ground black pepper, to taste
finely chopped fresh basil or Italian parsley**

Short Cut Risotto with Seafood

Heat 1 tbs olive oil in a large broad 4-qt saucepan over low heat. Add the onion and cook, stirring, until tender, about 5 minutes. Stir in the rice and stir to coat with the oil.

Add the wine, if using; heat to boiling; stir over high heat until almost evaporated. Stir in 1 cup of the chicken broth; cover and cook over low heat 5 minutes. Uncover and stir in an additional 1 cup of broth; heat to boiling. Cover and cook over low heat 10 minutes. Uncover and stir in remaining 1 cup broth, the seafood, peas and lemon zest. Cook uncovered, stirring constantly, until the rice is tender to the bite, the dish is moist and creamy and the seafood are cooked through, 5-8 minutes. Add remaining broth as needed to keep rice creamy. Add remaining 1 tbs olive oil and lemon juice; stir in salt and black pepper, to taste.

Spoon into serving bowls and sprinkle with fresh parsley and/or basil. Serves 4.

Approximate nutritional analysis per serving:
Calories 402, Protein 22 g, Carbohydrates 55 g, Fat 10 g,
Cholesterol 28 mg, Sodium 479 mg

SAVORY PIES & PIZZAS

Savory pies have long been part of Western food tradition. They are also perfect foods to prepare ahead as they store well and reheat easily. Combined with a salad and soup, they make a delightful meal. In the past decade pizza has joined the ranks of flexible foods. Usually round, though not always, it has become a canvas for flavors, garnishes and sauces to please the cook.

CHILI PUFF

2 - 4 oz cans (240 g) diced green chilies
1 lb (455 g) Monterey Jack cheese, grated
1 cup (240 ml) CALIFORNIA ripe olives, halved
1 cup (240 ml) half and half
2 eggs
⅓ cup (80 ml) flour
1 - 8 oz can (240 ml) tomato sauce, unsalted

Set aside ½ cup jack cheese for topping. Layer chilies with remaining cheese and olives in deep 1½-qt baking dish, making 3 layers of each. Whisk half and half with eggs and flour; slowly pour into baking dish. Top with tomato sauce and sprinkle with remaining cheese. Bake uncovered at 400 °F (205°C) for 1 hour or until hot and set in center. Serves 4.

Approximate nutritional analysis per serving:
Calories 563, Protein 31 g, Carbohydrates 21 g, Fat 41 g,
Cholesterol 101 mg, Sodium 120 mg

CRUSTLESS VEGETABLE QUICHE

1 cup (240 ml) cooked brown or white rice
¾ cup (3 oz) (90 g) lowfat Swiss cheese, shredded
1 tbs (15 ml) flour
1 - 10 oz pkg (300 g) frozen chopped broccoli,
    thawed and well drained
½ cup (120 ml) mushrooms, sliced
¼ cup (60 ml) green onion, sliced
1 red pepper, thinly sliced
1½ cups (355 ml) HEALTHY CHOICE
    Cholesterol Free Egg Product
1 cup (240 ml) skim milk
½ tsp (3 ml) hot pepper sauce
¾ tsp (4 ml) salt
½ tsp (3 ml) basil
¼ tsp (1 ml) pepper
2 tbs (30 ml) Parmesan cheese, grated

In large bowl, combine rice, Swiss cheese, flour, broccoli, mushrooms and onion. Place in 10-inch pie plate sprayed with vegetable oil spray. Top vegetable mixture with red pepper slices. In medium bowl, combine egg product, milk, hot pepper sauce, salt, basil and pepper. Pour egg product mixture over vegetable mixture. Sprinkle Parmesan cheese on top. Bake in 350°F (180°C) oven for 55 minutes. Serves 8.

Approximate nutritional analysis per serving:
Calories 120, Protein 13 g, Carbohydrates 13 g, Fat 3 g,
Cholesterol 10 mg, Sodium 350 mg

SAVORY VEGETABLE TART

CRUST:
2 cups (480 ml) all purpose flour
¾ cup (180 ml) butter or margarine, melted
1 tsp (5 ml) dried dill weed
½ tsp (3 ml) salt

FILLING:
3 tbs (45 ml) olive oil
8 oz (240 g) parsnips, peeled and thinly sliced
4 oz (120 g) broccoli florets
¼ lb (115 g) mushrooms, thinly sliced
1 small leek, sliced and well rinsed
1 small red bell pepper, seeded and
    cut into thin strips
1 tsp (5 ml) salt
1 cup (240 ml) heavy cream
½ cup (120 ml) cheddar cheese, shredded
1 large egg
1½ tsp (8 ml) Tabasco pepper sauce

Preheat oven to 375°F (190°C). In a large bowl combine flour butter, dill and salt. Press mixture into fluted 9-inch tart pan with removable bottom or a fluted ceramic quiche pan. Bake 10 minutes.

Meanwhile, in a 12-inch skillet over medium heat, in hot oil, cook parsnips and broccoli for 3 minutes. Add mushrooms, leek, red pepper, and salt; cook 7 minutes longer or until vegetables are crisp-tender.

In medium bowl, combine heavy cream, cheddar cheese, egg, and Tabasco pepper sauce. Spoon vegetables into pie crust; pour cheese mixture over the vegetables. Bake 35-40 minutes until knife inserted in the center of the pie comes out clean. Serves 6.

Approximate nutritional analysis per serving:
Calories 660, Protein 11 g, Carbohydrates 45 g, Fat 49 g,
Cholesterol 160 mg, Sodium 870 mg

Opposite: Savory Vegetable Tart

TAMALE PIE WITH CORNMEAL CRUST

CRUST:
1 cup (240 ml) yellow cornmeal
1 tsp (5 ml) sugar
1 cup (4 oz) (120 g) HEALTHY CHOICE Fat Free
    Natural Shredded Cheddar Cheese
⅓ cup (80 ml) skim milk
¼ cup (60 ml) HEALTHY CHOICE
    Cholesterol Free Egg Product
2 tsp (10 ml) vegetable oil

FILLING:
½ lb (230 g) ground turkey breast
½ cup (120 ml) green pepper, chopped
½ cup (120 ml) onion, chopped
1 tsp (5 ml) minced garlic
1 tsp (5 ml) jalapeño pepper, finely chopped
1 - 8 oz can (240 ml) tomato sauce
1 cup (240 ml) whole kernel corn, drained
2 tsp (10 ml) chili powder
1½ tsp (8 ml) ground cumin
⅛ tsp (.5 ml) cayenne pepper
1 cup (4 oz) (120 g) HEALTHY CHOICE
    Fat Free Natural Shredded Cheddar Cheese
light sour cream
salsa

Heat oven to 350°F (180°C). Combine cornmeal and sugar; stir in 1 cup cheese, milk, egg product and vegetable oil. Stir just until moistened. Press mixture on bottom and up sides of 9-inch pie plate sprayed with non-stick cooking spray.

In 10-inch skillet, cook ground turkey, green pepper, onion, garlic and jalapeño pepper over medium heat until turkey is no longer pink. Drain. Stir in tomato sauce, corn, chili powder, cumin and cayenne pepper. Spoon turkey mixture into cornmeal crust. Bake 30-35 minutes. Remove from oven; sprinkle with 1 cup cheese. Return to oven and bake until cheese melts. Let stand 5 minutes before serving. Serve with light sour cream and salsa if desired. Serves 8.

Approximate nutritional analysis per serving:
Calories 202, Protein 21 g, Carbohydrates 23 g, Fat 3 g,
Cholesterol 25 mg, Sodium 469 mg

LEEK AND MUSHROOM PIE WITH KIDNEY BEAN CRUST

1½ cups (12 oz) (360 g) canned light or dark red
    kidney beans, drained and rinsed
1 tbs (15 ml) butter or margarine, unsalted
2½ cups (590 ml) whites of leek, finely chopped
1½ cups (355 ml) mushrooms, thinly sliced
1 tbs (15 ml) fresh dill, snipped
    or 1 tsp (5 ml) dried dill
1 tsp (5 ml) dry mustard
¼ cup (60 ml) dry white wine
3 large eggs
¼ cup (60 ml) bread crumbs
½ cup (120 ml) sharp cheddar cheese, shredded
salt to taste
white pepper, freshly ground

Pat the beans dry on paper towels, place them between 2 layers of wax paper, and crush them with a rolling pin. Scrape the beans into an 8-inch pie plate and press them all around the bottom and sides to make a crust, just as you would with graham cracker crumbs.

Preheat the oven to 350°F (180°C). In a large skillet, melt the butter over moderately low heat, add the leeks, mushrooms, dill, and mustard, and sauté until the leeks are just tender. Remove from heat and cool slightly.

In a mixing bowl, beat the eggs well, add the wine, bread crumbs, cheddar, and leek mixture. Stir well and add salt and pepper to taste. Pour the mixture into the pie plate and bake 30-40 minutes, or until the filling is set and browned on top. Serves 4.

Approximate nutritional analysis per serving:
Calories 311, Protein 18 g, Carbohydrates 32 g, Fat 12 g,
Cholesterol 182 mg, Sodium 222 mg

Courtesy of the American Dry Bean Board.

Opposite: Tamale Pie with Cornmeal Crust

OREGON HAZELNUT VEGETABLE PIE

1 cup (240 ml) fresh broccoli, chopped
1 cup (240 ml) fresh cauliflower, sliced
2 cups (480 ml) fresh spinach, chopped
½ cup (120 ml) onion, chopped
¼ cup (60 ml) green pepper, chopped
1 cup (4 oz) (120 g) cheddar cheese, grated
1 cup (240 ml) OREGON Hazelnuts, coarsely chopped
1½ cups (355 ml) milk
1 cup (240 ml) BISQUICK
4 eggs
1 tsp (5 ml) garlic salt
¼ tsp (1 ml) pepper

Precook broccoli and cauliflower until almost tender, about 5 minutes. Drain well. Combine broccoli, cauliflower, spinach, onion, green pepper and cheese. Divide into 2 well-greased 8-inch pie pans. Top with OREGON Hazelnuts. Beat together milk, BISQUICK, eggs, garlic salt and pepper; pour over vegetable mixture. Bake at 400°F (205°C) for 35-40 minutes, until golden brown. Allow to stand for 5 minutes before cutting. Serves 8.

Approximate nutritional analysis per serving:
Calories 255, Protein 9 g, Carbohydrates 19 g, Fat 17 g,
Cholesterol 112 mg, Sodium 204 mg

IMPOSSIBLE CHICKEN 'N BROCCOLI PIE

1 - 10 oz pkg (300 g) chopped broccoli, thawed
1½ cups (6 oz) (180 g) mozzarella, shredded
1½ cups (355 ml) cooked chicken, cut up
⅔ cup (160 ml) onion, chopped
½ cup (120 ml) red bell pepper, chopped
1 cup (240 ml) skim milk
4 egg whites *or*
    ½ cup (120 ml) cholesterol free egg product
1 cup (240 ml) BISQUICK Reduced Fat bake mix
¾ tsp (4 ml) salt
¼ tsp (1 ml) pepper

Heat oven to 400°F (205°C). Grease glass pie plate, 10x1½ inches. Drain broccoli thoroughly. Mix broccoli, 1 cup of the cheese, the chicken, onion and bell pepper in pie plate. Beat remaining ingredients in blender on high speed 15 seconds, with hand beater or wire whisk 1 minute or until smooth. Pour into pie plate. Bake 25-35 minutes or until knife inserted in center comes out clean. Sprinkle with remaining cheese. Bake 1-2 minutes or until cheese melts. Cool 10 minutes. Serves 6-8.
    High altitude: 3500-6500 feet: Bake 35-45 minutes.

Approximate nutritional analysis per serving:
Calories 260, Protein 25 g, Carbohydrates 20 g, Fat 9 g,
Cholesterol 50 mg, Sodium 740 mg

BEAN PIE

3 - 16 oz cans (1.4 kg) of any bean, mashed
3 large eggs
¾ cup (180 ml) unsalted butter, melted
1 tbs (15 ml) cornstarch
1 tsp (5 ml) ground cinnamon
1 tsp (5 ml) ground ginger
½ tsp (3 ml) ground cloves
1 tbs (15 ml) fresh lemon or orange juice
1 cup (240 ml) evaporated milk
1 cup (240 ml) brown sugar
1 unbaked 9-inch pie shell

Preheat oven to 450°F (230°C). Combine all ingredients except pie shell. Stir to blend. When well combined, pour into pie shell. Place in preheated oven and bake for 15 minutes. Lower heat to 350°F (180°C) and bake for an additional 30 minutes or until center is set. When serving, add a dollop of freshly whipped cream to each slice. Serves 8.

Approximate nutritional analysis per serving:
Calories 610, Protein 18 g, Carbohydrates 71 g, Fat 30 g,
Cholesterol 135 mg, Sodium 381 mg

BLACK BEAN TAMALE PIE WITH CHEESE CRUST

½ lb (230 g) lean ground beef
½ cup (120 ml) onion, chopped
½ cup (120 ml) green bell pepper, chopped
1 - 15 oz can (450 g) black beans, drained
1 cup (240 ml) CHI-CHI'S Salsa
2 tbs (30 ml) CHI-CHI'S Whole Green Jalapeño
    Peppers, chopped
1 - 8½ oz pkg (255 g) corn muffin mix
2 cups (480 ml) sharp cheddar cheese, shredded
¼ cup (60 ml) milk
1 egg
ripe olives, additional salsa, sour cream, if desired

Heat oven to 375°F (190°C). Grease 9-inch glass pie plate. In 10-inch skillet, cook ground beef, onion and green pepper until beef is no longer pink. Stir in beans, salsa and chopped jalapeño peppers; set aside. In medium bowl, combine corn muffin mix, 1 cup shredded cheese, milk and egg. Stir just until moistened. Press mixture on bottom and up sides of greased 9-inch pie plate. Spoon beef mixture into crust. Bake 20-30 minutes or until set. Remove from oven; sprinkle with remaining 1 cup shredded cheese. Bake 2-5 minutes or until cheese is melted. Let stand 5 minutes. Cut into wedges. Serve with olives, salsa and sour cream, if desired. Serves 6.

Approximate nutritional analysis per serving:
Calories 490, Protein 24 g, Carbohydrates 44 g, Fat 23 g,
Cholesterol 100 mg, Sodium 710 mg

Tuna Vegetable Round

TUNA VEGETABLE ROUND

2 cups (480 ml) BISQUICK Reduced Fat Baking Mix
⅔ cup (160 ml) cold water
3 oz (90 g) light cream cheese (Neufchâtel), softened
½ cup (120 ml) reduced calorie mayonnaise
½ cup (120 ml) green onion, sliced
2 tsp (10 ml) prepared horseradish
⅛ tsp (.5 ml) red pepper sauce
2 - 6½ oz cans (390 g) tuna in water, drained
2 medium stalks celery, cut diagonally
   into ¼-inch slices
assorted fresh vegetables (sliced mushrooms,
   cherry tomato halves, chopped broccoli)

Heat oven to 450°F (230°C). Mix baking mix in water until soft dough forms; beat vigorously 20 strokes. Pat dough in ungreased 12-inch pizza pan with floured hands, forming ½-inch rim. Bake about 10 minutes or until crust is light brown. Cool 20 minutes. Mix cream cheese, mayonnaise, onions, horseradish, pepper sauce and tuna; spread evenly over crust. Top with vegetables. Cover and refrigerate at least 1 hour. Serves 8.

High altitude: 3500-6500 feet: Lightly grease pizza pan. Decrease baking mix to 1½ cups (355 ml) and add ½ cup (120 ml) GOLD MEDAL All-Purpose Flour.

Approximate nutritional analysis per serving:
Calories 240, Protein 15 g, Carbohydrates 23 g, Fat 10 g,
Cholesterol 40 mg, Sodium 630 mg

OLD BAY ONION PIE

3 tbs (45 ml) butter
6 medium onions, peeled and sliced
1 tsp (5 ml) OLD BAY Seasoning
¼ tsp (1 ml) salt
1½ cups (355 ml) milk
5 eggs, beaten
1 - 9-inch pie shell
2 tbs (30 ml) parsley
12 slices bacon, cooked, drained and crumbled

Preheat oven to 350°F (180°C). In a medium saucepan, melt butter and sauté onions, OLD BAY Seasoning and salt over low heat for 15 minutes, stirring occasionally. Drain. Add milk and stir in eggs. Pour mixture in pie shell; top with parsley and bacon. Bake for 50 minutes until done. Serves 8.

Approximate nutritional analysis per serving:
Calories 319, Protein 9 g, Carbohydrates 32 g, Fat 18 g,
Cholesterol 26 mg, Sodium 429 mg

Courtesy of McCormick/Schilling Spices.

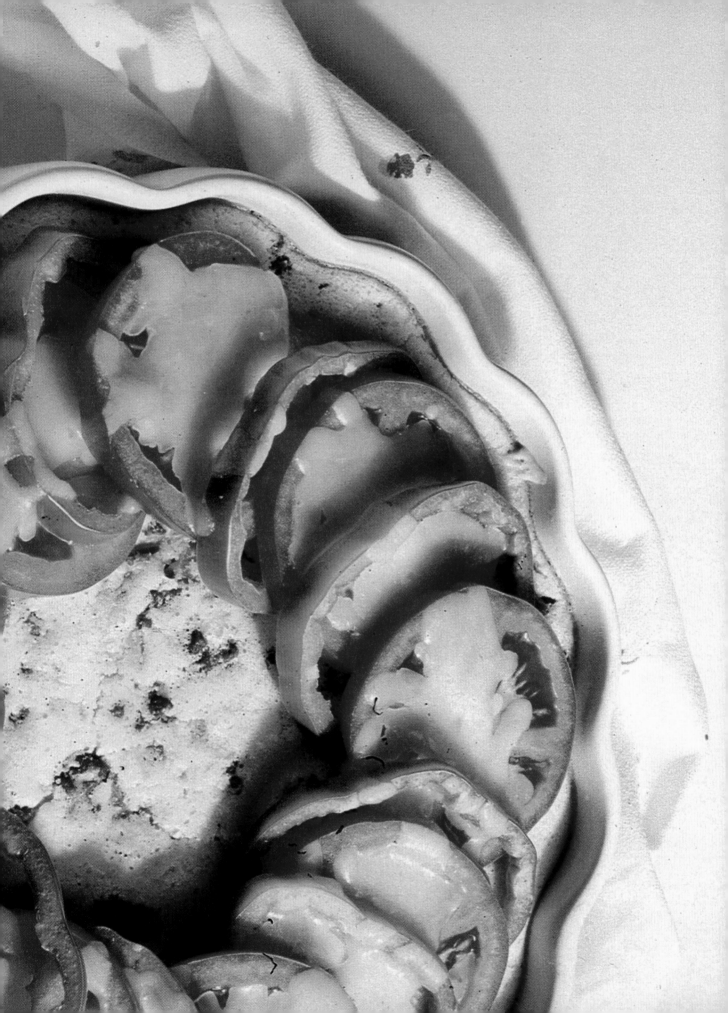

IMPOSSIBLE CHEESEBURGER PIE

1 lb (455 g) lean ground beef
1½ cups (355 ml) onion, chopped
1¼ cups (295 ml) skim milk
4 egg whites *or*
    ½ cup (120 ml) Cholesterol free egg product
1 cup (240 ml) BISQUICK Reduced Fat Baking Mix
½ tsp (3 ml) salt
¼ tsp (1 ml) pepper
1 green bell pepper, cut into rings
2 tomatoes, sliced
½ cup (2 oz) (60 g) mozzarella cheese, shredded

Heat oven to 400°F (205°C). Grease pie plate, 10x1½ inches, square baking dish, 8x8x2 inches, or six 10-oz custard cups. Cook ground beef and onion in 10-inch skillet over medium heat, stirring occasionally, until beef is brown; drain. Spread in pie plate. Beat milk, egg whites, baking mix, salt and pepper in blender on high speed 15 seconds, with hand beater or wire whisk 1 minute or until smooth. Pour into pie plate. Bake 25 minutes. Arrange pepper rings and tomato slices on pie; sprinkle with cheese. Bake 5-8 minutes longer or until knife inserted in center comes out clean. Cool at least 10 minutes. Serves 6-8.

High altitude: 3500-6500 feet: For pie plate or square baking dish, increase first bake time to 30 minutes. For custard cups, first bake time should remain 25 minutes.

Approximate nutritional analysis per serving:
Calories 290, Protein 23 g, Carbohydrates 23 g, Fat 12 g,
Cholesterol 55 mg, Sodium 570 mg

MEAT PIES

PASTRY:
2 tsp (10 ml) IMPERIAL Granulated Sugar
2 cups (480 ml) all purpose flour
4 tsp (60 ml) baking powder
½ tsp (3 ml) salt
½ cup (120 ml) shortening
⅔ cup (160 ml) beef broth or milk

MEAT FILLING:
¼ cup (½ stick) (60 ml) butter, margarine or oil
1 medium potato, diced in ½-inch cubes
1 clove garlic
½ cup (120 ml) onion, diced in ½-inch cubes
¼ cup (60 ml) raisins, optional
1 tsp (5 ml) salt
dash pepper
½ cup (120 ml) beef broth
1 cup (½ lb) (230 g) beef loin, in ½-inch cubes

Pastry: Cut shortening into mixture of dry ingredients until crumbly; stir in liquid with fork and form into ball of dough. Set aside.

Meat filling: Cook potatoes, garlic, onions and 2 tbs butter, margarine or oil until almost done; add raisins, salt, pepper, beef broth and simmer until almost all of liquid is gone; reserve. In heavy skillet, cook diced beef in 2 tbs butter, margarine or oil until beef is browned on all sides; combine meat with first mixture. Divide pastry into 8 portions. Roll each in 5-inch circle; place about 3 tbs meat filling on half of each pastry circle. Fold other half of each pastry circle over filling to make an oval pie. Crimp edges with fork dipped into cold water. Bake pies in preheated 450°F (230°C) oven on ungreased baking sheet about 12 minutes, or until browned. Serves 8.

Approximate nutritional analysis per serving:
Calories 372, Protein 9 g, Carbohydrates 30 g, Fat 24 g,
Cholesterol 19 mg, Sodium 751 mg

QUICHE ITALIENNE

1 - 28 oz can (840 g) LIBBY'S Whole Peeled
    Tomatoes in juice
¾ lb (340 g) Italian sausage
1 - 9 -inch unbaked pie shell
1 tbs (15 ml) oil
1 medium yellow onion, cut into rings
2 cloves garlic, minced
1 cup (240 ml) mushrooms, sliced
¼ cup (60 ml) parsley, chopped
½ cup (120 ml) ripe olives, sliced
¼ cup (60 ml) butter
¼ cup (60 ml) flour
3 eggs
1 cup (240 ml) sour cream
¼ tsp (1 ml) salt
⅛ tsp (.5 ml) white pepper
2 cups (480 ml) Swiss cheese, grated

Drain tomatoes well, save ½ cup juice. Cut tomatoes in half. Remove skin from Italian sausage. Break sausage apart with fork in frying pan; cook until browned. Drain on paper towel and place in bottom of pie shell. Add oil to pan and sauté onion, garlic and mushrooms until lightly browned; spoon over meat layer. Sprinkle parsley and olives as next layer and top with tomatoes. Melt butter in skillet over low heat; sprinkle with flour. Cook stirring constantly until well browned. Remove form heat and stir in ½ cup saved tomato juice. Spoon over tomato layer. In mixing bowl beat eggs slightly; stir in sour cream, salt, pepper and Swiss cheese. Pour egg mixture over all. Bake in preheated 350°F (180°C) oven about 35-40 minutes or until golden brown. Serves 8.

Approximate nutritional analysis per serving:
Calories 491, Protein 12 g, Carbohydrates 24 g, Fat 40 g,
Cholesterol 137 mg, Sodium 778 mg

Opposite: Impossible Cheeseburger Pie

FRESH HERB, OLIVE AND RICOTTA PIE

1 frozen pie shell
1 pt (480 ml) lowfat ricotta cheese
2 eggs
2 tbs (30 ml) flour
2 tbs (30 ml) fresh oregano leaves, chopped
1 tbs (15 ml) fresh thyme leaves, chopped
½ tsp (3 ml) salt
½ tsp (3 ml) pepper
¾ cup (180 ml) CALIFORNIA olives, chopped
1 small tomato, thinly sliced

Transfer pie shell to ovenproof glass pie plate. Bake as package directs until golden. Meanwhile, mix ricotta, eggs, flour, herbs, salt, pepper and ½ cup olives. Turn evenly into pie shell. Place on rack or inverted saucer in microwave oven. Bake at 50% (medium) power for 10-15 minutes, rotating pie one-quarter turn ever 3 minutes or until baked through but slightly soft-set in center. Top pie with overlapping tomato slices and a ring of remaining ¼ cup olives. Sprinkle with a few fresh herbs if desired. Let stand 5-10 minutes before cutting. Serves 6.

Approximate nutritional analysis per serving:
Calories 336, Protein 14 g, Carbohydrates 23 g, Fat 21 g, Cholesterol 96 mg, Sodium 645 mg

EMPANADA GALLEGA

1 small green pepper, chopped
1 onion, chopped
1 tbs (15 ml) GOYA Olive Oil
½ lb (230 g) ground pork
1 GOYA Chorizo, chopped fine
¼ tsp (1 ml) thyme
¼ tsp (1 ml) oregano
pinch of rosemary
1 packet Sazón GOYA sin Achiote
1 tsp (5 ml) crushed red pepper
1 tbs (15 ml) GOYA Sofrito
½ cup (120 ml) LA VINA White Cooking Wine
1 tbs (15 ml) GOYA Tomato Sauce
pepper to taste
1 pkg refrigerated pie crust dough
1 egg, beaten

In a skillet, sauté green pepper and onion in olive oil until soft. Add pork, and sauté until browned. Add chorizo, thyme, oregano, rosemary, Sazón , crushed pepper, Sofrito, wine and tomato sauce, and pepper to taste.Boil gently for about 10 minutes, until wine is almost evaporated. Remove from heat. Preheat oven to 350°F (180°C). Spread bottom pie crust dough flat on cookie sheet. Spread pork mixture on dough, mounding slightly in the center and leaving a 1-inch edge empty. Paint edges with beaten egg, and place top pie crust over pork mixture. Paint top crust with beaten egg and crimp edges closed with fork. Bake in bottom of oven about 20 minutes, or until dough is brown and completely cooked. Serves 6.

Approximate nutritional analysis per serving:
Calories 368, Protein 15 g, Carbohydrates 18 g, Fat 25 g, Cholesterol 76 mg, Sodium 478 mg

VIDALIA ONION TART

2 large VIDALIA Onions, peeled, sliced and in rings
1½ tsp (8 ml) olive oil
2 tbs (30 ml) minced fresh chives
1 cup (240 ml) skim milk
¼ cup (60 ml) egg substitute
2 egg whites
1 tsp (5 ml) sage

Heat olive oil in a 10-inch cast iron skillet and add the VIDALIA Onions and chives. Cook slowly over low heat until the onions are soft, approximately 3 minutes. In a bowl, whisk the milk, egg substitute, egg whites and sage together. Pour the egg mixture over the onions and bake until set, approximately 30 minutes. Slice into 4 wedges and serve warm. Serves 4.

Approximate nutritional analysis per serving:
Calories 145, Protein 9 g, Carbohydrates 23 g, Fat 3 g, Cholesterol 1 mg, Sodium 94 mg

RICOTTA-CHICKEN PIE

DOUGH:
½ cup (120 ml) ricotta cheese
⅓ cup (80 ml) butter or margarine, melted
1 cup (240 ml) all purpose flour, sifted
½ tsp (3 ml) salt

FILLING:
4 PREMIUM YOUNG 'N TENDER Brand boneless,
    skinless split chicken breasts, cut into
    bite-sized pieces
8 oz (240 g) bulk pork sausage
¼ cup (60 ml) onion, chopped
1 cup (240 ml) ricotta cheese
¾ cup (180 ml) milk
4 eggs
¼ tsp (1 ml) salt
¼ tsp (1 ml) pepper
⅔ cup (160 ml) Swiss cheese, shredded
⅛ cup (.5 ml) fresh parsley, chopped

Dough: Combine ricotta cheese and butter; beat with mixer or in food processor until smooth; blend in flour and salt. Form into a ball and chill about 30 minutes. Roll dough and fit into a 9-inch deep pie plate. Prick holes in bottom with fork; chill 10-15 minutes. Bake in preheated 450°F (230°C) oven for 5 minutes.

    Filling: Preheat oven to 375°F (190°C). Combine chicken, sausage and onion in a 10-inch skillet and cook until done, stirring to break up sausage. Remove and drain. In a medium bowl, beat together ricotta cheese, milk, eggs, salt and pepper. Stir in meat mixture, Swiss cheese and parsley. Pour into baked pie shell. Bake for 40-50 minutes or until filling is set. Let stand 5 minutes before serving. Serves 6.

Approximate nutritional analysis per serving:
Calories 683, Protein 43 g, Carbohydrates 22 g, Fat 47 g,
Cholesterol 300 mg, Sodium 835 mg

VEGETABLE PIZZA

1 small zucchini, sliced
1 medium onion, cut into eighths
1 small green pepper, cut into thin strips
2 cloves garlic, minced
½ tsp (3 ml) dried oregano leaves, crushed
½ tsp (3 ml) dried basil leaves, crushed
⅛ tsp (.5 ml) pepper
2 tbs (30 ml) olive oil
¾ cup (180 ml) HEINZ Chili Sauce
¼ cup (60 ml) Parmesan cheese, grated
1 - 12-inch pre-baked pizza shell
1½ cups (355 ml) mozzarella cheese, shredded

In 2-qt saucepan, sauté first 7 ingredients in oil until vegetables are tender-crisp. Stir in chili sauce and Parmesan cheese; simmer 5 minutes, stirring occasionally. Place pizza shell on baking sheet. Spoon vegetable mixture evenly over pizza shell; sprinkle mozzarella cheese on top. Bake in preheated 425°F (220°C) oven, 8-10 minutes or until shell is lightly browned. Cut pizza into 8 wedges. Serves 4.

Approximate nutritional analysis per serving:
Calories 458, Protein 17 g, Carbohydrates 48 g, Fat 22 g,
Cholesterol 37 mg, Sodium 265 mg

SUN GARDEN PIZZA

CONTADINA Refrigerated Pizza Kit
1½ tsp (8 ml) fresh tarragon leaves, chopped *or*
    ½ tsp (3 ml) dried tarragon leaves, crushed
¼ tsp (1 ml) garlic powder
¼ cup (60 ml) sun-dried tomatoes in oil, julienned
¼ cup (60 ml) red onion, thinly sliced
8 asparagus spears, blanched, in 1-inch lengths
½ cup (2 oz) (60 g) feta cheese, crumbled

Place oven rack in middle of oven; preheat to 425°F (220°C). Spread pizza sauce over crust to within 1 inch of edge. Sprinkle with tarragon, garlic powder, and ⅔ of cheese package. Add tomatoes and onion. Arrange asparagus on pizza. Sprinkle with feta cheese and remainder of cheese package. Bake on oven rack for 10-12 minutes or until crust is crisp and cheese is melted. Serves 8.

Nutritional analysis not available.

MEXICAN PIZZA

1 CONTADINA Refrigerated Cheese Pizza Kit:
    Crust, Pizza Sauce, Cheese
8 oz (240 g) lean ground beef
2 tbs (30 ml) (half of 1¼ oz pkg) taco seasoning mix
¼ cup (60 ml) water
¼ cup (60 ml) tomatoes, diced
¼ cup (60 ml) ripe olives, sliced, drained
¼ cup (60 ml) corn
¼ cup (60 ml) cheddar cheese, shredded
2 tbs (30 ml) green bell pepper, diced

Place oven rack in middle of oven; preheat to 425°F (220°C). In medium skillet, brown ground beef; drain. Add taco seasoning mix and water; cook for about 1 minute or until most of water has evaporated. Spread pizza sauce over crust to within 1 inch of edge. Sprinkle meat and cheese over; top with tomatoes, olives, corn, cheddar cheese and bell pepper. Bake on oven rack for 10-12 minutes or until crust is crisp and cheese is melted. Serves 8.

Nutritional analysis not available.

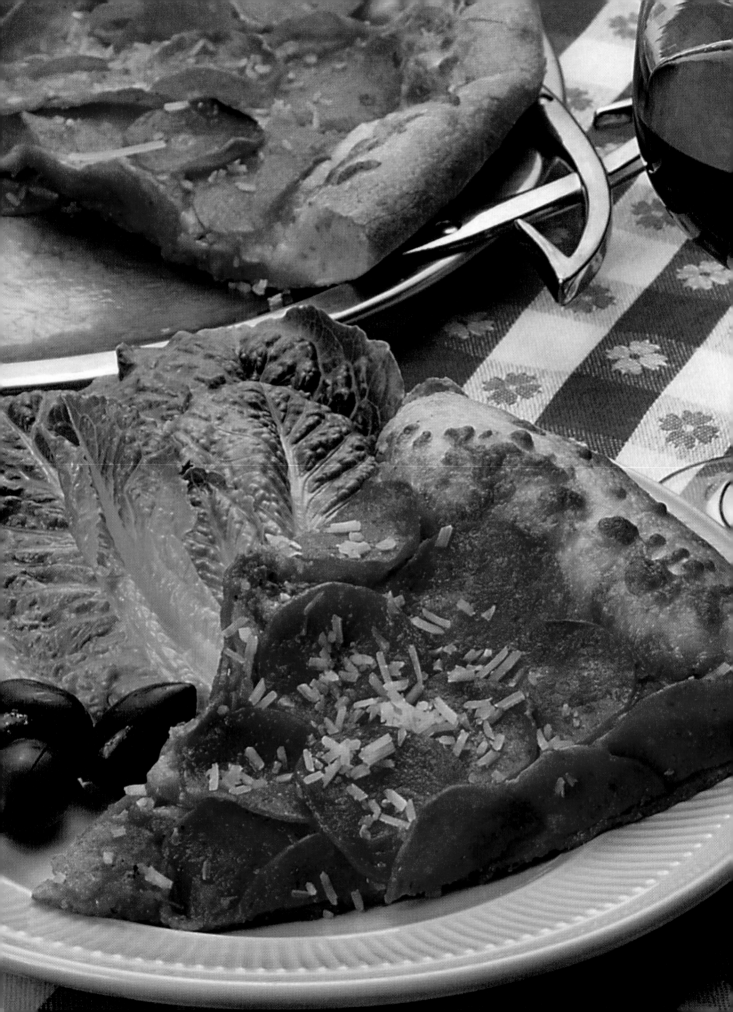

FRESH TOMATO SKILLET PIZZA

2 lbs (910 g) fresh FLORIDA tomatoes
¼ cup (60 ml) olive oil
2⅔ cups (640 ml) yellow onions, chopped
2 tbs (30 ml) garlic, minced
1 tsp (5 ml) Italian seasoning, crushed
¼ tsp (1 ml) black pepper
1¾ lbs (795 g) prepared pizza dough
2 cups (480 ml) mozzarella cheese,
    part skim, shredded
1 cup (240 ml) canned sliced mushrooms, drained
½ cup (120 ml) Parmesan cheese, grated
½ cup (120 ml) red onions, sliced

Use tomatoes held at room temperature until fully ripe. Core; slice off ends (reserve for soups or sauces). Slice ¼ inch thick; set aside. In a skillet heat 2 tbs oil until hot; add onions and garlic; sauté until tender, 6-7 minutes. Stir in Italian seasoning and black pepper; set aside.

For each pizza: Stretch or roll 7-oz pizza dough into a 10-inch circle. In a greased 8-inch oven-proof skillet fit dough into the bottom and sides. Bake in a preheated 400°F (205°C) oven until surface is dried, about 5 minutes. Remove from oven; spread 2 oz (⅓ cup) prepared onion mixture over bottom; sprinkle with 2 oz (½ cup) mozzarella, 1½ oz (¼ cup) mushrooms, 2 tbs grated Parmesan cheese, 4-5 reserved tomato slices and ¾ oz (2 tbs) red onion. Brush or drizzle with 1½ tsp olive oil.

Bake until crust is browned, about 20 minutes. Garnish with fresh basil and sprinkle with additional Parmesan, if desired. Serves 24.

Approximate nutritional analysis per serving:
Calories 924, Protein 40 g, Carbohydrates 112 g, Fat 33 g,
Cholesterol 54 mg, Sodium 600 mg

QUICK CHICKEN FAJITA PIZZA

2 tsp (10 ml) olive oil or oil
2 whole chicken breasts, skinned, boned,
    cut into 2x½-inch strips
1-2 tsp (5-10 ml) chili powder
½ tsp (3 ml) salt
½ tsp (3 ml) garlic powder
1 cup (240 ml) onions, thinly sliced
1 cup (240 ml) green or red bell pepper strips,
    2x¼ inch
1 - 10 oz can (300 g) PILLSBURY Refrigerated
    All Ready Pizza Crust
½ cup (120 ml) prepared mild salsa or picante sauce
4 oz (1 cup) (120 g) Monterey Jack cheese, shredded

Heat oil in large skillet over medium-high heat until hot. Add chicken; cook and stir 5 minutes or until lightly browned. Stir in chili powder, salt and garlic powder. Add onions and bell pepper; cook and stir an additional 1 minute or until vegetables are crisp-tender.

Heat oven to 425°F (220°C). Grease 12-inch pizza pan or 13x9-inch pan. Unroll dough; place in greased pan. Starting at center, press out with hands. Bake for 6-8 minutes or until very light golden brown. Spoon chicken mixture over partially baked crust, spoon salsa over chicken; sprinkle with cheese. Bake an additional 14-18 minutes or until crust is golden brown. Serves 8.

Approximate nutritional analysis per serving:
Calories 260, Protein 21 g, Carbohydrates 20 g, Fat 11 g,
Cholesterol 49 mg, Sodium 600 mg

MARINATED CHICKEN FAJITA PIZZA

MARINADE:
½ cup (120 ml) onion, chopped
½ cup (120 ml) lime juice
½ cup (120 ml) vegetable oil
1½ tsp (8 ml) fresh garlic, minced
1 tsp (5 ml) ground cumin
1 tsp (5 ml) grated lime peel
1 tsp (5 ml) paprika
¼ tsp (1 ml) coarsely ground pepper
2 tbs (30 ml) fresh cilantro, chopped

PIZZA:
1 lb (455 g) chicken boneless breasts, cur in strips
1 tbs (15 ml) cornmeal
1 - 10 oz can (300 g) refrigerated pizza dough
    ***or* 1 lb (455 g) prepared pizza dough**
1 cup (240 ml) CHI-CHI'S Salsa
½ cup (120 ml) ripe olives, sliced
2 cups (480 ml) hot pepper Monterey Jack cheese,
    shredded
guacamole, sour cream, sliced green onions

In large reclosable plastic food bag, place all marinade ingredients. Add chicken; seal bag and turn several times to coat. Place bag in 13x9-inch pan. Refrigerate, turning bag occasionally, 4 hours or overnight. Heat oven to 400°F (205°C). Sprinkle 12-inch pizza pie pan with 1 tbs (15 ml) cornmeal. Press pizza crust to within 1 inch from edge of pan. Remove chicken from marinade. On large skillet, cook chicken strips until no longer pink. Drain. Spread salsa on top of pizza crust. Top with chicken strips and ripe olives. Sprinkle with cheese. Bake 18-20 minutes or until cheese melts and crust is browned. Serve with guacamole, sour cream and green onions. Serves 6.

Approximate nutritional analysis per serving:
Calories 420, Protein 30 g, Carbohydrates 26 g, Fat 21 g,
Cholesterol 80 mg, Sodium 750 mg

Opposite: Fresh Tomato Skillet Pizza

SLOPPY JOE PIZZA BREAD

1 lb (455 g) ground beef
¾ cup (180 ml) frozen corn, defrosted
¾ cup (180 ml) prepared barbecue sauce
½ cup (120 ml) green onions, sliced
½ tsp (3 ml) salt, optional
1 prepared pizza crust
 or 1 - 16 oz (480 g) Italian bread shell
1½ cups (6 oz) (180 g) cheddar cheese, shredded

Heat oven to 425°F (220°C). In large nonstick skillet, brown ground beef over medium heat 8-10 minutes or until no longer pink, stirring occasionally. Pour off drippings. Stir in corn, barbecue sauce, green onions and salt, if desired; heat through. Place pizza crust on large baking sheet. Top evenly with beef mixture; sprinkle with cheese. Bake for 12-15 minutes or until cheese melts; cut into 6 wedges. Serves 6.

Approximate nutritional analysis per serving:
Calories 483, Protein 32 g, Carbohydrates 43 g, Fat 20 g,
Cholesterol 82 mg, Sodium 878 mg

Courtesy of the National Livestock and Meat Board.

HEARTY DEEP DISH PIZZA

1 loaf frozen bread dough,
 thawed to room temperature
1 cup (240 ml) HEALTHY CHOICE Pasta Sauce
1 clove garlic, minced
1 tsp (5 ml) dried oregano leaves, crushed
1 tsp (5 ml) dried basil leaves, crushed
1 - 8 oz ball (240 g) HEALTHY CHOICE Fat Free
 Natural Mozzarella Cheese, sliced
1 cup (240 ml) onion rings
1 cup (240 ml) green pepper strips
1 cup (240 ml) mushroom slices
1 - 8 oz pkg (240 g) HEALTHY CHOICE Fat Free
 Natural Fancy Shredded Pizza Cheese

Heat oven to 450°F (230°C). Press bread dough onto bottom and 1 inch up sides of 13x9-inch baking pan that has been sprayed with nonstick cooking spray. Bake 10 minutes. Top with mozzarella cheese. Combine pasta sauce, garlic, oregano and basil; spread over cheese. Top with onions, green peppers and mushrooms; sprinkle with shredded pizza cheese. Continue baking at 450°F (230°C) 10-15 minutes or until cheese melts and crust is deep golden brown. Serves 12.

Approximate nutritional analysis per serving:
Calories 206, Protein 16 g, Carbohydrates 24 g, Fat 1 g,
Cholesterol 10 mg, Sodium 469 mg

SPINACH CALZONE PIZZAS

1 loaf frozen white bread dough,
 thawed to room temperature
1 - 8 oz pkg (240 g) HEALTHY CHOICE Fat Free
 Natural Shredded Mozzarella Cheese
1 - 10 oz pkg (300 g) frozen chopped spinach,
 thawed, well drained
1 - 6 oz can (180 g) tomato paste
¼ cup (60 ml) onion, finely chopped
1 - 4 oz can (120 g) mushroom stems and pieces,
 drained
1 clove garlic, minced
2 tbs (30 ml) red wine

Heat oven to 375°F (190°C). Divide bread dough into 6 equal pieces. On baking sheets sprayed with nonstick cooking spray, pat each piece into 7-inch circle. Combine remaining ingredients; mix lightly. Spoon approximately ½ cup mixture onto half of each circle. Fold dough over filling; moisten edges and press together with fork to seal. Cut small slit in top of each calzone; lightly spray with cooking spray. Bake 15-18 minutes or until golden brown. Serves 6.

Approximate nutritional analysis per serving:
Calories 322, Protein 22 g, Carbohydrates 46 g, Fat 2 g,
Cholesterol 7 mg, Sodium 616 mg

SOUTH OF THE BORDER BEAN AND BACON PIZZA

1 - 10 oz can (300 g) refrigerated pizza crust
1 - 15 oz can (450 g) spicy or extra spicy
 chili beans, undrained
3-4 slices bacon, crisply cooked, crumbled
1 small onion, thinly sliced
2 cups (8 oz) (240 g) Colby/Monterey Jack
 blend cheese, shredded

Heat oven to 425°F (220°C). Place oven rack at lowest position. Grease 12-inch pizza pan or 13x9-inch pan. Unroll dough and place in greased pan; starting at center, press out with hands. Bake for 5-8 minutes or until crust begins to brown.

In medium bowl, combine beans, bacon and onion slices; mix well. Spread bean mixture over partially baked pizza crust; sprinkle with cheese. Bake 8-12 minutes or until crust is brown and cheese is bubbly. Serves 6.

Approximate nutritional analysis per serving:
Calories 366, Protein 19 g, Carbohydrates 37 g, Fat 16 g,
Cholesterol 39 mg, Sodium 745 mg

Opposite: Sloppy Joe Pizza Bread

GRAPE PESTO PIZZA

½ cup (120 ml) lowfat ricotta cheese
Pesto (below)
1 - 10-inch Italian bread shell
1 cup (240 ml) red CALIFORNIA seedless
    grapes, halved
¾ cup (180 ml) sweet red pepper, julienned
3 tbs (45 ml) Parmesan cheese, grated
2 tbs (30 ml) pistachios, toasted

PESTO:
1 cup (240 ml) fresh basil
2 tbs (30 ml) Parmesan cheese, grated
1 clove garlic
1 tbs (15 ml) olive oil

Combine ricotta cheese and pesto; mix well. Spread cheese mixture over top of bread shell. Top with grapes and pepper; sprinkle Parmesan cheese and pistachios. Bake at 375°F (190°C) 20-25 minutes or until golden. Serves 8.

Approximate nutritional analysis per serving:
Calories 245, Protein 9 g, Carbohydrates 39 g, Fat 5 g,
Cholesterol 8 mg, Sodium 426 mg

Courtesy of the California Table Grape Commission.

SAUSAGE ROLLS

1 pkg dry yeast or 1 cake yeast
1 tbs (15 ml) warm water
1 tsp (5 ml) IMPERIAL Granulated Sugar
½ cup (120 ml) shortening
½ cup (120 ml) IMPERIAL Granulated Sugar
1 tsp (5 ml) salt
1 cup (240 ml) hot water
3 eggs, beaten
4-4½ cups (960-1080 ml) all purpose flour
1-1½ lbs (455-685 g) Polish sausage cut in
    1½ -inch lengths, then quartered

Combine yeast, warm water, 1 tsp IMPERIAL Granulated Sugar; set aside. Combine shortening, ½ cup IMPERIAL Granulated Sugar, salt, hot tap water, eggs; beat well. Add yeast mixture. Add 2 cups flour and beat well. Stir in another 2-2½ cups flour to make soft dough. Refrigerate covered dough in large mixing bowl overnight. Divide dough into three portions. Roll one portion of dough into circle ¼-inch thick and cut with biscuit cutter into 2-inch diameter circles. Simmer sausages in small amount of water in covered pan about 5 minutes. Drain sausages on paper towel then place in centers of circles of dough. Moisten edges of dough with water, lap one side of dough over sausage and press edges of dough together to seal. Repeat with remaining dough.

Place rolls on greased cookie sheet and let rise about 1½ hours, or until doubled. Bake in preheated 350°F (180°C) oven about 10-12 minutes, or until golden brown. Yields 36 rolls.

Approximate nutritional analysis per roll:
Calories 126, Protein 3 g, Carbohydrates 15 g, Fat 6 g,
Cholesterol 23 mg, Sodium 160 mg

MEAT PIES

PASTRY:
2 tsp (10 ml) IMPERIAL Granulated Sugar
2 cups (480 ml) all purpose flour
4 tsp (60 ml) baking powder
½ tsp (3 ml) salt
½ cup (120 ml) shortening
⅔ cup (160 ml) beef broth or milk

MEAT FILLING:
¼ cup (½ stick) (60 ml) butter,
    margarine or oil, divided
1 medium potato, diced in ½-inch cubes
1 clove garlic
½ cup (120 ml) onion, diced in ½-inch cubes
¼ cup (60 ml) raisins, optional
1 tsp (5 ml) salt
dash pepper
½ cup (120 ml) beef broth
1 cup (½ lb) (230 g) beef loin, diced in ½-inch cubes

Pastry: Cut shortening into mixture of dry ingredients until crumbly; stir in liquid with fork and form into a ball of dough. Set aside.

Meat Filling: Cook potatoes, garlic, onions in 2 tbs butter, margarine or oil until almost done; add raisins, salt, pepper, beef broth and simmer until most of the liquid is gone; reserve. In heavy skillet, cook diced beef in 2 tbs butter, margarine or oil until beef is lightly browned on all sides; combine meat with first mixture. Divide pastry into 8 portions. Roll each portion in 5-inch circle; place about 3 tbs meat filling on half of each pastry circle. Fold remaining half of each pastry circle over filling to make an oval pie. Crimp edges with fork dipped into cold water. Bake pies in preheated 450°F (230°C) oven on ungreased baking sheet about 12 minutes, or until nicely browned. Serves 8.

Note: Can be frozen. There should be some meat filling left over; serve over hot meat pies.

Approximate nutritional analysis per serving:
Calories 372, Protein 9 g, Carbohydrates 30 g, Fat 24 g,
Cholesterol 19 mg, Sodium 751 mg

Opposite: Grape Pesto Pizza

GREEK FRESH TOMATO PIZZA

2 medium fresh **FLORIDA** tomatoes
3 small pita bread pockets
1 egg white
1 tsp (5 ml) water
1 tbs (15 ml) vegetable oil
1 cup (240 ml) mozzarella cheese
1 cup (240 ml) sweet green bell pepper, thinly sliced
½ cup (120 ml) feta or cream cheese, crumbled
⅓ cup (80 ml) oil-cured ripe olives, pitted and halved
½ tsp (3 ml) oregano leaves, crushed

Preheat oven to 400°F (205°C). Use tomatoes held at room temperature until fully ripe. Core tomatoes; cut in ¼-inch thick slices; set aside. In a small bowl lightly beat egg white and water. On a 12-inch round pizza pan* arrange pita halves around pan, overlapping slightly to form a crust. Lightly brush egg white mixture under overlapped pitas, pressing down gently. Bake 3-4 minutes, remove from oven. Using a potholder or towel, press down on overlapped pitas so they will hold together; return to oven. Bake until crisp, 3-4 minutes longer. Lightly brush crust with oil; sprinkle with mozzarella cheese; arrange green pepper and reserved tomato slices over mozzarella, overlapping slightly. Sprinkle with feta cheese, olives and oregano. Bake until tomatoes are softened and mozzarella is melted, 10-15 minutes. Serves 8.

    * Or use a cookie sheet, arranging pita halves in a 12-inch circle.

Approximate nutritional analysis per serving:
Calories 350, Protein 14 g, Carbohydrates 35 g, Fat 18 g,
Cholesterol 37 mg, Sodium 977 mg

WEST COAST PIZZAS

2 medium flour tortillas
vegetable oil cooking spray
1 - 8 oz ball (240 g) **HEALTHY CHOICE Fat Free**
    Natural Mozzarella Cheese, cut into 16 slices
2 cups (480 ml) fresh tomato, chopped
½ cup (120 ml) fresh basil, chopped
¼ cup (60 ml) green onions, sliced
¼ cup (60 ml) ripe olives, chopped
cracked black pepper

Heat oven to 400°F (205°C). Lightly spray both sides of each tortilla with non-stick cooking spray. Place on baking sheet and bake 2 minutes on each side or until crisp and golden brown. Remove from oven and reduce temperature to 350°F (180°C). Top each tortilla with half of the tomato, basil, onion, olives and 8 slices of cheese. Sprinkle with pepper to taste. Bake 5 minutes or until cheese melts. Cut each pizza into 8 wedges. Serves 8.

Approximate nutritional analysis per serving:
Calories 113, Protein 11 g, Carbohydrates 13 g, Fat 3 g,
Cholesterol 5 mg, Sodium 355 mg

INDIVIDUAL MEXICAN PIZZAS

8 small corn tortillas
1 - 15 oz can (450 g) pinto beans, drained, rinsed
½ lb (230 g) **HEALTHY CHOICE Fat Free**
    Pasteurized Process Cheese Product, cubed
2 tbs (30 ml) onion, finely chopped
1 cup (240 ml) tomato, chopped
1 - 10 oz pkg (300 g) frozen corn, cooked
½ cup (120 ml) green pepper, finely chopped
¼ cup (60 ml) fresh cilantro, chopped
1 - 8 oz pkg (240 g) **HEALTHY CHOICE Fat Free**
    Natural Shredded Mexican Cheese

Heat oven to 400°F (205 °C). Lightly spray both sides of each tortilla with nonstick cooking spray. Place on baking sheet and bake 2 minutes on each side or until crisp. Remove from oven and reduce oven temperature to 350°F (180°C). In bowl of food processor, combine beans, process cheese cubes and onion; process until blended. Spread ¼ cup of bean mixture on each tortilla. Combine tomatoes, corn, green pepper and cilantro; toss lightly. Top each tortilla with ¼ cup vegetable mixture and ¼ cup Mexican cheese. Return to oven and bake 6-8 minutes or until cheese melts. Serves 8.

Approximate nutritional analysis per serving:
Calories 241, Protein 22 g, Carbohydrates 37 g, Fat 2 g,
Cholesterol 10 mg, Sodium 603 mg

Greek Fresh Tomato Pizza

Opposite: West Coast Pizzas

PICCADILLY PIZZAS

½ cup (120 ml) zucchini, finely chopped
2 tbs (30 ml) onion, finely chopped
½ tsp (3 ml) dried oregano, crushed
8 English muffin halves, toasted
8 tomato slices
8 slices HEALTHY CHOICE Fat Free Pasteurized
   Process Cheese Singles Product

Mix together zucchini, onion and oregano. For each pizza, top muffin half with tomato slice and 1 tbs zucchini mixture; cover with cheese slice. Broil until cheese melts. Serves 8.

Approximate nutritional analysis per serving:
Calories 102, Protein 7 g, Carbohydrates 16 g, Fat .5 g,
Cholesterol 3 mg, Sodium 451 mg

CHILI PIZZAS

1 cup (240 ml) DANNON Plain Nonfat or
   Lowfat Yogurt
4 medium flour tortillas
1 cup (240 ml) canned chili without beans
1 tbs (15 ml) instant minced onion
1 cup (4 oz) (120 g) cheddar cheese, shredded
1 cup (240 ml) iceberg lettuce, shredded
1 large tomato, seeded and diced

Spoon yogurt into large strainer lined with double thickness of cheesecloth or a coffee filter. Place bowl beneath, but not touching strainer to catch the liquid. Let stand 15 minutes. Discard liquid.

Preheat oven to 400°F (205°C). Place tortillas on lightly greased baking sheet. Bake 3 minutes, turning once. In a small bowl combine chili and onion. Spread ¼ cup chili mixture on each crisped tortilla leaving a ½-inch border around edge. Divide cheese evenly among tortillas. Return to oven. Bake 5 minutes or until cheese is melted. Top evenly with lettuce, tomato and drained yogurt. Serve immediately. Serves 4.

Approximate nutritional analysis per serving:
Calories 228, Protein 10 g, Carbohydrates 34 g, Fat 7 g,
Cholesterol 14 mg, Sodium 514 mg

POULTRY

In a world watching its waistline and its timeline, chicken and turkey have become the most popular choices for fat-conscious quickly-prepared meals. The quantity of recipes included reflect the practicality and versatility of these noble fowls. Ground or flattened, roasted or braised, there is no limit to your flavorful choices.

CHICKEN VERONIQUE

2 - 2-2½ lb (910-1140 ml) EMPIRE KOSHER
  Rock Cornish Chickens
pepper to taste
grated rind of 4 lemons
2 tbs (30 ml) oil
2 tbs (30 ml) lemon juice
1 lb (455 g) seedless grapes, use red for more color
1-2 tbs (15-30 ml) kosher port
2 tsp (10 ml) kosher parve margarine

Preheat oven to 425°F (220°C). Rinse poultry, pat dry. Pepper the inside and outside of the birds, and sprinkle with lemon zest. Mix together the oil and lemon juice, rub outside of chickens. Wash the grapes, remove stems and fill cavities with the grapes. Truss chickens; place in large shallow casserole big enough just to hold the chickens, roast for 25 minutes at 425°F (220°C). Reduce heat to 350°F (180°C), baste. Roast another 25 minutes, turn the birds carefully and roast. Roast another 20 minutes. Remove chickens. Skim the fat from the pan juices, add the port, whisk in the margarine and correct seasoning. Cut each chicken in half, dividing the grapes between the halves. Pour pan juices over; serve with rice or potatoes. Serves 4.

Approximate nutritional analysis per ½ chicken:
Calories 1245, Protein 165 g, Carbohydrates 22 g, Fat 52 g, Cholesterol 502 mg, Sodium 514 mg

CRISP POTATO CHICKEN

1 - 3 lb (1.4 kg) EMPIRE KOSHER Chicken,
  cut in half, backbone and skin removed
1 tsp (5 ml) olive oil
1 tbs (15 ml) whole mustard seeds or caraway seeds
2 medium baking potatoes, peeled
1 onion, grated
1 egg, beaten
1 tbs (15 ml) prepared grainy mustard

Preheat oven to 425°F (220°C). Put the cut chicken, skin removed, meat side down, in an oven safe dish, sprinkle with mustard or caraway. Roast for 10 minutes. While the chicken is roasting, grate the potatoes on the coarse side of grater, place in a piece of gauze and wring out excess moisture. Grate the onion, add to the potatoes along with the beaten egg. Mix well. Remove the chicken from the oven, turn, spread the mustard over the chicken.Spread a thin, even layer of the potato-onion mixture over the chicken, return to the oven and bake 25 minutes. If a crisper crust is desired, place under the broiler for a few minutes until brown. Serves 4.

Approximate nutritional analysis per serving:
Calories 709, Protein 102 g, Carbohydrates 16 g, Fat 27 g, Cholesterol 304 mg, Sodium 361 mg

HERB ROASTED CUTLETS

4 EMPIRE KOSHER Chicken Breasts,
  boned, skin left on
olive oil
2 tbs (30 ml) lemon juice
small bunch either fresh rosemary, oregano,
  tarragon, basil or parsley, snipped finely
4 slices day-old Challah or other firm-textured
  bread, sliced
½-inch thick clove of garlic
freshly ground pepper

Preheat broiler. Line a broiler pan with foil; place the bread, trimmed to fit each breast, on the pan. Rub each slice of bread with the cut garlic clove, drizzle lightly with oil. Broil for 30 seconds to firm bread. Remove and top with the chicken breast, skin side down. Trim the bread if needed so that the edges are covered and don't burn. Brush the breasts with oil, squeeze lemon top, and sprinkle with herbs. Broil for about 4 minutes. Turn chicken, brush with oil and lemon, sprinkle with more herbs and broil for another 5-6 minutes or until tender and juices run clear. Remove carefully, season with pepper andserve with a green, mixed or tomato salad. Serves 4.

Approximate nutritional analysis per serving:
Calories 235, Protein 30 g, Carbohydrates 18 g, Fat 4 g, Cholesterol 74 mg, Sodium 227 mg

BRANDIED APRICOT-GLAZED CORNISH GAME HENS

4 small Cornish game hens
½ cup (120 ml) apricot preserves
1 tbs (15 ml) Dijon-style mustard
1 tsp (5 ml) McCORMICK or SCHILLING
  Brandy Extract
1 tbs (15 ml) soy sauce
2 tsp (1 ml) grated orange zest
3 tbs (45 ml) orange juice
1 tbs (15 ml) honey

Preheat oven to 375°F (190°C). Rinse game hens and lightly salt inside of cavity. Bake 15 minutes. Purée remaining ingredients in a blender or food processor. Brush game hens with glaze and continue cooking for a total of 50 minutes, brushing with glaze several times. Serves 4.

Approximate nutritional analysis per serving:
Calories 995, Protein 132 g, Carbohydrates 34 g, Fat 34 g, Cholesterol 402 mg, Sodium 667 mg

---

Previous page: Country Roasted Chicken Dinner

Basil-Crusted Chicken Oriental

BASIL-CRUSTED CHICKEN ORIENTAL

6 PREMIUM YOUNG 'N TENDER Brand
Boneless, Skinless Split Chicken Breasts
4 tbs (60 ml) butter or margarine, melted
2 tbs (30 ml) Hoisin sauce*
1 tbs plus 1 tsp (20 ml) Chinese-style hot mustard
²/₃ cup (180 ml) Panko Japanese-style bread
crumbs* or plain bread crumbs
3 tbs (45 ml) chopped fresh basil *or*
1 tbs (15 ml) dried basil
2 tbs (30 ml) grated Parmesan cheese
2 small plum tomatoes, peeled and diced
fresh basil and plum tomatoes for garnish

TOMATO MUSTARD CREAM SAUCE:
¹/₂ cup (120 ml) light or regular dairy sour cream
2 tbs (30 ml) tomato paste
2 tsp (10 ml) Chinese-style hot mustard
1 tsp (5 ml) light soy sauce

Preheat oven to 500°F (260°C). Rinse chicken breasts and pat dry. Combine butter, Hoisin sauce and mustard in a wide, shallow dish. Dip each chicken breast in butter mixture, then in bread crumb mixture, coating well on all sides. Place in a single layer in a shallow, non-stick baking pan. Bake uncovered for 15 minutes or until crumb coating is golden brown and chicken tests done.

Tomato Mustard Cream Sauce: Combine sour cream, tomato paste, mustard and soy sauce. Blend well then stir in half the diced tomatoes. Heat in microwave oven on HIGH power for 30 seconds, or heat in a saucepan just until warmed.

Spoon sauce onto warmed serving platter. Place whole chicken breasts over sauce, or cut breasts crosswise into thick slices and arrange over sauce. Sprinkle chicken with remaining diced tomato. Garnish with basil and plum tomatoes if desired. Serves 6.

* Available in specialty stores.

Approximate nutritional analysis per serving:
Calories 315, Protein 30 g, Carbohydrates 11 g, Fat 16 g,
Cholesterol 104 mg, Sodium 399 mg

TANDOORI-STYLE CHICKEN

1 cup (240 ml) DANNON Plain Nonfat or
    Lowfat Yogurt
3 tbs (45 ml) distilled white vinegar
2 tsp (10 ml) minced garlic
1¾ tsp (9 ml) garam masala*
1¼ tsp (6 ml) ground ginger
¼ tsp (1 ml) ground red pepper
6 boneless skinless chicken breast halves,
    trimmed of all visible fat
1¼ tsp (6 ml) salt
3 tsp (15 ml) olive oil, divided
2 cups (480 ml) sliced onions

* Garam masala is available in most Indian specialty shops or make your own from common kitchen spices.

In small bowl combine:
1½ tsp (8 ml) ground cumin
1 tsp (5 ml) ground coriander
1 tsp (5 ml) ground cardamom
1 tsp (5 ml) pepper
¼ tsp (1 ml) ground bay leaves (If ground bay
    leaves are not available, grind whole leaves
    to a fine powder with a mortar and pestle.)
pinch of ground cloves

In a large glass bowl combine yogurt, vinegar, garlic, garam masala, ginger and red pepper. Cut 4½-inch -deep diagonal slashes in top of each chicken breast. Sprinkle salt in slashes. Add chicken to yogurt mixture. Cover; chill at least 8 hours or overnight.

Preheat oven to 375°F. Brush 13x9-inch baking dish with 1 tsp oil. Remove chicken from marinade and arrange in a single layer, cut side up, in baking dish. Spoon some of the marinade over chicken; discard remainder. Sprinkle onions over chicken and drizzle with remaining 2 tsp oil. Bake 25-30 minutes or until chicken is no longer pink. Place chicken under broiler 3-5 minutes to brown onions. Serve immediately. Serves 6.

Approximate nutritional analysis per serving:
Calories 283, Protein 44 g, Carbohydrates 8 g, Fat 8 g,
Cholesterol 115 mg, Sodium 570 mg

OVEN-FRIED CHICKEN

2½-3½ lb (1.1-1.6 kg) cut-up broiler-fryer chicken
1 tbs (15 ml) margarine
⅔ cup (160 ml) BISQUICK Reduced Fat Baking Mix
1½ tsp (8 ml) paprika
1¼ tsp (6 ml) salt
¼ tsp (1 ml) pepper

Heat oven to 425°F (220°C). Remove skin from chicken. Heat margarine in rectangular pan, 13x9x2 inches, in oven until melted. Mix baking mix, paprika, salt and pepper; coat chicken. Place pieces, meaty sides down, in pan (pan and margarine should be hot). Bake 35 minutes. Turn; bake about 15 minutes longer or until done. Serves 6.

Mexican Oven-Fried Chicken: Decrease baking mix to ½ cup. Add 2 tbs yellow cornmeal and 1-2 tbs chili powder.

Approximate nutritional analysis per serving Oven-Fried Chicken:
Calories 230, Protein 27 g, Carbohydrates 9 g, Fat 10 g,
Cholesterol 80 mg, Sodium 700 mg

Approximate nutritional analysis per serving Mexican Oven-Fried Chicken:
Calories 220, Protein 27 g, Carbohydrates 8 g, Fat 9 g,
Cholesterol 80 mg, Sodium 670 mg

BAKED CHICKEN BREASTS WITH VIDALIA ONIONS

1¼ lbs (570 g) VIDALIA Onions, cut in ¼-inch slices
2 tbs (30 ml) all purpose flour
6 boneless, skinless chicken breasts
2 tbs (30 ml) olive oil
½ cup (120 ml) water
2 chicken bouillon cubes
1½ cups (355 ml) carrots, cut in ¼-inch slices
1½ lbs (685 g) red-skinned potatoes,
    cut in ½-inch slices
salt and freshly ground pepper to taste

Preheat oven to 375°F (190°C). In a large bowl or plastic bag, toss onions with flour and set aside. Heat oil in large nonstick skillet. Add chicken and brown on both sides, about 4 minutes per side. Deglaze the skillet by adding water and bouillon cubes. Stir until cubes are dissolved. Place half the onions in the bottom of a 2-qt baking dish. Add chicken and pour the liquid, from the skillet, on top. Top with remaining onions, carrots and potatoes. Season to taste. Cover and bake 1 hour or until vegetables are tender. Serve with crusty bread and a green salad. Serves 6.

Approximate nutritional analysis per serving:
Calories 390, Protein 40 g, Carbohydrates 37 g, Fat 9 g,
Cholesterol 97 mg, Sodium 453 mg

DIAMOND JIM'S CHICKEN HASH WITH CHAMPAGNE RAISINS

¼ cup (60 ml) raisins
⅓ cup (80 ml) Champagne
3 tbs (45 ml) flour
2½ tbs (38 ml) butter or margarine
¾ cup (180 ml) chicken stock or broth
⅓ cup (80 ml) whipping cream or half and half
3 cups (720 ml) diced, cooked chicken
2 tbs (30 ml) chopped parsley
salt and pepper to taste

In small bowl plump raisins in Champagne ½ hour or longer. In heavy saucepan stir in flour over low heat until brown. Mix in butter; cook until mixture is bubbly. Gradually whisk in stock and cream; cook and stir until mixture begins to thicken. Mix in chicken, parsley, ½ cup of the raisins and all of the Champagne (reserve remaining raisins for garnish). Cook and stir until mixture is thickened. Season with salt and pepper. Butter four 1-1½ cup individual baking dishes (or 1-qt baking dish); spoon in chicken mixture. Bake in 375°F (190°C) oven 15 minutes or until bubbly and edges are golden. Loosen edges and unmold onto serving plates. Garnish with reserved raisins and additional parsley. Serve with toast points. Serves 4.

Approximate nutritional analysis per serving:
Calories 447, Protein 32 g, Carbohydrates 27 g, Fat 22 g,
Cholesterol 139 mg, Sodium 176 mg

Yogurt-Marinated Chicken

YOGURT-CHICKEN MARINADE

½ cup (120 ml) low-sodium chicken broth
½ cup (120 ml) dry white wine
¾ cup (180 ml) sliced leeks
2 tbs (30 ml) lemon juice
½ tsp (3 ml) grated lemon peel
¼ tsp (1 ml) ground allspice
4 boneless skinless chicken breast halves,
    trimmed of all visible fat
1 cup (240 ml) DANNON Plain Nonfat or
    Lowfat Yogurt
1 tbs (15 ml) Dijon-style mustard
1 tbs (15 ml) snipped fresh parsley

In a large shallow dish combine chicken broth, wine, leeks, lemon juice, lemon peel and allspice; add chicken. Cover; chill several hours or overnight. Remove chicken from marinade and place on broiler pan; reserve marinade. Broil 4-6 inches from heat 8-12 minutes or until lightly brown.

Preheat oven to 350°F (180°C). Place chicken in shallow baking pan; set aside. In a small saucepan bring reserved marinade to a boil; reduce heat and simmer, covered, 5 minutes. Cool 10 minutes. Whisk in yogurt, mustard and parsley. Spoon over chicken. Bake 15 minutes or until chicken is no longer pink in center. Serves 4.

Approximate nutritional analysis per serving:
Calories 259, Protein 39 g, Carbohydrates 8 g, Fat 5 g,
Cholesterol 100 mg, Sodium 248 mg

THAI CHICKEN WITH PEANUT SAUCE

3 tbs (45 ml) olive oil
2 tbs (30 ml) soy sauce
1 tbs (15 ml) lemon juice
1 tbs (15 ml) honey
1 tbs (15 ml) McCORMICK Thai Seasoning
1 lb (455 g) boneless skinless chicken breasts

PEANUT SAUCE:
1 tbs (15 ml) honey
2 tbs (30 ml) water
2 tbs (30 ml) soy sauce
2 tsp (10 ml) McCORMICK Thai Seasoning
2 tbs (30 ml) peanut butter
3 tbs (45 ml) rice vinegar

Combine first 5 ingredients in large self-closing plastic bag or shallow dish. Cut chicken into 1-inch wide strips. Add to marinade. Refrigerate 3 or more hours. Remove chicken; discard marinade. Thread chicken on skewers. Broil 4 minutes per side. Meanwhile, combine peanut sauce ingredients in small saucepan. Cook over medium heat until mixture boils, stirring frequently with a whisk. Reduce heat and simmer 2-3 minutes. Serve warm with chicken skewers. Serves 4.

Approximate nutritional analysis per serving:
Calories 283, Protein 38 g, Carbohydrates 7 g, Fat 11 g,
Cholesterol 96 mg, Sodium 893 mg

CHICKEN IN RASPBERRY SAUCE

4 boneless chicken breasts
1 cup (240 ml) fresh orange sections

MARINADE:
1 cup (240 ml) POMPEIAN 100% Pure Olive Oil
1 tsp (5 ml) thyme
1 tsp (5 ml) sage
zest of 1 orange, julienned
¼ cup (60 ml) POMPEIAN Red Wine Vinegar
½ cup (120 ml) finely chopped shallots
1 cup (240 ml) whole fresh raspberries

Marinate chicken breasts for 2 hours. Remove the breasts from the marinade and oven roast at 350°F (180°C) for 10 minutes on each side, until done. Transfer to a serving platter and deglaze roasting pan with the marinade. Transfer the marinade to a saucepan and reduce it to thicken slightly. Finish the sauce with orange sections. Slice each chicken breast lengthwise into strips. Arrange them in a fan-like pattern on each dinner plate and top with the reduced raspberry marinade sauce. Serves 4.

Approximate nutritional analysis per serving:
Calories 650, Protein 28 g, Carbohydrates 8 g, Fat 57 g,
Cholesterol 73 mg, Sodium 66 mg

SAUCY HERBED CHICKEN BREASTS

2 tbs (30 ml) margarine or butter
2 tbs (30 ml) shortening or vegetable oil
4 chicken breasts, cut in half
½ cup (120 ml) finely chopped onion
1 large clove garlic, finely chopped
4 oz (120 g) mushrooms, sliced
¼ cup (60 ml) margarine or butter
¾ cup (180 ml) dry white wine
3 tbs (45 ml) cornstarch
¼ cup (60 ml) water
2 cups (480 ml) YOPLAIT Fat Free Plain Yogurt
1 tsp (5 ml) salt
½ tsp (3 ml) dried tarragon leaves

Heat oven to 350°F (180°C). Heat 2 tbs margarine and the shortening in rectangular baking dish, 13x9x2 inches, in oven until melted. Place chicken in dish; turn to coat with margarine mixture. Arrange chicken, skin sides up, in dish. Bake uncovered 1 hour; drain.

Cook onion, garlic and mushrooms in ¼ cup margarine in 10-inch skillet until onion is tender; stir in wine. Stir cornstarch into water until smooth; stir into wine mixture. Heat to boiling, stirring constantly. Boil and stir 1 minute; remove from heat. Stir in yogurt, salt and tarragon leaves; pour over chicken. Cover tightly with aluminum foil. Bake 10-15 minutes longer or until chicken is done. Remove chicken to warm platter. Stir sauce; spoon over chicken. Sprinkle with additional tarragon leaves if desired. Serves 8.

High altitude: 3500-6500 ft: Increase first bake time to 1½ hours.

Approximate nutritional analysis per serving:
Calories 240, Protein 27 g, Carbohydrates 10 g, Fat 10 g,
Cholesterol 65 mg, Sodium 440 mg

Opposite: Chicken in Raspberry Sauce

GOLDEN GLAZED CHICKEN AND PEARS

1 - 16 oz can (480 g) **LIBBY'S LITE** Pear Halves
2 tbs (30 ml) lemon juice
2 tsp (10 ml) soy sauce
2 tsp (10 ml) cornstarch
½ tsp (3 ml) dry mustard
¼ tsp (1 ml) grated lemon peel
1 - 2½-3 lb (1.1-1.4 kg) fryer chicken,
    cut into serving-sized pieces
chopped parsley
lemon wedges

Drain pears; reserve juice. Combine juice with lemon juice, soy sauce, cornstarch, mustard and lemon peel. Cook and stir over medium heat until thickened; keep warm. Remove skin from chicken parts; place in baking pan. Brush chicken with lemon juice mixture. Bake at 350°F (180°C) for 30 minutes; baste frequently with lemon juice mixture. Turn chicken pieces. Bake 20 minutes longer or until chicken is tender; add pears during last 10 minutes. Arrange chicken and pears on serving patter. Garnish with chopped parsley and lemon wedges. Serves 4.

Approximate nutritional analysis per serving:
Calories 617, Protein 83 g, Carbohydrates 20 g, Fat 21 g,

ALMOND-CRUSTED CHICKEN BREASTS

1½ cups (355 ml) **BLUE DIAMOND**
    Sliced Natural Almonds, lightly toasted
2 whole chicken breasts, skinned, boned,
    and cut in half
salt
pepper
¼ cup (60 ml) flour
1 egg, beaten with:
2 tsp (10 ml) water
¼ cup (60 ml) butter, melted
1 tsp (5 ml) lemon juice
1½ tsp (8 ml) chopped fresh basil
    or ½ tsp (3 ml) dried basil

With hands, lightly crush almonds into small pieces; reserve. Lightly flatten chicken breasts. Season with salt and pepper. Dredge chicken with flour. Pat off excess flour. Dip chicken in beaten egg. Press each chicken breast in almonds, covering chicken well. Place on buttered baking sheet. Bake at 425°F (220°C) for 10-15 minutes or until chicken is just firm and almonds are golden. Meanwhile, combine butter, lemon juice, and basil. Drizzle over cooked chicken breasts. Serves 4.

Approximate nutritional analysis per serving:
Calories 577, Protein 39 g, Carbohydrates 16 g, Fat 41 g,
Cholesterol 157 mg, Sodium 202 mgCholesterol 251 mg, Sodium 762 mg

TURKEY BREAST WITH PARSLEY-LIME SAUCE

1 **EMPIRE KOSHER** Turkey Breast, bone in

MARINADE:
⅓ cup (80 ml) sesame oil
4 tbs (60 ml) lemon juice
⅓ cup (80 ml) soy sauce
⅔ cup (160 ml) kosher white wine
4 tsp (20 ml) minced garlic
1 tsp (5 ml) dried thyme
1 tsp (5 ml) hot sauce

SAUCE:
4 egg yolks
2 tsp (10 ml) minced garlic
1 tbs (15 ml) fresh hot peppers,
    seeds removed, chopped
1½ tsp (8 ml) Dijon mustard
1 tbs (15 ml) soy sauce
3 tbs (45 ml) lime juice
2 cups fresh parsley leaves
2 cups (480 ml) vegetable oil

Cut meat off bone, remove skin. You should have 2 half breasts. Mix the ingredients for the marinade in a glass dish. Reserve ¼ cup of the marinade for basting. Add turkey breast pieces, turn to coat. Cover, marinate overnight in the refrigerator.

For the sauce, combine all ingredients except for the oil in a food processor or blender. Process for a few seconds. With the motor running, add a few drops of oil at a time until the mixture thickens, then in a small stream. If the sauce becomes too thick, add a little hot water. May be made ahead and refrigerated.

Preheat oven to 375°F (190°C). Place turkey breast in shallow roasting pan, baste with marinade, and roast for 45 minutes to an hour, or until juice runs clear. Remove, cool a few minutes before slicing. Serve the sauce on the side. Serves 12.

Approximate nutritional analysis per serving:
Calories 664, Protein 64 g, Carbohydrates 2 g, Fat 43 g,
Cholesterol 249 mg, Sodium 388 mg

CORNISH GAME HENS WITH ROASTED VEGETABLES

2 - 1 lb (910 g) Cornish game hens, cleaned
1 small onion, cut into 4 wedges
2 cloves garlic, cut in half
2 baking potatoes, each cut into 4 wedges
2 carrots, cut into 2-inch pieces
1½ cups (355 ml) water
1 - 11½ oz jar (345 ml) CHI-CHI'S Pico de Gallo
1 tsp (5 ml) dried oregano leaves
¼ tsp (1 ml) coarsely ground pepper

Heat oven to 350°F (180°C). Place hens in 13x9-inch baking pan. Stuff each hen with 2 onion wedges and 2 pieces garlic. Place potato wedges and carrot pieces around hens. Pour in water. Spoon Pico de Gallo over hens and vegetables. Sprinkle with oregano and pepper. Bake 1-1½ hours or until internal temperature reaches 180-185°F (82-85°C) and juices run clear, basting hens occasionally. Remove onion and garlic from hens. Serve with roasted vegetables. Serves 4.

Approximate nutritional analysis per serving:
Calories 270, Protein 26 g, Carbohydrates 30 g, Fat 6 g,
Cholesterol 65 mg, Sodium 400 mg

CHICKEN ALMOND RICE
WITH RED AND GREEN PEPPERS

1 - 3½ lb chicken, cut up
salt , white pepper
1 cup (240 ml) BLUE DIAMOND
Blanched Slivered Almonds
3 tbs (45 ml) olive oil, divided
1 onion, chopped
1 red bell pepper, cut in half crosswise
and then into strips
2 cloves garlic, chopped finely
1 cup (240 ml) long grain rice
½ cup (120 ml) tomato sauce
2 cups (480 ml) chicken broth
½ cup (120 ml) golden raisins
pinch cinnamon

Season chicken pieces with salt and white pepper; reserve. In a large oven proof skillet, sauté almonds in 1 tbs oil until golden; remove and reserve. Sauté chicken in remaining 2 tbs oil until browned on both sides; remove and reserve. In oil remaining in pan, sauté onion, red and green bell pepper, and garlic until onion is translucent. Add rice and sauté 1 minute. Stir in tomato sauce, chicken broth, raisins, cinnamon, and 1½ tsp salt. Bring to a boil. Bake, uncovered, at 350°F (180°C) on lowest rack in oven for 15 minutes. Arrange chicken pieces on top. Continue baking 15 minutes or until all liquid is absorbed and chicken is cooked through. Remove from oven and sprinkle almonds over top. Let stand 5 minutes. Serves 6.

Approximate nutritional analysis per serving:
Calories 878, Protein 85 g, Carbohydrates 47 g, Fat 38 g,
Cholesterol 235 mg, Sodium 611 mg

STUFFED INDONESIAN CHICKEN

¼ cup (60 ml) Dijon mustard
¼ cup (60 ml) honey
1 tbs (15 ml) curry powder
1 - 4 lb (1.8 kg) chicken
1 cup (240 ml) long grain white rice
2 cups (480 ml) orange juice
½ cup (120 ml) pitted CALIFORNIA ripe olives,
coarsely chopped
1 - 8 oz can (240 g) water chestnuts, chopped
½ cup (120 ml) chopped red bell pepper
½ tsp (3 ml) ground cloves

Mix mustard, honey and curry powder in dish, place chicken in mixture and rub with sauce, inside and out. Cover and refrigerate for several hours or overnight. For stuffing, combine rice and orange juice in saucepan, bring to a boil and simmer gently for 20-25 minutes or until plumped. Stir in olives, water chestnuts, bell pepper and cloves. Spoon rice stuffing into cavities of chicken. Skewer close and roast at 375°F (190°C) for 1 hour or until tender. Cover bird loosely with foil if it begins to get too dark. Serves 6.

Approximate nutritional analysis per serving:
Calories 814, Protein 91 g, Carbohydrates 52 g, Fat 25 g,
Cholesterol 268 mg, Sodium 519 mg

Cornish Game Hens with Roasted Vegetables

TURKEY WITH VEGETABLE RICE

2 turkey tenderloins, cut into 1½-inch cubes
2 tbs (30 ml) olive oil
1 cup (240 ml) chopped onion
½ cup (120 ml) chopped green bell pepper
½ cup (120 ml) chopped red bell pepper
2 cloves garlic, minced
1 cup (240 ml) long grain brown rice
1 tsp (5 ml) ground cumin
2 - 16 oz jars (960 ml) CHI-CHI'S Salsa Verde
2 cups (480 ml) chicken broth
1 - 10 oz pkg (300 g) frozen artichoke hearts, thawed
½ cup (120 ml) frozen peas
⅓ cup (80 ml) sliced pimiento-stuffed green olives
salt and pepper

In Dutch oven, cook and stir turkey in oil until lightly browned. Remove turkey, leaving juices in pan. Add onion, bell peppers and garlic to pan. Cook and stir until tender. Stir in rice, coating well with pan juices. Stir in cumin, 1 cup salsa verde and chicken broth. Bring to a boil. Reduce heat to low; place turkey on top of sauce. Cover; simmer 40-45 minutes or until liquid is absorbed. Sprinkle artichoke hearts, peas and olives over turkey; remove from heat. Cover; let stand 10 minutes. Toss mixture with fork. Add salt and pepper to taste. Serve with remaining salsa verde. Serves 6.

Approximate nutritional analysis per serving:
Calories 370, Protein 30 g, Carbohydrates 46 g, Fat 8 g,
Cholesterol 55 mg, Sodium   300 mg

CHICKEN WITH TOMATO MANGO RELISH

1 lb (455 g) boneless skinless chicken breasts
1 cup (240 ml) CHI-CHI'S Salsa

TOMATO MANGO RELISH:
1 large mango, peeled, cut into ¾-inch chunks
1 large tomato, cut into chunks
3 tbs (45 ml) sliced green onions
1 tbs (15 ml) fresh lime juice
2 tsp (10 ml) grated fresh ginger root
1½ tsp (8 ml) vegetable oil
½ tsp (3 ml) grated lime peel

In large recloseable plastic food bag, place chicken and salsa; seal bag and turn several times to coat. Place bag in a 13x9-inch baking pan. Refrigerate, turning bag occasionally, 3 hours. In large bowl, combine all Tomato Mango Relish ingredients. Mix well; set aside. Heat broiler. Remove chicken from salsa marinade; reserve marinade. Place chicken on broiler pan. Broil 7-8 inches from heat source 6-8 minutes on each side or until chicken is no longer pink in center, basting occasionally with reserved salsa marinade. Serve with Tomato Mango Relish. Serves 4.

Approximate nutritional analysis per serving:
Calories 200, Protein 25 g, Carbohydrates 13 g, Fat 5 g,
Cholesterol 65 mg, Sodium 130 mg

HOT AND SWEET TURKEY

SEASONING MIX:
1 tbs plus 1 tsp (20 ml) CHEF PAUL PRUDHOMME'S Poultry Magic
½ tsp (3 ml) ginger
¼ tsp (1 ml) ground nutmeg
¼ tsp (1 ml) ground coriander

1 lb (455 g) turkey breast, cut into 2x¼-inch julienne strips
3 tbs (45 ml) cornstarch
2½ cups (590 ml) defatted chicken stock, in all
¼ cup (60 ml) thinly sliced fresh ginger
1 small onion, peeled and cut into julienne strips
¾ cup (180 ml) carrots, scrubbed and sliced diagonally ¼ inch thick
¾ cup (180 ml) julienne yellow bell peppers
¾ cup (180 ml) julienne green bell peppers
2 tsp (10 ml) thinly sliced fresh garlic
¼ cup (60 ml) tamari*
¼ cup (60 ml) balsamic vinegar
1 - 8 oz can (240 ml) tomato sauce
6 - 1 g packets artificial sweetener, optional
4 cups (960 ml) cooked long grain white rice

* Tamari is a very flavorful kind of soy sauce, available in specialty markets and the international or ethnic food sections of many supermarkets. If you cannot find it where you shop, substitute the best soy sauce available.

Combine the seasoning mix ingredients in a small bowl. Sprinkle all surfaces of the turkey evenly with 2 tsp of the seasoning mix and rub it in well. Dissolve the cornstarch in 4 tbs of the stock and set aside.

    Preheat a heavy 12-inch skillet, preferably nonstick, over high heat to 350°F (180°C), about 5 minutes. Add turkey, stir, and cook until it starts to brown, about 2 minutes. Add the fresh ginger and onions, stir and cook for 2 minutes. Add the remaining vegetables and seasoning mix, and cook for 3 minutes. Stir in the tamari and vinegar, and cook 2 minutes. Stir in the tomato sauce and remaining stock, bring to a boil, and cook 2 minutes. Add the cornstarch mixture, cook for 2 minutes, remove from the heat, and, if desired, add artificial sweetener. Serve over the rice. Serves 4.

Approximate nutritional analysis per serving:
Calories 530, Protein 44 g, Carbohydrates 76 g, Fat 5 g,
Cholesterol 98 mg, Sodium   739 mg

Opposite: Chicken with Tomato Mango Relish

CITRUS-TOMATO CHICKEN

SEASONING MIX:
1 tbs (15 ml) CHEF PAUL PRUDHOMME'S
    Poultry Magic
1 tsp (5 ml) dill weed
½ tsp (3 ml) ground ginger

MARINADE:
2 tbs (30 ml) apple juice
2 tbs (30 ml) orange juice
1 tbs (15 ml) lemon juice
1 tbs (15 ml) balsamic vinegar
1½ tsp (8 ml) Seasoning Mix (above)

1 - 3-4 lb (1.4-1.8 kg) chicken, all skin and
    visible fat removed, cut into 8 pieces
2 cups (480 ml) apple juice
1½ cups (355 ml) chopped onions
1 cup (240 ml) chopped green bell peppers
½ cup (120 ml) grated carrots
1 tsp (5 ml) minced fresh garlic
1 - 8 oz can (240 ml) tomato sauce
1 cup (240 ml) peeled, diced fresh tomatoes
    or 7 oz (210 ml) canned diced tomatoes
1 cup (240 ml) defatted chicken stock
4 cups (960 ml) cooked long grain white rice

Combine the seasoning mix ingredients in small bowl.

Blend the marinade ingredients. Place the chicken in a large bowl, pour the marinade over the chicken, cover and refrigerate at least 4 hours, but preferably overnight.

Preheat the broiler. Remove the chicken from the marinade and reserve the marinade. Place the chicken in a baking pan and broil until brown on both sides, about 7 minutes in all. Remove the chicken and set aside. While the chicken is broiling, place the apple juice in a saucepan, bring to a boil, reduce to 1 cup, and set aside.

Preheat a heavy 5-qt pot, preferably nonstick, over high heat to 350°F (180°C), about 4 minutes. Add the onion, bell peppers, carrots and 1 tsp of the seasoning mix, cover, and cook 3 minutes. At this point, the vegetables will start to stick and turn light brown. Add garlic, mix in well, and scrape the bottom of the pot to clear it of all brown bits. Re-cover and cook 3 more minutes. Add the reduced apple juice and remaining seasoning mix, and scrape the bottom clear. By now the mixture will have turned medium brown. Cook 4 minutes. Stir in the tomato sauce, diced tomatoes, stock, and reserved marinade. Add the chicken to the pot, bring to boil, reduce the heat to medium, and cook until the chicken is tender, about 20 minutes. Serve over the rice. Serves 4.

Approximate nutritional analysis per serving:
Calories 661, Protein 77 g, Carbohydrates 83 g, Fat 13 g,
Cholesterol 289 mg, Sodium 751 mg

Citrus Tomato Chicken

CURRIED PAPAYA CHICKEN BAKE

1 cup (240 ml) flour
1 tsp (5 ml) seasoned salt
¼ tsp (1 ml) garlic powder
2 tsp (10 ml) curry powder
2½-3 lbs (910-1365 g) boned, skinned chicken thighs
⅓ cup (80 ml) brown sugar
1 heaping tbs (15 ml) cornstarch
2 tsp (10 ml) curry powder
1½ cups (355 ml) orange juice
1 tbs (15 ml) lemon juice
1 tbs (15 ml) soy sauce
2 cups (480 ml) sliced papaya

Combine flour, seasoned salt, garlic powder and 2 tsp curry powder and dredge chicken. In a large baking dish arrange chicken. Bake at 400°F (205°C) for 20 minutes; turn and bake 20 minutes longer. While chicken is baking, in a saucepan combine sugar, cornstarch and 2 tsp curry powder, mix. Add orange juice, lemon juice, soy sauce, mix well and cook until slightly thickened. Fold in papaya. Spread mixture over chicken and bake 10-15 minutes more until chicken is glazed. Serves 6.

Approximate nutritional analysis per serving:
Calories 458, Protein 48 g, Carbohydrates 39 g, Fat 12 g,
Cholesterol 134 mg, Sodium 662 mg

FIDEUA

Pan-Fried Noodles and Chicken

6 oz (180 g) GOYA Fideos or angel-hair pasta
2 cups (480 ml) GOYA Vegetable Oil
½ lb (230 g) boneless chicken breast, in small chunks
1 tbs (15 ml) GOYA Olive Oil
1 tsp (5 ml) GOYA Adobo with Pepper
1 clove garlic, minced
1 packet GOYA Chicken Bouillon
    mixed with: 2 cups (480 ml) water
chopped parsley

In a large skillet, fry uncooked pasta in hot vegetable oil until golden brown. Drain pasta and set aside, reserving oil for future use. Preheat oven to 400°F (205°C). In a flame-proof, oven-proof casserole, lightly sauté chicken in olive oil. Add Adobo and garlic and sauté until garlic is golden. Add fried pasta into chicken mixture; add enough prepared bouillon to just cover the pasta. Bring to a boil, and boil 3-4 minutes. Place on the bottom of pre-heated oven and bake, uncovered, until liquid is evaporated and noodles are soft, 6-7 minutes. Garnish with chopped parsley. Serves 2, as a main dish.

Approximate nutritional analysis per serving:
Calories 1053, Protein 47 g, Carbohydrates 65 g, Fat 67 g,
Cholesterol 97 mg, Sodium 914 mg

HAZELNUT TROPICAL CHICKEN

½ cup (120 ml) raisins
¾ cup (180 ml) orange juice
2 lb (910 g) cut-up chicken
½ cup (120 ml) flour
seasoning salt to taste
3 tbs (45 ml) olive oil
1 cup (240 ml) Hazelnuts, cracked
2 tbs (30 ml) brown sugar
¼ tsp (1 ml) cinnamon
½ tsp (3 ml) salt
½ cup (120 ml) mandarin oranges
1 cup (240 ml) sliced mushrooms
½ cup (120 ml) drained pineapple chunks
¼ tsp (1 ml) cloves
¼ cup (60 ml) sherry

Soak raisins in orange juice for at least 1 hour. Dust chicken pieces in seasoned flour, then sauté in olive oil in heavy frying pan with remaining ingredients. Bake at 350°F (180°C) for 45 minutes, basting frequently with juices. Serves 4.

Approximate nutritional analysis per serving:
Calories 903, Protein 73 g, Carbohydrates 49 g, Fat 46 g,
Cholesterol 201 mg, Sodium 471 mg

CHEESY TURKEY DIVAN

SAUCE:
½ lb (230 g) HEALTHY CHOICE Fat Free
    Pasteurized Process Cheese Product,
    cut into 1-inch cubes
¼ cup (80 ml) skim milk
1 tbs (15 ml) sherry
½ tsp (3 ml) nutmeg
1 lb (455 g) fresh broccoli spears, cooked, drained
¾ lb (340 g) turkey breast slices, cooked
1 tbs (15 ml) shredded Parmesan cheese

Heat oven to 375°F (190°C). In 2-qt saucepan place cheese cubes and milk. Cook over medium heat, stirring frequently, until cheese melts. Stir in sherry and nutmeg. In 12x7-inch baking dish sprayed with nonstick cooking spray, place broccoli spears. Arrange turkey slices on top. Pour sauce over turkey slices. Sprinkle with Parmesan cheese. Bake at 375°F (190°C), for 15-18 minutes or until cheese is lightly browned. Serves 6.

Approximate nutritional analysis per serving:
Calories 162, Protein 28 g, Carbohydrates 7 g, Fat 2 g,
Cholesterol 47 mg, Sodium 604 mg

CHICKEN BREASTS WITH RICE PRIMAVERA

1 tbs (15 ml) margarine or butter
1 small zucchini, diced*
1 small yellow squash, diced*
2 cups (480 ml) water
1 pkg LIPTON Rice and Sauce - Chicken Flavor
1 small tomato, chopped
4 boneless skinless chicken breast halves
¼ cup (60 ml) WISH - BONE Italian Dressing
2 tbs (30 ml) chopped fresh basil leaves
     or 1 tsp (5 ml) chopped dried basil leaves

* Substitution: Use 2 cups (480 ml) frozen vegetables, partially thawed.

In medium saucepan, melt margarine over medium-high heat and cook zucchini and yellow squash, stirring frequently, 3 minutes or until almost tender. Add water, rice and sauce (chicken flavor) and tomato; bring to a boil. Reduce heat and simmer uncovered, stirring occasionally, 10 minutes or until rice is tender.

   Meanwhile, on broiler pan sprayed with nostick cooking spray, arrange chicken. Brush chicken with ½ of the Italian dressing. Broil, turning chicken once and brushing with remaining dressing, 10 minutes or until chicken is done. Stir basil into rice mixture. Arrange chicken over rice. Serves 4.

Approximate nutritional analysis per serving:
Calories 336, Protein 31 g, Carbohydrates 30 g, Fat 10 g,
Cholesterol 74 mg, Sodium 856 mg

Courtesy of The Lipton Kitchens.

COUNTRY ROASTED CHICKEN DINNER

1 envelope LIPTON Recipe Secrets Savory Herb
     with Garlic Soup Mix, or Golden Herb with
     Lemon, or Golden Onion Soup Mix
2 tbs (30 ml honey
1 tbs (15 ml) water
1 tbs (15 ml) margarine or butter, melted
5-6 lb (2.3-2.7 kg) roasting chicken
3 lbs (1.4 kg) all purpose and/or sweet potatoes,
     cut into chunks

Preheat oven to 350°F (180°C). In small bowl, blend Savory Herb with Garlic Soup Mix, honey, water and margarine. In 18x12-inch roasting pan, arrange chicken, breast side up; brush with soup mixture. Cover loosely with aluminum foil. Roast 30 minutes; drain. Arrange potatoes around chicken and continue roasting covered, stirring potatoes occasionally, 1 hour or until meat thermometer reaches 175°F (79°C) and potatoes are tender. Serves 8.

Approximate nutritional analysis per serving:
Calories 709, Protein 85 g, Carbohydrates 40 g, Fat 21 g,
Cholesterol 251 mg, Sodium 517 mg

Courtesy of The Lipton Kitchens.

CHICKEN BREASTS WITH MUSHROOMS

3 boneless, skinless chicken breasts, split
¾ cup (180 ml) matzah meal
½ tsp (3 ml) dried thyme leaves
salt and pepper to taste
2 egg whites
vegetable spray
2 tsp (10 ml) olive oil
1 large onion, finely chopped
3 cloves garlic, minced
2 lbs (910 g) mushrooms, thinly sliced
½ cup (120 ml) kosher-for-Passover sherry
¼ cup (60 ml) kosher chicken stock
juice of 1 large orange
½ tsp (3 ml) paprika
2 tbs (30 ml) chopped Italian parsley
fresh ground pepper
parsley to garnish

In blender, or food processor fitted with metal blade, pulse/chop the matzah meal, thyme, salt and pepper until meal is "powdery". Place in a shallow dish, set aside.

   In another shallow bowl, whisk egg whites until light in color. Dip chicken breast pieces in egg whites, then dredge in matzah meal. Place in lightly oiled baking dish, 9x12 inches; lightly spray one side of breasts with oil and place in 400°F (205°C) oven for 3 minutes. Remove from oven and turn oven down to 350°F (180°C).

   In a large skillet, sauté garlic and onions in olive oil until the onions are translucent. Add mushrooms and sauté for 3 minutes. With slotted spoon, remove mushrooms and spoon over breasts. With remaining juices still in skillet, return the skillet to the flame, pour in sherry, stock, orange juice and paprika. Simmer for 3-5 minutes. Stir in parsley, pour over mushrooms and chicken. Cover and bake for 45 minutes. Garnish with more parsley and serve. Serves 6.

Approximate nutritional analysis per serving:
Calories 329, Protein 34 g, Carbohydrates 24 g, Fat 9 g,
Cholesterol 1 mg, Sodium 184 mg

Courtesy of the Empire Kosher Poultry Test Kitchens.

ROAST CHICKEN WITH FENNEL AND TOMATOES

2 chickens, cut in eighths, skin removed
6 cloves garlic, crushed
2 tbs (30 ml) full-flavored olive oil
1 tsp (5 ml) crushed fennel seeds
½ cup (120 ml) fresh squeezed lemon juice
4 bay leaves
salt and pepper to taste
4 fresh fennel bulbs (remove fronds, set aside),
    cut in eighths
2 large onions, peeled, sliced very thin
16 fresh or canned tomatoes, quartered
4 tbs (60 ml) chopped fresh parsley
1 cup (240 ml) kosher chicken broth
2 tbs (30 ml) parsley to garnish

In a large bowl, combine all ingredients. Marinate overnight. One hour before you begin to cook, remove the marinating chicken and vegetables from the refrigerator and bring to room temperature. Preheat oven to 375°F (190°C). Place chicken and vegetables in a single layer into a large 2-inch deep roasting pan (an oven-to-table dish works well). Place in oven and roast 45 minutes. Garnish with additional parsley and serve.

Approximate nutritional analysis per serving:
Calories 825, Protein 104 g, Carbohydrates 34 g, Fat 31 g,
Cholesterol 301 mg, Sodium 484 mg

Courtesy of the Empire Kosher Poultry Test Kitchens.

Roast Chicken

ROAST TURKEY WITH FENNEL-CORNBREAD STUFFING
(Closed Foil Method)

STUFFING:
2 tbs (30 ml) olive oil
4 onions, sliced very thin
6 cloves garlic, minced
2 fennel bulbs, chopped, reserve fronds
2 lbs (910 g) fresh mushrooms,
**   1 lb sliced, 1 lb chopped**
4 cups (960 ml) dry French bread cubes
5 cups (1.2 L) cornbread cubes, dry
2-3 tsp (10-15 ml) thyme leaves
1 tsp (5 ml) sage
1 cup (240 ml) chopped Italian parsley
½ cup (120 ml) sun-dried tomatoes,
**   chopped and soaked in:**
½ cup (120 ml) kosher sherry
1 tsp (5 ml) crushed fennel seeds
fresh ground pepper
2 cups (480 ml) kosher chicken broth

TURKEY:
1 - 18-20 lb (8-9 kg) turkey, fresh or completely
**   defrosted, neck and giblet reserved**
1 fennel bulb, sliced into 6 pieces, reserve fronds
1 onion, quartered
2 carrots, peeled and quartered
1 tbs (15 ml) vegetable oil
8 cloves garlic, crushed
1 cup (240 ml) apricot preserves
1-2 tbs (15-30 ml) soy sauce
1 tsp (5 ml) thyme leaves, dried
fresh ground pepper
2 cups (480 ml) kosher chicken broth (additional
**   broth may be needed for extra stuffing or gravy)**
½ cup (120 ml) orange juice
½ cup (120 ml) kosher sherry wine
½ tsp (3 ml) cornstarch

Stuffing: Heat oil in a large skillet. Sauté the onions, garlic and fennel over low heat until soft, about 10 minutes. Add the chopped and sliced mushrooms. Sauté 2 minutes more. Transfer the vegetables to a large bowl and set aside. Add dry cubes of bread, herbs, chopped sun-dried tomatoes with their soaking liquid, fennel seeds and fresh ground pepper. Lightly toss ingredients together. Add chicken stock and toss again, lightly. Set stuffing aside while preparing turkey.

Turkey: Preheat oven to 400°F (205°C). Rinse the turkey well, trim all visible fat, pat dry and stuff the cavity loosely with stuffing, allowing for expansion. Stuff the neck area and secure with neck skin. Put any remaining stuffing in oven proof baking dish and set aside.

In the bottom of a large roasting pan, arrange a bed of the fennel slices, reserved fronds, carrot and onion pieces. Gently place the turkey on top, breast side up. Rub oil all over the bird. Pour 1 cup of the broth in the pan, place pan in hot oven and roast turkey for 30 minutes to seal in the juices.

Meanwhile, prepare the basting glaze; combine the garlic, preserves, soy sauce, thyme, pepper, 1 cup broth and orange juice in a bowl and set aside.

After 30 minutes, remove or pull turkey out on rack, brush on glaze, covering entire surface. Create a tent with 2 large pieces of foil that allow 3-4 inches of air space so that you can open to baste and then reclose. Return covered turkey to oven and reduce to 350°F (180°C). Roast the turkey for 4 hours, basting every hour with basting mixture and pan juices. After 4 hours, uncover the turkey to allow it to further brown. Bake 1 more hour, basting 2-3 times. (Approximately 5 hours total cooking time). If you have extra stuffing to bake, stir in a bit of broth or pan juices, loosely cover and bake for the last 40-50 minutes.

Transfer the turkey to a heated platter, cover loosely and allow it to rest 15-20 minutes before carving. While the turkey rests, strain and de-fat the pan juices - you should have 4 cups (add broth if necessary). Place in a saucepan. Heat to simmer.

In a small bowl, combine the sherry and cornstarch. Then whisk into saucepan, simmer 5-7 minutes, add salt and pepper to taste and serve with turkey, passed in a sauce boat. Serves 18.

Approximate nutritional analysis per serving:
Calories 998, Protein 131 g, Carbohydrates 46 g, Fat 28 g, Cholesterol 343 mg, Sodium 604 mg

Courtesy of the Empire Kosher Poultry Test Kitchens.

GENERAL GUIDELINES:
TURKEY TIMETABLE ROASTING GUIDE

325°F (165°C) uncovered	350°F (180°C) foil covered
up to 6 lbs (2.7 kg)	allow 20-25 minutes/lb
up to 15 lbs (6.8 kg)	allow 15-20 minutes/lb
over 16 lbs (7.3 kg)	allow 13-15 minutes/lb

If stuffed, add 3-5 minutes more per lb cooking time.

OPEN PAN ROAST TURKEY

fresh or thawed turkey (1 lb per person)
vegetable oil
4 cups (960 ml) cut up vegetables
   (onions, leeks, celery, carrots)
1 cup (240 ml) fresh herbs
   (rosemary, parsley, basil, sage, some or all)
½ cup (120 ml) fruit preserves
   (apricot, peach, strained berry)
more broth as needed for gravy
2 tsp (10 ml) cornstarch, optional

BASTING MIXTURE:
12 cups (480 ml) kosher chicken stock
4 cloves garlic, crushed
2 tsp (10 ml) paprika
pepper to taste
½ cup (120 ml) orange juice
1 tsp (5 ml) ground ginger
1 tsp (5 ml) dried thyme leaves
1 tbs (15 ml) Dijon mustard
1 tbs (15 ml) oil

Preheat oven to 400°F (205°C). Reserve neck and giblet, wrap and store in refrigerator or freezer.

Rinse/drain turkey. Pat dry, inside and out. Fill the cavity with cut up vegetables and fresh herb sprigs, or, stuff the neck and body cavity with your desired stuffing. Turn wings back to hold the neck skin in place. Place turkey breast side up on a flat rack in open roasting pan that is about 2½ inches deep. If using meat thermometer insert it into the deepest part of the thigh next to the body, being careful not to touch the bone. Rub/brush the skin with vegetable oil to help brown turkey evenly. Place turkey in hot oven, then turn temperature down to 325°F (165°C).

Whisk together basting mixture ingredients and baste turkey every hour with basting mixture.

When the skin turns golden, about ⅔ the way through, brush the apricot or other fruit preserves on turkey. Shield the breast loosely with lightweight foil to protect breast and prevent over-browning. Continue to baste turkey every 30 minutes. When turkey is done, thermometer should read 180-185°F (82-85°C). Let stand 15-20 minutes before carving.

Drain pan juices (should have 4 cups - add broth), de-fat and simmer with giblet and neck for 30 minutes. Remove neck and giblet, discard. If you want to thicken gravy, whisk in 2 tsp cornstarch and simmer 15 more minutes. Or, serve as is - a natural juice sauce.

STUFFING TIPS: RULES OF THUMB

under 10 lbs (< 4.6 kg)	estimate ½ cup (120 ml) stuffing per lb
over 10 lbs (> 4.6 kg)	estimate ¾ cup (180 ml) stuffing per lb

Unstuffed birds: If you cook the stuffing out of the bird in an oven to table casserole dish (which makes a lighter less caloric stuffing), estimate ½-¾ cup (120-180 ml) stuffing per person.

To save time: You can prepare stuffing ingredients ahead: measure, slice and chop, but keep wet and dry ingredients separate until just before ready to cook or stuff bird. If you are making your own stuffing, do not pre-stuff bird. After taking the turkey out of the oven, be sure to remove stuffing within 2 hours of roasting.

Courtesy of the Empire Kosher Poultry Test Kitchens.

CRANBERRY GLAZED TURKEY BREAST

1 - 6 lb (2.7 kg) NORBEST Turkey Breast, bone in
1 cup (240 ml) jellied cranberry sauce
1 cup (240 ml) orange marmalade
2 tsp (10 ml) dry mustard
2 tsp (10 ml) lemon juice
½ tsp (3 ml) ground cloves

In small roasting pan, fitted with meat rack, place turkey breast on rack. Bake at 325°F (165°C) 1¾-2 hours or until meat thermometer inserted in thickest part of breast reaches 170-175°F (78-79°C).

In small saucepan, over medium heat, combine cranberry sauce, marmalade, mustard, juice and cloves. Cook 4-5 minutes or until sauce is smooth. Brush 2-3 tbs sauce over turkey breast during last 20 minutes of baking. Serve remaining sauce over turkey slices. Serves 10.

Approximate nutritional analysis per serving:
Calories 476, Protein 54 g, Carbohydrates 32 g, Fat 14 g,
Cholesterol 138 mg, Sodium 144 mg

Apricot-Ginger Chicken

APRICOT-GINGER CHICKEN

1 whole kosher chicken, cut up
12 cloves garlic, peeled and minced
1x½-inch piece of ginger, grated
1 tbs (15 ml) dried thyme leaves
⅓ cup (80 ml) kosher red wine vinegar
juice of 1 lemon
2 tbs (30 ml) oil
3 bay leaves
1 cup (240 ml) dried apricots
fresh ground pepper to taste
½ cup (120 ml) light brown sugar
½ cup (120 ml) dry white wine
¼ cup (60 ml) chopped fresh parsley

Marinate chicken overnight in a large bowl in a mixture of the first nine ingredients. Cover tightly. Preheat oven to 375°F (190°C). Arrange chicken in a single layer on two large foil-covered pans. Spoon marinade over chicken. Sprinkle chicken with brown sugar and pour wine over it. Bake for 45 minutes then remove from the oven and drain juices. Skim the fat, discard and serve remaining liquid as sauce on the side. Sprinkle the parsley on top. Serves 8.

Approximate nutritional analysis per serving:
Calories 686, Protein 83 g, Carbohydrates 28 g, Fat 25 g,
Cholesterol 251 mg, Sodium 251 mg

Courtesy of the Empire Kosher Poultry Test Kitchens.

ROASTED HOLIDAY CHICKEN WITH GRAPES

1-4½ lb (1.8 kg) roasting chicken
1 lemon, cut in half
2 tbs (30 ml) Dijon mustard
2 tsp (10 ml) ground ginger
salt and pepper to taste
1 tbs (15 ml) chopped fresh basil
    or 1 tsp (5 ml) dried basil
1-2 sprigs fresh rosemary
    or 1 tsp (5 ml) dried rosemary
6 onions, peeled and quartered
2 cups (480 ml) kosher chicken broth
½ cup (120 ml) orange juice
2 cups (480 ml) seedless red and green grapes
¼ cup (60 ml) chopped fresh basil or
    Italian parsley for garnish

Preheat oven to 425°F (220°C). Rinse chicken, pat dry and squeeze the juice of 1 lemon all over chicken. Place the lemon halves in chicken cavity. Combine the mustard, ginger, salt, pepper and dried herbs, making a paste. Rub this mixture all over the chicken. Place the fresh herb sprigs in the cavity and put the chicken in a roasting pan, scatter 4 of the onions in a pan. Roast 30 minutes in hot oven.

While the chicken is roasting combine the giblet, neck, remaining onion, chicken broth and orange juice in a saucepan and simmer 25 minutes, set aside. Reduce oven temperature to 375°F (190°C) and ladle ¾ cup of simmered broth into roasting pan. Roast 30 minutes more, basting 2-3 times. Strain remaining broth, add another ½-1 cup to pan and continue to roast chicken 30 more minutes, basting 2 more times. Remove chicken from pan, let set 15 minutes and cut into serving pieces. Discard herbs and lemon rind. Place chicken in roasting pan, spoon juices and onions over chicken. Scatter grapes over the chicken and add any remaining broth, cover and bake 15 minutes. Serve on a large platter with grapes and juices as sauce. Garnish with fresh chopped herbs. Serves 4.

Approximate nutritional analysis per serving:
Calories 1169, Protein 153 g, Carbohydrates 46 g, Fat 39 g, Cholesterol 452 mg, Sodium 548 mg

Courtesy of the Empire Kosher Poultry Test Kitchens.

TURKEY IN SPICY NUT SAUCE

1 tbs (15 ml) flour
1 cup (240 ml) chopped onion
1 tsp (5 ml) minced garlic
2-2½ lb (910-1138 g) NORBEST Turkey Thighs,
    skin removed
¼ tsp (1 ml) cayenne pepper
1 - 1 lb 13 oz can (845 g) potatoes, drained
    and cut into ¼-inch slices
1 - 10 oz can (300 g) mild enchilada sauce
1 - 4 oz can (120 g) chopped green chilies
¼ cup (60 ml) Parmesan cheese
1 - 4 oz can (120 g) sliced black olives, drained
¼ cup (60 ml) chopped walnuts
1 egg, hard-cooked, peeled and quartered

In regular size oven cooking bag, coated with flour, add onion, garlic, turkey and pepper. Place bag in 9-inch square micro-wave-safe baking dish. Using plastic twist tie close bag securely. Cut 6 - ½-inch slits in top of bag. Cook in microwave oven at MEDIUM-HIGH (70% power) 30-35 minutes or until meat thermometer reaches 180°F (82°C) when inserted in thighs. Turn dish halfway through cooking time. Remove from microwave and allow to stand 10-15 minutes for heat to equalize. Remove turkey from bone and cut into ½-inch cubes; discard bones.

In 7x11-inch microwave-safe dish layer potatoes and turkey. Top with sauce, green chilies, cheese, olives and walnuts. Cover with vented plastic wrap and cook in micro-wave oven at HIGH (100% power) 3-4 minutes or until heated throughout. To serve, garnish with egg. Serves 6.

Approximate nutritional analysis per serving:
Calories 356, Protein 33 g, Carbohydrates 24 g, Fat 14 g, Cholesterol 123 mg, Sodium 887 mg

SUNSHINE ORANGE CHICKEN

3 tbs (45 ml) water
½ cup (120 ml) cider vinegar
¼ cup (60 ml) olive oil
3 tbs (45 ml) honey
½ tsp (3 ml) McCORMICK or SCHILLING
    Pure Orange Extract
1 tsp (5 ml) McCORMICK or SCHILLING Rosemary
½ tsp (3 ml) McCORMICK or SCHILLING Nutmeg
¼ tsp (1 ml) salt
1 lb (455 g) boneless, skinless chicken breasts

Combine all ingredients except chicken. Mix well. Marinate chicken 2 hours. Broil or grill. Serves 4.

Approximate nutritional analysis per serving:
Calories 358, Protein 35 g, Carbohydrates 15 g, Fat 18 g, Cholesterol 96 mg, Sodium 218 mg

FLORENTINE-STUFFED TURKEY BREAST HALF

**1 - 1-3 lb (455-1365 g) NORBEST
Turkey Breast Half, skin removed**
2 tbs (30 ml) margarine, divided
1 tsp (5 ml) thyme
2 fresh cloves garlic, sliced
1 cup (240 ml) chopped onion
1 cup (240 ml) chopped celery
**1 - 10 oz pkg (300 g) frozen chopped spinach,
thawed and well drained**
¾ cup (180 ml) chicken broth or water
3 slices wheat bread, cubed
½ cup (120 ml) walnut pieces, toasted
**½ cup (120 ml) coarsely chopped
Granny Smith apples**
½ tsp (3 ml) salt
¼ tsp (1 ml) nutmeg
¼ tsp (1 ml) pepper

Rub turkey breast with 1 tbs margarine, thyme and garlic. In large non-stick skillet, over medium-high heat, sauté onion and celery in 1 tbs margarine 4-5 minutes or until soft. Fold in spinach, broth, bread, walnuts, apple, salt, nutmeg and pepper until mixture is well combined. Spoon dressing into mound in center of 9x13x2-inch roasting pan. Place turkey, breast-side-up, over dressing.

Bake at 350°F (180°C) 1½-2 hours or until meat thermometer reaches 170-175°F (77-79°C) and juices run clear. Serves 6.

Approximate nutritional analysis per serving:
*Calories 280, Protein 29 g, Carbohydrates 14 g, Fat 13 g,
Cholesterol 65 mg, Sodium 537 mg*

SOUTH AMERICAN-STYLE TURKEY THIGHS

1 tbs (15 ml) flour
**1 - 14½ oz can (435 g) Italian plum tomatoes,
drained, juice reserved, tomatoes coarsely
chopped**
1 cup (240 ml) chopped onions
1 tsp (5 ml) minced garlic
½ tsp (3 ml) cumin
½ tsp (3 ml) salt
**2-2½ lbs (910-1138 g) NORBEST
Turkey Thighs, skin removed**

BLACK BEANS:
1 - 16 oz can (480 g) black beans, drained and rinsed
½ cup (120 ml) reserved tomato juice
2 tbs (30 ml) chopped fresh cilantro
1 tbs (15 ml) green pepper flakes
1 tbs (15 ml) instant minced onion
½ tsp (3 ml) dried instant garlic

SPICY RICE:
2¼ cups (540 ml) instant rice
2 tsp (10 ml) olive oil
2¼ cups (540 ml) water
1 tsp (5 ml) instant minced onion
1 tsp (5 ml) green pepper flakes
½ tsp (3 ml) salt

PLANTAINS:
2 ripe plantains, peeled
vegetable cooking spray

In regular size oven cooking bag, coated with flour, add tomatoes, onion, garlic, cumin and salt. Squeeze mixture to combine. Add turkey, turn bag and squeeze to coat. Using plastic twist tie close bag securely and place bag in 2-qt microwave-safe dish. Cut 6 - ½-inch slits in top of bag. Cook in microwave oven at MEDIUM-HIGH (70% power) 25-30 minutes or until meat thermometer reaches 180°F (82°C) when inserted into thighs. Turn dish halfway through cooking time.

Remove dish from microwave and allow to stand 10-15 minutes to allow heat to equalize. Transfer turkey and tomato mixture to bowl. Using two forks, shred turkey meat from bone; reserve turkey meat and discard bones. To serve, place turkey in center of large platter. Alternate mounds of black beans and rice around turkey and garnish with plantain slices. Serves 6.

Black Beans: In small saucepan, over medium heat, combine beans, juice, cilantro, green pepper flakes, onion and garlic and cook 10 minutes or until heated throughout.

Spicy Rice: In medium saucepan, over medium-high heat, sauté rice in oil 3 minutes or until golden brown, stirring constantly. Remove pan from heat and slowly add water, onion, green pepper and salt. Return pan to heat, cover and bring to boil. Remove pan from heat and allow rice to stand 5 minutes or until all liquid is absorbed and rice is fluffy.

Plantains: Cut plantains in half crosswise and cut lengthwise into ⅛-inch slices. Arrange plantain slices on 10x15x2-inch baking sheet, lightly sprayed with vegetable cooking spray. Spray top of plantains with vegetable cooking spray. Bake at 425°F (220°C) 15 minutes or until lightly browned and crisp.

Approximate nutritional analysis per serving:
*Calories 482, Protein 35 g, Carbohydrates 64 g, Fat 10 g,
Cholesterol 85 mg, Sodium 684 mg*

Orange Chicken

ORANGE CHICKEN

4 EMPIRE KOSHER Chicken Breast Cutlets
1 cup (240 ml) orange juice
¼ cup (60 ml) brown sugar (syrup at Passover)
grated orange rind
1 tbs (15 ml) cornstarch (potato starch at Passover)

Cook all ingredients for the sauce over medium heat, stirring constantly until thick and glossy. Pour sauce over frozen chicken breast cutlets, bake uncovered approximately 30 minutes at 350°F (180°C). This sauce may also be used for microwaved cutlets. If using fresh chicken cutlets, adjust time accordingly. Serves 4.

Approximate nutritional analysis per serving:
Calories 192, Protein 21 g, Carbohydrates 22 g, Fat 2 g,
Cholesterol 55 mg, Sodium 53 mg

 ## HOT AND SOUR KEBABS

1½ lbs (685 g) EMPIRE KOSHER Chicken
Cutlets, cut into ¾-inch cubes

MARINADE:
¼ cup (60 ml) margarine
¼ cup (60 ml) peanut oil
4 tbs (60 ml) fresh lime or lemon juice
4 cloves garlic, minced
2 tbs (30 ml) crushed red pepper flakes or hot sauce

Melt the margarine, add the oil and remaining ingredients, simmer to blend flavors. Pour marinade over chicken cubes, refrigerate for a couple of hours. Thread the chicken on skewers, broil or grill over charcoal until done. Serves 4.

Approximate nutritional analysis per serving:
Calories 336, Protein 53 g, Carbohydrates < 1 g, Fat 12 g,
Cholesterol 145 mg, Sodium 164 mg

SALSA VERDE CHICKEN KABOBS

1 - 16 oz jar (480 g) CHI-CHI'S Salsa Verde
¼ cup (60 ml) oil
2 tbs (30 ml) lime juice
3 cloves garlic
4 boneless skinless chicken breasts, in cubes
2 cups (480 ml) finely shredded cabbage
1½ cups (355 ml) finely julienned jicama
1 cup (240 ml) shredded carrot
⅓ cup (80 ml) coarsely chopped fresh cilantro
salt and pepper
2 large firm ripe bananas

In blender container or food processor bowl fitted with metal blade, combine salsa verde, oil, lime juice and garlic. Process until smooth. Remove ⅔ cup of salsa verde mixture; set aside. Place chicken in reclosable plastic food storage bag; pour remaining salsa verde mixture over chicken. Seal bag and turn several times to coat. Place bag in 13x9-inch pan. Refrigerate, turning bag occasionally, at least 4 hours or overnight.

In large bowl, combine cabbage, jicama, carrot and cilantro. Stir in reserved ⅔ cup salsa verde mixture. Add salt and pepper to taste; set aside. Thread chicken pieces onto 8 long bamboo skewers. Over medium-hot coals, grill kabobs 5 minutes on each side or until no longer pink in center. Slice bananas lengthwise; grill 2 minutes on each side. Serve chicken and bananas on top of cabbage mixture. Serves 4.

Approximate nutritional analysis per serving:
Calories 330, Protein 27 g, Carbohydrates 34 g, Fat 10 g,
Cholesterol 65 mg, Sodium 370 mg

MEXICAN CHICKEN SKEWERS
WITH SPICY YOGURT SAUCE

1 - 1¼ oz pkg (38 ml) taco seasoning mix, divided
6 boneless skinless chicken breast halves,
    cut into 1-inch cubes
1 large clove garlic
¼ tsp (1 ml) salt
2 tbs (30 ml) olive oil
1 cup (240 ml) DANNON Plain Nonfat or
    Lowfat Yogurt
1 red bell pepper, cut into chunks
1 green bell pepper, cut into chunks
1 yellow bell pepper, cut into chunks

In a large bowl combine 3 tbs seasoning mix and chicken; toss to coat well. Cover; chill 2 hours.

Spicy Yogurt Sauce: In a mortar and pestle or with a large knife press garlic and salt together until a smooth paste forms. Place in a small bowl with olive oil; mix well. Stir in yogurt and remaining taco seasoning mix. Cover; chill 30 minutes before serving.

Thread chicken onto skewers alternately with peppers; grill over hot coals 10-12 minutes, turning occasionally. Serve with Spicy Yogurt Sauce. Serves 12.

Approximate nutritional analysis per serving:
Calories 132, Protein 19 g, Carbohydrates 3 g, Fat 5 g,
Cholesterol 49 mg, Sodium 145 mg

CHEAP CALORIE GRILLED CHICKEN
IN SPICY LEMON SAUCE

1 tbs (15 ml) CHEF PAUL PRUDHOMME'S
    Meat Magic, in all
4 - 4 oz (480 g) boned, skinned chicken breasts
1¾ cup (420 ml) defatted chicken stock, in all
¼ tsp (1 ml) lemon zest
2 tbs (30 ml) lemon juice
1 tbs (15 ml) julienne jalapeño peppers
20 green peppercorns
1 tbs (15 ml) cornstarch
1-2 packets EQUAL

Preheat 8-inch skillet over high heat for 4 minutes. On each side of each chicken breast sprinkle ¼ tsp Meat Magic, and place them on hot skillet. Cook 4-5 minutes, turning once or twice. Remove chicken from skillet and set aside.

Immediately add ½ cup stock to skillet and deglaze it, then add carrot, lemon zest and juice, pepper and peppercorns. Cook and reduce liquid about 2 minutes. Add 1 cup stock and cook 3-4 minutes. Add cornstarch to the remaining ¼ cup stock and stir until dissolved. Add this mixture to the pan and whisk it thoroughly into the sauce. Let come to a boil, reduce the heat, add chicken and simmer 4-5 minutes, turning chicken once. Remove skillet from heat and whisk in EQUAL, 1-2 packets to taste. Serve immediately over rice. Serves 4.

Approximate nutritional analysis per serving:
Calories 202, Protein 36 g, Carbohydrates 3 g, Fat 4 g,
Cholesterol 96 mg, Sodium 217 mg

Opposite: Salsa Verde Chicken Kabobs

GRILLED CHICKEN AND SHRIMP

1 lb (455 g) medium shrimp, peeled and deveined
4 boneless, skinless chicken breast halves

SPICY MARINADE:
⅔ cup (180 ml) white wine vinegar
½ cup (120 ml) soy sauce
2 tbs (30 ml) minced ginger
2 tbs (30 ml) olive oil
2 tbs (30 ml) sesame oil
2 large cloves garlic, minced
2 tsp (10 ml) Tabasco pepper sauce
2 scallions, sliced

Place shrimp on skewers. If using wooden skewers, soak in water while preparing marinade. In 13x9-inch baking dish combine Spicy Marinade ingredients. Place skewered shrimp and chicken breasts in mixture; toss to mix well. Cover and refrigerate at least 2 hours and up to 24 hours, turning occasionally.

About 30 minutes before serving, preheat grill to medium heat, placing rack 5-6 inches above coals. Place skewered shrimp and chicken on grill rack. Grill shrimp 3-4 minutes; grill chicken breasts 6 minutes, turning once and brushing with marinade occasionally. Serves 4.

OR: Preheat broiler. Place skewered shrimp and chicken on broiler pan. Broil 4 inches from the heat as above.

Approximate nutritional analysis per serving:
Calories 341, Protein 59 g, Carbohydrates 2 g, Fat 9 g,
Cholesterol 269 mg, Sodium 637 mg

HONEY-MUSTARD CHICKEN

½ cup (120 ml) MIRACLE WHIP Salad Dressing
2 tbs (30 ml) Dijon Mustard
1 tbs (15 ml) honey
4 boneless skinless chicken breast halves

Heat grill. Mix salad dressing, mustard and honey. Brush chicken with ½ of the salad dressing mixture. Place chicken on greased grill over medium coals. Grill 9 minutes. Brush with remaining salad dressing mixture. Turn; continue grilling 7-9 minutes or until chicken is cooked through. Serves 4.

Approximate nutritional analysis per serving:
Calories 304, Protein 46 g, Carbohydrates 10 g, Fat 8 g,
Cholesterol 138 mg, Sodium 437 mg

TURKEY FAJITAS

1¼ cups (300 ml) olive oil
⅓ cup (80 ml) lime juice
3 tbs (45 ml) soy sauce
1 clove garlic, minced
2 tsp (10 ml) oregano
2 fresh hot peppers, seeded and minced
**   *or* ¼ cup (60 ml) canned chopped chilies**
1 tsp (5 ml) ground cumin
2 medium onions
1½ lbs (685 g) EMPIRE KOSHER Turkey Tenders
**   *or* 2 lbs (910 g) EMPIRE KOSHER Turkey**
**   Thighs, boned**
2 green peppers
12 kosher parve flour tortillas

Combine 1 cup of the olive oil, lime juice, soy sauce, garlic, hot peppers, seasonings. Remove ¼ cup marinade and save for basting. Flatten the turkey into ½-inch thick cutlets. Add the turkey to marinade, mix to coat well. Cover tightly and refrigerate for about 2-4 hours. Discard marinade.

Cut the onions into ½-inch rounds, leaving them in rings. Cut the peppers in sixths. Marinate onion and peppers in oil until ready to grill.

Wrap tortillas in foil and set on outside edge of grill, turning often until heated through. Drain cutlets and grill along with the onions and peppers over medium heat, basting with reserved marinade, and turning often. Allow about 6-8 minutes for turkey to cook through, then transfer to serving platter, and cut into ¼-inch wide strips.

Unwrap tortillas, and place a few slices of grilled turkey and some cooked onions and peppers on each tortilla. Top with salsa and/or guacamole, roll up and enjoy! Serves 6.

Approximate nutritional analysis per serving:
Calories 849, Protein 40 g, Carbohydrates 50 g, Fat 56 g,
Cholesterol 86 mg, Sodium 865 mg

Opposite: Honey-Mustard Chicken

HERBED LIME CHICKEN

2-3 lbs (910-1365 g) chicken pieces
½ cup (120 ml) vegetable oil
⅓ cup (80 ml) lime juice
¼ cup (60 ml) chopped onion
2 cloves garlic, crushed
1-1½ tsp (5-8 ml) TABASCO pepper sauce
¾ tsp (4 ml) dried rosemary, crumbled
½ tsp (3 ml) dried leaf marjoram, crumbled
½ tsp (3 ml) salt

Pierce chicken skin several places with fork. In shallow dish or plastic bag combine chicken and remaining ingredients. Cover. Refrigerate overnight in lime mixture. Drain chicken; reserve marinade. Place chicken over hot coals. Cook about 20 minutes per side, or until chicken is done. Turn chicken several times during grilling, brushing with reserved marinade each time. Serve with additional TABASCO pepper sauce, if desired. Serves 4.

Approximate nutritional analysis per serving:
Calories 391, Protein 21 g, Fat 32 g, Cholesterol 65 mg, Sodium 339 mg

WISH-BONE MARINADE ITALIANO

½ cup (120 ml) WISH - BONE Italian, Robusto
    Italian, Lite Italian or Honey Dijon Dressing
2½-3 lbs (1.1-1.4 kg) chicken pieces*

*Variations:
1 - 2½ lb (1.1 kg) T-bone, boneless sirloin or top sirloin steak *or*
    4 boneless skinless chicken breast halves *or*
    2½ lbs (1.1 kg) center cut pork chops, about 1-inch thick

In large shallow baking dish or plastic bag, pour Italian dressing over chicken. Cover, or close bag, and marinate in refrigerator, turning occasionally, 3 hours or overnight. Remove chicken, reserving marinade.

Grill or broil chicken, turning or basting frequently with reserved marinade, until chicken is done. Do not brush with marinade last 5 minutes of cooking. Serves 4.

Approximate nutritional analysis per serving:
Calories 490, Protein 46 g, Carbohydrates 3 g, Fat 32 g, Cholesterol 180 mg, Sodium 720 mg

Courtesy of The Lipton Kitchens.

CHICKEN-VEGETABLE KABOBS

½ cup (120 ml) WISH - BONE Italian, Robusto
    Italian or Lite Italian Dressing
¼ cup (60 ml) dry white wine or WISH - BONE
    Italian Dressing
1 lb (455 g) boneless skinless chicken breasts, cubed
1 large zucchini or yellow squash,
    cut into ½-inch slices
1 large red, green or yellow bell pepper,
    cut into chunks

In large shallow baking dish or plastic bag, blend Italian dressing with wine. Add chicken and vegetables; turn to coat. Cover, or close bag, and marinate in refrigerator, turning occasionally, up to 3 hours. Remove chicken and vegetables, reserving marinade.

On skewers, alternately thread chicken and vegetables. Grill or broil, turning and basting frequently with reserved marinade, until chicken is done. Do not brush with marinade last 5 minutes of cooking. Serves 4.

Approximate nutritional analysis per serving:
Calories 300, Protein 36 g, Carbohydrates 4 g, Fat 13 g, Cholesterol 95 mg, Sodium 670 mg

Courtesy of The Lipton Kitchens.

Herbed Lime Chicken

SUMMER CHICKEN AND SQUASH

¾ cup (180 ml) WISH - BONE Italian, Robusto
    Italian or Lite Italian Dressing
¼ cup (60 ml) grated Parmesan cheese
4 boneless skinless chicken breast halves
2 medium zucchini or yellow squash, quartered

In large shallow baking dish or plastic bag, combine Italian
dressing with cheese. Add chicken and zucchini; turn to coat.
Cover, or close bag, and marinate in refrigerator, turning
occasionally, up to 3 hours.

    Grill or broil chicken and zucchini, turning and basting
frequently with reserved marinade, until chicken is done. Do
not brush with marinade last 5 minutes of cooking. Serves 4.

Approximate nutritional analysis per serving:
Calories 370, Protein 32 g, Carbohydrates 5 g, Fat 24 g,
Cholesterol 85 mg, Sodium 107 mg

Courtesy of The Lipton Kitchens.

GRILLED SUMMER CHICKEN AND VEGETABLES

1 cup (240 ml) WISH - BONE Italian, Robusto
    Italian, or Lite Italian Dressing
4 chicken breast halves
4 ears fresh or frozen corn
2 large tomatoes, halved crosswise

In large shallow baking dish or plastic bag, pour ½ cup Italian
dressing over chicken. In another large shallow baking dish or
plastic bag, pour remaining ½ cup Italian dressing over corn
and tomatoes. Cover, close bag, and marinate chicken and
vegetables in refrigerator, turning occasionally, 3 hours or
overnight. Remove chicken and vegetables from marinades,
reserving marinades.

    Grill or broil chicken and corn 20 minutes, turning and
basting frequently with reserved marinades. Arrange tomato
halves cut-side-up on grill or broiler pan and continue cooking
chicken and vegetables, turning and basting frequently with
reserved marinades, 10 minutes or until chicken and corn are
done. Do not brush with marinade last 5 minutes of cooking.
Serves 4.

Approximate nutritional analysis per serving:
Calories 490, Protein 33 g, Carbohydrates 30 g, Fat 28 g,
Cholesterol 80 mg, Sodium 127 mg

TURKEY SCALLOPINI

1¼ lb (570 g) EMPIRE KOSHER Turkey Tenders
    or ¼ inch thick slices cut from deboned
    EMPIRE KOSHER Turkey Breast
kosher white wine
orange juice

MARINADE:
¼ cup (60 ml) low sodium soy sauce
2 tsp (10 ml) minced garlic
1 tbs (15 ml) oil

Butterfly the turkey tenders, pound thin. Marinate overnight in
the refrigerator.

    To cook: Preheat broiler or grill. Brush cutlets with kosher
white wine, orange juice, season with pepper, salt if desired,
sprinkle with paprika. Broil or grill until tender. Serves 4.

Approximate nutritional analysis per serving:
Calories 251, Protein 52 g, Carbohydrates < 1 g, Fat 3 g,
Cholesterol 146 mg, Sodium 352 mg

Turkey Scallopini

Chicken Barbecue with Sherry Marinade

HOT AND SOUR KEBABS

1 ½ lbs (685 g) **EMPIRE KOSHER**
   Chicken Cutlets, cut into ¾-inch cubes

MARINADE:
¼ cup (60 ml) **margarine**
¼ cup (60 ml) **peanut oil**
4 tbs (60 ml) **fresh lime or lemon juice**
4 cloves garlic, minced
2 tbs (30 ml) **crushed red pepper flakes or hot sauce**

Melt the margarine, add the oil and remaining ingredients, simmer to blend flavors. Pour marinade over chicken cubes, refrigerate for a couple of hours. Thread the chicken on skewers, broil or grill over charcoal until done. Serves 4.

Approximate nutritional analysis per serving:
Calories 335, Protein 53 g, Carbohydrates < 1 g, Fat 12 g,
Cholesterol 145 mg, Sodium 164 mg

CHICKEN BARBECUE WITH SHERRY MARINADE

¼ cup (60 ml) **POMPEIAN Extra Virgin Olive Oil**
2 tbs (30 ml) **soy sauce**
1 cup (240 ml) **dry sherry**
½ tsp (3 ml) **oregano**
1 clove garlic, crushed
4 boneless chicken breasts

Combine the olive oil, soy sauce, sherry, oregano and garlic. Pour over the chicken breasts and refrigerate overnight, turning several times. Place marinated chicken on the barbecue grill over medium heat. Turn and baste frequently until the breasts are golden brown and slightly firm to touch, about 7 minutes on each side. Serves 4.

Approximate nutritional analysis per serving:
Calories 178, Protein 27 g, Carbohydrates < 1 g, Fat 6 g,
Cholesterol 73 mg, Sodium 321 mg

GRILLED MARINATED CHICKEN BREASTS

**3 chicken breasts, boneless, skinless,
    split and well trimmed of fat**
juice of 4 limes
1 tbs (15 ml) olive oil
**¼ cup (60 ml) fresh coriander or
    Italian parsley, finely chopped**
½ tsp (3 ml) cumin powder
2 cloves garlic, minced
black pepper, to taste

Combine the lime juice, olive oil, black pepper, coriander and cumin in a glass bowl. Mix well and add the chicken breasts. Cover and marinate for 1-2 hours, turn occasionally. Grill or broil chicken 3-5 minutes on each side. Serves 6.

Approximate nutritional analysis per serving:
Calories 148, Protein 27 g, Carbohydrates 4 g, Fat 4 g,
Cholesterol 73 mg, Sodium 64 mg

Courtesy of the Empire Kosher Poultry Test Kitchens.

GRILLED HONEY-MUSTARD CHICKEN

¼ cup (60 ml) GREY POUPON Dijon Mustard
3 tbs (45 ml) honey
2 tbs (30 ml) FLEISCHMANN'S Margarine, melted
1 tbs (15 ml) lemon juice
1 garlic clove, crushed
8 - 4 oz (960 g) boneless chicken breasts

Variation:
¼ cup (60 ml) PLANTERS Slivered Almonds, toasted

In small bowl, combine mustard, honey, margarine, lemon juice and garlic. Grill or broil chicken 6 inches from heat source for 10-15 minutes, turning occasionally and brushing with mustard mixture frequently. Serves 8.
    Variation: Sprinkle with almonds before serving.

Approximate nutritional analysis per serving:
Calories 199, Protein 27 g, Carbohydrates 7 g, Fat 6 g,
Cholesterol 72 mg, Sodium 312 mg

Approximate nutritional analysis per serving plus almonds:
Calories 209, Protein 28 g, Carbohydrates 8 g, Fat 7 g,
Cholesterol 66 mg, Sodium 324 mg

GRILLED CHICKEN BREASTS WITH KIWI SAUCE

¼ cup (60 ml) FLEISCHMANN'S Margarine, melted
**⅓ cup plus 3 tbs (115 ml) GREY POUPON
    Specialty Mustard: Honey**
**3 whole boneless chicken breasts,
    halved and pounded to ¼ inch thickness**
⅔ cup (160 ml) orange juice
1 tsp (5 ml) minced fresh ginger root
**2 small kiwi fruit, peeled,
    halved lengthwise and sliced**

Blend margarine and 3 tbs mustard. Grill chicken for 8-10 minutes or until done, turning and basting with mustard mixture. Meanwhile in small saucepan, heat orange juice, remaining mustard and ginger to a boil; remove from heat. Stir in kiwi slices. Serve with grilled chicken. Serves 6.

Approximate nutritional analysis per serving:
Calories 257, Protein 28 g, Carbohydrates 8 g, Fat 9 g,
Cholesterol 66 mg, Sodium 138 mg

PEANUT CHICKEN IN ORANGE SAUCE

1 tsp (5 ml) chili powder
1 tsp (5 ml) salt
¼ tsp (1 ml) black pepper
1 - 3 lb (1.4 kg) chicken, cut up
5 tbs (75 ml) butter
**1 cup (240 ml) FLORIDA'S NATURAL
    Brand Orange Juice**
⅔ cup (160 ml) chopped, salted, roasted peanuts
1 medium orange, thinly sliced
¼ cup (60 ml) finely minced fresh cilantro

Rub chili powder, salt and pepper into chicken. In a large frying pan, heat butter and sauté chicken on both sides until golden brown. Cover, reduce heat and cook until chicken is tender, about 30 minutes. Remove chicken to platter and keep warm. Add FLORIDA'S NATURAL Brand Orange Juice to frying pan. Stir to loosen all the browned particles; pour sauce over chicken and sprinkle with peanuts. Garnish with orange slices and top with finely minced cilantro. Serves 4.

Approximate nutritional analysis per serving:
Calories 956, Protein 106 g, Carbohydrates 15 g, Fat 52 g,
Cholesterol 340 mg, Sodium 1076 mg

CHICKEN HAVANA

**8 PREMIUM YOUNG 'N TENDER Brand
   Boneless, Skinless Split Chicken Breasts**
¼ cup (60 ml) fresh lime juice
4 tbs (60 ml) chili powder
2 tbs (30 ml) vegetable oil
1 tbs (15 ml) minced garlic
½ tsp (3 ml) ground cumin
½ tsp (3 ml) crushed red pepper flakes, optional

BLACK BEAN AND HOMINY RELISH:
2 tbs (30 ml) vegetable oil
2 small onions, thinly sliced, in rings
½ cup (120 ml) thin strips of red bell pepper
1 - 16 oz can (480 g) black beans, drained
1 - 15½ oz can (465 g) white hominy, drained
1 - 15½ oz can (465 g) yellow hominy, drained

SOUR CREAM CHILI SAUCE:
2 - 4 oz cans (240 g) chopped green chilies, undrained
¾ cup (180 ml) heavy cream
¾ cup (180 ml) dairy sour cream
2 tbs (30 ml) minced fresh cilantro

GARNISH:
lime wedges
cilantro sprigs
red bell pepper strips

Rinse chicken breasts, pat dry and place in a shallow glass dish. Combine lime juice, chili powder, vegetable oil, garlic and cumin. Add red pepper flakes if spicier flavor is desired. Spoon over chicken breasts and toss to coat all sides. Cover and refrigerate at least 4 hours or overnight.

Black Bean Hominy Relish: Heat oil in a large non-stick skillet. Add onion and red bell pepper strips. Cook and stir over medium heat 3-4 minutes or until onions are transparent. Stir in black beans, white and yellow hominy. Cook 2-3 minutes or until just heated. Spoon relish onto a large ovenproof serving platter; cover with foil and set aside to keep warm.

Preheat oven to 375°F (190°C). Add chicken to skillet used to cook relish. (May need to add a small amount of vegetable oil.) Cook chicken 4-5 minutes per side or until it tests done. Arrange chicken over relish, cover with foil and bake for 15-20 minutes.

Sour Cream Chili Sauce: Purée green chilies in blender or food processor. Combine chilies, heavy cream in a medium saucepan. Bring to a gentle boil; stir in sour cream and cilantro. Cook just until blended and heated. Garnish chicken with lime wedges, cilantro and red bell pepper strips if desired. Serve Sour Cream Chili Sauce over chicken or on the side. Serves 8.

Approximate nutritional analysis per serving:
Calories 451, Protein 35 g, Carbohydrates 33 g, Fat 22 g,
Cholesterol 113 mg, Sodium 417 mg

Chicken Havana

Chicken with Apple-Pepper Sauce

CHICKEN WITH APPLE-PEPPER SAUCE

**4 PREMIUM YOUNG 'N TENDER Brand
  Boneless, Skinless Split Chicken Breasts**
¼ **cup (60 ml) all purpose flour**
1 ½ **tsp (8 ml) lemon pepper seasoning**
½ **tsp (3 ml) salt**
¼ **tsp (1 ml) garlic powder**
2 **tbs (30 ml) vegetable oil**
½ **cup (120 ml) apple juice**
⅓ **cup (80 ml) hot jalapeño pepper jelly**
apple slices
parsley

Rinse chicken breasts and pat dry. Combine flour, lemon pepper, salt and garlic powder in a shallow dish. Dredge chicken in flour mixture to coat well. Heat oil in a medium skillet and add chicken. Cook until chicken is brown on all sides and tender, about 10-12 minutes. Remove chicken from skillet and keep warm.

Add apple juice and jelly to skillet drippings. Cook and stir until jelly melts and sauce thickens slightly about 4 minutes. Spoon some of sauce on platter or serving plates, top with chicken and spoon remaining sauce over chicken. Garnish with apple slices and parsley if desired. Serves 4.

Approximate nutritional analysis per serving:
Calories 316, Protein 28 g, Carbohydrates 28 g, Fat 10 g,
Cholesterol 73 mg, Sodium 334 mg

CREAMY PESTO CHICKEN WITH WALNUTS

2 tbs (30 ml) chopped walnuts
2 tsp (10 ml) vegetable oil
1 lb (455 g) boneless, skinless chicken breast halves
½ cup (120 ml) GILROY FARMS Pesto Sauce
6 tbs (90 ml) heavy cream
2 tbs (30 ml) dry sherry

Sauté walnuts in large skillet over medium-low heat until toasted; remove and set aside. In same skillet heat oil over medium heat. Add chicken breasts and cook about 7 minutes per side or until no longer pink in center. Remove and keep warm. Wipe skillet of excess oil. Add pesto, cream and sherry. Simmer over low heat 3-4 minutes, stirring occasionally. To serve, spoon pesto mixture over chicken and sprinkle with walnuts. Serve 4.

Approximate nutritional analysis per serving:
Calories 408, Protein 38 g, Carbohydrates 2 g, Fat 26 g,
Cholesterol 129 mg, Sodium 152 mg

Courtesy of McCormick/Schilling Spices.

OPEN SESAME CHICKEN

4 EMPIRE KOSHER Chicken Breast Cutlets
2 tbs (30 ml) kosher mayonnaise
¼ cup (60 ml) sesame seeds
2 tbs (30 ml) vegetable oil
lemon wedges to squeeze over cutlets
juice of ½ lemon
pepper

Season the cutlets, which may be flattened slightly, with pepper. Brush mayonnaise over both sides. Dredge cutlets in sesame seeds, coating well on all sides. Heat oil in a large non-stick frying pan, and cook cutlets over medium heat for about 5 minutes per side. Serve with lemon wedges. Serves 4.

Approximate nutritional analysis per serving:
Calories 338, Protein 18 g, Carbohydrates 9 g, Fat 26 g,
Cholesterol 64 mg, Sodium 249 mg

HERBED CHICKEN AND MUSHROOMS

1 lb (455 g) boneless, skinless chicken breasts
salt and black pepper
1 tbs (15 ml) flour
1 tbs (15 ml) vegetable oil
1 tbs (15 ml) butter
½ lb (230 g) fresh mushrooms, sliced
¼ cup (60 ml) dry white wine
¼ cup (60 ml) chicken broth
1 tsp (5 ml) McCORMICK Herbes de Provence
½ tsp (3 ml) McCORMICK Garlic Powder

Pound chicken to ½-inch thickness. Season with salt and pepper. Lightly coat with flour. Heat oil and butter in large skillet over medium-high heat. Add chicken and cook 3-4 minutes per side. Remove and keep warm. Add remaining ingredients to skillet and cook 3-4 minutes. Serve over chicken. Serves 4.

Approximate nutritional analysis per serving:
Calories 274, Protein 37 g, Carbohydrates 4 g, Fat 11 g,
Cholesterol 104 mg, Sodium 122 mg

Courtesy of McCormick/Schilling Spices.

STIR-FRIED CHICKEN CACCIATORE

1 green pepper, cut into strips
1 medium onion, cut into wedges
3 tbs (45 ml) olive oil
1 lb (455 g) boneless, skinless chicken breasts,
  cut into narrow strips
2-3 tbs (30-45 ml) bottled or fresh minced garlic
1 cup (240 ml) CALIFORNIA ripe olive wedges
1½ tsp (8 ml) thyme
1½ tsp (8 ml) sage
2 tomatoes, diced
¼ cup (60 ml) red wine vinegar
1 cup (240 ml) white wine mixed with:
1 tbs (15 ml) flour
12 oz (360 g) spaghetti

Sauté green pepper and onion in oil in large skillet for 6 minutes or until nearly tender. Push to side of pan, add chicken and garlic and cook, stirring over high heat for 3 minutes or until evenly cooked. Stir in olives, thyme, sage, tomato, vinegar and wine-flour mixture and cook, stirring until glossy and thickened. Season with salt and pepper to taste. Serve over hot, cooked pasta. Serves 4.

Approximate nutritional analysis per serving:
Calories 709, Protein 37 g, Carbohydrates 78 g, Fat 18 g,
Cholesterol 96 mg, Sodium 275 mg

Opposite: Herbed Chicken and Mushrooms

CHICKEN FAJITAS

4 boneless, skinless chicken breast halves
2 tsp (10 ml) ground cumin
1½ tsp (8 ml) TABASCO pepper sauce
1 tsp (5 ml) chili powder
½ tsp (3 ml) salt
8 flour tortillas
1 tbs (15 ml) vegetable oil
3 large green onions, cut into 2-inch pieces

SPICY TOMATO SALAD:
1 large ripe tomato, diced
1 tbs (15 ml) chopped cilantro
1 tbs (15 ml) lime juice
¼ tsp (1 ml) TABASCO pepper sauce
¼ tsp (1 ml) salt

CORN RELISH:
1 -11 oz can (330 g) corn, drained
½ cup (120 ml) diced green bell pepper
1 tbs (15 ml) lime juice
¼ tsp (1 ml) TABASCO pepper sauce
¼ tsp (1 ml) salt

ACCOMPANIMENTS:
½ cup (120 ml) shredded cheddar cheese
½ cup (120 ml) sliced avocado
½ cup (120 ml) sour cream

Cut chicken breasts into ½-inch strips. In large bowl toss chicken strips with cumin, TABASCO pepper sauce, chili powder, and salt. Set aside.

Spicy Tomato Salsa: In a medium bowl toss tomato, cilantro, lime juice, TABASCO pepper sauce, and salt.

Corn Relish: In medium bowl toss corn, green pepper, lime juice, TABASCO pepper sauce, and salt.

Wrap tortillas in foil; heat in preheated 350°F (180°C) oven 10 minutes or until warm. Meanwhile, in a large skillet, heat vegetable oil over medium-high heat. Add chicken mixture; cook 4 minutes, stirring frequently. Add green onions; cook 12 minute longer or until chicken is browned and tender.

To serve, set out the warmed tortillas along with the chicken, salsa, corn relish, cheddar cheese, avocado, and sour cream. To eat, place strips of chicken in center of each tortilla, add salsa, relish and toppings, then fold the bottom quarter and both sides of the tortilla to cover the filling. Serves 4.

Approximate nutritional analysis per serving:
Calories 632, Protein 41 g, Fat 28 g, Cholesterol 101 mg,
Sodium   236 mg

CHICKEN CUTLETS CONTINENTAL

4 EMPIRE KOSHER Chicken Breast Cutlets
2 tbs (30 ml) parve margarine
1 cup (240 ml) sliced mushrooms
1 small clove garlic, crushed
½ cup (120 ml) dry white kosher wine
pinch Italian herbs
1 tsp (5 ml) fresh lemon juice
1 tbs (15 ml) chopped parsley
pepper, salt if desired

Brown frozen cutlets briefly on both sides over medium-high heat. Remove. Add garlic and mushrooms, sauté until mushrooms are golden and pan is virtually dry. Add remaining ingredients and cutlets. Simmer over low heat for about 5 minutes per side, or until cooked through. Serves 4.

If using fresh cutlets, adjust cooking times accordingly.

Approximate nutritional analysis per serving:
Calories 218, Protein 27 g, Carbohydrates 1 g, Fat 9 g,
Cholesterol 73 mg, Sodium 143 mg

FRIED CHICKEN OLD BAY STYLE

1 - 2½-3 lb (1.1-1.4 kg) chicken, cut up
1 cup (240 ml) flour
¼ cup (60 ml) OLD BAY Seasoning
2 cups (480 ml) cooking oil
2 tbs (30 ml) water
1 egg, beaten

Wash chicken and pat dry. Mix flour and OLD BAY Seasoning. Heat cooking oil in a large skillet. In mixing bowl, combine water and egg. Dip chicken in egg mixture, then in flour (a few pieces at a time). Fry over medium heat until golden brown, about 20 minutes on each side. Serves 4.

Approximate nutritional analysis per serving:
Calories 413, Protein 58 g, Carbohydrates 3 g, Fat 17 g,
Cholesterol 177 mg, Sodium 171 mg

Courtesy of McCormick/Schilling Spices.

Opposite: Chicken Fajitas

FLORENTINE CHICKEN

2 tbs (30 ml) CHEF PAUL PRUDHOMME'S
    Poultry Magic
1 tsp (5 ml) dry mustard
½ tsp (3 ml) ground sage
½ tsp (3 ml) ground nutmeg
8 chicken breast halves
½ cup (120 ml) all purpose flour
3 eggs
¼ cup (60 ml) plus 3 tbs (45 ml) half and half, in all
¾ cup (180 ml) bread crumbs
½ cup (120 ml) grated Parmesan cheese, in all
½ cup (120 ml) plus 1-2 tbs (15-30 ml)
    unsalted butter, in all
1½ lbs (685 g) fresh or frozen (thawed) spinach,
    rinsed, drained and toweled dry

Make a seasoning mix by combining the Poultry Magic with the mustard, sage and nutmeg. You should have 8 tsp in all.

Place the chicken breasts on a flat surface and pound a few times with the flat side of a cleaver or a heavy knife. Sprinkle the breasts with 4 tsp of the seasoning mix, distributing evenly on both sides and patting it in with your hands.

In a shallow bowl, combine the flour with 1 tsp seasoning mix. In another bowl, combine the eggs with 3 tbs half and half and ½ tsp seasoning mix. Beat thoroughly with a fork. In a third bowl, combine the bread crumbs with 1 tsp seasoning mix and ¼ cup Parmesan cheese.

Preheat a large heavy skillet over high heat, and while it's heating, dredge the chicken in the seasoned flour, dip in the egg mixture and then dredge in the breadcrumb mixture, shaking off all excess. Add the remaining ¼ cup half and half to the remaining egg mixture, beat briefly with a fork and set aside.

When the skillet is hot, add ¼ cup butter. Add the chicken right away, because the butter will begin to brown almost immediately and you don't want it to burn. Add the chicken breasts in one layer and brown on both sides, about 30-45 seconds each side. Remove the pieces as they brown and add 1-2 tbs butter around the sides of the skillet, if needed. When all chicken is brown and removed from skillet, add the remaining ¼ cup butter to the pan, along with the remaining 1½ tsp seasoning mix. When hot, add the spinach, push down gently while it heats for 1 minute. Pour the remaining egg mixture over the spinach and stir well. Sprinkle with the remaining ¼ cup Parmesan cheese. Place the chicken breasts on top, cover and turn heat down to medium-low. Cook 13 minutes and turn off heat. Sere immediately. Serves 8.

Approximate nutritional analysis per serving:
Calories 428, Protein 37 g, Carbohydrates 19 g, Fat 23 g,
Cholesterol 203 mg, Sodium 422 mg

HONEY-PECAN GLAZED FRIED CHICKEN

Seasoned flour (below)
10 - 5 oz (1.5 kg) boneless skinless chicken
breasts, pounded to uniform thickness, about ½ inch
3 cups (720 ml) buttermilk
vegetable oil for frying

SEASONED FLOUR:
12 oz (360 g) flour
1 tbs (15 ml) salt
1 tbs (15 ml) garlic powder
1 tbs (15 ml) cayenne pepper
1 tbs (15 ml) white pepper

HONEY-PECAN GLAZE:
¼ lb (115 g) clarified butter or butter flavored oil
¼ cup (60 ml) pecans, chopped
¾ cup (180 ml) honey

Mix all seasoned flour ingredients together. Press chicken into flour, dip in buttermilk, then in flour again. Place each chicken breast in 350°F (180°C) deep-fat fryer for 2-3 minutes or until golden and cooked thoroughly. Drain briefly and serve each breast topped with ½-1 oz of Honey-Pecan Glaze. Serves 10.

Honey-Pecan Glaze: Melt butter or oil in pan. Add pecans and heat together briefly. Add honey and mix well. Hold in double boiler if not serving immediately.

Approximate nutritional analysis per serving:
Calories 587, Protein 54 g, Carbohydrates 41 g, Fat 23 g,
Cholesterol 161 mg, Sodium 598 mg

Courtesy of The Pecan Marketing Board.

TURKEY WITH OLIVES, ROSEMARY AND BASIL

1 lb (455 g) thinly sliced turkey (uncooked)
3 tbs (45 ml) olive oil
3 tbs (45 ml) butter or margarine
¾ cup (180 ml) dry white wine
2 tsp (10 ml) basil, crumbled finely
2 tsp (10 ml) rosemary, crumbled finely
½ cup (120 ml) pitted CALIFORNIA
    ripe olives, halved

Sauté turkey, a few slices at a time, in oil and butter until browned. Transfer to a platter and keep warm. Loosen drippings in pan, add wine, herbs and olives and cook rapidly, stirring for 2-3 minutes until saucy. Pour over turkey. Serves 4.

Approximate nutritional analysis per serving:
Calories 366, Protein 35 g, Carbohydrates 1 g, Fat 21 g,
Cholesterol 120 mg, Sodium 246 mg

Opposite: Honey-Pecan Glazed Fried Chicken

CHICKEN BREASTS WITH ORANGE-LIME SAUCE

2 whole chicken breasts, skinned, boned,
    and cut in half
salt and white pepper
7 tbs (105 ml) butter, divided
1 cup (240 ml) orange juice
1 tbs (15 ml) lime juice
¼ tsp (1 ml) grated orange peel
⅔ cup (160 ml) BLUE DIAMOND
    Sliced Natural Almonds, toasted

Lightly flatten chicken breasts. Season with salt and pepper. Sauté breasts in 1 tbs butter, 2-3 minutes on each side or until cooked through. Remove and keep warm. Add orange juice, lime juice, and orange peel to pan. Remove over high heat until mixture thickens to a syrupy consistency. Add ½ tsp salt and ⅛ tsp pepper. Over low heat, whisk in remaining 6 tbs butter until sauce is thick and glossy. Add almonds and pour over chicken. Serves 4.

Approximate nutritional analysis per serving:
Calories 474, Protein 32 g, Carbohydrates 11 g, Fat 35 g,
Cholesterol 127 mg, Sodium 69 mg

THREE PEPPER CHICKEN

20 PREMIUM Crackers, any variety, crushed
1 tsp (5 ml) Italian seasoning
4 - 4 oz (480 g) boneless chicken breasts
¼ cup (60 ml) EGG BEATERS Real Egg Product
1 cup (240 ml) red, yellow or green pepper strips
1 medium onion, cut in strips
1 clove garlic, crushed
3 tbs (45 ml) FLEISCHMANN'S Margarine
1 cup (240 ml) COLLEGE INN Chicken Broth
1 tbs (15 ml) all purpose flour
2 cups (480 ml) hot cooked bow tie pasta
chopped parsley, for garnish

In shallow bowl, combine crackers and Italian seasoning. Dip each chicken breast in egg product and coat with cracker mixture; set aside.

In large nonstick skillet, over medium-high heat, cook peppers, onion and garlic in 1 tbs margarine until tender-crisp; remove from skillet. In same skillet, cook chicken in 1 tbs margarine until golden brown on both sides, adding remaining margarine as needed, about 5-10 minutes. Remove chicken to serving platter; keep warm. Blend chicken broth and flour; stir into pan drippings. Heat until mixture thickens and begins to boil; stir in pepper mixture and heat through. Serve over chicken with pasta. Garnish with parsley. Serves 4.

Approximate nutritional analysis per serving:
Calories 398, Fat 13 g, Cholesterol 67 mg, Sodium 511 mg

OLD BAY SESAME CHICKEN

1 lb (455 g) chicken breast meat
2 oz (60 g) sesame seeds
2 tbs (30 ml) butter or margarine
4 tsp (20 ml) OLD BAY Seasoning

Chop the chicken meat into bite size pieces. Toast sesame seeds in a toaster oven or heavy frying pan until golden.

In a frying pan, melt butter and add OLD BAY Seasoning. Add chicken to pan and cook at medium heat until the chicken is white throughout. Stir in the sesame seeds; serve immediately over rice. Serves 4.

Approximate nutritional analysis per serving:
Calories 437, Protein 29 g, Carbohydrates 11 g, Fat 31 g,
Cholesterol 113 mg, Sodium 444 mg

Courtesy of McCormick/Schilling Spices.

CHICKEN BREASTS WITH HONEY MUSTARD

4 boneless, skinless EMPIRE KOSHER
    Chicken Breast Cutlets
flour for coating
2 tbs (30 ml) oil

SAUCE:
3 tbs (45 ml) Dijon -style mustard
2 tbs (30 ml) chopped onion
2 tbs (30 ml) margarine
½ cup (120 ml) kosher white wine
1 cup (240 ml) kosher chicken broth
1 tbs (15 ml) honey
1 tbs (15 ml) kosher cider vinegar
⅓ cup (80 ml) chopped walnuts, optional

Dust the chicken cutlets with flour. In large saucepan, cook chicken cutlets in margarine over medium heat until done. Remove cutlets, and keep warm. Wipe out the pan, and sauté the onion until soft and golden. Add the flour, whisk well and let flour become lightly brown. Add the wine, stir. Combine the honey, mustard, vinegar and broth, and gradually stir into flour mixture. Simmer until thickened. Add the walnuts if desired, pour the sauce over the chicken, serve with rice or pasta. Serves 4.

Approximate nutritional analysis per serving without walnuts:
Calories 270, Protein 28 g, Carbohydrates 6 g, Fat 13 g,
Cholesterol 73 mg, Sodium 358 mg

Grecian Chicken Breasts

GRECIAN CHICKEN BREASTS

6 PREMIUM YOUNG 'N TENDER Brand
Boneless Split Chicken Breasts
1 - 10 oz pkg (300 g) frozen chopped spinach, thawed
1 - 8 oz pkg (240 g) feta cheese, crumbled
½ cup (120 ml) mayonnaise
1 clove garlic, minced
¼ cup (60 ml) all purpose flour
½ tsp (3 ml) paprika
12 strips bacon

Preheat oven to 325°F (165°C). Cut a pocket into each chicken breast. Salt and pepper to taste; set aside.

Thoroughly drain and squeeze any liquid from thawed spinach. Do not cook. Combine with feta cheese, mayonnaise and garlic; stuff into chicken breast pockets.

Combine flour and paprika and lightly coat stuffed chicken breasts. Wrap 2 strips of bacon around each and place on a baking rack in baking dish. Bake uncovered for 1 hour or until chicken tests done. Serves 6.

Note: May be prepared ahead. Cover well; refrigerate or freeze and bake later. If frozen, thaw in refrigerator before baking.

Approximate nutritional analysis per serving:
Calories 422, Protein 38 g, Carbohydrates 13 g, Fat 24 g,
Cholesterol 123 mg, Sodium 866 mg

MULACALONG CHICKEN

2 cups (480 ml) corn kernels, preferably fresh,
    about 4 ears
5½ cups (1.3 L) defatted chicken stock, in all
8 boneless skinless chicken breasts,
    all visible fat removed
Seasoning Mix (below)
olive oil spray
2 cups (480 ml) chopped onions
2 tsp (10 ml) grated lemon peel
juice of 1 lemon
1 red bell pepper, seeded, stemmed and
    cut into strips
2 packets EQUAL or other low calorie sweetener

SEASONING MIX:
2 tbs (30 ml) CHEF PAUL PRUDHOMME'S
    Poultry Magic
1½ tsp (8 ml) turmeric
1½ tsp (8 ml) dried leaf cilantro
½ tsp (3 ml) ground ginger
1 tsp (5 ml) dry mustard
1 tsp (5 ml) curry powder

Place the corn kernels with ½ cup stock in a blender and process about 2 minutes. Mixture should be somewhat coarse, not smooth.

Place chicken breasts in a bowl, coat them with 2 tbs of the seasoning mixture, and rub in thoroughly with your hands. Preheat a large pot or Dutch oven, preferably cast iron, over high heat. Lightly spray each chicken breast with olive oil spray on one side, and place sprayed-side-down in a single layer in the heated pot. When brown on the first side, turn (no need to spray again) and brown the second side. While the second side is browning, add the chopped onions. Remove the chicken when brown. Cover the brown on the bottom of the pot with the onions and cook about 2 minutes, or until onions are sticking hard. Stir the pureed corn into the onions, add 2 tsp seasoning mix and scrape the bottom of the pot well. (You may need a metal spatula to do this properly.) Cook, scraping from time to time, 6-7 minutes or until corn looks almost like a golden brown roux. Add the remaining seasoning mix, the lemon peel and lemon juice and cook 1 minute. Stir in 2 cups stock, scrape the pot bottom and bring to boil. Add the remaining 3 cups stock, stir well and cook, uncovered, 15 minutes. Add the chicken breasts and red peppers, cover and cook 5 minutes, or until chicken is tender and juicy. Turn off heat and stir in EQUAL.

To serve, place one chicken breast on each plate and add ½ cup of sauce. Top with 2-3 strips of red pepper. Serves 8.

Approximate nutritional analysis per serving:
Calories 208, Protein 31 g, Carbohydrates 13 g, Fat 4 g,
Cholesterol 79 mg, Sodium 547 mg

SAVORY CHICKEN WITH MUSHROOMS AND SPINACH

2 tbs (30 ml) olive or vegetable oil
1 lb (455 g) boneless skinless chicken breast
halves, pounded thin
8 oz (240 g) fresh spinach leaves, rinsed and drained
    or 1 - 10 oz pkg (300 g) frozen leaf spinach,
thawed and squeezed dry
1½ cups (355 ml) sliced fresh or canned mushrooms
1 envelope LIPTON Recipe Secrets Savory Herb
    with Garlic, Golden Herb with Lemon, or
    Golden Onion Soup Mix
1 cup (240 ml) water

In 12-inch skillet, heat 1 tbs oil over medium-high heat and cook chicken until done; remove and keep warm. In same skillet, heat remaining 1 tbs oil over medium heat and cook spinach and mushrooms, stirring frequently, 3 minutes. Stir in savory herb with garlic soup mix blended with water. Bring to a boil over high heat; continue boiling, stirring occasionally, 1 minute or until sauce is thickened. To serve, arrange chicken over vegetable mixture. Serves 4.

Courtesy of The Lipton Kitchens.

TOMATO CHICKEN

4 EMPIRE KOSHER Chicken Breast Cutlets
2 tbs (30 ml) olive oil
½ cup (120 ml) chopped shallots or red onion
3 very ripe tomatoes, diced
½ cup (120 ml) dry kosher vermouth
1 tsp (5 ml) oregano
1 tsp (5 ml) tarragon
1 tsp (5 ml) basil
pepper to taste

In large frying pan, sauté frozen chicken breast cutlets in olive oil, about 2 minutes per side over medium-high heat. Remove chicken. Add the shallots or onions and sauté for 3 minutes. Add tomatoes and vermouth. Cook until tomatoes are soft and tender, about 10 minutes. Return chicken to pan, add herbs and pepper, cover. Simmer until chicken is tender, about 5-7 minutes. If using fresh cutlets, adjust cooking times accordingly. Serves 4.

Approximate nutritional analysis per serving:
Calories 256, Protein 28 g, Carbohydrates 8 g, Fat 10 g,
Cholesterol 73 mg, Sodium 78 mg

LEMON CHICKEN SAUTÉ

¾ cup (180 ml) water
3 tbs (45 ml) lemon juice
3 tbs (45 ml) dry sherry
3 tbs (45 ml) soy sauce
3 tbs (45 ml) sugar
1½ tsp (8 ml) grated lemon peel
1½ tsp (8 ml) cornstarch
1 tsp (5 ml) salt
¼ tsp (1 ml) white pepper
1 - ¾ lb (340 g) whole chicken breast,
    skinned and boned
¾ cup (180 ml) BLUE DIAMOND
    Blanched Slivered Almonds
3 tbs (45 ml) butter
1 tbs (15 ml) vegetable oil
2 carrots, julienned
2 zucchini, julienned
1 clove garlic, chopped finely
1 cup (240 ml) chopped fresh parsley

Combine first 9 ingredients. Slice chicken into 2x½-inch strips. Marinate strips in mixture for 10 minutes; reserve. Sauté almonds in butter and oil until golden. Drain chicken, reserving marinade. Add chicken to pan and cook 1 minute. Add vegetables and garlic and cook 1 minute. Add marinade and cook 2-3 minutes until liquid thickens to a syrupy consistency. Sprinkle with parsley. Serves 4.

Approximate nutritional analysis per serving:
Calories 434, Protein 15 g, Carbohydrates 26 g, Fat 31 g, Cholesterol 54 mg, Sodium 142 mg

CRANBERRY-ORANGE CHICKEN BREASTS

4 skinless, boneless chicken breast halves
2 tsp (10 ml) vegetable oil
¼ cup (60 ml) HEINZ Tomato Ketchup
¼ cup (60 ml) packaged cranberry-orange crushed
    fruit sauce
dash ground cloves
dash pepper

Lightly flatten chicken to uniform thickness. In large skillet, brown chicken in oil. Combine ketchup and remaining ingredients; pour over chicken. Cover; simmer 8-10 minutes, turning and basting once. Serves 4.

Approximate nutritional analysis per serving:
Calories 208, Protein 27 g, Carbohydrates 12 g, Fat 5 g, Cholesterol 73 mg, Sodium 251 mg

LOW-CALORIE CHICKEN STIR-FRY

1 lb (455 g) EMPIRE KOSHER Chicken Breast Cutlets
1 - 8 oz can (240 g) pineapple chunks in juice
1 tbs (15 ml) cornstarch
½ tsp (3 ml) ground ginger *or*
    2 tsp (10 ml) fresh grated ginger
1 clove garlic, crushed
2 tbs (30 ml) parve unsalted margarine
1 onion, cut into thin rings
2 medium carrots, cut into thin diagonal slices
1 medium pepper, cut into squares
2 cups (480 ml) broccoli florets
¼ cup (60 ml) chicken broth

Drain pineapple, reserve ¼ cup of juice. Stir in the cornstarch, ginger and garlic into the juice. Combine chicken and juice mixture and marinate in the refrigerator for 30 minutes.

Melt 1 tbs of margarine in skillet over high heat, add the vegetables and stir fry until tender-crisp. Remove. In the same skillet, melt remaining margarine and add chicken. Stir fry until tender, return vegetables to skillet with the pineapple chunks and broth. Heat through, serve over hot rice. Serves 4.

Approximate nutritional analysis per serving:
Calories 323, Protein 38 g, Carbohydrates 34 g, Fat 5 g, Cholesterol 96 mg, Sodium 109 mg

SOUTHWESTERN TURKEY CUTLETS

1 lb (455 g) boneless turkey cutlets
¾ cup (180 ml) all purpose flour
3 eggs, slightly beaten
½ cup (120 ml) WISH - BONE Italian or
    Robusto Italian Dressing
½ cup (120 ml) chopped green onions
½ cup (120 ml) chicken broth
1 tbs (15 ml) butter or margarine
1 tsp (5 ml) lime juice

Dip turkey in flour, then eggs, then again in flour. In large skillet, heat ¼ cup Italian dressing and cook ½ of the turkey over medium heat, turning once, 5 minutes or until done; drain on paper towels and keep warm. Heat remaining ¼ cup Italian dressing and repeat with remaining turkey.

In skillet, add green onions and cook 1 minute. Stir in remaining ingredients, then bring to a boil to heat through. Serve over turkey. Serve, if desired, with freshly ground black pepper. Serves 4.

Approximate nutritional analysis per serving:
Calories 367, Protein 36 g, Carbohydrates 21 g, Fat 14 g, Cholesterol 238 mg, Sodium 679 mg

Courtesy of The Lipton Kitchens.

Blue Bayou Chicken Breasts

BLUE BAYOU CHICKEN BREASTS

6 PREMIUM YOUNG 'N TENDER Brand
 Boneless Chicken Breasts or Boneless Thighs
 with skin attached
2 medium onions, chopped
6 tbs (90 ml) butter, divided
5 scallions or green onions, chopped
2 cloves garlic, minced
12 oz (360 g) fresh mushrooms, chopped
6 oz (180 g) bleu cheese, crumbled
1 cup (240 ml) fresh bread crumbs
1 lb (455 g) linguine, freshly cooked
1 - 10 oz pkg (300 g) frozen chopped spinach,
 defrosted and squeezed dry
2 tbs (30 ml) minced parsley
parsley sprigs, garnish
sliced tomatoes or tomato roses, garnish

Preheat oven to 350°F (180°C). Rinse and pat dry chicken breasts. Separate skin from flesh of each breast, leaving one side attached; set aside.

Melt 2 tbs of the butter in a large skillet and sauté onions until transparent. Add scallions and garlic and continue to sauté until onions are lightly browned. Using a slotted spoon, transfer the onion mixture to a large bowl. Add the mushrooms to the drippings in the skillet. Sauté, stirring often until most of the liquid evaporates. Add the mushrooms to the onion mixture. Stir in the bleu cheese and bread crumbs, mixing well.

Spoon cheese mixture between the skin and the flesh of each chicken breast. Tuck skin edges under the breast; secure with wooden picks if necessary. Place breasts skin side up in a shallow baking dish. Melt remaining 4 tbs butter and brush on each breast. Bake uncovered for 40-45 minutes, basting occasionally with pan juices. Remove chicken breasts from the baking pan; set aside to keep warm.

Add the freshly cooked linguine to the drippings in the baking dish and toss along with the chopped spinach. Spread linguine on a serving platter and arrange chicken breasts on top. Sprinkle chicken with minced parsley and garnish with the parsley sprigs and tomatoes. Serves 6.

Approximate nutritional analysis per serving:
Calories 753, Protein 49 g, Carbohydrates 83 g, Fat 25 g,
Cholesterol 126 mg, Sodium 752 mg

SAUTÉED CHICKEN BREASTS WITH MICHIGAN DRIED CHERRY SAUCE

2 whole skinless boneless chicken breasts
2 tbs (30 ml) olive oil
salt and pepper

MICHIGAN DRIED CHERRY SAUCE:
½ cup (120 ml) butter softened
⅓ cup (80 ml) MICHIGAN Dried Cherries
¼ cup (60 ml) whipping cream
½ cup (120 ml) dry white wine
⅛ tsp (.5 ml) ground cardamon

Cut chicken breasts into halves. Pound chicken breast to flatten to an even thickness. Heat olive oil in skillet over medium heat. Sauté chicken breasts about 4 minutes per side until done. Lightly season with salt and pepper; keep warm. If unpounded chicken breasts are used, sauté for about 6 minutes per side. Chicken breasts may also be grilled. To serve, place ½ cup Michigan Dried Cherry Sauce on platter, place chicken breasts on top of sauce. Pour remaining ½ cup sauce over chicken breasts. Serves 4.

Michigan Dried Cherry Sauce: Process butter and Michigan Dried Cherries in a food processor with steel attachment until smooth. Chill until firm. Combine whipping cream, white wine and cardamom in a saucepan. Bring to a boil and reduce to ⅓ cup, about 7 minutes. Whisk in Michigan Dried Cherry-butter mixture, 1 tbs at a time. Yield 1 cup.

Approximate nutritional analysis per serving:
Calories 501, Protein 28 g, Carbohydrates 7 g, Fat 39 g, Cholesterol 155 mg, Sodium 74 mg

PARMESAN CHICKEN

½ cup (120 ml) fine dry bread crumbs
3 tbs (45 ml) grated Parmesan cheese
1 tsp (5 ml) dried oregano leaves
2 boneless chicken breasts, split and pounded
2 tbs (30 ml) all purpose flour
¼ cup (60 ml) EGG BEATERS Real Egg Product
1 clove garlic, crushed
3 tbs (45 ml) FLEISCHMANN'S Margarine
1 cup (240 ml) no salt added spaghetti sauce, heated

Mix bread crumbs, Parmesan cheese and oregano; set aside. Coat chicken pieces with flour, dip into the egg product, then coat with bread crumb mixture.

In nonstick skillet, over medium-high heat, cook garlic in margarine for 1 minute. Add chicken and cook until golden brown and chicken is tender, about 5-7 minutes on each side. Serve warm with spaghetti sauce. Serves 4.

Approximate nutritional analysis per serving:
Calories 344, Fat 15 g, Cholesterol 69 mg, Sodium 341 mg

MEDITERRANEAN LEMON CHICKEN

4 boneless skinless chicken breasts, trimmed,
    split and lightly pounded
¼ cup (60 ml) chopped parsley
2 tsp (10 ml) olive oil
1 cup (240 ml) chopped onion
5 cloves garlic, minced
2 tbs (30 ml) flour
2 tbs (30 ml) crushed coriander seeds
    (can crush using a mortar and pestle)
¼ tsp (1 ml) ground coriander
pinch saffron threads, optional
½ cup (120 ml) fresh chopped parsley or
    fresh coriander
1½ cups (355 ml) kosher chicken stock
salt and pepper to taste
juice of ½ lemon
1½ lemons thinly sliced, seeded
½ lb (230 g) small fresh white mushrooms, quartered

Place the chicken pieces, boned side up, on a flat surface, sprinkle with chopped parsley, and roll, starting at one end; skewer with a toothpick to secure. Place rolled breasts seam side down in a deep oven-to-table baking dish. Set aside.

In a medium skillet, heat oil, add garlic and onions, sauté until lightly golden and translucent over low heat. Add flour, sauté 2 more minutes; add crushed coriander, saffron and remaining parsley or fresh coriander. Stir and remove from heat.

Spoon ¼ of the mixture into a small bowl and set aside. Add the chicken broth to remaining mixture in the skillet, stir to incorporate. Pour this over rolled chicken breasts in oven dish. Cover, place in preheated oven to poach. After 25 minutes, uncover, remove toothpicks, stir in mushrooms, lemon slices and reserved onion mixture. Return dish to oven, for 10 more minutes. Serves hot. Serves 8.

Approximate nutritional analysis per serving:
Calories 179, Protein 28 g, Carbohydrates 6 g, Fat 4 g, Cholesterol 73 mg, Sodium 103 mg

Courtesy of the Empire Kosher Poultry Test Kitchens.

APPLE-STUFFED CHICKEN BREASTS

6 PREMIUM YOUNG 'N TENDER Brand
  Boneless, Skinless Chicken Breasts
1½ cups (355 ml) finely diced red or green apples
¼ cup (60 ml) golden seedless raisins
¼ cup (60 ml) pecans or walnuts
3 tbs (45 ml) minced onion
⅔ tsp (3.3 ml) rubbed sage

APPLE GLAZE:
¼ cup (60 ml) orange juice concentrate
¼ cup 960 ml) butter or margarine
⅓ cup 980 ml) apple jelly
¼ cup (60 ml) dry sherry

Place chicken breasts between sheets of waxed paper and pound with rolling pin or meat mallet until ¼-inch thick. Make apple stuffing by combining apples, raisins, nuts, onion and sage. Place a spoonful of stuffing on each chicken breast and roll, tucking in all sides; secure wooden picks if necessary. Bake chicken, uncovered, in a preheated 350°F (180°C) oven for about 45 minutes, brushing frequently with Apple Glaze. Serves 6.

Apple Glaze: Combine all ingredients in a small saucepan and simmer 2-3 minutes. Yields 1 cup.

Approximate nutritional analysis per serving:
Calories 356, Protein 28 g, Carbohydrates 27 g, Fat 14 g,
Cholesterol 94 mg, Sodium 147 mg

Apple-Stuffed Chicken Breasts

CHICKEN CREOLE

1 cup (240 ml) CALIFORNIA ripe olives wedges
1 cup (240 ml) frozen peas
1 tsp (5 ml) brown sugar
¼ tsp (1 ml) cinnamon
½ tsp (3 ml) garlic salt
¼ tsp (1 ml) black pepper
1 tsp (5 ml) hot pepper sauce
2 cups (480 ml) quick-cooking rice
1 tbs (15 ml) olive oil
½ cup (120 ml) diced onion
1 cup (240 ml) diced green pepper
½ tsp (3 ml) turmeric
1¾ cups (415 ml) tomato juice
1 lb (455 g) chicken breast, skinless

Combine first seven ingredients in small bowl. Measure rice into small bowl. Mix olive oil, onion and green pepper in 12x8-inch glass baking dish. Microwave on HIGH for 3 minutes. Add all ingredients except chicken. Stir well. Place chicken breasts on top. Cover with plastic wrap. Microwave on HIGH for 10 minutes. Turn chicken over. Rotate dish ¼ turn. Cover with plastic wrap. Microwave on HIGH until chicken is cooked, about 7-10 more minutes. Serves 6.

Approximate nutritional analysis per serving:
Calories 436, Protein 30 g, Carbohydrates 61 g, Fat 7 g, Cholesterol 64 mg, Sodium 530 mg

CUMIN TURKEY TENDERLOINS

1 cup (240 ml) fresh cilantro leaves
¼ cup (60 ml) chopped onion
2 tbs (30 ml) lemon juice
½ tsp (3 ml) cumin
¼ tsp (1 ml) salt
¼ tsp (1 ml) pepper
1 lb (455 g) NORBEST Turkey Tenderloins,
    cut into 10-inch medallions
2 tsp (10 ml) olive oil

In food processor, fitted with metal blade, process cilantro, onion, lemon juice, cumin, salt and pepper until smooth. In small saucepan, over medium heat, cook mixture 1-2 minutes or until heated throughout. In large non-stick skillet, over medium heat, saute turkey medallions in oil 4-5 minutes per side or until turkey is no longer pink in center. To serve, spoon 2 tbs sauce on each of 4 plates; place medallions over sauce. Serves 4.

Approximate nutritional analysis per serving:
Calories 153, Protein 28 g, Carbohydrates 2 g, Fat 3 g, Cholesterol 70 mg, Sodium 194 mg

CHICKEN CACCIATORE

1¼ oz (38 g) dried mushrooms
1 cup (240 ml) water
3 whole chicken breasts, split in half
½ cup (120 ml) olive oil
3 beef bouillon cubes
1 medium size onion, chopped
4-6 cloves garlic, sliced
2 tsp (10 ml) sweet basil
½ tsp (3 ml) salt
pinch of freshly ground pepper
1 - 6 oz can (180 g) LIBBY'S Tomato Paste
1 bay leaf
1 - 16 oz can (480 g) LIBBY'S Stewed Tomatoes
1 cup (240 ml) rosé wine
2 green peppers, sliced

Preheat oven to 350°F (180°C). Soak mushrooms in water at least 15 minutes. Brown chicken in olive oil, takes about 5 minutes. Remove chicken, leaving oil in pan. Add bouillon cubes, onion and drained mushrooms; save mushroom liquid. Cook and stir onion mixture a few minutes; push to side of pan and add garlic and sauté. Stir in basil, salt, pepper and tomato paste. Then add saved mushroom liquid, bay leaf, stewed tomatoes and wine. Place chicken in shallow baking dish; cover with sauce. Bake covered for 30 minutes. Remove cover; add green pepper rings and continue cooking uncovered for additional 10 minutes or until chicken is tender. Serves 6.

Approximate nutritional analysis per serving:
Calories 339, Protein 31 g, Carbohydrates 21 g, Fat 13 g, Cholesterol 73 mg, Sodium 906 mg

Opposite: Chicken Cacciatore

YAM-STUFFED CHICKEN BREAST

2 cups (480 ml) cooked yams
½ cup (120 ml) finely chopped tasso
½ cup (120 ml) chopped fresh shrimp
½ cup (120 ml) seasoned bread crumbs
1 medium chicken breast
1½ cups (355 ml) chopped onions
1 medium bell pepper
3 cloves garlic
½ tsp (3 ml) salt
¼ tsp (1 ml) red pepper

Stuffing: Mix onions, garlic, bell pepper, salt and pepper into medium saucepan with shrimp and tasso. Smother down approximately 15 minutes or until shrimp and tasso are cooked. Add cooked yams and bread crumbs to mixture and stir well.

Stuff mixture into chicken breast and sew together to hold stuffing in. Bake at 350°F (180°C) oven for 1 hour in greased baking pan. Serve hot. Serves 2.

Approximate nutritional analysis per serving:
Calories 377, Protein 30 g, Carbohydrates 52 g, Fat 5 g,
Cholesterol 118 mg, Sodium   357 mg

Courtesy of Louisiana Sweet Potatoes.

GARLIC LOVER'S CHICKEN

2 EMPIRE KOSHER Fryers, cut into serving
    pieces, skin removed
¼ cup (60 ml) olive oil
40 cloves garlic (3-4 heads), peeled but left whole
4 stalks of celery, cut into 1-inch strips
2 tbs (30 ml) parsley
1 tbs (15 ml) tarragon
¼ tsp (1 ml) nutmeg
salt and pepper
⅓ cup (80 ml) kosher cognac or white wine

Peel garlic - easiest if hit with a knife handle or mallet. Place garlic in 5-qt casserole and cook in microwave on HIGH for 3 minutes. Add olive oil, celery, parsley, tarragon and nutmeg. Stir well. Season chicken with pepper. Place in casserole and turn to coat well. Add cognac or wine and turn chicken in mixture again. Cover with plastic wrap and cook on high for 20 minutes, rearranging pieces after 10 minutes. Reduce setting to medium power, cook another 40 minutes, stirring every 15 minutes. Serve with French bread, dipped in the cooking juices. Serves 8.

Approximate nutritional analysis per serving:
Calories 631, Protein 83 g, Carbohydrates 6 g, Fat 28 g,
Cholesterol 251 mg, Sodium 263 mg

EMPAÑADAS GRANDE

1 tbs (15 ml) olive oil
1 lb (455 g) ground turkey
½ cup (120 ml) chopped onion
2 cloves garlic, minced
1 cup (240 ml) CHI-CHI'S Pico de Gallo
½ cup 9120 ml) cooked garbanzo beans
½ cup (120 ml) chopped tart apple
¼ cup (60 ml) golden raisins
2 tbs (30 ml) slivered almonds
2 tbs (30 ml) chopped fresh mint
2 tbs (30 ml) chopped fresh basil
1 - 16 oz pkg (480 g) hot roll mix
1¼ cups (294 ml) water
2 tbs (30 ml) vegetable oil
1¾ cups (415 ml) shredded sharp cheddar cheese
CHI-CHI'S Salsa, if desired
sour cream, if desired

In large skillet, heat oil over medium-high heat. Cook turkey, onion and garlic until turkey is no longer pink; drain. Stir in Pico de Gallo, beans, apple, raisins, almonds, mint and basil. Cook and stir over low heat until heated through. Stir in 1 cup shredded cheese. Set aside.

Prepare hot roll mix according to package directions except eliminate the egg and 1¼ cups (295 ml) water and 2 tbs (30 ml) oil. After mixing dough and kneading 4 times, gradually knead in ¾ cup of shredded cheese. Cover dough with bowl; let rise 5 minutes. Heat oven to 425°F (220°C). Grease 2 large baking sheets. Divide dough in half. Roll each piece into 10-inch circle. Place dough circles on baking sheets. Spoon half of turkey mixture and half of the remaining cheese onto half of one circle. Repeat with remaining dough circle, turkey mixture and cheese. Brush edge of dough circles with water. Fold dough in half; seal edges with finger, fork or pastry crimper.

Bake on empañada at a time on lower oven rack 12-18 minutes or until golden brown. Keep second empañada in refrigerator; covered with plastic wrap, until ready to bake. Cut into wedges to serve. Serve with salsa and sour cream, if desired. Serves 6.

Approximate nutritional analysis per serving:
Calories 640, Protein 32 g, Carbohydrates 70 g, Fat 26 g,
Cholesterol 80 mg, Sodium 660 mg

Opposite: Empañadas Grande

PARISIAN WALNUT-DIJON CHICKEN

6 PREMIUM YOUNG 'N TENDER Brand
   Boneless, Skinless Split Chicken Breasts
2 tbs (30 ml) butter, divided
1 clove garlic, minced
½ cup (120 ml) minced onion
2 oz (60 g) cream cheese
¾ cup (180 ml) finely chopped walnuts
½ tsp (3 ml) salt
¼ tsp (1 ml) black pepper
¼ cup (60 ml) Dijon mustard, divided
½ cup (120 ml) half and half cream
½ cup (120 ml) seeded, chopped tomatoes
2 tbs (30 ml) chopped parsley
1 cup (240 ml) sliced onions, optional

Place chicken breasts between sheets of plastic wrap or waxed paper and flatten with meat mallet until ¼-inch thick. Melt 1 tbs butter in small sauté pan. Add garlic and minced onion; sauté until tender. Add cream cheese, walnuts, salt and pepper. Sauté about 1 minute until blended. Divide mixture, reserving half for later use.

Preheat broiler. Place about 1 tbs walnut mixture on each breast; fold chicken over filling and place on baking pan. Reserve 1 tbs Dijon mustard. Brush remaining mustard on both sides of chicken. Broil 4-6 inches from heat source for 6-8 minutes per side, or until done.

Prepare sauce by combining remaining half of walnut mixture, reserved tbs Dijon mustard, cream, tomatoes and parsley. Simmer on low heat until slightly thickened, about 2-3 minutes.

If desired, melt remaining tbs butter in small skillet and sauté 1 cup sliced onions about 10 minutes or until golden. Place chicken on platter top with sauce then with sautéed onions as garnish. Serve with rice or pasta. Serves 6.

Approximate nutritional analysis per serving:
Calories 370, Protein 31 g, Carbohydrates 9 g, Fat 24 g, Cholesterol 107 mg, Sodium 451 mg

CHEESE-STUFFED RED PEPPERS

½ lb (230 g) ground turkey breast
1 tsp (5 ml) minced fresh garlic
3 large red peppers
4 cups (960 ml) water
1 - 8 oz pkg (240 g) HEALTHY CHOICE Fat Free
   Natural Fancy Shredded Pizza Cheese
¾ cup (180 ml) cooked brown rice
¾ cup (180 ml) cooked wild rice
⅓ cup (80 ml) sliced green onions
1 - 2 oz jar (60 g) chopped pimiento
⅛ tsp (.5 ml) cayenne pepper

Heat oven to 350°F (180°C). In 10-inch skillet, cook turkey and garlic until browned; drain. Cut red peppers lengthwise in halves. Remove seeds and membranes; rinse. In Dutch oven bring water to a boil; cook pepper halves 2 minutes; drain. In large bowl stir together 1 cup cheese, brown rice, green onions, pimiento, cayenne pepper and turkey mixture. Loosely stuff each pepper half. Arrange in 12x7-inch baking dish sprayed with non-stick cooking spray. Cover and bake at 350°F (180°C), 30 minutes. Uncover; sprinkle with remaining cheese. Continue baking until cheese melts. Serves 6.

Approximate nutritional analysis per serving:
Calories 176, Protein 26 g, Carbohydrates 15 g, Fat 2 g, Cholesterol 33 mg, Sodium 299 mg

STUFFED GRAPE LEAVES

1 lb (455 g) ground chicken or turkey
1 cup (240 ml) finely chopped onion
1 tbs (15 ml) tomato paste, diluted with:
2 tbs (30 ml) kosher chicken broth
½ tsp (3 ml) dried mint
⅛ tsp (.5 ml) allspice
fresh ground pepper
1 cup (240 ml) cooked short grain brown rice
¼ cup (60 ml) chopped Italian parsley
1 cup (240 ml) tomatoes, fresh or canned,
   drained and chopped
juice of 1 lemon
1 cup (240 ml) kosher chicken broth
1 - 8 oz jar (240 g) grape leaves packed in brine

In a large mixing bowl, thoroughly combine ground chicken or turkey, onion, diluted tomato paste, dried mint leaves, allspice, pepper, rice and chopped parsley. Set aside.

Rinse the grape leaves under cold running water, carefully separating each leaf. Place the leaves, shiny side down, a few at a time on a flat work surface. Fill each by placing one heaping tbs of filling on each grape leaf near the base. Starting at the base, fold the bottom of leaf over filling, fold sides over filling to center, then roll tightly toward tip.

In heavy 3-qt saucepan, sprinkle ½ the chopped tomatoes on bottom of pan, then arrange rolls in layers, scattering more tomato. Add a few torn grape leaves between layers. When all the rolls are in the pan, add enough chicken broth to cover rolls and squeeze in lemon juice. Weigh them down using a heavy plate just large enough to cover top of rolls. Bring to a boil, cover saucepan and cook over very low heat for 45 minutes. Add additional broth if needed. Serve hot. Serves 8.

Approximate nutritional analysis per serving:
Calories 176, Protein 15 g, Carbohydrates 10 g, Fat 8 g, Cholesterol 39 mg, Sodium 204 mg

Courtesy of the Empire Kosher Poultry Test Kitchens.

Crab-Stuffed Turkey

CRAB-STUFFED TURKEY

1 lb (455 g) crab meat
1 egg
1 tsp (5 ml) OLD BAY Seasoning
1 tsp (5 ml) mustard
1 tsp (5 ml) Worcestershire sauce
1 tsp (5 ml) mayonnaise
2 slices bread, diced
8 thin turkey breast slices, uncooked

DIPPING MIXTURE:
1 egg
1 tbs (15 ml) milk
2 tsp (10 ml) OLD BAY Seasoning, divided
½ cup (120 ml) bread crumbs
½ cup (120 ml) crushed frosted flakes

Preheat oven to 400°F (205°C). In a large bowl, mix crab meat, egg, OLD BAY Seasoning, mustard, Worcestershire sauce, mayonnaise and bread. Roll the crab mixture into balls and place on turkey slices. Fold or roll turkey around crab mixture. Set aside.

In a bowl, beat egg, milk and 1 tsp OLD BAY Seasoning. In another bowl, blend the bread crumbs, corn flakes and remaining tsp OLD BAY Seasoning. Dip turkey crab rolls in egg and milk mixture, then in bread crumbs-corn flakes mixture. Place balls on lightly greased or nonstick pan. Cook at 400°F (205°C) for 20-30 minutes. Yields 8 turkey crab balls.

Approximate nutritional analysis per turkey crab ball:
Calories 173, Protein 23 g, Carbohydrates 11 g, Fat 3 g,
Cholesterol 135 mg, Sodium 303 mg

Courtesy of McCormick/Schilling Spices.

THE CHARLESTON

1 - 8¾ oz can (265 g) whole kernel corn, drained
¾ cup (180 ml) raisins
½ cup (120 ml) cider vinegar
¼ cup (60 ml) chopped onion
¼ cup (60 ml) chopped red and/or green bell pepper
2 tbs (30 ml) sugar
1 tsp (5 ml) mustard seeds
1 tsp (5 ml) dry mustard
½ tsp (3 ml) salt
⅛ tsp (.5 ml) red pepper flakes
torn greens (spinach, mustard, dandelion)
4 boned chicken breast halves, fried or broiled

To make corn relish, in saucepan combine corn, raisins, vinegar, onion, bell pepper, sugar, mustard seeds, dry mustard, salt and pepper flakes. Bring to a boil; cover and simmer 15 minutes, stirring occasionally. Cool. For each serving, line plate with greens; cut breast diagonally and fan out on greens. Top with relish; serve remaining relish on the side. Serves 4.

Approximate nutritional analysis per serving:
Calories 290, Protein 29 g, Carbohydrates 38 g, Fat 4 g,
Cholesterol 73 mg, Sodium 466 mg

Courtesy of The California Raisin Advisory Board.

The Charleston

MESQUITE CHICKEN BURGERS

1 lb (455 g) PREMIUM YOUNG 'N TENDER
Brand Boneless, Skinless Chicken Thighs, ground
½ lb (120 g) bulk pork sausage, spicy or hot
1¼ tsp (6 ml) mesquite seasoning salt, or to taste

APRICO- PEPPER CHUTNEY:
¾ cup (180 ml) apricot preserves
2 tbs (30 ml) balsamic vinegar
1 tbs (15 ml) Dijon mustard
1 tsp (5 ml) grated fresh ginger
or ¼ tsp (1 ml) ground ginger
1 tsp (5 ml) minced garlic
1 tsp (5 ml) fresh thyme or ¼ tsp (1 ml) dried thyme
¼ cup (60 ml) finely chopped red bell pepper
¼ cup (60 ml) finely chopped sweet onions
2 tsp (10 ml) finely chopped jalapeño peppers
4 Kaiser or onion rolls, split
Dijon mustard

Combine chicken, sausage and mesquite salt. Shape into four patties, chill at least 20 minutes.

Chutney: combine preserves, vinegar, mustard, ginger and garlic in a small saucepan. Heat to simmering and cook about 3 minutes. Remove from heat and add thyme, red pepper, onion and jalapeño pepper. Set aside.

Grill chicken burgers over medium coals until juices run clear, turning as needed. Lightly toast rolls on grill and spread with mustard. Serve chicken burgers with chutney. Serves 4.

Note: You may have butcher grind thighs for you or use food processor with metal blade attachment. Burgers may be cooked in oven broiler or on stove top if preferred.

Approximate nutritional analysis per serving:
Calories 760, Protein 55 g, Carbohydrates 78 g, Fat 25 g, Cholesterol 138 mg, Sodium 171 mg

MICROWAVE TURKEY MEAT BALLS

1 lb (455 g) EMPIRE KOSHER Ground Turkey
¼ tsp (1 ml) minced garlic
½ tsp (3 ml) minced onion
2 tbs (30 ml) dry kosher parve bread crumbs
2 tbs (30 ml) parve spaghetti
salt and pepper, if desired

Mix all ingredients together, shape into meat balls a little larger than a golf ball. Cook in microwave on HIGH for 3 minutes. Spoon additional spaghetti sauce over top, cook another 4 minutes on HIGH. Season with salt and pepper if desired.

Approximate nutritional analysis per serving:
Calories 276, Protein 28 g, Carbohydrates 3 g, Fat 16 g, Cholesterol 78 mg, Sodium 119 mg

MEDITERRANEAN TURKEY AND EGGPLANT STIR-FRY

1 lb (455 g) EMPIRE KOSHER Ground Turkey
or Ground Chicken
1 cup (240 ml) onion thinly sliced
2 cloves garlic, minced
1½ tsp (8 ml) oregano or 3 tsp (15 ml) fresh oregano
pepper and salt to taste
4 cups (960 ml) eggplant or zucchini, in cubes
1 cup (240 ml) green pepper, cut into ½-inch strips
1 tbs (165 ml) olive oil
1 tsp (5 ml) sugar
1 medium ripe tomato, peeled, in wedges

In large skillet, sauté ground turkey or chicken over medium-high heat with onion, garlic, oregano, mint and pepper 5-6 minutes or until meat is no longer pink. Remove turkey mixture from skillet and set aside. In the same skillet, over medium-high heat, sauté eggplant and green pepper in oil 4 minutes or until vegetables are crisp-tender. Combine turkey mixture with vegetable mixture and add tomato and sugar. Cook over medium-high heat, about 5 minutes, or until heated through. Serves 4.

Approximate nutritional analysis per serving:
Calories 348, Protein 30 g, Carbohydrates 14 g, Fat 19 g, Cholesterol 78 mg, Sodium 103 mg

SWEDISH MEATBALLS

1 lb (455 g) EMPIRE KOSHER Ground Turkey
1 lb (455 g) EMPIRE KOSHER Ground Chicken
2 eggs
½ cup (120 ml) seltzer or soda water
½ cup (120 ml) kosher parve bread crumbs
2 onions, grated
salt and pepper to taste

Soak the bread crumbs in seltzer or soda water for 15 minutes. Leftover mashed potatoes may be used rather than bread crumbs. Mix with ground meats, add the grated onion and the eggs. Mix briefly. Do not overmix or meat balls will be tough. Wet hands, roll meatballs between the palms of your hand about the size of large walnuts. Place on lightly oiled plate. Melt margarine in heavy skillet, add a little vegetable oil. Over medium heat, add meatballs to pan, shaking constantly so that meatballs turn and brown on all sides while keeping their shape. Do not overcrowd. Serve with mashed potatoes, green beans and cranberry sauce, like the Swedes do. Serves 4.

Approximate nutritional analysis per serving:
Calories 607, Protein 67 g, Carbohydrates 20 g, Fat 27 g, Cholesterol 285 mg, Sodium 318 mg

GINGERED TURKEY BURGERS

vegetable cooking spray
2 lbs (910 g) NORBEST Ground Turkey
2 tbs (30 ml) minced ginger
2 tsp (10 ml) minced garlic
1 tsp (5 ml) sage
1 tsp (5 ml) thyme
1 tsp (5 ml) salt
½ tsp (3 ml) pepper
8 hamburger buns, toasted
Chinese hot mustard

Spray cold grill rack with vegetable cooking spray. Preheat charcoal grill for direct-heat cooking.

In medium bowl, combine turkey, ginger, sage, thyme, salt and pepper. Evenly divide turkey mixture into 8 burgers, approximately 3½ inches in diameter. Grill turkey burgers 5-6 minutes per side or until 160°F (71°C) is reached on meat thermometer and meat is no longer pink in center. To serve, spread bottom half of each bun with Chinese mustard. Place burger on bun and top with other half of buns. Serves 8.

Approximate nutritional analysis per serving:
Calories 321, Protein 24 g, Carbohydrates 23 g, Fat 14 g, Cholesterol 57 mg, Sodium 584 mg

OLIVE TURKEY TAMALE BAKE

4 ears corn, with husks
1 lb (455 g) ground turkey
2 tbs (30 ml) vegetable oil
1 cup (240 ml) CALIFORNIA ripe olive wedges
½ cup (120 ml) chopped green onion,
    half green, half bulbs
1 tbs (15 ml) chili powder
1½ cups (355 ml) grated pepper jack or Monterey
    Jack cheese

Husk corn, tearing husk as little as possible. Save outer husks, cleaning off the silk. Drop the corn and saved husks into large pot of boiling water. Return to boil and simmer 5 minutes. Drain through colander. Meanwhile, sauté turkey in oil in skillet over high heat until browned. Using large knife, quickly slice corn kernels from cobs and add olives, onion and chili powder to turkey. Sauté 2 minutes longer. Remove from heat and stir in cheese. Line bottom 1½-qt casserole with half the softened husks. Turn turkey filling over husks and make a layer of remaining husks on top, tucking in at edges. Cover and bake at 425°F (220°C) for 20 minutes or until hot in center. Serves 4.

Approximate nutritional analysis per serving:
Calories 540, Protein 40 g, Carbohydrates 11 g, Fat 38 g, Cholesterol 116 mg, Sodium 511 mg

SOUTH AMERICAN CHICKEN AND POTATO PLATTER

POTATOES AND CHICKEN:
6 cups (1.5 L) chicken broth, fresh or canned
2 lbs (910 g) potatoes, cut into 1-inch chunks
2 lemons, halved
3 fresh or canned jalapeño peppers,
    quartered lengthwise
1 tbs (15 ml) ground cumin
½ lb (230 g) boned and skinned chicken
    breast halves
1 bunch cilantro

SALSA ACCOMPANIMENTS:
2 cups (480 ml) diced tomatoes
¼ cup (60 ml) fresh or canned diced
    mild green chilies
1 tbs (15 ml) chopped cilantro
1 tbs (15 ml) white wine vinegar
¼ tsp (1 ml) salt
¼ tsp (1 ml) pepper
3 hard-cooked eggs, quartered
1 red bell pepper, julienned
1 cup (240 ml) pimiento-stuffed green olives
6 whole green onions

OPTIONAL ACCOMPANIMENTS:
crumbled feta cheese
raisins
peanuts
sour cream and/or
tortilla chips

Potatoes and Chicken: In large saucepan or Dutch oven combine broth, potatoes, lemons, jalapeño peppers and cumin. Bring to a boil, reduce heat and simmer 8 minutes. Add chicken; simmer about 7 minutes longer until potatoes are just tender and chicken is cooked. Remove from heat; add cilantro to saucepan. Cool potatoes and chicken in broth 30 minutes. Meanwhile, make salsa.

Salsa: In small bowl combine tomatoes, chilies, cilantro, vinegar, salt and pepper. Drain potatoes and chicken, reserving 1 cup broth. To assemble, mound potatoes in center of large platter. Shred chicken and arrange on platter with remaining ingredients. Pour ½ cup broth over potatoes; serve remaining ½ cup broth in sauce boat. Serve immediately with salsa in bowl on the side. Serves 6.

Approximate nutritional analysis per serving:
Calories 310, Protein 21 g, Carbohydrates 41 g, Fat 8 g, Cholesterol 125 mg, Sodium 770 mg

Courtesy of The Potato Board.

Opposite: South American Chicken and Potato Platter

Camp Tacos

CAMP TACOS

8 taco shells
1 lb (455 g) ground turkey or lean ground beef
1 - 15 oz can (450 g) pinto beans, drained
4 oz (120 g) "mild Mexican" pasteurized
    process cheese spread*
½ cup (120 ml) chopped CALIFORNIA ripe olives
shredded lettuce
chopped tomato
extra chopped olives for topping

* The cheese spread is usually found on grocery shelf, not
under refrigeration.

To warm taco shells, place them on metal camp plate, cover
with foil and set plate on top of pot of water that has been
brought to a boil then removed from heat, or warm in oven.
Sauté ground turkey in well-oiled skillet over high heat until
cooked. Stir in pinto beans, the cheese spread and chopped
olives. Heat, stirring until hot through. To serve, spoon turkey
mixture into taco shells. Add lettuce, tomato and extra olives
to shells. Serves 4.

Approximate nutritional analysis per serving:
Calories 604, Protein 43 g, Carbohydrates 40 g, Fat 32 g,
Cholesterol 105 mg, Sodium   152 mg

TURKEY BARBECUE MEAT LOAF

1 lb (455 g) NORBEST Ground Turkey
1 cup (240 ml) chopped onion
½ cup (120 ml) seasoned bread crumbs
½ cup (120 ml) grated carrots
½ cup (120 ml) bottled barbecue sauce, divided
2 tsp (10 ml) Worcestershire sauce
1 tsp (5 ml) minced garlic
¾ tsp (4 ml) pepper
vegetable cooking spray

In medium bowl combine turkey, onion, bread crumbs, carrots, ¼ cup barbecue sauce, Worcestershire, garlic and pepper. In 9-inch pie plate, sprayed with vegetable cooking spray, shape meat mixture into round loaf. Drizzle top of loaf with remaining barbecue sauce. Bake at 350°F (180°C) 35-40 minutes or until meat thermometer reaches 160°F (71°C) when inserted in center of meat loaf, juices run clear and meat is no longer pink. Serves 6.

Approximate nutritional analysis per serving:
Calories 178, Protein 16 g, Carbohydrates 14 g, Fat 7 g,
Cholesterol 55 mg, Sodium 528 mg

STUFFED CABBAGE

1 large head cabbage
1 can tomatoes
2 chopped onions
1 lb (455 g) EMPIRE KOSHER Ground Turkey
  or Ground Chicken
2 chicken bouillon cubes
1 grated onion
1 tsp (5 ml) salt
½ cup (120 ml) rice, partially cooked and drained
1 beaten egg
4 tbs (60 ml) lemon juice
3 tbs (45 ml) brown sugar

Pour boiling water over the cabbage and cook for 10 minutes. Drain well. Carefully separate the leaves, so that you have 12 large leaves.

Cook the tomatoes, chopped onions and chicken broth cubes over medium heat in a heavy saucepan while you prepare the stuffed cabbage. Mix ground poultry with grated onion, salt, pepper, rice and the egg. Mix until well blended. Place a heaping tbs of the mixture on each cabbage leaf, fold over the sides and carefully roll up. Place seam side down in the tomato mixture, cover and cook over low heat for an hour. Add the lemon juice and sugar, cook uncovered for another 30 minutes. Serves 4.

Approximate nutritional analysis per serving:
Calories 647, Protein 39 g, Carbohydrates 83 g, Fat 19 g,
Cholesterol 132 mg, Sodium 448 mg

CAJUN TURKEY BURGERS

vegetable cooking spray
2 lbs (910 g) NORBEST Ground Turkey
2 tbs (30 ml) Worcestershire sauce
4 tsp (60 ml) Creole seasoning, divided
1 - 14½ oz can (435 g) stewed tomatoes, drained
1 tsp (5 ml) minced garlic
8 hamburger buns, toasted

Spray cold grill rack with vegetable cooking spray. Preheat charcoal grill for direct-heat cooking.

In medium bowl combine turkey, Worcestershire sauce and 2 tsp Creole seasoning. Evenly divide turkey mixture into 8 burgers, approximately 3½ inches in diameter. Grill turkey burgers 5-6 minutes per side or until 160°F (71°C) is reached on meat thermometer and meat is no longer pink in center.

In small saucepan, over medium-high heat, combine tomatoes, remaining Creole seasoning and garlic. Cook 5 minutes or until most of liquid is evaporated. To serve, place burger on bottom half of each bun, drizzle 3 tbs sauce over burger and top with other half of buns. Serves 8.

Approximate nutritional analysis per serving:
Calories 337, Protein 25 g, Carbohydrates 27 g, Fat 14 g,
Cholesterol 57 mg, Sodium 782 mg

BURRITO TURKEY BURGERS

vegetable cooking spray
2 lbs (910 g) NORBEST Ground Turkey
1 - 4 oz can (120 g) chopped green chilies, drained
1 cup (240 ml) chopped onions
1 - 1¼ oz pkg (47 g) taco seasoning mix
8 medium flour tortillas
1 - 16 oz can (480 g) nofat refried beans
shredded lettuce
½ cup (120 ml) grated nofat cheddar cheese
salsa, optional

Spray cold grill rack with vegetable cooking spray. Preheat charcoal grill for direct-heat cooking.

In medium bowl combine turkey, chilies, onion and seasoning mix. Evenly divide turkey mixture into 8 - 9x2-inch rectangular-shaped burgers. Grill burgers 3-4 minutes, turn and continue cooking 2-3 minutes or until 160°F (71°C) is reached on meat thermometer and meat is no longer pink in center. Remove and keep warm. Heat tortillas according to pkg directions. Spread each tortillas with ¼ cup refried beans and sprinkle with lettuce. Place burgers in center of each tortilla and sprinkle 1 tbs of cheese over top. Fold sides of tortilla over burger to create a burrito. Serve with salsa. Serves 8.

Approximate nutritional analysis per serving:
Calories 387, Protein 29 g, Carbohydrates 33 g, Fat 14 g,
Cholesterol 58 mg, Sodium 946 mg

CHICKEN CACCIATORE WITH TORTELLONI

2 tbs (30 ml) olive oil, divided
8 oz (240 g) boneless skinless chicken breast
halves, cut into ¼-inch strips
¾ cup (180 ml) thinly sliced onion
1 cup (240 ml) sliced green or yellow bell pepper
⅔ cup (160 ml) sliced fresh mushrooms
1 - 12 oz container (360 ml) CONTADINA
   Refrigerated Marinara or Plum Tomato Sauce
½ cup (120 ml) dry vermouth or chicken broth
½ cup (120 ml) sliced ripe olives, drained
2 tsp (10 ml) chopped fresh rosemary
½ tsp (3 ml) salt
¼ tsp (1 ml) ground black pepper
1 - 9 oz pkg (270 g) CONTADINA Refrigerated
   Cheese and Basil Tortelloni, cooked,
   drained and kept warm
grated Parmesan or Romano cheese, optional

In medium skillet, heat 1 tbs olive oil; sauté chicken over medium-high heat until lightly browned. Remove. Heat remaining oil in skillet. Sauté onion, bell pepper and mushrooms for 3 minutes. Stir in cooked chicken, sauce, vermouth, olives, rosemary, salt and pepper. Simmer for 5 minutes. Toss mixture with pasta; sprinkle with cheese. Serves 4.

Approximate nutritional analysis per serving:
Calories 472, Protein 29 g, Carbohydrates 55 g, Fat 13 g,
Cholesterol 53 mg, Sodium 527 mg

GREEK MARINATED CHICKEN

4 PREMIUM YOUNG 'N TENDER Brand
   Boneless, Skinless Split Chicken Breasts
⅔ cup (160 ml) white wine
⅓ cup (80 ml) water
¼ cup (60 ml) olive oil
3 tbs (45 ml) red wine vinegar
3 tbs (45 ml) capers
1 tbs (15 ml) lemon juice
1 tsp (5 ml) dried oregano
1 tsp (5 ml) black pepper
1 clove garlic, crushed
feta cheese or Chevret cheese
black olives

Place chicken breasts in a sauce pan with white wine and water. Simmer about 15 minutes or until chicken is done. Remove chicken; set aside to cool, then cut into 1-inch strips.

Combine oil, vinegar, capers, lemon juice, oregano, pepper and garlic to make a marinade. Add chicken strips, cover and refrigerate at least 1 hour, preferably longer.

To serve, drain chicken from marinade and arrange on platter or four individual plates with cheese and black olives. Serve with a crusty, hot bread. May also be served as an appetizer. Serves 4.

Approximate nutritional analysis per serving w/o cheese and olives:
Calories 290, Protein 27 g, Carbohydrates 1 g, Fat 17 g,
Cholesterol 73 mg, Sodium 66 mg

PINEAPPLE FRUIT SCHOONER WITH GINGER CHICKEN

6 whole pineapples, cut in half
½ cup (120 ml) lemon juice
1½ cups (355 ml) water
2 cups (480 ml) pineapple juice
1 cup (240 ml) sugar
2 lbs (910 g) papaya wedges
½ lb (230 g) medium diced honeydew melon
½ lb (230 g) medium diced cantaloupe
½ lb (230 g) orange sections
½ lb (230 g) black red grapes

GINGER CHICKEN SALAD:
6 lbs (2.7 kg) cooked chicken breast,
   skin removed, cut into large cubes
6 oz (180 g) fresh ginger, diced small
6 oz (180 g) Chinese parsley, chopped
1½ oz (45 g) fresh garlic, chopped
3 tbs (45 ml) lime juice
1 cup (240 ml) peanut oil
salt and pepper to taste
4 tbs (60 ml) chicken base

Scoop out the fruit from pineapple halves, leaving a rim of fruit ½ inch from the skin. Cut scooped out fruit into medium-size cubes.

In large mixing bowl, combine lemon juice, water, pineapple juice and sugar. Mix well until sugar dissolves, then add remaining fruit ingredients. Marinate for about 10-15 minutes. Fill pineapple halves with marinated fruits and 1 scoop of warm ginger chicken. Garnish with papaya wedges and mint. Serves 12.

GINGER CHICKEN SALAD: Place all ingredients in a large mixing bowl. Mix well. Correct seasoning to taste. Marinate, refrigerated, 1-6 hours. Broil or grill.

Approximate nutritional analysis per serving:
Calories 727, Protein 73 g, Carbohydrates 80 g, Fat 14 g,
Cholesterol 193 mg, Sodium 180 mg

Courtesy of The Papaya Administrative Committee and Pineapple Growers Association of Hawaii.

CLASSIC CHICKEN AND MUSHROOM STEW

3 tbs (45 ml) butter or margarine
3½ lbs (1.6 kg) boneless skinless chicken breast
   cut into 1-inch cubes
1 cup (240 ml) coarsely chopped onions
1 lb (455 g) mushrooms, cleaned and quartered
¾ cup (180 ml) flour
3 cups (720 ml) water
2 tbs (30 ml) GOYA Sofrito
2 packets GOYA Chicken Bouillon
1 tsp (5 ml) GOYA Adobo
1 packet Sazón GOYA sin Achiote
1 can GOYA Pink Beans, rinsed and drained

In large skillet, melt butter on medium flame and sauté
chicken. If necessary, sauté in batches. Add onions and sauté
5 minutes. Add mushrooms and sauté 5 minutes more.
Sprinkle flour over mixture and cook, tossing well, for
3 minutes. Add remaining ingredients, except beans, cover
and bring to boil. Lower flame and simmer 20 minutes, stirring
occasionally, until gravy becomes thick. Add beans and
simmer, uncovered, 10 minutes. Serves 8.

Approximate nutritional analysis per serving:
Calories 486, Protein 68 g, Carbohydrates 24 g, Fat 12 g,
Cholesterol 181 mg, Sodium 714 mg

CHILAQUILES

1 - 16 oz jar (480 g) CHI-CHI'S Salsa
1 cup (240 ml) CHI-CHI'S Salsa Verde
¼ cup (60 ml) chopped fresh cilantro
10 small corn tortillas, cut into 1x2-inch pieces
1 - 15 oz can (450 g) CHI-CHI'S Refried Beans
1 cup (240 ml) shredded cooked chicken
2 cups (480 ml) shredded Co-Jack cheese
additional salsa or salsa verde, if desired

Heat oven to 350°F (180°C). Grease 9x9x2-inch baking dish.
In medium bowl, combine salsa, salsa verde and cilantro. Mix
well. Spread ½ cup salsa mixture in bottom of greased baking
dish. Layer half of tortillas, beans, chicken, remaining salsa
mixture and cheese in baking dish. Repeat layering. Bake,
uncovered, 30 minutes or until cheese is melted and casserole is
bubbling. Serve with additional salsa or salsa verde, if desired.
Serves 8.

Approximate nutritional analysis per serving:
Calories 340, Protein 18 g, Carbohydrates 35 g, Fat 15 g,
Cholesterol 40 mg, Sodium 990 mg

Classic Chicken and Mushroom Stew

SAVORY CHICKEN STEW OVER RICE

3-3½ lbs (1.4-1.6 kg) PREMIUM YOUNG 'N
    TENDER Brand Chicken Breasts, boned,
    skinned and cut into 2-inch pieces
2-3 tbs (30-45 ml) vegetable oil
1 large red onion, chopped
6-8 cloves garlic, crushed
1 cup (240 ml) chopped green pepper
1½ tsp (8 ml) curry powder, or to taste
2 - 28 oz cans (1.7 kg) whole peeled tomatoes,
    cut into pieces, undrained
1½ tbs (25 ml) Kitchen Bouquet or other
    gravy browning liquid
½ tsp (3 ml) salt
½ tsp (3 ml) pepper
¼ tsp (1 ml) mace
3 tbs (45 ml) chopped parsley
⅓ cup (80 ml) raisins or currants
⅓ cup (80 ml) slivered almonds

In a large heavy pan, brown chicken pieces in hot vegetable oil. Remove chicken and set aside. Add onion, garlic, green pepper and curry powder to drippings in pan. Sauté over low heat until onions are tender. Return chicken to pan. Add remaining ingredients except almonds. Simmer 30 minutes or until chicken is tender. Sprinkle with almonds and serve over steamed rice. Serves 8.

Approximate nutritional analysis per serving:
Calories 397, Protein 56 g, Carbohydrates 14 g, Fat 13 g,
Cholesterol 145 mg, Sodium 584 mg

TURKEY IN MUSHROOM SAUCE

2 cups (480 ml) sliced mushrooms
¼ cup 960 ml) margarine
1½ lbs (685 g) boneless turkey cutlets
1 cup (240 ml) COLLEGE INN Chicken Broth
¼ tsp (1 ml) ground black pepper
¼ tsp (1 ml) poultry seasoning
1 tbs (15 ml) all purpose flour
¼ cup (60 ml) dairy sour cream
3 cups (720 ml) hot-cooked rice
sliced scallions, for garnish

In large skillet, over medium heat, cook mushrooms in 2 tbs margarine just until tender; remove from pan. In same skillet, in remaining margarine, brown turkey cutlets on both sides. Return mushrooms to pan with ¾ cup broth, pepper and poultry seasoning. Heat to boil; reduce heat to low. Cover; simmer 15-20 minutes or until turkey is done. Remove turkey from skillet; keep warm.

Blend flour into remaining broth; slowly stir mushroom mixture in pan. Cook over medium-high heat, stirring constantly until mixture thickens and begins to boil. Remove from heat; stir in sour cream. Arrange turkey on rice; spoon sauce over turkey. Top with scallions if desired; serve immediately. Serves 6.

Approximate nutritional analysis per serving:
Calories 354, Fat 11 g, Cholesterol 70 mg, Sodium 369 mg

TURKEY DRUMS AND SAUERKRAUT

2 tbs (30 ml) vegetable oil
1 medium onion, sliced thin
1 medium green apple, cored, sliced thin
2 small carrots, divided
1 minced garlic clove
2 lbs (910 g) sauerkraut, rinsed, squeezed dry
¾ cup (180 ml) dry kosher white wine
¾ cup (180 ml) kosher chicken broth
2 tbs (30 ml) gin
½ tsp (3 ml) salt
¼ tsp (1 ml) pepper
2 turkey drumsticks
1 lb (455 g) EMPIRE KOSHER Turkey Kielbasa,
    cut into 2-inch pieces

In a large 4-qt pot heat the oil, add onion, apple, carrots and garlic. Cook until onion is soft, about 3 minutes. Add half the sauerkraut, place drums and kielbasa on top of sauerkraut. Top with remaining sauerkraut. Pour in wine, broth, gin, season with salt and pepper. Cover, simmer until drumsticks are tender, about 1½ hours. Serves 4.

Approximate nutritional analysis per serving:
Calories 711, Protein 71 g, Carbohydrates 24 g, Fat 32 g,
Cholesterol 205 mg, Sodium 210   mg

TURKEY MEAT LOAF

1 lb (455 g) EMPIRE KOSHER Ground Turkey
5 tbs (75 ml) jellied cranberry sauce
⅓ cup (80 ml) instant oatmeal
1 tbs (15 ml) minced dry onion
parsley and dill to taste

Mix all ingredients together. Bake at 350°F (180°C) for about 45 minutes. May be made in the microwave: Cook about 15-18 minutes on HIGH, turning at least once. Serves 4.

Approximate nutritional analysis per serving:
Calories 316, Protein 29 g, Carbohydrates 13 g, Fat 16 g,
Cholesterol 78 mg, Sodium 101 mg

TURKEY NOODLE CASSEROLE

2 lbs (910 g) EMPIRE KOSHER Turkey Thighs
2 tbs (30 ml) oil
3 large stalks celery, diced
4 green onions, chopped
1 medium onion, chopped
2 cloves garlic, minced
parsley
1 can pitted black olives, drained and cut up, optional
¼ cup (60 ml) mushrooms, sliced
1 small can tomato paste
1 lb (455 g) medium noodles
1 tbs (15 ml) lemon juice
½ cup (120 ml) water
½ cup (120 ml) white kosher wine

Boil the turkey thighs in water with pepper to make about 1 qt of stock, about 1½ hours, or until very tender. Remove thighs from pot, reserve stock for noodles. Let cool, take meat off bones, set aside. Sauté celery , onions, garlic and mushrooms until tender. Add parsley, olives, pepper to taste.

Boil noodles in the reserved turkey stock until just done. Drain. In a large pot, mix the turkey thigh meat, tomato paste, olives, water, wine, and the sautéed vegetables with the noodles. Cook covered for about 45 minutes over low heat, stirring once or twice. Freezes well. Serves 6.

Approximate nutritional analysis per serving:
Calories 660, Protein 54 g, Carbohydrates 64 g, Fat 18 g, Cholesterol 129 mg, Sodium 302 mg

TURKEY WINGS WITH ARTICHOKES

2 lbs (910 g) EMPIRE KOSHER Turkey Wings,
**   cut at joint, tip discarded**
1 tsp (5 ml) olive oil
¾ cup (180 ml) kosher white wine
1 tsp (5 ml) rosemary, crushed
1 tsp (5 ml) leaf sage, crushed
6 whole black peppercorns
1 can artichoke hearts, drained
2 onions, sliced

In heavy Dutch oven, sauté wings over medium heat in oil. Remove. Drain. Add wine, herbs, artichokes and onions to pan, bring to a boil. Reduce heat, return wings to pan and simmer about 1 hour, covered until done. Serve with rice, couscous or barley pilaf as main course. May also be refrigerated and served cold for an appetizer. Serves 4.

Approximate nutritional analysis per serving:
Calories 540, Protein 68 g, Carbohydrates 17 g, Fat 18 g, Cholesterol 193 mg, Sodium 221 mg

CHICKEN SANTA FE

2-2½ lbs (910-1138 g) broiler-fryer pieces
1 tbs (15 ml) vegetable oil
1 cup (240 ml) quartered fresh mushrooms
1 medium onion, sliced
2 tbs (30 ml) all purpose flour
1 tbs (15 ml) chili powder
¼ tsp (1 ml) salt
¼ tsp (1 ml) pepper
1 cup (240 ml) water
½ cup (120 ml) HEINZ Tomato Ketchup
hot cooked rice

In large skillet, brown chicken in oil; remove. In same skillet, sauté mushrooms and onion until onion is tender. Stir in flour, chili powder, salt and pepper. Slowly stir in water and ketchup. Return to skillet; baste with sauce. Cover; simmer 30-40 minutes or until chicken is tender, basting occasionally. Skim excess fat from sauce. Serve chicken and sauce with rice. Serves 4.

Approximate nutritional analysis per serving without rice:
Calories 417, Protein 36 g, Carbohydrates 17 g, Fat 23 g, Cholesterol 126 mg, Sodium 797 mg

Approximate nutritional analysis per serving with ⅔ cup rice:
Calories 537 , Protein 38 g, Carbohydrates 45 g, Fat 23 g, Cholesterol 126 mg, Sodium 797 mg

CRANBERRY CHICKEN

1 - 3-4 lb (1.4-1.8 kg) EMPIRE KOSHER Chicken
1 cup (240 ml) flour
salt and pepper to taste
dash cayenne pepper
1 cup (240 ml) oil for frying
1 can whole cranberry sauce
¼ cup (60 ml) chopped onion
¾ cup (180 ml) orange juice
¼ tsp (1 ml) ground cinnamon
¼ tsp (1 ml) ginger

Cut the chicken into serving pieces, rinse in cold water and pat dry. Mix the flour with salt and peppers and dust each piece. Pan-fry in the oil until brown, turning once. Remove chicken, drain all but 1 tbs of the fat. Mix all remaining ingredients in a small saucepan and bring to a boil. Return chicken to pan, pour the sauce over the chicken, cover and simmer for 45 minutes or until the chicken is very tender. Serves 4.

Approximate nutritional analysis per serving:
Calories 773, Protein 100 g, Carbohydrates 15 g, Fat 32 g, Cholesterol 301 mg, Sodium 295 mg

NORTH CAROLINA STEWED CHICKEN

3 tbs (45 ml) parve margarine
1 - 3-4 lb (1.4-1.8 kg) EMPIRE KOSHER
    Chicken, cut up
2 cups (480 ml) water
2½ cups (590 ml) canned or fresh tomatoes,
chopped, with juice
2 onions, sliced
½ tsp (3 ml) sugar
½ cup (120 ml) kosher dry white wine
1 - 10 oz pkg (300 g) frozen lima beans
1 - 10 oz pkg (300 g) frozen corn
1 - 10 oz pkg (300 g) frozen sliced okra
1 cup (240 ml) toasted parve bread crumbs
black pepper
½ tsp (3 ml) hot sauce
1 tsp (5 ml) Liquid Smoke
    or 1 tsp (5 ml) hickory-flavored salt

Melt margarine in a large heavy pot. Fry chicken until lightly brown; drain off fat. Add water, tomatoes, onions, sugar and wine. Cover and bring to a boil. Simmer for 1 hour or until chicken is very tender. Remove chicken from the pot, cool. Add remaining ingredients to the pot and bring to a boil, simmer for 30 minutes, uncovered. Meanwhile, debone chicken into small pieces. Add the chicken and cook another 10 minutes. Serve over hot-cooked rice or riced potatoes. Serves 8.

Approximate nutritional analysis per serving:
Calories 483, Protein 54 g, Carbohydrates 30 g, Fat 15 g,
Cholesterol 151 mg, Sodium 529 mg

QUICK CHICKEN CACCIATORE

1 - 2½-3½ lb (1.1-1.6 kg) EMPIRE KOSHER
    Fryer Chicken
1 pkg kosher parve onion soup mix
1 can stewed tomatoes
¼ lb (60 ml) fresh mushrooms, sliced
½ tsp (3 ml) rosemary
½ tsp (3 ml) thyme

Cut the fryer in serving pieces; remove skin. Place in large microsafe casserole, add remaining ingredients. Cover with plastic wrap or wax paper. Cook on HIGH 20-25 minutes, turning dish at least once. Serve with noodles or brown rice. Serves 6.

   Conventional oven: Preheat oven to 325°F (165°C). Proceed as above, but do not cover. Bake for 1 hour or until juices run clear and chicken is tender.

Approximate nutritional analysis per serving:
Calories 485, Protein 67 g, Carbohydrates 5 g, Fat 17 g,
Cholesterol 201 mg, Sodium 665 mg

GREEN CHILI AND CHICKEN STEW

1 cup (240 ml) chopped onion
1 tsp (5 ml) minced fresh garlic
2 tbs (30 ml) vegetable oil
1 - 16 oz jar (480 ml) CHI-CHI'S Salsa Verde
1 - 10½ oz can (315 ml) CHI-CHI'S Salsa
1 cup (240 ml) water
1 cup (240 ml) diced carrots
1 - 4¼ oz can (128 g) CHI-CHI'S
    Diced Green Chilies, drained
1 tsp (5 ml) dried oregano leaves
½ tsp (3 ml) coarsely ground pepper
3 cups (720 ml) shredded cooked chicken
1 - 15 oz can (450 g) pinto beans, drained

In Dutch oven, cook onion and garlic in oil until onion is tender. Add remaining ingredients except chicken and beans. Bring to a boil. Reduce heat to low. Cover; simmer 15 minutes, stirring occasionally. Add chicken and beans. Cook 15 minutes, stirring occasionally. Serves 9.

Approximate nutritional analysis per serving:
Calories 200, Protein 18 g, Carbohydrates 17 g, Fat 7 g,
Cholesterol 40 mg, Sodium 430 mg

ARROZ CON POLLO
Chicken with Yellow Rice

2 tbs (30 ml) GOYA Olive Oil
4-6 cut-up chicken pieces
2 cups (480 ml) water
1 pkg GOYA Yellow Rice
½ cup (120 ml) frozen peas
1 whole GOYA Pimiento, sliced

Heat olive oil in a skillet and sauté chicken pieces until browned. Drain excess oil, add 2 cups water to a skillet and bring to a boil. Add rice, and contents of seasoning packet. Cover and simmer 25 minutes. A few minutes before done, add peas. Garnish with pimientos. Serves 4.

Approximate nutritional analysis per serving:
Calories 793, Protein 87 g, Carbohydrates 43 g, Fat 28 g,
Cholesterol 251 mg, Sodium 513 mg

GINGER CHICKEN AND BEANS

4 small skinless chicken breast halves
flour
1 tbs (15 ml) olive oil
2 cups (480 ml) chopped onions
¾ cup (180 ml) sliced red pepper
¾ cup (180 ml) sliced green pepper
1 tbs (15 ml) very finely chopped fresh ginger root
 or ½-¾ tsp (3-4 ml) ground ginger
1 clove garlic, minced
1 tbs (15 ml) flour
1 tsp (5 ml) ground allspice
½ tsp (3 ml) ground cumin
¼ tsp (1 ml) ground nutmeg
¼ tsp (1 ml) pepper
1 - 16 oz can (480 g) red kidney beans, drained
1 - 15½ oz can (465 g) pinto beans, drained
1 - 15 oz can (450 g) garbanzo beans, drained
1 - 14½ oz can (435 g) low salt chicken broth
minced parsley

Cut chicken breasts into halves; coat lightly with flour. Cook chicken in oil in large skillet or Dutch oven until brown on all sides, 8-10 minutes; remove from skillet. Drain excess fat from skillet; add onions, peppers, ginger root and garlic, and sauté 2-3 minutes. Stir in 1 tbs (15 ml) flour, spices and pepper; sauté until onions are tender, 2-3 minutes longer. Stir beans and chicken broth into skillet; add chicken and heat to boiling. Reduce heat and simmer, covered, until chicken is cooked and tender, about 20 minutes. Serve on rimmed serving platter; sprinkle with parsley. Serves 8.

Approximate nutritional analysis per serving:
Calories 300, Protein 30 g, Carbohydrates 37 g, Fat 6 g,
Cholesterol 48 mg, Sodium 577 mg

Courtesy of the Bean Education and Awareness Network.

Ginger Chicken and Beans

CHICKEN MICRO POT AU FEU

4 boneless skinless chicken breast halves,
    rinsed well and cut into 1-inch cubes
1 large onion, coarsely chopped
3 cloves garlic, minced
1½ cups (355 ml) chicken broth
½ cup (120 ml) dry white wine
½ tsp (3 ml) TABASCO pepper sauce
3 medium carrots, trimmed, peeled and
    cut into 2x¼x¼-inch sticks
1 stalk celery, sliced ½-inch thick
1 tbs (15 ml) cornstarch
1 cup (240 ml) peas, fresh, canned or frozen
½ cup (120 ml) finely chopped parsley
    or 2 tsp (10 ml) dried parsley flakes
1½ tbs (25 ml) fresh rosemary leaves
    or 1 tsp (5 ml) dried rosemary
¼ tsp (1 ml) salt
¼ tsp (1 ml) black pepper

In a 2-qt microwave-safe casserole place chicken, onion, garlic, chicken broth, wine, TABASCO pepper sauce, carrots and celery. Cover and cook at 100% (HIGH) for 15 minutes, or until meat and vegetables are tender, stirring once. Uncover. Dissolve cornstarch in ¼ cup cooking liquid. Add to chicken mixture and stir thoroughly until blended. Add peas, parsley and rosemary. Cover. Cook at 100% (HIGH) for 3 minutes, or until sauce has thickened. Remove from oven. Season to taste with salt, pepper and additional TABASCO pepper sauce as desired. Serves 4.

Approximate nutritional analysis per serving:
Calories 390, Protein 57 g, Carbohydrates 19 g, Fat 7 g,
Cholesterol 145 mg, Sodium 571 mg

Opposite: Chicken Micro Pot au Feu

POLLO CON NARANJA Y MENTA
Chicken with Orange and Mint

3 skinless, boneless chicken breasts, cut in half
all purpose flour, for coating
¼ cup (60 ml) GOYA Olive Oil
1 cup (240 ml) sherry
1½ cups (355 ml) orange juice
½ cup (120 ml) chicken broth
2 tbs (30 ml) chopped mint
¼ tsp (1 ml) GOYA Adobo with Pepper
1 packet Sazón GOYA sin Achiote

Coat chicken lightly with flour. In a large skillet, sauté floured chicken lightly in olive oil; remove chicken and set aside. In same skillet, simmer sherry over medium heat for 2-3 minutes, until lightly reduced. Add orange juice and chicken broth to skillet and simmer, uncovered, for 10 minutes. Return chicken to skillet, stir in mint, and cook, uncovered, over high heat for 10-15 minutes, or until chicken is done. Remove chicken from skillet to serving plate. Stir Adobo and Sazón into sauce, strain sauce from skillet and pour over chicken. Salt and pepper to taste. Garnish with mint leaves and serve with rice. Serves 6.

Approximate nutritional analysis per serving:
Calories 260, Protein 27 g, Carbohydrates 7 g, Fat 12 g,
Cholesterol 73 mg, Sodium 243 mg

POLLO ESCABECHADO
Marinated Chicken

1 - 3-4 lb (1.4-1.8 kg) chicken, cut up
2 packets Sazón GOYA con Azafrán
1½ cups (355 ml) GOYA Olive Oil
3 medium onions, thinly sliced
10 cloves garlic, peeled and crushed
1 tbs (15 ml) paprika
2 cups (480 ml) La Vina White Cooking Wine
1½ cups (355 ml) GOYA Red Wine Vinegar
4 bay leaves
1 tbs (15 ml) chopped fresh thyme
8 whole cloves

Sprinkle chicken evenly with Sazón. In a large saucepan, sauté chicken in olive oil until browned. Remove chicken. In the same pan, lightly sauté onion and carrot; add garlic and paprika, stirring in quickly to prevent burning. Add wine and simmer, uncovered, for 2-3 minutes until slightly reduced. Add vinegar, bay leaves, thyme and cloves. Bring to a boil, return chicken to pot and simmer, uncovered, for 30-40 minutes. Serve cold, sliced on a bed of lettuce or re-heat and serve with rice or potatoes. Garnish with fresh thyme. Serves 4.

Approximate nutritional analysis per serving:
Calories 1868, Protein 151 g, Carbohydrates 27 g, Fat 119 g,
Cholesterol 452 mg, Sodium 726 mg

COUSCOUS WITH CURRIED CHICKEN

CHICKEN MIXTURE:
1 tbs (15 ml) olive oil
1 lb (455 g) boneless skinless chicken breasts,
        cut into strips
1 - 16 oz pkg (480 g) frozen blend of cauliflower,
        carrots and asparagus, thawed, drained
1 - 15 oz can (450 g) Garbanzo Beans, drained
1 tsp (5 ml) chicken flavor instant bouillon
1 cup (240 ml) water
2-3 tsp (10 -15 ml) curry powder
1 tsp (5 ml) cumin

COUSCOUS:
1½ cups (355 ml) water
2 tbs (30 ml) margarine or butter
1 tsp (5 ml) chicken flavor instant bouillon
1 cup (240 ml) uncooked couscous
1 tbs (15 ml) fresh parsley, chopped

Heat oil in large skillet or Dutch oven over medium-high heat. Add chicken; cook and stir 6-9 minutes or until chicken is no longer pink, stirring constantly. Add vegetables, beans, bouillon, water, curry and cumin. Bring to boil. Reduce heat; cover and simmer 8 minutes or until vegetables are tender.

Couscous: Meanwhile, in medium saucepan combine water, margarine and bouillon; bring to boil. Stir in couscous. Cover; remove from heat. Let stand 5 minutes. Before serving, fluff mixture with fork; spoon onto platter. Top with chicken mixture; sprinkle with parsley. Serves 6.

Approximate nutritional analysis per serving:
Calories 397, Protein 34 g, Carbohydrates 44 g, Fat 10 g,
Cholesterol 64 mg, Sodium 610 mg

Courtesy of the American Dry Bean Board.

ONE-POT CHICKEN COUSCOUS

¼ cup (60 ml) olive oil
2 lbs (910 g) boneless skinless chicken breasts,
        cut into 1-inch chunks
4 large carrots, peeled and sliced
2 medium onions, diced
2 large garlic cloves, minced
2 - 13¾ oz cans (825 ml) chicken broth
2 cups (480 ml) precooked couscous
2 tsp (10 ml) TABASCO pepper sauce
½ tsp (3 ml) salt
1 cup (240 ml) raisins or currants
1 cup (240 ml) slivered almonds, toasted
¼ cup (60 ml) fresh chopped parsley or mint

In 12-inch skillet over medium-high heat, in hot oil, cook chicken until well browned on all sides. With slotted spoon, remove chicken to plate. Reduce heat to medium. In drippings remaining in skillet cook carrots and onion 5 minutes. Add garlic; cook 2 minutes longer, stirring frequently.

Add chicken broth, couscous, TABASCO pepper sauce, salt and chicken chunks. Heat to boiling, then reduce heat to low, cover and simmer 5 minutes. Stir in raisins or currants, almonds and parsley or mint. Serves 8.

Approximate nutritional analysis per serving:
Calories 422, Protein 33 g, Carbohydrates 21 g, Fat 18 g,
Cholesterol 67 mg, Sodium 530 mg

ALMOND CHICKEN WITH GRAPES

⅔ cups (160 ml) BLUE DIAMOND
        Blanched Slivered Almonds
2 tbs (30 ml) vegetable oil, divided
3 whole chicken breasts, skinned, boned,
        and cut in half
1 small onion, chopped
1 clove garlic, chopped finely
1 tbs (15 ml) flour
2 cups (480 ml) chicken broth
½ cup (120 ml) heavy cream
¼ tsp (1 ml) white pepper
2 oz (60 g) Brie cheese or 1 oz (30 g) blue cheese
1 cup (240 ml) seedless green grapes,
        cut in half lengthwise

In large skillet, sauté almonds in 1 tbs oil until golden; remove and reserve. Add remaining 1 tbs oil to skillet and brown chicken breasts 1 minute on each side. Remove and reserve. In oil remaining in pan, sauté onion until translucent. Add garlic and flour and sauté 1 minute longer. Stirring constantly, whisk in chicken broth, cream and pepper. Reduce over medium-high heat, 8-10 minutes, until sauce is thickened and coats the back of a spoon. Stir in cheese, then place chicken pieces on top and cook, covered, over low heat 5-7 minutes or until chicken is tender. Add almonds and grapes. Serves 6.

Approximate nutritional analysis per serving:
Calories 402, Protein 33 g, Carbohydrates 12 g, Fat 25 g,
Cholesterol 110 mg, Sodium 319 mg

Opposite: One-Pot Chicken Couscous

CHICKEN IN WINE SAUCE

¼ cup (60 ml) all purpose flour
1 tsp (5 ml) garlic and herb, no-salt seasoning mix
4 boneless skinless chicken breasts,
    cut in ½-inch cubes
vegetable oil spray
2 cups (480 ml) sliced mushrooms
½ tsp (3 ml) minced garlic
1 - 26 oz jar (780 ml) HEALTHY CHOICE
    Traditional Pasta Sauce
¼ cup (60 ml) dry white wine
1 tsp (5 ml) dried basil
½ lb (230 g) pasta noodles or shells,
    cooked and drained

In paper bag, combine flour and seasoning mix. Shake chicken in bag until lightly coated with flour mixture. Spray Dutch oven or large nonstick saucepan with pan coating; add chicken. Lightly brown chicken over medium heat. Add mushrooms and garlic; cook and stir until mushrooms are tender. Mix in pasta sauce, wine and basil. Simmer, covered, 10 minutes. Serve over pasta. Serves 6.

Approximate nutritional analysis per serving:
Calories 357, Protein 13 g, Carbohydrates 42 g, Fat 10 g,
Cholesterol 62 mg, Sodium 445 mg

HUNTER-STYLE CHICKEN

4 slices bacon, cut into 1-inch pieces
1 medium onion, sliced
1 tbs (15 ml) vegetable oil
2-2½ lbs (910-1138 g) broiler-fryer pieces
1 - 16 oz can (480 g) tomatoes,
    cut into bite-size pieces
⅓ cup (80 ml) HEINZ 57 Sauce
⅛ tsp (.5 ml) pepper
hot-cooked rice or noodles

In large skillet, sauté bacon until crisp. Remove bacon; drain fat. Sauté onion in oil until tender; remove. In same skillet, brown chicken adding more oil if necessary. Drain excess fat. Combine bacon, onion, tomatoes, 57 Sauce and pepper; pour over chicken. Cover; simmer 20-25 minutes or until chicken is tender, basting occasionally. Remove chicken. Skim excess fat from sauce. If thicker sauce is desired, gradually stir in mixture of equal parts flour and water, simmering until thickened. Serve chicken and sauce with rice or noodles. Serves 4.

Approximate nutritional analysis per serving w/o skin:
Calories 410, Protein 44 g, Carbohydrates 20 g, Fat 17 g,
Cholesterol 129 mg, Sodium 754 mg

CHILI-CRANBERRY CHICKEN

½ cup (120 ml) HEINZ Chili Sauce
½ cup (120 ml) packaged cranberry-
    orange crushed fruit
1 tbs (15 ml) orange marmalade
⅛ tsp (.5 ml) ground allspice
6 skinless boneless chicken breast halves
½ tbs (8 ml) vegetable oil

Combine first 4 ingredients; set aside. In large skillet, slowly brown chicken on both sides in oil. Pour reserved chili sauce mixture over chicken. Simmer, uncovered, until chicken is cooked and sauce is desired consistency, stirring occasionally and turning chicken once. Serves 6.

Approximate nutritional analysis per serving:
Calories 263, Protein 36 g, Carbohydrates 17 g, Fat 5 g,
Cholesterol 96 mg, Sodium 395 mg

TANGY CHICKEN AND HERBS

1 medium onion, sliced
2 cloves garlic, minced
½ tsp (3 ml) dried rosemary leaves
½ tsp (3 ml) dried basil leaves
½ tsp (3 ml) dried thyme leaves
1 tbs (15 ml) vegetable oil
1 - 16 oz can (480 g) tomatoes, drained,
    cut into bite-size pieces
½ cup (120 ml) HEINZ Tomato Ketchup
¼ cup (60 ml) HEINZ Apple Cider Vinegar
½ tsp (3 ml) salt
⅛ tsp (.5 ml) pepper
2½-3 lbs (1.1-1.4 kg) broiler-fryer pieces, skinned
cornstarch-water mixture
hot cooked noodles

In Dutch oven or large skillet, sauté onion, garlic and herbs in oil until onion is tender-crisp. Stir in tomatoes and next 4 ingredients. Add chicken. Bring to a boil; reduce heat and simmer, covered, 35-40 minutes or until chicken is tender, turning and basting occasionally. Remove chicken. To thicken sauce, gradually stir in mixture of equal parts cornstarch and water, simmering until thickened. Serve chicken and sauce with noodles. Serves 6.

Approximate nutritional analysis per serving:
Calories 349, Protein 50 g, Carbohydrates 12 g, Fat 10 g,
Cholesterol 159 mg, Sodium 824 mg

SOUTHWESTERN CHICKEN CASSEROLE

**4 PREMIUM YOUNG 'N TENDER Brand
  Boneless Chicken Breasts**
2 oz (60 g) olive oil, divided
1 medium onion, chopped
3 cloves garlic, minced
1 - 4 oz can (120 g) green chilies, chopped
**1 - 14 oz can (420 g) plum tomatoes,
  drained and chopped**
1 tbs (15 ml) red wine vinegar
4 tsp (20 ml) ground cumin
½ tsp (3 ml) dried oregano leaves
¼ tsp (1 ml) pepper
salt to taste
1 - 15 oz can (450 g) black beans, drained and rinsed
4 oz (120 g) shredded Monterey Jack cheese
4 oz (120 g) shredded cheddar cheese

In large skillet, sauté chicken breasts in 1 oz of the olive oil for 2 minutes each side; remove. Add remaining olive oil to skillet and sauté onions, garlic and green chilies. Cook, stirring occasionally until tender, about 5 minutes. Stir in tomatoes, red wine vinegar and all seasonings. Cover and simmer about 5 minutes. Add black beans and cook 5 minutes more.

Layer chicken breasts in a medium casserole dish. Top with black bean mixture and sprinkle with cheeses. Cover with aluminum foil and bake in a preheated 350°F (180°C) oven for 30 minutes. Serves 4.

Note: Chicken chunks may be substituted for boneless chicken breasts.

Approximate nutritional analysis per serving:
Calories 649, Protein 50 g, Carbohydrates 32 g, Fat 36 g,
Cholesterol 128 mg, Sodium 591 mg

Southwestern Chicken Casserole

TURKEY BREAST BRAISED WITH GARLIC AND RICE

1 cup (240 ml) long-grain rice
1 - 14½ oz can (435 ml) chicken broth
½ cup (120 ml) white wine
2 tsp (10 ml) dried parsley
½ tsp (3 ml) dried rosemary
½ tsp (3 ml) dried thyme
½ tsp (3 ml) dried sage
1 bay leaf
1 - 6 lb (2.7 kg) bone-in NORBEST Turkey Breast
paprika
3 garlic bulbs, root end cut off

In 5 qt Dutch oven combine rice, broth, wine, parsley, rosemary, thyme, sage and bay leaf. Place turkey over rice mixture and sprinkle turkey generously with paprika. Place whole garlic bulbs, cut end up, in rice around turkey breast. Cover top of Dutch oven with foil and lid. Bake at 350°F (180°C) 2½-3 hours or until meat thermometer inserted in thickest part of breast registers 170-175°F (77-79°C). Allow to stand 10-15 minutes before serving. To serve, carve turkey into slices and place on platter. Spoon rice mixture into serving bowl. Squeeze garlic from skins onto turkey and rice. Serves 4.

Approximate nutritional analysis per serving:
Calories 590, Protein 59 g, Carbohydrates 56 g, Fat 11 g,
Cholesterol 150 mg, Sodium 549 mg

PLUM CHUTNEY CHICKEN

**2 - 16 oz cans (960 g) THANK YOU Purple Plums,
  drained, juice reserved**
2 tsp (10 ml) grated fresh ginger root
3 cloves garlic, minced
1 medium onion, coarsely chopped
¼ cup (60 ml) rice wine vinegar
⅓ cup (80 ml) sugar
¾ cup (180 ml) dried fruit bits
2 tbs (30 ml) chili sauce
1½ tsp (8 ml) curry powder
4 drops hot pepper sauce
**4 boneless skinless chicken breast halves,
  cut into 2-inch pieces**

Pour reserved juice into large skillet. Remove pits and halve plums. Add plums and remaining ingredients to skillet. Simmer, covered, for 20 minutes. Simmer, uncovered, for 15-20 minutes longer, or until chicken is cooked and sauce is thickened. Serve with rice. Serves 4.

Approximate nutritional analysis per serving:
Calories 468, Protein 38 g, Carbohydrates 73 g, Fat 4 g,
Cholesterol 96 mg, Sodium 204 mg

CHICKEN PAPRIKASH

¾ cup (180 ml) DANNON Plain Nonfat or
  Lowfat Yogurt
2 tbs (30 ml) olive oil
2 cups (480 ml) sliced onions
1 cup (240 ml) red bell pepper strips
1½ tsp (8 ml) minced garlic
1 tbs plus 1½ tsp (23 ml) all purpose flour
1-2 tsp (5-10 ml) Hungarian paprika
1 cup (240 ml) chicken broth
1 lb (455 g) chicken cutlets, trimmed of all
  visible fat, cut into 2x1-inch strips
½ tsp (3 ml) salt
hot-cooked noodles, optional
snipped fresh parsley, optional

Spoon yogurt into large strainer lined with double thickness of cheesecloth or a coffee filter. Place bowl beneath, but not touching strainer to catch liquid. Let stand at room temperature 15 minutes. Scrape yogurt into a small bowl. Discard liquid.

In a large heavy saucepan or Dutch oven heat oil over medium-low heat. Add onions, bell pepper and garlic; stir well. Cook, covered, 10-15 minutes or until tender, stirring occasionally. Reduce heat if vegetables start to brown. Sprinkle in flour and paprika; cook uncovered 1 minute, stirring constantly. Pan will seem dry.

Add broth; increase heat to medium-high. Cook, stirring constantly, until sauce thickens and boils. Add chicken; stir well and return to a boil. Reduce heat to low; simmer, covered, 8-10 minutes or until chicken is cooked through. Remove from heat; uncover and let cool slightly. Stir a little of hot chicken sauce into yogurt then slowly add yogurt to chicken, stirring constantly. Stir in salt and pepper. If desired, serve over hot cooked noodles and garnish with parsley. Serves 4.

Approximate nutritional analysis per serving:
Calories 328, Protein 39 g, Carbohydrates 15 g, Fat 12 g,
Cholesterol 99 mg, Sodium 396 mg

SMALL WHITE BEANS AND CHICKEN

2 cans GOYA Small White Beans, not drained
2 lbs (910 g) chicken, cut in pieces
¼ cup (60 ml) GOYA Corn Oil or Butter
¼ cup (60 ml) onion, minced
½ lb (230 g) mushrooms. sliced
2 cloves garlic, minced
¼ tsp (1 ml) black pepper
1 tbs (15 ml) parsley, chopped
½ tsp (3 ml) tarragon
½ cup (120 ml) dry white wine
1 large tomato, chopped

Brown chicken pieces in corn oil or butter and remove. Sauté onion, mushrooms and garlic. Add beans and remaining ingredients. Set browned chicken pieces in bean mixture; bring to boil. Cover, simmer 20-30 minutes. Serves 4.

Approximate nutritional analysis per serving:
Calories 825, Protein 83 g, Carbohydrates 47 g, Fat 32 g,
Cholesterol 201 mg, Sodium 206 mg

CARIBBEAN TURKEY STEW

2 lb (910 g) NORBEST Turkey Thighs
1 tbs (15 ml) oil
3 cups (720 ml) thinly sliced onion
½ tsp (3 ml) red pepper flakes
½ tsp (3 ml) salt
¼ cup (60 ml) sweetened flaked coconut
1 cup (240 ml) turkey broth or
  reduced-sodium chicken bouillon
1 - 16 oz can (480 g) stewed tomatoes, drained
1 - 16 oz can (480 g) black beans, drained*
1 lb (455 g) butternut squash, peeled and
  cut into 1-inch cubes
1 lb (455 g) sweet potatoes, peeled and
  cut into 1-inch cubes

CONDIMENTS:
2 medium bananas, sliced
1 bunch green onions, sliced
½ cup (120 ml) sweetened flaked coconut
1-2 limes, cut in wedges

* If canned beans are unavailable, soak 8 oz (240 g) of dried black beans according to package directions. Add beans at beginning of cooking with all of other ingredients.

In 5-qt saucepan, over medium-high heat, brown thighs in oil about 3 minutes per side. Remove and set aside. In same saucepan, sauté onions 2-3 minutes, or until translucent. Add red pepper, salt, coconut, broth, tomatoes, black beans, squash, sweet potatoes and turkey thighs. Bring mixture to boil; reduce heat, cover and simmer 1¼-1½ hours, or until turkey thighs register 180-185°F (82-85°C) in thickest portion.

Ten minutes before serving, remove turkey thighs from stew and strip meat from bones with fork; return meat strips to stew. Heat throughout. To serve, spoon stew into bowl and garnish with bananas, green onions and coconut. Squeeze juice of lime over top. Serve 6.

Approximate nutritional analysis per serving:
Calories 388, Protein 30 g, Carbohydrates 49 g, Fat 9 g,
Cholesterol 81 mg, Sodium 887 mg

QUICK TURKEY CURRY WITH RICE

3 tbs (45 ml) butter
¼ cup (60 ml) minced onion
2-3 tsp (10-15 ml) curry powder
¼ tsp (1 ml) ground ginger
3 tbs (45 ml) flour
½ tsp (3 ml) salt
1 cup (240 ml) milk
1 cup (240 ml) chicken broth
2 cups (480 ml) diced cooked turkey
½ tsp (3 ml) lemon juice
1 cup (240 ml) Natural or Golden Raisins
4 cups (960 ml) cooked rice

CONDIMENTS, CHOICE OF:
crumbled crisp bacon
shredded hard-cooked eggs
chopped green onion
chopped nuts
coconut
chopped raw vegetables

In 2-qt bowl, place butter, onion, curry powder and ginger; microwave on HIGH 2 minutes. Stir in flour and salt; microwave 90 seconds longer on HIGH, stirring after 45 seconds. Gradually stir in broth and milk. Microwave on HIGH 6-8 minutes, stirring every minute until thick and bubbly. Stir in turkey, lemon juice and raisins; microwave on HIGH for 1 minute longer. Serve over rice, or serve rice and curry in separate bowls. Offer condiments for each person to add on top. Serves 4.

Approximate nutritional analysis per serving:
Calories 514, Protein 10 g, Carbohydrates 94 g, Fat 12 g, Cholesterol 32 mg, Sodium 532 mg

Courtesy of The California Raisin Advisory Board.

TURKEY JAMBALAYA

2 tbs plus 2 tsp (40 ml) CHEF PAUL PRUDHOMME'S Poultry Magic
3 cups (720 ml) chopped onions, in all
3 cups (720 ml) chopped green bell peppers, in all
1 cup (240 ml) julienned turkey tasso
2 cups (480 ml) turkey andouille sausage, cut into ¼-inch rounds, in all
1 cup (240 ml) chopped celery
3 bay leaves
6 cups (1.4 L) defatted chicken stock, in all
2 cups (480 ml) peeled, chopped fresh tomatoes
8 oz (240 g) julienned turkey breasts
3 cups (720 ml) uncooked long grain white rice

Preheat a heavy 5-qt pot, preferably a nonstick, over high heat to 150°F (180°C), about 4 minutes. Add 2 cups of the onions, 2 cups of the bell peppers, the celery, tasso, 1 cup of the andouille, the bay leaves, and 3 tbs of the seasoning mix. Cook scraping the bottom of the pot frequently, until the crust seems in danger of burning, about 12 minutes. Stir in 1 cup of the stock, scrape the bottom of the pot to clear it of all brown bits, and cook for 10 minutes more. Add the remaining onions, peppers, andouille, and stock, and bring to a boil. Stir in the rice and return to a boil. Reduce the heat to a slow simmer, cover, and cook until the liquid is completely absorbed, about 15 minutes. Serves 8.

Approximate nutritional analysis per serving:
Calories 424, Protein 23 g, Carbohydrates 67 g, Fat 6 g, Cholesterol 53 mg, Sodium 795 mg

QUICK CHICKEN MOLE

1 - 8 oz can (240 ml) tomato sauce
½ cup (120 ml) water
1 pkg taco seasoning mix
2 tsp (10 ml) sugar
dash ground cinnamon
¼ oz (8 g) unsweetened chocolate
½ cup (120 ml) Natural Raisins
2½-3 lb (1.1-1.4 kg) fryer chicken, cut up, or all chicken breasts
2 tsp (10 ml) cornstarch
1 tbs (15 ml) cold water

In 1-qt bowl mix tomato sauce, water, taco seasoning, sugar and cinnamon. Microwave on HIGH 8 minutes, until bubbling throughout. Stir in chocolate to melt, and stir in raisins. Place chicken pieces in 12x8x2-inch baking dish, largest parts to outside of dish. Pour sauce over all, coating each piece. Cover and microwave on MEDIUM-HIGH (70%) for 25 minutes, re-arranging chicken pieces once. Test for doneness and continue microwaving as necessary. Remove chicken to platter. In small cup, stir cornstarch into water; stir into sauce. Microwave 3-4 minutes on HIGH, stirring each minute, until slightly thickened and bubbling. Pour over chicken and serve. Serve with flour tortillas and a cool green salad. Serves 4.

Approximate nutritional analysis per serving:
Calories 634, Protein 84 g, Carbohydrates 23 g, Fat 22 g, Cholesterol 251 mg, Sodium 393 mg

Courtesy of The California Raisin Advisory Board.

Opposite: Turkey Jambalaya

LEMON-DILL CHICKEN

SEASONING MIX:
2 tsp (10 ml) CHEF PAUL PRUDHOMME'S
  Poultry Magic
1 tsp (5 ml) dill weed
1 tsp (5 ml) dried sweet basil leaves

8 - 2-3 oz (480-720 g) boneless, skinless
  chicken breasts
1 tbs plus 2 tsp (25 ml) cornstarch
1 cup (240 ml) apple juice, in all
1½ cups (355 ml) defatted chicken stock, in all
2 cups (480 ml) julienne onions
½ cup (120 ml) fresh lemon juice, in all
2 - 1 g packets artificial sweetener, optional

Combine the seasoning mix ingredients in a small bowl. Sprinkle all surfaces of the chicken evenly with 2 tsp of the seasoning mix and rub it in well.

Dissolve the cornstarch in ¼ cup of the apple juice and set aside.

Preheat a heavy 10-inch skillet, preferably nonstick, over high heat to 350°F (180°C), about 4 minutes. Place 4 of the chicken breasts in the skillet, lower the heat to medium, and brown them for at least 1 minute per side. Remove these 4 breasts, brown the other 4, and set all the chicken aside.

Return the heat to high and stir in ½ cup of the stock, scraping the bottom of the skillet to clear it of all the browned bits. Add the onions and the remaining seasoning mix, stir and cook until all the liquid evaporates, about 3-4 minutes. Stir in ¼ cup of the lemon juice, scrape the bottom of the skillet again to clear it, and cook until liquid evaporates, about 3-4 minutes.

Add ½ cup of the apple juice, clear the bottom and sides of the skillet, and cook until about half the liquid evaporates, about 2-3 minutes. Stir in the remaining 1 cup of stock, the ¼ cup lemon juice, and the ¼ cup apple juice. Bring to boil (will take 2-3 minutes), whisk in the cornstarch/apple juice mixture, and return to a boil. Return the chicken to the skillet, lower the heat to medium, and cook until the chicken is done all the way through, about 4-5 minutes. Turn off the heat, remove the chicken, and, if desired, whisk in the artificial sweetener. Serves 4.

Approximate nutritional analysis per serving:
Calories 274, Protein 38 g, Carbohydrates 19 g, Fat 5 g, Cholesterol 136 mg, Sodium 400 mg

CHILI BLANCO

½ lb (230 g) diced turkey breast or ground
  turkey, optional
1 tbs (15 ml) vegetable oil
½ cup (120 ml) diced celery
½ cup (120 ml) fresh or canned Anaheim chilies
½ cup (120 ml) chopped onion
2 cups (480 ml) water
1 - 16 oz can (480 g) white small or
  white kidney beans, drained
1 cup (240 ml) seeded and diced fresh tomatoes
1 cup (240 ml) seeded and diced fresh zucchini
½ tsp (3 ml) salt
½ tsp (3 ml) ground cumin
⅛ tsp (.5 ml) black pepper
⅛ tsp (.5 ml) cayenne pepper
corn or flour tortillas

CONDIMENTS:
shredded lowfat cheese
chopped onion
chopped cilantro
diced tomatoes

Brown ground turkey in oil in medium saucepan; drain excess drippings. Add celery, chilies and onion and cook until tender. Add remaining ingredients except tortillas and condiments; mix well. Bring mixture to boil, reduce heat and simmer 30 minutes or until flavors are blended. Serve with tortillas and condiments. Serves 4.

Approximate nutritional analysis per serving:
Calories 288, Protein 25 g, Carbohydrates 38 g, Fat 5 g, Cholesterol 36 mg, Sodium 317 mg

Courtesy of the California Table Grape Commission.

POULTRY-ON-THE-GRILL: TIPS

In general, when using poultry on the grill and a basting sauce containing anything sweet such as honey or brown sugar or preserves, you may want to precook chicken pieces and simply finish browning the chicken on the grill. Not only does this cut total cooking time, but it prevents burning of the food. Many people like to line their grills with heavy aluminum foil and cook the poultry over lower heat.

A word about marinades: Because some cuts of poultry are very lean (boneless chicken cutlets, turkey tenderloins) marinating the poultry add moisture and flavor. When mixing marinades, set aside ⅓ for brushing poultry while grilling. Discard used liquid in which the raw poultry has marinated prior to cooking, and do not use this for basting.

About food safety: Always rinse uncooked poultry with cold water inside and out before cooking. It's particularly important to make absolutely sure that chicken or turkey is completely done and cooked throughout when grilling. Handle brushes and sauces with common sense and do not taste anything that has come in contact with raw poultry. While studies have shown that many bacteria are intolerant to the salt and cold water used in kosher poultry processing, proper handling of raw poultry by the consumer at home is urged.

COOKING DIRECTIONS

TURKEY

Open pan roasting: Whole turkey, completely defrosted, in preheated 325°F (165°C) oven. Allow approximately 20 minutes per lb (455 g). The larger the bird, the shorter the time per lb.

Ready To Cook Weight (lbs)	Unstuffed Roasting Time (hours)	Stuffed Roasting Time (hours)
6-8	2¼-3¼	3-3½
8-12	3-4	3½-4½
12-16	3½-4½	4-5
16-20	4-5	4½-5½
20-24	4½-5½	5-6½

TURKEY BREAST

Open pan roasting: Allow 22-25 minutes per lb (455 g), 325°F (165°C).

DEFROSTING INSTRUCTIONS

Allow 24 hours for every 5 lbs (2.3 kg) of frozen poultry in the refrigerator. NEVER DEFROST FROZEN POULTRY AT ROOM TEMPERATURE. Quick defrost by immersing in cold water, changing the water every half hour. This will speed up thawing to about 30 minutes per lb.

FREEZER LIFE

Whole frozen poultry may be kept at 0°F (-18°C) for up to 18 months. Frozen poultry parts may be kept up to 12 months. Cooked products should be used within 4 months. After that time, flavor and/or texture loss as well as freezer burn may occur.

KOSHER FOR PASSOVER

The easiest rule of thumb to remember is that all EMPIRE KOSHER raw (uncooked) chicken, turkey and duck is kosher for Passover all year round. This is true of fresh poultry, frozen poultry or fresh-pack poultry. No special designation is required on uncooked poultry. The only exception may be ground turkey in plastic casings. Cooked products, such as barbecue, rendered chicken fat, or delicatessen products, require special designation. Such products are marked Kosher for Passover.

Courtesy of The Empire Kosher Poultry Test Kitchens.

Barbecued Chicken

MEAT

While Americans were struggling with mixed messages about the role of meat in their diets, farmers and breeders were raising leaner animals to produce leaner cuts of meat. So whether you prefer to grill or stew, roast or sauté, there is a place for beef, lamb, pork and veal in your diet. Just watch those side dishes!

Savory Mushroom-Stuffed Steak

SAVORY MUSHROOM-STUFFED STEAK

**3 lbs (1.4 g) boneless beef tip sirloin steak,
   cut 2-inches thick**
1 tbs (15 ml) olive oil
1 cup (240 ml) finely chopped fresh mushrooms
¼ cup (60 ml) minced shallots or green onions
1 tbs (15 ml) dry red wine
¼ tsp (1 ml) salt
¼ tsp (1 ml) dried thyme leaves
¼ tsp (1 ml) pepper

Heat oil in heavy nonstick skillet over medium-high heat. Add mushrooms and shallots; cook 4-5 minutes or until vegetables are tender, stirring occasionally. Add wine and cook until evaporated. Stir in salt, thyme and pepper. Remove from heat; cool thoroughly. Meanwhile trim excess fat from beef top sirloin steak. To cut pocket in steak, make horizontal cut through center of steak, parallel to surface of meat, approximately 1 inch from each side. Cut to, but not through, opposite side. Spoon cooled stuffing into pocket, spreading evenly. Secure opening with wooden picks. Place steak on rack in broiler pan so surface of meat is 4-5 inches from heat. Broil 26-32 minutes for rare to medium, turning once. Place on warm serving platter. Cover with aluminum foil tent and allow to stand 10-15 minutes. Remove wooden picks. Trim excess fat from steak; carve steak into ½-inch thick slices. Serves 12.

Note: A boneless beef top sirloin steak will yield 4 - 3 oz (90 g each) cooked, trimmed servings per lb (455 g).

Approximate nutritional analysis per serving:
Calories 180, Protein 26 g, Carbohydrates 1 g, Fat 7 g,
Cholesterol 76 mg, Sodium 102 mg

Courtesy of the National Live Stock and Meat Board.

ORIENTAL BEEF STEAKS AND NOODLES

**4 - 4 oz (480 g) beef eye round steaks,
    cut ½-inch thick**
¼ cup (60 ml) water
3 tbs (45 ml) hoisin sauce
1 tbs (15 ml) red wine vinegar
vegetable oil
1 small cucumber, peeled, halved, seeded and sliced
1 small red bell pepper, cut into thin strips
¼ cup (60 ml) sliced green onion
**3 oz (90 g) Chinese noodles, broken,
    cooked and drained**
4 tsp (20 ml) chopped fresh cilantro, divided

Oriental Beef Steaks and Noodles

Combine water, hoisin sauce and wine vinegar; reserve. Heat large non-stick skillet over medium-high heat. Brush skillet lightly with oil. Add cucumber, bell pepper and green onion; cook and stir 1 minute. Stir in noodles, 1 tbs cilantro and half of reserved hoisin mixture. Remove to warm platter. Heat same skillet over medium-high heat until hot. Pan-broil beef eye round steaks 2-4 minutes, turning once. Do not overcook. Add remaining hoisin mixture to skillet, turning steaks to coat. Place steaks on noodle mixture. Spoon warm sauce over steaks. Sprinkle with remaining 1 tsp cilantro. Serves 4.

Approximate nutritional analysis per serving:
Calories 272, Protein 28 g, Carbohydrates 22 g, Fat 7 g,
Cholesterol 59 mg, Sodium 439 mg

Courtesy of the National Live Stock and Meat Board.

STEAK DIJON

1 lb (455 g) boneless beef steak (flank, sirloin)
**1 - 12 oz jar (360 ml) HEINZ Home Style Brown
    or Mushroom Gravy**
3 tbs (45 ml) milk
1½ tbs (25 ml) Dijon-style mustard
chopped fresh parsley

In large skillet, quickly cook steaks in butter to desired doneness, turning once. Remove; keep warm. Reduce heat; add gravy, milk and mustard. Heat, stirring, until bubbly. To serve, spoon sauce over steaks, sprinkle with parsley. Serves 4.

Approximate nutritional analysis per serving:
Calories 271, Protein 24 g, Carbohydrates 5 g, Fat 16 g,
Cholesterol 61 mg, Sodium 607 mg

POMPEIAN BEEF BROCHETTES

1½ lbs (685 g) beef round steak,
    cut into 1¼-inch cubes

GRILLING SAUCE:
⅔ cup (160 ml) POMPEIAN Extra Virgin Olive Oil
½ cup (120) ml finely chopped onion
1 tsp (5 ml) salt
1 tsp (5 ml) dried thyme
1 cup (240 ml) red wine
2 garlic cloves, minced
1 tsp (5 ml) freshly ground black pepper
¼ cup (60 ml) fresh parsley, chopped

BROCHETTES:
4 small onions, parboiled or microwaved 5 minutes
    on HIGH
8 ripe, firm cherry tomatoes
1 green bell pepper, cut into 8 squares
1 zucchini squash, peeled and sliced into
    1-inch pieces
8 large mushrooms, washed
1 red bell pepper, cut into 8 squares
4 cups (960 ml) cooked white or saffron rice

Cover beef with marinade in a deep dish overnight in the refrigerator. Preheat the broiler or the barbecue grill. Remove the meat from the marinade and alternate the meat and vegetables on skewers. Brush with the marinade and broil or grill 5 minutes on each side, continuing to brush with the marinade throughout the cooking. Serve on a bed of cooked rice if desired. Serves 8.

Approximate nutritional analysis per serving w/o rice:
Calories 164, Protein 25 g, Carbohydrates < 1 g,
Fat 7 g, Cholesterol 59 mg, Sodium 86 mg

GRILLED ITALIAN STEAK

¾ cup (180 ml) WISH - BONE Italian,
    Robusto Italian or Lite Italian
    Dressing
2 tbs (30 ml) grated Parmesan cheese
2 tsp (10 ml) dried basil leaves,
    crushed
¼ tsp (1 ml) cracked black pepper
2-3 lbs (910-1365 g) boneless sirloin or
    London broil steak

In large shallow baking dish or plastic bag, combine all ingredients, except steak; mix well. Add steak; turn to coat. Cover or close bag, and marinate in refrigerator, turning occasionally,

3 hours or overnight. Remove steak, reserving marinade. Grill or broil steak until done. Meanwhile, in small saucepan, bring reserved marinade to a boil, then pour over steak. Serves 8.

Approximate nutritional analysis per serving:
Calories 310, Protein 32 g, Carbohydrates 3 g, Fat 19 g,
Cholesterol 75 mg, Sodium 560 mg

ORIENTAL FLANK STEAK

½ cup (120 ml) WISH -BONE Italian, Robust Italian
    or Lite Italian Dressing
2 tbs (30 ml) soy sauce
2 tbs (30 ml) firmly-packed brown sugar
½ tsp (3 ml) ground ginger
1-1½ lb (455-685 g) flank steak

In large shallow baking dish or plastic bag, combine all ingredients, except steak; mix well. Add steak; turning to coat. Cover, or close bag, and marinate in refrigerator, turning occasionally, 3 hours or overnight. Remove steak, reserving marinade. Grill or broil steak until done. Meanwhile, in small saucepan, bring reserved marinade to boil, then pour over steak. Serves 6.

Approximate nutritional analysis per serving:
Calories 241, Protein 21 g, Carbohydrates 7 g, Fat 14 g,
Cholesterol 51 mg, Sodium 800 mg

STEAK TACOS

1 medium onion, cut into strips
1 medium green or red pepper, cut into strips
1 tbs (15 ml) FLEISCHMANN'S Sweet
    Unsalted Margarine
½ cup (120 ml) ORTEGA Mild, Medium,
    or Hot Thick and Chunky Salsa
4 curly green leaf lettuce leaves
8 slices leftover cooked round steak
4 corn tortillas, warmed

In nonstick skillet, over medium heat, cook onion and pepper in margarine until tender-crisp; stir in salsa and heat through. Place a lettuce leaf, 2 slices steak and ¼ of the pepper mixture on each tortilla; roll up to serve. Serves 4.

Approximate nutritional analysis per serving:
Calories 143, Protein 6 g, Carbohydrates 19 g, Fat 5 g,
Cholesterol 11 mg, Sodium 231 mg

BEEF FAJITAS WITH FRESH TOMATOES

1¼ lbs (680 g) fresh FLORIDA tomatoes
1¼ lbs (680 g) flank steak (or chicken breast)
½ cup (120 ml) white wine
⅓ cup (60 ml) lime juice
1 tsp (5 ml) grated lime peel
1 tsp (5 ml) crushed garlic
½ tsp (3 ml) salt
½ tsp (3 ml) ground red pepper
¾ cup (180 ml) sliced onion
¾ cup (180 ml) sweet green pepper
¾ cup (180 ml) sweet yellow pepper
6 medium flour tortillas, warmed
shredded cheddar or Monterey Jack cheese
sour cream, optional
sliced avocado, optional

Use tomatoes held at room temperature until fully ripe. Slice tomatoes into wedges; set aside. Cut beef into ¼-inch thick slices. In a shallow pan combine wine, lime juice and peel, garlic, salt and red pepper. Stir in beef, onion, and green and yellow peppers; mix gently; let stand 20 minutes. Preheat broiler to hot. Using slotted spoon remove beef and vegetables from marinade; place on a broiler pan in a single layer. Broil 3-4 inches from heat until beef is browned. Using a spatula, turn beef and vegetables; place reserved tomatoes on broiler pan. Broil until beef reaches desired doneness. Serve in tortillas with shredded cheddar or Monterey Jack cheese, sour cream and avocado slices, if desired. Serves 3.

Approximate nutritional analysis per serving:
Calories 542, Protein 42 g, Carbohydrates 39 g, Fat 25 g,
Cholesterol 96 mg, Sodium 595 mg

BEEF PROVENÇALE

¼ cup (60 ml) olive oil
1 lb (455 g) tender beef, cut into strips
1 large onion, cut into narrow wedges
2 tsp (10 ml) bottled or fresh minced garlic
2 tbs (30 ml) fresh minced rosemary, no stems
2 tbs (30 ml) fresh minced thyme
1 cup (240 ml) halved cherry tomatoes, diced
    or 1 large tomato, cubed
½ cup (120 ml) pitted CALIFORNIA ripe olives,
    halved

Heat half the oil in skillet. Sauté beef in oil in skillet over highest heat just until brown, about 1 minute, stirring a little. Remove from pan. Add remaining oil and the onion to pan; sauté for 4 minutes. Add remaining ingredients and cook, stirring for 2 minutes until hot. Return beef to pan and warm through for ½ minute. Don't overcook or beef will toughen. Serves 4.

Approximate nutritional analysis per serving:
Calories 406, Protein 36 g, Carbohydrates 10 g, Fat 24 g,
Cholesterol 101 mg, Sodium 174 mg

STEAK WITH WAHOO SAUCE

6 - ¼ lb (115 g each) steaks, tenderized
1 - 15 oz can (450 g) tamales, drained (reserve sauce)
1 egg, beaten mixed with:
1 tbs (15 ml) water
flour
bread or cracker crumbs
salt and pepper
½ tsp (3 ml) chili powder
oil
½ cup (120 ml) tomato juice or sauce
1 tsp (5 ml) chili powder

Wrap each steak around a tamale and secure with toothpicks. Dip steak rolls in beaten egg, then in flour seasoned with salt, pepper, chili powder. Dip again in egg, then in bread or cracker crumbs. Brown steak rolls on all sides in hot fat; reduce heat and drain off excess fat. Cook steaks until tender, about 10 minutes. Remove steaks to platter and keep hot. Add tamale sauce and tomato sauce and chili powder. Taste for seasonings. Bring to boil and pour over hot steaks. Serves 6.

Approximate nutritional analysis per serving:
Calories 478, Protein 41 g, Carbohydrates 28 g, Fat 22 g,
Cholesterol 149 mg, Sodium 890 mg

ALMOND BEEF GAUCHO

¼ cup (60 ml) orange juice
2 tbs (30 ml) lime juice
2 cloves garlic, chopped finely
1½ tsp (8 ml) tomato paste
1 tsp (5 ml) chili powder
1 tsp (5 ml) cornstarch
¼ tsp (1 ml) cinnamon
⅛ tsp (.5 ml) ground cloves
½ tsp (3 ml) salt
¼ tsp (1 ml) pepper
¾ cup (180 ml) BLUE DIAMOND Blanched
    Slivered Almonds
3 tbs (45 ml) olive oil
1 cup (240 ml) diced red onions
1½ lbs (685 g) round steak, sliced thinly into
3x½-inch strips
½ cup (120 ml) sliced pimiento-stuffed olives
½ cup (120 ml) raisins, soaked in boiling water
    for 20 minutes and drained

Combine first 10 ingredients; reserve. Sauté almonds in oil until golden. Add onion and sauté over medium heat just until tender, about 5 minutes. Add steak and sauté until brown, 1-2 minutes. Add orange juice mixture; simmer until thickened, about 1 minute. Stir in olives and raisins. Garnish with lime wedges. Serves 4.

Approximate nutritional analysis per serving:
Calories 627, Protein 56 g, Carbohydrates 27 g, Fat 34 g,
Cholesterol 117 mg, Sodium 502 mg

WESTERN-STYLE BEEF SKILLET

¾ lb (340 g) thin strips top sirloin
1 tbs (15 ml) oil
1 - 16 oz pkg (480 g) GREEN GIANT AMERICAN
    MIXTURES Western Style Frozen Vegetables
½ cup (120 ml) chili sauce
1-2 tsp (5-10 ml) chili powder

In large skillet brown beef in oil. Add remaining ingredients. Cover; simmer 7-9 minutes until vegetables are crisp-tender, stirring occasionally. Serves 4.

Approximate nutritional analysis per serving:
Calories 280, Protein 23 g, Carbohydrates 23 g, Fat 10 g,
Cholesterol 58 mg, Sodium 530 mg

LOUISIANA YAM-B-CUE

4 lbs (1.8 kg) spareribs (have butcher crack bones)
2 - 8 oz cans (480 ml) tomato sauce
1 envelope onion salad dressing mix
⅔ cup (160 ml) apple jelly
1½ cups (355 ml) celery, cut into ¾-inch
    diagonal slices
2 medium green peppers, cut in strips
1 lb (455 g) zucchini squash, cut in ½-inch slices
2 - 16 oz cans (960 g) LOUISIANA yams, drained
    or 4 medium LOUISIANA yams, cooked,
    peeled and quartered

Place spareribs on grill over low coals; barbecue 1 hour, turning ribs every 15 minutes. Meanwhile prepare barbecue sauce. Stir tomato sauce, dry salad dressing mix and jelly in saucepan over medium heat until smooth. Remove from heat.

Cook celery, green peppers and squash in large pot with boiling salted water 5-7 minutes or just until tender; drain. Place vegetables and yams on a large piece of heavy duty foil; spoon about ½ of the barbecue sauce on top. Carefully toss vegetables until coated with sauce. Secure ends of foil so that vegetables are completely enclosed. Place over low coals during last 30 minutes of cooking spareribs.

About 5 minutes before spareribs are done, brush some of the remaining barbecue sauce over bony side of ribs; barbecue until sauce starts to brown. Turn ribs over and repeat. Serves 4.

To judge the temperature of a charcoal briquette fire, cautiously hold your hand, palm side down, just above the grill. For a "low coal" temperature, you should be able to keep your hand in position for 5 seconds. To lower temperature, raise grill or separate coals; to raise temperature, tap the outer gray layer from coals and push coals together.

Note: To prepare the recipe indoors, place spareribs 8-10 inches from low broiler flame. Broil for 1 hour, turning every 15 minutes. Follow above procedure for barbecuing ribs with barbecue sauce. Boil vegetables as given above. Add yams and ½ of barbecue sauce to drained vegetables in pot; simmer just until heated through. Occasionally stir gently.

Approximate nutritional analysis per serving:
Calories 1226, Protein 61 g, Carbohydrates 124 g, Fat 54 g,
Cholesterol 214 mg, Sodium 235   mg

Opposite: Louisiana Yam-B-Cue

ORANGE GINGER BEEF STIR-FRY

½ cup (120 ml) orange juice
¼ cup (60 ml) HEINZ 57 Sauce
2 tsp (10 ml) cornstarch
¼ tsp (1 ml) salt
⅛ tsp (.5 ml) crushed red pepper
2 cups (480 ml) broccoli flowerets
1 cup (240 ml) julienne carrots
1 medium onion, cut into eighths
2 tbs (30 ml) vegetable oil, divided
1 - 1 lb (455 g) flank steak, cut into thin strips
1 tsp (5 ml) grated ginger root

Combine first 5 ingredients; set aside. In large skillet, stir-fry broccoli, carrots and onion in 1 tbs oil until tender-crisp, about 2 minutes; remove. Quickly stir-fry half of beef and ginger root in remaining 1 tbs oil just until steak loses its red color; remove. Repeat with remaining beef, adding more oil if necessary. Return all beef and vegetables to skillet. Stir in reserved 57 Sauce mixture; heat until thickened. Serves 4.

Approximate nutritional analysis per serving:
Calories 331, Protein 35 g, Carbohydrates 13 g, Fat 15 g,
Cholesterol 92 mg, Sodium 230 mg

PEPPER STEAK

1 lb (455 g) round steak, cut in thin strips
2 tbs (30 ml) butter or margarine
1 cup (240 ml) sliced green pepper
1 cup (240 ml) sliced mushrooms
1 cup (240 ml) sliced onion
½ cup (120 ml) coarsely chopped celery
1-1½ tsp (5-8 ml) OLD BAY Seasoning, to taste
1 tsp (5 ml) salt
1 tbs (15 ml) cornstarch
1 cup (240 ml) water
2 tbs (30 ml) soy sauce

In a 10-inch skillet, brown round steak lightly in butter or margarine. Add vegetables, OLD BAY Seasoning and salt. Stir-fry about 5 minutes. In a small bowl, mix cornstarch with water and soy sauce. Pour over vegetables. Continue cooking and stir until sauce thickens and becomes slightly transparent. Serve over hot rice. Serves 6.

Approximate nutritional analysis per serving:
Calories 392, Protein 25 g, Carbohydrates 5 g, Fat 30 g,
Cholesterol 135 mg, Sodium 750 mg

GRILLED SOUTHWESTERN TOP ROUND STEAK AND COLORFUL VEGETABLES

1½ lbs (685 g) beef top round steak cut 1-inch thick
¼ cup (60 ml) fresh lime juice
¼ cup (60 ml) bottled steak sauce
¼ cup (60 ml) prepared salsa, mild, medium or hot
1 tbs (15 ml) vegetable oil
1 clove crushed garlic
½ tsp (3 ml) coarse grind black pepper
salt, if desired

COLORFUL VEGETABLES:
2 tbs (30 ml) margarine or butter
2 medium zucchini, sliced
2 cups (480 ml) sliced fresh mushrooms
½ green bell pepper, cut into 2x¼-inch strips
1 tsp (5 ml) cumin seeds *or*
    ½ tsp (3 ml) ground cumin
½ tsp (3 ml) salt
¼ tsp (1 ml) coarse grind black pepper
1 cup (240 ml) finely chopped tomato
¼ cup (60 ml) chopped green onion

Combine lime juice, steak sauce, salsa, oil, garlic and pepper in small saucepan. Bring to boil; reduce heat. Simmer, uncovered, 5 minutes, stirring occasionally. Cool. Place beef top round steak in plastic bag; add cooled marinade, turning to coat. Close bag securely and marinate in refrigerator 8 hours, or overnight, turning occasionally. Remove steak from marinade; discard marinade. Place steak on grid over medium coals*. Grill steaks 12-14 minutes for rare to medium, turning once. Season with salt, if desired. Meanwhile prepare Colorful Vegetables. Trim excess fat from steak; carve steak into thin slices. Serve with Colorful Vegetables. Serves 6.

Colorful Vegetables: Melt margarine in large heavy skillet with heat-proof handle on grid over medium coals. Add zucchini, mushrooms, bell pepper, cumin seeds, salt and black pepper. Cook 4-5 minutes or until vegetables are crisp-tender, stirring occasionally. Add tomato and green onion; continue to cook and stir 1 minute. Yields 3 cups.

To check temperature, cautiously hold hand about 4 inches above coals. Medium coals will force removal of hand in 4 seconds.

Approximate nutritional analysis per 3 oz cooked, trimmed serving steak:
Calories 171, Protein 27 g, Carbohydrates 2 g, Fat 5 g,
Cholesterol 71 mg, Sodium 180 mg

Approximate nutritional analysis per ½ cup serving vegetable:
Calories 57, Protein 2 g, Carbohydrates 5 g, Fat 4 g,
Cholesterol 0 mg, Sodium 233 mg

Courtesy of the National Live Stock and Meat Board.

Opposite: Grilled Southwestern Top Round Steak and Colorful Vegetables

CHOW

2 - 3½ lb (1.6 kg each) beef back ribs
¾ cup (180 ml) soy sauce
juice of 2 large lemons
6 tbs (90 ml) Dijon-style mustard
6 tbs (90 ml) packed brown sugar
4-6 shallots, finely chopped
2 tbs (30 ml) grated fresh ginger
2 tbs (30 ml) finely chopped jalapeño or
    serrano peppers
Chinese greens and vegetables (cabbage,
    spinach, sugar peas, bean sprout, etc.)
chopped fresh cilantro leaves

Combine soy sauce, lemon juice, mustard, sugar, shallots, ginger and jalapeño peppers; whisk to blend thoroughly. Reserve half of marinade for dressing. Place beef back ribs in large plastic bag or utility dishes; add remaining marinade, turning to coat. Close bag securely or cover dishes and marinate in refrigerator 1-4 hours, turning occasionally. Remove ribs from marinade; discard marinade. Place ribs on grid over hot mesquite coals. Grill until crisp and browned outside, but still pink inside, turning once and brushing with some of reserved marinade before turning. Serve ribs with Chinese greens and vegetables; sprinkle with cilantro. Serve with reserved dressing/marinade. Serves 6.

To check temperature, cautiously hold hand about 4 inches above coals. Hot coals will force removal of hand in 2 seconds.

Note: Beef back ribs will yield 1¼ - 3 oz (90 g each) cooked, trimmed servings per lb (455 g).

Approximate nutritional analysis not available.

SPICY PEPPER STEAK

1 lb (455 g) sirloin tip beef steak, cut ½-inch thick
2 tbs (30 ml) soy sauce
1 tbs (15 ml) cornstarch
¼ cup (60 ml) water
½ cup (120 ml) HEINZ Chili Sauce
¼ tsp (1 ml) salt
⅛ tsp (.5 ml) red pepper
⅛ tsp (.5 ml) black pepper
1 medium onion, halved, sliced
2 tbs (30 ml) vegetable oil, divided
3 large bell peppers (green, red, yellow or
    combination), cut into ¼-inch strips

Slice steak diagonally across the grain into ¼x2-inch pieces. Sprinkle soy sauce over steak and toss to coat; set aside. In small bowl, combine cornstarch and water; stir in chili sauce, salt, red pepper and black pepper and set aside.

In large skillet or wok, stir-fry onion in 1 tbs oil 1 minute. Add bell peppers and stir-fry until peppers are tender-crisp, about 3 minutes; remove. Stir-fry steak in remaining 1 tbs oil 2 minutes; stir in chili sauce mixture. Simmer 1 minute until thickened, stirring constantly. Stir in pepper mixture; heat. Serve with rice, if desired. Serves 4.

Approximate nutritional analysis per serving:
Calories 379, Protein 37 g, Carbohydrates 21 g, Fat 3 g,
Cholesterol 101 mg, Sodium 1182 mg

Chow

MANDARIN STEAK STIR-FRY

⅔ cup (160 ml) chicken broth
2 tbs (30 ml) rice vinegar
4 tsp (20 ml) cornstarch
2 cloves fresh garlic, minced
1 tbs (15 ml) soy sauce
1 tsp (5 ml) McCORMICK or SCHILLING
    Pure Orange Extract
1 tbs (15 ml) sesame oil
2 tsp (10 ml) vegetable oil
12 oz (360 g) beef, cut in ½-inch strips
1 cup (240 ml) frozen baby carrots
1 medium golden or red bell pepper,
    cut into ¼-inch strips
1 - 5 oz can (150 g) sliced water chestnuts, drained
1 cup (240 ml) snow peas, strings removed
2 tbs (30 ml) minced fresh ginger

Mix chicken broth, vinegar, cornstarch, garlic, soy sauce and
extract. Set aside. In large skillet, heat sesame and vegetable
oils over medium-high heat. When hot, add beef strips and stir-
fry 30 seconds. Remove to platter and hold. In the same skillet
add frozen carrots and cook 1 minute. Add remaining ingredients and stir-fry 2 minutes. Add liquid mixture and stir-fry
about
4 minutes or until sauce has thickened. Add beef, toss well and
serve over rice or cellophane noodles. Pass soy sauce at the
table if desired. Serves 4.

Approximate nutritional analysis per serving:
Calories 283, Protein 28 g, Carbohydrates 14 g, Fat 13 g,
Cholesterol 76 mg, Sodium 411 mg

PECOS STEAKS ON OLIVE TOAST

4 tender loin or rib steaks
2 tbs (30 ml) minced garlic
½-1 tsp (3-5 ml) bottled red chili flakes
½ tsp (3 ml) black pepper
1 loaf French bread
2 tbs (30 ml) butter or margarine
2 tbs (30 ml) chopped CALIFORNIA ripe olives
1 tbs (15 ml) minced cilantro

Trim steaks well. Mix 1 tbs garlic with chili flakes and black
pepper with back of spoon, making paste. Rub on both sides of
steaks. Cut 4 thick ½-inch slices of bread on a sharp diagonal.
Melt butter and mix in olives, cilantro and remaining 1 tbs
garlic. Grill or broil steaks until done as desired. Grill or broil
bread just long enough to toast both sides. Spoon olive butter
over bread. Place toast on plates and top with steaks. Serves 4.

Approximate nutritional analysis per serving:
Calories 655, Protein 60 g, Carbohydrates 50 g, Fat 22 g,
Cholesterol 170 mg, Sodium 652 mg

FLANK STEAK WITH CREAMY GARLIC WINE SAUCE

MARINADE:
1½-2 lbs (685-1365 g) beef flank steaks, pounded thin
1 - 10 oz can (300 g) CHI-CHI'S Diced Tomatoes
    and Green Chilies
2 tsp (10 ml) minced fresh garlic
2 bay leaves

SAUCE:
3 tbs (45 ml) butter
2-3 tsp (10-15 ml) minced fresh garlic
1 tbs (15 ml) all-purpose flour
½ cup (120 ml) beef broth
⅓ cup (80 ml) dry white wine
1 - 4¼ oz can (128 g) CHI-CHI'S Diced Green
    Chilies, drained
1 - 8 oz carton (240 g) sour cream

In large reclosable plastic food bag, place flank steak and
marinade ingredients; seal bag and turn several times to coat.
Place bag in 13x9-inch pan. Refrigerate, turning bag occasionally, 8 hours or overnight. Heat broiler. Remove meat from
marinade, remove bay leaves; reserve marinade. Place meat on
broiler pan. Broil 7-8 inches from heat source 6-8 minutes on
each side for medium doneness, basting with reserved marinade. In medium saucepan, sauté garlic in butter 1 minute.
Stir in flour; cook and stir 1 minute or until bubbling. Stir in
beef broth, wine and chilies. Cook 1-2 minutes or until sauce
thickens, stirring frequently. Add 2 tbs hot sauce to sour cream;
mix well. Add sour cream mixture to sauce. Cook and stir 2-3
minutes just until sauce is heated through, do not overheat.
Spoon sauce over flank steak. Serves 8.

Approximate nutritional analysis per serving:
Calories 270, Protein 19 g, Carbohydrates 4 g, Fat 19 g,
Cholesterol 70 mg, Sodium 190 mg

CARNE ASADA

1 - 16 oz jar (480 g) CHI-CHI'S Salsa
2 tbs (30 ml) lime juice
1 tbs (15 ml) chopped fresh sage
1 tbs (15 ml) tequila, if desired
4 - 6 oz (180 g) boneless rib-eye steaks, ¾-inch thick
¾ cups (180 ml) shredded co-jack cheese

In medium saucepan, combine salsa, lime juice, sage and
tequila. Cook and stir over medium heat until heated through.
Broil steaks 6 inches from heat source 4-5 minutes on each side
for medium-rare doneness. Spoon hot salsa over steaks;
sprinkle with cheese. Serves 4.

Approximate nutritional analysis per serving:
Calories 330, Protein 32 g, Carbohydrates 7 g, Fat 19 g,
Cholesterol 95 mg, Sodium 730 mg

SPICY GRILLED SHORT RIBS

1 ½ lbs (685 g) well-trimmed beef rib short rib,
    cut crosswise ⅜-½ inch thick*
½ cup (120 ml) barbecue sauce
¼ cup (60 ml) fresh lemon juice
3 jalapeños peppers, minced**
3 tbs (45 ml) minced green onion
salt and pepper, if desired

Combine barbecue sauce, lemon juice, jalapeño peppers and green onion. Reserve ¼ cup marinade. Place beef rib short ribs in large plastic bag; add remaining marinade, turning to coat. Close bag securely and marinate in refrigerator 6-8 hours or overnight, turning occasionally. Remove ribs from marinade; discard marinade. Place ribs on grid over medium coals. Grill 10-12 minutes, turning once and brushing with marinade before turning. Season with salt and pepper, if desired. Serves 4.

   * Beef rib short ribs, cut ⅜-½ inch thick may be special ordered from your meat retailer. Each rib piece should contain 3 crosscut rib bones and come from the 6th, 7th and 8th rib.

   ** To reduce the heat of jalapeño peppers, membranes and seeds may be removed.

   To check temperature, cautiously hold hand about 4 inches above coals. Medium coals will force removal of hand in 4 seconds.

Approximate nutritional analysis per serving:
Calories 283, Protein 27 g, Carbohydrates 6 g, Fat 16 g,
Cholesterol 79 mg, Sodium 308 mg

Courtesy of the National Live Stock and Meat Board.

Spicy Grilled Short Ribs

HONEY MUSTARD-GLAZED STEAK WITH GRILLED ONIONS

2 boneless beef top loin steaks, cut 1-inch thick*
⅓ cup (80 ml) coarse grain or regular
    Dijon-style mustard
1 tbs (15 ml) chopped fresh parsley
1 ½ tbs (25 ml) honey
1 tbs (15 ml) cider vinegar
1 tbs (15 ml) water
¼ tsp (1 ml) hot pepper sauce
⅛ tsp (.5 ml) coarse grind black pepper
1 large onion, cut into ½-inch slices

Combine mustard, parsley, honey, vinegar, water, pepper sauce and black pepper. Place beef top loin steaks and onions on grid over medium coals; brush both sides liberally with glaze. Grill steaks and onions 9-12 minutes for rare to medium and until onions are tender, turning steaks and onions once and brushing with glaze. Trim excess fat from steaks before carving into slices. Serve steak with onions.

   * Recipe may also be prepared using 1 lb boneless beef sirloin steak, cut 1 inch thick. Grill steaks 16-20 minutes for rare to medium, turning once.

   To check temperature, cautiously hold hand about 4 inches above coals. Medium coals will force removal of hand in 4 seconds.

   Note: Boneless beef top loin steaks and onion may also be cooked in covered cooker (direct method) 8-11 minutes, turning once and brushing with glaze.

   Boneless beef top loin steaks will yield 3-4 - 3 oz (90 g each) cooked, trimmed servings per lb (455 g).

Approximate nutritional analysis per serving:
Calories 229, Protein 26 g, Carbohydrates 11 g, Fat 8 g,
Cholesterol 65 mg, Sodium 314 mg

Courtesy of National Live Stock and Meat Board.

Spicy Beef Back Ribs

SPICY BEEF BACK RIBS

5 lbs (2.3 kg) beef back ribs, cut into 3-4 rib sections
1 cup (240 ml) catsup
½ cup (120 ml) water
1 medium onion, grated
2 tbs (30 ml) fresh lemon juice
1 tsp (5 ml) hot pepper sauce
½-1 tsp (3-5 ml) crushed red pepper pods

Combine catsup, water, onion, lemon juice, pepper sauce and pepper pods in small saucepan. Bring to a boil; reduce heat. Cook slowly, uncovered, 10-12 minutes, stirring occasionally; keep warm. Prepare grill for indirect cooking. Place beef back ribs , meat side up, on grid centered over drip pan. Cover cooker. Grill ribs 45-60 minutes or until tender, turning occasionally. Brush reserved sauce over ribs and continue grilling, covered, 10 minutes. Serves 6.

To prepare grill for indirect cooking, arrange equal amount of briquettes on each side of grill. Place aluminum foil drip pan in center between coals. Coals are ready when ash-covered, approximately 30 minutes. Make sure coals are burning equally on both sides.

Uncovered Grilling Directions: Place ribs, meat side down, in center of double-thick rectangle of heavy duty aluminum foil. Sprinkle 2 tbs water over rib bones. To form packets, bring two opposite sides of aluminum foil together over top of ribs. Fold edges over 3-4 times pressing crease in tightly each time. Allow some air space. Flatten aluminum at both ends; crease to form triangle and fold each end over several times toward packet, pressing tightly to seal. Place packets on grid over low to medium coals. Grill 2 hours or until tender, turning packets over every ½ hour. Remove ribs from packets and place on grid. Continue grilling 10-20 minutes, turning once. Brush sauce over ribs; continue cooking 10 minutes.

To check temperature, cautiously hold hand about 4 inches above coals. Low to medium coals will force removal of hand in 4-5 seconds.

Note: Beef back ribs will yield 1¼ - 3 oz (90 g each) cooked, trimmed servings per lb (455 g).

Approximate nutritional analysis not available.

Courtesy of the National Live Stock and Meat Board.

MINTED LAMB CHOPS AND PEARS

1 cup (240 ml) CHI-CHI'S Salsa
½ cup (120 ml) firmly packed brown sugar
2 tsp (10 ml) dry mustard
4 lamb shoulder chops, ½-inch thick
2 large firm ripe pears, cored and cut into quarters
2 tbs (30 ml) chopped fresh mint

In blender container, combine salsa, brown sugar and mustard. Process until smooth. Place lamb chops in reclosable plastic food storage bag. Pour salsa mixture over lamb. Seal bag and turn several times to coat. Place bag in 13x9-inch pan. Refrigerate, turning bag occasionally, at least 4 hours or overnight. Remove lamb from marinade; reserve marinade. Over medium coals, grill lamb 5 minutes on each side for medium doneness. Grill pears, turning every 2 minutes. In saucepan, bring reserved marinade to boil; boil 2 minutes. Stir in mint. Serve marinade with lamb and pears. Serves 4.

Approximate nutritional analysis per serving:
Calories 450, Protein 24 g, Carbohydrates 49 g, Fat 19 g, Cholesterol 90 mg, Sodium 350 mg

HONEY-CITRUS GLAZED VEAL CHOPS

4 - 8 oz (240 g each) veal rib chops, cut 1-inch thick
3 tbs (45 ml) fresh lime juice
2 tbs (30 ml) honey
2 tsp (10 ml) grated fresh ginger
½ tsp (3 ml) grated lime peel

Combine lime juice, honey, ginger and lime peel. Place veal rib chops in utility dish just large enough to hold chops. Brush marinade liberally over both sides of chops; reserve any remaining marinade. Cover and marinate in refrigerator 30 minutes while preparing coals. Remove chops from dish; brush with reserved marinade. Place chops on grid over medium coals. Grill 12-14 minutes for medium, turning once. Serves 4.

To check temperature, cautiously hold hand about 4 inches above coals. Medium coals will force removal of hand in 4 seconds.

Broiler Directions: marinate chops as directed above. Place chops on rack in broiler pan so surface of meat is 4 inches from heat. Brush with reserved marinade. Broil 14-16 minutes for medium, turning once.

Approximate nutritional analysis per serving:
Calories 186, Protein 22 g, Carbohydrates 10 g, Fat 6 g, Cholesterol 97 mg, Sodium 84 mg

Courtesy of the National Live Stock and Meat Board.

LEMON-ROSEMARY VEAL STEAKS WITH GRILLED POLENTA

3 veal arm or blade steaks, cut ¾-inch thick
⅓ cup (80 ml) fresh lemon juice
⅓ cup (80 ml) water
1½ tsp (8 ml) vegetable oil
1 tsp (5 ml) dried rosemary leaves, crushed
¾ tsp (4 ml) minced garlic
¼ tsp (1 ml) coarse ground black pepper
½ tsp (3 ml) salt

GRILLED POLENTA:
2¾ cups (660 ml) water
¾ cup (180 ml) yellow cornmeal
½ tsp (3 ml) salt
2 oz (60 g) shredded mozzarella or fontina cheese
2 tbs (30 ml) grated Parmesan cheese

Combine lemon juice, water, oil, rosemary, garlic and pepper. Place veal arm or blade steaks in plastic bag; add marinade, turning to coat. Close bag securely and marinate in refrigerator at least 6 hours or overnight, turning occasionally. Prepare polenta for Grilled Polenta. Remove steaks from marinade; discard marinade. Place steaks on grid over medium coals. Grill 16-18 minutes for medium, turning once. Season with salt. Serve with Grilled Polenta. Serves 6.

Broiler Directions: marinate veal arm or blade steaks as directed above. Place steaks on rack in broiler pan so surface of meat is 4 inches from heat. Broil 14-15 minutes for medium, turning once. Arrange polenta on rack in broiler pan with steaks 10-12 minutes before end of cooking time broil until lightly browned on both sides, turning once. Sprinkle polenta with cheese.

Grilled Polenta: Combine water, cornmeal and salt in 2-qt microwave-safe dish. Cover and microwave on HIGH 10-12 minutes, stirring once. Stir in mozzarella cheese. Let stand, covered, 2 minutes. Spread cornmeal mixture into lightly greased 9-inch round pan; cool slightly. Cover and refrigerate at least 1 hour or overnight. Cut into 6 wedges. Place wedges on grid over medium coals. Grill 12-15 minutes or until lightly browned, turning once. Sprinkle cheese over warm polenta wedges. Serves 6.

To check temperature, cautiously hold hand about 4 inches above coals. Medium coals will force removal of hand in 4 seconds.

Note: A veal arm or blade steak will yield 2 - 3 oz (90 g each) cooked, trimmed servings per lb (455 g).

Approximate nutritional analysis per serving veal:
Calories 146, Protein 22 g, Carbohydrates 1 g, Fat 6 g, Cholesterol 93 mg, Sodium 261 mg

Approximate nutritional analysis per serving polenta:
Calories 238, Protein 8 g, Carbohydrates 45 g, Fat 3 g, Cholesterol 6 mg, Sodium 267 mg

Opposite: Honey-Citrus Glazed Veal Chops

GRILLED LAMB KABOBS WITH COUSCOUS TABBOULEH

COUSCOUS TABBOULEH:
½ cup (120 ml) couscous
¾ cup (180 ml) boiling water
2 medium tomatoes, coarsely chopped
⅓ cup (80 ml) chopped fresh parsley
¼ cup (60 ml) chopped green onion
3 tbs (45 ml) fresh lemon juice
1 tbs (15 ml) finely chopped fresh mint *or*
       ¼ tsp (1 ml) dried mint leaves, crushed
½ tsp (3 ml) salt
freshly ground black pepper, as desired

GRILLED LAMB KABOBS:
1 medium onion, cut in half crosswise
2 tbs (30 ml) olive oil
2 cloves garlic, crushed
1 tsp (5 ml) dried basil leaves, crushed
¼ tsp (1 ml) ground cinnamon
1 lb (455 g) well-trimmed boneless lamb leg,
       cut into 1¼-inch pieces
1 small lemon, cut into 8 wedges
¼ cup (60 ml) apple jelly
2 tbs (30 ml) fresh lemon juice
1 tsp (5 ml) chopped fresh mint OR
¼ tsp (1 ml) dried mint leaves, crushed

Couscous Tabbouleh: Combine couscous and boiling water; cover and let stand 5 minutes. Cool. Crumble couscous with fingers. Combine couscous, tomatoes, parsley, green onion, lemon juice, mint, salt and pepper in bowl. Serve at room temperature. Yields 3 cups.

Cut each onion half into quarters; separate into pieces. Combine oil, garlic, basil and cinnamon. Place lamb leg pieces, onion and lemon wedges in plastic bag; add marinade, turning to coat. Close bag securely and marinate in refrigerator in refrigerator 1 hour. Meanwhile combine apple jelly, lemon juice and mint in small saucepan. Cook over low heat until jelly melts, stirring occasionally. Remove lamb cubes from marinade; discard marinade. Alternately thread lamb cubes, onion pieces and lemon wedges on each of four 12-inch metal skewers. Place kebobs on grid over medium coals. Grill 8-12 minutes for medium, turning and brushing with jelly mixture occasionally. Serve kabobs with Couscous Tabbouleh. Serves 4.

Approximate nutritional analysis per ¾ cup serving Couscous Tabbouleh:Calories 106, Protein 4 g, Carbohydrates 18 g, Fat < 1 g, Cholesterol 0 mg, Sodium 281 mg

Approximate nutritional analysis per kabob: Calories 280, Protein 23 g, Carbohydrates 18 g, Fat 13 g, Cholesterol 79 mg, Sodium 83 mg

SOUTHWEST BLACKENED PORK CHOPS

4 boneless pork loin or rib chops, ½-inch thick
1 tsp (5 ml) vegetable oil
1½ tsp (8 ml) chili powder
1 tsp (5 ml) crushed fennel seed
½ tsp (3 ml) ground cumin
1¼ cups (295 ml) CHI-CHI'S Salsa
2 small oranges, peeled, segmented and
       coarsely chopped
¼ cup (60 ml) sliced green onions

Rub both sides of pork chops with oil. Combine chili powder, fennel seed and cumin. Pat seasoning mixture onto both sides of each pork chop. Over medium-hot coals, grill pork 5 minutes on each side or until no longer pink in center. In medium bowl, combine salsa, oranges and green onions. Mix well. Serve with pork chops. Serves 4.

Approximate nutritional analysis per serving: Calories 310, Protein 34 g, Carbohydrates 14 g, Fat 13 g, Cholesterol 90 mg, Sodium 420 mg

BONELESS CHUCK ROAST

3 lbs (1.4 kg) rolled boneless beef chuck roast
all-purpose flour
fat for browning
1 cup (240 ml) water
salt and pepper

Dust meat lightly with flour. Brown slowly on all sides in hot fat in Dutch oven. Salt and pepper to suit personal preference, about 2 tsp salt. Add water, cover, cook in preheated 300°F (150°C) oven about 2 hours, or until meat is very tender. Add more water and turn meat halfway through cooking time, if desired. Remove meat and thicken liquid with a flour and water paste. If desired, potatoes, onions, carrots may be added when meat is turned. Serves 6.

Approximate nutritional analysis per serving w/o vegetables: Calories 446, Protein 53 g, Carbohydrates 0 g, Fat 24 g, Cholesterol 180 mg, Sodium 811 mg

Courtesy of Imperial Sugar.

Opposite: Grilled Lamb Kabobs with Couscous Tabbouleh

BEEF TENDERLOIN AU POIVRE

3-3½ lbs (1.4-1.6 kg) beef tenderloin roast
⅔ cup (160 ml) Rhine wine
⅓ cup (80 ml) vegetable oil
1 small onion, chopped
1½ tsp (8 ml) salt
1 clove garlic, crushed
1-2 tbs (15-30 ml) cracked black pepper

Combine wine, oil, onion, salt and garlic. Place beef tenderloin roast in plastic bag; add marinade, turning to coat. Close bag securely and marinate in refrigerator 6-8 hours or overnight, turning occasionally. Remove roast from marinade; discard marinade. Pat dry roast with paper towels. Roll roast in pepper, lightly pressing into surface of roast. Place roast, fat side up, on rack in shallow roasting pan. Insert meat thermometer into thickest part of roast, not touching fat. Do not add water. Do not cover. Roast in hot, 425°F (220°C), oven approximately 45-50 minutes or until meat thermometer registers 135°F (57°C) for rare. Cover roast with aluminum foil tent and allow to stand 15 minutes. Roast will continue to rise approximately 5°F (3°C) in temperature to reach 140°F (60°C) for rare. Trim excess fat from roast before carving. Serves 9-14.

Note: A beef tenderloin roast will yield 3-4 - 3 oz (90 g each) cooked, trimmed servings per lb (455 g).

Approximate nutritional analysis per serving:
Calories 217, Protein 24 g, Carbohydrates < 1 g, Fat 13 g,
Cholesterol 73 mg, Sodium 75 mg

Beef Tenderloin au Poivre

PRONTO SPICY BEEF AND BLACK BEAN SALSA

SEASONING:
1 tbs (15 ml) chili powder
1 tsp (5 ml) ground cumin
1 tsp (5 ml) salt
½ tsp (3 ml) ground red pepper

1 beef tri-tip (bottom sirloin) or top sirloin steak,
    cut 1½ inches thick
1 - 15 oz can (450 g) black beans, rinsed and drained
1 medium tomato, chopped
1 small red onion, finely chopped
3 tbs (45 ml) coarsely chopped fresh cilantro
fresh cilantro sprigs, optional

Combine seasoning ingredients; reserve 2 tbs for salsa. Trim fat from beef roast. Press remaining seasoning mixture evenly into surface of roast. Place tri-tip on grid over medium coals (medium-low coals for top sirloin). Grill tri-tip 30-35 minutes (top sirloin 22-30 minutes) for rare to medium doneness, turning occasionally. Let stand 10 minutes before carving.

Meanwhile in medium bowl, combine beans, tomato, onion, chopped cilantro and reserved seasoning mixture; mix until blended. Carve roast across the grain into slices. Arrange beef and bean salsa on serving platter; garnish with cilantro sprigs, if desired. Serves 6.

To check temperature, cautiously hold hand about 4 inches above coals. Low to medium coals will force removal of hand in 4-5 seconds.

Approximate nutritional analysis per serving using beef tri-tip:
Calories 252, Protein 29 g, Carbohydrates 14 g, Fat 9 g,
Cholesterol 48 mg, Sodium 439 mg

Approximate nutritional analysis per serving using beef top sirloin:
Calories 242, Protein 30 g, Carbohydrates 14 g, Fat 7 g,
Cholesterol 76 mg, Sodium 428 mg

Pronto Spicy Beef and Black Bean Salsa

WONDERFULLY QUICK BEEF TENDERLOIN

**1 - 5¾ lb (2.6 kg) whole beef tenderloin,
    trimmed, preferably heavy aged beef***
3 tbs (45 ml) extra virgin olive oil
**2 tbs (30 ml) CHEF PAUL PRUDHOMME'S
    Blackened Steak Magic**
nonstick vegetable oil spray

* Ask your butcher to trim the tenderloin. If you want to trim it yourself, remove all the silver skin from the meat. Then remove the back strap: To find it, lay the tenderloin down with the larger end to your right; the back strap is on the back side of the tenderloin and is immediately evident when you remove the silver skin. It can be removed with your fingers. Don't remove the marbled fat from the bottom side; it will keep the tenderloin from sticking to the pan. The trimmings can be browned off and used for gravy.

Spray a heavy roasting pan (without rack) with vegetable spray. Place the tenderloin in the roasting pan, fat side down. Pour the olive oil directly in the pan and use it to oil the tenderloin really well. The three tbs will coat the meat and leave enough remaining to coat the pan. This is necessary because the tenderloin has so little fat on it.

    Sprinkle the Blackened Steak Magic lightly and evenly over the tenderloin - on every surface - and pat it in. Refrigerate the tenderloin and baking pan for 1 hour. Don't remove it from the refrigerator until you're ready to place it in the oven. It's important for the tenderloin to be cold when you place it in the hot oven.

    While the meat is chilling, preheat the oven to 550°F (288°C). Be sure to check your oven temperature with a free standing oven thermometer to see if it registers accurately; most home ovens vary somewhat from the temperature you set.

    Place roasting pan in the middle of the oven and bake until a probe inserted into the thickest part of the meat registers 127°F (53°C) for a true rare (cool red center), about 25 minutes. Increase the cooking time in very small increments to reach medium rare (138°F (59°C)), medium (148°F (64°C)), medium well (158°F (70°C)). Any temperature in excess of 165°F (74°C) is considered well done - but don't do this to a fine cut of beef. Remove from oven and transfer meat to a cutting board or platter; let sit 15-20 minutes. Carve and serve immediately. Serves 10.

Approximate nutritional analysis per serving:
Calories 561, Protein 80 g, Carbohydrates 0 g, Fat 25 g,
Cholesterol 232 mg, Sodium 279 mg

PARTY BARBECUE

3-3½ lb (1.4-1.6 kg) beef brisket
¼ cup (60 ml) water
2 tbs (30 ml) liquid smoke
½ tsp (3 ml) garlic salt
¼ tsp (1 ml) pepper
2½ cups (590 ml) HEINZ Tomato Ketchup
⅓ cup (80 ml) firmly packed brown sugar
2 tbs (30 ml) Worcestershire sauce
1 tbs (15 ml) HEINZ Apple Cider Vinegar
1 tsp (5 ml) prepared mustard
½ tsp (3 ml) garlic salt
½ tsp (3 ml) onion salt
¼ tsp (1 ml) black pepper
¼ tsp (1 ml) red pepper
semi-hard rolls or sandwich buns

Place beef and next 4 ingredients in Dutch oven. Cover tightly; cook over low heat 2 hours. Remove beef; reserve ½ cup meat juices. Allow beef to cool slightly for easier slicing. Thinly slice beef diagonally across the grain. In same Dutch oven, combine reserved meat juices, ketchup and remaining ingredients except rolls; simmer covered, 5 minutes. Add sliced beef; heat. Serve in rolls. Serves 12.

Approximate nutritional analysis per serving w/o bread:
Calories 286, Protein 33 g, Carbohydrates 19 g, Fat 8 g,
Cholesterol 92 mg, Sodium 819 mg

BARBECUE BEEF BRISKET

8 lb (3.6 kg) boneless beef brisket
coarse ground pepper
salt
Worcestershire sauce
paprika
liquid smoke

The best briskets for outdoor cooking are packer-trimmed and sealed in Cryovac. Brisket should be smoked long and slow over low heat. For added flavor, soak mesquite or hickory chips in water overnight and place on hot coals.

    To prepare brisket, rub lightly with pepper, salt, Worcestershire sauce, paprika, liquid smoke. Place on grill, fat side up and away from coals. Cover tightly and let smoke 1½ hours per lb (455 g). Do not turn over as fat will drip through meat for self-basting action. Add briquettes and wood chips as needed during cooking but keep fire steady and slow. Brisket is done when no pink is showing in thickest part of meat. Cut away fat, slice against grain and serve with warm barbecue sauce. Serves 15.

Approximate nutritional analysis per serving meat only:
Calories 439, Protein 54 g, Carbohydrates 0 g, Fat 23 g,
Cholesterol 169 mg, Sodium 127 mg

TENDERLOIN OF BEEF POMPEIAN

4 lbs (1.8 kg) tenderloin of beef
salt and freshly ground pepper to taste
2 tbs (30 ml) POMPEIAN Red Wine Vinegar
2 tbs (30 ml) crushed fresh garlic
½ cup (120 ml) POMPEIAN Extra Virgin Olive Oil
fresh rosemary sprigs

Generously rub the tenderloin of beef with the crushed garlic. Sprinkle with salt and fresh pepper to taste. Combine the olive oil and red wine vinegar and brush the beef with the mixture. Top with the fresh rosemary sprigs and roast at 400°F (205°C) for 20 minutes, then 350°F (180°C) for 20 minutes, or until meat thermometer registers medium rare. The tenderloin should be pink when sliced. Serves 10.

Approximate nutritional analysis per serving:
Calories 413, Protein 55 g, Carbohydrates 0 g, Fat 20 g, Cholesterol 162 mg, Sodium 120 mg

Chili-Roasted Sirloin with Corn Pudding

Opposite: Tenderloin of Beef Pompeian

CHILI-ROASTED SIRLOIN WITH CORN PUDDING

CORN PUDDING:
1 - 20 oz bag (600 g) frozen whole kernel corn, defrosted
1 small onion, quartered
2 cups (480 ml) 2% milk
2 eggs, beaten
1 - 8½ oz box (255 g) corn muffin mix
½ tsp (3 ml) salt
4 oz (120 g) shredded cheddar cheese
1 cup (240 ml) thinly sliced Romaine lettuce
½ cup (120 ml) julienned radishes

3 lb (1.4 kg) boneless beef top sirloin steak, cut 2 inches thick
2 large garlic cloves, crushed
2 tsp (10 ml) chili powder
¾ tsp (4 ml) dried oregano leaves, crushed
½ tsp (3 ml) ground cumin
salt and pepper, as desired

Corn Pudding: Combine corn and onion in food processor bowl fitted with steel blade; cover and process until corn is broken but not puréed, scraping side of bowl as necessary. Add milk and eggs; process until just blended. Add muffin mix and salt; process only until mixed. Pour mixture into greased 11¾x7½-inch baking dish. Bake 45-50 minutes or until outside crust is golden brown. Broil until cheese is melted and top is crusty. Top with Romaine lettuce and radishes before serving. Serves 8.

Combine garlic, chili powder, oregano and cumin; press into both sides of beef top sirloin steak. Place steak on rack in shallow roasting pan. Do not add water. Do not cover. Roast in moderate, 350°F (180°C), oven to desired doneness. Allow 16-20 minutes per lb (455 g) for rare. Remove steak when meat thermometer registers 135°F (57°C) for rare. Season with salt and pepper to taste. Cover steak with aluminum foil tent and allow to stand 10 minutes. Thick-cut steaks will continue to rise approximately 5°F (3°C) in temperature to 140°F (60°C) for rare. Trim excess fat from steak; carve into thin slices. Serve with Corn Pudding. Serves 12.

Note: A boneless beef top sirloin steak will yield 4 - 3 oz (90 g each) cooked, trimmed servings per lb (455 g) .

Approximate nutritional analysis per serving Corn Pudding:
Calories 270, Protein 10 g, Carbohydrates 39 g, Fat 9 g, Cholesterol 81 mg, Sodium 545 mg

Approximate nutritional analysis per 3 oz cooked, trimmed serving meat:
Calories 180, Protein 26 g, Carbohydrates 1 g, Fat 7 g, Cholesterol 76 mg, Sodium 61 mg

Courtesy of the National Live Stock and Meat Board.

VEAL STEAKS RIO GRAND WITH FRESH SALSA

2 - 1 lb (910 g) veal blade or arm steaks,
    cut ¾-inch thick
1 cup (240 ml) picante sauce
1 tbs (15 ml) fresh lime juice
2 tsp (10 ml) vegetable oil
¼ tsp (1 ml) salt
⅛ tsp (.5 ml) freshly ground black pepper

FRESH SALSA:
8 oz (240 g) medium tomatoes, seeded
    and finely chopped
¼ cup (60 ml) finely chopped onion
2 tbs (30 ml) finely chopped fresh cilantro
2 tbs (30 ml) fresh lime juice
1 fresh serrano or jalapeño pepper, seeded
    and finely chopped
1 clove garlic, crushed
½ tsp (3 ml) salt

Combine picante sauce, lime juice, oil, salt and pepper. Place veal blade or arm steaks in plastic bag; add marinade, turning to coat. Close bag securely and marinate in refrigerator at least 6 hours or overnight, turning occasionally. Remove steaks from marinade, discard marinade. Place steaks on rack in broiler pan so surface of meat is 4 inches from heat. Broil 14-15 minutes for medium, turning once. Serve chops with Fresh Salsa. Serves 4.

Fresh Salsa: Combine tomatoes, onion, cilantro, lime juice, serrano pepper, garlic and salt in medium glass bowl. Cover and refrigerate at least 2 hours. Let stand at room temperature 1 hour before serving. Yields 1 cup.

Note: A veal blade or arm steak will yield 2 - 3 oz (180 g) cooked trimmed servings per lb (455 g) .

Grilling Directions: Marinate veal blade or arm steaks as directed above. Place steaks on grid over medium coals. Grill 16-18 minutes for medium, turning once. To check temperature of coals, cautiously hold hand about 4 inches above coals. Medium coals will force removal of hand in 4 seconds.

Approximate nutritional analysis per serving veal plus ¼ cup salsa:
Calories 200, Protein 31 g, Carbohydrates 7 g, Fat 5 g,
Cholesterol 135 mg, Sodium 508 mg

Courtesy of the National Live Stock and Meat Board.

VEAL RIB ROAST WITH CRANBERRY-PORT SAUCE

4-5 lb (1.8-2.3 kg) veal rib roast, cap removed
1¼ cup (295 ml) fresh bread crumbs
3 tbs (45 ml) minced fresh parsley
2 tbs (30 ml) butter or margarine, melted
2 medium cloves garlic, crushed
1¼ tsp (6 ml) dried marjoram leaves, crushed
2 tbs (30 ml) Dijon-style mustard
1 - 16 oz can (480 g) whole berry cranberry sauce
⅓ cup (80 ml) Ruby port wine

Place veal rib roast, rib ends down, in shallow roasting pan. Insert meat thermometer into thickest part of roast, not touching bone or fat. Do not add water. Do not cover. Roast in slow, 325°F (165°C) oven until meat thermometer registers 150°F (66°C) for medium. Allow approximately 25-27 minutes per pound for medium. Approximately 30 minutes before end of cooking time, combine bread crumbs, parsley, butter, garlic and marjoram; reserve. Remove roast from oven. Spread mustard evenly over top surface of roast. Coat with crumb mixture, patting firmly into mustard. Return roast to oven and continue roasting 25 minutes or until meat thermometer registers 155°F (68°C) for medium. Do not overcook. Cover roast with aluminum foil tent and allow to stand 15 minutes. Roast will continue to rise approximately 5°F (3°C) in temperature to reach 160°F (71°C) for medium. Meanwhile skim and discard fat from drippings, if necessary. Add wine to drippings, stirring to dissolve browned meat juices from pan. Add cranberry sauce and cook over medium-high heat 10 minutes or until sauce is thickened, stirring frequently. Trim excess fat and remove back bone from roast; carve roast. Serve with sauce. Serves 8-10.

Note: Ask meat retailer to loosen the chine bone (back bone) by sawing across the rib bones. After roasting, the back bone can be removed easily by running the carving knife along the edge of the roast before the meat is placed on the platter to be carved.

A veal rib roast, cap removed, will yield 2 - 3 oz (180 g) cooked, trimmed servings per lb (455 g).

Approximate nutritional analysis per serving:
Calories 348, Protein 24 g, Carbohydrates 39 g, Fat 9 g,
Cholesterol 116 mg, Sodium 300 mg

Courtesy of the National Live Stock and Meat Board.

Opposite: Veal Steaks Rio Grande with Fresh Salsa

HERBED VEAL ROAST PROVENCAL

3 lb (1.4 kg) boneless veal leg rump roast
¼ cup (60 ml) finely chopped parsley, divided
2 tsp (10 ml) olive oil or vegetable oil
1¼ tsp (6 ml) dried thyme leaves
¼ tsp (1 ml) garlic powder
¼ tsp (1 ml) coarsely ground pepper
¼ tsp (1 ml) salt
1 - 14½ oz can (435 g) whole peeled tomatoes
⅓ cup (80 ml) dry white wine

Do not preheat oven. Reserve 1 tbs parsley. Combine remaining parsley, oil, thyme, garlic powder, pepper and salt; rub over veal leg rump roast. Place roast, fat side up, on rack in shallow roasting pan. Insert meat thermometer into thickest part of roast, not touching bone or fat. Do not add water. Do not cover. Roast in slow 325°F (165°C) oven until thermometer registers 155°F (68°C), approximately 33-35 minutes per lb. Transfer roast to warm platter; let stand 15-20 minutes while preparing sauce. Temperature should rise to 160°F (71°C) during standing. For sauce, drain tomatoes, reserving liquid. Seed and chop tomatoes. Drain fat from roasting pan if necessary. Add tomatoes, reserved liquid and wine to roasting pan, scraping to loosen browned bits. Bring to boil. Reduce heat to medium-high and cook until slightly thickened, about 3 minutes. Stir in reserved parsley. Carve roast and serve with sauce and couscous or barley. Serves 12.

Approximate nutritional analysis per serving:
Calories 186, Protein 27 g, Carbohydrates 2 g, Fat 6 g,
Cholesterol 100 mg, Sodium 178 mg

Courtesy of the National Live Stock and Meat Board.

VEAL STEW WITH MUSHROOMS

½ cup (120 ml) chopped onion
¼ cup (60 ml) chopped celery
¼ cup (60 ml) diced carrot
1 garlic clove, finely chopped
2 tsp (10 ml) BERTOLLI Classico Olive Oil
1 lb (455 g) well-trimmed veal shoulder or leg,
cut into 1-inch cubes
3 large white button or shitake mushroom caps,
quartered
salt and freshly ground black pepper
1 - 14½ oz can (435 g) Italian plum tomatoes
with juices
1 cup (240 ml) chicken broth
1 strip orange zest, 2x½ inch
½ tsp (3 ml) dried rosemary
8 oz (240 g) potatoes, peeled and cut into 1-inch cubes
2 cups (480 ml) thick sliced zucchini

In large non-stick skillet combine the onion, celery, carrot, garlic and olive oil. Cook, stirring, over low heat until vegetables are tender, about 10 minutes. Add veal and mushrooms; season with salt and pepper; cook, turning, 5 minutes. Add the tomatoes, broth, orange zest and rosemary. Cover and cook over medium-low heat, stirring occasionally, until the veal is tender, about 45 minutes. Add the potatoes; cover and cook until potatoes are almost tender, about 10 minutes. Add zucchini, cook 5 minutes. Season to taste. Serves 4.

Approximate nutritional analysis per serving:
Calories 234, Protein 26 g, Carbohydrates 18 g, Fat 7 g,
Cholesterol 98 mg, Sodium 447 mg

SUMMER SWISS STEAK

1½ lbs (685 g) boneless veal round steak,
cut ½-inch thick
8 oz (240 g) shitake mushrooms or
button mushrooms
1 tbs (15 ml) olive oil
salt and freshly ground black pepper, as desired
⅓ cup (80 ml) dry white wine
2 medium tomatoes, seeded and diced
⅓ cup (80 ml) thinly sliced fresh basil leaves

Cut small mushrooms in half, large mushrooms into quarters; reserve. Cut veal round steak into six pieces. Pound steak pieces to ⅛-inch thickness. Heat oil in 12-inch non-stick skillet. Brown veal pieces, a few at a time; remove and keep warm. Return veal to skillet; season with salt and pepper to taste. Cook, uncovered, over medium heat 4-5 minutes or until tender, turning occasionally. Remove veal to platter; keep warm. Add wine and mushrooms to skillet, stirring to dissolve browned meat juices attached to pan. Cook over medium-high heat 3 minutes or until mushrooms are tender, stirring frequently. Add tomato and basil; heat through. Spoon vegetable mixture over veal. Serves 6.

Note: A veal round steak will yield 4 - 3 oz (360 g) cooked, trimmed servings per lb (455 g).

Approximate nutritional analysis per serving:
Calories 175, Protein 26 g, Carbohydrates 5 g, Fat 5 g,
Cholesterol 91 mg, Sodium 263 mg

Courtesy of the National Live Stock and Meat Board.

Opposite: Summer Swiss Steak

Braised Veal Brisket with Dried Fruit

BRAISED VEAL BRISKET WITH DRIED FRUIT

2-2½ lb (910-1138 g) veal brisket
1 tbs (15 ml) vegetable oil, divided
2 medium onions, thinly sliced
1 large clove garlic, crushed
1 tsp (5 ml) salt
½ tsp (3 ml) coarse grind black pepper
apple juice
water
3 large carrots, cut into 3x¼x¼-inch strips
2 medium parsnips, cut into 3x¼x¼-inch strips
¾ cup (80 ml) dried pitted prunes
½ cup (120 ml) dried apricot halves
2 tsp (10 ml) cornstarch

Heat 2 tbs oil in Dutch oven over medium-high heat; brown veal brisket on both sides. Remove brisket; reserve. Add remaining 1 tsp oil to Dutch oven, if necessary. Add onions and garlic; cook over medium-low heat 5 minutes or until onions are tender, stirring occasionally. Place brisket, fat side up, on top of onions. Sprinkle with salt and pepper. Pour 6 tbs each apple juice and water around veal. Cover tightly and cook in very hot, 450°F (230°C) oven 30 minutes. Reduce heat to 325°F (165°C) and continue to cook 1 hour. Add carrots, parsnips, prunes and apricots; continue cooking 30 minutes or until veal and vegetables are tender. Remove brisket to warm serving platter; surround with carrots, parsnips and fruit. Keep warm. Pour cooking liquid into 1-cup glass measure. Skim and discard fat from cooking liquid. Add enough apple juice to equal 1 cup. Dissolve cornstarch in combined liquids; return to Dutch oven. Cook over medium-high heat until thickened, stirring constantly. Trim excess fat from brisket; carve brisket across the grain into thin slices. Serve with vegetables, fruit and sauce. Serves 6.

Approximate nutritional analysis per serving:
Calories 344, Protein 30 g, Carbohydrates 39 g, Fat 8 g,
Cholesterol 100 mg, Sodium 470 mg

Courtesy of the National Live Stock and Meat Board.

VEAL PARMIGIANA

1 clove garlic, minced
1 cup (240 ml) chopped mushrooms
olive oil
2 tbs (30 ml) LIBBY'S Tomato Paste
1 - 16 oz can (480 g) LIBBY'S Stewed Tomatoes
¼ tsp (1 ml) salt
⅛ tsp (.5 ml) pepper
¼ cup (60 ml) white wine
¼ tsp (1 ml) thyme
1 tbs (15 ml) sugar
1 cup (240 ml) fresh bread crumbs
½ cup (120 ml) finely grated Parmesan cheese
¼ cup (60 ml) finely chopped parsley
grated peel of 1 lemon, optional
1 egg, slightly beaten
2 tbs (30 ml) water
¼ tsp (1 ml) salt
⅛ tsp (.5 ml) pepper
8 veal cutlets
8 slices mozzarella cheese

Sauté garlic and mushrooms in 2 tbs hot olive oil. Stir in tomato paste; add next 6 ingredients. Cook over low heat about 15 minutes, stirring occasionally. In shallow baking dish combine bread crumbs, Parmesan cheese, parsley and lemon peel. In separate bowl mix together egg, water, salt and pepper. Dip each cutlet into egg mixture, then into bread crumbs. Heat 2 tbs oil in frying pan, cook breaded veal until golden brown on both sides. Arrange in shallow baking dish, topping each cutlet with a slice of cheese. Pour sauce over cutlets. Bake at 350°F (180°C) about 20 minutes or until cheese is melted and sauce heated through. Serves 8.

Approximate nutritional analysis per serving:
Calories 398, Protein 34 g, Carbohydrates 15 g, Fat 21 g,
Cholesterol 143 mg, Sodium 572 mg

BRONZED VEAL CHOPS

1 tbs plus 1½ tsp (23 ml) CHEF PAUL
    PRUDHOMME'S Pork and Veal Magic
6 veal chops, all visible fat removed
vegetable oil cooking spray

Lay the veal chops on a cutting board, take the point of a boning knife and, following the curve of the bone, cut through the meat a little less than half the thickness of the bone; do this on both sides. This step helps reduce the thickness of the meat while keeping it still attached to the bones, so the chops will cook very quickly over high heat and retain maximum moisture. Pound the entire meaty part of the chop with a meat mallet, reducing the thickness of the chops to no more than ½ inch. Sprinkle surfaces of the chops evenly with Pork and Veal Magic.

Preheat a 12-inch skillet, preferably non-stick, over high heat to 400°F (205°C), about 5 minutes. While the skillet is heating, spray each chop lightly with the vegetable oil spray. Place the chops in the skillet 2 at a time, and cook 1 minute. Turn the chops over and cook 2 minutes, then turn back to the other side and cook 1 minute more. Remove the cooked chops, wipe the skillet clean, place back over high heat, and repeat the process with the remaining chops. Serves 4.

Approximate nutritional analysis per serving:
Calories 791, Protein 127 g, Carbohydrates 2 g, Fat 29 g,
Cholesterol 312 mg, Sodium 327 mg

OVEN-BRAISED VEAL MEDITERRANEAN-STYLE

2 - 1 lb (1.4 kg) veal shoulder arm or blade steaks,
    cut 1-inch thick
2 small onions, quartered
1 large clove garlic, cut into thin slivers
¼ cup (60 ml) dry white wine
¾ tsp (4 ml) dried basil leaves, crushed
¾ tsp (4 ml) salt
¼ tsp (1 ml) dried thyme leaves, crushed
⅛ tsp (.5 ml) pepper
1 medium red bell pepper, cut into 1-inch squares
2 tbs (30 ml) thinly sliced ripe olives
1 tbs (15 ml) finely chopped fresh parsley

Place veal shoulder arm or blade steaks in single layer in 13x9-inch baking pan. Arrange onions in pan around veal. Add garlic, placing some slivers on veal; add wine. Sprinkle basil, salt, thyme and pepper over veal and vegetables. Cover tightly with aluminum foil. Bake in slow, 325°F (165°C) oven 45 minutes. Carefully remove aluminum foil; add bell pepper to pan. Cover and continue baking 45 minutes to 1 hour or until veal is tender. Sprinkle with olives and parsley. Serves 4.

Approximate nutritional analysis per serving:
Calories 203, Protein 31 g, Carbohydrates 5 g, Fat 5 g,
Cholesterol 135 mg, Sodium 550 mg

Oven-Braised Veal Mediterranean-Style

ORIENTAL PORK POT STICKERS

1 cup (240 ml) finely chopped cooked pork tenderloin
⅓ cup (80 ml) finely chopped bok choy or cabbage
⅓ cup (80 ml) finely chopped celery
¼ cup (60 ml) finely chopped green onion
1 tbs (15 ml) soy sauce
1 tbs (15 ml) dry sherry
1 tsp (5 ml) cooking oil
1½ tsp (8 ml) cornstarch
36 won ton wrappers
6 tbs (90 ml) cooking oil
1 cup (240 ml) water
Chinese mustard
soy sauce

In a mixing bowl combine pork, bok choy, celery and green onion; mix well. Combine 1 tbs soy sauce, sherry and 1 tsp oil; stir in cornstarch until dissolved. Pour soy sauce mixture over pork mixture; toss to coat. Cover and chill 30 minutes.

Cut won ton wrappers into 4-inch circles with cookie cutter. Keep won ton wrappers covered with a dry cloth when not working with wrappers. Spoon about 2 tsp filling in center of one round. Bring up sides and seal edges with water. Transfer to a baking sheet and cover with a dry cloth. Repeat with remaining rounds and filling.

In a large skillet heat 2 tbs of the oil. Carefully place half the pot stickers in skillet. Do not let the pot stickers touch. Cook over medium heat 1 minute or until bottoms are browned. Carefully add ½ cup water to skillet. Reduce heat; cover and simmer 10 minutes. Uncover and cook 3-5 minutes or until water evaporates. Add more oil if necessary. Cook, uncovered, 1 minute. Transfer pot stickers to a baking sheet. Place in a 250°F (121°C) oven to keep warm. Repeat procedure with remaining pot stickers, oil and water. Serve with Chinese mustard and soy sauce. Serves 36.

Approximate nutritional analysis per serving:
Calories 39, Protein 2 g, Fat 2 g, Cholesterol 4 mg, Sodium 59 mg

Courtesy of the National Pork Producers Council.

JERK RIBS

2 lbs (480 ml) pork back ribs
1 tbs (15 ml) onion powder
4 tsp (20 ml) ground thyme
2 tsp (10 ml) salt
2 tsp (10 ml) ground allspice
½ tsp (3 ml) ground nutmeg
½ tsp (3 ml) ground cinnamon
1 tbs (15 ml) sugar
2 tsp (10 ml) black pepper
1 tsp (5 ml) cayenne

In a small jar with a tight-fitting lid, shake together all dry ingredients until well blended. Rub dry mixture onto all surfaces of the ribs. Grill ribs over indirect heat in covered grill, turning occasionally, until ribs are very tender, about 1½ hours *or* roast ribs on rack in shallow pan in 350°F (180°C) oven for 1½ hours). Cut into 1-2 rib portions to serve. Serves 10.

Approximate nutritional analysis per serving:
Calories 155, Protein 10 g, Carbohydrates 26 g, Fat 10 g,
Cholesterol 43 mg, Sodium 461 mg

Courtesy of the National Pork Producers Council.

Jerk Ribs

Opposite: Oriental Pork Pot Stickers

Cowboy Barbecued Ribs

COWBOY BARBECUED RIBS

5 lbs (2.3 kg) pork spareribs
1 cup (240 ml) water
⅓ cup (80 ml) butter or margarine
2 tbs (30 ml) fresh lemon juice
¼ cup (60 ml) dry mustard
¼ cup (60 ml) chili powder
1 tbs (15 ml) sugar
1 tbs (15 ml) paprika
2 tsp (10 ml) salt
1 tsp (5 ml) onion powder
1 tsp (5 ml) garlic powder
¼ tsp (1 ml) cayenne pepper

Place spareribs on broiler pan. Cover with foil. Roast at 400°F (205°C) for 1½ hours. Meanwhile, combine remaining ingredients in medium saucepan; mix well. Bring to boil. Reduce heat; simmer for 30 minutes. Brush sauce on ribs. Broil 5 inches from heat for 7-10 minutes on each side. Serve ribs with additional sauce. Serves 6.

Approximate nutritional analysis per serving:
Calories 706, Protein 45 g, Carbohydrates < 1 g, Fat 55 g,
Cholesterol 204 mg, Sodium 1126 mg

Courtesy of the National Pork Producers Council.

IMPERIAL PORK STIR-FRY

1 - 16 oz can (480 g) LIBBY'S Lite Cling Peach Slices
¼ cup (60 ml) cider vinegar
¼ cup (60 ml) ketchup
2 tbs (30 ml) soy sauce
1 tbs (15 ml) grated fresh ginger
1 large clove garlic, minced
2 tbs (30 ml) cornstarch
1 lb (455 g) pork butt, cut into strips
2 tbs (30 ml) sesame oil
1 onion, cut into wedges
1 large bunch broccoli, cut into flowerettes
1 red pepper, cut into strips

Drain peaches, reserving all juice. Combine reserved juice with vinegar, ketchup, soy sauce, ginger and garlic. Blend in cornstarch; set aside. Heat oil in wok or large skillet to 400°F (205°C). Stir-fry pork in oil until brown, a few pieces at a time. Remove meat; set aside. Stir fry onion 1 minute. Add broccoli and red pepper; stir-fry 2 minutes. Return meat to wok. Pour sauce over all. Cook until sauce is thickened. Stir in peaches. Serve on bed of shredded iceberg lettuce or hot cooked rice. Serves 6.

Approximate nutritional analysis per serving:
Calories 255, Protein 16 g, Carbohydrates 22 g, Fat 12 g,
Cholesterol 53 mg, Sodium 517 mg

OKTOBERFEST RIBS

2 lbs (910 g) pork ribs
2 - 32 oz jars (1.9 kg) sauerkraut, drained
2 yellow onions, peeled and cut in half
2 tart green apples, cored and wedged
¼ cup (60 ml) brown sugar
8 juniper berries *or* 1 tbs (15 ml) caraway seed

Layer ingredients into a large Dutch oven in this order: sauerkraut, onions, apples, brown sugar (sprinkle evenly over) and ribs. Bury juniper berries or caraway seed evenly in the sauerkraut layer. Bring to boil, lower heat, cover and simmer gently for 2-3 hours, until ribs are very tender. Serves 6.

Approximate nutritional analysis per serving:
Calories 315, Protein 19 g, Carbohydrates 29 g, Fat 14 g,
Cholesterol 54 mg, Sodium 1130 mg

Courtesy of the National Pork Producers Council.

Opposite: Oktoberfest Ribs

GLAZED FRESH HAM AND LOUISIANA YAMS

**6-7 lb (2.7-3.2 kg) pork leg (fresh ham)
   shank half
2½ cups (590 ml) cranberry apple juice
¾ cup (180 ml) dark corn syrup
dash ground allspice
6 medium LOUISIANA yams, cooked, peeled and
   halved *or* 3 - 16 oz cans (1.4 g) LOUISIANA Yams,
   drained
salt, to taste**

Trim excess fat from surface of ham; score if desired. Bake ham in shallow pan in 325°F (165°C) oven 35-40 minutes per lb (455 g) or until meat thermometer registers 170°F (77°C).

Meanwhile prepare glaze. Boil cranberry apple juice and corn syrup in large skillet until thick and syrupy; stir in allspice and remove from heat.

Pour off fat from roasting pan. Sprinkle yams lightly with salt and place around ham about 30 minutes before end of baking period. Pour glaze over ham and yams; bake 30 minutes longer. Remove ham and yams to warm serving platter; pour glaze over ham and yams, strain if desired. Serves 12 (ham) and serves 6 (vegetables).

Approximate nutritional analysis per serving ham and yams:
Calories 404, Protein 35 g, Carbohydrates 48 g, Fat 8 g,
Cholesterol 73 mg, Sodium 1855 mg

Glazed Fresh Ham and Louisiana Yams

SPRINGTIME HAM WITH RHUBARB SAUCE

**3-4 lb (1.4-1.8 kg) boneless fully-cooked
   smoked ham half
½ cup (120 ml) water
1 - 16 oz pkg (480 g) frozen cut rhubarb, defrosted
   or 3 cups (720 ml) sliced fresh rhubarb
1¼ cups (295 ml) sugar
⅓ cup (80 ml) orange juice
2 tsp (10 ml) grated orange peel
¾ tsp (4 ml) dry mustard
1 cinnamon stick**

Do not preheat oven. Place smoked ham half, straight from the refrigerator, on rack in shallow roasting pan. Add water. Insert meat thermometer into thickest part of ham, not touching fat. Cover pan tightly with aluminum foil, leaving thermometer dial exposed. Roast in slow, 325°F (165°C), oven until meat thermometer registers 135°F (57°C), approximately 19-23 minutes per lb (455 g)

Meanwhile combine rhubarb, sugar, orange juice, orange peel, mustard and cinnamon stick in large saucepan. Bring to a boil; reduce heat to medium. Cook, uncovered, 15 minutes, stirring occasionally. Remove and discard cinnamon stick. Remove aluminum foil and spoon small amount of sauce over ham 15 minutes before end of cooking time. Remove ham when meat thermometer registers 135°F (57°C). Cover ham with aluminum foil tent and allow to stand approximately 10 minutes or until meat thermometer registers 140°F (60°C). Serve ham with remaining sauce. Serves 12-20.

Note: A boneless fully-cooked smoked ham half will yield 4-5 - 3 oz (90 g each) cooked, trimmed servings per lb (455 g).

Approximate nutritional analysis per serving:
Calories 193, Protein 18 g, Carbohydrates 19 g, Fat 5 g,
Cholesterol 45 mg, Sodium 1025 mg

Courtesy of the National Live Stock and Meat Board.

GLAMOUR GLAZE FOR BAKED HAM

**1 cup (240 ml) IMPERIAL Brown Sugar
1 tsp (5 ml) dry mustard
2-4 tbs (30-60 ml) orange or pineapple juice**

Mix IMPERIAL Brown Sugar and dry mustard with enough orange juice or pineapple juice to moisten. About 30 minutes before end of baking, trim off rind from ham; spread with glaze and return to oven.

Approximate nutritional analysis for entire recipe of glaze only:
Calories 857, Protein 2 g, Carbohydrates 216 g, Fat 2 g,
Cholesterol 0 mg, Sodium 67 mg

Opposite: Springtime Ham with Rhubarb Sauce

GLAMOUR GLAZE # 2

¾ cup (180 ml) IMPERIAL Brown Sugar
¾ cup (180 ml) crushed pineapple

Combine IMPERIAL Brown Sugar and pineapple and use to glaze ham as directed above.

Approximate nutritional analysis for entire recipe of glaze only:
Calories 728, Protein 1 g, Carbohydrates 188 g, Fat 1 g,
Cholesterol 0 mg, Sodium 51 mg

BAVARIAN CHOPS

4 boneless pork loin chops, ½-¾-inch thick
2 tbs (30 ml) flour
1 tsp (5 ml) butter
½ cup (120 ml) chopped green onion
2 garlic cloves, minced
½ tsp (3 ml) thyme
8 oz (240 ml) beer, room temperature
freshly ground black pepper
buttered noodles, optional
minced fresh parsley, optional

Lightly flour chops. Melt butter in non-stick skillet over medium-high heat until foaming. Brown chops quickly on both sides. Remove; reserve. Add green onion, garlic, mushrooms and thyme and sauté an additional minute. Return chops to skillet, add beer; bring to boil. Reduce heat, cover and simmer 7-8 minutes. Season with salt and pepper. Serve with noodles, garnished with parsley, if desired. Serves 4.

Approximate nutritional analysis per serving:
Calories 226, Protein 27 g, Fat 8 g, Cholesterol 73 mg, Sodium 123 mg

PORK 'N TOMATO SAUERKRAUT

2 tbs (30 ml) oil
2 cloves garlic, minced
4 center cut pork chops
1 - 6 oz can (180 ml) LIBBY'S Tomato Paste
1 cup (240 ml) sour cream
¼ cup (60 ml) brown sugar
1 - 29 oz can (870 g) sauerkraut

Heat oil in skillet, sauté garlic; add pork chops and brown well. In 2-qt casserole blend tomato paste, sour cream and brown sugar. Stir in sauerkraut. Arrange pork chops on top of sauerkraut. Bake uncovered for 20 minutes at 350°F (180°C) or until meat is done. Serves 4.

Approximate nutritional analysis per serving:
Calories 475, Protein 28 g, Carbohydrates 33 g, Fat 26 g,
Cholesterol 96 mg, Sodium 1742 mg

PORK CHOP AND ONION DUET

4 large pork chops (end or center-cut chops)
flour
6 cups (1.4 L) thickly sliced onions
1½ tsp BELL'S Seasoning
salt and black pepper
¼ cup (60 ml) water

Sprinkle chops with flour and brown slowly in skillet without added fat. Remove chops and brown onions lightly, stirring often. Add Seasoning, 1 tsp salt and ⅛ tsp pepper. Put chops on top. Add ¼ cup water. Sprinkle chops with salt and pepper, cover and cook very slowly , for 40 minutes. Add more water if necessary to prevent sticking. Serve chops with onion on top. Serves 4.

Approximate nutritional analysis per serving:
Calories 342, Protein 34 g, Carbohydrates 27 g, Fat 10 g,
Cholesterol 93 mg, Sodium 620 mg

FIESTA PORK CHOPS

4 pork chops, ¾-inch thick
1 tbs (15 ml) vegetable oil
1 - 6.8 oz pkg (204 g) RICE-A-RONI Spanish Rice
2 tbs (30 ml) margarine or butter
2 cups (480 ml) hot water
1 - 8 oz can 240 ml) tomato sauce
2 tomatoes, seeded, chopped
1 medium onion, chopped
1-2 jalapeño peppers, chopped

In large skillet, brown pork chops in oil. Drain; set aside. In same skillet, combine rice-vermicelli mix and margarine. Sauté until golden brown. Stir in water, contents of seasoning packet, tomato sauce, tomatoes, onion and pepper. Layer pork chops over rice mixture in skillet; bring to a boil. Cover; reduce heat. Simmer 30 minutes or until liquid is absorbed and rice and chops are tender. Serves 4.

Approximate nutritional analysis per serving:
Calories 475, Protein 35 g, Carbohydrates 47 g, Fat 16 g,
Cholesterol 80 mg, Sodium 975 mg

Opposite: Bavarian Chops

LOUISIANA YAM, APPLE, PORK CHOP SKILLET

3 medium red apples
6 tbs (90 ml) butter or margarine
2 medium onions, sliced
4 rib pork chops
1 tbs (15 ml) cornstarch
½ cup (120 ml) cold water
¼ tsp (1 ml) curry powder
¼ tsp (1 ml) ground ginger
¼ tsp (1 ml) ground nutmeg
2½ cups (590 ml) chicken bouillon or broth
salt and pepper
2 - 16 oz cans (960 g) LOUISIANA Yams, drained
    ***or* 4 medium LOUISIANA Yams cooked,**
      peeled and halved

Core unpared apples and cut into ½-inch rings. Melt 4 tbs butter in large skillet; add apple and onion slices. Sauté until lightly browned; remove from skillet and set aside. Add remaining 2 tbs butter to skillet; add chops and brown well on all sides.

Blend cornstarch into water. Stir cornstarch mixture, curry powder, ginger and nutmeg into chicken bouillon; pour into skillet with chops. Cover skillet; simmer 40-45 minutes or until chops are tender. Season sauce to taste with salt and pepper. Add yams, apple rings and onion slices to skillet and cook just until heated through. Remove to warm serving platter and garnish with parsley sprigs. Serves 4.

Approximate nutritional analysis per serving:
Calories 668, Protein 29 g, Carbohydrates 78 g, Fat 27 g,
Cholesterol 115 mg, Sodium 904 mg

ISLAND BARBECUE PORK CHOPS

½ cup (120 ml) KRAFT Original Barbecue Sauce
¼ cup (60 ml) orange juice
1 tsp (5 ml) ground allspice
1 tsp (5 ml) vanilla
½ tsp (3 ml) garlic powder
6 pork loin chops, ½-inch thick

Heat broiler. Mix barbecue sauce, juice, allspice, vanilla and garlic powder. Place chops on greased rack of broiler pan. Broil 3-5 inches from heat 8-10 minutes on each side or until cooked through, brushing frequently with barbecue sauce mixture. Serves 6.

Approximate nutritional analysis per serving:
Calories 187, Protein 24 g, Carbohydrates 4 g, Fat 7 g,
Cholesterol 70 mg, Sodium 230 mg

Island Barbecue Pork Chops

Opposite: Louisiana Yam, Apple, Pork Chop Skillet

LOIN CHOPS CHAMPIGNON

**4 - 7-8 oz (210-240 g each) pork loin chops,
     1¼-inch thick**
1 egg yolk, beaten
2 tbs (30 ml) dry white wine
1 tbs (15 ml) soy sauce
½ cup (120 ml) finely chopped fresh mushrooms
2 tbs (30 ml) finely chopped green onion
1 tbs (15 ml) parsley, snipped
½ tsp (3 ml) dried thyme, crushed
¼ tsp (1 ml) ground black pepper
8-12 large mushroom caps

In bowl stir together egg yolk, wine and soy sauce. Add chopped mushrooms, green onion, parsley, thyme and pepper; mix well.

Broil chops 5 inches from heat for 12 minutes. Turn chops over and broil 4 minutes more. Spoon 2-3 tbs mushroom mixture evenly on each chop. If desired, spoon a small amount of mixture into each mushroom cap and place them alongside the chops. Broil 3-5 minutes more until chops are done (slightly pink in center and 155-160°F (68-71°C) internal temperature). Serve mushroom caps with chops. Serves 4.

Approximate nutritional analysis per serving: Calories 243, Protein 37 g, Fat 9 g, Cholesterol 141 mg, Sodium 353 mg

Courtesy of the National Pork Producers Council.

PORK PICCATA

**1 lb (455 g) pork tenderloin or boneless loin,
     cut into ¼-inch slices**
1 tbs (15 ml) vegetable oil
1 - 12 oz jar (360 ml) HEINZ Pork Gravy
2 tbs (30 ml) water
1 tbs (15 ml) lemon juice
4 thin lemon slices
1 tbs (15 ml) drained capers

In large skillet, quickly sauté pork in oil until lightly browned and cooked; remove and set aside. In same skillet, stir in gravy, water and lemon juice; heat until bubbly. Add lemon, capers and reserved pork; heat. Garnish with chopped parsley and serve with rice, if desired. Serves 4.

Approximate nutritional analysis per serving:
Calories 199, Protein 26 g, Carbohydrates 5 g, Fat 8 g,
Cholesterol 72 mg, Sodium 519 mg

PORK TENDERLOIN WITH APPLE WINE SAUCE

1¼ lbs (570 g) pork tenderloin
2½ tbs (38 ml) vegetable oil
2 tbs (30 ml) butter
1 small onion, chopped
¾ cup (180 ml) white or blush wine
10½ oz (315 g) COMSTOCK Apple Filling or Topping
salt and pepper to taste

Preheat oven to 375°F (190°C). Place pork on rack in roasting pan. Brush with oil and cook 45-55 minutes or until internal temperature reaches 155-160°F (68-71°C).

Sauté onion in butter over medium-low heat until soft and transparent. Stir in wine. Bring to gentle boil and boil 3-5 minutes until reduced to ½ cup. Stir in Apple Filling. Transfer to a food processor or blender and process until smooth. Add salt and pepper to taste. Stir in remaining oil. Use as a basting sauce for tenderloin, basting every 10 minutes.

When roast reaches 155-160°F (68-71°C), remove from oven and tent with foil. Return apple mixture to saucepan and bring to a boil for 2 minutes. Slice pork and serve with apple mixture. Serves 4.

Approximate nutritional analysis per serving:
Calories 380, Protein 29 g, Carbohydrates 14 g, Fat 20 g,
Cholesterol 99 mg, Sodium 138 mg

PORK AND BELL PEPPER VINAIGRETTE

4 well-trimmed thin-sliced boneless pork cutlets
¼ tsp (1 ml) dried thyme
salt and freshly ground black pepper
2 tsp (10 ml) BERTOLLI Classico Olive Oil
½ sweet white onion, cut into thin strips
**½ green bell pepper, seeds and stem removed,
     cut into thin strips**
**½ red bell pepper, seeds and stem removed,
     cut into thin strips**
1 tbs (15 ml) red wine vinegar
16 oz (480 g) potatoes, peeled, cubed and boiled

Sprinkle the pork with the thyme, salt and pepper. Heat 1 tsp of the olive oil in a large non-stick skillet. Add the pork and brown on both sides. Remove to a side dish. Add the remaining olive oil, onion and peppers to skillet. Cook, stirring, over low heat, until the vegetables are tender. Return the pork and any meat juices to skillet; add the vinegar and heat to boiling. Place the potatoes in serving dish and roughly mash with fork. Top with pork and peppers. Serves 4.

Approximate nutritional analysis per serving:
Calories 217, Protein 20 g, Carbohydrates 18 g, Fat 7 g,
Cholesterol 58 mg, Sodium 54 mg

Opposite: Loin Chops Champignon

IMPERIAL PORK CUTLETS

¼ cup (60 ml) rice vinegar or white vinegar
3 tbs (45 ml) 62%-less-sodium soy sauce
2 tbs (30 ml) honey
4-6 drops hot pepper sauce
2 tsp (10 ml) vegetable oil
2 tsp (10 ml) sesame oil
4 boneless pork loin chops, trimmed
6 cloves garlic, coarsely crushed
1 tbs (15 ml) grated fresh ginger
cilantro sprigs, optional

In small bowl, stir together vinegar, soy sauce, honey and hot pepper sauce; set aside. Heat oils in 10-inch heavy skillet over medium-high heat. Add chops; cook about 2 minutes on each side or until browned. Add garlic and ginger; cook for 2-3 minutes, stirring constantly. Reduce heat to low. Add vinegar mixture; cover and cook until chops are fork tender, about 10 minutes. Uncover and cook an additional 2-3 minutes or until sauce is slightly thickened. Garnish with chopped cilantro, if desired. Serves 4.

Approximate nutritional analysis per serving: Calories 252, Protein 27 g, Fat 11 g, Cholesterol 66 mg, Sodium 444 mg

Courtesy of the National Pork Producers Council.

MICROWAVED HERBED PORK ROAST

3 lb (1.4 kg) boneless double-loin pork roast, rolled and tied
paprika
3 tbs (45 ml) snipped fresh parsley
½ tsp (3 ml) snipped fresh oregano
¼ tsp (1 ml) snipped fresh tarragon
¼ tsp (1 ml) snipped fresh thyme
¼ tsp (1 ml) snipped fresh dill
¼ tsp (1 ml) snipped fresh chervil
additional fresh herbs, optional
lemon slices, optional

Sprinkle roast lightly with paprika; rub into surface. Combine parsley, oregano, tarragon, thyme, dill and chervil; rub mixture over surface of roast.

Place roast in a 10x16-inch oven cooking bag in a microwave-safe dish; tie bag loosely. Cook 35-40 minutes at MEDIUM-LOW (30% power), invert roast and rotate dish one half turn. Cook 30-35 minutes more at MEDIUM-LOW Cover roast in cooking bag with foil and let stand 10 minutes. Remove roast from bag and place on serving platter. Garnish with herbs and lemon slices, if desired. Serves 10.

Approximate nutritional analysis per serving:
Calories 161, Protein 26 g, Fat 6 g, Cholesterol 66 mg, Sodium 59 mg

Above: Microwaved Herbed Pork Roast

Opposite: Imperial Pork Cutlets

SAUCY PORK BARBECUE

1½ cups (355 ml) HEINZ Tomato Ketchup
¾ cup (180 ml) water
¾ cup (180 ml) chopped onions
3 tbs (45 ml) HEINZ Vinegar
2 tbs (30 ml) brown sugar
1½ tbs (25 ml) HEINZ Worcestershire Sauce
1 small bay leaf
⅛ tsp (.5 ml) celery seed
⅛ tsp (.5 ml) hot pepper sauce
12 oz (360 g) cooked pork, cut into strips
6-8 sandwich buns, split

In saucepan, combine Ketchup and next 8 ingredients. Simmer 20 minutes or until thickened, stirring occasionally. Remove bay leaf. Stir in pork; heat. Meanwhile, toast buns. To serve, spoon pork mixture over buns. Serves 6.

Approximate nutritional analysis per serving:
Calories 381, Protein 23 g, Carbohydrates 57 g, Fat 7 g,
Cholesterol 47 mg, Sodium 1267 mg

CORIANDER-PEPPER CHOPS

2 cloves garlic, crushed
1 tbs (15 ml) crushed coriander seeds
1 tbs (15 ml) coarsely ground black pepper
1 tbs (15 ml) brown sugar
3 tbs (45 ml) soy sauce
4 boneless pork chops, about 1-inch thick

Combine all ingredients except pork chops. Place chops in a shallow dish and pour marinade over; let marinate 30 minutes. Prepare medium-hot coals, banked, in grill bed. Remove pork from marinade, discarding marinade, and grill chops over indirect heat for 12-15 minutes, turning once. Juices should run clear and chops should be tender and juicy. Serves 4.

Approximate nutritional analysis per serving:
Calories 204, Protein 26 g, Fat 6 g, Cholesterol 66 mg, Sodium 255 mg

Courtesy of the National Pork Producers Council.

PORK TENDERLOIN WITH BOURBON SAUCE

1 - 10 oz can (300 g) CHI-CHI'S Diced Tomatoes
**   and Green Chilies, drained**
⅓ cup (80 ml) bourbon
⅓ cup (80 ml) soy sauce
⅓ cup (80 ml) Worcestershire sauce
½ cup (120 ml) chopped onion
2 tbs (30 ml) honey
2 tbs (30 ml) Dijon mustard
¼ tsp (1 ml) pepper
2 lbs (910 g) pork tenderloin

In a large recloeable plastic food bag, combine all ingredients except meat. Mix well. Add meat; seal bag and turn several times to coat. Place bag in 13x9-inch pan. Refrigerate, turning bag occasionally, 8 hours or overnight.

Heat broiler. Remove meat from marinade; reserve marinade. Place meat on broiler pan. Broil 7-8 inches from heat source 7-9 minutes on each side. In small saucepan, bring marinade to boil 1 minute. Serve marinade with meat. Serves 8.

Approximate nutritional analysis per serving:
Calories 210, Protein 27 g, Carbohydrates 9 g, Fat 5 g,
Cholesterol 70 mg, Sodium 1050 mg

STUFFED PORK LOIN WITH TROPICAL SALSA

3 tbs (45 ml) butter or margarine
6 large yellow onions, thinly sliced
1 cup (240 ml) pine nuts, lightly toasted
1 - 3 lb (1.4 kg) boneless pork top loin roast
**   (double loin tied)**
1 - 16 oz jar (480 ml) CHI-CHI'S Salsa
1 - 8 oz can (240 g) crushed pineapple, well drained

Heat oven to 350°F (180°C). Grease 13x9-inch baking dish. In large skillet, melt butter. Add onion; cook and stir over medium heat until golden brown. Stir in pine nuts; cool mixture slightly. Untie and stuff roast with about 2 cups onion mixture. Retie roast. Spread remaining onion mixture evenly on bottom of greased baking dish. Place roast on top of onion mixture.

In medium saucepan, combine salsa and pineapple. Cook and stir just until hot. Pour mixture over roast. Bake about 1½ hours or until internal temperature reaches 160°F (71°C), 25 minutes per lb (455 g). Let roast rest 10 minutes. Slice roast and serve with salsa-onion mixture. Serves 6.

Approximate nutritional analysis per serving:
Calories 480, Protein 40 g, Carbohydrates 27 g, Fat 26 g,
Cholesterol 95 mg, Sodium 470 mg

Opposite: Coriander-Pepper Chops

SWEET AND SOUR PORK LOIN

4-5 lb (1.8-2.3 kg) boneless pork loin roast
    (double loin, rolled and tied)
1 cup (240 ml) packed brown sugar
¾ cup (180 ml) teriyaki sauce
¾ cup (180 ml) dry red wine
¾ cup (180 ml) chili sauce
½ tsp (3 ml) ground cloves
¼ tsp (1 ml) pepper
⅛ tsp (.5 ml) garlic powder

For marinade, combine brown sugar, teriyaki sauce, wine, chili sauce, cloves, pepper, and garlic powder; mix well. Place roast in a plastic bag; set in shallow baking dish. Pour marinade over roast; close bag and tie securely. Marinate in refrigerator 8 hours or overnight, turning roast occasionally.

Make a foil drip pan and position drip pan under meat. Drain the roast, reserving marinade. Place roast on grill over low coals. Close grill hood. Grill 1-1½ hours or until meat thermometer registers 155-160°F (68-71°C), brushing frequently with marinade during last 45 minutes of grilling. Let roast stand 10-15 minutes before carving. Serves 12.

Approximate nutritional analysis per serving:
Calories 235, Protein 27 g, Fat 6 g, Cholesterol 66 mg, Sodium 677 mg

Courtesy of the National Pork Producers Council.

Sweet & Sour Pork Loin

SPICY PORK WITH PEACH SAUCE

1 tsp (5 ml) McCORMICK/SCHILLING
    Marjoram Leaves
1 tsp (5 ml) McCORMICK/SCHILLING
    Thyme Leaves
1 tsp (5 ml) McCORMICK/SCHILLING
    Garlic Powder
¼ tsp (1 ml) McCORMICK/SCHILLING
    ground Red Pepper
1 lb (455 g) boneless lean pork chops

PEACH SAUCE:
½ tsp (3 ml) cornstarch
½ tsp (3 ml) water
1 - 16 oz can (480 g) juice-packed sliced peaches,
    drained
2 tbs (30 ml) brown sugar
2 tsp (10 ml) cider vinegar
½-1 tsp (3-5 ml) cooking sherry
¼ tsp (1 ml) McCORMICK/SCHILLING
    ground Cinnamon

Combine first 4 ingredients. Rub on both sides of pork chops. Broil or grill until thoroughly cooked. Meanwhile, prepare sauce. Add cornstarch to small saucepan. Mix in ½ tsp water to dissolve cornstarch. Add remaining ingredients and simmer 8-10 minutes, stirring occasionally. Serves 4.

Approximate nutritional analysis per serving:
Calories 279, Protein 28 g, Carbohydrates 21 g, Fat 9 g,
Cholesterol 84 mg, Sodium 75 mg

PEPPERED PORK ROAST

2-4 lb (910-1820 g) boneless pork roast
1-2 tsp (5-10 ml) garlic pepper
1-2 tsp (5-10 ml) dried rosemary, crushed

Coat roast with seasoning mixture of garlic pepper and rosemary. Place roast in a shallow pan in a preheated 350°F (180°C) oven for 45 minutes-1½ hours, until meat thermometer inserted registers 155°F (68°C). Remove from oven and let roast rest for 5-10 minutes before slicing to serve. Serves 6.

Approximate nutritional analysis per serving:
Calories 167, Protein 24 g, Fat 6 g, Cholesterol 66 mg, Sodium 78 mg

Courtesy of the National Pork Producers Council.

Opposite: Peppered Pork Roast

SINGAPORE SAMPLINGS

1½ lbs (685 g) boneless pork loin, sliced into
    4x1x⅛-inch strips
8 wooden skewers
¼ cup (60 ml) soy sauce
3 tbs (45 ml) rice vinegar
1 tbs (15 ml) grated fresh ginger
    or 1 tsp (5 ml) dry ginger
1 clove garlic, minced
½ tsp (3 ml) crushed red pepper

PEPPERED TOFU: (OPTIONAL)
1 tbs (15 ml) sesame oil
½ tsp (3 ml) dried red pepper
1 thin slice fresh ginger
1 tbs (15 ml) oyster sauce
8 oz (240 g) tofu, cubed

Soak skewers for 20-30 minutes in water. Thread pork onto skewers. Place in a 12x9-inch baking dish. Combine remaining ingredients and pour over skewers, turning to coat. Marinate at room temperature for 30 minutes, turning once or twice. Broil 6 inches from heat for 10 minutes, turning to cook all sides. Baste occasionally with remaining marinade. Serve with Peppered Tofu, if desired. Serves 6.

Peppered Tofu: Heat sesame oil in frying pan, add dried red pepper and ginger. Cook and stir over medium heat for 2-3 minutes. Stir in oyster sauce; add tofu and stir to heat through and coat with sauce.

Approximate nutritional analysis per serving:
Calories 171, Protein 27 g, Fat 6 g, Cholesterol 66 mg, Sodium 746 mg

CREAMY PORK ENCHILADAS

1 tbs (15 ml) olive oil
1 lb (455 g) pork loin roast, cut into thin strips,
    ½x2-inches
¾ cup (180 ml) CHI-CHI'S Salsa
1 tbs (15 ml) dried marjoram leaves, crushed
1 tsp (5 ml) dried rosemary leaves, crushed
1 - 3 oz pkg (90 g) cream cheese
2 - 16 oz jars (960 ml) CHI-CHI'S Salsa Verde,
    divided
12 small flour tortillas, warmed
2 cups (480 ml) shredded Monterey Jack cheese
additional salsa, if desired.

Heat oven to 350°F (180°C). In large skillet, heat oil over medium-high heat. Sauté pork until no longer pink. Reduce heat to medium-low; stir in salsa, marjoram and rosemary. Simmer 2 minutes. Stir in cream cheese until melted; simmer 1-2 minutes or until mixture is thickened and bubbling. Cool slightly.

Spread ¾ cup salsa verde in bottom of 13x9-inch baking dish. Working with 1 tortilla at a time (keep remaining tortillas wrapped), spoon about 2 tbs pork mixture down center of each tortilla; sprinkle with 1 tbs cheese. Roll up tightly; place seam side down over salsa verde in baking dish. Pour 1½ cups salsa verde over enchiladas; sprinkle with remaining cheese. Bake, uncovered, 25-35 minutes or until heated through and bubbling. Serve with additional salsa, if desired, and remaining salsa verde. Serves 6.

Approximate nutritional analysis per serving:
Calories 580, Protein 34 g, Carbohydrates 48 g, Fat 29 g,
Cholesterol 100 mg, Sodium 1450 mg

CORDERO ASADO
Roast Lamb

1 - 4 lb (1.8 kg) leg of lamb
1 tbs (15 ml) GOYA Adobo with Pepper
¾ cup (180 ml) GOYA Olive Oil
½ cup (120 ml) pearl onions, peeled
1 bay leaf
1 carrot, cut in ½-inch slices
½ cup (120 ml) sherry
1½ cups (355 ml) La Vina White Cooking Wine
2 cups (480 ml) water
1 packet GOYA Chicken Bouillon
2 - 16 oz cans (960 g) GOYA Small White Beans,
    drained and rinsed

Sprinkle lamb evenly with Adobo. In a large flame-proof casserole, sear lamb in olive oil over high heat, turning frequently until browned. Add pearl onions, bay leaf, and carrot; lower heat to medium, add sherry and white wine, and cook over medium heat for 30 minutes, turning and basting lamb frequently. Meanwhile, preheat oven to 350°F (180°C). Stir water and bouillon into casserole around lamb. Add beans, bring to a boil, and boil for 2-3 minutes. Cover with aluminum foil and bake for 1 hour, or until lamb is done to taste. Remove bay leaf. Serves 6.

Approximate nutritional analysis per serving:
Calories 1041, Protein 97 g, Carbohydrates 30 g, Fat 51 g,
Cholesterol 269 mg, Sodium 403 mg

Opposite: Singapore Samplings

MUSTARD-BOURBON KABOBS

1 lb (455 g) boneless pork, cut into ¾-inch cubes
4 tbs (60 ml) Dijon-style mustard
4 tbs (60 ml) brown sugar
2 tbs (30 ml) bourbon
2 tbs (30 ml) soy sauce

In self-sealing plastic bag, combine all ingredients and mix well. Refrigerate overnight (6-24 hours). Remove pork from marinade and thread pork cubes onto skewers. Broil or grill kabobs about 4 inches from heat source, turning occasionally, for 8-10 minutes, until nicely browned. Serves 4.

Approximate nutritional analysis per serving:
Calories 234, Protein 24 g, Fat 7 g, Cholesterol 66 mg, Sodium 432 mg

Courtesy of the National Pork Producers Council.

CAROLINA BARBECUE

5 lb (2.3 kg) Boston Butt roast
2 tsp (10 ml) vegetable oil
1½ cups (355 ml) water
1 - 8 oz can (240 ml) tomato sauce
¼ cup (60 ml) cider vinegar
¼ cup (60 ml) Worcestershire sauce
¼ cup (60 ml) brown sugar
salt and pepper to taste
1 tsp (5 ml) celery seeds
1 tsp (5 ml) chili powder
dash hot pepper sauce

Randomly pierce the surface of the roast with a sharp knife. In a Dutch oven, brown roast on all sides in hot oil. In a mixing bowl, combine remaining ingredients and mix well. Pour sauce over roast and bring to boil. Reduce heat, cover and simmer 2 hours or until pork is fork-tender. Baste roast with sauce during cooking time. Slice or chop to serve. Serves 20.

Approximate nutritional analysis per serving:Calories 229, Protein 21 g, Fat 13 g, Cholesterol 82 mg, Sodium 168 mg

Courtesy of the National Pork Producers Council.

ITALIAN PORKETTA

2-4 lb (910-1820 g) boneless pork roast
3 tbs (45 ml) dill seed
1 tbs (15 ml) fennel seed
¼ tsp (1 ml) oregano
1 tsp (5 ml) lemon pepper
¼ tsp (1 ml) onion powder
¼ tsp (1 ml) garlic powder

Combine seasonings together and coat roast with mixture. Roast in a shallow pan at 325°F (165°C) for 45 minutes to 1 hour, until meat thermometer registers 155-160°F (68-71°C). Let roast rest 5-10 minutes before carving. Serves 8.

Approximate nutritional analysis per serving:
Calories 171, Protein 26 g, Fat 6 g, Cholesterol 66 mg, Sodium 160 mg

Courtesy of the National Pork Producers Council.

Italian Porketta

HAM AND POTATO CASSEROLE

1 cup (240 ml) diced cooked ham
2 cups (240 ml) diced cooked potato
¼ cup (60 ml) margarine, melted or oil
1 small onion, minced
3 tbs (45 ml) all purpose flour
1½ cups (355 ml) milk
salt and pepper to taste
½ cup (120 ml) grated sharp cheddar cheese
¼ cup (60 ml) fine, dry bread crumbs
2-2½ cups (480-600 ml) canned or fresh cooked
    green beans, drained

Put ham and potato into shallow 1½-qt baking dish. Add onion to melted margarine or oil and cook until onion is golden. Blend in flour. Add milk and cook, stirring, until thickened. Season with salt and pepper, then pour over ham and potato. Sprinkle with cheese and crumbs. Dot with remaining 1 tbs margarine. Bake in preheated 400°F (205°C) oven about 20 minutes. Add heated green beans in ring around edge of casserole. Serves 4.

Approximate nutritional analysis per serving:
Calories 424, Protein 18 g, Carbohydrates 32 g, Fat 9 g,
Cholesterol 49 mg, Sodium 920 mg

BAKED IDAHO APPLE 'N LAMB CHOPS

6 IDAHO loin lamb chops, 1 inch thick
½ tsp (3 ml) salt
3 large IDAHO ROME or Red Delicious Apples
5 tbs (75 ml) flour
3 tbs (45 ml) molasses
2 cups (480 ml) hot water
1 tbs (15 ml) cider vinegar
⅓ cup (80 ml) golden raisins

Score fat edges of chops; brown fat edges in frying pan, then brown chops on both sides. Arrange in shallow baking dish. Sprinkle with salt. Core apples; do not peel; cut into thick rings. Place on chops. Add flour to fat in frying pan; stir until browned. Combine molasses and water; add; stir over low heat until mixture thickens. Add vinegar and raisins; pour over chops and apples. Cover; bake at 350°F (180°C) for 1 hour. Serves 6.

Approximate nutritional analysis per serving:
Calories 599, Protein 69 g, Carbohydrates 27 g, Fat 22 g,
Cholesterol 215 mg, Sodium 371 mg

Courtesy of the Idaho Apple Commission.

LAMB RIB ROAST DIJON

1½-1¾ lb (685-795 g) 6-rib lamb rib roast
1 tbs (15 ml) Dijon-style mustard
⅓ cup (80 ml) soft bread crumbs
½ tsp (3 ml) dried basil leaves
dash garlic powder
lemon slices, if desired
Italian parsley, if desired

Trim excess fat from lamb rib roast; spread roast with mustard. Combine bread crumbs, basil and garlic powder; pat mixture over mustard. Place roast, fat side up, on rack in shallow roasting pan. Insert meat thermometer into thickest part of roast, not touching in bone or fat. Do not add water. Do not cover. Roast in moderate, 375°F (190°C), oven to desired degree of doneness. Allow 30-35 minutes per lb (455 g) for rare; 35- 40 minutes for medium. Remove roast when meat thermometer registers 135°F (57°C) for rare; 155°F (68°C) for medium. Cover roast with aluminum foil tent and allow to stand 15-20 minutes before carving. Roast will continue to rise approximately 5°F (3°C) in temperature to reach 140°F (60°C) for rare; 160°F (71°C) for medium. Garnish with lemon slices and Italian parsley, if desired. Serves 3.

Note: A lamb roast will yield 2 - 3 oz (180 g), cooked trimmed servings per lb (455 g) .

Approximate nutritional analysis per serving:
Calories 218, Protein 23 g, Carbohydrates 3 g, Fat 12 g,
Cholesterol 75 mg, Sodium 242 mg

Courtesy of the National Live Stock and Meat Board.

Opposite: Lamb Rib Roast Dijon

Spring Lamb Crown Roast with Vegetable Stuffing

SPRING LAMB CROWN ROAST WITH VEGETABLE STUFFING

3-3½ lb (1.4-1.6 kg) 14-16-rib lamb crown roast
3 tbs (45 ml) butter or margarine
1 medium onion, chopped
1 large bell pepper, cut into thin strips
8 oz (240 g) mushrooms, coarsely chopped
1 large clove garlic, crushed
3 - 10 oz pkgs (900 g) frozen chopped spinach,
**   defrosted, drained well**
¾ tsp (4 ml) salt
⅛ tsp (.5 ml) pepper

Place lamb crown roast, rib ends down, on rack in shallow roasting pan. Do not add water. Do not cover. Roast in moderate, 375°F (190°C), oven 20 minutes. Meanwhile melt butter in large skillet. Add onion; cook 4-5 minutes or until onion is transparent, stirring occasionally. Add bell pepper, mushrooms and garlic; continue cooking 5 minutes, stirring occasionally. Stir in spinach, salt and pepper. Remove roast from oven. Turn roast so rib ends are up. Insert meat thermometer into thickest part of roast, not touching bone or fat. Fill cavity of roast with spinach stuffing. Continue roasting 25-35 minutes or until meat thermometer registers 135°F (57°C) for rare to 155°F (68°C) for medium. Cover roast with aluminum foil tent and allow to stand 10-15 minutes. Roast will continue to rise approximately 5°F (3°C) in temperature to reach 140°F (60°C) for rare and to 160°F (71°C) for medium. Trim excess fat from roast; carve roast between ribs. Serves 5-7.

Note: A lamb crown roast will yield 1½-2 - 3 oz (150-180 g) cooked, trimmed servings per lb (455 g).

Approximate nutritional analysis per serving:
Calories 656, Protein 33 g, Carbohydrates 10 g, Fat 54 g,
Cholesterol 147 mg, Sodium 484 mg

Courtesy of the National Live Stock and Meat Board.

LAMB PASTITSIO

1½ cups (355 ml) uncooked elbow macaroni
5 tbs (75 ml) butter or margarine, divided
⅓ cup (80 ml) all-purpose flour
3 cups (720 ml) milk
½ cup (120 ml) grated kefalotiri or Parmesan cheese
1 tbs (15 ml) olive oil
1 lb (455 g) ground lamb
½ cup (120 ml) finely chopped onion
2 cloves garlic, crushed
½ tsp (3 ml) dried oregano leaves, crushed
¼ tsp (1 ml) salt
¼ tsp (1 ml) ground cinnamon
⅛ tsp (.5 ml) freshly ground black pepper
dash ground nutmeg
1 - 10 oz can (300 g) peeled whole tomatoes,
    undrained
¼ cup (60 ml) tomato paste
4 eggs, divided
⅓ cup (80 ml) soft bread crumbs

Prepare macaroni according to package directions; drain. Rinse with cold water; drain. Meanwhile melt 4 tbs butter in heavy saucepan; stir in flour. Gradually stir in milk; cook until thickened, stirring occasionally. Add cheese; stir until melted. Cover; cool slightly. Heat oil in large skillet; brown ground lamb, onion and garlic; stirring occasionally to break up lamb.. Pour off drippings. Sprinkle oregano, salt, cinnamon, pepper and nutmeg over lamb. Drain liquid from tomatoes into small bowl; break up and reserve tomatoes. Combine tomato liquid and tomato paste; stir into lamb mixture. Cook over medium heat 5 minutes; stir in tomatoes. Separate 1 egg; combine yolk and 1 cup white sauce in large bowl; reserve. Beat together egg white, remaining 3 eggs and remaining white sauce in large bowl; gently stir in macaroni. Place half of the macaroni mixture in bottom of buttered 8x8-inch baking dish. Spoon lamb mixture evenly over macaroni; spoon remaining macaroni mixture over lamb. Pour reserved egg yolk mixture over macaroni. Melt remaining 1 tbs butter; stir in bread crumbs. Sprinkle over macaroni mixture. Bake in moderate, 375°F (190°C), oven 45 minutes. Reduce heat to moderate, 325°F (165°C); continue baking 15 minutes. Let stand 15 minutes before serving. Serves 6.

Approximate nutritional analysis per serving:
Calories 543, Protein 32 g, Carbohydrates 40 g, Fat 28 g,
Cholesterol 288 mg, Sodium 618 mg

Lamb Pastitsio

Butterflied Leg of Lamb with Orange Sauce

BUTTERFLIED LAMB LEG WITH ORANGE SAUCE

3½-4 lb (1.6-1.8 kg) butterflied lamb leg
⅔ cup (160 ml) fresh orange juice
½ cup (120 ml) orange marmalade
1 tbs (15 ml) butter or margarine
½ tsp (3 ml) grated fresh ginger
¼ tsp (1 ml) dry mustard
1 tbs (15 ml) cornstarch
2 tbs (30 ml) fresh lemon juice

Thread 2 long metal skewers through butterflied lamb leg to secure and facilitate turning roast. Place on grid over medium coals*. Grill 40-60 minutes for rare, 140°F (60°C), to medium, 160°F (71°C), turning several times. Meanwhile combine orange juice, marmalade, butter, ginger and mustard in small saucepan. Cook over medium-low heat until marmalade is melted, stirring occasionally. Dissolve cornstarch in lemon juice; stir into orange juice mixture. Cook until thickened, stirring frequently. Remove from heat; reserve. Brush leg with ⅓ cup reserved sauce during last 10 minutes of cooking time. Remove leg to warm platter. Remove skewers and separate leg into 3 sections along natural seams. Trim excess fat; carve each section across the grain into thin slices. Serve carved lamb with remaining sauce. Serves 14-16.

   * To check temperature, cautiously hold hand about 4 inches above coals. Medium coals will force removal of hand in 4 seconds.

Approximate nutritional analysis per serving:
Calories 175, Protein 19 g, Carbohydrates 12 g, Fat 6 g, C holesterol 116 mg, Sodium 59 mg

MOROCCAN LAMB WITH CURRIED CARROT-SPINACH SALAD

1½-2 lb (685-910 g) boneless lamb loin
    double roast, tied
1 cup (240 ml) plain yogurt, divided
¼ cup (60 ml) thinly sliced onion
2 tbs (30 ml) chopped fresh cilantro
2 tbs (30 ml) fresh orange juice
2 cloves garlic
½ tsp (3 ml) ground cardamom
½ tsp (3 ml) ground cumin
¼ tsp (1 ml) ground cinnamon
¼ tsp (1 ml) ground ginger
¼ tsp (1 ml) coarsely ground black pepper
Curry Vinaigrette (below)
8 cups (1.9 L) thinly sliced mixed greens,
    such as spinach and Romaine
3 cups (720 ml) diagonally sliced carrots
cilantro and orange slices, if desired

CURRY VINAIGRETTE:
2 tbs (30 ml) olive oil
1 tbs (15 ml) fresh orange juice
1 tsp (5 ml) minced fresh ginger
¼ tsp (1 ml) sugar
¼ tsp (1 ml) curry powder
salt and pepper to taste

Combine yogurt, onion, cilantro, orange juice, garlic, carda-mom, cumin, cinnamon, ginger and pepper in blender container; process until smooth. Add salt to taste. Combine ½ cup yogurt mixture and remaining plain yogurt for sauce; cover and refrigerate. Place lamb loin double roast in plastic bag: add remaining yogurt mixture from blender, turning to coat. Close bag securely and marinate in refrigerator 2 hours, turning occasionally. Remove roast from marinade; discard marinade. Place roast on grid over medium coals.* Grill approximately 20 minutes for rare, 135°F (57°C), turning ¼ turn every 5 minutes. Cover roast with aluminum foil tent and allow to stand 10 minutes. Roast will continue to rise approximately 5°F (3°C) to reach 140°F (60°C) for rare. Meanwhile prepare Curry Vinaigrette. Toss greens and carrots with vinaigrette; place on large serving platter. Trim excess fat from roast. Carve roast slices; arrange over salad. Garnish with cilantro and orange slices. Serve with reserved yogurt sauce. Serves 6-8.

Curry Vinaigrette: Whisk together first 5 ingredients; season with salt and pepper to taste.

* To check temperature, cautiously hold hand about 4 inches above coals. Medium coals will force removal of hand in 4 seconds.

Approximate nutritional analysis per serving:
Calories 264, Protein 28 g, Carbohydrates 8 g, Fat 13 g,
Cholesterol 84 mg, Sodium 124 mg

GREEK-STYLE LAMB AND BEAN SKILLET DINNER

1 lb (455 g) ground lamb
1 tsp (5 ml) garlic salt
1 tsp (5 ml) Italian seasoning, crushed
1 - 15 oz can (450 g) great northern beans, drained
2 medium tomatoes, chopped
1 cup (240 ml) dry white wine
1 tbs (15 ml) chopped fresh parsley
1 tsp (5 ml) grated lemon peel

Combine ground lamb, garlic salt and Italian seasoning; mix lightly but thoroughly. Pinch off 1½-inch pieces of lamb mixture to make approximately 16 free-form meatballs. Brown meatballs in large non-stick skillet over medium heat. Pour off drippings. Add beans, tomatoes and wine; cook, uncovered, over medium heat 15 minutes, stirring occasionally. Garnish with parsley and lemon peel. Serves 4.

Microwave directions: Reduce wine to ½ cup (120 ml) . Use ½ tsp garlic salt in lamb mixture; reserve remaining ½ tsp garlic salt for bean mixture. Place free-form meatballs around sides of 11¾x7½-inch microwave-safe baking dish. Cover with waxed paper and microwave at HIGH 4-5 minutes, rotating dish ¼ turn after 3 minutes. Remove meatballs with slotted spoon; keep warm. Pour off drippings. Combine beans, tomatoes, wine and reserved ½ tsp garlic salt in same baking dish. Microwave, uncovered, at HIGH 5 minutes, stirring once. Return meatballs to baking dish; continue to microwave at MEDIUM 2 minutes. Garnish with parsley and lemon peel. Serves 4.

Approximate nutritional analysis per serving:
Calories 321, Protein 33 g, Carbohydrates 20 g, Fat 11 g,
Cholesterol 91 mg, Sodium 879 mg

Courtesy of the National Live Stock and Meat Board.

Greek-Style Lamb and Bean Skillet Dinner

STUFFED CABBAGE ROLLS WITH YOGURT-DILL SAUCE

1 - 3 lb (1.4 kg) head green cabbage, cored
2 tbs (30 ml) olive oil
3 large green onions, sliced
2 large garlic cloves, minced
1 lb (455 g) ground lamb
2 cups (480 ml) plain yogurt
4 tbs (60 ml) fresh snipped dill
1½ tsp (8 ml) Tabasco pepper sauce
1½ tsp (8 ml) salt

Over high heat, heat a large pot of water to boiling. Add cabbage, core-end down. Reduce heat to medium. Cover and simmer until leaves are softened, 10-12 minutes. Remove cabbage to bowl of cold water. Separate 16 large leaves from the head of the cabbage. Trim the tough ribs on the back of leaves so that they will roll up easily. Chop enough of the remaining cabbage to make 3 cups.

In 12-inch skillet over medium heat, in hot oil, cook chopped cabbage, green onions and garlic until tender, about 10 minutes, stirring occasionally. With slotted spoon, remove to bowl. In drippings remaining in skillet over high heat, cook ground lamb until well browned on all sides, stirring frequently. Remove to bowl with cabbage.

In food processor, blend lamb mixture until finely ground. In large bowl toss lamb mixture with ½ cup yogurt, 2 tbs dill, Tabasco pepper sauce, and salt to mix well. Place 3 tbs lamb mixture at bottom of cabbage leaf and roll up tightly to form a 3-inch-long roll, tucking ends in as you roll. Repeat with remaining lamb and leaves.

Preheat oven to 400°F (205°C). Place cabbage rolls on rack in a roasting pan. Add 1 cup boiling water; cover pan tightly with foil. Bake 20 minutes or until rolls are hot. Meanwhile, in medium bowl combine remaining 1½ cups yogurt and 2 tbs dill. To serve, remove cabbage rolls to platter; top with Yogurt-Dill Sauce. Serves 4.

Approximate nutritional analysis per serving:
Calories 309, Protein 28 g, Carbohydrates 18 g, Fat 14 g,
Cholesterol 66 mg, Sodium 971 mg

ZESTY HAMBURGERS

1 lb (455 g) ground beef (or ground turkey)
1½ tsp (8 ml) OLD BAY Seasoning

In a medium bowl, mix together ground beef and OLD BAY Seasoning. Shape into patties. Fry or broil as usual. Serves 6.

Approximate nutritional analysis per serving:
Calories 216, Protein 17 g, Carbohydrates 0 g, Fat 16 g,
Cholesterol 66 mg, Sodium 134 mg

HAMBURGER UPDATE

¼ cup plus 1 tbs (75 ml) plain nonfat yogurt
1 oz (30 g) crumbled feta cheese
½ tsp (3 ml) ground cumin
1 lb (455 g) HEALTHY CHOICE Extra Lean
    Low Fat Ground Beef Product
¼ cup (60 ml) minced green onion
¼ cup (60 ml) cilantro leaves, minced
1 large clove garlic, minced
1 tbs (15 ml) grated fresh ginger root
4 lettuce leaves
20 very thin slices peeled cucumber
2 onion rolls, split and toasted

Combine yogurt, cheese and cumin; blend with a fork until cheese is finely crumbled. Cover and chill at least 1 hour. Combine low fat ground beef and next 4 ingredients, mixing well. Shape into 4 - ½-inch-thick patties. Cook in non-stick skillet or grill 3 inches from heat 6-7 minutes on each side or until meat and juices are no longer pink. Place a lettuce leaf, 5 slices of cucumber, and beef patty on each bun half. Top each patty with 2 tbs yogurt mixture. Serve immediately. Serves 4.

Approximate nutritional analysis per serving:
Calories 232, Protein 27 g, Carbohydrates 21 g, Fat 7 g,
Cholesterol 62 mg, Sodium 458 mg

SPICED MEATBALLS AND MAPLE-Y BEANS

MEATBALLS:
½ lb (230 g) lean ground beef
½ lb (230 g) Italian sausage, skinned
1 cup (240 ml) fine bread crumbs
½ cup (120 ml) milk
2 tbs (30 ml) onion, chopped
2 eggs, lightly beaten
1 tsp (5 ml) salt
½ tsp (3 ml) nutmeg
¼ tsp (1 ml) black pepper
¼ tsp (1 ml) allspice
3 tbs (45 ml) GOYA Vegetable Oil for frying

2 cans GOYA Pinto Beans, drained
¼ cup (60 ml) GOYA Cider Vinegar
¼ cup (60 ml) maple syrup

Combine all ingredients for meatballs; mix thoroughly. Shape into 16 - 1-inch balls. Heat oil in large frying pan; brown meatballs and remove. Combine beans, vinegar and maple syrup in fryimg pan. Arrange meatballs on top of beans; bring to boil. Cover and simmer 30 minutes. Serves 4.

Approximate nutritional analysis per serving:
Calories 834, Protein 46 g, Carbohydrates 75 g, Fat 39 g,
Cholesterol 208 mg, Sodium 241   mg

Opposite: Stuffed Cabbage Rolls with Yogurt-Dill Sauce

BRONZED HAMBURGERS

4 tbs (60 ml) unsalted butter or margarine
2 small yellow onions, coarsely chopped
2 lbs (910 g) ground round, ground chuck,
    ground veal, or very lean ground beef,
    at room temperature
2 tbs (30 ml) CHEF PAUL PRUDHOMME'S
    Meat Magic
6 hamburger buns or onion rolls
shredded lettuce
sliced tomatoes
sliced red onions
mayonnaise
Creole mustard, or Dijon or yellow mustard

Melt the butter in a small sauté pan over medium heat. Add the coarsely chopped onion and sauté until transparent. Reduce the heat and continue to cook until the onions are golden brown, about 15 minutes. You should end up with about ¾ cup caramelized onions. Set aside.

Place the ground meat in a large mixing bowl. Sprinkle 1 tbs of the Meat Magic over the meat and work it in well. Sprinkle the remaining 1 tbs Meat Magic into the meat and mix well until thoroughly incorporated. Add the onions to the meat mixture and combine. Form the meat into 6 patties about 6 oz each and about ¾-inch thick.

Heat a heavy griddle or large, heavy aluminum or electric skillet to 350°F (180°C). Hamburgers will not stick to the surface if griddle is very hot. Place about 4 patties on the griddle or skillet surface and cook for 3 minutes. Turn and cook another 3 minutes for medium rare. For medium, cook 4 minutes per side. Place the patties on a serving platter, then wipe the griddle or skillet surface thoroughly before cooking the remaining patties. Serve immediately with all the traditional trimmings. Serves 6.

* About Bronzing: Bronzing is a good technique that works wonderfully for meat and fish - and it's so simple. In order to lock in juices, you actually brown very quickly one side of the meat or fish at a time on a heavy griddle or in a large, heavy aluminum skillet or electric fry-pan heated to 350°F (180°C). If you omit the butter stages, bronzing is an exceptional way to cook delicious reduced fat diet food. Just coat the meat or seafood with a non-stick vegetable spray and season as recipe indicates.

Approximate nutritional analysis per serving:
Calories 391, Protein 36 g, Carbohydrates 21 g, Fat 17 g,
Cholesterol 114 mg, Sodium 342 mg

Bronzed Hamburgers

SWEET AND SOUR CRANBERRY MEATBALLS

1½ lbs (685 g) lean ground meat (beef, pork,
    mutton, or a mixture of any)
⅔ cup (160 ml) fine dry bread crumbs
½ cup (120 ml) milk
2 medium eggs
½ tsp (3 ml) garlic powder
½ tsp (3 ml) pepper
1 tsp (5 ml) salt

SWEET AND SOUR SAUCE:
1 - 16 oz can (480 g) whole berry cranberry sauce
1 - 8 oz can (240 g) crushed pineapple
1 - 12 oz bottle (360 ml) chili sauce

Mix first 7 ingredients together, blending thoroughly, and set
aside to "ripen" while mixing Sweet and Sour Sauce. Mix fruit
and chili sauce well; heat slowly in large shallow pan so that
meatballs are not piled too deeply. Shape meat mixture into
1-inch balls. DO NOT BROWN; place gently in heated sauce
and simmer until well cooked and sauce is thickened. During
early stages of cooking, stir meatballs very gently so they will
hold their shape. Yields 70 meatballs, serves 6.

Approximate nutritional analysis per serving:
Calories 576, Protein 33 g, Carbohydrates 57 g, Fat 24 g,
Cholesterol 173 mg, Sodium 1038 mg

Courtesy of the Cape Cod Cranberry Growers' Association.

SAUCY MEATBALLS

1 lb (455 g) lean ground beef
⅔ cup (160 ml) grated Parmesan cheese
½ cup (120 ml) seasoned dry bread crumbs
½ cup (120 ml) milk
1 egg, slightly beaten
1 tbs (15 ml) vegetable oil
2 - 14½ oz cans (840 g) stewed tomatoes,
    cut into bite-size pieces
⅓ cup (80 ml) HEINZ 57 Sauce
½ tsp (3 ml) salt
⅛ tsp (.5 ml) pepper
hot buttered noodles

Combine first 5 ingredients. Form into 20 meatballs using a
rounded tbs for each. Brown oil; drain excess fat. Combine
tomatoes, 57 Sauce, salt and pepper; pour over meatballs.
Simmer, uncovered, 15-20 minutes or until sauce is desired
consistency, stirring occasionally. Serve meatballs and sauce
over noodles. Serves 5.

Approximate nutritional analysis per serving w/o noodles:
Calories 382, Protein 28 g, Carbohydrates 17 g, Fat 23 g,
Cholesterol 126 mg, Sodium 709 mg

MEATBALLS WITH CRANBERRY-APRICOT SAUCE

1 lb (455 g) ground turkey
½ cup (120 ml) dry bread crumbs
⅓ cup (80 ml) onion, finely chopped
¼ cup (60 ml) milk
1 egg
2 tbs (30 ml) dried parsley flakes
1 tsp (5 ml) poultry seasoning
1 tsp (5 ml) Worcestershire sauce
dash salt and pepper

SAUCE:
1 cup (240 ml) ketchup
1 - 12 oz jar (360 g) apricot preserves
½ cup (120 ml) Dried Cranberries

Mix together ground turkey, bread crumbs, onion, milk, egg,
parsley flakes, poultry seasoning, Worcestershire sauce, salt and
pepper. Shape into 1-inch balls. Brown meatballs in a large
non-stick skillet over medium heat until done. Remove
meatballs from pan. Remove any fat from pan. Heat ketchup
and apricot preserves in skillet, stirring until blended. Add
Dried Cranberries to the sauce mixture. Add meatballs and stir
until coated with sauce. Simmer uncovered 30 minutes, stirring
occasionally. Yields 30-40 meatballs.

Approximate nutritional analysis per meatball:
Calories 67, Protein 4 g, Carbohydrates 8 g, Fat 2 g,
Cholesterol 15 mg, Sodium 108 mg

QUARTERBACK MEATLOAF

1 egg or egg substitute
1 lb (455 g) lean ground beef *or*
    ½ lb (230 g) *each* ground beef and pork
1 tsp (5 ml) salt
1 tsp (5 ml) IMPERIAL Granulated Sugar
⅛ tsp (.5 ml) pepper
1 tsp (5 ml) lemon juice
¼ cup (60 ml) chopped onion
½ cup (120 ml) bread crumbs
½ cup (120 ml) pork and beans
12 strips pimiento
¼ cup (60 ml) catsup

Set oven at 400°F (205°C). Beat egg in mixing bowl. Add all
ingredients except pimiento and catsup. Mix lightly with fork.
Shape into four loaves shaped like footballs. Place loaves on
baking sheet and brush with catsup mixed with 1 tbs water.
Bake 25 minutes. Lift with large spoon onto serving dish. Put
strips of pimiento on top of each loaf in X design. Serves 4.

Approximate nutritional analysis per serving:
Calories 396, Protein 33 g, Carbohydrates 20 g, Fat 20 g,
Cholesterol 156 mg, Sodium 101 mg

CAJUN-STUFFED TOMATOES

4 large fresh FLORIDA Tomatoes
1 lb (455 g) Italian hot or sweet sausage,
  casing removed, coarsely chopped
½ cup (120 ml) chopped green pepper
½ cup (120 ml) chopped celery
2 tsp (10 ml) minced garlic
2 tsp (10 ml) thyme leaves, crushed
2 eggs, lightly beaten

Use tomatoes held at room temperature until fully ripe.
Preheat oven to 350°F (180°C). Cut off stem end of each
tomato. Scoop out pulp (save for stews, soups, etc.) leaving
¼-inch thick shells. Turn tomatoes upside down to drain; set
aside. In a large skillet cook sausage until browned, about
3 minutes. Remove any excess fat from the pan with a spoon
and discard. Add green pepper, celery, garlic and thyme. Cook
and stir until vegetables are tender, about 2 minutes. Remove
from heat. Stir in eggs. Spoon meat mixture into reserved
tomato shells. Place in a shallow baking pan containing ½-inch
water. Cover and bake until tomatoes are tender, 20-25
minutes. Garnish with yellow pepper, if desired. Serves 4.

Approximate nutritional analysis per serving:
Calories 451, Protein 20 g, Carbohydrates 6 g, Fat 38 g,
Cholesterol 193 mg, Sodium 880 mg

SCANDINAVIAN MEATBALLS

1½ cups (355 ml) DANNON Plain Nonfat or
  Lowfat Yogurt, divided
½ cup (120 ml) soft bread crumbs
1 lb (455 g) lean ground beef
1 egg
¼ cup (60 ml) finely chopped onion
¼ tsp (1 ml) salt, optional
2 tbs (30 ml) all-purpose flour
1 - 3½ g envelope instant beef broth mix
1 tsp (5 ml) Worcestershire sauce
snipped fresh parsley, optional

In a large bowl combine ½ cup yogurt and bread crumbs; let
stand 5 minutes. Add ground beef, egg, onion and salt. Mix
well and shape into 1¼-inch meatballs. Spray a large nonstick
skillet with vegetable cooking spray. Cook meatballs over
medium heat until brown and cooked through, turning often;
drain. Wipe skillet dry.

   In a small bowl, combine 1 cup yogurt, flour, beef broth
mix and Worcestershire sauce until smooth. Add to skillet.
Cook over medium-low heat, stirring constantly, until thickened. Do not boil. Reduce heat to low. Add meatballs; mix
with sauce and cook until just heated through. If desired,
garnish with parsley. Serves 6.

Approximate nutritional analysis per serving:
Calories 301, Protein 24 g, Carbohydrates 13 g, Fat 16 g,
Cholesterol 105 mg, Sodium 429 mg

STUFFED CABBAGE

1 - 2 lb (910 g) head cabbage
½ cup (120 ml) water
1 lb (455 g) lean ground pork or beef
¼ cup (60 ml) packaged dry bread crumbs
1 tsp (5 ml) oregano
1 cup (240 ml) sliced CALIFORNIA ripe olives
1⅔ cups (400 ml) spaghetti sauce

Place cabbage in microwave-safe dish or bowl large enough to
hold it. Add water, cover with plastic wrap and cook at HIGH
for 6-8 minutes, turning once halfway through, or until outer
leaves flex easily. Drain and run under cold water to cool
enough to handle. Gently remove 8 large outer leaves. Chop
enough of remaining cabbage to get about 1 cup. Save any
leftover for other uses. Combine chopped cabbage with pork,
bread crumbs, oregano and half the olives and sauce. Roll
leaves around filling to make closed packages. Cover with
plastic wrap and heat at HIGH for 14-16 minutes, or until hot,
rearranging rolls halfway through. Heat remaining sauce in
large measuring cup, covered with paper towel to prevent
splattering, for 1½-2 minutes. Transfer rolls to platter or plates,
ribbon sauce over and sprinkle with remaining olives. Serves 4.

Approximate nutritional analysis per serving:
Calories 401, Protein 41 g, Carbohydrates 22 g, Fat 17 g,
Cholesterol 130 mg, Sodium 401 mg

FIESTA MEAT LOAF

1 lb (455 g) HEALTHY CHOICE Extra Lean
Ground Beef
¾ cup (180 ml) quick oats
½ cup (120 ml) HEALTHY CHOICE
  Cholesterol Free Egg Product
¼ cup (60 ml) salsa
½ cup (120 ml) diced green pepper
¼ cup (60 ml) diced onion
1 tbs (15 ml) chili powder
½ tsp (3 ml) salt
¼ cup (60 ml) salsa

In medium bowl, combine beef, oats, egg product, ¼ cup salsa,
green pepper, onion, chili powder and salt. Form meat mixture
into loaf shape and place in a 8x4x3-inch loaf dish sprayed with
vegetable oil spray. Top with ¼ cup salsa. Bake in 350°F
(180°C) oven for 55 minutes. Serves 6.

Approximate nutritional analysis per serving:
Calories 150, Protein 18 g, Carbohydrates 8 g, Fat 4 g,
Cholesterol 35 mg, Sodium 400 mg

SOUTHWEST MEATLOAF

1 lb (455 g) lean ground beef
½ lb (230 g) chorizo or Italian sausage
½ cup (120 ml) quick-cooking or regular rolled oats
½ cup (120 ml) chopped onion
2 eggs, beaten
1 - 16 oz jar (480 ml) CHI-CHI'S Salsa, divided
1½ cups (355 ml) CHI-CHI'S Refried Beans
1 cup (240 ml) shredded cheddar cheese
2 tbs (30 ml) CHI-CHI'S Diced Green Chilies

Heat oven to 350°F (180°C), Line 9x5-inch loaf pan with enough foil so that it extends beyond the pan edges. Coat foil with nonstick cooking spray. In medium bowl, combine ground beef, sausage, oats, onion, eggs and 2 tbs salsa. Press half of the mixture into prepared pan. Form a 1-inch deep indentation down center of meat mixture, leaving a 1-inch border of meat on all sides. In a small bowl, combine refried beans, cheese and chilies. Mix well. Spoon bean mixture into indentation, mounding mixture if necessary. Press remaining meat mixture evenly over beans and meat, sealing edges. Bake 1¼ hours or until well done. Let stand 15 minutes. Lift loaf from pan using foil. Remove foil. Spoon remaining salsa on top of meatloaf. Serves 6.

Approximate nutritional analysis per serving:
Calories 530, Protein 33 g, Carbohydrates 19 g, Fat 35 g,
Cholesterol 170 mg, Sodium 230 mg

PIMIENTOS RELLENOS
Stuffed Peppers

1 small onion, minced
¼ cup (60 ml) GOYA Olive Oil
1 clove garlic, minced
¼ lb (115 g) ground beef
¼ lb (115 g) ground veal
1 GOYA Chorizo, chopped
2 tbs (30 ml) GOYA Sofrito
1 packet Sazón GOYA sin Achiote
1 tbs (15 ml) pine nuts
2 tbs (30 ml) GOYA Tomato Sauce
¼ cup (60 ml) GOYA Medium Rice, cooked
salt and pepper to taste
6 whole medium bell peppers, tops cut off,
    seeds and veins removed

In skillet, sauté onion slowly in 2 tbs olive oil until translucent. Add garlic, ground beef, veal, chorizo, Sofrito, Sazón, pine nuts and tomato sauce. Cook 5-10 minutes over medium heat, until meat is done. Stir in cooked rice; add salt and pepper to taste. Spoon meat mixture into peppers. Place into a shallow greased pan and bake at 350°F (180°C) for 5-10 minutes. Serve drizzled with olive oil if desired. Serves 6.

Approximate nutritional analysis per serving:
Calories 512, Protein 26 g, Carbohydrates 12 g, Fat 40 g,
Cholesterol 96 mg, Sodium 136 mg

Southwest Meatloaf

CORN AND SAUSAGE CASSEROLE

2 cups (480 ml) whole kernel corn
1 can Vienna sausage, cut in thirds crosswise
½ cup (120 ml) chopped green pepper
½ tsp (3 ml) salt
½ tsp (3 ml) IMPERIAL Granulated Sugar
dash white pepper
2 cups (480 ml) medium white sauce
1½ cups (355 ml) cracker crumbs or bread crumbs

Combine corn, sausages, green pepper. Add seasonings. Place alternate layers of corn mixture, crumbs, white sauce in oven proof casserole, topping with crumbs. Bake in 350°F (180°C) oven about 30 minutes. Serves 6.

Approximate nutritional analysis per serving:
Calories 332, Protein 10 g, Carbohydrates 36 g, Fat 17 g,
Cholesterol 45 mg, Sodium 863 mg

MEATLOAF RING WITH FRENCH ONION SAUCE

1½ lbs (685 g) ground beef *or* 1 lb (455 g) ground beef
   plus ½ lb (230 g) ground pork
1 small onion, chopped
1 cup (240 ml) fine dry bread crumbs
2 eggs, beaten
⅔ cup (160 ml) milk
1 tsp (5 ml) seasoned salt
freshly ground pepper

SAUCE:
2 large onions, thinly sliced
1 tbs (15 ml) butter
1 tsp (5 ml) dried tarragon
½ cup (120 ml) ketchup
¼ cup (60 ml) cider vinegar
reserved meatloaf juices (skim off fat)
½ cup (120 ml) Natural raisins

Lightly mix first 7 ingredients and fill a 9-inch microwaveable ring mold, or make a ring by placing a custard cup in the center of a 9-inch baking dish. Cover meat with waxed paper; microwave on MEDIUM-HIGH for 12-14 minutes, rotating dish a quarter turn after 7 minutes and again after 11 minutes. Pour off liquid and fat and save; let meatloaf stand 5-10 minutes while making sauce. Standing allows meat to set-up for easier slicing. Serves 6.

   Sauce: Place onions, butter and tarragon in 1-qt bowl; cover and microwave on HIGH for 5-6 minutes stirring once or twice. Stir in ketchup, vinegar, meat juices and raisins. Cook, uncovered, on HIGH for 2 minutes, until bubbling throughout. Pour on top of entire meatloaf, guiding most of the sauce that drips down into the open center of the ring.

Approximate nutritional analysis per serving:
Calories 531, Protein 35 g, Carbohydrates 39 g, Fat 27 g,
Cholesterol 179 mg, Sodium 847 mg

Courtesy of the California Raisin Advisory Board.

MEXICAN CORN CASSEROLE

½ lb (230 g) lean ground beef
¾ cup (180 ml) CALIFORNIA ripe olive wedges
2 eggs
1 - 17 oz can (510 g) cream-style corn
1 - 4 oz can (120 g) diced green chilies
¼ cup (60 ml) yellow cornmeal
2 tsp (10 ml) oregano
1 tsp (5 ml) thyme
½ tsp (3 ml) salt
½ cup (120 ml) Monterey Jack cheese

Crumble beef into microwave-safe baking dish. Cover with paper towel and microwave on HIGH for 2-3 minutes or until cooked. Break up with fork. Combine ½ cup olives with eggs, corn, chilies, cornmeal, herbs and salt. Turn into 1½-qt baking dish. Top with beef then cheese and remaining olives. Microwave uncovered at MEDIUM-HIGH for 15 minutes, or until hot in center. Serves 4.

Approximate nutritional analysis per serving:
Calories 388, Protein 21 g, Carbohydrates 40 g, Fat 17 g,
Cholesterol 62 mg, Sodium 875 mg

FANTASTIC KIELBASA AND BEAN CASSEROLE

2 tbs (30 ml) GOYA Olive Oil
2 cups (480 ml) chopped onion
1½ cups (355 ml) dark brown sugar
2 cups (480 ml) ketchup
2 tbs (30 ml) maple syrup
2 tbs (30 ml) molasses
¼ cup (60 ml) Worcestershire sauce
1 tsp (5 ml) GOYA Adobo
1 packet GOYA Ham Concentrate
2 lbs (910 g) kielbasa, cut into 2-inch slices
2 - 16 oz cans (960 g) GOYA White Beans, drained

Heat oil in large stock pot and sauté onions over medium heat until golden. Add sugar and dissolve. Add remaining ingredients one at a time, except beans and meat. Stir after adding each one. Bring to boil, lower flame and simmer 5 minutes. Add beans and meat and simmer, covered, for 30 minutes to 1 hour, stirring occasionally. Serves 8.

Approximate nutritional analysis per serving:
Calories 746, Protein 23 g, Carbohydrates 88 g, Fat 35 g,
Cholesterol 76 mg, Sodium 527 mg

SAUSAGE-OLIVE SAUCE ON RICE

1 lb (455 g) Polish sausage, bratwurst (casing
   removed), hot dogs or other smoked ready-
   to-eat sausage
1⅔ cups (400 ml) no-salt-added spaghetti sauce
1 - 1 lb can (455 g) zucchini with Italian-style
   tomato sauce
½ cup (120 ml) CALIFORNIA ripe olive wedges
4 cups (960 ml) hot cooked rice
grated Romano or Parmesan cheese

Slice sausages. Combine with spaghetti sauce, zucchini and olive in saucepan. Heat through and serve over rice. Pass cheese. Serves 4.

Approximate nutritional analysis per serving:
Calories 664, Protein 22 g, Carbohydrates 69 g, Fat 33 g,
Cholesterol 76 mg, Sodium 342 mg

Opposite: Kielbasa and Bean Casserole

BUTIFARRA CON ALUBIAS
White Beans with Sausage

1 lb (455 g) sweet sausage
1 tbs (15 ml) GOYA Olive Oil
1 small onion, chopped
4 cloves garlic, minced
3 strips bacon, chopped
2 - 16 oz cans (960 g) GOYA Small White Beans
2 tbs (30 ml) GOYA Sofrito
1 bay leaf
½ tsp (3 ml) GOYA Adobo with Pepper
2 tbs (30 ml) chopped parsley
1 whole GOYA Pimiento, cut into strips

Puncture sausages with fork, and sauté in a large skillet in olive oil until well browned. Remove sausages and set aside. In the same pan, sauté onion, garlic and bacon until bacon is browned. Add beans, Sofrito and bay leaf, and simmer 2-3 minutes over low-medium heat, stirring often. Stir in Adobo and parsley. Arrange pimiento strips on top. Remove bay leaf. Serves 6.

Approximate nutritional analysis per serving:
Calories 478, Protein 25 g, Carbohydrates 31 g, Fat 28 g,
Cholesterol 66 mg, Sodium   789 mg

SMOKED SAUSAGE AND CARIBBEAN BEANS

vegetable cooking spray
1 tsp (5 ml) minced garlic
¼ tsp (1 ml) dried pepper flakes
1 cup (240 ml) salt-free chicken broth
¼ tsp (1 ml) ground allspice
2½ cups (590 ml) cooked black beans
1 - 14 oz pkg (420 g) HEALTHY CHOICE Low Fat
    Smoked Sausage Product, cut in ½-inch pieces
3 cups (720 ml) cooked rice

ORANGE SALSA:
1 tbs (15 ml) minced onion
1½ tbs (25 ml) minced jalapeño pepper
⅔ cup (160 ml) peeled, seeded and chopped tomato
¼ cup (60 ml) chopped orange segments
1 tbs (15 ml) chopped cilantro
2 tsp (10 ml) orange juice
1 tbs (15 ml) cider vinegar
⅛ tsp (.5 ml) salt

Coat a large skillet with cooking spray; heat over medium heat. Add garlic and red pepper; cook 1 minute. Add chicken broth, allspice and beans. Bring to boil over medium heat, add sausage, cover and cook 10 minutes. Serve beans on rice with Orange Salsa. Serves 6.
    Orange Salsa: Combine ingredients and refrigerate.

Approximate nutritional analysis per serving:
Calories 339, Carbohydrates 48 g, Fat 3 g, Cholesterol 23 mg,
Sodium 693 mg

MEXICAN BEANS AND CHORIZO

1 lb (455 g) chorizo or Italian sausage,
    cut into 1-inch pieces
1 - 16 oz can (480 g) baked beans
1 - 15½ oz can (465 g) Great Northern beans, drained
1 - 16 oz can (480 g) pinto beans, drained
1 - 8 oz jar (240 g) CHI-CHI'S Thick and Chunky
    Taco Sauce
8 oz (240 g) cooked, crumbled bacon
1 cup (240 ml) chopped onion
¼ cup (60 ml) firmly packed brown sugar
2 tbs (30 ml) coarse grain mustard
1 tbs (15 ml) red wine vinegar
2 tsp (10 ml) minced fresh garlic

In Dutch oven, brown chorizo. Drain. Add remaining ingredients. Bring to a boil. Cover; reduce heat to low. Simmer, stirring occasionally, 20 minutes. Serves 20.

Approximate nutritional analysis per serving:
Calories 210, Protein 10 g, Carbohydrates 18 g, Fat 11 g,
Cholesterol 25 mg, Sodium 500 mg

SAUSAGE LINK STIR-FRY

1 LIGHT & LEAN 97 Smoked Dinner Link,
    cut in ½-inch slices
2 tbs (30 ml) olive oil , divided
1 - 16 oz pkg (480 g) frozen mixed vegetables,
    thawed and drained
½ cup (120 ml) beef broth
1 tbs plus 2 tsp (25 ml) cornstarch
1 tbs (15 ml) low sodium soy sauce
1 tbs (15 ml) hot sauce
5 cups (1.2 L) hot cooked rice

In large skillet, cook meat in 1 tbs oil until lightly browned. Remove from skillet; keep warm. Add remaining oil and vegetables to skillet; sauté until tender. Return meat to skillet. Combine broth, cornstarch, soy sauce and hot sauce. Add to skillet. Cook, stirring constantly until mixture is thickened. Serve over rice. Serves 5.

Approximate nutritional analysis per serving:
Calories 537, Protein 27 g, Carbohydrates 70 g, Fat 12 g,
Cholesterol 40 mg, Sodium 714 mg

Opposite: Sausage Stir-Fry

YAMBILEE BEEF STEW

⅓ cup (80 ml) all-purpose flour
1½ tsp (8 ml) salt, divided
2 lbs (190 g) stew beef, cut into 1-inch cubes
¼ cup (60 ml) salad oil
1 - 10½ oz can (315 ml) condensed beef broth
    (bouillon), undiluted
1 - 8 oz can (240 ml) tomato sauce
⅓ cup (80 ml) chopped fresh parsley
1 clove garlic, minced
½ tsp (3 ml) thyme leaves
½ tsp (3 ml) pepper
½ bay leaf
1 large onion, chopped
12 small whole white onions
3 cloves
½ cup (120 ml) dry sherry
4 medium uncooked **LOUISIANA** yams*,
    pared and cut into 2-inch pieces
1 lb (455 g) fresh green beans**, cut in half
1 cup (240 ml) celery pieces

* 2 - 16 oz cans (960 ml) LOUISIANA yams, drained and quartered, may be substituted for fresh yams. Add during last 20 minutes of cooking time.
** 2 - 9 oz pkgs (540 g) frozen cut green beans may be substituted for fresh beans. Add during last 20 minutes of cooking time.

Combine ⅓ cup flour and ½ tsp salt in a small bag; add meat, a few pieces at a time, shake until evenly coated. In large Dutch oven, heat salad oil. Add meat and cook, a few pieces at a time, until well browned, removing pieces as they brown. Drain fat from Dutch oven.

Return meat to Dutch oven; add condensed beef broth, tomato sauce, parsley, garlic, thyme, 1 tsp salt, the pepper, bay leaf and chopped onion. In one small onion place 3 cloves and add to Dutch oven; set aside remaining 11 small whole white onions. Heat to boiling. Reduce heat to low; cover and simmer 1¼ hours, stirring occasionally. Add sherry, remaining 11 small whole white onions, the yams, green beans and celery; continue cooking for 45 minutes more or until vegetables are fork-tender.

If desired, thicken stew by removing ½ cup liquid from stew to a small bowl; blend in 1 tbs flour with the ½ cup liquid until smooth. Slowly stir flour mixture into stew. Stir frequently and simmer 5 minutes more or until stew is slightly thickened. Remove and discard cloves from onion. Serve stew in bowls. Serves 8.

Approximate nutritional analysis per serving:
Calories 517, Protein 39 g, Carbohydrates 33 g, Fat 24 g,
Cholesterol 120 mg, Sodium 248 mg

HEARTY BEEF VEGETABLE STEW

2 tsp (10 ml) **OLD BAY** Seasoning, divided,
    or more to taste
3 lbs (1.4 kg) beef chuck roast, trimmed of fat
4 large potatoes, peeled and cut into chunks
3 carrots, scraped and sliced
1 cup (240 ml) water

Sprinkle 1 tsp OLD BAY Seasoning over beef. Sprinkle remaining tsp OLD BAY Seasoning over vegetables. To crockpot, add water, chuck roast and vegetables; cook on high for 6 hours. Serves 10.

Approximate nutritional analysis per serving:
Calories 417, Protein 44 g, Carbohydrates 14 g, Fat 20 g,
Cholesterol 144 mg, Sodium 161 mg

GYPSY GOULASH

1 lb (455 g) lean ground beef
4 tsp (20 ml) vegetable oil
3 green bell peppers, halved and sliced
2 tbs (30 ml) paprika
1 lb (455 g) tomatoes, halved and sliced
½ cup (120 ml) sliced **CALIFORNIA** ripe olives
salt and pepper

Sauté beef in large skillet in 2 tsp oil over high heat until browned. Remove meat from pan, leaving drippings. Add 2 tsp oil, the peppers and onion to pan and sauté over high heat about 5 minutes or until tender. Stir in paprika. Return beef to pan, add tomatoes and olives and heat through. Salt and pepper to taste. Serve in wide soup bowls with thickly sliced boiled potatoes, if desired. Serves 4.

Approximate nutritional analysis per serving:
Calories 448, Protein 31 g, Carbohydrates 21 g, Fat 27 g,
Cholesterol 99 mg, Sodium 195 mg

Opposite: Gypsy Goulash
Sausages and Olives with Tomato Sauce

PIQUANT BEEF STEW WITH RICE

3 lbs (1.4 kg) beef stew meat, cut into 1-inch cubes
1 tbs (15 ml) olive oil
1 - 16 oz jar (480 ml) CHI-CHI'S Salsa
1 cup (240 ml) beef broth
2 cups (480 ml) quartered fresh mushrooms
1½ cups (355 ml) chopped onion
1 tbs (15 ml) minced fresh garlic
1½ tsp (8 ml) cumin seeds, crushed
1 tsp (5 ml) dried oregano leaves
¼ tsp (1 ml) coarsely ground pepper
2 tbs (30 ml) chopped CHI-CHI'S Whole Green
    Jalapeño Peppers
2 cups (480 ml) hot cooked rice
¼ cup (60 ml) chopped fresh cilantro
ripe olives

Heat oven to 325°F (165°C). In Dutch oven, brown beef in oil over medium-high heat, stirring occasionally. Add salsa, broth, mushrooms, onion, garlic, cumin, oregano, pepper and jalapeño peppers. Bring to boil. Cover; place in oven. Bake about 3 hours or until meat is tender, stirring occasionally. Serve over hot cooked rice. Garnish with cilantro and olives. Serves 6.

Approximate nutritional analysis per serving plus ⅓ cup rice:
Calories 450, Protein 55 g, Carbohydrates 29 g, Fat 11 g,
Cholesterol 135 mg, Sodium 590 mg

GUMBO WITH BEEF AND OLIVES

1 lb (455 g) boneless beef chuck, trimmed
    and finely cubed
2 tbs (30 ml) bottled or fresh minced garlic
1 medium onion, cut into narrow wedges
1 - 1 lb 13 oz can (845 g) whole peeled tomatoes
1 cup (240 ml) water
½ cup (120 ml) tomato sauce
1 tsp (5 ml) Tabasco pepper sauce
½ tsp (3 ml) salt
¼ cup (60 ml) Worcestershire sauce
1 cup (240 ml) whole pitted CALIFORNIA ripe olives
5 oz (150 g) frozen baby okra
1 tsp (5 ml) gumbo filé, if available

Combine all ingredients except olives, okra and filé in large saucepan. Cover, bring to boil and simmer 1 hour or until beef is falling-apart tender. Add olives, okra and filé and heat through. Serves 7.

Approximate nutritional analysis per serving:
Calories 187, Protein 21 g, Carbohydrates 12 g, Fat 6 g,
Cholesterol 53 mg, Sodium 472 mg

Gumbo with Beef and Olives

BEEF STROGANOFF

1 tbs (15 ml) butter or margarine
½ cup (120 ml) chopped onion
1 clove garlic, finely chopped
1 lb (455 g) lean beef sirloin, ½-inch thick,
    cut into 3x½-inch strips
8 oz (240 g) mushrooms, sliced
¼ cup (60 ml) dry red wine
2 tbs (430 ml) cornstarch
1 cup (240 ml) condensed beef broth
¼ tsp (1 ml) pepper
1 cup (240 ml) YOPLAIT Fat Free Plain Yogurt
hot cooked noodles or rice

Heat margarine in 10-inch skillet until melted. Add onion and garlic; cook and stir over medium-high heat until tender. Add beef and mushrooms; cook and stir about 7 minutes or until beef is no longer pink. Stir in wine; reduce heat. Cover and simmer 10 minutes. Stir cornstarch into broth until smooth; stir into beef mixture. Cook and stir over medium-high heat until thickened; remove from heat. Stir in pepper and yogurt; heat through over low heat if necessary - do not boil. Serve over noodles. Serves 4.

    High altitude: 3500-6500 ft: Thinly slice beef.

Approximate nutritional analysis per serving:
Calories 500, Protein 42 g, Carbohydrates 57 g, Fat 11 g,
Cholesterol 130 mg, Sodium 580 mg

COCIDO MADRILEÑO
Chick Pea Stew

1 - 16 oz can (480 g) GOYA Chick Peas,
    drained and rinsed
1 gal (3.8 kg) water
4 new potatoes, peeled
1 lb (455 g) beef chunks
2 chicken thighs
¼ lb (115 g) bacon
1 GOYA Chorizo sausage
2 soup bones
1 ham hock, cut in pieces
1 small pork sparerib
1 sweet sausage
3 whole medium onions, peeled
1 large carrot, cut into 3 pieces
2 cloves garlic
1 leek, split (green and white parts)
1 bay leaf
1 sprig fresh thyme
1 packet Sazón GOYA sin Achiote
2 tsp (10 ml) GOYA Adobo with Pepper
1 - 12 oz pkg (360 g) GOYA Fideos, broken up

In a large saucepan or soup pot, combine water, potatoes, beef, chicken, bacon, chorizo, soup bones, ham hock, spare rib, sausage, onions, carrot, garlic, leek, bay leaf, thyme, Sazón and Adobo. Bring to a boil, reduce heat and simmer, covered, an additional 20 minutes. With a slotted spoon, carefully remove the chick peas, vegetables, and pieces of meat and bones from soup and arrange on platter. Discard bay leaf. Return soup to a boil, and cook pasta in soup until done. Serve soup next to platter of meat. Serves 8.

Approximate nutritional analysis per serving:
Calories 728, Protein 50 g, Carbohydrates 39 g, Fat 40 g,
Cholesterol 169 mg, Sodium   479 mg

PORK STEW WITH CORNBREAD DUMPLINGS

STEW:
1½ lbs (685 g) boneless pork, cut in 1-inch cubes
1 large onion, cut in wedges
1 clove garlic, minced
2 large carrots, cut in 1-inch cubes
2 large potatoes, peeled and cut into large chunks
1 - 16 oz can (480 g) tomatoes, coarsely chopped
¼ cup (60 ml) strong coffee or beef broth
2 tbs (30 ml) molasses
1 tsp (5 ml) Worcestershire sauce
2 tsp (10 ml) salt
½ tsp (3 ml) oregano, crushed
½ tsp (3 ml) thyme, crushed
dash cayenne pepper
¾ cup (180 ml) Natural raisins

DUMPLINGS:
1 - 15 oz pkg (450 g) cornbread mix
1 small can corn, drained

In 3-qt casserole combine all stew ingredients except raisins. Cover and microwave on HIGH until boiling, about 10 minutes. Reduce power to MEDIUM and continue cooking, covered, for 1 hour. Stir in raisins.

    Dumplings: Mix cornbread as directed, reducing liquid called for by ¼ cup. Stir in drained corn. Drop tablespoonfuls of corn batter over surface of hot stew, leaving center open. Microwave, uncovered, on MEDIUM-HIGH for 5-6 minutes, rotating dish a half turn after 3 minutes. Dumplings expand and blend into each other. Test dumplings for doneness using a pick. Serves 6.

Approximate nutritional analysis per serving stew only:
Calories 435, Protein 40 g, Carbohydrates 37 g, Fat 14 g,
Cholesterol 129 mg, Sodium 972 mg

Approximate nutritional analysis per serving dumplings only:
Calories 192, Protein 5 g, Carbohydrates 41 g, Fat 1 g,
Cholesterol 0 mg, Sodium 909 mg

FARMER'S STEW ARGENTINA

3 cups (720 ml) water
1 lb (455 g) lean ground beef
2 tbs (30 ml) vegetable oil
1 medium onion, chopped
1 green bell pepper, diced into ½-inch pieces
1 red bell pepper, diced into ½-inch pieces
1 small sweet potato, peeled, diced in ½-inch pieces
1 large garlic clove, minced
1 tbs (15 ml) fresh parsley, chopped
½ tsp (3 ml) granulated sugar
⅛ tsp (.5 ml) cumin
1 tsp (5 ml) salt
3 cups (720 ml) beef broth, heated
½ lb (230 g) zucchini, diced into ½-inch pieces
1 cup (240 ml) whole kernel corn
2 tbs (30 ml) raisins
½ tsp (3 ml) Tabasco sauce
1 small pear, firm, but ripe, diced into 1-inch pieces
6 cups (1.5 L) cooked white rice

In a large saucepan, boil water. Remove the saucepan from heat. Add the ground beef, stirring to break meat into little pieces. Let sit 5 minutes, stirring once or twice, until most of the pink disappears from the meat. Drain meat well, discarding the water. In a large deep-sided skillet or Dutch oven, heat the oil over medium-high heat. Add onions and cook 4-5 minutes, stirring constantly, until all liquid has evaporated from the pan and the meat is lightly browned, about 10 minutes. Reduce heat to medium. Add the bell peppers, sweet potato and garlic. Continue cooking and stirring the mixture for 5 minutes, or until peppers and potatoes are slightly tender. Add the parsley, sugar, cumin and salt. Stir and cook for one minute to blend flavors. Pour beef broth into the skillet. Add the zucchini, corn, raisins and Tabasco pepper sauce. Simmer gently for 10 minutes. Add pear and simmer for 10 minutes, or until all the fruits and vegetables are tender. Ladle over rice. Serves 6.

Approximate nutritional analysis per serving:
Calories 505, Protein 21 g, Carbohydrates 70 g, Fat 16 g, Cholesterol 47 mg, Sodium 796 mg

LAMB STEW WITH BUTTER BEANS

2 cans GOYA Butter Beans, drained
3 lbs (1.4 g) lamb, cubed
3 tbs (45 ml) GOYA Corn Oil
2 cups (480 ml) water
1 carrot, chopped
2 cloves garlic, minced
1 bay leaf
1 large onion, chopped
½ tsp (3 ml) thyme
few grains black pepper
2 tbs (30 ml) parsley, chopped

Brown lamb in oil in large skillet. Combine remaining ingredients and simmer 40 minutes, or until lamb is tender. Add beans and simmer 30 minutes longer. Serves 6.

Approximate nutritional analysis per serving:
Calories 664, Protein 74 g, Carbohydrates 33 g, Fat 25 g, Cholesterol 202 mg, Sodium 742 mg

A QUICKIE CASSOULET

2 cans GOYA White Kidney Beans, drained
3 tbs (45 ml) GOYA Corn Oil or Butter
2 cups (480 ml) tomatoes, chopped
6 shallots, sliced
2 cloves garlic, minced
2 tbs (30 ml) parsley, chopped
1 lb (455 g) Italian sausage, cooked

Heat corn oil or melt butter in skillet; add tomatoes, shallots, garlic and parsley. Sauté until tender. Combine with beans in a 2-qt casserole, top with sausage and bake at 350°F (180°C) for 30 minutes. Serves 4.

Approximate nutritional analysis per serving:
Calories 758, Protein 37 g, Carbohydrates 48 g, Fat 47 g, Cholesterol 94 mg, Sodium   348 mg

Opposite: Farmer's Stew Argentina

CASSOULET OF SMOKED MEATS AND KRAUT

1 lb (455 g) new red potatoes
1 - 16 oz jar (480 g) sauerkraut, drained
½ medium cabbage, cut in 1-inch wedges
1 large leek, only, sliced
½ cup (120 ml) Golden raisins
½ cup (120 ml) wine or chicken broth
1 tsp (5 ml) salt
1 tsp (5 ml) thyme
1 tsp (5 ml) fresh ground pepper
8 oz (240 g) cooked smoked sausage, cut in 2-inch pieces
8 oz (240 g) smoked ham, in 1-inch sliced

Peel center of potatoes leaving a white band (or, cut large potatoes into pieces). Place in large dish and microwave 4-6 minutes until almost done. Place sauerkraut on top of potatoes; top with cabbage and leek, then raisins. In a measuring cup, stir wine with salt, thyme and pepper; pour over all. Cover and microwave on HIGH for 2 minutes. Arrange sausage and ham on top alternating in spoke-style pattern. Loosely cover and microwave on MEDIUM-HIGH for 8 minutes, rotating dish a quarter turn after 4 minutes. Cabbage should be slightly crisp in thick parts. Serves 6.

Approximate nutritional analysis per serving:
Calories 300, Protein 15 g, Carbohydrates 25 g, Fat 15 g, Cholesterol 47 mg, Sodium 795 mg

CALERETA DE PASTOR

Shepherd's Lamb Stew

2 cloves garlic, peeled
3 tbs (45 ml) GOYA Olive Oil
1½ lbs (685 g) boneless lamb, cut into 1-inch cubes
1 tsp (5 ml) GOYA Adobo with Cumin
1 onion, chopped
1 bay leaf
1 tomato, cut in chunks
2 carrots, peeled and sliced
1 cup (240 ml) LA VINA Red Cooking Wine
1 cup (240 ml) water
1 packet GOYA Chicken Bouillon
1 clove
1 peppercorn
1 tsp (5 ml) chopped GOYA Green Jalapeños
1½ tsp (8 ml) ground almonds
1 slice toasted bread
1 tbs (15 ml) GOYA Red Wine Vinegar
2 tsp (10 ml) paprika
1 whole GOYA Pimiento
1 packet Sazón GOYA sin Achiote
½ tsp (3 ml) fresh thyme, minced

In a large flame-proof casserole or Dutch oven, sauté garlic in olive oil until brown. Remove garlic with a slotted spoon and set aside. Sprinkle lamb cubes evenly with Adobo. In same casserole or Dutch oven, sauté lamb cubes, onion and bay leaf until lamb is browned. Add tomato, carrots, red cooking wine, bouillon and water. Bring to a boil, reduce heat, and simmer, uncovered, for 30 minutes.

In separate bowl, mash together clove, peppercorn, jalapeños, almonds, toasted bread, vinegar, paprika, pimiento, browned garlic and Sazón. Remove ⅓ cup of stew liquid from casserole, add to spice mixture in bowl, and stir. Add this mixture back into casserole and stir. Bring to a boil, and boil, uncovered, for 3-4 minutes. Remove bay leaf. Garnish with fresh thyme and serve. Serves 6.

Approximate nutritional analysis per serving:
Calories 350, Protein 34 g, Carbohydrates 10 g, Fat 3 g, Cholesterol 101 mg, Sodium 370 mg

CHOUCROUTE GARNI

4-6 lbs (1.8-2.7 kg) refrigerated sauerkraut
½ lb (230 g) bacon, diced
2 large onions, peeled and coarsely chopped
3 carrots, pared and sliced
½ cup (120 ml) chopped parsley
2 bay leaves
10 black peppercorns
10 juniper berries
4 whole cloves
2-4 cups (480-960 ml) fruity white wine
3-4 cups (720-960 ml) chicken broth
1 lb (455 g) lean pork loin, cubed
½ lb (230 g) ham, cubed
1 lb (455 g) smoked sausage, sliced
1 lb (455 g) bratwurst, sliced
2 tart green apples, cored and coarsely chopped

In a large Dutch oven, over medium-low heat, render bacon fat; add onion and carrots and sauté slowly; stirring occasionally, about 8-10 minutes. Place parsley , bay leaves, peppercorns, juniper berries and cloves in cheesecloth bag or large tea strainer. Add to pot along with sauerkraut, wine and broth. Bring to boil; cover and simmer 1 hour. Add meats to pot, stir, cover and simmer another hour. Add apples and simmer an additional 20 minutes. Serve immediately with pumpernickel or Jewish rye bread. Or refrigerate overnight and reheat to serve. Serves 10.

Approximate nutritional analysis per serving:
Calories 602, Protein 34 g, Carbohydrates 9 g, Fat 44 g, Cholesterol 111 mg, Sodium 206 mg

Opposite: Cassoulet of Smoked Meats and Kraut

JAMBALAYA

2 tbs (30 ml) vegetable oil
4 oz (120 g) smoked ham, diced
1 smoked sausage, sliced ½-inch thick
1 lb (455 g) boneless pork loin, cubed
1½ cups (355 ml) chopped onion
1 cup (240 ml) chopped celery
1 large green pepper, chopped
2 cloves garlic, minced
½ tsp (3 ml) hot pepper sauce
2 bay leaves
1½ tsp (8 ml) salt
1½ tsp (8 ml) dried oregano
1 tsp (5 ml) white pepper
½ tsp (3 ml) black pepper
1 tsp (5 ml) thyme
4 medium tomatoes, peeled and chopped
1 - 8 oz can (240 ml) tomato sauce
1 - 14½ oz can (435 ml) chicken broth
½ cup (120 ml) chopped green onion
2 cups (480 ml) rice

In a large Dutch oven, heat oil over medium heat. Stir in ham, sausage and pork; sauté until lightly browned, stirring frequently, 4-8 minutes. Stir in onion, celery and pepper, sauté until crisp-tender, about 5 minutes. Stir in next 8 ingredients. Cook over medium heat, stirring constantly and scraping pan bottom for 5 minutes. Stir in tomatoes, cook for 5-8 minutes. Stir in tomato sauce and chicken broth, bring to boil. Stir in green onion and rice. Bake, covered, in 350°F (180°C) oven until rice is tender, about 20-25 minutes. Remove bay leaves and serve immediately. Serves 10.

Approximate nutritional analysis per serving:
Calories 382, Protein 23 g, Carbohydrates 48 g, Fat 14 g,
Cholesterol 54 mg, Sodium 121 mg

SANTA FE PORK STEW

3 tbs (45 ml) GOYA Olive Oil
3 lbs (1.4 g) pork shoulder, cut into 1-inch cubes
3 tbs (45 ml) flour
1½ cups (355 ml) chopped onion
2 sweet potatoes, peeled and cut in 1-inch cubes
2 tbs (30 ml) cumin
1 tsp (5 ml) GOYA Adobo
1 packet Sazón GOYA sin Achiote
3 cups (720 ml) water
2 packets GOYA Chicken Bouillon
2 tbs (30 ml) GOYA Recaito
½ tsp (3 ml) sugar
1 can GOYA Black Beans, rinsed and drained

In large skillet, over medium flame, sauté pork in oil until slightly browned. Sauté in small batches if necessary. Sprinkle flour over pork and cook, tossing well, for 3 minutes. Add remaining ingredients, except beans, mix well and cover. When mixture boils, lower flame and simmer 30 minutes, stirring occasionally. Add beans and simmer uncovered 10 minutes. Serves 8.

Approximate nutritional analysis per serving:
Calories 587, Protein 60 g, Carbohydrates 25 g, Fat 26 g,
Cholesterol 194 mg, Sodium 809 mg

MOUNTAIN CHILI

2 lbs (910 g) beef sirloin, cut into 1-inch pieces
12 oz (360 g) pork sausage links,
    cut into 1-inch pieces
2 tbs (30 ml) vegetable oil
2 - 16 oz jars (960 g) CHI-CHI'S Salsa
1 - 10½ oz can (315 ml) beef consommé
1 cup (240 ml) beer
1 cup (240 ml) chopped green bell pepper
1 cup (240 ml) chopped red bell pepper
1 cup (240 ml) chopped onion
1 - 6 oz can (180 g) tomato paste
2 bay leaves
1 tbs plus 1½ tsp (23 ml) chili powder
4 tsp (20 ml) ground cumin
4 tsp (20 ml) minced fresh garlic
1 tsp (5 ml) dried oregano leaves
1 tsp (5 ml) sugar
¾ tsp (4 ml) pepper
sour cream
shredded cheddar cheese
chopped avocado

In Dutch oven, brown beef and sausage in oil. Drain. Stir in remaining ingredients except sour cream, cheese, and avocado. Bring to a boil; reduce heat to low. Simmer, stirring occasionally, 1½ hours or until beef is tender. Serve with sour cream, shredded cheese and chopped avocado. Serves 9.

Approximate nutritional analysis per serving:
Calories 280, Protein 24 g, Carbohydrates 16 g, Fat 13 g,
Cholesterol 65 mg, Sodium 108 mg

Opposite: Jambalaya

PIEDMONT PORK STEW

1 lb (455 g) boneless pork loin, cut into 1-inch cubes
1 tbs (15 ml) oil
1 medium onion, coarsely chopped
2 carrots, sliced
8 oz (240 g) mushrooms, coarsely chopped
1 - 8 oz can (240 ml) tomato sauce
1 cup (240 ml) dry red wine
1 tsp (5 ml) thyme
1 tsp (5 ml) oregano
¼ tsp (1 ml) cinnamon
¼ tsp (1 ml) salt
½ cup (120 ml) raisins

Brown pork in oil in large pot over medium-high heat until browned, about 4 minutes. Stir in vegetables, cook and stir 2 minutes more. Add tomato sauce, wine seasonings. Bring to boil; lower heat to a simmer, cover and cook gently, 15-20 minutes. Stir in raisins; heat through. Serve over hot cooked rice or orzo, if desired. Serves 6.

Approximate nutritional analysis per serving:
Calories 237, Protein 19 g, Carbohydrates 17 g, Fat 7 g,
Cholesterol 44 mg, Sodium 371 mg

MIKI'S CHILI

2 cans GOYA Red Kidney Beans, drained
1½ lbs (685 g) ground beef
3 tbs (45 ml) GOYA Vegetable Oil
2 large onions, chopped
2 green peppers, chopped
2 red peppers, chopped
3 cloves garlic, whole
1 - 2 lb can (910 g) whole tomatoes, cut up
dash cayenne pepper
2 tbs (30 ml) chili powder
2 tbs (30 ml) chili seasoning
1 tsp (5 ml) sugar

Heat oil in large skillet, brown meat. Add onions, red and green pepper, garlic, tomatoes and seasonings. Bring to boil, and simmer at least 2 hours. Add beans before last half hour. Serves 6.

Approximate nutritional analysis per serving:
Calories 593, Protein 40 g, Carbohydrates 45 g, Fat 29 g,
Cholesterol 99 mg, Sodium 919 mg

CHILI WITH BLACK BEANS

2 cans GOYA Black Beans, not drained
3 lbs (1.4 kg) chuck steak cut in ½-inch cubes
¼ cup (60 ml) GOYA Extra Virgin Olive Oil
2 onions, chopped
1 canned jalapeño, seeded and minced
1 - 8 oz can (240 ml) GOYA Tomato Sauce
3 tbs (45 ml) chili powder
¼ cup (60 ml) red wine
1 tsp (5 ml) dry mustard
2 cloves garlic, minced
½ tsp (3 ml) ground cumin
black pepper to taste

In large heavy casserole, heat oil and sauté onions and pepper. Add beef and brown lightly. Add remaining ingredients except beans and simmer 30-45 minutes. Add beans, cover and simmer 30 minutes. Serves 8.

Approximate nutritional analysis per serving:
Calories 695, Protein 47 g, Carbohydrates 9 g, Fat 51 g,
Cholesterol 168 mg, Sodium 204 mg

CHILI AND THEN SOME

2 cans GOYA Red Kidney Beans, drained
1 lb (455 g) ground beef
1 lb (455 g) Italian hot sausage, skinned
2 tbs (30 ml) GOYA Extra Virgin Olive Oil
2 cups (480 ml) onion, chopped
1 cup (240 ml) green pepper, chopped
1 cup (240 ml) celery, chopped
2 cloves garlic, minced
3 tbs (45 ml) chili powder
1 tbs (15 ml) oregano
2 bay leaves
2 tsp (10 ml) ground cumin
3 cups (720 ml) canned tomatoes in purée
1 cup (240 ml) beef broth
salt and pepper to taste

Heat oil in heavy skillet; add meat and brown. Add remaining ingredients except beans, and blend well. Bring to boil and simmer 20 minutes, stirring frequently. Add beans and simmer 15 minutes longer. Serves 8.

Approximate nutritional analysis per serving:
Calories 552, Protein 33 g, Carbohydrates 30 g, Fat 34 g,
Cholesterol 97 mg, Sodium   503 mg

Opposite: Piedmont Pork Stew

FIERY POT TEXAS CHILI

2 lbs (910 g) chili meat*
¼ cup (60 ml) cooking oil, divided
1½ cups (355 ml) water or beer
1 - 8 oz can (240 ml) tomato sauce
2 small onions, chopped
1 medium green pepper, finely chopped
5-6 cloves garlic, minced
1 tsp (5 ml) oregano
1 tbs (15 ml) ground cumin, or to taste
4 tbs (60 ml) chili powder
1 tsp (5 ml) salt
½ tsp (3 ml) IMPERIAL Granulated Sugar
red pepper (cayenne) to taste
4-5 medium jalapeño peppers, chopped

* Chili meat is coarsely ground round steak or well-trimmed chuck steak.

In large skillet, brown meat in one half of the oil. Transfer the meat to a large kettle or electric slow-cooker, leaving liquid in skillet. Add water or beer and tomato sauce to meat; sauté onion, green pepper, garlic in remaining oil and liquid in skillet. Add remaining dry ingredients and chopped jalapeño peppers. Simmer about 30 minutes, then transfer to kettle. Simmer about 2 hours. Dip off grease that rises to top. Serves 8.

    Note: Red pepper and jalapeño peppers are the "zingers" in this recipe. Add both with caution.

Approximate nutritional analysis per serving:
Calories 409, Protein 30 g, Carbohydrates 8 g, Fat 28 g,
Cholesterol 95 mg, Sodium 804 mg

BLACK BEAN CHILI

1½ lbs (685 g) ground beef
1 cup (240 ml) chopped onions
1 clove garlic, minced
2 - 16 oz cans (960 ml) black beans, drained
1 - 1¼ oz packet (38 g) ORTEGA Taco Seasoning Mix
1 - 12 oz jar (360 g) ORTEGA Mild, Medium or
    Hot Thick and Chunky Salsa
1 cup (240 ml) water
1 cup (240 ml) shredded cheese

In large saucepan, over medium-high heat, cook beef, onions and garlic until beef is no longer pink, stirring occasionally to break up meat; drain. Add black beans, taco seasoning mix, salsa and water. Cover; heat to boil. Reduce heat; simmer 20 minutes. Serve chili topped with cheese. Serves 8.

Approximate nutritional analysis per serving:
Calories 331, Protein 27 g, Carbohydrates 14 g, Fat 18 g,
Cholesterol 66 mg, Sodium 898 mg

SMOKY CHILI

1 cup (240 ml) sliced celery
1 tbs (15 ml) vegetable oil
½ lb (230 g) Polish smoked sausage, quartered
    lengthwise, cut into ¼-inch slices
1 large green bell pepper, coarsely chopped
1 tbs (15 ml) chili powder
1 - 14½ oz can (435 g) tomatoes, cut into
    bite-size pieces
1 - 15 oz can (450 g) spicy chili beans
½ cup (120 ml) HEINZ Chili Sauce
hot cooked rice

In 4-qt Dutch oven, sauté celery in oil 5 minutes. Add sausage, bell pepper and onion; sauté until vegetables are tender, about 4 minutes stirring occasionally. Stir in chili powder, tomatoes, beans and chili sauce; simmer, uncovered, 15 minutes, stirring occasionally. Serve over rice. Serves 4.

Approximate nutritional analysis per serving:
Calories 395, Protein 17 g, Carbohydrates 40 g, Fat 20 g,
Cholesterol 38 mg, Sodium   724 mg

Fiery Pot Texas Chili

SEAFOOD

From the water comes an appetizing array of choices. These days, everything from clean-tasting catfish to sparkling mussels and salmon are farm-raised and readily available in most supermarkets. So even if you live inland, good seafood is to be had both fresh and frozen. Filets cook quickly, their delicate flavors a ready partner for a wide range of sauces.

SWEET AND SOUR CRAB PATTIES

1 lb (455 g) crab meat, picked
½ lb (230 g) ground turkey
1 green onion, chopped
2 tsp (10 ml) OLD BAY Seasoning
1 egg white
2 tsp (10 ml) cornstarch
1 cup (240 ml) flour
½ cup (120 ml) vegetable oil

SWEET AND SOUR SAUCE:
1½ cups (355 ml) water
2 tbs (30 ml) cornstarch
2 tbs (30 ml) catsup
2 tbs (30 ml) soy sauce
½ cup (120 ml) packed brown sugar
½ cup (120 ml) apple cider vinegar

Patties: In a large bowl, blend crab meat, turkey, onion, OLD BAY Seasoning, egg white and cornstarch. Shape 24 patties and dust with flour. Set patties on wax paper and chill while making the sauce.

Sweet and Sour Sauce: In a bowl, whisk together water and cornstarch until thoroughly blended. Stir in catsup, soy sauce, brown sugar and vinegar. Bring to a boil in a saucepan, stirring until mixture thickens, about 1 minute. Remove from heat. Use hot or cold.

In wok or heavy skillet, heat vegetable oil, and cook patties over high heat. Serve patties with Sweet and Sour Sauce. Serves 24.

Approximate nutritional analysis per patty plus 1 tbs sauce:
Calories 124, Protein 7 g, Carbohydrates 10 g, Fat 6 g,
Cholesterol 25 mg, Sodium 188 mg

CLASSIC CRAB CAKES

2 slices bread, crusts removed
milk, sufficient to moisten bread
1 lb (455 g) crab meat, picked
¼ tsp (1 ml) salt
1 tsp (5 ml) OLD BAY Seasoning
1 tbs (15 ml) baking powder
1 tbs (15 ml) chopped parsley
1 tbs (15 ml) Worcestershire sauce
1 tbs (15 ml) mayonnaise or salad dressing
3-4 tbs (45-60 ml) vegetable oil, for frying

Break bread into small pieces and moisten with milk; combine with remaining ingredients. Shape into patties. Fry patties quickly in hot oil until brown. Serves 4.

Approximate nutritional analysis per serving:
Calories 248, Protein 25 g, Carbohydrates 11 g, Fat 11 g,
Cholesterol 117 mg, Sodium 805 mg

OLD BAY CLAM BAKE

4 eggs
2 cups (480 ml) milk
3½ cups (840 ml) saltine crackers, crushed
⅓ cup (80 ml) melted butter or margarine
¼ cup (60 ml) minced onion
2 tbs (30 ml) minced seeded green pepper
1 tsp (5 ml) Worcestershire sauce
2 tbs (30 ml) OLD BAY Seasoning
2 - 10 oz cans (600 g) minced clams with liquid
salt and pepper to taste

In a mixing bowl, beat eggs. Stir in milk and cracker crumbs and let stand for 20 minutes. Stir in remaining ingredients. Pour mixture into lightly oiled 9x9x2-inch baking pan and place in refrigerator to chill. One hour before serving time, remove from refrigerator. Bake in preheated oven at 350°F (180°C) for 25-30 minutes. Cut into squares or strips and serve immediately. Serves 4.

Approximate nutritional analysis per serving:
Calories 778, Protein 47 g, Carbohydrates 77 g, Fat 30 g,
Cholesterol 341 mg, Sodium 209 mg

CRAB CAKES WITH SPICY OLIVE SAUCE

½ lb (230 g) fresh crab meat, lumps broken up
2 tbs (30 ml) Worcestershire sauce
6 tbs (90 ml) minced fresh parsley
½ cup (120 ml) packaged fine bread crumbs
2 eggs
1 tbs (15 ml) butter or margarine
1 tbs (15 ml) vegetable oil

SPICY OLIVE SAUCE:
1 - 8 oz can (240 ml) unsalted tomato sauce
½ cup (120 ml) slivered pitted CALIFORNIA
     ripe olives
1-2 tsp (5-10 ml) Louisiana hot sauce or Tabasco

Mix crab with Worcestershire sauce, parsley, bread crumbs and eggs. Shape into 8 small cakes. Prepare Spicy Olive Sauce. Sauté cakes in butter and oil over medium-low heat until golden, turning once, about 2 minutes on each side. Serve with sauce. Serves 4.

Spicy Olive Sauce: Combine tomato sauce, olives and hot sauce in saucepan. Heat.

Approximate nutritional analysis per serving:
Calories 232, Protein 17 g, Carbohydrates 15 g, Fat 12 g,
Cholesterol 171 mg, Sodium 391 mg

Opposite: Classic Crab Cakes

CRAB CAKES WITH SATISFYING (LOW FAT) SAUCE

1 medium potato, peeled and cut into 1-inch dice
4 cups (960 ml) defatted seafood stock
3 eggs, hard-boiled, whites only
1¼ cups (295 ml) onion, finely minced
1¼ cups (295 ml) celery, finely minced
½ cup (120 ml) green bell pepper, finely minced
1 tbs plus ½ tsp (18 ml) CHEF PAUL
    PRUDHOMME'S Seafood Magic
⅝ cup (150 ml) green onions, green part only,
    finely minced
1 lb (455 g) crab meat, picked over for cartilage
4 tbs (60 ml) plain, dry bread crumbs
1 - 12 oz pkg (360 g) 1% low fat cottage cheese
1 tbs plus ½ tsp (18 ml) Worcestershire sauce
1 tsp (5 ml) salt
1 tbs (15 ml) imitation butter flakes

Crab Mixture: Bring the seafood stock to a boil. Peel and cut the potato into a 1-inch dice, add it to the boiling stock and cook until just tender, about 7 minutes. Remove from heat. Strain off and reserve the liquid, and mash the potato with a fork. Set aside. Cut the hard-boiled egg whites into thin shreds.

Place a 10-inch skillet over high heat. Add 1 cup onions, ½ cup celery, ¼ cup bell pepper and let it begin to soften, about 1 minute. Add 2 tsp Seafood Magic, cook 2 minutes, then turn heat down to medium and continue cooking 1 minute, stirring and shaking occasionally to brown all sides. Add ¼ cup onions, ¼ cup celery and ½ cup of the seafood stock-potato liquid. Turn heat back up to high and use the stock to help you scrape up all of the brown on the bottom of the skillet. Scrape and stir occasionally for 4 minutes. Add another ½ cup stock and continue cooking 8 minutes, scraping pan bottom occasionally. We're adding the stock in small amounts because the liquid evaporates more quickly in this way, causing the mixture to brown and caramelize for a lot of rich flavor. It should stick, and you should scrape it up, but don't let it burn! After 4 more minutes add another ½ cup stock and 1 tbs Worcestershire sauce. Continue cooking another 5 minutes, stirring and scraping occasionally, and remove from heat.

Place the vegetable mixture and the mashed potatoes in a food processor and blend until it's the consistency of thick mashed potatoes. Turn into a bowl and combine with the crab meat, blending gently with your hands. Add 1 tsp Seafood Magic, ½ tsp salt, ½ cup green onions, ½ cup celery, ¼ cup bell pepper and egg whites. Blend again. Yields 5 cups.

Sauce: Put the cottage cheese into blender and process until the consistency of sour cream.

Place a small pan over high heat. Add ½ cup crab meat mixture and cook about 2 minutes, until mixture starts sticking to pan. Stir and scrape up pan bottom, adding remaining seafood-potato stock, including the potato starch that has probably settled to the bottom. Continue cooking over high heat 2 minutes, add the remaining ½ tsp Seafood Magic and cook until it comes to a boil, about 1 more minute. Turn heat down to a simmer and slowly add 1 cup of the whipped cottage cheese cream, whisking constantly. Add ½ tsp Worcestershire, ½ tsp salt, the imitation butter flakes and the remaining 2 tbs green onions. Continue whisking until mixture bubbles, and turn off heat.

To serve: Place Teflon skillet over high heat. For each portion, scoop ¾ cup crab mixture and form 2 patties. Press each side of each patty in ½ tsp bread crumbs. Brown in skillet about 3-4 minutes on each side. Serves 6.

Approximate nutritional analysis per serving, 2 patties plus ¼ cup sauce: Calories 184, Protein 26 g, Carbohydrates 14 g, Fat 2 g, Cholesterol 78 mg, Sodium 968 mg

MEDITERRANEAN CATCH

2 medium onions, sliced
1 small green pepper, cut into thin strips
1 small red pepper, cut into thin strips
2 tbs (30 ml) olive oil
2 large tomatoes, cut into thin wedges
3 cloves garlic, minced
2 lbs (910 g) firm-textured fish filets
1 - 8 oz pkg (240 g) ATHENOS Feta Natural
    Cheese or Feta Natural Cheese with
    Peppercorns, crumbled
1 tbs (15 ml) chopped fresh parsley
salt and pepper to taste

Heat oven to 375°F (190°C). Cook and stir onions and peppers in oil in large skillet on medium-high heat 5 minutes or until tender-crisp. Add tomatoes and garlic; mix lightly. Arrange fish in a single layer in 13x9-inch baking dish. Spoon vegetable mixture over fish; sprinkle with cheese. Bake 25 minutes or until fish flakes easily with fork. Sprinkle with parsley. Season to taste with salt and pepper. Serves 6.

Approximate nutritional analysis per serving: Calories 321, Protein 34 g, Carbohydrates 15 g, Fat 14 g, Cholesterol 99 mg, Sodium 513 mg

STEAMED CRABS

12 crabs
vinegar and water
2½ tbs (38 ml) OLD BAY Seasoning
3 tbs (45 ml) salt

Use a large pot with a raised rack at least 2 inches high. Add equal quantities vinegar and water to just below level of rack. Layer the crabs in the pot, sprinkling each layer with mixture of OLD BAY Seasoning and salt. Cover and steam until crabs are red. Serves 3-4.

Opposite: Medterranean Catch

SAUTÉED SOFT-SHELL CRABS

4 soft shell crabs
2 tbs (30 ml) flour
1 tsp (5 ml) OLD BAY Seasoning,
    or more to taste
½ cup (120 ml) butter or margarine

Wash and thoroughly dry soft shell crabs. In small bowl, mix flour and OLD BAY Seasoning together. In a large frying pan, melt butter or margarine. Spoon flour mixture over crabs lightly. Sauté crabs in butter about 8 minutes on each side. Serves 2.

Nutritional analysis not available.

Pompeian Broiled Fish Steaks

POMPEIAN BROILED FISH STEAKS

4 fresh fish steaks, such as swordfish

MARINADE:
¼ cup (60 ml) POMPEIAN Extra Virgin Olive Oil
½ tsp (3 ml) salt
2 tsp (10 ml) oregano
⅓ cup (80 ml) fresh lemon juice
¼ tsp (1 ml) freshly ground black pepper
1 tsp (5 ml) basil
fresh orange slices to garnish

Wipe the steaks with a damp cloth or paper towel and place in a shallow dish. Combine the marinade ingredients and pour over fish. Marinate 30 minutes, turning once. Remove the fish from marinade and broil or grill at medium-high heat, turning once and brushing with marinade at intervals, about 5 minutes on each side. Brush again with the marinade and broil 3 minutes more, or until fish flakes easily with a fork. Garnish with the orange slices and serve with a fresh green salad. Serves 4.

Approximate nutritional analysis per serving:
Calories 237, Protein 34 g, Carbohydrates < 1 g, Fat 10 g,
Cholesterol 66 mg, Sodium 220 mg

CRAB AND MOZZARELLA WITH SWEET PEPPERS

1 tsp (5 ml) olive oil
1 small red onion
1 small red pepper
1 small yellow pepper
3 cups (720 ml) tomatoes
12 oz (360 g) crab-style surimi seafood blend
⅓ cup (80 ml) chopped fresh basil
2 tsp (10 ml) minced fresh garlic
¼ tsp (1 ml) pepper
2 cups (480 ml) cooked wild rice
1 - 8 oz ball (240 g) HEALTHY CHOICE Fat Free
    Natural Mozzarella Cheese, cubed

In large non-stick skillet, cook onion, peppers and garlic in olive oil over medium heat until tender. Add tomatoes, surimi, basil and pepper. Cover and continue to cook until tomatoes are softened and heated through. Place wild rice and cheese cubes on a serving plate. Pour crab mixture over wild rice and cheese. Serve immediately. Serves 6.

Approximate nutritional analysis per serving:
Calories 145, Protein 20 g, Carbohydrates 14 g, Fat 2 g,
Cholesterol 17 mg, Sodium 658 mg

ALMOND CHIVE BAKED SOLE

¾ cup (180 ml) BLUE DIAMOND
    Sliced Natural Almonds, lightly toasted
6 tbs (90 ml) butter
¼ cup (60 ml) flour
2 tbs (30 ml) lemon juice
1 tbs (15 ml) chopped fresh chives
    or 1 tsp (5 ml) dried chives
¼ tsp (1 ml) paprika
pinch cayenne
salt
white pepper
1½ lbs (685 g) sole filets

With hands, lightly crush almonds into small pieces; reserve. Combine next 6 ingredients, ½ tsp salt and ¼ tsp pepper. Add almonds; reserve. Butter an ovenproof pan. Fold sole filets in half; season lightly with salt and pepper. Distribute almond topping evenly over filets. Bake at 500°F (260°C) for 12-15 minutes or until fish is firm and top is golden. Serves 5.

Approximate nutritional analysis per serving:
Calories 385, Protein 30 g, Carbohydrates 9 g, Fat 26 g,
Cholesterol 103 mg, Sodium 253 mg

BAJA SEAFOOD TACOS

CORAL SAUCE:
½ cup (120 ml) low fat yogurt
¼ cup (60 ml) mayonnaise
2 tbs (30 ml) CHI-CHI'S Thick and
    Chunky Taco Sauce

TACOS:
⅔ cup (160 ml) plain dry bread crumbs
6 tbs (90 ml) sesame seed
4 tbs (60 ml) finely chopped fresh parsley
2 egg whites
1 tbs (15 ml) water
¼ cup (60 ml) olive oil, divided
1 lb (455 g) red snapper or cod filets,
    cut into 1½-inch pieces
4 warm corn or flour tortillas
finely shredded cabbage
additional taco sauce, if desired

Combine all Coral Sauce ingredients; set aside. In shallow dish, combine bread crumbs, sesame seed and parsley. Mix well. In another shallow dish, beat egg whites with water. In large skillet, over medium-high heat, heat 2 tbs oil. Dip half the fish pieces in egg mixture, then in bread mixture. Fry fish in hot oil until browned and flakes easily with fork; keep warm. Repeat with remaining fish and oil. Serve fish folded in warm tortillas with cabbage, Coral Sauce and additional taco sauce, if desired. Serves 4.

Approximate nutritional analysis per serving:
Calories 560, Protein 33 g, Carbohydrates 34 g, Fat 33 g,
Cholesterol 55 mg, Sodium 500 mg

COUNTRY-FRIED CATFISH

2½ lbs (1.1 kg) Farm Fresh Catfish
1 tsp (5 ml) salt
¼ tsp (1 ml) pepper
2 cups (480 ml) self-rising cornmeal
    in brown paper bag
1 qt (960 ml) peanut oil

Sprinkle catfish over lightly with salt and pepper. When ready to cook, drop pieces into bag of meal to cover completely. Use a deep pot or skillet filled half full with cooking oil. Heat fat until just under "smoking hot". Place each piece into fat separately. Cook on high until the catfish floats to top and reaches a golden brown. Drain well and place on paper towel. Serve hot. Serves 4.

Approximate nutritional analysis per serving:
Calories 643, Protein 57 g, Carbohydrates 54 g, Fat 20 g,
Cholesterol 164 mg, Sodium 796 mg

MEXICAN BASS WITH RED SALSA AND OLIVES

1½ lbs (685 g) sea bass or other firm white fish filets
1 - 6 oz can (180 ml) tomato paste
6 tbs (90 ml) water
¼ cup (60 ml) chopped onion
2 tsp (10 ml) bottled or fresh minced garlic
½-1 tsp (3-5 ml) bottled crushed red pepper
1 tsp (5 ml) ground cumin
½ tsp (3 ml) chili powder
½ cup (120 ml) sliced CALIFORNIA ripe olives

If fish filets are more than 1-inch thick, butterfly them (cut crosswise not quite all the way through) and spread open to make them thinner. Place fish in a single layer in microwave-safe baking dish. Combine tomato paste, water, onion, garlic and spices in electric blender or food processor. Process until puréed. Spoon over fish. Top with olives. Cover and micro-wave at MEDIUM for 12-15 minutes or until just cooked in center. Serve with lime wedges and with rice. Serves 4.

Approximate nutritional analysis per serving:
Calories 248, Protein 38 g, Carbohydrates 12 g, Fat 6 g,
Cholesterol 54 mg, Sodium 217 mg

Courtesy of the California Olive Board.

SALMON GRILL WITH SUN-COOKED SALSA

4 salmon steaks
POMPEIAN Extra Virgin Olive Oil

SUN-COOKED SALSA:
2 lbs (910 g) chopped fresh tomatoes
2 tbs (30 ml) chopped fresh parsley
2 tbs (30 ml) POMPEIAN Extra Virgin Olive Oil
¼ tsp (1 ml) salt
¼ tsp (1 ml) pepper
¼ tsp (1 ml) sugar
½ cup (120 ml) chopped red onion
½ cup (120 ml) chopped fresh basil
1 tbs (15 ml) POMPEIAN Red Wine Vinegar

Lightly baste salmon steaks with POMPEIAN Extra Virgin Olive Oil and grill over hot coals and mesquite chips on your barbecue. Turn the fish once, baste again, and continue to cook until it flakes easily with fork. Prepare a bed of sun-cooked salsa on each plate and place a grilled salmon steak on top. Garnish with a sprig of fresh herb. Serves 4.

Sun-Cooked Salsa: Combine all ingredients in a large jar. Cover jar tightly with a layer of cheesecloth and place in a sunny spot for 4 hours.

Approximate nutritional analysis per serving:
Calories 359, Protein 36 g, Carbohydrates 13 g, Fat 18 g,
Cholesterol 94 mg, Sodium 232 mg

SPICY PAN-FRIED CATFISH

3 lbs (1.4 kg) whole catfish or filets
1 cup (240 ml) yellow cornmeal
1½ tsp (8 ml) paprika
1 tsp (5 ml) salt
½ tsp (3 ml) celery salt
½ tsp (3 ml) pepper
¼ tsp (1 ml) dry mustard
½ tsp (3 ml) onion powder
oil for frying
lemon wedges

Combine cornmeal and seasonings. Roll fish in seasoned cornmeal. Place fish in a single layer in hot fat in a 12-inch fry pan. Fry at a moderate heat 4-5 minutes or until brown. Turn carefully. Fry 4-5 minutes longer or until fish are brown and flake easily when tested with a fork. Drain on absorbent paper. Serve with lemon wedges. Serves 6.

Approximate nutritional analysis per serving:
Calories 387, Protein 43 g, Carbohydrates 18 g, Fat 15 g,
Cholesterol 132 mg, Sodium 577 mg

Courtesy of The Catfish Institute.

CLASSIC FRIED FISH

¾ cup (180 ml) yellow cornmeal
¼ cup (60 ml) flour
2 tsp (10 ml) salt
1 tsp (5 ml) cayenne pepper
¼ tsp (1 ml) garlic powder
4 Mississippi farm-raised catfish filets
    or whole catfish
vegetable oil

Combine cornmeal, flour, salt, cayenne pepper and garlic powder. Coat catfish with mixture, shaking off excess. Fill deep pot or 12-inch skillet half full with vegetable oil. Heat to 350°F (180°C). Add catfish in single layer, and fry until golden brown, about 5-6 minutes, depending on size. Remove and drain on paper towels. Serves 4.

Approximate nutritional analysis per serving:
Calories 315, Protein 24 g, Carbohydrates 26 g, Fat 12 g,
Cholesterol 66 mg, Sodium 605 mg

Opposite: Salmon Grill with Sun-Cooked Salsa

OLD BAY CATFISH

2 lbs (910 g) catfish
½-1 cup (120-240 ml) yellow cornmeal
3 tbs (45 ml) butter or margarine
1½ tbs (25 ml) OLD BAY Seasoning
1 tsp (5 ml) paprika
1 tsp (5 ml) parsley flakes
½ tsp (3 ml) garlic salt

Roll catfish in cornmeal. In large frying pan, melt butter or margarine. Add catfish to pan. Shake OLD BAY Seasoning over catfish until covered. Sprinkle paprika, parsley flakes and garlic salt over catfish. Fry until golden brown, about 10-15 minutes each side. Serves 6.

Approximate nutritional analysis per serving:
Calories 279, Protein 29 g, Carbohydrates 13 g, Fat 11 g,
Cholesterol 88 mg, Sodium 273 mg

POACHED SALMON WITH YOGURT-DILL SAUCE

2 cups (480 ml) water
1 cup (240 ml) dry white wine
1 lemon, sliced
1 small onion, sliced, optional
2 bay leaves
8 black peppercorn
4 dill sprigs
1 tsp (5 ml) TABASCO pepper sauce
¼ tsp (1 ml) salt
4 - 8 oz (240 g each) salmon or halibut steaks

YOGURT DILL SAUCE:
1 cup (240 ml) plain low fat yogurt
1 tbs (15 ml) chopped fresh dill
1 tbs (15 ml) Dijon mustard
1 tsp (5 ml) lemon juice
½ tsp (3 ml) TABASCO pepper sauce

In large skillet combine water, wine, lemon, onion, bay leaves, peppercorn, dill, TABASCO pepper sauce and salt. Bring to a boil. Reduce heat to low; simmer covered 15 minutes. Add salmon to skillet. Simmer covered 12-15 minutes or until fish flakes easily when tested with fork. Serve warm or chilled with Yogurt Dill Sauce. Serves 4.

 Yogurt-Dill Sauce: In a small bowl stir together ingredients until well blended. Yields 1 cup.

Approximate nutritional analysis per serving:
Calories 329, Protein 42 g, Carbohydrates 8 g, Fat 13 g,
Cholesterol 110 mg, Sodium 279 mg

CRISP SKILLET TROUT

6 small trout, perch, snapper or other fish, dressed
½ cup (120 ml) flour
vegetable oil
2 egg whites, slightly beaten
2 tbs (30 ml) milk
1 tsp (5 ml) TABASCO pepper sauce
½ tsp (3 ml) salt
1 cup (240 ml) yellow cornmeal

Pat fish dry with paper towels. Dredge in flour; set aside. Coat the bottom of large heavy skillet with ⅛-inch oil. Heat over medium-high heat. In shallow dish combine egg whites, milk, TABASCO pepper sauce and salt. Dip flour-coated fish in egg white-milk mixture; turn to coat all surfaces. Dredge in cornmeal; turn to coat well. Shake off excess. Gently place fish in hot oil. Fry 5 minutes on each side or until golden and crisp. Drain on paper towels. Serve hot with additional TABASCO pepper sauce. Serves 6.

Approximate nutritional analysis per serving:
Calories 367, Protein 28 g, Carbohydrates 21 g, Fat 17 g,
Cholesterol 66 mg, Sodium 261 mg

BROILED CATFISH

4 Mississippi farm-raised catfish fillets
½ tsp (3 ml) garlic salt
½ tsp (3 ml) lemon pepper

Sprinkle catfish with garlic salt and lemon pepper. Preheat broiler. Place fish on the greased rack of an unheated broiler pan. Tuck under any thin edges. Broil 3 inches from the heat for 4-6 minutes or until fish flakes easily with fork. Serve with warm Mustard Dill Sauce or fresh, chilled Lemon-Watercress Sauce (recipes follow). Serves 4.

Approximate nutritional analysis per serving fish only:
Calories 197, Protein 31 g, Carbohydrates 0 g, Fat 7 g,
Cholesterol 99 mg, Sodium 240 mg

Courtesy of The Catfish Institute.

Opposite: Poached Salmon with Yogurt-Dill Sauce

MUSTARD-DILL SAUCE

2 tbs (30 ml) butter or margarine
2 tbs (30 ml) all purpose flour
1¼ cups (295 ml) milk
¼ cup (60 ml) chopped fresh dill
    or 1 tsp (5 ml) dried dillweed
3 tbs (45 ml) Dijon mustard
¼ tsp (1 ml) salt

In a small saucepan melt butter or margarine. Stir in flour. Add milk all at once. Cook and stir until thickened and bubbly. Cook and stir 1 minute more. Stir in parsley, dill, mustard and salt. Yields 1½ cups.

Approximate nutritional analysis per 1 tbs serving:
Calories 81, Protein 2 g, Carbohydrates 5 g, Fat 6 g,
Cholesterol 17 mg, Sodium 252 mg

Courtesy of The Catfish Institute.

CATFISH MEUNIÈRE

1 egg
¼ cup (60 ml) milk
½ cup (120 ml) all-purpose flour
½ tsp (3 ml) salt
½ tsp (3 ml) ground red pepper
4 Mississippi farm-raised catfish fillets
¼ cup (60 ml) butter or margarine
¼ cup (60 ml) cooking oil
¼ cup (60 ml) butter or margarine
2 tbs (30 ml) lemon juice
2 tbs (30 ml) chopped parsley
½ tsp (3 ml) Worcestershire sauce
parsley sprigs
lemon wedges

In a shallow bowl combine egg and milk. In another shallow bowl or pie plate stir together flour, salt and red pepper. Dip catfish fillets in milk mixture, then coat with flour mixture, shaking off excess. Melt ¼ cup butter or margarine and heat cooking oil in a large skillet. Add fish to hot butter mixture. Cook about 4 minutes on each side or until fish is golden brown and flakes easily. Drain on paper towels.

Meanwhile, melt ¼ cup butter or margarine. Stir in lemon juice, parsley and Worcestershire sauce. Transfer fillets to a serving plate. Pour mixture over fillets. Garnish with parsley and lemon. Serves 4.

Approximate nutritional analysis per serving:
Calories 506, Protein 35 g, Carbohydrates 14 g, Fat 34 g,
Cholesterol 185 mg, Sodium 514 mg

LEMON-WATERCRESS SAUCE

1 egg yolk
¼ cup (60 ml) packed watercress or parsley sprigs
¼ cup (60 ml) packed parsley sprigs
2 tsp (10 ml) finely shredded lemon peel
2 tbs (30 ml) lemon juice
2 tbs (30 ml) Dijon mustard
1 clove garlic, quartered
¼ tsp (1 ml) salt
⅛ tsp (.5 ml) pepper
⅔ cup (160 ml) vegetable oil

In a food processor or blender combine egg yolk, watercress, parsley, lemon peel, lemon juice, mustard, garlic, salt and pepper. Process or blend until smooth. With machine running, slowly add oil in a thin stream, processing or blending until well combined. Cover and chill. Yields ¾ cup.

Approximate nutritional analysis per serving:
Calories 114, Protein < 1 g, Carbohydrates < 1 g, Fat 13 g,
Cholesterol 18 mg, Sodium 79 mg

Courtesy of The Catfish Institute.

CATFISH PARMESAN

6 pan-dressed whole Mississippi farm-raised
    catfish or catfish fillets
2 cups (480 ml) dry bread crumbs
¾ cup (180 ml) Parmesan cheese
¼ cup (60 ml) chopped parsely
1 tsp (5 ml) paprika
½ tsp (3 ml) oregano
¼ tsp (1 ml) basil
2 tsp (10 ml) salt
½ tsp (3 ml) pepper
¾ cup (180 ml) margarine or cooking oil
lemon wedges

Combine bread crumbs, Parmesan cheese, parsley, paprika, oregano, basil, salt and pepper. Dip catfish in melted margarine or oil and roll in breadcrumb mixture. Arrange fish in a well greased baking dish 14x9x2 inches. Bake in a 375°F (190°C) oven for 25 minutes or until fish flakes easily. Cooking time will be less if using fillets. Garnish with lemon wedges. Serves 6.

Approximate nutritional analysis per serving:
Calories 587, Protein 51 g, Carbohydrates 25 g, Fat 30 g,
Cholesterol 143 mg, Sodium 1359 mg

GRILLED CATFISH

**4 Mississippi farm-raised
  catfish fillets**
½ tsp (3 ml) garlic salt
½ tsp (3 ml) pepper

Sprinkle catfish with garlic salt and pepper.
Place catfish in a well-oiled grill basket or on
a well-oiled grill rack. Grill on an uncovered
grill directly over medium-hot coals about
5 minutes per side or until fish flakes easily.
Serve either Fresh Homemade Salsa or Spicy
Black Bean Relish (recipes follow) over catfish
fillets hot off the grill. Serves 4.

Approximate nutritional analysis per serving fish only:
Calories 197, Protein 31 g, Carbohydrates 0 g,
Fat 7 g, Cholesterol 99 mg, Sodium 240 mg

Courtesy of The Catfish Institute.

FRESH HOMEMADE SALSA

1 tsp (5 ml) salt
3 medium tomatoes, chopped
¼ cup (60 ml) chopped onion
2 medium jalapeño peppers, chopped
2 tbs (30 ml) white wine vinegar

In a bowl combine tomatoes, onion, jalapeño
peppers, vinegar and salt. Stir well. Let
stand at room temperature for about
30 minutes before serving. Chill to store.
Yields 3 cups.

Approximate nutritional analysis per ½ cup serving:
Calories 28, Protein 1 g, Carbohydrates 6 g,
Fat < 1 g, Cholesterol 0 mg, Sodium 365 mg

Fresh Homemade Salsa

BLACK BEAN RELISH

¼ cup (60 ml) chopped onion
¼ cup (60 ml) chopped celery
¼ cup (60 ml) chopped carrot
3 cloves garlic, minced
2 jalapeño peppers, chopped
2 tbs (30 ml) butter or margarine
1 - 15 oz can (450 g) black beans, undrained
¼ cup (60 ml) diced ham
¼ cup (60 ml) chopped cilantro or parsley
½ tsp (3 ml) salt

In a medium saucepan cook onion, celery, carrot, garlic and
jalapeño peppers in butter or margarine until onion is tender.
Stir in black beans, ham, cilantro or parsley and salt. Bring to
boil; reduce heat. Simmer, uncovered, for 10 minutes or until
desired consistency. Yields 2 cups.

Approximate nutritional analysis per ½ cup serving:
Calories 159, Protein 8 g, Carbohydrates 32 g, Fat < 1 g,
Cholesterol 1 mg, Sodium 170 mg

CATFISH COURT BOUILLON

½ cup (120 ml) cooking oil
½ cup (120 ml) all-purpose flour
1 cup (240 ml) chopped onion
1 cup (240 ml) chopped celery
1 cup (240 ml) chopped green pepper
4 cloves garlic, minced
6 cups (1.4 L) chicken broth, fish stock or water
1 - 15 oz can (450 ml) tomato sauce
1 - 10 oz can (300 g) ROTEL Tomatoes
2 bay leaves
3 lbs (1.4 kg) Mississippi farm-raised catfish fillets
creole seasoning
8 cups (1.8 L) hot cooked rice

In large kettle or Dutch oven stir together oil and flour until smooth. Cook over medium-high heat until mixture boils, stirring constantly about 10 minutes or until mixture turns a medium brown. Add onions, celery, green pepper and garlic. Cook and stir until tender. Stir in chicken broth, fish stock or water. Add tomato sauce, tomatoes and bay leaves. Bring to boil; reduce heat. Cover and simmer for 30 minutes.

Meanwhile, cut fish into bite-size pieces. Sprinkle lightly with creole seasoning. Add catfish to tomato mixture. Cover and simmer for 25 minutes or until fish flakes easily. Season to taste with creole seasoning. Remove and discard bay leaves. Mound 1 cup rice on each serving plate. Spoon catfish mixture over rice. Serves 8.

Approximate nutritional analysis per serving:
Calories 654, Protein 39 g, Carbohydrates 73 g, Fat 22 g, Cholesterol 99 mg, Sodium 477 mg

Courtesy of The Catfish Institute.

Opposite: Grilled Salmon with Creamy Tarragon Sauce

FRESH CHARD BUNDLED FISH

1 lb (455 g) fresh chard
2 tbs (30 ml) olive oil or vegetable oil
2 tbs (30 ml) sliced garlic
1 large onion, cut into narrow wedges
2 large tomatoes, cubed, seeded and drained
1 cup (240 ml) whole CALIFORNIA ripe olives,
    cut in wedges
1½ lbs (685 g) lean white fish fillets (sea bass,
    haddock, cod, sole, halibut, flounder)
salt and pepper

Cut leaves from chard and sauté in 1 tbs oil in large skillet for 1-2 minutes, or just until limp. Remove from pan and lay in 2-qt shallow casserole to line bottom and sides, with extra part of leaves hanging out over sides of dish. Slice chard stems crosswise and sauté in 1 tbs oil with garlic, onion and tomato in skillet over high heat for 4 minutes or until tender-crisp. Stir in olives. Lay fish in chard-lined casserole, overlapping fillet as necessary. Sprinkle with salt and pepper and top with sautéed vegetables. Fold leaves over top, cover dish and bake at 450°F (230°C) for 25 minutes or until hot in center. To heat in microwave, use microwave dish and cook covered at HIGH for 5 minutes or until hot. Serve with rice. Serves 4.

Approximate nutritional analysis per serving:
Calories 309, Protein 36 g, Carbohydrates 19 g, Fat 11 g, Cholesterol 73 mg, Sodium 320 mg

GRILLED SALMON WITH CREAMY TARRAGON SAUCE

1 cup (240 ml) DANNON Plain Nonfat or
    Lowfat Yogurt
1 tbs (15 ml) reduced-calorie mayonnaise
¼ cup (60 ml) minced green onions
1 tbs (15 ml) minced fresh tarragon or dill weed
2 tsp (10 ml) lime juice
1 tsp (5 ml) hot pepper sauce
16 oz (480 g) salmon fillet, 1-inch thick, skinned
1 tbs (15 ml) olive oil

In a small glass bowl combine yogurt, mayonnaise, green onions, tarragon, lime juice and hot pepper sauce. Cover; chill at least 1 hour. Cut salmon into 4 equal portions; brush with olive oil. Grill salmon over medium-hot coals 5 minutes on each side or until fish flakes easily with fork. Serve with tarragon sauce. Serves 4.

Note: Fish may be broiled 4-6 inches from heat source 3-4 minutes on each side or until fish flakes easily with fork.

Approximate nutritional analysis per serving:
Calories 236, Protein 26 g, Carbohydrates 5 g, Fat 12 g, Cholesterol 68 mg, Sodium 95 mg

GRILLED SEAFOOD FAJITAS

SEASONING MIX:
1 tbs plus 2 tsp (25 ml) CHEF PAUL PRUDHOMME'S
Seafood Magic
½ tsp (3 ml) ground coriander
¼ tsp (1 ml) ground cardamom
1 tsp (5 ml) dry mustard
¾ tsp (4 ml) ground cumin
¼ tsp (1 ml) nutmeg
½ tsp (3 ml) ground cinnamon

CITRUS SOAK:
juice of 1 lime
juice of 1 lemon
1 tbs (15 ml) white vinegar
½ tsp (3 ml) Tabasco sauce

FAJITAS:
1 lb (455 g) firm-fleshed fish (such as swordfish,
fresh tuna, sole, red snapper, grouper) or shrimp
1 tsp (5 ml) minced fresh garlic
2 cups (480 ml) onions, cut into strips
1 cup (240 ml) green bell peppers, cut in strips
1 cup (240 ml) red bell peppers, cut in strips
1 cup (240 ml) yellow bell peppers, cut in strips
2 cups (480 ml) sliced mushrooms
large flour tortillas
vegetable oil spray

Prepare charcoal grill so that coals reach the grill itself and get coals very hot. Place a piece of stainless steel mesh (can be purchased at cooking supply or hardware store) over grill to prevent fish and vegetables form sliding through rungs of the grill. Dampenend wood chips such as mesquite or hickory can be mixed into the coals to give the dish extra flavor.

While grill is heating, place seafood in one bowl, onions and mushrooms in another and peppers in another. Divide the citrus soak in three and add ⅓ to each of the three bowls, mix thoroughly with your hands. Add 2¼ tsp seasoning mix to the peppers, 2 tsp seasoning mix to the onions and mushrooms, and 4 tsp seasoning mix to the seafood and combine well.

Have tortillas softening on a grid over a double boiler, or for 1-2 mintes in a very slow oven, or follow directions on the package.

When grill is very hot (flames should be visible), spray the peppers once with the vegetable spray, mix in with your hands and place them on the mesh. Grill about 4 minutes, turning once or twice. Spray the onions and mushrooms with vegetable spray, mix with your hands and place them on the mesh with the peppers. Continue cooking another 6-7 minutes or until all are brown, turning once to distribute well and brown evenly. Remove from grill to a bowl and keep warm. Spray the seafood with the vegetable spray and mix well with your hands. Place on the mesh and grill, turning once, until brown on both sides, about 3-4 minutes. Don't overcook!

Mix the seafood with the vegetables and fill the tortillas with the mixture. Serve immediately. Serves 6.

Approximate nutritional analysis per serving:
Calories 267, Protein 20 g, Carbohydrates 39 g, Fat 6 g,
Cholesterol 30 mg, Sodium 562 mg

BLACKENED CATFISH

2 tbs (30 ml) paprika
2½ tsp (13 ml) salt
2 tsp (10 ml) lemon pepper
1½ tsp (8 ml) garlic powder
1½ tsp (8 ml) ground red pepper
1½ tsp (8 ml) dried basil, crushed
1 tsp (5 ml) onion powder
1 tsp (5 ml) dried thyme
6 Mississippi farm-raised catfish fillets
1 cup (240 ml) unsalted butter or margarine, melted
lemon wedges

Heat a large cast iron skillet or heavy aluminum skillet over high heat for 10 minutes. In a small bowl stir together paprika, salt, lemon pepper, garlic powder, ground red pepper, basil, onion powder and thyme.

Dip catfish fillets into melted butter or margarine. Coat both sides of fish with spice mixture, using about 1 tbs spice mixture for each fillet. Place coated fillets on waxed paper.

Place 3 fillets at a time in hot skillet. Drizzle each fillet with 1 tbs of the melted butter or margarine. Cook over high heat about 2 minutes per side or until fish flakes easily. Serve with lemon wedges. Serves 6.

Approximate nutritional analysis per serving:
Calories 418, Protein 41 g, Carbohydrates 22 g, Fat 10 g,
Cholesterol 132 mg, Sodium 1035 mg

Courtesy of The Catfish Institute.

Opposite: Grilled Seafood Fajitas

Magic Grilled Fish

MAGIC GRILLED FISH

6 - 8-10 oz (240-300 g each) firm-fleshed fish fillets
  (such as redfish, pompano, tilefish, golden tile,
  red snapper, wall-eyed pike, or sac-a-lait) or
  salmon or tuna steaks (or other freshwater or
  saltwater fish), cut about ½-inch thick
¾ cup (180 ml) unsalted butter, melted
3 tbs plus 2 tsp (55 ml) CHEF PAUL PRUDHOMME'S
  Blackened Redfish Magic
CHEF PAUL PRUDHOMME'S Magic Pepper
  Sauce, to taste.

Heat grill as hot as possible and have flames reaching above the
grate before putting the fish on grill. Add dry wood chunks to
glowing coals to make the fire hotter.

Dip each fillet in the melted butter so that both sides are
well coated, then sprinkle Blackened Redfish Magic generously
and evenly on both sides of fillets, patting it in by hand. Place
fillets directly over flame on very hot grill and pour 1 tsp of the
melted butter on top of each. (Be careful; the butter may flame
up. Cook, uncovered, directly in flames until underside looks
blackened, about 2 minutes. Time will vary according to the
fillet's thickness and heat of grill.) Turn fish over and grill until
cooked through, about 2 minutes more. Serve piping hot with
assorted grilled vegetables. Have Magic Pepper Sauce available
as a table-top condiment to sprinkle on fish according to taste.
Serves 6.

Approximate nutritional analysis per serving:
Calories 530, Protein 67 g, Carbohydrates < 1 g, Fat 27 g,
Cholesterol 182 mg, Sodium 558 m

BLACKENED HALIBUT À LA OLD BAY

4 - 8-10 oz (240-300g each) halibut fillets
  (or salmon steaks, redfish or shark steaks),
  cut about ½-¾-inch thick
4 tbs (60 ml) unsalted butter, divided
¾ cup (180 ml) OLD BAY Seasoning

Heat a large cast iron skillet over very high heat for at least 10 minutes.

In a small skillet melt 4 tbs butter. When melted, remove from stove. Dip each fillet into the melted butter so that both sides are well coated; then sprinkle the OLD BAY Seasoning generously and evenly on both sides of fillets, pressing it into fish with your hand.

Place one fillet in the hot skillet; cook uncovered over high heat until the underside of fish looks charred, about 2 minutes. Turn the fillet over and repeat for 2 minutes. Keep fillet hot on warming tray while repeating process for remaining fillets. Serves 4.

Note: This procedure can produce some smoke, so make sure your kitchen is well ventilated with an overhead fan or windows. The great taste is worth a little smoke.

Approximate nutritional analysis per serving:
Calories 399, Protein 56 g, Carbohydrates 3 g, Fat 17 g,
Cholesterol 104 mg, Sodium 240 mg

Grilled Red Snapper Veracruz

GRILLED RED SNAPPER VERACRUZ

2 cups (480 ml) julienned green bell pepper, 1x¼ inch
1 cup (240 ml) chopped onion
3 cloves garlic
1 tbs (15 ml) olive oil
2 - 11½ oz jar (690 ml) CHI-CHI'S Pico de Gallo
⅓ cup (80 ml) dry red wine
3 tbs (45 ml) lemon juice
2 tsp (10 ml) dried oregano, crushed
1 tsp (5 ml) ground cumin
1 cup (240 ml) pitted ripe olives, halved
2 tbs (30 ml) capers
1 lb (455 g) red snapper fillets
lemon wedges

Prepare grill; arrange hot coals around outside edge of grill. In large skillet, sauté green pepper, onion and garlic in oil until tender. Stir in Pico de Gallo, wine, lemon juice, oregano and cumin. Bring to a boil. Reduce heat to low; simmer 8 minutes. Stir in olives and capers. Cool slightly. Cut aluminum foil into 8 - 12-inch lengths. Place ¼ of red snapper fillets on top of each ¼ of sauce. Cover each with another piece of foil; seal edges tightly. Place packets on baking sheet to transfer to and from grill. Place foil packets in center of prepared grill. Cover; cook 30 minutes or until fish flakes easily in center. Remove fish sauce from foil. Serve with lemon wedges. Serves 4.

Approximate nutritional analysis per serving:
Calories 280, Protein 28 g, Carbohydrates 22 g, Fat 9 g,
Cholesterol 40 mg, Sodium 1010 mg

CAPRI'S ROASTED HALIBUT
WITH WHITE WINE BEAN CRUST AND PANCETTA

24 oz (720 g) center cut Alaskan Halibut
¾ lb (340 g) dry Great Northern beans
    or 2 - 16 oz cans (480 g each) Great Northern
    beans, drained and rinsed
10 vine ripe tomatoes
2 cloves garlic
2 shallots
2 bouquet garnis (each one is 4 thyme sprigs,
    2 bay leaves, 10 black peppercorns wrapped
    in cheesecloth)
4 very thin slices pancetta or apple-smoked bacon
½ cup (120 ml) white wine, or vegetable stock
1 bunch flat leaf parsley
8 oz (240 ml) chicken stock
4 oz (120 ml) water
5 tbs (75 ml) olive oil
salt and pepper

Preparation: Soak beans for 3 hours in cold water; drain and rinse. Chop 1 clove garlic and 1 shallot. Set aside. Core tomatoes and cut a small "X" at the top. Blanch in boiling water for 30-45 seconds. Remove tomatoes from water and place in ice water for 1-2 minutes. Peel, seed and chop tomatoes. Set aside. Chop parsley and set aside. Chop halibut into 4 - 6-oz squares (180 g each) (or ask butcher to do it). Prepare bouquets.

Cooking: Tomatoes: Heat a 10-inch saucepan on moderate heat, add 1 tbs of olive oil, and the diced shallots and diced garlic. Cook for 1-1½ minutes (be sure not to brown), then add chopped tomatoes, a touch of salt and pepper and 1 bouquet garni. Cook over low heat for 1 hour. When finished, set aside and keep warm. Great Northern beans: Heat another 10-inch saucepan, add 1 tbs olive oil, chopped shallots and chopped garlic. Cook for 1 minute, then add beans, chicken stock, water and the other bouquet garni. Bring to boil, turn down to a simmer and cook for 1½ hours (if using canned beans cook for 20 minutes), stirring often. Check beans to make sure they are cooked through. Season to taste with salt and pepper. Cook 2 more minutes, strain beans, saving liquid. Puree beans in a food processor, adding cooking liquid as needed to obtain a fine puree. Transfer to a bowl and keep warm.

Finishing: Heat oven and broiler to 400°F (205°C). Season fish with salt and pepper, then neatly spread ¼-inch layer of the bean puree over the fish. Place the pancetta on top of the bean puree. Heat a 10-inch skillet on stove at high heat. Put the fish in the skillet, pancetta side up. Add 1 tbs olive oil. Cook 45 seconds on stove at high heat. Remove from heat. Add wine to fish in skillet, place skillet in preheated oven 4 minutes, then in broiler for 2 minutes to make the pancetta crispy. Take fish out of skillet and keep warm. Add the prepared, warm tomatoes to white wine left in skillet. Heat, season to taste with salt and pepper, and add chopped parsley and 2 tbs of olive oil.

Presentation: Heat 4 dinner plates. Put a bed of the tomatoes on plate. Place fish with pancetta and puree facing up on the bed of tomatoes. Serve immediately. Serves 4.

Approximate nutritional analysis per serving:
Calories 756, Protein 61 g, Carbohydrates 70 g, Fat 25 g,
Cholesterol 68 mg, Sodium 499 mg

GRILLED FISH WITH AVOCADO SALSA

4 - 6-8 oz (180-240 g each) fish steaks, such as
    halibut, swordfish or tuna, 1-inch thick
1 - 11½ oz jar (345 ml) CHI-CHI'S
    Pico de Gallo or CHI-CHI'S Salsa
1 avocado, peeled and diced
2 tbs (30 ml) fresh lime juice
fresh cilantro leaves and lime wedges, if desired

Over medium-hot coals, grill fish 5 minutes on each side or until fish flakes easily in center. In medium bowl, combine Pico de Gallo, avocado and lime juice. Spoon avocado salsa over hot fish. Serve with cilantro and lime wedges, if desired. Serves 4.

Approximate nutritional analysis per serving:
Calories 270, Protein 33 g, Carbohydrates 10 g, Fat 11 g,
Cholesterol 45 mg, Sodium 420 mg

SUMMER VEGETABLE AND FISH BUNDLES

4 - ¼ lb (115 g each) fish fillets
1 lb (455 g) thinly sliced vegetables
    (any combination of zucchini, yellow squash,
    mushrooms or tomatoes)
1 envelope LIPTON Recipe Secrets Savory Herb
    with Garlic or Golden Onion Soup Mix
½ cup (120 ml) water

On 2 - 18x18-inch pieces heavy duty aluminum foil, divide fish equally; top with vegetables. Evenly pour savory herb with garlic soup mix blended with water over fish. Wrap foil loosely around fillets and vegetables, sealing edges airtight with double fold. Grill or broil seam-side-up 15 minutes or until fish flakes. Serve, if desired, over hot cooked rice. Serves 4.

Approximate nutritional analysis per serving:
Calories 206, Protein 24 g, Carbohydrates 15 g, Fat 5 g,
Cholesterol 66 mg, Sodium 669 mg

Courtesy of The Lipton Kitchens.

Grilled Swordfish

GRILLED SWORDFISH WITH TOMATO RELISH

1 cup (240 ml) granulated sugar
1 cup (240 ml) HEINZ Apple Cider Vinegar
⅓ cup (80 ml) HEINZ 57 Sauce
2 tsp (10 ml) minced fresh ginger root
1½ lbs (685 g) tomatoes, peeled, chopped
1½ cups (355 ml) chopped onions
½ cup (120 ml) golden raisins
1 clove garlic, crushed
½ tsp (3 ml) coriander
¼ tsp (1 ml) crushed red pepper
2 tbs (30 ml) vegetable oil
1 tbs (15 ml) lemon juice
¼ tsp (1 ml) lemon pepper seasoning
⅛ tsp (.5 ml) garlic powder
6 swordfish steaks, cut ¾-inch thick
vegetable cooking spray

Tomato Relish: Combine first 11 ingredients in large saucepan. Cook over medium-low heat for 1 hour or until thick. Chill. (Mixture may be stored in refrigerator for up to 3 weeks.) Let relish stand at room temperature 1 hour before serving.

Swordfish: Combine oil, lemon juice, lemon pepper seasoning and garlic powder. Brush on swordfish. Spray grill rack with vegetable cooking spray. Place swordfish on grill over medium-hot coals and grill 5 minutes on each side or until fish flakes easily when tested with fork. Serve swordfish with Tomato Relish. Serves 6.

Approximate nutritional analysis per serving:
Calories 421, Protein 29 g, Carbohydrates 54 g, Fat 11 g, Cholesterol 55 mg, Sodium 132 mg

SOLE AU GRATIN

GARLIC CRUMBS:
2 tbs (30 ml) firm margarine
¾ cup (180 ml) BISQUICK Reduced Fat Baking Mix
¼ tsp (1 ml) garlic powder

2 tbs (30 ml) margarine
2 tbs (30 ml) BISQUICK Reduced Fat Baking Mix
1 tsp (5 ml) chicken bouillon granules
½ tsp (3 ml) dry mustard
1 cup (240 ml) skim milk
¼ cup (60 ml) grated Parmesan cheese
1 - 10 oz pkg (300 g) frozen chopped broccoli,
  thawed and well drained
1 tbs (15 ml) lemon juice
1½ lbs (685 g) sole or other lean white fish fillets

Heat oven to 350°F (180°C). Prepare Garlic Crumbs. Heat margarine in 1½-qt saucepan over medium heat until melted. Stir in baking mix, bouillon granules and mustard. Cook over medium heat, stirring constantly, until mixture is hot and bubbly; remove from heat. Stir in milk. Heat to boiling, stirring constantly. Boil and stir 1 minute. Stir in cheese until melted.

Spread broccoli in ungreased square baking dish, 9x9x2 inches; sprinkle with lemon juice. Place fish on broccoli. (If fillets are large, cut into 4 serving pieces; pat dry.) Spread cheese sauce over fish; sprinkle with Garlic Crumbs. Bake about 30 minutes or until fish flakes easily with fork. Remove fish with slotted spoon. Serves 4.

Garlic Crumbs: Cut margarine into baking mix and garlic powder until crumbly. Spread evenly in ungreased square pan, 9x9x2 inches. Bake 9 minutes; stir.

High Altitude: 3500-6500: Heat oven to 375°F (190°C).

Approximate nutritional analysis per serving:
Calories 310, Protein 28 g, Carbohydrates 20 g, Fat 13 g,
Cholesterol < 5 mg, Sodium 580 mg

BAKED VEGETABLE-STUFFED FISH

½ lb (230 g) bacon slices, divided
1 small onion, chopped
2 stalks celery, chopped
1 small red or green pepper, chopped
1 medium carrot, shredded
½ cup (120 ml) plain bread crumbs
2 tbs (30 ml) chopped parsley
2 tbs (30 ml) lemon juice
1 tsp (5 ml) lemon rind
1 tsp (5 ml) Tabasco pepper sauce
½ tsp (3 ml) dried thyme leaves
4 - ¾ lb (340 g each) trout, drawn *or*
  3-4 lbs (1.4-1.8 kg) whole bass, bluefish
  or salmon, drawn and cleaned

Preheat oven to 375°F (190°C). Reserve 4 slices of the bacon. Cut up remaining bacon slices. Heat large skillet over medium heat. Cut up bacon. Cook until crisp; drain on paper towels. Drain bacon drippings reserving 2 tbs. Return bacon to skillet; add onion, celery, pepper and carrot. Cook 10 minutes or until soft. Remove from heat; stir in bread crumbs, parsley, lemon juice and rind, Tabasco pepper sauce and thyme until well blended. Grease a large shallow baking pan. Place trout in prepared pan. Stuff each trout with ¼ of stuffing and bake 45 minutes or until fish flakes easily with fork. Discard bacon slices and skin before carving. Serves 4.

Approximate nutritional analysis per serving:
Calories 1004, Protein 124 g, Carbohydrates 17 g, Fat 46 g,
Cholesterol 339 mg, Sodium 1156 mg

HERBED FISH ROLL-UPS

8 - 4-5 oz (120 -150 g each) white fish fillets,
  such as sole or haddock
8 HEALTHY CHOICE Fat Free Natural
  Mozzarella Cheese Snack Stix
paprika

FILLING:
1 cup (240 ml) cooked wild rice
1 cup (240 ml) shredded zucchini
2 tbs (30 ml) chopped fresh parsley
1 tsp (5 ml) Dijon mustard
1 tsp (5 ml) lemon juice
1 tsp (5 ml) Worcestershire sauce
½ tsp (3 ml) garlic powder
¼ tsp (1 ml) pepper
¼ tsp (1 ml) dried tarragon leaves
¼ tsp (1 ml) dried thyme

Heat oven to 375°F (190°C). Combine all filling ingredients. Place about 2 tbs of filling in center of each fish fillet; top with cheese stick. Roll up and place seam side down in 12x7-inch baking dish sprayed with nonstick cooking spray. Bake 20-25 minutes until fish flakes with a fork and cheese is melted. Sprinkle fish with paprika before serving, if desired. Serves 8.

Approximate nutritional analysis per serving:
Calories 144, Protein 26 g, Carbohydrates 6 g, Fat 1 g,
Cholesterol 50 mg, Sodium 310 mg

Opposite: Herbed Fish Roll-Ups

VEGETABLE-TOPPED FISH POUCHES

4 - ¼ lb (115 g each) firm fish fillets
   (flounder, cod or halibut)
1 carrot, cut into very thin strips
1 rib celery, cut into very thin strips
1 medium red onion, cut into thin wedges
1 medium zucchini or yellow squash, sliced
8 mushrooms, sliced
2 oz (60 g) shredded Swiss cheese
½ cup (120 ml) WISH - BONE Italian,
   Robusto Italian or Lite Italian Dressing

On 4 - 9x18-inch pieces heavy duty aluminum foil, divide fish equally. Evenly top with vegetables, then cheese, then Italian dressing. Wrap foil loosely around fillets and vegetables, sealing edges airtight with double fold. Let stand to marinate 15 minutes. Grill or broil pouches seam-side-up 15 minutes or until fish flakes. Serves 4.

Approximate nutritional analysis per serving:
Calories 290, Protein 31 g, Carbohydrates 10 g, Fat 14 g,
Cholesterol 75 mg, Sodium 730 mg

Courtesy of The Lipton Kitchens.

BAKED FISH DIJON

juice from 1 lemon
1 tbs (15 ml) olive oil
1 tbs (15 ml) Dijon mustard
1 tsp (5 ml) McCORMICK/SCHILLING Dill Weed
½ tsp (3 ml) McCORMICK/SCHILLING
   Black Pepper
¼ tsp (1 ml) McCORMICK/SCHILLING
   Garlic Powder
1½ lbs (685 g) fresh fish fillets
   (such as flounder, sole, cod or pollack)
1 carrot, peeled and shredded
3 tbs (45 ml) grated Parmesan cheese

Preheat oven to 350°F (180°C). Whisk together first 6 ingredients. Brush over both sides of fish. Arrange fish, overlapping thinner portions, in 9x13-inch baking dish. Drizzle remaining mustard mixture over fish. Layer carrots over top and sprinkle with cheese. Bake 10-15 minutes or until fish flakes easily. Serves 6.

Approximate nutritional analysis per serving:
Calories 146, Protein 23 g, Carbohydrates 2 g, Fat 5 g,
Cholesterol 56 mg, Sodium 210 mg

HERB SEASONED FISH FILLETS

3 tbs (45 ml) melted unsalted margarine
1 tsp (5 ml) fresh lemon juice
½ tsp (3 ml) McCORMICK/SCHILLING
   Tarragon Leaves
½ tsp (3 ml) McCORMICK/SCHILLING
   Freeze-Dried Chives
1 lb (455 g) fresh fish fillets or steaks

In a small bowl, combine margarine, lemon juice, tarragon and chives. Brush over fish. Broil, grill or bake until fish flakes easily, brushing with remaining margarine mixture. Serves 4.

Approximate nutritional analysis per serving:
Calories 141, Protein 21 g, Carbohydrates 0 g, Fat 5 g,
Cholesterol 54 mg, Sodium 92 mg

ITALIAN CORN-CRUSTED BAKED FISH WITH OLIVES

2 cups (480 ml) chopped tomato
½ cup (120 ml) sliced CALIFORNIA ripe olives
2 tbs (30 ml) bottled or fresh minced garlic
¼ cup (60 ml) olive oil
1 tbs (15 ml) thyme or oregano, crumbled
1 lb (455 g) fresh fish fillets
½ cup (120 ml) yellow cornmeal, mixed with
   ½ tsp (3 ml) each, salt and pepper
grated Parmesan cheese

Mix tomato, olives, garlic, olive oil and oregano in bottom of 1½-qt baking dish. Separate fish fillets, cut smaller if they are large and dip each into seasoned cornmeal. Place in casserole. Bake at 450°F (230°C) for 20-25 minutes or until baked and crusty. Serve with Parmesan cheese on top. Serves 4.

Approximate nutritional analysis per serving:
Calories 319, Protein 24 g, Carbohydrates 19 g, Fat 17 g,
Cholesterol 54 mg, Sodium 460 mg

FISHERMAN'S LIGHT FILLETS

½ cup (120 ml) WISH - BONE Italian Dressing
1 small green bell pepper, cut into strips
1 small onion, thinly sliced
1 lb (455 g) fish fillets
1 medium tomato, coarsely chopped

In large skillet, heat Italian dressing over medium heat and cook green pepper and onion, stirring occasionally, 5 minutes or until tender. Add fish and tomato, then simmer covered 10 minutes or until fish flakes. Serves 4.

Approximate nutritional analysis per serving:
Calories 272, Protein 23 g, Carbohydrates 10 g, Fat 16 g,
Cholesterol 54 mg, Sodium 329 mg

Opposite: Vegetable-Topped Fish Bundles

NORTHWEST SALMON WITH HAZELNUT AND JUNIPER BERRY SAUCE

4 - ½ lb (230 g each) salmon steaks
¼ cup (60 ml) Hazelnuts, broken
3 juniper berries, crushed
½ cup (120 ml) brandy
½ cup (120 ml) cream
salt

Sauté salmon steak. Remove from pan. Add Hazelnuts and juniper berries, then deglaze with brandy. When mixture is reduced and alcohol is gone, add cream. Cook until thickened. Salt to taste. Pour over warm salmon steak and enjoy! Serves 4.

Approximate nutritional analysis per serving:
Calories 538, Protein 47 g, Carbohydrates 12 g, Fat 30 g,
Cholesterol 165 mg, Sodium 112 mg

BUTTERY HERB FISH

¼ cup (60 ml) reduced calorie mayonnaise
1½ tsp (8 ml) McCORMICK/SCHILLING
**   Butter Flavor**
1 lb (455 g) flounder fillets
McCORMICK/SCHILLING Dill Weed
McCORMICK/SCHILLING Paprika

Combine mayonnaise and butter flavor. Spread thinly over fish fillets. Sprinkle lightly with dill weed and paprika. Broil until fish flakes easily. Serves 4.

Approximate nutritional analysis per serving:
Calories 124, Protein 22 g, Carbohydrates < 1 g, Fat 3 g,
Cholesterol 62 mg, Sodium 110 mg

Buttery Herb Fish

PINK LADY

½ cup (120 ml) orange juice
¼ cup (60 ml) lemon juice
2 tbs (30 ml) lime juice
⅓ cup (80 ml) natural or golden raisins
¼ cup (60 ml) minced onion
2 tbs (30 ml) honey
1 tbs (15 ml) grated fresh ginger
1 tsp (5 ml) grated orange peel
1 tsp (5 ml) grated lemon peel
1 tsp (5 ml) grated lime peel
dash salt and cayenne pepper
4 small salmon steaks, 1½ lbs (685 g) total

In bowl mix juices, raisins, onion, honey, ginger, peels, salt and pepper. Pour over salmon in shallow dish. Cover and chill 30 minutes; transfer to buttered baking dish, reserving marinade. Bake in 425°F (220°C) oven, allowing about 10 minutes per inch thickness of salmon. Season with additional salt. Meanwhile, simmer marinade in broad skillet to reduce by half. Taste; correct seasonings. Spoon over cooked salmon. Serves 4.

Approximate nutritional analysis per serving:
Calories 333, Protein 35 g, Carbohydrates 24 g, Fat 11 g,
Cholesterol 94 mg, Sodium 78 mg

SHRIMPOREE CREOLE

1 lb (455 g) shrimp, uncooked
½ cup (120 ml) chopped onion
½ cup (120 ml) chopped green pepper
2 cloves garlic, minced
¼ cup (60 ml) minced celery
3 tbs (45 ml) butter, margarine or oil
1 tbs (15 ml) all-purpose flour
1 - 1 lb can (455 g) sliced stewed tomatoes
⅛ tsp (.5 ml) dried thyme
1 bay leaf
½ tsp (3 ml) IMPERIAL Granulated Sugar
1 tsp (5 ml) Worcestershire sauce
several whole allspice berries, salt and pepper
minced parsley
hot, freshly cooked rice

Cook shrimp. Remove shells and devein. To make Creole sauce, sauté onion, green pepper, garlic, celery in butter, margarine or oil until limp; add flour, cook and stir until flour is light tan. Add all other ingredients except parsley and rice. Cook until sauce is thickened. Taste for salt and pepper and add more if needed. Stir in parsley. Serve over hot, freshly cooked rice. Serves 4.

Approximate nutritional analysis per serving:
Calories 361, Protein 28 g, Carbohydrates 39 g, Fat 10 g,
Cholesterol 221 mg, Sodium 1192 mg

Opposite: Pink Lady

Baked Salmon with Almonds and Lime-Parsley Sauce

BAKED SALMON WITH ALMONDS AND LIME-PARSLEY SAUCE

1 large clove garlic, chopped finely
1 egg yolk
1 tsp (5 ml) lime juice
½ tsp (3 ml) cumin
salt
white pepper
½ cup (120 ml) vegetable oil
4½ tsp (23 ml) olive oil, divided
6 tbs (90 ml) chopped, fresh parsley
4 - 6 oz pieces (180 g each) salmon fillet
¾ cup (180 ml) BLUE DIAMOND
    Sliced Natural Almonds, lightly toasted

In food processor, combine garlic, egg yolk, lime juice, cumin, ¼ tsp salt, and a pinch pepper. With machine running, slowly pour in vegetable oil and 1½ tsp olive oil.

To prepare by hand, beat egg yolk until thick and lemon-colored. Beat in garlic, lime juice, cumin, ¼ tsp salt, and a pinch pepper. Combine vegetable oil and 1½ tsp olive oil. Whisking constantly, add oils one drop at a time until mixture begins to thicken and emulsify. Pour remaining oil in a thin steady stream, whisking constantly.

Mixture will resemble mayonnaise. Fold on chopped parsley. Brush salmon with remaining 3 tbs olive oil; season with salt and pepper. Spread parsley down center of each fillet. Top with almonds. Bake at 400°F (205°C) for 8-12 minutes or until fish is just firm. Serves 4.

Approximate nutritional analysis per serving:
Calories 770, Protein 51 g, Carbohydrates 6 g, Fat 61 g,
Cholesterol 178 mg, Sodium 107 mg

ZARZUELA DE MARISCOS

Shellfish Stew

8 mussels, scrubbed
18 small clams, scrubbed
1 small onion, finely chopped
¼ cup (60 ml) GOYA Olive Oil
2 cloves garlic, minced
1 tbs (15 ml) GOYA Sofrito
1 bay leaf
4 oz (120 ml) GOYA Tomato Sauce
1 oz (30 ml) brandy or cognac
1 cup (240 ml) LA VINA White Cooking Wine
1 lb (455 g) sea scallops
all-purpose flour for coating
½ tbs (8 ml) ground almonds
½ tsp (3 ml) GOYA Adobo
12 large shrimp in shells
1 packet Sazón GOYA con Azafrán
1 cup (240 ml) fish stock *or* ½ cup (120 ml) water *plus*
    ½ cup (120 ml) clam juice
salt and pepper to taste

In large skillet, boil or steam mussels and clams until they are open. Remove open mussels and clams from pot with slotted spoon and set aside. In a large saucepan or soup pot, sauté onion or olive oil over low heat until golden brown. Add garlic and Sofrito and simmer, uncovered, for 10 minutes. Add bay leaf, tomato sauce and brandy or cognac. Raise heat to medium and cook, uncovered, for 2-3 minutes. In a separate saucepan, heat fish stock. Set on back burner over low heat to keep hot until needed. Add ⅓ cup of white wine to tomato-vegetable mixture. Dust scallops with flour and stir into mixture with additional ⅓ cup wine. Add almonds, Adobo, shrimp and remaining wine; stir well, and cook uncovered, over medium heat for 2-3 minutes until wine is reduced. Add Sazón, heated stock, opened clams and mussels to stew and heat through. Salt and pepper to taste. Serves 6.

Approximate nutritional analysis per serving:
Calories 261, Protein 27 g, Carbohydrates 10 g, Fat 12 g,
Cholesterol 97 mg, Sodium 275 mg

ZUPPA DI PESCE

¼ cup (60 ml) chopped onion
¼ cup (60 ml) chopped celery or fennel
2 tsp (10 ml) BERTOLLI Extra Virgin Olive Oil
1 cup (240 ml) dry white wine
1 - 28 oz can (840 g) Italian plum tomatoes
1 bay leaf
½ tsp (3 ml) dried oregano
freshly ground black pepper
1 lb (455 g) cod, ocean perch or other lean white
    fillet, cut into 1-inch pieces

12 medium shrimp, shelled and deveined
4 crostini or toasted Italian bread
1 tbs (15 ml) finely chopped Italian parsley

Combine the onion, celery or fennel and olive oil in a large broad saucepan. Cook, stirring over low heat until the vegetables are tender, about 10 minutes. Add the wine and heat to boiling; boil 5 minutes. Add the tomatoes, bay leaf, oregano and pepper; stir to break up tomatoes. Cook uncovered, 5 minutes.

Add the fish and shrimp. Cover and cook over low heat until the fish is cooked through, about 5 minutes. Place a crostini in each bowl. Divide fish and broth evenly among the bowls. Sprinkle with parsley. Serves 4.

Approximate nutritional analysis per serving:
Calories 324, Protein 32 g, Carbohydrates 27 g, Fat 6 g,
Cholesterol 101 mg, Sodium 612 mg

SEAFOOD STEW

1 cup (240 ml) shredded carrots
1 cup (240 ml) sliced celery
1 cup (240 ml) sliced leeks
2 tsp (10 ml) minced fresh garlic
¼ cup (60 ml) butter or margarine
2 cups (480 ml) water
1 - 8 oz jar (240 ml) CHI-CHI'S Salsa
1 cup (240 ml) dry white wine
2 cups (480 ml) cubed baking potatoes, 1 inch
2 bay leaves
½ tsp (3 ml) seafood seasoning mix
½ tsp (93 ml) dried thyme leaves
¼ tsp (1 ml) coarsely ground pepper
1 lb (455 g) fresh or frozen raw shrimp,
    deveined and rinsed
1 lb (455 g) white fish fillets (halibut, scrod, etc.),
    cut into 1-inch pieces
1 - 6 oz pkg (180 g) frozen cooked crab meat, thawed
½ lb (230 g) bacon, cooked and crumbled

In Dutch oven , cook carrot, celery, leeks and garlic in butter 8-10 minutes or until vegetables are softened. Add water, clam juice, salsa, wine, potatoes, bay leaves, seasoning mix, thyme and pepper. Bring to a boil. Reduce heat to medium-low. Cover; cook 30-40 minutes or until potatoes are just tender, stirring occasionally. Add shrimp, fish and crab meat. Cook 4-5 minutes or just until shrimp turn pink, stirring occasionally. Stir in bacon. Remove bay leaves. Serves 9.

Approximate nutritional analysis per serving:
Calories 270, Protein 26 g, Carbohydrates 12 g, Fat 11 g,
Cholesterol 105 mg, Sodium 650 mg

SUPER SEAFOOD GUMBO

1 large onion, sliced vertically in long thin strips
1 large green pepper, chopped
2 stalks celery, chopped
3 garlic cloves, minced
2 tbs (30 ml) parsley, chopped
½ cup (120 ml) butter, margarine or oil
1 tsp (5 ml) salt
1 tsp (5 ml) black pepper
1 tsp (5 ml) white pepper
1 tsp (5 ml) IMPERIAL Granulated Sugar
2 tsp (10 ml) coarse ground black pepper
2 bay leaves
2 tbs (30 ml) chili powder
1 pinch dried thyme
1½ tsp (8 ml) crushed basil
½ tsp (3 ml) dried rosemary
½ tsp (3 ml) red pepper (cayenne)
1 tbs (15 ml) paprika
¼ tsp (1 ml) red pepper sauce
1 tbs (15 ml) Worcestershire sauce
6 tbs (90 ml) all-purpose flour
3 - 15 oz cans (1.4 kg) okra or okra gumbo
1 - 15 oz can (450 g) tomatoes, cut up
1 - 16 oz can (480 ml) tomato paste
3 cups (720 ml) chicken broth (canned or stock
    from cooking chicken)
1 - 15 oz can (450 g) oyster stew
1 - 4 oz can (120 g) chopped mushrooms
1 cup (240 ml) cubed cooked chicken
1 lb (455 g) crab meat, rinsed (remove any
    small pieces of shell)
2 lbs (910 g) shrimp, cooked, shelled, deveined
2 pts (960 ml) oysters, undrained
2 tbs (30 ml) gumbo filé
hot cooked rice

In large soup kettle, sauté onion, green pepper, celery, garlic, parsley in butter, margarine or oil until transparent. Add seasonings except gumbo filé. Cover and simmer 30 minutes. Stir in flour and cook until golden. Add okra, tomatoes, tomato paste, chicken broth, oyster stew, mushrooms and chicken; cook over low-medium heat. Simmer about 1 hour, stirring occasionally. Add crab meat, shrimp, oysters and about 1 cup water, if needed; simmer an additional 30 minutes, stirring frequently. Shortly before serving, stir in gumbo filé, but do not allow gumbo to boil after filé is added. Serve gumbo over mounds of hot rice in large soup bowls. Serves 20.

Approximate nutritional analysis per serving plus ½ cup rice:
Calories 337, Protein 25 g, Carbohydrates 40 g, Fat 8 g,
Cholesterol 143 mg, Sodium 901 mg

CLASSIC PAELLA VALENCIANA

8 small clams, scrubbed
8 mussels, scrubbed
6 cups (1.4 L) water
3 packets GOYA Chicken Bouillon
½ cup (120 ml) GOYA Olive Oil
8 large shrimp, peeled and deveined
1 - 3-4 lb (1.4-1.8 kg) chicken, cut up
8 GOYA Chorizos, cut into ½-inch slices
8 cloves garlic, minced
3 cup (720 ml) GOYA Valencia Rice
    or Medium Grain Rice
4 oz (120 ml) GOYA Tomato Sauce
1 packet Sazón GOYA con Azafrán
1 tsp (5 ml) GOYA Adobo with Pepper
1 cup (240 ml) peas
1 - 6½ oz jar (195 g) GOYA Pimientos, diced

In a saucepan, mix water and bouillon. Add clams and mussels and simmer until they open. Remove open clams and mussels with a slotted spoon and set aside, reserving broth. In a paella pan or 8-qt Dutch oven, heat olive oil until very hot. Sauté shrimp 1-2 minutes and remove; sauté chicken until well browned and remove; sauté chorizos until lightly browned and remove; set these aside.

Lower heat to medium, and sauté garlic until browned. Add uncooked rice and sauté for 1 minute. Add tomato sauce, Sazón, Adobo, and reserved broth; bring to a rapid boil, gently shaking and turning the pan so all ingredients heat evenly.

Reduce heat to a gentle boil, and simmer until most of the liquid has been absorbed. Stir gently, and salt to taste.

Add peas, shrimp, clams, mussels, chicken, chorizos and pimientos. Simmer until rice is done to desired consistency. Remove from heat and let sit for three minutes. Garnish with parsley and lemon wedges.
Serves 8.

Approximate nutritional analysis per serving:
Calories 996, Protein 77 g, Carbohydrates 65 g, Fat 45 g,
Cholesterol 235 mg, Sodium   354 mg

Opposite: Classic Paella Valenciana

SHRIMP RATATOUILLE

1 cup (240 ml) onion, diced
½ cup (120 ml) green bell pepper, diced
1 tbs plus 1 tsp (20 ml) **CHEF PAUL PRUDHOMME'S**
    Seafood Magic, in all
1 large eggplant, peeled, stemmed and
    cut into a large, 1½-inch dice
1 medium green bell pepper,
    cut roughly into large pieces
1 medium onion, cut in a very large dice
5 oz (150 g) zucchini, cut in a large dice
5 oz (150 g) yellow squash, cut in a large dice
6 medium tomatoes, peeled, and cut in wedges
1¼ cups (295 ml) defatted seafood stock
¼ cup (60 ml) defatted veal glaze*
4 bay leaves
1 tsp (5 ml) minced garlic
½ tsp (3 ml) salt
32 medium-large shrimp, peeled
2 cups (480 ml) hot cooked rice

* If you don't have veal glaze, use 2 cups (480 ml) of defatted chicken stock and cook over high heat until it reduces to ½ cup (120 ml) . Use ¼ cup (60 ml) of this.

In a large hot skillet over high heat, place the 1 cup chopped onion and the ½ cup green bell pepper. Cook 4 minutes, stirring occasionally, until slightly brown. Add 1 tbs Seafood Magic; stir and cook 3 minutes. Add ½ cup seafood stock and scrape up the brown bits sticking to the pan bottom. Cook 3 minutes. Add another ½ cup stock, scraping and stirring so mixture doesn't burn, and cook 5 minutes more. Add the remaining vegetables and bay leaves. Mix thoroughly, breaking up the tomatoes, and cook 2 minutes. Stir in the veal glaze and the remaining Seafood Magic, and cook over high heat 10 minutes, stirring occasionally, and being careful not to let the mixture stick to the pan. Add garlic, cook 3 minutes, then add the salt. Cook 15 minutes more, stirring occasionally. Gently fold the shrimp into the mixture, add the remaining ¼ cup seafood stock, and cook about 5 minutes.

    To serve, place ½ cup of cooked rice on a plate and spoon the ratatouille around it, being sure each portion has 8 shrimp. Serves 4.

Approximate nutritional analysis per serving:
Calories 333, Protein 20 g, Carbohydrates 61 g, Fat 3 g,
Cholesterol 89 mg, Sodium 520 mg

SOUTHWESTERN JAMBALAYA

1 lb (455 g) chorizo or Italian sausage links
1 cup (240 ml) sliced celery
1 cup (240 ml) chopped onion
1 cup (240 ml) chopped green bell pepper
1 cup (240 ml) chopped red bell pepper
2 tsp (10 ml) minced fresh garlic
1 cup (240 ml) long-grain rice
2 cups (480 ml) cooked chicken, cubed ¾-inch
2 cups (480 ml) water
2 - 16 oz jars (960 ml) **CHI-CHI'S Salsa**
2 tsp (10 ml) paprika
¼ tsp (1 ml) ground red pepper (cayenne)
¼ tsp (1 ml) coarsely ground pepper
¼ tsp (1 ml) dried thyme leaves
1 bay leaf
1 lb (455 g) fresh or frozen raw shrimp, shelled,
    deveined and rinsed
    or 12 oz (360 g) frozen cooked shrimp
¼ cup (60 ml) chopped fresh cilantro

In Dutch oven, cook chorizo over medium heat until browned and cooked through. Remove from heat; cut into ¼-inch slices. Set aside. Drain all but 2 tbs fat. In same pan, add celery, onion, bell peppers and garlic. Cook over medium heat until vegetables are tender. Add remaining ingredients except shrimp and cilantro. Bring to a boil. Cover; reduce heat to low. Simmer, stirring occasionally, 20-25 minutes or until rice is tender. Add shrimp and cilantro; cook 3-4 minutes or until shrimp turn pink. Remove bay leaf. Serves 10.

Approximate nutritional analysis per serving:
Calories 400, Protein 29 g, Carbohydrates 25 g, Fat 20 g,
Cholesterol 115 mg, Sodium 108   mg

STEAMED SHRIMP

½ cup (120 ml) vinegar
1 tbs (15 ml) **OLD BAY Seasoning**
1 tsp (5 ml) salt
½ cup (120 ml) water
1 lb (455 g) shrimp

In a saucepan, combine first 4 ingredients; bring to boil. Add shrimp, stir gently. Cover, steam until tender. Drain, remove shells and devein. Serves 3-4.

Approximate nutritional analysis per serving:
Calories 120, Protein 23 g, Carbohydrates 1 g, Fat 2 g,
Cholesterol 172 mg, Sodium 434 mg

MARMITAKO

Tuna Stew

1 large potato, peeled and cut into ½-inch cubes
1 lb (455 g) fresh tuna steak, cut into 1-inch cubes
2 tsp (10 ml) salt
¼ tsp (1 ml) GOYA Adobo with Pepper
1 tbs (15 ml) GOYA Olive Oil
1 cup (240 ml) chopped onion
1½ cups (355 ml) chopped green pepper
1 clove garlic, chopped
1 bay leaf
1 cup (240 ml) LA VINA White Cooking Wine
2 cups (480 ml) fish stock *or* ½ cup (120 ml) water
    plus ½ cup (120 ml) clam juice
1 GOYA Pimiento, chopped
1 tbs (15 ml) minced parsley

In a large bowl, soak potato cubes in cold water. Sprinkle tuna evenly with salt and Adobo. In a large saucepan or soup pot, lightly sauté tuna in olive oil; remove tuna and set aside. In same pan, sauté onion until soft. Add green pepper, garlic, bay leaf, drained potato cubes, and white wine. Bring to a boil, reduce heat and simmer, uncovered, for 2-3 minutes. Add fish stock and simmer, covered, for 10 minutes or until potatoes are tender. Add tuna and pimientos to stew and simmer, covered, for an additional 3-4 minutes. Remove bay leaf. Salt to taste. Garnish with parsley. Serves 4.

Approximate nutritional analysis per serving:
Calories 389, Protein 37 g, Carbohydrates 19 g, Fat 12 g,
Cholesterol 58 mg, Sodium 781 mg

MICROWAVE BOUILLABAISSE

2 medium potatoes, cut into ¼-inch slices
1 small onion, sliced
1 large clove garlic, minced
1½ tbs (25 ml) olive oil
½ lb (230 g) firm white fish fillets (sea bass, cod, halibut, haddock) cut into 1-inch cubes
¼ lb (115 g) medium shrimp, peeled
8 mussels, scrubbed and debearded
1 - 8 oz can (240 g) stewed tomatoes
⅓ cup (80 ml) dry white wine or chicken stock
1 tbs (15 ml) tomato paste
¾ tsp (4 ml) dried basil
¼ tsp (1 ml) fennel seeds
⅛ tsp (.5 ml) saffron
salt and pepper to taste

In a 1½-qt microwave safe dish, arrange potatoes around the edge and the onion and garlic in the center; drizzle with oil. Cover tightly and microwave on HIGH for 3 minutes. Arrange fish and shrimp over onions; place mussels over potatoes. In a small bowl mix together 7 remaining ingredients, except salt and pepper; pour over contents of dish. Cover tightly; microwave on HIGH for 8 minutes. Stir; season with salt and pepper and serve. Serves 2.

Approximate nutritional analysis per serving:
Calories 534, Protein 47 g, Carbohydrates 48 g, Fat 14 g,
Cholesterol 159 mg, Sodium 601 mg

SMUCKER'S MANDARIN SHRIMP AND VEGETABLE STIR-FRY

1 cup (240 ml) SMUCKER'S Orange Marmalade
24 fresh jumbo shrimp, peeled and deveined
3 tbs (45 ml) soy sauce
2 tbs (30 ml) white vinegar
2 tsp (10 ml) Tabasco pepper sauce
1½ tbs (25 ml) cornstarch
2 tbs (30 ml) vegetable oil
1 tbs (15 ml) fresh ginger, chopped
1 tbs (15 ml) fresh garlic, chopped
1 red bell pepper, chopped
1 yellow or green bell pepper, chopped
3 cups (720 ml) broccoli florettes, about 1 bunch
½ cup (120 ml) water
1 cup (240 ml) scallions, chopped, about 1 bunch

Combine the SMUCKER'S Orange Marmalade, soy sauce, vinegar, Tabasco and cornstarch in small bowl. Stir to dissolve the cornstarch and set aside

Place a large skillet or wok over high heat. Heat the pan for 1 minute then add the vegetable oil. Heat the oil for 30 seconds then add the ginger, garlic and shrimp. Stir-fry the shrimp for 2-3 minutes until they begin to turn rosy pink in color. Remove the shrimp from the pan and set aside.

Add the peppers and broccoli florettes to the pan and cook on high heat for 1 minute. Add water, cover, and reduce heat to medium. Cook vegetables 4-5 minutes, or until tender. Uncover pan and return the heat to high. Add shrimp and SMUCKER'S Orange Marmalade mixture. Cook shrimp for another 2 minutes until sauce is thickened and shrimp are completely cooked. Correct seasoning with salt and fresh ground black pepper as needed. Stir in scallions and serve with boiled rice. Serves 4-6.

Approximate nutritional analysis per serving:
Calories 278, Protein 12 g, Carbohydrates 47 g, Fat 6 g,
Cholesterol 62 mg, Sodium 633 mg

BRAZILIAN CORN AND SHRIMP MOQUECA CASSEROLE

1 lb (455 g) medium cooked shrimp
2 tbs (30 ml) olive oil
½ cup (120 ml) chopped onion
2 tbs (30 ml) chopped parsley
¼ cup (60 ml) chopped green bell pepper
¼ cup (60 ml) tomato sauce
½ tsp (3 ml) TABASCO pepper sauce
salt
2 tbs (30 ml) all-purpose flour
1 cup (240 ml) milk
1 - 16 oz can (480 g) cream-style corn
grated Parmesan cheese

In a large oven-proof skillet over medium-high heat, heat oil. Add onion, parsley, bell pepper, TABASCO pepper sauce and tomato sauce and cook, stirring occasionally, for 5 minutes. Add shrimp and salt. Cover and reduce heat to low, and simmer for 2-3 minutes. Preheat oven to 375°F (190°C). Sprinkle flour over shrimp, stir, and add milk gradually, stirring after each addition. Cook over medium heat until mixture thickens. Remove from heat. Pour the corn over the mixture without stirring. Sprinkle with Parmesan cheese. Bake for 30 minutes, or until browned. Serves 4.

Approximate nutritional analysis per serving:
Calories 315, Protein 28 g, Carbohydrates 30 g, Fat 10 g, Cholesterol 226 mg, Sodium 713 mg

BASQUE PAELLA

1 cup (240 ml) chopped onion
3 tbs (45 ml) olive oil
1 cup (240 ml) long or medium grain white rice
2 garlic cloves, pressed
1 tsp (5 ml) ground cumin
1 - 15 oz can (450 g) whole tomatoes,
    halved, undrained
1 - 13¾ oz can (413 ml) reduced-sodium
    chicken broth
1 cup (240 ml) Sonoma dried tomato halves,
    cut into strips with kitchen shears
12 oz (360 g) shelled shrimp, deveined,
    with or without tails
1 - 15 oz can (450 g) pinto beans, rinsed and drained
    or 1½ cups (355 ml) cooked light
    red kidney beans
1 cup (240 ml) zucchini, trimmed and diced ¼ inch
1 cup (240 ml) fresh, frozen or canned corn kernels
salt, to taste
¼ cup (60 ml) chopped cilantro leaves
2 tbs (30 ml) finely chopped red bell pepper
2 tsp (10 ml) finely chopped, seeded jalapeño pepper

In 12-inch skillet over medium heat, sauté onions in olive oil about 5 minutes until golden. Add rice, garlic and cumin; stir over low heat 1 minute. Add canned tomatoes with juice, broth and dried tomatoes; heat to boiling, stirring once. Cover; cook over medium-low heat 15 minutes.

Meanwhile, mix shrimp, beans, zucchini and corn in bowl. Add to skillet; mix. Cover and cook over low heat about 10-15 minutes (depending on size of shrimp), mixing often until shrimp is opaque throughout. Season with salt.

Transfer to serving dish; sprinkle with cilantro, bell pepper and jalapeño just before serving. Serves 6.

Approximate nutritional analysis per serving:
Calories 440, Protein 26 g, Carbohydrates 65 g, Fat 10 g, Cholesterol 110 mg, Sodium 710 mg

Courtesy of the American Dry Bean Board.

SEAFOOD ONE POT MEAL

1 cup (240 ml) brown or white rice,
    or a mixture of both
2 cups (480 ml) boiling water
1-2 tsp (5-10 ml) olive oil
2-3 cloves garlic, minced
½ cup (120 ml) chopped red or yellow onion
1 stalk celery, sliced
1 medium green or red pepper, sliced
1 - 16 oz can (480 g) stewed tomatoes
    or 1 cup (240 ml) diced fresh tomatoes
¼ tsp (1 ml) Tabasco sauce, optional
1 tsp (5 ml) saffron or dried oregano leaves
8 slices spicy turkey sausage, chorizo
    or other spicy sausage
1 - 12¼ oz can (368 g) BUMBLE BEE Tuna,
    White or Light
1 - 6½ oz can (195 g) BUMBLE BEE Skinless
    Boneless Salmon, Red or Pink
1 - 8 oz can (240 g) BUMBLE BEE Oysters,
    Boiled or Smoked, optional
1 lb (455 g) medium-size raw shrimp, in shells,
    or mussels and/or clams

Place rice in sieve under cold water until water runs clear. In a large skillet or paella pan, heat oil and sauté garlic, onion, celery and pepper just until softened, about 3 minutes. Add remaining ingredients, except seafood. Bring to a boil, reduce heat, cover and simmer about 25 minutes. Arrange seafood over rice, cover and cook through 4-5 minutes. Toss with a fork, if desired, to fluff rice and distribute seafood. Serves 6.

Approximate nutritional analysis per serving w/o oysters:
Calories 418, Protein 47 g, Carbohydrates 31 g, Fat 11 g, Cholesterol 63 mg, Sodium 772 mg

BAYOU JAMBALAYA

1 medium onion, sliced
½ cup (120 ml) chopped green pepper
1 clove garlic, minced
1 cup (240 ml) uncooked white rice
2 tbs (30 ml) vegetable oil
¾ cup (180 ml) HEINZ Tomato Ketchup
2 cups (480 ml) water
1 tbs (15 ml) HEINZ Vinegar
⅛ tsp (.5 ml) black pepper
⅛ tsp (.5 ml) red pepper
1 medium tomato, coarsely chopped
1 cup (240 ml) cooked ham
½ lb (230 g) raw shrimp, shelled and deveined

Microwave Directions: Place onion, green pepper, garlic and butter in 3-qt casserole. Cover dish with lid or vented plastic wrap; microwave at HIGH 3-4 minutes, stirring once. Stir in rice, ketchup, water, vinegar, black pepper, red pepper, tomato and ham. Cover; microwave on HIGH 10-12 minutes or until mixture comes to a boil. Microwave on MEDIUM 18-20 minutes until rice is cooked, stirring once. Stir in shrimp; cover. Microwave on HIGH 2-3 minutes or until shrimp turn pink. Let stand, covered, 5 minutes before serving.

In large skillet, sauté first 4 ingredients in oil until onion is transparent. Stir in ketchup and remaining ingredients except shrimp. Cover; simmer 20-25 minutes or until rice is tender. Add shrimp; simmer uncovered 3-5 minutes or until shrimp turn pink, stirring occasionally. Serves 6.

Approximate nutritional analysis per serving:
Calories 243, Protein 29 g, Carbohydrates 18 g, Fat 6 g,
Cholesterol 66 mg, Sodium   148 mg

BAKED STUFFED SHRIMP

12 jumbo shrimp shelled and deveined
3 tsp (15 ml) BERTOLLI Classico or
    Extra Virgin Olive Oil
1 cup (240 ml) coarse bread crumbs from
    day-old Italian bread
1 garlic clove, crushed through a press
1 tbs (15 ml) finely chopped Italian parsley
1 tsp (5 ml) grated lemon zest
1 tbs (15 ml) fresh lemon juice
4 sprigs parsley

Split shrimp along the backs but not all the way through. Spray a baking pan with olive oil cooking spray. Arrange shrimp on the pan. Heat 2 tsp of the olive oil in a large nonstick skillet. Add the bread crumbs and cook, stirring over medium-low heat until the bread is golden. Add 1 tbs of the parsley, the garlic and lemon zest; cook, stirring 1 minute. Remove from heat.

Preheat oven to 450°F (230°C). Carefully pack the bread mixture into opening in each shrimp, dividing evenly. Brush or drizzle each shrimp with the remaining oil. Bake until shrimp are cooked through, about 5 minutes. Sprinkle with lemon juice before serving. Serves 4.

Approximate nutritional analysis per serving:
Calories 137, Protein 15 g, Carbohydrates 7 g, Fat 5 g,
Cholesterol 106 mg, Sodium 158 mg

EASY SHRIMP PAELLLA

2½ cups (590 ml) water
1 tbs (15 ml) butter or margarine
1 cup (240 ml) long grain rice
3 tbs (45 ml) McCORMICK Mediterranean
    Rice Seasoning
1 lb (455 g) large shrimp, peeled and deveined
1 cup (240 ml) frozen peas
1 - 2.2 oz can (66 g) sliced ripe olives, drained

Bring water and butter to a boil in 2-qt saucepan. Stir in rice and seasoning. Cover and simmer 20 minutes. Remove from heat and let stand 5 minutes. Meanwhile, sauté shrimp in nonstick skillet over medium-high heat 4 minutes. Add peas and olives and sauté 2 minutes or until heated throughout. Stir in cooked rice. Serves 6.

Approximate nutritional analysis per serving:
Calories 246, Protein 19 g, Carbohydrates 31 g, Fat 5 g,
Cholesterol 120 mg, Sodium 224 mg

Courtesy of McCormick/Schilling Spices.

Baked Stuffed Shrimp

BUTTERFLY SHRIMP

1 lb (455 g) large shrimp
1 egg, beaten
¼ cup (60 ml) cornstarch
¼ cup (60 ml) all-purpose flour
¼ cup (60 ml) chicken broth
½ tsp (3 ml) salt
oil for deep frying
1 large green pepper, diced
1 cup (240 ml) thinly sliced carrots
1 clove garlic, minced
2 tbs (30 ml) cooking oil
1 cup (240 ml) chicken broth
½ cup (120 ml) IMPERIAL Granulated Sugar
⅓ cup (80 ml) cider vinegar
2 tsp (10 ml) soy sauce
¼ cup (60 ml) water
2 tbs (30 ml) cornstarch
freshly cooked rice

Shell and devein shrimp, leaving tails on. Combine egg, cornstarch, flour, chicken broth, salt; beat until smooth. Dip shrimp in batter and fry in deep hot fat, 375°F (190°C), about 5 minutes, until golden brown. Drain and keep warm. In skillet, sauté green pepper, carrot, garlic in cooking oil until tender but still crisp. Add broth, IMPERIAL Granulated Sugar, vinegar, soy sauce to vegetables. Bring to boil and boil 1 minute. Blend water slowly into cornstarch and stir into vegetables. Cook and stir until thickened and bubbling. To serve, arrange hot shrimp over rice and pour sauce over shrimp and rice. Serves 4.

Approximate nutritional analysis per serving:
Calories 605, Protein 29 g, Carbohydrates 75 g, Fat 22 g, Cholesterol 200 mg, Sodium 767 mg

SHRIMP STIR-FRY

1 lb (455 g) shrimp, peeled
3 scallions, chopped
1 tbs (15 ml) McCORMICK/SCHILLING Arrowroot
1 tbs (15 ml) McCORMICK/SCHILLING
    Pure Sherry Extract
1 tbs (15 ml) soy sauce
¼ cup (60 ml) water
¼ lb (115 g) snow peas

Sauté shrimp and scallions in oil until shrimp are pink. Combine next 4 ingredients. Add to shrimp with snow peas. Cook until sauce thickens. Serve over rice. Serves 4.

Approximate nutritional analysis per serving:
Calories 169, Protein 24 g, Carbohydrates 5 g, Fat 5 g, Cholesterol 172 mg, Sodium 428 mg

BISTRO SHRIMP WITH POTATO MATCHSTICKS

½ tsp (3 ml) McCORMICK or SCHILLING
    Pure Vanilla Extract
1 - 13¾ oz can (413 ml) chicken broth
½ tsp (3 ml) McCORMICK or SCHILLING
    Saffron Stigmas
1 tsp (5 ml) McCORMICK or SCHILLING
    Garlic Powder
½ lb (230 g) medium shrimp, peeled
1 cup (240 ml) heavy cream
3 tbs (45 ml) cornstarch mixed with:
3 tbs (45 ml) water
3 medium redskin potatoes, cut in matchsticks
3 Italian plum tomatoes, seeded and
    cut into ½-inch dices
salt to taste

Combine first 4 ingredients in 2-qt saucepan. Bring to low boil. Add shrimp and poach 1 minute. Remove shrimp and keep warm. Add cream and cornstarch mixture to broth. Cook over medium-high heat while stirring with a whisk until mixture thickens slightly. Reduce heat and simmer 10 minutes. Add potato matchsticks and cook 7 minutes more. Add diced tomatoes and cook 7 minutes more. Add shrimp and toss until all ingredients are warm. Serve in warm bowls. Serves 4.

Approximate nutritional analysis per serving:
Calories 408, Protein 16 g, Carbohydrates 35 g, Fat 24 g, Cholesterol 168 mg, Sodium 399 mg

GAMBAS AL AJILLO
Garlic Shrimp

3 cloves garlic, sliced
¾ cup (180 ml) GOYA Olive Oil
¾ lb (340 g) medium shrimp, shelled and deveined
½ tsp (3 ml) crushed chili pepper
    or 1 small chili pepper, chopped
2 tbs (30 ml) chopped parsley
1 tbs (15 ml) GOYA Adobo

In a skillet, sauté sliced garlic in olive oil until golden. Add shrimp and chili peppers and sauté for 3 minutes. Remove shrimp and garlic slices from oil with slotted spoon, reserving oil. Sprinkle with parsley and Adobo and serve drizzled with reserved oil. Serves 3.

Approximate nutritional analysis per serving:
Calories 603, Protein 23 g, Carbohydrates 2 g, Fat 56 g, Cholesterol 172 mg, Sodium 347 mg

Opposite: Gambas al Ajillo

SEAFOOD SUPREME

½ cup (120 ml) margarine
1 cup (240 ml) chopped green pepper
1 cup (240 ml) chopped celery
1 medium onion, chopped
1½ lbs (685 g) fresh shrimp, shelled
3 tbs (45 ml) flour
3 cups (720 ml) milk
1 cup (240 ml) mayonnaise
2 tbs (30 ml) mustard
3 tbs (45 ml) Worcestershire sauce
2-3 tbs (30-45 ml) OLD BAY Seasoning, to taste
1½ lbs (685 g) sea legs (imitation crab meat)
½ cup (120 ml) cracker crumbs
OLD BAY Seasoning for topping

In a large skillet, melt margarine; add green pepper, celery, onion and shrimp; sauté over medium heat until vegetables are tender and shrimp is done. Add flour to skillet and stir until flour is absorbed. Add milk, stirring until mixture thickens. Take skillet off heat and cool.

Preheat oven to 350°F (180°C). In a large 6-qt casserole dish, add mayonnaise, mustard, Worcestershire sauce, OLD BAY Seasoning and imitation crab meat. Mix well. Stir in the cooled shrimp mixture with the crab mixture; top with cracker crumbs and sprinkle with more OLD BAY Seasoning. Bake for 30-35 minutes until the top is browned. Serves 10.

Approximate nutritional analysis per serving:
Calories 411, Protein 34 g, Carbohydrates 19 g, Fat 22 g, Cholesterol 185 mg, Sodium 709 mg

GARLICKY TOMATO AND SHRIMP KABOBS

1¼ lbs (570 g) fresh FLORIDA tomatoes
⅓ cup (80 ml) olive oil
2 tbs (30 ml) red wine vinegar
1 tsp (5 ml) crushed garlic
1 tsp (5 ml) Italian seasoning, crushed
¾ tsp (4 ml) salt
⅛ tsp (.5 ml) ground black pepper
1 lb (455 g) shrimp, peeled and deveined
    (12 oz (360 g) peeled) *or*
    12 oz (360 g) boned and skinned chicken
    breast cutlets, cut in chunks
1⅓ cups (320 ml) zucchini cut in
    ¼-inch thick slices
1¼ cups (300 ml) mushrooms

Use tomatoes held at room temperature until fully ripe. Cut into wedges; set aside. In a shallow baking dish combine oil, vinegar, garlic, Italian seasoning, salt and black pepper. Add shrimp, turning to coat. Let stand at room temperature for 10 minutes. Preheat broiler to hot. Thread shrimp onto skewers alternating with zucchini, mushrooms and reserved tomatoes. Place on broiler pan; broil 4-5 inches from heat until shrimp are just cooked through, 8-10 minutes, turning once and brushing occasionally with marinade. Serve with steamed rice, if desired. Serves 4.

Approximate nutritional analysis per serving:
Calories 290, Protein 20 g, Carbohydrates 10 g, Fat 20 g, Cholesterol 129 mg, Sodium 556 mg

CITRUS SHRIMP KABOBS

3 medium oranges
¼ cup (60 ml) WISH - BONE Italian, Robust
Italian or Lite Italian Dressing
2 tbs (30 ml) snipped fresh dill
    or 1 tsp (5 ml) dried dill weed
1 lb (455 g) large shrimp, peeled and deveined

Grate 1 tsp peel from orange, then squeeze out ¼ cup juice. Cut remaining 2 oranges into 16 wedges; set aside.

In shallow baking dish or plastic bag, combine orange peel, ¼ cup orange juice, Italian dressing and dill. Add shrimp; turn to coat. Cover, or close bag, and marinate in refrigerator, turning occasionally, 30 minutes. Remove shrimp. Bring reserved marinade to a boil.

On 8 skewers, alternately thread shrimp and orange wedges. Grill or broil, turning and basting with reserved marinade, until shrimp turn pink. If desired, bring remaining reserved marinade to a boil and serve over kabobs or toss with hot cooked rice. Serves 4.

Approximate nutritional analysis per serving:
Calories 210, Protein 25 g, Carbohydrates 13 g, Fat 6 g, Cholesterol 220 mg, Sodium 550 mg

Courtesy of The Lipton Kitchens.

Opposite: Citrus Shrimp Kabobs

RED AND GREEN SEAFOOD ENCHILADAS

RED ENCHILADAS:
1 - 16 oz jar (480 ml) CHI-CHI'S Salsa
1 tbs (15 ml) chili powder
1 tsp (5 ml) ground cumin
1 tsp (5 ml) dried oregano leaves
4 medium flour tortillas, warmed
¾ lb (340 g) white fish (halibut, scrod, etc.),
    cooked and cut into small pieces
2 cups (480 ml) shredded cheddar cheese

GREEN ENCHILADAS:
1 - 16 oz jar (480 ml) CHI-CHI'S Salsa Verde
½ cup (120 ml) sour cream
¼ tsp (1 ml) coarsely ground pepper
4 medium flour tortillas, warmed
¾ lb (340 g) fresh or frozen cooked shrimp,
shelled and deveined
2 cups (480 ml) shredded hot pepper
    Monterey Jack cheese
sour cream
chopped fresh cilantro

Red Enchiladas: Grease 9x9x2-inch baking dish. In small saucepan, combine salsa, chili powder, cumin and oregano. Bring to a boil. Cook 5 minutes, stirring occasionally. Pour into shallow bowl; cool slightly. Dip each tortilla into sauce to coat. Fill each with ¼ of fish and 3 tbs shredded cheddar cheese. Roll up. Place seam-side-down in greased baking dish. Pour remaining red sauce over enchiladas. Sprinkle with remaining shredded cheddar cheese.

Green Enchiladas: Grease 9x9x2-inch baking dish. In shallow bowl, combine salsa verde, sour cream and pepper. Dip each tortilla into sauce to coat. Fill each with ¼ of shrimp and 3 tbs shredded Monterey Jack cheese. Roll up. Place seam-side-down in greased baking dish. Pour remaining green sauce over enchiladas. Sprinkle with remaining shredded cheese.

Heat oven to 350°F (180°C). Bake enchiladas 18-22 minutes or until lightly browned and cheese is melted. Place 1 red and 1 green enchilada on each serving plate. Serve with sour cream and cilantro. Serves 4.

Approximate nutritional analysis per enchilada:
Calories 1030, Protein 73 g, Carbohydrates 68 g, Fat 52 g, Cholesterol 315 mg, Sodium 243 mg

VEGETABLES

Save room for vegetables. When you eat them all you will have added vitamins, minerals, fiber and flavor to your diet, with little fat — except for butter or sauces, of course. Balance your diet and you balance your plate as well. Nothing looks so enticing as bright bunches of green broccoli coupled with deep orange disks of sweet potato or the confetti yellow of corn. And don't forget rice and beans; they combine with many flavorings and other vegetables, and are an excellent source of dietary fiber.

GRILLED VEGETABLES AND FRUITS

VEGETABLE BASTING SAUCE
1 cup (240 ml) CHI-CHI'S Salsa Verde
2 cloves garlic
2 tbs (30 ml) olive oil
1 tbs (30 ml) lime juice
½ tsp (3 ml) dried rosemary leaves

FRUIT BASTING SAUCE
1 cup (240 ml) CHI-CHI'S Salsa Verde
¼ cup (60 ml) Jalapeño Pepper Jelly (below)
1 tbs (15 ml) lime juice
1 tbs (15 ml) melted butter or margarine

JALAPEÑO PEPPER JELLY
1 - 7 oz jar (210 g) CHI-CHI'S Whole Red
    or Green Jalapeño Peppers
1 - 4¼ oz can (128 g) CHI-CHI'S Whole
    or Diced Green Chilies, drained
2 cups (480 ml) white vinegar, divided
7 cups (1.7 L) sugar
2 - 3 oz pouches (180 ml) liquid pectin

SAUCES: In blender container, combine all ingredients. Process until smooth.

Jalapeño Pepper Jelly: Remove pepper stems; halve and seed peppers. In blender container, place jalapeño peppers, green chilies and 1 cup vinegar. Process until smooth. In 6-8 qt saucepan, combine pepper mixture, remaining 1 cup vinegar and sugar. Bring to a full rolling boil, stirring occasionally. Stir in liquid pectin. Bring to a full rolling boil; boil 1 minute, stirring constantly. Remove from heat. Skim off any foam. Immediately fill hot sterilized half-pint jars, leaving ¼-inch head space. Wipe jar tops and threads clean. Place hot lids on jars and screw bands on firmly. Process in boiling water canner for 5 minutes. Yields 7 half-pints.

To grill vegetables: Prepare a bed of medium-hot coals. Prepare vegetables by either cutting into chunks for skewers or into ½-inch slices to lay on grill rack or in grill basket. Some vegetables grill well whole, such as corn-on-the-cob, cherry tomatoes, pattypan squash and baby-sized vegetables. Turn vegetables frequently and baste with sauce until tender and browned.
Bell peppers (green, red, yellow, orange): leave whole
    or cut in half: 10 minutes.
Green onions: whole: 10-12 minutes
Corn: whole, shucked ears: 15-20 minutes
Eggplant: ½-inch sliced: 10-15 minutes on each side
    (total 20-30 minutes).
Red or yellow onions: wedges or ½-inch slices: 12-18 minutes.
Jicama: kabobs or ½-inch slices: 20 minutes.
Squashes (zucchini, pattypan, chayote, yellow crook neck):
    8-12 minutes.

Tomatoes: halved large or cherry: 8-10 minutes.
Potatoes (baking or sweet): ½-inch slices: 14-16 minutes.

To grill fruit: Prepare a bed of low-heat coals. Cut fruits into chunks for skewers, into ½-inch slices or cut in half. Turn fruit at least once during cooking and baste with sauce during last 5 minutes only (sauce can burn if grilled too long).
Melon: slices or kabobs: 10 minutes.
Pineapple: slices or kabobs: 15 minutes.
Apples/Pears: slices, kabobs, halved fruit: 10 minutes.
Papaya: kabobs or halved (remove seeds): 15 minutes.

Approximate nutritional analysis per 1 tbs serving Vegetable Basting Sauce: Calories 18, Protein 0 g, Carbohydrates 1 g, Fat 1 g, Cholesterol 0 mg, Sodium 60 mg

Approximate nutritional analysis per 1 tbs serving Fruit Basting Sauce: Calories 20, Protein 0 g, Carbohydrates 4 g, Fat 1 g, Cholesterol 0 mg, Sodium 65 mg

Approximate nutritional analysis per 1 tbs serving Jalapeño Pepper Jelly: Calories 50, Protein 0 g, Carbohydrates 13 g, Fat 0 g, Cholesterol 0 mg, Sodium 0 mg

BASIL-TINGED FRESH VEGETABLES IN PAPILLOTE

4 - 12-inch squares parchment paper
½ cup (120 ml) whole pitted CALIFORNIA ripe olives
1 lb (455 g) fresh summer squash (zucchini,
    crookneck or pattypan), sliced
4 small tomatillos, halved *or*
½ basket cherry tomatoes, halved
½ cup (120 ml) onion wedges or sliced fresh leek
¼ cup (60 ml) slivered fresh basil leaves
1½ tsp (8 ml) bottled or fresh minced garlic
3 tbs (45 ml) olive oil

Spread out parchment squares on counter. Pile olives, squash, tomatillos, onion, basil and garlic in center of each, with olives on bottom, to keep them moist. One by one, drizzle with olive oil then bring up 2 edges of parchment together at top of bundle and fold tightly together to seal. Tuck paper ends underneath package. Place in wide, shallow microwave-safe baking pan and microwave on HIGH for 14-16 minutes or until tender-crisp. Serve with fresh salmon or other fish and boiled red potatoes. The juices sauce the fish, too. Serves 4.

Approximate nutritional analysis per serving:
Calories 138, Protein 2 g, Carbohydrates 9 g, Fat 12 g,
Cholesterol 0 mg, Sodium 101 mg

Preceding page: Galley Yams and Apples   *Opposite: Grilled Vegetables and Fruit*

GRILLED VEGETABLES AL FRESCO

2 large red peppers
2 medium zucchini
1 large eggplant

SPICY MARINADE
⅔ cup (160 ml) white wine vinegar
½ cup (120 ml) soy sauce
2 tbs (30 ml) minced ginger
2 tbs (30 ml) olive oil
2 tbs (30 ml) sesame oil
2 large garlic cloves, minced
2 tsp (10 ml) TABASCO pepper sauce

Seed red peppers; cut each pepper into quarters. Cut each zucchini lengthwise into ¼-inch-thick strips. Slice eggplant into ¼-inch-thick rounds.

In 13x9-inch baking dish combine Spicy marinade ingredients. Place vegetable pieces in mixture; toss well to mix. Cover and refrigerate at least 2 hours and up to 24 hours, turning occasionally.

About 30 minutes before serving, preheat grill to medium heat, placing rack 5-6 inches above coals. Place red peppers, zucchini and eggplant slices on grill rack. Grill vegetables 4 minutes, turning once and brushing with marinade occasionally. Serves 4.

To Broil: Preheat oven to broil, and broil vegetables 5-6 inches below broiler flame for 4 minutes on each side.

Approximate nutritional analysis per serving:
Calories 100, Protein 3 g, Carbohydrates 17 g, Fat 4 g,
Cholesterol 0 mg, Sodium 523 mg

ITALIAN ASPARAGUS MEDLEY

1 - 10 oz pkg (300 g) frozen asparagus cuts
3 hard-cooked eggs, chopped
3 tbs (45 ml) bottled Italian salad dressing
3 tbs (45 ml) fine dry Italian-style bread crumbs
3 tbs (45 ml) grated Parmesan cheese

Cook asparagus according to package directions. Stir in eggs and 2 tbs of the dressing. Pour into 1-qt casserole. Stir together remaining dressing, crumbs and cheese until well combined. Sprinkle evenly over asparagus. Bake in preheated 350°F (180°C) oven, until hot throughout, about 10-15 minutes. Serves 3.

Microwave: In 1-qt casserole, cook asparagus according to package directions. Add remaining ingredients as above. Cook, uncovered, on full power, until hot throughout, about 2-3 minutes.

Approximate nutritional analysis per serving:
Calories 218, Protein 12 g, Carbohydrates 11 g, Fat 14 g,
Cholesterol 217 mg, Sodium 477 mg

ALMOND-BROCCOLI STIR-FRY

1 lb (455 g) broccoli
¾ cup (180 ml) BLUE DIAMOND
    Chopped Natural Almonds
3 tbs (45 ml) vegetable oil
3 cloves garlic, sliced thinly
2 tbs (30 ml) soy sauce
1 tbs (15 ml) sugar
1 tsp (5 ml) grated, fresh ginger *or*
¼ tsp (1 ml) powdered ginger
1 tsp (5 ml) lemon juice

Cut broccoli into flowerets. Trim and peel stalks; cut diagonal into thin slices; reserve. Sauté almonds in oil 1 minute. Add broccoli and stir-fry until barely tender, about 2 minutes. Add garlic and stir-fry until just tender, about 1 minute. Stir in soy sauce, sugar, and ginger. Continue stir-frying until sugar dissolves, about 1 minute. Add lemon juice. Serves 4.

Approximate nutritional analysis per serving:
Calories 286, Protein 9 g, Carbohydrates 16 g, Fat 23 g,
Cholesterol 0 mg, Sodium 548 mg

CAULIFLOWER WITH CREAMY CHIVE SAUCE

1 head cauliflower, washed
1 cup (240 ml) DANNON Plain Nonfat or
    Lowfat Yogurt
1 tbs (15 ml) chopped fresh chives *or*
½ tsp (3 ml) dried chives
1 tsp (5 ml) dry mustard

Steam cauliflower, covered, over boiling water 15-20 minutes or until tender. In a small bowl, combine yogurt, chives and mustard. Blend well with wire whisk or fork. Spoon over cooked cauliflower, allowing steam to heat sauce. Serves 6.

Approximate nutritional analysis per serving:
Calories 42, Protein 3 g, Carbohydrates 6 g, Fat < 1 g,
Cholesterol 2 mg, Sodium 39 mg

Opposite: Almond-Broccoli Stir Fry

MUSTARD-GLAZED CARROTS

3 tbs (45 ml) firmly packed, dark brown sugar
2 tbs (30 ml) Dijon mustard
¾ tsp (4 ml) salt
⅔ cup (160 ml) BLUE DIAMOND
    Blanched Slivered Almonds
2 tbs (30 ml) butter, divided
1 tbs (15 ml) vegetable oil
1 lb (455 g) carrots, peeled and
    sliced thinly on diagonal
2 large stalks celery, sliced thinly on diagonal
2 cloves garlic, chopped finely
1 tbs (15 ml) chopped, fresh parsley

Combine first 3 ingredients and reserve. Sauté almonds in
butter and oil until golden. Add carrots and sauté over medium
heat until barely tender, about 3 minutes. Add celery and garlic
and sauté until vegetables are just tender, about 1 minute. Stir
in mustard mixture and continue cooking, stirring constantly,
until carrots are glazed, about 1 minute. Stir in parsley.
Serves 6.

Approximate nutritional analysis per serving:
Calories 187, Protein 4 g, Carbohydrates 14 g, Fat 14 g,
Cholesterol 10 mg, Sodium 374 mg

CORN MEDITERRANEAN STYLE

3 tsp (15 ml) BERTOLLI Extra Virgin Olive Oil
½ garlic clove, crushed through a press
2 cups (240 ml) corn kernels
¼ tsp (1 ml) finely chopped fresh thyme
freshly ground black pepper, to taste

Combine the oil and garlic in a small skillet. Heat over low heat
just until the garlic begins to sizzle. Add the corn and stir to
blend and heat through, about 1 minute. Add thyme or
rosemary and a light grinding of black pepper. Serve at once.
Serves 4.

Approximate nutritional analysis per serving:
Calories 97, Protein 2 g, Carbohydrates 15 g, Fat 4 g,
Cholesterol 0 mg, Sodium 12 mg

CORN ON THE COB

6 ears corn
½ cup (120 ml) softened butter
1 tbs (15 ml) McCORMICK/SCHILLING
    Season-All Seasoned Salt
½ tsp (3 ml) McCORMICK/SCHILLING
    Black Pepper

Put 6 ears corn on individual sheets of heavy-duty aluminum
foil. Brush with a mixture of butter, Season-All Seasoned Salt
and Black Pepper. Wrap tightly. Cook on grill 20 minutes.
Turn occasionally. Serves 6.

Approximate nutritional analysis per serving:
Calories 207, Protein 3 g, Carbohydrates 17 g, Fat 16 g,
Cholesterol 41 mg, Sodium 183 mg

SALSA CORN NIBBLERS

4 fresh or frozen ears of corn
1 - 16 oz jar (480 ml) CHI-CHI'S Salsa

In Dutch oven, bring 3 qts of water to a boil. Add corn; cook 5-
8 minutes or until tender. Cool corn slightly; cut into 2-inch
slices. In large bowl, combine corn and salsa. Mix well. Cover;
refrigerate at least 4 hours or up to 24 hours. Serve chilled or at
room temperature. Serves 4.

Approximate nutritional analysis per serving:
Calories 110, Protein 4 g, Carbohydrates 26 g, Fat 1 g,
Cholesterol 0 mg, Sodium 550 mg

GREEN PEAS, POTATOES AND PROSCIUTTO

2 cups (480 ml) diced peeled potatoes
1 cup (240 ml) fresh or frozen tiny green peas
1 tbs (15 ml) minced prosciutto or ham
2 tsp (10 ml) BERTOLLI Classico or
    Extra Virgin Olive Oil
freshly ground black pepper

Cook the potatoes in boiling salted water until almost tender,
about 8 minutes. Add the peas and cook 1 minute. Drain.
Add the prosciutto and olive oil to the vegetable mixture.
Season with black pepper and serve.

Approximate nutritional analysis per serving:
Calories 115, Protein 4 g, Carbohydrates 19 g, Fat 3 g,
Cholesterol 1 mg, Sodium 34 mg

Opposite: Mustard-Glazed Carrots

SPANISH SWEET ONION SLICES
WITH PINEAPPLE SALSA

3 large Idaho-Oregon Spanish Sweet onions, peeled
1 - 15½ oz can (465 g) pineapple tidbits, drained
2 tbs (30 ml) chopped cilantro
2 tbs (30 ml) lime juice
1 tbs (15 ml) sugar
1 tbs (15 ml) olive oil
¾ tsp (4 ml) grated ginger root, optional
⅛ tsp (.5 ml) ground white pepper

Cut 2 - ½-inch slices from center of each onion; cover and refrigerate. Chop end pieces of onions to equal 2½ cups. Microwave chopped onions in 1-qt microwave-safe measure at HIGH 3-4 minutes or until softened. Cool. Combine 1½ cups pineapple and remaining ingredients in food processor or blender container and process ingredients, on pulse setting, just until mixture is blended and pineapple is finely chopped. Stir in remaining pineapple tidbits. Cover and refrigerate until served. For each serving, top one center-cut onion slice with ⅓ cup salsa. Serves 6.

Approximate nutritional analysis per serving:
Calories 141, Protein 3 g, Carbohydrates 29 g, Fat 3 g,
Cholesterol 0 mg, Sodium 7 mg

SWEET AND SPICY ALMOND GREEN BEANS

1 lb (455 g) green beans, cut into lengthwise strips
½ cup (120 ml) **BLUE DIAMOND**
    Chopped Natural Almonds
1 tbs (15 ml) vegetable oil
2 tbs (30 ml) butter
1 clove garlic, chopped finely
1 tbs (15 ml) firmly packed, brown sugar
2-3 tsp (10-15 ml) lemon juice
¼ tsp (1 ml) red pepper flakes
¼ tsp (1 ml) salt

Plunge green beans into salted, boiling water. Cook until just tender, about 3-4 minutes. Drain and rinse in cold water. Sauté almonds in oil until crisp. Add butter to pan and add green beans. Stir to coat and heat. Stir in garlic, sugar, lemon juice, red pepper flakes, and salt. Cook, stirring constantly, until sugar dissolves and beans are glazed, about 30 seconds. Serves 6.

Approximate nutritional analysis per serving:
Calories 151, Protein 4 g, Carbohydrates 10 g, Fat 12 g,
Cholesterol 10 mg, Sodium 96 mg

Above: Onion Slices with Pineapple Salsa

CREAMED PEAS

1 cup (240 ml) **DANNON Plain Nonfat or
    Lowfat Yogurt**
2 tbs (30 ml) **all-purpose flour**
2 tbs (30 ml) **finely chopped fresh dill weed** *or*
1 tsp (5 ml) **dried dill weed**
1 - 2 oz jar (60 g) **diced pimiento, drained**
½ tsp (3 ml) **salt**
¼ tsp (1 ml) **pepper**
1½ cups (355 ml) **fresh or frozen English peas**
3 tbs (45 ml) **chicken broth**

In a small bowl combine yogurt, flour, dill weed, pimiento, salt and pepper; stir until smooth. Set aside.

In small saucepan combine peas and broth; cover and bring to a boil. Reduce heat and simmer 5 minutes or until peas are tender. Stir in yogurt mixture; cook over low heat until thickened, stirring constantly. Serves 4.

Approximate nutritional analysis per serving:
Calories 103, Protein 7 g, Carbohydrates 17 g, Fat 1 g,
Cholesterol 3 mg, Sodium 310 mg

GUISANTES EXTREMEÑO

Peas with Ham

1 - 16 oz can (480 g) **GOYA Green Peas, drained**
2 tbs (30 ml) **minced onion**
4 tbs (60 ml) **minced carrot**
2 tbs (30 ml) **GOYA Olive Oil**
¼ lb (115 g) **prosciutto, diced**
pepper to taste

In a skillet, sauté onions and carrots in olive oil until onions are soft. Add prosciutto and sauté very lightly. Add peas, and pepper to taste. Heat, and serve. Serves 4.

Approximate nutritional analysis per serving:
Calories 165, Protein 10 g, Carbohydrates 12 g, Fat 9 g,
Cholesterol 15 mg, Sodium 618 mg

CASHEW SUGAR SNAP PEAS

1 - 16 oz pkg (480 g) **GREEN GIANT SELECT
    Frozen Sugar Snap Peas**
⅓ cup (80 ml) **orange juice**
1 tbs (15 ml) **honey**
1 tsp (5 ml) **cornstarch**
⅛ tsp (.5 ml) **salt**
½ tsp (3 ml) **grated orange peel, if desired**
¼ cup (60 ml) **cashews**

Cook peas to desired doneness as directed on package; drain. Meanwhile, in small saucepan, mix orange juice, honey, cornstarch and salt until well blended. Cook over medium heat until mixture boils and thickens, stirring constantly. Stir in orange peel and cashews; gently stir into peas. Serves 6.

Approximate nutritional analysis per serving:
Calories 90, Protein 3 g, Carbohydrates 14 g, Fat 3 g,
Cholesterol 0 mg, Sodium 85 mg

VEGETABLE CHEESE BAKED POTATO

3 - 3 oz (540 g) **large baking potatoes**
2 tbs (30 ml) **skim milk**
¼ cup (60 ml) **sliced green onion**
¼ tsp (1 ml) **pepper**
½ cup (120 ml) **broccoli flowerettes**
½ cup (120 ml) **sweet red pepper, cut into strips**
½ cup (120 ml) **cauliflower flowerettes**
½ cup (120 ml) **water**
½ lb (230 g) **HEALTHY CHOICE Fat Free
    Pasteurized Process Cheese Product,
    cut into 1-inch cubes**
½ cup (120 ml) **skim milk**
¼ tsp (1 ml) **dill weed**

Heat oven to 350°F (180°C). Clean and scrub potatoes. Prick several times with fork. Bake directly on oven rack for 1 hour or until softened. Remove from oven and cut potatoes lengthwise in half. Holding each potato half in a towel, scoop out center leaving ¼-inch shell. With mixer, beat together cooked potato, 2 tbs skim milk, green onions, and pepper; beat until smooth. Fill potato shells with potato mixture and keep warm.

Cook broccoli, red pepper slices and cauliflower in water until crisp-tender. Drain. In same saucepan, place cheese cubes and milk. Cook over medium heat, stirring occasionally, until cheese melts. Stir in vegetables and dill weed. Serve over potatoes. Serves 6.

Approximate nutritional analysis per serving:
Calories 103, Protein 10 g, Carbohydrates 16 g, Fat 0 g,
Cholesterol 7 mg, Sodium 547 mg

POTATO AND APPLE SAUTÉ

2 medium baking potatoes, peeled and diced
4 strips bacon, diced
3 tbs (45 ml) olive oil
½ cup (120 ml) BLUE DIAMOND
    Chopped Natural Almonds
1 cup (240 ml) chopped onion
1 small, tart green apple, peeled, cored, and diced
1 tsp (5 ml) sugar
½ tsp (3 ml) salt
1 tsp (5 ml) black pepper

Cook potatoes in salted, boiling water until barely tender. Drain and reserve. Sauté bacon in oil until it begins to soften and turns translucent. Add almonds and sauté until almonds are crisp. Remove bacon and almonds with a slotted spoon. Drain on paper towel. In fat remaining in pan, sauté onion until translucent. Add potatoes and sauté until potatoes and onions start to turn golden. Add apples and continue to cook until apples are cooked but still hold their shape. Return bacon and almonds to pan. Sprinkle with sugar and salt. Sauté 1-2 minutes longer until sugar dissolves. Stir in pepper. Serves 6.

Approximate nutritional analysis per serving:
Calories 213, Protein 5 g, Carbohydrates 18 g, Fat 15 g,
Cholesterol 4 mg, Sodium 249 mg

ZUCCHINI POTATO LATKES

2 zucchini
4 large potatoes, peeled, quartered or cut to fit
    processor feed tube. (Place in bowl of water
    to avoid browning.)*
1 large onion, peeled and quartered
3 large eggs
3 tbs (45 ml) flour
1 tbs (15 ml) chopped dill
salt and pepper to taste
vegetable oil to fry

*Note: If using food processor, use steel blade on half and grater on rest to get best consistency.

In food processor, fitted with the grater, grate the zucchini. Squeeze out extra liquid and place in a large bowl. Grate half the potatoes and squeeze out liquid. Quickly add this to the zucchini, add eggs and flour. In the processor fitted with the metal blade, grate onion and remaining potato. Add this to the zucchini potato mixture. Add dill, salt and pepper to taste. Stir to blend well.

In a large heavy skillet heat ⅛-¼-inch vegetable oil. With a tablespoon, spoon mixture into hot oil, brown on both sides. Drain on brown paper or paper towels. Serve hot with applesauce. Serves 8.

Approximate nutritional analysis per serving w/o applesauce:
Calories 145, Protein 5 g, Carbohydrates 20 g, Fat 6 g,
Cholesterol 80 mg, Sodium 29 mg

Courtesy of the Empire Kosher Poultry Test Kitchens.

NEW POTATOES WITH OLIVE AIOLI

2 lbs (910 g) small red-skinned potatoes
2 tbs (30 ml) lemon juice
1 tbs (15 ml) Dijon mustard
1 egg yolk
1 tsp (5 ml) minced garlic
⅔ cup (160 ml) olive oil
1 tsp (5 ml) chopped fresh rosemary leaves
½ cup (120 ml) whole pitted CALIFORNIA ripe olives
chopped fresh parsley or herbs

Cover potatoes with water in large saucepan, cover, bring to boil and simmer for 15-20 minutes, or until barely tender. Meanwhile, combine lemon juice, mustard, egg yolk and garlic in electric blender and whir until smooth. Continue whirring, slowly adding oil. Turn off blender, add rosemary and olives then "pulse", off and on, until olives are finely chopped but not pureed. Slice hot cooked potatoes, turn onto serving platter and ribbon sauce down center. Sprinkle with parsley. Serves 6.

Approximate nutritional analysis per serving:
Calories 363, Protein 3 g, Carbohydrates 32 g, Fat 26 g,
Cholesterol 35 mg, Sodium 103 mg

HERBED CHEESE MASHED POTATOES

2 tbs (30 ml) FLEISCHMANN'S Margarine
¼ cup (60 ml) chopped scallions
2 cloves garlic, minced
2 lbs (910 g) potatoes, peeled, cubed and cooked
½ cup (120 ml) nonfat yogurt
½ cup (120 ml) skim milk
2 oz (60 g) reduced fat Jarlsberg cheese, grated

In large saucepan, melt margarine. Add scallions and garlic; cook until tender. Add hot cooked potatoes, yogurt, milk and cheese. Mash until smooth and well blended. Serve immediately. Serves 6.

Approximate nutritional analysis per serving:
Calories 214, Protein 6 g, Carbohydrates 33 g, Fat 5 g,
Cholesterol 5 mg, Sodium 105 mg

Golden Parmesan Potatoes

GOLDEN PARMESAN POTATOES

2 lbs (910 g) new potatoes, cut into quarters
¹⁄₃ cup (80 ml) olive oil
1 ¹⁄₂ tsp (8 ml) Italian seasoning
2 cloves garlic, minced
1 cup (240 ml) KRAFT 100% Grated
    Parmesan Cheese

Heat oven to 400°F (205°C). Toss potatoes with oil, seasoning and garlic. Add cheese; mix lightly. Place in 15x10x1-inch baking pan. Bake 45 minutes. Serves 8.

Approximate nutritional analysis per serving:
Calories 234, Protein 7 g, Carbohydrates 23 g, Fat 13 g,
Cholesterol 10 mg, Sodium 238 mg

TEXAS POTATO TOPPER

1 cup (240 ml) DANNON Plain Nonfat or
    Lowfat Yogurt
¹⁄₃ cup (80 ml) mild or medium chunky salsa
¹⁄₃ cup (80 ml) chopped stuffed green olives

In a small bowl combine yogurt, salsa and olives. Cover; chill until ready to serve. To serve, spoon onto baked potato halves. Serves 10.

Approximate nutritional analysis per 1 tbs serving:
Calories 10, Protein 1 g, Carbohydrates 2g, Fat < 1 g,
Cholesterol 1 mg, Sodium 91 mg

CALIFORNIA CHEESE POTATOES

1 cup (240 ml) **CALIFORNIA ripe olive wedges**
½ cup (120 ml) **minced red bell pepper**
1 tsp (5 ml) **minced jalapeño pepper**
3 cups (720 ml) **sliced cooked red skin potatoes**
1 tsp (5 ml) **garlic salt**
½ tsp (1 ml) **white pepper**
¼ cup (60 ml) **butter or margarine**
3 tbs (45 ml) **flour**
1¾ cups (415 ml) **milk**
1 cup (240 ml) **grated cheddar cheese**

Combine first 6 ingredients. Stir gently to mix well. Melt butter over medium heat. Add flour. Stir just until mixture is golden, about 5 minutes. Add milk gradually, stirring with wire whip. Heat to boil. Reduce heat to simmer. Simmer, stirring occasionally, for 20 minutes. Add cheese. Stir just until melted. Add sauce to reserved olive mixture. Transfer to shallow casserole dish sprayed with nonstick spray. Bake uncovered in preheated 350°F (180°C) oven until golden brown and bubbly, about 25-30 minutes. Serves 6.

Approximate nutritional analysis per serving:
Calories 140, Protein 2 g, Carbohydrates 14 g,
Fat 9 g, Cholesterol 21 mg, Sodium 305 mg

DAKOTA POTATO TOPPER

1 cup (240 ml) **DANNON Plain Nonfat or**
  Lowfat Yogurt
3 tbs (45 ml) **bacon bits**
2 tsp (10 ml) **prepared white horseradish**

In a small bowl combine yogurt, bacon bits and horseradish. Cover; chill until ready to serve. To serve, spoon onto baked potato halves. Serves 8.

Approximate nutritional analysis per 1 tbs serving:
Calories 10, Protein 2 g, Carbohydrates 2 g, Fat 0 g,
Cholesterol 3 mg, Sodium 46 mg

SAVORY MASHED POTATOES

1 tbs (15 ml) **olive oil**
1 tbs (15 ml) **minced garlic**
4 cups (960 ml) **water**
4 medium russet, **peeled and cut into quarters**
1 cup (240 ml) **DANNON Plain Nonfat or**
  Lowfat Yogurt
¼ cup (60 ml) **milk**
¼ cup (60 ml) **sliced scallions or green onions**
1 tsp (5 ml) **salt**
¼ tsp (1 ml) **freshly ground pepper**

In a large heavy saucepan or Dutch oven heat oil over medium-low heat. Add garlic; cook and stir 1 minute, stirring constantly, until fragrant but not browned. Add water and potatoes. Cover and bring to a boil over high heat. Reduce heat to medium-low and simmer 15-20 minutes or until potatoes are very tender. Drain well. Return potatoes to saucepan and mash. Add yogurt and milk and stir until creamy. Stir in scallions, salt and pepper. Serve immediately. Serves 8.

Approximate nutritional analysis per serving:
Calories 138, Protein 4 g, Carbohydrates 26 g, Fat 3 g,
Cholesterol 3 mg, Sodium 296 mg

SALINAS VALLEY POTATO TOPPER

1 tbs (15 ml) **margarine or butter**
½ cup (120 ml) **chopped fresh broccoli flowerets**
1 cup (240 ml) **DANNON Plain Nonfat or**
  Lowfat Yogurt
¼ cup (60 ml) **shredded part-skim mozzarella cheese**
paprika

In a small heavy saucepan over medium heat melt margarine. Add broccoli; cook and stir just until tender. Remove from heat. Stir in yogurt and mozzarella. To serve, spoon onto baked potato halves and sprinkle with paprika. Serves 10.

Approximate nutritional analysis per 1 tbs serving:
Calories 10, Protein 2 g, Carbohydrates 2 g, Fat 2 g,
Cholesterol 6 mg, Sodium 31 mg

LITTLE ITALY POTATO TOPPER

1 cup (240 ml) **DANNON Plain Nonfat or**
  Lowfat Yogurt
½ cup (120 ml) **tomato, chopped**
2 tbs (30 ml) **grated Parmesan cheese**
1 tbs (15 ml) **chopped fresh basil leaves *or***
  ½ tsp (3 ml) **dried basil**
1 tbs (15 ml) **fresh oregano *or***
  ¼ tsp (1 ml) **dried oregano**
¼ tsp (1 ml) **salt**

In small bowl combine yogurt, tomato, cheese, basil, oregano and salt. Cover; chill until ready to serve. To serve, spoon onto baked potato halves. Serves 10.

Approximate nutritional analysis per 1 tbs serving:
Calories 10, Protein 2 g, Carbohydrates 2 g, Fat < 1 g,
Cholesterol 2 mg, Sodium 93 mg

MASHED GREEN CHILI POTATOES

12 medium red new potatoes, peeled
2 tsp (10 ml) beef bouillon granules
4 large garlic cloves
1 - 4¼ oz can (135 g) CHI-CHI'S
Diced Green Chilies, drained
2 tbs (30 ml) butter or margarine, if desired

In Dutch oven or large saucepan, place potatoes, bouillon and whole garlic cloves. Cover with water; bring to a boil. Reduce heat to low. Simmer 30-35 minutes or until potatoes are very tender. Remove potatoes and garlic to a large bowl. Mash with potato masher until there are few lumps, adding some of the cooking water as necessary to keep mixture moist. Stir in chilies. Stir in butter, if desired. Serves 5.

Approximate nutritional analysis per serving:
Calories 90, Protein 3 g, Carbohydrates 20 g, Fat 0 g,
Cholesterol 0 mg, Sodium 140 mg

YAMS WITH ORANGES

6 yams or sweet potatoes, fully cooked and cooled
2 navel oranges, thinly sliced
¼-¾ cup (120-180 ml) butter
¾ cup (180 ml) brown sugar
1 cup (240 ml) FLORIDA'S NATURAL
Brand Orange Juice
1 cup (240 ml) chopped fresh or frozen cranberries
2 tbs (30 ml) fresh lemon juice, or more to taste

Preheat oven to 375°F (190°C).

Peel the sweet potatoes and slice thinly. Place one layer in a shallow buttered baking dish. Top with a layer of orange slices. Dot generously with butter and sprinkle with sugar. Continue, making 3 layers, ending with a layer of potatoes, butter and sugar.

Mix the FLORIDA'S NATURAL Brand Orange Juice and cranberries with the lemon juice and pour over the potatoes. Bake until a pleasant syrup has formed and the top is tinged with brown, 1½ hours. Serves 8.

Approximate nutritional analysis per serving:
Calories 341, Protein 3 g, Carbohydrates 58 g, Fat 12 g,
Cholesterol 31 mg, Sodium 23 mg

Yams with Oranges

OVEN-ROASTED POTATOES

1 lb (455 g) small, new potatoes
1 red bell pepper, coarsely chopped
2 tbs (30 ml) soy oil
2 tbs (30 ml) chopped fresh rosemary
4 cloves garlic, minced
¼ cup (60 ml) sliced shallots
salt and pepper to taste

Preheat oven to 475°F (246°C). Cut potatoes into wedges. In a bowl, combine the rest of the ingredients. Toss well with the potatoes. Arrange the potatoes in a single layer on cookie sheet and bake for 30-35 minutes until tender and lightly browned, tossing 2-3 times during baking. Serves 4.

Approximate nutritional analysis per serving:
Calories 161, Protein 4 g, Carbohydrates 28 g, Fat 4 g,
Cholesterol 0 mg, Sodium 8 mg

MASHED SWEET NEW YEAR POTATOES

1 lb (455 g) sweet potatoes, peeled and cubed
2 lbs (910 g) all-purpose potatoes, peeled and cubed
1 tbs (15 ml) margarine
¾-1 cup (180-240 ml) kosher chicken broth
salt and pepper, to taste
1 tbs (15 ml) chopped fresh Italian parsley

Place the potatoes in a large saucepan, cover with cold water and bring to a boil. Reduce heat, maintain a slight boil and cook 20-30 minutes or until tender. Drain potatoes, return them to saucepan and shake pan over low heat to remove remaining moisture. Transfer potatoes to a large bowl or an electric mixer and begin mashing by hand or slowly with mixer. Add broth, margarine, salt and pepper to the mixture. Beat until just smooth, lumps are O.K. Stir in parsley and serve at once or keep warm in a pan over hot water. Serves 8.

Approximate nutritional analysis per serving:
Calories 170, Protein 3 g, Carbohydrates 37 g, Fat 2 g,
Cholesterol 0 mg, Sodium 32 mg

Courtesy of the Empire Kosher Poultry Test Kitchens.

BAKED YAMS

Scrub, trim and dry well. Rub with fat or oil. Arrange on baking sheet. Preheat oven to 400°F (205°C). Bake for 15 minutes, reduce temperature to 375°F (190°C), and bake medium size potatoes about 1½ hours, or until soft. Large potatoes may require longer time. Fresh, uncured potatoes will not bake successfully.

Oven-Roasted Potatoes

MICROWAVING LOUISIANA YAMS

Microwaved yams have a different texture and flavor from yams cooked conventionally. They do not develop the sweet, syrupy taste of yams baked conventionally. Some people like them and others prefer baking yams conventionally, freezing them and reheating in the microwave. Yams may be microwaved for use in recipes calling for cooked yams.

To microwave yams, scrub them and prick with a fork or knife. This allows steam to escape and prevents the potato from popping. Arrangement is most important. To cook evenly, yams are placed in a circular arrangement with the smaller ends toward the center. Place in microwave on paper towel. Rearrange once during cooking time. Let stand three minutes to complete cooking. Dry or old potatoes do not microwave well whole. Peel and dice them before microwaving.

MICROWAVE TIME ON HIGH

1 potato	4-6 minutes
2 potatoes	6-8 minutes
3 potatoes	8-12 minutes
4 potatoes	12-16 minutes

Approximate nutritional analysis per yam:
Calories 158, Protein 2 g, Carbohydrates 37 g, Fat 0 g,
Cholesterol 0 mg, Sodium 20 mg

Courtesy of the Louisiana Sweet Potato Commission.

SWEET POTATO TOPPER

1 cup (240 ml) **LAND O LAKES No-Fat,**
  Light or Regular Sour Cream
2 tsp (10 ml) dried basil leaves
1 cup (240 ml) water
2 cups (480 ml) coarsely chopped broccoli
2 medium carrots, thinly sliced
2 tsp (10 ml) **LAND O LAKES Butter, softened**
½ tsp (3 ml) Italian herb seasoning*
½ tsp (3 ml) garlic powder
1 small onion, coarsely chopped
1 small red pepper, cut into ½-inch pieces
4 hot roasted sweet potatoes, cut in half lengthwise
2 oz (60 g) light cheddar or mozzarella cheese,
  shredded

In small bowl stir together No-Fat Sour Cream and basil; set aside. In 10-inch nonstick skillet bring water to a full boil; add broccoli and carrots. Cook until crispy tender, 2-3 minutes; drain. In same skillet melt butter until sizzling; stir in Italian herb seasoning and garlic powder. Add broccoli, carrots, onion and red pepper. Cook over medium heat, stirring constantly until vegetables are crisply tender, 2-3 minutes. Set aside; keep warm. Heat broiler. Place roasted potatoes on broiler pan. Spread No-Fat Sour Cream mixture evenly over potato halves. Divide vegetable mixture evenly among potato halves; top each with 1 tbs shredded cheese. Broil 3-5 inches from heat until cheese is melted, 1-3 minutes. Serves 8.

Approximate nutritional analysis per serving:
Calories 130, Protein 6 g, Carbohydrates 23 g, Fat 2 g,
Cholesterol 10 mg, Sodium 120 mg

TWICE-BAKED SWEET POTATOES

2 sweet potatoes
2 tsp (10 ml) reduced fat butter or margarine
⅓ cup (80 ml) skim milk
¼ tsp (1 ml) cinnamon
¼ tsp (1 ml) nutmeg
dash ginger

Wrap sweet potatoes in aluminum foil, pierce, and bake in an iron skillet, Dutch oven, or pan. Bake 20 minutes at 500°F (260°C), lower oven to 400°F (205°C), bake until tender. Let sweet potato cool. Cut in half, remove pulp, save skins. Mix pulp with ⅓ cup skim milk, cinnamon, nutmeg, and ginger. Add 2 tsp of reduced fat butter or margarine to pulp mixture. Beat pulp mixture with an electric mixer until smooth. Spoon pulp into shells, bake on baking sheet for 10-15 minutes at 350°F (180°C). Serves 4.

Approximate nutritional analysis per serving:
Calories 133, Protein 2 g, Carbohydrates 29 g, Fat 1 g,
Cholesterol 3 mg, Sodium 24 mg

CANDIED SWEET POTATOES

2 large sweet potatoes
3 tbs (45 ml) brown sugar
1 tbs (15 ml) reduced fat butter or margarine
¼ cup (60 ml) orange juice
¼ tsp (1 ml) cinnamon
¼ tsp (1 m l) nutmeg

Wash sweet potatoes, peel and slice into ½-inch slices. Place sweet potatoes in baking pan. Arrange slices in a single layer, ½-inch apart. Mix brown sugar, orange juice, spices together. Pour mixture on top of sweet potato slices. Dot sweet potatoes with reduced fat butter or margarine. Cover and bake at 375°F (190°C) for 30 minutes, or until tender. Serves 4.

Approximate nutritional analysis per serving:
Calories 141, Protein 1 g, Carbohydrates 30 g, Fat 2 g,
Cholesterol 5 mg, Sodium 13 mg

Courtesy of the Louisiana Sweet Potato Commission.

BAKED HONEY SWEET POTATO

Wrap sweet potato in foil. Bake at 500°F (260°C) for 20 minutes, lower oven to 400°F (205°C), bake until tender. Let potato cool. Cut potato in half. Scoop out pulp, saving the shell. Add to pulp 1 tsp (5 ml) honey, cinnamon, ginger, nutmeg to taste. Beat potato mixture with electric mixer until smooth. Spoon mixture back into shells. Bake at 350°F (180°C) for 20 minutes.

Approximate nutritional analysis per serving:
Calories 90, Protein 1 g, Carbohydrates 21 g, Fat < 1 g,
Cholesterol 0 mg, Sodium 10 mg

Courtesy of the Louisiana Sweet Potato Commission.

WHIPPED YAMS

Whipped yams form the basis for many interesting dishes. Fresh or canned yams may be used. Bake or boil yams in skins, or pare thin, cut and cook in small amount of water until tender. If canned yams are used, boil gently until most of the liquid has evaporated before whipping (gives a better flavor, retains some of the minerals and vitamins). Whip while hot. Do not scrape beaters because all the undesirable fibers cling to them.

PRUNE-STUFFED YAMS

6 medium LOUISIANA yams
1 tbs (15 ml) grated orange peel
½ cup (120 ml) orange juice
¼ tsp (1 ml) salt
¼ cup (60 ml) butter or margarine
1 cup (240 ml) cooked prunes, pitted and halved
2 tbs (30 ml) slivered almonds

Bake yams in 400°F (205°C) oven 15 minutes. Lower temperature to 375°F (190°C) and bake 45 minutes or until tender. Score lengthwise and crosswise and scoop out yam centers, leaving ¼-inch shells. Mash yams; add orange peel and juice, salt and butter; whip well. Fold in prunes. Divide equally among yam shells; sprinkle with almonds. Return to oven to heat through, about 5-10 minutes. Serves 6.

Approximate nutritional analysis per serving:
Calories 289, Protein 4 g, Carbohydrates 49 g, Fat 10 g,
Cholesterol 21 mg, Sodium 111 mg

LOUISIANA YAM PATTYCAKES

4 medium LOUISIANA yams, cooked, peeled and
**   mashed *or* 2 - 16 oz cans (960 g) LOUISIANA**
**   yams, drained and mashed**
1 cup (240 ml) toasted rice cereal, Rice Krispies
⅓ cup (80 ml) finely chopped celery
¼ cup (60 ml) finely chopped onion
2 tbs (30 ml) flour, plus extra for baking sheet
¾ tsp (4 ml) salt
dash pepper
1 egg
3 tbs (45 ml) butter or margarine
3 tbs (45 ml) salad oil
apple butter or apple sauce

Combine yams, cereal, celery, onion, 2 tbs flour, salt, pepper and the egg; mix well. Drop by rounded tablespoonfuls onto lightly floured baking sheet; shape into patties. Chill for about 1 hour to firm.

In large skillet, heat butter and oil together. With spatula, lift each patty off baking sheet and lightly coat with flour. Fry in butter and oil over medium-low heat until lightly browned on each side, about 2-3 minutes per side, turning once. Serves 20.

Approximate nutritional analysis per patty:
Calories 78, Protein 1 g, Carbohydrates 9 g, Fat 4 g,
Cholesterol 15 mg, Sodium 106 mg

GALLEY YAMS AND APPLES

1 cup (240 ml) diagonally slice celery
¼ cup (60 ml) butter or margarine
4 LOUISIANA yams, cooked, peeled and halved *or*
**   2 - 16 oz cans (960 g) LOUISIANA yams, drained**
2½ cup s (590 ml) canned apple slices
1 tbs (15 ml) chopped chives
½ tsp (3 ml) grated lemon peel

In same skillet, sauté celery in butter 5 minutes. Add remaining ingredients and cook covered 5 minutes or until heated through. Serves 8.

Approximate nutritional analysis per serving:
Calories 175, Protein 2 g, Carbohydrates 30 g, Fat 6 g,
Cholesterol 16 mg, Sodium 26 mg

SWEET POTATO PONE

2 cups (480 ml) grated raw yams
½ cup (120 ml) sugar
¼ cup (60 ml) Karo or Cane syrup
½ tsp (3 ml) cinnamon
1 egg
¼ cup (60 ml) flour
½ tsp (3 ml) baking powder
½ stick butter
¼ cup (60 ml) evaporated milk
½ tsp (3 ml) vanilla extract

Mix all ingredients. Pour into casserole and bake at 350°F (180°C) for 45 minutes to 1 hour. Serves 10.

Approximate nutritional analysis per serving:
Calories 194, Protein 2 g, Carbohydrates 34 g, Fat 6 g,
Cholesterol 36 mg, Sodium 44 mg

Courtesy of Louisiana Sweet Potatoes.

Caramelized Spanish Sweet Onion Slices

CARAMELIZED SPANISH SWEET ONION SLICES

3 large IDAHO-OREGON Spanish Sweet Onions
¼ cup (60 ml) vegetable oil, margarine or butter
¾ cup (180 ml) granulated sugar
3 tbs (45 ml) packed brown sugar
2 tsp (10 ml) dried thyme, crushed
½ tsp (3 ml) salt
⅛ tsp (.5 ml) pepper

Peel and cut onions into ¾-1-inch slices. Microwave slices at HIGH 5 minutes. Heat oil in large skillet; add onion slices. Combine sugars, thyme, salt and pepper. Sprinkle 1 tbs sugar mixture over each slice; cook over medium-low heat about 10 minutes on first side. Turn slices, sprinkle each with 1 tbs sugar mixture and cook 10 minutes longer. Turn slices and cook 1 minute to caramelize sugar topping. Keep warm and repeat procedure for remaining onion slices. Serves 4.

Approximate nutritional analysis per serving:
Calories 433, Protein 4 g, Carbohydrates 77 g, Fat 14 g,
Cholesterol 0 mg, Sodium 280 mg

BROWN SUGARED TOMATOES

6 medium tomatoes
3 slices bread, trimmed, cubed
⅓ cup (80 ml) butter or margarine, melted
⅓ cup (80 ml) IMPERIAL Brown Sugar
¾ tsp (4 ml) salt
dash pepper
chopped parsley

Slice top fourth of tomatoes on stem end. Scoop out tomato pulp and reserve, leaving shells. Place shells in greased baking pan. Combine bread cubes, 1 cup tomato pulp, melted butter, IMPERIAL Brown Sugar, seasonings. Blend. Fill tomato shells with mixture. Bake at 350°F (180°C) for 30 minutes. Garnish with chopped parsley. Serves 6.

Approximate nutritional analysis per serving:
Calories 200, Protein 2 g, Carbohydrates 25 g, Fat 11 g,
Cholesterol 0 mg, Sodium 489 mg

FRIED GREEN TOMATOES

4 large green FLORIDA tomatoes
¼ cup (60 ml) flour
1 tbs (15 ml) sugar
1½ tsp (8 ml) salt
⅛ tsp (.5 ml) ground black pepper
2 tbs (30 ml) bacon drippings or vegetable oil

Cut green tomatoes into ½-inch slices; set aside. Combine flour, sugar, salt, and black pepper. Lightly coat tomatoes on both sides with flour mixture. In a large skillet heat bacon drippings. Place tomatoes in skillet in single layer. Fry until brown on both sides; remove to hot platter and repeat with remaining tomatoes, adding additional bacon drippings, if needed. Serves 6.

Approximate nutritional analysis per serving:
Calories 35, Protein 1 g, Carbohydrates 6 g, Fat 1 g,
Cholesterol 0 mg, Sodium 10 mg

CHEESY BAKED SPINACH

4 slices bacon, cut into 2-inch pieces
1 lb (455 g) fresh spinach *or*
   1 - 12 oz pkg (360 g) frozen spinach, drained
½ tsp (3 ml) IMPERIAL Granulated Sugar
salt and pepper
½ lb (115 g) Swiss cheese, sliced

Cook bacon until crisp and drain on paper towel. Wash fresh spinach thoroughly and remove tough stems; or pour boiling water over frozen spinach to thaw. Arrange spinach over bottom of greased 1½-qt shallow bake-and-serve dish. Sprinkle spinach with IMPERIAL Granulated Sugar, salt and pepper. Cover with cheese slices. Distribute bacon over cheese. Bake in preheated 375°F (190°C) oven about 15 minutes, or until cheese is melted and spinach is tender. Serves 4.

Approximate nutritional analysis per serving:
Calories 166, Protein 13 g, Carbohydrates 6 g, Fat 11 g,
Cholesterol 31 mg, Sodium 514 mg

Fried Green Tomatoes

EASY TOMATO CREOLE

1 - 28 oz can (840 g) LIBBY'S Whole Peeled
    Tomatœs in juice
2 tbs (30 ml) butter
2-3 tsp (10-15 ml) curry powder
1 large onion, cut into rings
1 green pepper, cut into rings
¾ tsp (4 ml) salt
¼ tsp (1 ml) paprika
1 tbs (15 ml) brown sugar
1½ tbs (25 ml) flour
2 tbs (30 ml) white wine

Drain tomatoes, saving ½ cup juice. Melt butter over medium heat in skillet; add curry and cook a few minutes. Add tomatoes, onion and green pepper; cook until onion is translucent. Stir in salt, paprika and sugar. Stir flour into saved tomato juice; add to Creole, continue cooking until thickened. Add wine and serve hot. Serves 6.

Approximate nutritional analysis per serving:
Calories 101, Protein 2 g, Carbohydrates 14 g, Fat 4 g,
Cholesterol 10 mg, Sodium 498 mg

MATZAH SPINACH KUGEL

2 - 10 oz pkgs (600 g) frozen chopped spinach,
    defrosted
2 cups (480 ml) chopped leeks (white part only)
1 tbs (15 ml) vegetable oil
6 egg whites
2 whole eggs
1 tbs (15 ml) chopped parsley
1 tbs (15 ml) chopped dill
4 cups (960 ml) kosher for Passover matzah farfel
salt and pepper to taste
pinch of nutmeg
vegetable oil spray for pan
1 tbs (15 ml) matzah meal

Preheat oven to 350°F (180°C). Drain spinach in colander; squeeze out any extra water and set aside in a large bowl. In a skillet, sauté the leeks and/or onions in oil until soft. Remove from heat and add to drained spinach. In the work bowl of a food processor fitted with a metal blade, chop the herbs, add the 2 whole eggs, salt, pepper and nutmeg. Process for 2 minutes. Scrape down sides, pulse chop until greens are specks. Pour into the spinach mixture. Mix in matzah farfel. Beat egg whites, fold into mixture. Spray pan with oil, dust lightly with matzah meal. Pour mixture into pan and bake for 45 minutes. Cut into wedges and serve. Serves 8.

Approximate nutritional analysis per serving:
Calories 225, Protein 11 g, Carbohydrates 34 g, Fat 5 g,
Cholesterol 2 mg, Sodium 394 mg

SAUTÉED SPINACH WITH BASIL

1 tbs (15 ml) olive oil
3 cloves finely chopped garlic
4½ lbs (2 kg) fresh spinach, well rinsed and trimmed
1 cup (240 ml) fresh basil leaves
1 pinch red pepper flakes
1 tbs (15 ml) toasted pine nuts

In a large skillet, lightly brown the chopped garlic in oil. Add the washed spinach, cooking with just the water that clings to the leaves after washing. Add basil leaves, cook until just tender. Add red pepper and pine nuts and serve. Serves 6.

Approximate nutritional analysis per serving:
Calories 117, Protein 11 g, Carbohydrates 15 g, Fat 5 g,
Cholesterol 0 mg, Sodium 270 mg

Courtesy of the Empire Kosher Poultry Test Kitchens.

SQUASH WITH RIPE OLIVES

1 lb (455 g) zucchini
1 lb (455 g) yellow crookneck squash
1 - 10 oz can (300 g) whole kernel corn, drained
    or kernels cut from 2 ears fresh corn
1 small onion, chopped
2 tbs (30 ml) vegetable or olive oil
1 - 4 oz can (120 g) diced green chilies, drained
½ cup (120 ml) halved CALIFORNIA ripe olives
2 tsp (10 ml) ground cumin
8 yellow or blue corn tortillas, steamed

Dice unpared zucchini and crookneck. Sauté with corn and onion in oil in large skillet over high heat for 4 minutes or until nearly tender. Add chilies, olives and cumin and sauté 5 minutes longer. Serve with hot tortillas, to accompany grilled or broiled fish. Serves 6.

Approximate nutritional analysis per serving:
Calories 145, Protein 4 g, Carbohydrates 23 g, Fat 5 g,
Cholesterol 0 mg, Sodium 131 mg

SUPER ZUCCHINI CAKES

2 cups (480 ml) grated zucchini
2 eggs, beaten
1 cup (240 ml) seasoned bread crumbs
1 tbs (15 ml) mayonnaise
1 tbs (15 ml) OLD BAY Seasoning
2 tbs (30 ml) grated onion
flour for coating
oil for frying

Drain zucchini for 2 hours. In a large bowl mix all ingredients except flour and oil together. Form into cakes. Coat with flour. Fry in oil until brown on both sides. Serves 3.

Approximate nutritional analysis per serving:
Calories 294, Protein 9 g, Carbohydrates 29 g, Fat 16 g,
Cholesterol 144 mg, Sodium 325 mg

ZUCCHINI AND CORN SAUTÉ

1 tbs (15 ml) olive oil
½ cup (120 ml) chopped onion
1 clove garlic, minced
1½ cups (355 ml) zucchini, diced ½-inch
1 cup (240 ml) fresh or frozen whole kernel corn
1½ cups (355 ml) CHI-CHI'S Salsa
2 tbs (30 ml) chopped fresh cilantro

In large skillet, heat oil over medium-high heat until hot. Sauté onion and garlic 2 minutes. Stir in zucchini, corn and salsa. Reduce heat to low. Simmer, uncovered, about 8 minutes or until vegetables are tender. Stir in cilantro. Serve hot or at room temperature. Serves 6.

Approximate nutritional analysis per serving:
Calories 70, Protein 2 g, Carbohydrates 10 g, Fat 3 g,
Cholesterol 0 mg, Sodium 270 mg

PUREED CARROTS AND CELERY ROOT

2 lbs (910 g) carrots, peeled and sliced
1 lb (455 g) celery root, peeled and cut into cubes
6 sprigs parsley, tied with string
2 pears, or apples, peeled and cut into large pieces
juice of 1 lemon
3 cups (720 ml) kosher chicken broth
nutmeg, salt and pepper to taste

Note: Squeeze lemon juice in bowl of cold water. As you cut up pear and celery root, place in the water to retard oxidation (browning).

Drain celery root and pears, discard water. Place pieces in a large saucepan and add the carrots. Cover with the broth and bring to boil. Reduce heat, simmer until carrots are very tender. Drain, reserving ½ cup liquid. Transfer mixture to food processor in small batches and puree until smooth. Add broth as needed. Add nutmeg, salt and pepper to taste. At this point the puree can be refrigerated for a day.

To serve, heat in saucepan over low heat for 3-5 minutes *or* transfer puree to a baking dish, cover with lid or foil and bake in preheated 350°F (180°C) oven for 20-30 minutes until steaming hot. Serves 6.

Approximate nutritional analysis per serving:
Calories 120, Protein 3 g, Carbohydrates 28 g, Fat 1 g,
Cholesterol 0 mg, Sodium 305 mg

Courtesy of the Empire Kosher Poultry Test Kitchens.

MICROWAVED BROCCOLI-STUFFED VIDALIA ONIONS

3 large VIDALIA Onions
1 - 10 oz pkg frozen chopped broccoli
1 cup (240 ml) cheddar cheese, grated
¼ cup (60 ml) mayonnaise
1 can cream of celery soup
1 egg, beaten
¾ cup (180 ml) RITZ crackers, crushed

Remove stem and root ends of VIDALIAS, then cut in half and carefully press out center rings leaving a 2-3 ring shell. Place shells in baking dish and set aside. Chop the removed portion of VIDALIAS and set aside. Place broccoli in a bowl and microwave on HIGH 4 minutes, stirring once. Add chopped VIDALIAS and microwave on HIGH 2 minutes. Add remaining ingredients, mixing well. Stuff onion halves with filling, mounding slightly. Microwave uncovered on HIGH 11-13 minutes, or until shells are tender. Let stand 2 minutes. Serves 6.

Approximate nutritional analysis per serving:
Calories 248, Protein 11 g, Carbohydrates 29 g, Fat 11 g,
Cholesterol 61 mg, Sodium 555 mg

Opposite: Microwaved Broccoli-Stuffed Vidalia Onions

MEDITERRANEAN BAKED ZUCCHINI

1 cup (240 ml) CALIFORNIA ripe olive wedges
2 tbs (30 ml) chopped parsley
1 tbs (15 ml) chopped scallion greens
1 tbs (15 ml) lemon juice
6 Roma tomatoes, sliced
3 medium zucchini, sliced
2 tbs (30 ml) olive oil
½ tsp (3 ml) salt
¼ tsp (1 ml) black pepper

Combine first 4 ingredients in small bowl. Layer tomato and zucchini slices in casserole dish sprayed with non-stick spray. Sprinkle with olive mixture over the top. Sprinkle with olive oil, salt and pepper. Bake in preheated 350°F (180°C) oven until zucchini is tender, about 15-20 minutes. Serves 6.

Approximate nutritional analysis per serving:
Calories 92, Protein 2 g, Carbohydrates 9 g, Fat 7 g,
Cholesterol 0 mg, Sodium 314 mg

SUMMER HARVEST RATATOUILLE

1 tbs (15 ml) olive oil
1 cup (240 ml) chopped onion
4 cloves garlic, minced
2 small zucchini, cut into ½-inch pieces
1 small eggplant, peeled and cut into ½-inch cubes
1 red or yellow bell pepper, in ½-inch cubes
1 small green bell pepper, cut into ½-inch pieces
1 - 16 oz jar (480 ml) CHI-CHI'S Salsa
1 tsp (5 ml) dried thyme leaves, crushed
1 tsp (5 ml) dried rosemary leaves, crushed
1 tsp (5 ml) dried basil leaves, crushed
½ tsp (3 ml) salt
unsalted hulled pumpkin seeds, if desired

In large saucepan, sauté onion and garlic in oil 2 minutes. Stir in remaining ingredients except pumpkin seeds. Bring to a boil. Partially cover pan; reduce heat to low. Simmer 20-25 minutes or until vegetables are very tender and mixture is thick, stirring frequently. Serve vegetables hot or at room temperature sprinkled with pumpkin seeds, if desired. Serves 4.

Approximate nutritional analysis per serving:
Calories 110, Protein 3 g, Carbohydrates 17 g, Fat 4 g,
Cholesterol 0 mg, Sodium 810 mg

QUICK SUMMER SQUASH SAUTÉ

1 tbs (15 ml) butter
1 medium zucchini, sliced
1 large yellow squash, sliced
¼ cup (60 ml) chopped onion
1½ tsp (8 ml) fresh chopped basil leaves or
½ tsp (3 ml) McCORMICK/SCHILLING
    Basil Leaves
1 tsp (5 ml) GILROY FARMS Minced Garlic
¼-½ tsp (1-3 ml) salt
¼ tsp (1 ml) McCORMICK/SCHILLING
    Coarse Grind Black Pepper

Melt butter in large skillet over medium-high heat. Add zucchini, yellow squash and onion; sauté 2 minutes. Add remaining ingredients and sauté 2 minutes. Serves 4.

Approximate nutritional analysis per serving:
Calories 45, Protein 1 g, Carbohydrates 4 g, Fat 3 g,
Cholesterol 8 mg, Sodium 137 mg

OVEN-ROASTED VEGETABLES

1 envelope LIPTON Recipe Secrets Savory Herb
    with Garlic, Golden Herb with Lemon,
    Italian Herb with Tomato, Onion or Golden
    Onion Soup Mix
1½ lbs (685 g) assorted fresh vegetables (sliced:
    zucchini, yellow squash, red or green bell
    peppers, carrots, celery and mushrooms)
2 tbs (30 ml) olive or vegetable oil

Preheat oven to 450°F (230°C). In a large plastic bag or bowl, add all ingredients. Close bag and shake, or toss in bowl, until all vegetables are evenly coated. Empty vegetables into 13x9-inch baking or roasting pan; discard bag. Bake, stirring once, 20 minutes or until vegetables are tender. Serves 4.

Approximate nutritional analysis per serving:
Calories 69, Protein 2 g, Carbohydrates 6 g, Fat 5 g,
Cholesterol < 1 mg, Sodium 282 mg

Courtesy of The Lipton Kitchens.

Opposite: Oven-Roasted Vegetables

SANTA FE VEGETABLE MEDLEY

1 cup (240 ml) **CALIFORNIA** ripe olive wedges
½ cup (120 ml) tomato sauce
½ cup (120 ml) canned mushroom slices
½ cup (120 ml) canned sliced green chilies
2 tsp (10 ml) brown sugar
½ tsp (3 ml) onion powder
½ tsp (3 ml) garlic powder
2 tsp (10 ml) olive oil
½ cup (120 ml) sliced celery
½ cup (120 ml) minced onion
1 cup (240 ml) seeded and chopped tomato
2 cups (480 ml) corn kernels

Combine first 7 ingredients in small pot. Heat to a simmer. Heat olive oil in small pan and sauté celery and onion for 3-4 minutes. Add tomatoes and corn. Simmer 5 minutes. Add this mixture to tomato sauce. Simmer 5 minutes. Serves 6.

Approximate nutritional analysis per serving:
Calories 102, Protein 3 g, Carbohydrates 19 g, Fat 3 g,
Cholesterol 0 mg, Sodium 198 mg

Grilled Vegetables with Lemon and Herbs

GRILLED VEGETABLES WITH LEMON AND HERBS

1 medium eggplant
1 large red onion
1 large red pepper
1 large zucchini
⅓ cup (80 ml) lemon juice
2 tbs (30 ml) **FLEISCHMANN'S** Margarine, melted
1 tsp (5 ml) rosemary leaves, crushed
1 tsp (5 ml) thyme leaves, crushed
8 large mushrooms
2 cups (480 ml) cooked brown rice

In large pot, over high heat, heat a 2-inch depth of water to a boil; add eggplant, onion, pepper and zucchini. Reduce heat to low; cover and simmer 5-10 minutes or until pepper and zucchini are tender-crisp. Remove pepper and zucchini to plate to cool. Cover pot; cook onion and eggplant for 10-15 more minutes or until fork tender. Remove to plate to cool.

Cut zucchini, pepper and onion lengthwise in half; discard seeds from pepper. Cut eggplant in half, then cut each half into 4 pieces.

In small bowl, combine lemon juice, margarine and herbs. Grill or broil eggplant, onion, pepper, zucchini and mushrooms 6 inches from heat source for 10-12 minutes, turning occasionally and basting with lemon mixture frequently. Serve over rice. Serves 8.

Approximate nutritional analysis per serving:
Calories 122, Protein 3 g, Carbohydrates 22 g, Fat 4 g,
Cholesterol 0 mg, Sodium 36 mg

RATATOUILLE

2 - 28 oz cans (1.7 kg) **LIBBY'S** Whole Tomatoes
2 eggplants, unpeeled, diced into 1-inch cubes
olive oil
⅔ cup (160 ml) rosé wine
2 tbs (30 ml) olive oil
4 large cloves garlic, sliced
5 zucchini, sliced

Drain tomatoes, cutting in half to release juice. In heavy skillet brown eggplant in ½ cup olive oil until almost tender, then add ⅓ cup rosé wine. Using a slotted spoon, transfer eggplant to large saucepan. Add 2 tbs olive oil to liquid in skillet, brown garlic slightly and add zucchini. Cook over high heat until half done, stirring constantly; then transfer to saucepan. Quickly sauté tomatoes over high heat and transfer to saucepan. Add remaining wine to vegetables. Cook another 10-15 minutes over low heat. Remove from stove and let stand for at least 1 hour before reheating to serve. Serves 8.

Approximate nutritional analysis per serving:
Calories 128, Protein 4 g, Carbohydrates 19 g, Fat 4 g,
Cholesterol 0 mg, Sodium 302 mg

ROASTED MIXED VEGETABLES

1 lb (455 g) VIDALIA Onions, cut into
    1-inch wedges and separated
1 red bell pepper, cut in 1-inch pieces
2 medium carrots, sliced ¼-inch
½ lb (230 g) snow peas, trimmed
3 oz (90 g) mushrooms, sliced ¼-inch
2 tbs (30 ml) toasted sesame seeds
rice wine vinegar or balsamic vinegar or lemon juice
olive oil pan spray
salt and freshly ground pepper to taste

Preheat oven to 400°F (205°C). Place aluminum foil on a flat baking pan or cookie sheet. Coat with pan spray. Combine vegetables in large bowl. Generously coat vegetables with pan spray. Mix thoroughly so that each vegetable is coated. Arrange in a single layer on baking sheet. Bake 10 minutes. Remove from oven and carefully stir. Return to oven and continue baking for 10 minutes or until vegetables are tender crisp. Remove from oven. Drizzle with rice wine vinegar and top with toasted sesame seeds. Serves 6.

Approximate nutritional analysis per serving:
Calories 76, Protein 3 g, Carbohydrates 13 g, Fat 2 g,
Cholesterol 0 mg, Sodium 23 mg

SYRIAN LENTILS WITH TOMATOES

1 cup (240 ml) lentils
1 tsp (5 ml) salt
¼ cup (60 ml) olive oil
1 large onion, chopped
2 cloves garlic, minced
⅛ tsp (.5 ml) pepper
1 tsp (5 ml) ground cumin
1 - 16 oz can (480 g) LIBBY'S Stewed Tomatoes
1 beef bouillon cube

Place lentils in large pan with 2 qts water and 1 tsp salt. Bring to boil and continue boiling for 2 minutes. Remove from heat; cover and allow to sit 1 hour. Drain lentils, saving ½ cup liquid. Heat oil in large saucepan. Add stewed tomatoes, drained lentils, bouillon cube and saved lentil liquid. Cover and refrigerate until half hour before serving time. Cook about 20 minutes or until lentils are tender. Transfer to bowl or vegetables dish and garnish with dollop of sour cream, if desired. Serves 6.

Approximate nutritional analysis per serving:
Calories 225, Protein 11 g, Carbohydrates 26 g, Fat 10 g,
Cholesterol < 1 mg, Sodium 749 mg

ZUCCHINI MUSHROOM SAUTÉ

½ cup (120 ml) BLUE DIAMOND
    Blanched Slivered Almonds
2 tbs (30 ml) butter, divided
1 lb (455 g) zucchini, sliced
½ lb (230 g) fresh mushrooms, quartered
1 clove garlic, chopped finely
1 tbs (15 ml) olive oil
1 tsp (5 ml) lemon juice
½ tsp (3 ml) chopped, fresh oregano *or*
¼ tsp (1 ml) dried oregano
½ tsp (3 ml) salt
¼ tsp (1 ml) pepper

Sauté almonds in 1 tbs butter until golden; remove and reserve. Sauté zucchini, mushrooms, and garlic in remaining 1 tbs butter and oil, 1-2 minutes, until vegetables are crisp-tender. Stir in lemon juice, oregano, salt, pepper and almonds. Serves 6.

Approximate nutritional analysis per serving:
Calories 139, Protein 4 g, Carbohydrates 7 g, Fat 12 g,
Cholesterol 10 mg, Sodium 183 mg

MEDITERRANEAN ROASTED VEGETABLE AND CHEESE CASSEROLE

2 large onions, cut into narrow wedges
2 lb (910 g) zucchini, sliced
¼ cup (60 ml) olive oil
¼ cup (60 ml) flour
1 lb (455 g) tomatoes, cut into wedges
2 red bell peppers, cut into squares
½ cup (120 ml) pine nuts
1 cup (240 ml) CALIFORNIA ripe olives, halved
⅓ cup (80 ml) minced fresh basil
1 cup (240 ml) grated fontina or other
    medium-soft cheese
¼ cup (60 ml) balsamic vinegar

Sauté onions and zucchini in oil until tender. Turn into wide, shallow baking dish that holds about 3 qts. Sprinkle with flour. Arrange tomato and bell peppers on top. Bake uncovered at 450°F (230°C) for 20 minutes or until fork-tender. Top with pine nuts and olives then basil then cheese. Bake 10-12 minutes longer. Drizzle with balsamic vinegar before serving. Serves 6.

Approximate nutritional analysis per serving:
Calories 354, Protein 13 g, Carbohydrates 27 g, Fat 25 g,
Cholesterol 22 mg, Sodium 291 mg

LAYERED VEGETABLE BAKE

2 slices day-old white bread, crumbled
2 tbs (30 ml) chopped fresh parsley, optional
2 tbs (30 ml) margarine or butter, melted
1 large all-purpose potato, thinly sliced
1 large yellow or red bell pepper, sliced
1 envelope LIPTON Recipe Secrets Savory Herb
    with Garlic or Golden Onion Soup Mix
1 large tomato, sliced

Preheat oven to 375°F (190°C). Spray 1½-qt round casserole or baking dish with non-stick cooking spray. In small bowl, combine bread crumbs, parsley and margarine; set aside.

In prepared baking dish, arrange potato slices; top with yellow pepper. Sprinkle with savory herb with garlic soup mix. Arrange tomato slices over pepper, overlapping slightly. Sprinkle with bread crumb mixture. Cover with aluminum foil and bake 45 minutes. Remove foil and continue baking 15 minutes or until vegetables are tender. Serves 6.

Approximate nutritional analysis per serving:
Calories 102, Protein 2 g, Carbohydrates 14 g, Fat 5 g,
Cholesterol < 1 mg, Sodium 390 mg

CHILI RELLENOS CASSEROLE

2 - 4¼ oz cans (255 g) CHI-CHI'S Whole
    Green Chilies, drained
1 cup (240 ml) shredded sharp cheddar cheese
1 cup (240 ml) shredded hot pepper
    Monterey jack cheese
2 eggs
¾ cup (180 ml) milk
⅔ cup (160 ml) all-purpose flour
½ tsp (3 ml) salt

SAUCE
1 - 10 oz can (300 g) CHI-CHI'S Diced Tomatoes
    and Green Chilies
4 slices bacon, cooked and crumbled
2 tbs (30 ml) chopped fresh cilantro
1 tsp (5 ml) minced fresh garlic
½ tsp (3 ml) dried oregano leaves
¼ tsp (1 ml) coarsely ground pepper
chopped fresh cilantro

Heat oven to 400°F (205°C). Lightly grease 8x8x2-inch baking dish. Cut slit in each chili lengthwise down one side. In small bowl, combine cheeses. Fill each chili with about 3 tbs cheese. Place cut-side-down in greased baking dish. In large mixing bowl, beat eggs, milk, flour and salt until well blended and frothy. Pour egg mixture over chilies. Bake 25-30 minutes or until light golden brown. In small saucepan, combine all Sauce ingredients except cilantro and sour cream. Bring to a boil. Cook 5 minutes, stirring occasionally. Spoon Sauce over chilies. Serve with cilantro and sour cream. Serves 6.

Approximate nutritional analysis per serving:
Calories 280, Protein 16 g, Carbohydrates 18 g, Fat 17 g,
Cholesterol 115 mg, Sodium 700 mg

EASY CHILI

1 pkg vegetarian burger mix
    (enough to make 4 burgers)
1 medium onion, coarsely chopped
1 green pepper, coarsely chopped
1 carrot, sliced
3 cloves garlic, finely minced
1 - 16 oz can (480 ml) crushed tomatoes
    or tomato puree
1 - 16 oz can (480 ml) tomato sauce
1 - 16 oz can (480 g) beans (kidney, pinto,
    garbanzo or black beans)
2 tbs (30 ml) chili powder
¾ tsp (4 ml) cumin
¼ tsp (1 ml) cayenne pepper

Cook the burgers according to package directions. Combine the rest of the ingredients in a large pot. Crumble the burgers with your fingers and add to chili sauce. Simmer 30 minutes. Serves 4.

Nutritional analysis not available.

Courtesy of the United Soybean Board.

East Chili

NACHO CASSEROLE

1 cup (240 ml) beef strip textured
   vegetable protein
12 oz (360 g) chunky salsa
1 cup (240 ml) sweet corn, canned, drained
I cup (180 ml) reduced calorie salad dressing
(made with soy oil)
1 tbs (15 ml) chili powder
1 tsp (5 ml) cilantro dried *or*
   1 tbs (15 ml) fresh cilantro
2 cups (480 ml) tortilla chips, baked,
   or homemade*, crushed
1 cup (240 ml) pinto beans
4 oz (120 g) lite Monterey jack cheese,
   or lite cheddar cheese, shredded

Heat oven to 350°F (180°C). Combine ⅞ cup of boiling water
and 1 cup of the beef strip textured vegetable protein, let stand
5 minutes. Cover the bowl with plastic wrap and microwave for
5 minutes. Check after 2 minutes. Add a little water if needed.
Combine the rehydrated textured vegetable protein, salsa,
corn, pinto beans, dressing, chili powder, cilantro. Layer
½ each of the textured vegetable protein mixture, tortilla chips,
and cheese in 2-qt casserole. Repeat layers. Bake 20 minutes
or until thoroughly heated. Top with shredded lettuce and
chopped tomato, if desired. Serves 6.
   * Homemade baked tortilla chips: 6 small corn tortillas.
Lightly spray tops of tortillas with no-stick vegetable (soy) spray.
Stack and cut into eighths. Spread out onto a baking sheet and
bake for 10 minutes at 350°F (180°C) until crisp and lightly
browned.

Approximate nutritional analysis per serving:
Calories 330, Protein 16 g, Carbohydrates 37 g, Fat 14 g,
Cholesterol 16 mg, Sodium 472 mg

Courtesy of the United Soybean Board.

COUSCOUS WITH VEGETABLES IN SAVORY BROTH

2 tbs (30 ml) butter or margarine
1 large onion, sliced
½ cup (120 ml) dry white wine or water
1 cup (240 ml) sliced carrots
1 medium zucchini, sliced
1 small red or green bell pepper, sliced
1 envelope LIPTON Recipe Secrets Savory Herb
   with Garlic Soup Mix
2 cups (480 ml) water
1⅓ cups (320 ml) couscous, cooked or penne
   or ziti pasta

In 12-inch skillet, melt butter over medium-high heat and cook
onion, stirring occasionally, 5 minutes or until golden. Add
wine and boil 1 minute. Stir in carrots, zucchini, red pepper
and savory herb with garlic soup mix blended with water.
Bring to boil over high heat. Reduce heat to low and simmer
uncovered, stirring occasionally, 15 minutes. To serve, spoon
over hot couscous. Serves 2.

Approximate nutritional analysis per serving:
Calories 258, Protein 5 g, Carbohydrates 25 g, Fat 13 g,
Cholesterol 32 mg, Sodium   550 mg

Courtesy of The Lipton Kitchens.

MARINATED TOFU KABOBS

8 pearl onions, peeled
8 medium fresh mushrooms
1 - 1 lb can (455 g) small, whole potatoes, drained
1 cup (240 ml) green pepper, cut into 1-inch squares
1 lb (455 g) firm tofu, cut into 1-inch cubes
8 cherry tomatoes

GINGER-SOY MARINADE
¼ cup (60 ml) apple cider vinegar
2 tbs (30 ml) low-sodium soy sauce
2 green onions, chopped
1 tsp (5 ml) gingeroot, grated
¼ cup (60 ml) frozen orange juice concentrate
2 tbs (30 ml) lemon juice

Place green onions, mushrooms, potatoes, green pepper and
tofu in a large bowl. Set cherry tomatoes aside. Pour Ginger
Soy Marinade over ingredients. Marinate for four hours in
refrigerator. Turn bag several times. Thread the marinated
ingredients, along with the cherry tomatoes, alternately, on
four skewers. Place on a broiler rack or outdoor grill. Cook
about eight minutes or until vegetables are tender-crisp. Turn
one time and baste several times with marinade. Serves 4.
   Ginger-Soy Marinade: Combine all ingredients; mix well.

Approximate nutritional analysis per 2 oz serving marinade:
Calories 48 , Protein < 1 g, Carbohydrates 9 g, Fat 1 g,
Cholesterol 0 mg, Sodium 198 mg

Opposite: Couscous with Vegetables in Savory Broth

GRILLED EGGPLANT "LASAGNE"

1 - 1¼ lb (570 g) eggplant
½ cup (120 ml) olive oil
1 tsp (5 ml) oregano
1 tsp (5 ml) basil
6 oz (180 g) sliced Mozzarella cheese
1 cup (240 ml) ricotta cheese
2 cups (480 ml) bottled spaghetti sauce
2 tsp (10 ml) fennel seed
1 cup (240 ml) CALIFORNIA ripe olive wedges

Slice eggplant ½-inch thick. Combine oil with herbs and brush onto both sides of eggplant. Lay in single layer in shallow baking pans; broil 2 inches from heat for 4-5 minutes or until cooked; turn, brush more oil on other side and broil until done. Layer half the eggplant slices, mozzarella, ricotta, spaghetti sauce, fennel seed and olives in wide, shallow 2-3-qt baking dish, in that order. Repeat layering. Cover and bake at 425°F (220°C) for 30 minutes or until hot and bubbly. Serves 6.

Approximate nutritional analysis per serving:
Calories 376, Protein 12 g, Carbohydrates 15 g, Fat 31 g,
Cholesterol 43 mg, Sodium 374 mg

CHILIES RELLENOS

2 - 4 oz cans (240 g) chopped green chilies
2 cups (480 ml) grated Monterey jack
    or cheddar cheese
6 eggs separated
cooking oil
1 - 28 oz can (840 g) LIBBY'S Concentrated
    Crushed Tomatoes
1 tbs (15 ml) sugar
1 tsp (5 ml) garlic powder
½ cup (120 ml) chopped onion
1 tbs (15 ml) chopped fresh parsley or cilantro

In bowl combine chilies and cheese. Beat egg whites in a deep bowl until stiff peaks form. Beat yolks and fold into egg whites. In a large skillet heat about 2 tbs cooking oil or bacon drippings until hot. Spoon egg batter into pan, approximately ⅓ cup. Spoon cheese and chilies into egg batter. Spread a little egg batter over the top just to cover chilies and cheese mixture. Let rellenos cook on one side until crisp brown. Flip with a large spatula. Don't worry if egg batter spreads a little, just push it back to the rellenos. Cook 2 at a time. When done, place rellenos onto a deep-set serving dish. Heat tomatoes, sugar and garlic powder in saucepan; pour over rellenos and sprinkle with chopped onion and parsley. Serves 6.

Approximate nutritional analysis per serving:
Calories 257, Protein 17 g, Carbohydrates 10 g, Fat 17 g,
Cholesterol 246 mg, Sodium 494 mg

EGGPLANT CASSEROLE

1 - 28 oz can (840 g) LIBBY'S Whole Peeled
    Tomatoes, in juice
1 large eggplant, unpeeled, diced
½ cup (120 ml) olive oil
12 slices Swiss cheese
1⅓ cups (320 ml) ricotta cheese or
    small curd cottage cheese
3 cloves garlic, sliced

Drain tomatoes; cut in half to release juice and discard juice. In skillet brown eggplant in olive oil; remove and place in baking dish or small casserole. Cover with 6 slices Swiss cheese. Spread ricotta over entire surface of cheese. In same skillet sauté garlic quickly and add tomatoes; heat through, then spoon over top of ricotta. Cover with remaining cheese slices. Bake in 375°F (190°C) oven 20-25 minutes. Serves 4.

Approximate nutritional analysis per serving:
Calories 706, Protein 31 g, Carbohydrates 26 g, Fat 55 g,
Cholesterol 98 mg, Sodium 623 mg

WESTERN TOSTADAS

1 - 28 oz can (840 g) LIBBY'S Whole Peeled
    Tomatoes, in juice
2 - 17 oz cans (1 kg) refried beans
2 - 4 oz cans (240 g) chopped green chilies
3 cups (720 ml) Monterey jack cheese, cubed
1 tsp (5 ml) garlic salt
1 head lettuce, shredded
½ cup (120 ml) chopped parsley or cilantro
3 lemons, cut into wedges
4-6 green onions, chopped
¾ cup (180 ml) shortening
8-10 corn tortillas

Drain tomatoes well, cutting in half to release extra juice. In large saucepan combine beans, chilies, 1 cup cheese, drained tomatoes, and garlic salt. Stir together and refrigerate. Place shredded lettuce, remaining cheese, parsley, lemons, and onions on plate; cover with plastic wrap and refrigerate until serving time. Just before dinner time, heat bean mixture. In heavy skillet melt shortening until very hot; fry tortillas until crisp; do not fold. Remove and drain on paper towels. Serve bean mixture in a bowl along with lettuce platter. Let everyone make their own tostadas. Serves 8.

Approximate nutritional analysis per serving:
Calories 452, Protein 22 g, Carbohydrates 44 g, Fat 22 g,
Cholesterol 38 mg, Sodium 109   mg

MEXICAN RICE

1 tbs (15 ml) olive oil
½ cup (120 ml) chopped onion
¼ cup (60 ml) carrot, diced ¼-inch
2 cloves garlic, minced
¾ cup (180 ml) long-grain rice
½ cup (120 ml) water
½ cup (120 ml) CHI-CHI'S Picante Sauce
1 - 10 oz can (300 g) CHI-CHI'S Diced Tomatoes
    and Green Chilies
½ cup (120 ml) green peas
½ cup (120 ml) cooked ham, diced ¼-inch

In medium saucepan, heat oil over medium-high heat until hot.
Sauté onion, carrot and garlic 3 minutes. Add rice; cook and
stir 1 minute. Stir in ½ cup water, picante sauce and diced
tomatoes and green chilies. Cover; reduce heat to low. Simmer
20-25 minutes or until all liquid is absorbed and rice is tender.
Let stand, covered, 5 minutes. Stir in peas. Stir in ham,
if desired. Serves 4.

Approximate nutritional analysis per serving:
Calories 200, Protein 5 g, Carbohydrates 38 g, Fat 4 g,
Cholesterol 0 mg, Sodium 520 mg

YELLOW RICE

½ cup (120 ml) CALIFORNIA ripe olive wedges
1 cup (240 ml) uncooked brown rice
1 tsp (5 ml) low-sodium instant chicken
    bouillon granules
1½ tsp (8 ml) oregano
½ tsp (3 ml) turmeric
⅛ tsp (.5 ml) bottled red pepper flakes
2½ cups (590 ml) hot water

Combine all ingredients in microwave-safe 2-qt baking dish.
Cover and microwave on HIGH for 5 minutes. Mix, return
cover to dish and microwave at MEDIUM (50% power) for 25
minutes or until liquid is absorbed and rice tender. Serve with
barbecued, broiled or baked shrimp, chicken or pork. Serves 4.

Approximate nutritional analysis per serving:
Calories 185, Protein 4 g, Carbohydrates 36 g, Fat 3 g,
Cholesterol < 1 mg, Sodium 235 mg

Above: *Yellow Rice*

WILD RICE AND OLIVE SKILLET CAKES

1 cup (240 ml) uncooked wild rice
2 cups (480 ml) water
1 egg
1 egg yolk
1½ tbs (25 ml) olive oil
⅓ cup (80 ml) flour
1 tsp (5 ml) finely chopped fresh sage
     or ½ tsp (3 ml) dried sage
1 tsp (5 ml) finely chopped fresh thyme
     or ½ tsp (3 ml) dried thyme
¼ cup (60 ml) finely chopped parsley
½ tsp (3 ml) pepper
1⅓ cups (320 ml) finely chopped California olives
olive oil for frying
sour cream, light sour cream or cream fraiche
minced chives or green onion

Combine wild rice with water in saucepan, cover and bring to boil. simmer gently for 50 minutes or until barely tender. Beat egg with egg yolk, olive oil, flour, sage, thyme, parsley and pepper. Add rice and olives. Heat 1 tbs oil in skillet, portion ⅓ cup (packed) measures of rice mixture into skillet; and shape gently with fork into 3-inch wide patties. Pan-fry 2-3 minutes over medium-high heat until crispy, turn and cook 2-3 minutes longer. Keep warm and repeat with remaining rice. Serve topped with sour cream and chives. Yields 10 cakes.

Approximate nutritional analysis per serving:
Calories 206, Protein 5 g, Carbohydrates 19 g, Fat 13 g,
Cholesterol 56 mg, Sodium 202 mg

PIEDMONT PECAN RICE

2 cups (480 ml) chicken broth
1 cup (240 ml) rice, not instant
3 tbs (45 ml) margarine
½ cup (120 ml) coarsely chopped pecans
4 scallions, chopped
1 cup (240 ml) sliced fresh mushrooms
½ red bell pepper, diced
1 cup (240 ml) petite peas, frozen
1 tsp (5 ml) McCORMICK or SCHILLING
     pure Orange Extract
2 tsp (10 ml) McCORMICK or SCHILLING
     pure Sherry Extract
1 tsp (5 ml) McCORMICK or SCHILLING
     Garlic Powder

In saucepan, bring chicken broth to a boil. Stir in rice, reduce heat to simmer, cover and cook 20 minutes. While rice is cooking, melt margarine in skillet. Add pecans and toss 2 minutes. Add scallions, mushrooms and pepper. Sauté 3 minutes. Add to cooked rice along with remaining ingredients. Toss to blend well. Serves 6.

Approximate nutritional analysis per serving:
Calories 257, Protein 5 g, Carbohydrates 33 g, Fat 12 g,
Cholesterol 0 mg, Sodium 82 mg.

ALMOND-RAISIN PILAF

⅔ cup (160 ml) BLUE DIAMOND Blanched
     Slivered Almonds
3 tbs (45 ml) butter, divided
1 cup (240 ml) chopped onion
2 cloves garlic, chopped finely
1 small, green bell pepper, diced
1 cup (240 ml) long-grain rice
½ cup (120 ml) raisins
1 tsp (5 ml) cumin
½ tsp (3 ml) salt
1¾ cups (415 ml) chicken broth

Sauté almonds in 1 tbs butter until golden; reserve. Sauté onion and garlic in remaining 2 tbs butter until translucent. Add green pepper, rice, raisins, cumin, and salt; sauté 2 minutes. Add chicken broth. Bring to a boil. Reduce heat to low, cover, and cook 20 minutes or until all liquid is absorbed. Remove from heat and let stand, covered, 5 minutes. Stir in almonds. Serves 6.

Approximate nutritional analysis per serving:
Calories 302, Protein 6 g, Carbohydrates 41 g, Fat 14 g,
Cholesterol 16 mg, Sodium 277 mg

HERB AND MUSHROOM RICE

2 cups (480 ml) chicken broth
2 tsp (10 ml) McCORMICK /SCHILLING
     Parsley Flakes
2 tsp (10 ml) McCORMICK/SCHILLING
     Instant Minced Onion
½ tsp (3 ml) McCORMICK/SCHILLING
     Oregano Leaves
1 cup (240 ml) uncooked long-grain or converted rice
1 tbs (15 ml) margarine or butter
1 - 4 oz can (120 g) sliced mushrooms, drained

In a 2-qt saucepan, combine broth, parsley, onion, and oregano. Bring to boil over high heat. Stir in rice and margarine. Cover and reduce heat to medium-low. Cook 20 minutes. Remove form heat and let stand 5 minutes. Fluff rice with fork. Gently toss in mushrooms and serve. Serves 6.

Approximate nutritional analysis per serving:
Calories 204, Protein 4 g, Carbohydrates 39 g, Fat 3 g,
Cholesterol < 1 mg, Sodium 263 mg

BAKED VIDALIA ONION AND RICE AU GRATIN

2½ lbs (1.1 kg) VIDALIA Onions, cut in 1-inch wedges
¼ cup (60 ml) water or chicken broth
2 cups (480 ml) cooled rice
1 cup (240 ml) finely shredded non-fat
 cheddar cheese
1 - 5 oz can (150 g) sliced water chestnuts, drained
¾ cup (180 ml) evaporated skim milk
salt to taste
fresh chopped chives for garnish

Preheat oven to 325°F (165°C). Coat an 8x8x2-inch or a
1½-qt baking dish with pan spray. Coat a large nonstick skillet
with pan spray. Heat skillet on medium heat and add the
onions. As onions begin to cook, stir, add the water or broth,
and cover. Cntinue to cook covered on medium heat until the
onions are clear, stirring 3-4 times. To the onions add the
cooked rice, cheese, water chestnuts and evaporated skim milk.
Mix well. Add salt to taste. Turn into baking dish and bake for
45 minutes. Garnish with chopped chives. Serves 6.

Approximate nutritional analysis per serving:
Calories 144, Protein 11 g, Carbohydrates 25 g, Fat 0 g,
Cholesterol 4 mg, Sodium 198 mg

BARBECUE BEANS

2 medium onions, chopped
2 jalapeño peppers, minced, seeds removed
¼ cup (60 ml) bacon drippings
1 lb (455 g) ground beef
3 - 15 oz cans (.4 kg) pinto beans and liquid
½ tsp (3 ml) IMPERIAL Granulated Sugar
salt and pepper, to taste

In heavy pot, sauté onion and jalapeños in bacon drippings.
Add beef and sauté, keeping ground meat in tiny pieces. Add
beans, IMPERIAL Granulated Sugar, along with salt and
pepper to taste. Simmer over low heat 2 hours, adding small
amounts of water to prevent scorching. Serves 8.

Approximate nutritional analysis per serving:
Calories 350, Protein 18 g, Carbohydrates 26 g, Fat 19 g,
Cholesterol 56 mg, Sodium 1143 mg

Barbecue Beans

BULGUR-OLIVE PILAF

2 tbs (30 ml) olive oil
½ cup (120 ml) bulgur wheat
½ cup (120 ml) chopped onion
1 cup (240 ml) chicken broth
½ cup (120 ml) pitted CALIFORNIA ripe olives, sliced
¼ cup (60 ml) toasted slivered almonds
1½ tsp (8 ml) lemon juice
1½ tsp (8 ml) chopped fresh mint
salt and pepper

Heat oil in large skillet. Add bulgur and onions and cook, stirring until onion is tender and bulgur starts to color. Stir in broth, cover and bring to boil. Simmer, covered, for about 20 minutes until liquid is absorbed and bulgur is tender. Stir in almonds, lemon juice, mint and salt and peppert o taste. Serves 4.

Approximate nutritional analysis per serving:
Calories 220, Protein 6 g, Carbohydrates 19 g, Fat 15 g,
Cholesterol < 1 mg, Sodium 712 mg

BARLEY-VEGETABLE PILAF

2 tbs (30 ml) margarine
1 medium onion, diced
4 oz (120 g) mushrooms, sliced
1 cup (240 ml) reduced-sodium chicken or beef broth
½ cup (120 ml) pearl barley
1 tsp (5 ml) TABASCO pepper sauce
1 medium red bell pepper, diced
1 medium zucchini, sliced

In a 10-inch skillet over medium heat, melt butter; cook onion and mushrooms 5 minutes, stirring occasionally. Add chicken broth, barley and TABASCO pepper sauce. Over high heat, brng to boil. Reduce to low; cover and simmer 20 minutes.

Add red pepper and zucchini; cover and simmer 15-20 minutes longer or until barley is tender, stirring occasionally. Serve mixture hot or cold. Serves 4.

Approximate nutritional analysis per serving:
Calories 174, Protein 5 g, Carbohydrates 26 g, Fat 6 g,
Cholesterol 0 mg, Sodium 96 mg

MOROCCAN COUSCOUS

¾ cup (180 ml) quick-cooking couscous
¾-1 cup (180-240 ml) dried tomato halves,
    cut into strips with kitchen shears
¼ cup (60 ml) raisins or dried currants
1¼ cups (295 ml) boiling water *or*
    reduced-sodium chicken broth
2 cups (480 ml) chopped onions
3 tbs (45 ml) olive oil, divided
1 - 16 oz can (480 g) small pink beans, drained
2 garlic cloves, pressed
2 tsp (10 ml) grated orange peel
salt and freshly ground black pepper, to taste
½ cup (120 ml) finely chopped parsley
⅓ cup (80 ml) orange juice
3 tbs (45 ml) lemon juice
1 tbs (15 ml) thinly sliced green onion tops

In bowl, stir couscous, tomatoes, raisins and boiling water; cover and let stand 15 minutes.

Meanwhile, in large skillet over medium heat, sauté onions in 2 tbs of olive oil about 10 minutes, stirring occasionally, until onions are golden. Add beans, garlic and orange peel. Cook, stirring, just until heated through. Season with salt and pepper.

Uncover couscous and stir with fork or chop sticks to fluff; add to skillet with parsley. In small bowl, whisk remaining 1 tbs olive oil, orange juice and lemon juice until blended; drizzle evenly over couscous mixture and fluff with fork. Spoon into serving bowl and sprinkle with green onion. Serves 6.

Approximate nutritional analysis per serving:
Calories 270, Protein 8 g, Carbohydrates 46 g, Fat 10 g,
Cholesterol 0 mg, Sodium 240 mg

BROWN RICE-BARLEY PILAF

4 cups (960 ml) beef broth or water
¾ cup (180 ml) long-grain brown rice
¾ cup (180 ml) pearl barley
1 - 4¼ oz can (128 g) CHI-CHI'S Diced Green
    Chilies, drained
¼ cup (60 ml) toasted pine nuts
1 tbs (15 ml) chopped fresh cilantro
2 tsp (10 ml) grated lemon peel

In large saucepan, bring broth to a boil. Stir in rice and barley. Reduce heat to low. Cover; simmer 40-50 minutes or until all liquid is absorbed and grains are tender. Let stand, covered, 5 minutes. Gently stir in chilies, pine nuts, cilantro and lemon peel. Cook over low heat 1-2 minutes or until heated through, stirring once or twice. Serves 6.

Approximate nutritional analysis per serving:
Calories 220, Protein 8 g, Carbohydrates 40 g, Fat 5 g,
Cholesterol 0 mg, Sodium 530 mg

Garbanzos con Espinacas

GARBANZOS CON ESPINACAS

½ lb (230 g) fresh spinach, stems removed
1 medium onion, chopped
1 clove garlic, chopped
2 tbs (30 ml) GOYA Olive Oil
1 bay leaf
1 tomato, chopped
1 packet GOYA Chicken Bouillon mixed with:
    2 cups (480 ml) water
1 whole clove
1 tsp (5 ml) paprika
1 tsp (5 ml) GOYA Adobo with Pepper
2 - 16 oz cans (960 g) GOYA Chick Peas.
    drained and rinsed
1-2 hard-boiled eggs, shelled and sliced in quarters

Place spinach in boiling water for 10 seconds. Remove spinach with tongs and immediately place in a bowl of ice water. When cold, squeeze water out of spinach and set aside. In a large skillet or saucepan, sauté onion and garlic in olive oil until soft. Add bay leaf, tomato, clove, and 1 tbs of prepared bouillon, and heat thoroughly. Add paprika, Adobo and remaining bouillon. Remove bay leaf and clove.

Stir in chick peas and cook over medium heat, uncovered, for 10 minutes. Remove 1 cup of chick pea mixture, puree the removed portion, and mix back into pan. Arrange chick peas evenly in a large pie plate or wide, shallow serving dish. Chop spinach. Arrange sliced eggs and chopped spinach on top of chick peas. Salt and pepper to taste. Serves 6.

Approximate nutritional analysis per serving:
Calories 236, Protein 13 g, Carbohydrates 33 g, Fat 7 g,
Cholesterol 53 mg, Sodium 817 mg

SOUTH-OF-THE-BORDER BLACK BEANS

2 -15 oz cans (900 g) black beans, rinsed and drained
1 cup (240 ml) CHI-CHI'S Salsa
¼ cup (60 ml) sliced green onions
1-2 tbs (15-30 ml) chopped CHI-CHI'S Whole
   Green or Red Jalapeño Peppers
3 cloves garlic, minced
½ tsp (3 ml) ground cumin
 crumbled feta cheese, if desired

In large saucepan, combine all ingredients except cheese.
Cook and stir over medium heat 5-10 minutes or until hot.
Serve sprinkled with feta cheese, if desired. Serves 4.

Approximate nutritional analysis per serving:
Calories 190, Protein 12 g, Carbohydrates 36 g, Fat 1 g,
Cholesterol 0 mg, Sodium 270 mg

BLACK BEANS AND YELLOW RICE

1 -14 oz can (420 ml) chicken broth
1 - 5 oz pkg (150 g) yellow rice mix
2 tbs (30 ml) olive oil
1 yellow onion, minced
2-3 cloves garlic, minced
½ yellow pepper, minced
½ green or red pepper, minced
1 - 15 oz can (450 g) Black or Red Beans, drained
salt and pepper to taste
garlic powder to taste, optional
onion powder to taste, optional

Bring chicken broth to a boil. Add rice and simmer on low,
covered, for 20 minutes.
    Meanwhile, heat olive oil in a frying pan and sauté onion,
garlic and peppers until soft, about 3-4 minutes. Drain excess
liquid. Add beans to sautéed vegetables and heat thoroughly.
Season to taste with salt, pepper, garlic powder, and onion
powder. Mix bean mixture with yellow rice and serve.
Serves 3-4.

Approximate nutritional analysis per serving:
Calories 312, Protein 12 g, Carbohydrates 48 g, Fat 8 g,
Cholesterol < 1 mg, Sodium 953 mg

Courtesy of the American Dry Bean Board.

SOUTHERN RICE 'N BLACK EYED PEAS

1 cup (240 ml) sliced CALIFORNIA ripe olives
1 - 16 oz can (480 g) black eyed peas, drained
1 cup (240 ml) seeded and diced tomato
3 cups (720 ml) cooked white rice
½ tsp (3 ml) garlic salt
2 tbs (30 ml) olive oil
½ cup (120 ml) minced onion
¼ cup (60 ml) minced green bell pepper
1 tsp (5 ml) minced garlic
1 seeded and minced jalapeño pepper
½ cup (120 ml) thinly sliced scallion greens

Combine first 5 ingredients in large bowl. Heat olive oil in
small pan. Add next 5 ingredients to hot oil. Sauté 5 minutes.
Add to rice mixture. Stir well. Transfer to shallow casserole
dish sprayed with nonstick spray. Sprinkle scallion greens on
top. Cover. Bake in preheated 350°F (180°C) oven until heated
through, about 25-30 minutes. Serves 6.

Approximate nutritional analysis per serving:
Calories 275, Protein 9 g, Carbohydrates 47 g, Fat 6 g,
Cholesterol 0 mg, Sodium 179 mg

HOPPIN' JOHN

2 cans GOYA Black Eye Peas, drained
2 ham hocks, cooked
½ cup (120 ml) onion, chopped
½ tsp (3 ml) salt
½ tsp (3 ml) pepper
dash cayenne pepper
1 cup (240 ml) uncooked CANILLA Long-Grain Rice
1 tbs (15 ml) GOYA Corn Oil or butter

Combine all ingredients except rice and oil or butter. Simmer
until heated thoroughly. Cook rice according to package
directions, using part of ham hock liquid for part of water. Add
oil or butter. Combine cooked rice with bean mixture. Serve
hot. Serves 4.

Approximate nutritional analysis per serving:
Calories 433, Protein 19 g, Carbohydrates 80 g, Fat 5 g,
Cholesterol 0 mg, Sodium 273 mg

SAUCES & CONDIMENTS

By the most traditional standards, what makes a poached salmon an elegant entrée? Why, it's the Hollandaise sauce. By today's standards what makes grilled Mahi Mahi suitable for company, or even a family dinner? Why, it's the kiwi-tangerine salsa. Some things never change. A simple sauce or chutney can transform a simple meal into something simply delicious.

ITALIAN STEAK MARINADE

3 tbs (45 ml) water
2 tbs (30 ml) red wine vinegar
1 tbs (15 ml) olive oil
1½ tsp (8 ml) McCORMICK/SCHILLING
    Seasoned Pepper
1¼ tsp (6 ml) McCORMICK/SCHILLING
    Italian Seasoning
½ tsp (3 ml) McCORMICK/SCHILLING Garlic Salt
½ tsp (3 ml) McCORMICK/SCHILLING
    Onion Powder
1 lb (455 g) sirloin steak or other steak,
    trimmed of fat

Combine all ingredients except steak in a self-closing plastic bag or shallow glass dish. Add steak and refrigerate 2 hours. Remove steak, discarding marinade. Broil or grill to desired doneness. Serves 4.

Approximate nutritional analysis per serving:
Calories 198, Protein 24 g, Carbohydrates 1 g, Fat 10 g,
Cholesterol 65 mg, Sodium 176 mg

CHUNKY SALSA

2 tbs (30 ml) olive oil
1 cup (240 ml) coarsely chopped onion
1 cup (240 ml) coarsely diced green bell pepper
1 - 35 oz can (1 kg) tomatoes, drained and
    coarsely chopped, reserve ½ cup (120 ml) juice
1 tbs (15 ml) freshly squeezed lime juice
2 tsp (10 ml) TABASCO pepper sauce
½ tsp (3 ml) salt
2 tbs (30 ml) chopped fresh cilantro or Italian parsley

Heat oil in a large heavy saucepan over high heat. Add onion and bell pepper and sauté 5-6 minutes, stirring frequently, until tender. Add tomatoes and juice; bring to a boil over high heat. Reduce heat to low and simmer 6-8 minutes, stirring occasionally, until salsa is slightly thickened. Remove from heat. Stir in lime juice, TABASCO pepper sauce to taste and salt. Cool to lukewarm; stir in cilantro. Spoon salsa into clean jars. Keep refrigerated for up to 5 days. Yields 3½ cups.

Approximate nutritional analysis per 1 tbs serving:
Calories 10, Protein 0 g, Carbohydrates 0 g, Fat 0 g,
Cholesterol 0 mg, Sodium 50 mg

TROPICAL HAM GLAZE

2 tbs (30 ml) cornstarch
1 - 15½ oz can (465 g) crushed pineapple with juice
1 cup (240 ml) raisins (chopped, if desired)
½ cup (120 ml) packed brown sugar
½ cup (120 ml) honey
⅓ cup (80 ml) cider vinegar
2 tbs (30 ml) lemon juice
1 tbs (15 ml) prepared mustard
1 tsp (5 ml) grated lemon rind

In saucepan, stir together cornstarch and 2 tbs pineapple and juice, to make a smooth paste. Add all remaining ingredients and blend. Cook, stirring frequently, until mixture thickens and bubbles. Spread half of glaze over baked ham ½ hour before baking time ends. After 15 minutes, drizzle on remaining glaze and bake 15 minutes longer to completion. Pour glaze and drippings from baking pan into serving dish to accompany ham. Yields 2½ cups.

Approximate nutritional analysis per ⅛ cup serving w/o drippings:
Calories 85, Protein < 1 g, Carbohydrates 22 g, Fat < 1 g,
Cholesterol 0 mg, Sodium 13 mg

Courtesy of The California Raisin Advisory Board.

APRICOT-ORANGE GLAZE FOR HAM

½ cup (120 ml) apricot jam
1½ tsp (8 ml) cornstarch
1 tsp (5 ml) grated orange peel
⅛ tsp (.5 ml) ground nutmeg
⅛ tsp (.5 ml) ground allspice
¼ cup (60 ml) FLORIDA'S NATURAL
    Brand Orange Juice

Mix together all ingredients. Cook over medium heat, stirring constantly until thickened and boiling. Yields ¾ cup.

Approximate nutritional analysis per ⅛ cup serving:
Calories 80, Protein < 1 g, Carbohydrates 20 g, Fat < 1 g,
Cholesterol 0 mg, Sodium 3 mg

Opposite: Chunky Salsa

BARBECUE BASTE

1 - 28 oz can (840 g) LIBBY'S
    Concentrated Crushed Tomatoes
juice of 3 lemons
3 tbs (45 ml) steak sauce
6 tbs (90 ml) Worcestershire sauce
1 tsp (5 ml) salt
2 tbs (30 ml) sugar

Combine all ingredients in saucepan. Boil about 10 minutes, stirring occasionally. Remove from heat and let cool. Chill until ready to use. For delicious oven barbecued hamburger patties use sauce liberally and baste often. Yields 4 cups.

Approximate nutritional analysis per ¼ cup serving:
Calories 18, Protein < 1 g, Carbohydrates 4 g, Fat < 1 g,
Cholesterol 0 mg, Sodium 281 mg

MAPLE-APPLE BARBECUE SAUCE AND GLAZE

⅔ cup (160 ml) chicken broth
1 tbs (15 ml) cornstarch
2 tbs (30 ml) maple syrup
2 tbs (30 ml) balsamic vinegar or apple cider vinegar
⅓ cup (80 ml) apple sauce
¼ tsp (1 ml) McCORMICK or SCHILLING
    Ground Ginger
2 tsp (10 ml) soy sauce
1½ tsp (8 ml) McCORMICK or SCHILLING
    Maple Flavor

In a small saucepan, combine all ingredients except maple flavor. Bring to a boil while stirring with a whisk. Continue to cook 10 minutes. Remove from heat and stir in maple flavor. Use immediately or store in refrigerator up to 2 weeks. Yields 1½ cups.

Approximate nutritional analysis per ⅛ cup serving:
Calories 18, Protein < 1 g, Carbohydrates 4 g, Fat 0 g,
Cholesterol 0 mg, Sodium 74 mg

KIWI FRUIT AND TANGERINE SALSA

3-4 CALIFORNIA kiwifruit, peeled and diced
2 medium tangerines, peeled and diced *or*
1 orange, peeled and diced
1 cup (240 ml) peeled and diced jicama
½ cup (120 ml) diced sweet yellow or red bell pepper
¼ cup (60 ml) chopped cilantro
1 tbs (15 ml) lime juice
1 tbs (15 ml) vegetable oil
½-1 small jalapeño pepper, minced
¼ tsp (1 ml) salt

In large bowl, combine all ingredients, mixing well. Chill briefly. Yields 2½ cups.

Approximate nutritional analysis per ¼ cup serving:
Calories 42, Protein < 1 g, Carbohydrates 7 g, Fat 2 g,
Cholesterol 0 mg, Sodium 56 mg

CHUCK WAGON BARBECUE SAUCE

¼ cup (60 ml) salad oil
¼ cup (60 ml) IMPERIAL Brown Sugar
⅔ cup (160 ml) catsup
⅓ cup (80 ml) water
2 tbs (30 ml) soy sauce
1 tbs (15 ml) mustard
1 medium onion, chopped
⅓ cup (80 ml) lemon juice
2 tbs (30 ml) liquid smoke
¼ tsp (1 ml) pepper
1½ tsp (8 ml) salt
1 cup (240 ml) Worcestershire sauce

Combine ingredients in saucepan and simmer slowly over low heat about 30 minutes, or until well blended, stirring occasionally. Store in tightly covered jar in refrigerator until needed. Heat gently before using. Serve at table with meat. Yields 2-3 cups.

Approximate nutritional analysis per 1 tbs serving:
Calories 31, Protein 0 g, Carbohydrates 4 g, Fat 1 g, Cholesterol 0 mg,
Sodium 239 mg

SMUCKER'S ORANGE-CHILI BARBECUE SAUCE

1 cup (240 ml) SMUCKER'S Sweet
    Orange Marmalade
1 cup (240 ml) tomato sauce,
    or crushed tomatoes packed puree
2 tbs (30 ml) red wine vinegar
2 tbs (30 ml) chili powder
1 tsp (5 ml) ground cumin
1 tsp (5 ml) fresh chopped garlic
½ tsp (3 ml) salt
¼ tsp (1 ml) cayenne pepper or
    hot pepper sauce (for spicier sauce)

Combine all ingredients in small saucepan and mix well. Heat the sauce until it comes to a boil, stirring constantly. Simmer 1 minute.

Use the sauce immediately as a marinade and baste for baked or grilled chicken, ribs, beef or pork. Or, cool and store in the refrigerator for future use.

Approximate nutritional analysis per serving:
Calories 160, Protein 1 g, Carbohydrates 42 g, Fat 1 g,
Cholesterol 0 mg, Sodium 459 mg

Opposite: Kiwi and Tangerine Salsa

SMUCKER'S LEMON-APRICOT MARINADE

½ cup (120 ml) SMUCKER'S Apricot Preserves
¼ cup (60 ml) pitted green olives, sliced into quarters
3 tbs (45 ml) fresh lemon juice
1 tbs (15 ml) grated lemon rind
1 tsp (5 ml) freshly ground black pepper
¼ tsp (1 ml) salt

Combine all ingredients in a small bowl and mix together. Use marinade for grilling shrimp, salmon, swordfish or chicken.

Approximate nutritional analysis per serving:
Calories 84, Protein 0 g, Carbohydrates 20 g, Fat 1 g,
Cholesterol 0 mg, Sodium 239 mg

FAT-FREE TARTAR SAUCE

1⅓ cups (320 ml) YOPLAIT Fat Free Plain Yogurt
¼ cup (60 ml) chopped dill pickle
1 tbs (15 ml) snipped parsley
1 tbs (15 ml) chopped pimiento
2 tsp (10 ml) instant minced onion

Mix all ingredients. Cover and refrigerate at least 1 hour. Store in refrigerator. Yields 1½ cups.

Variation: Mix in ⅛-¼ tsp (.5-1 ml) curry powder.

Approximate nutritional analysis per 1 tbs serving:
Calories 8 , Protein 1 g, Carbohydrates 1 g, Fat 0 g,
Cholesterol 0 mg, Sodium 35 mg

BACARDI MARINADE FOR CHICKEN

2 cups (480 ml) fresh orange juice
zest from 2 oranges
2 tbs (30 ml) chopped mint
curry powder
chopped cilantro
minced garlic
¼ cup (60 ml) soy sauce
½ cup (120 ml) BACARDI Dark Rum
1 whole cut up chicken

Combine all ingredients in a shallow baking dish. Place chicken in marinade overnight. Grill chicken, basting with marinade until done.

Bacardi Marinade for Chicken

TARTAR SAUCE

1-1¼ cups (240-295 ml) mayonnaise
2½ tbs (38 ml) finely chopped sweet pickle
1 tbs (15 ml) snipped fresh parsley
1½ tbs (25 ml) chopped onion *or*
1 tsp (5 ml) minced onion
1 tsp (5 ml) prepared mustard

In medium bowl, stir together all ingredients until well combined. Cover and chill if not using immediately.
Yields 1½ cups.

Courtesy of the American Egg Board.

COOKED HOLLANDAISE SAUCE

3 egg yolks
¼ cup (60 ml) water
2 tbs (30 ml) lemon juice
½ cup (120 ml) firm cold butter, cut into eighths
¼ tsp (1 ml) salt, optional
⅛ tsp (.5 ml) paprika

In small saucepan, beat together egg yolks, water and lemon juice. Cook over very low heat, stirring constantly, until yolk mixture bubbles at edges. Stir in butter, 1 piece at a time, until melted and sauce is thickened. Stir in seasonings. Remove from heat. Cover and chill if not using immediately. Yields ¾ cup.

Approximate nutritional analysis per ⅛ cup serving:
Calories 167, Protein 2 g, Carbohydrates < 1 g, Fat 18 g,
Cholesterol 147 mg, Sodium 94 mg

Courtesy of the American Egg Board.

BERNAISE SAUCE

3 tbs (45 ml) tarragon or white wine vinegar
    or white wine
2 tsp (10 ml) chopped onion
1 tsp (5 ml) tarragon leaves, crushed
¼ tsp (1 ml) ground pepper
¾ cup (180 ml) Hollandaise Sauce
    (see previous recipe)

In small saucepan, bring vinegar, onion and seasonings to boiling. Reduce heat and simmer, uncovered, until almost all liquid has evaporated. Stir hot mixture into Hollandaise Sauce. Cover and chill if not using immediately. Yields ¾ cup.

Approximate nutritional analysis per ⅛ cup serving:
Calories 168, Protein 2 g, Carbohydrates 1 g, Fat 18 g,
Cholesterol 147 mg, Sodium 94 mg

Courtesy of the American Egg Board.

ZUCCHINI AND RED PEPPER SAUCE

1 tbs (15 ml) FLEISCHMANN'S Margarine
½ small onion, sliced
2 cloves garlic, chopped
1 small zucchini, sliced
½ small red pepper, coarsely chopped
1 tbs (15 ml) balsamic vinegar

In medium skillet, melt margarine. Add onion and garlic; cook for 1 minutes. Add zucchini and red pepper; cook for 5 minutes or until vegetables are tender. Add vinegar. Spoon mixture into food processor or electric blender; process just until finely chopped. Serve warm over grilled sliced chicken. Makes enough sauce for approximately 1 lb chicken, meat or fish.

Approximate nutritional analysis per ¼ cup serving:
Calories 40, Protein < 1 g, Carbohydrates 3 g, Fat 3 g,
Cholesterol 0 mg, Sodium 40 mg

PAPAYA-MINT-BASIL BEURRE BLANC

2 whole papayas
2 oz (60 g) fresh basil
4 oz (120 ml) brandy
1 cup (240 ml)whipping cream
5 sprigs dill
2 oz (60 g) fresh mint
4 oz (120 g) butter
1 tsp (5 ml) shallots, chopped

Blend herbs with fruit on high speed until pureed. In a medium sauté pan, add brandy. Flame off alcohol until flame disappears. Add butter and melt for about 2 minutes. Add puree and sauté for 3-4 minutes. Ladle over broiled, steamed or sautéed fish. Yields 2 cups.

Approximate nutritional analysis per ⅛ cup serving:
Calories 134, Protein < 1 g, Carbohydrates 7 g, Fat 11 g,
Cholesterol 36 mg, Sodium 8 mg

CHILI BUTTER

¾ cup (180 ml) butter or margarine, softened
3 tbs (45 ml) CHI-CHI'S Diced Green Chilies
½ tsp (3 ml) minced fresh garlic
¼ tsp (1 ml) chili powder

In small bowl, beat butter until fluffy. Stir in remaining ingredients. Serve spread on warm bread or on top of hot vegetables. Yields 1 cup.

Approximate nutritional analysis per 1 tsp serving:
Calories 25, Protein 0 g, Carbohydrates 0 g, Fat 3 g,
Cholesterol 10 mg, Sodium 30 mg

HAZELNUT & SUN DRIED TOMATO PESTO

2 cups (480 ml) sun-dried tomatoes
3 garlic cloves
1¼ cups (295 ml) olive oil
½ cup (120 ml) Hazelnuts, chopped
½ cup (120 ml) Romano cheese
½ cup (120 ml) Parmesan cheese

Blend tomatoes, garlic and olive oil in food processor until smooth. Add Hazelnuts and cheese. Process to the consistency you prefer - either smooth or slightly chunky. Season to taste. Allow about ¼ cup pesto per serving. Great on pasta, vegetables, rice, potatoes, seafood, soup ... or just about anything.

Approximate nutritional analysis per ⅛ cup serving:
Calories 183, Protein 2 g, Carbohydrates 3 g, Fat 19 g,
Cholesterol 3 mg, Sodium 65 mg

GREEN PEPPER JELLY

3 - 4¼ oz cans (383 g) CHI-CHI'S
    Diced Green Chilies, drained
1-3 tbs (15-45 ml) finely chopped CHI-CHI'S
Whole Green or Red Jalapeño Peppers, if desired
1 cup (240 ml) cider vinegar
⅓ cup (80 ml) lemon juice
1 tsp (5 ml) salt
1 tsp (5 ml) chili powder
5 cups (1.2 L) sugar
1 - 3 oz pouch (90 ml) liquid pectin

In 6-8-qt saucepan, combine all ingredients except liquid pectin. Bring to full rolling boil; boil 1 minute, stirring constantly. Remove from heat. Skim off any foam. Immediately fill hot sterilized half pint jars, leaving ¼-inch-head space. Wipe jar tops and threads clean. Place hot lids on jars and screw bands on firmly. Process in boiling water canner for 5 minutes. Yields 6 half-pints.

Approximate nutritional analysis per 1 tbs serving:
Calories 40, Protein 0 g, Carbohydrates 11 g, Fat 0 g,
Cholesterol 0 mg, Sodium 25 mg

CRANBERRY SAUCE

3 cups (720 ml) fresh or frozen cranberries
1 cup (240 ml) water
1 cup (240 ml) sugar

Combine water and sugar in a saucepan, stir to dissolve sugar. Bring to a boil, add cranberries and cook until skins pop, about 8-10 minutes. Remove from heat. Cool completely at room temperature. Serve warm or chilled. Yields 2½ cups.

Approximate nutritional analysis per serving:
Calories 91, Protein < 1 g, Carbohydrates 24 g, Fat < 1 g,
Cholesterol 0 mg, Sodium < 1 mg

TROPICAL FRUIT SALSA

1 medium ripe mango, peeled,
    pitted and cut into ¼-inch cubes
1 medium ripe papaya, peeled,
    seeded and cut into ¼-inch cubes
1 medium ripe avocado, peeled, pitted
    and cut into ¼-inch cubes
3 tbs (45 ml) fresh lime juice
2 tbs (30 ml) fresh chopped cilantro
2 tsp (10 ml) brown sugar
1 tsp (5 ml) GILROY FARMS Chopped
    Jalapeño Peppers, drained
1 tsp (5 ml) GILROY FARMS Crushed Ginger

Combine all ingredients in medium bowl. Cover and refrigerate at least 1 hour to allow flavors to blend. Serve with grilled fish or chicken. Also good with tortilla chips. Yields 2 cups.

Approximate nutritional analysis per serving:
Calories 3 , Protein < 1 g, Carbohydrates 6 g, Fat 2 g,
Cholesterol 0 mg, Sodium 2 mg

PROVENÇALE FRESH TOMATO RELISH

1 lb (455 g) fresh FLORIDA tomatoes
3 tbs (45 ml) red wine vinegar
1 tbs (15 ml) Dijon-style mustard
2 tbs (30 ml) water
¾ tsp (4 ml) salt
½ cup (120 ml) chopped onion
3 tbs (45 ml) capers

Use tomatoes held at room temperature until fully ripe. Dice tomatoes; set aside. In a small bowl combine vinegar, mustard, water and salt. Add onion, capers and reserved diced tomatoes; mix well. Cover and refrigerate. Serve with chicken, fish or meat.

Approximate nutritional analysis per ¼ cup serving:
Calories 15, Protein < 1 g, Carbohydrates 3 g, Fat < 1 g,
Cholesterol 0 mg, Sodium 310 mg

Opposite: Provençale Fresh Tomato Relish

ORANGE CRANBERRY RELISH

**1 - 12 oz pkg (360 g) fresh cranberries,
   picked over and rinsed**
**1 seedless orange, peeled (reserve ¼ of the peel)
   and cut in quarters**
½-1 cup (120-240 ml) sugar
3 tbs (45 ml) lemon juice
¼ tbs (4 ml) allspice

In the bowl of a large food processor fitted with a metal blade, pulse-chop half the cranberries and orange pieces and peel. Repeat instructions using the second half of the ingredients. Combine the batches in a large bowl. Add remaining ingredients, mix all together. Yields 3½ cups.

   Note: Can be made 2-3 days ahead and refrigerated. Check sweetness as cranberries can vary in tartness; adjust lemon juice and/or sugar.

Approximate nutritional analysis per ¼ cup serving:
Calories 58, Protein < 1 g, Carbohydrates 15 g, Fat 0 g,
Cholesterol 0 mg, Sodium < 1 mg

Courtesy of The Empire Kosher Poultry Test Kitchens.

VIDALIA ONION PRESERVES

6-7 VIDALIA Onions
spray olive oil
¼ tsp (1 ml) allspice
1 bay leaf
1 tsp (5 ml) finely grated fresh ginger
3 tbs (45 ml) honey
¼ cup (60 ml) red wine vinegar

Peel VIDALIA Onions and slice in ½-inch slices. Spray a non-stick pan with olive oil and add the onions, allspice, bay leaf and ginger. Cook, stirring often, for approximately 10 minutes. Stir in honey and vinegar. Continue cooking and stirring for another 5 minutes. Spoon the preserves into a bowl and let cool. The preserves may be stored, tightly covered, indefinitely in the refrigerator. Serve hot with grilled meats or fish; in omelets or with ham and eggs. Serve cold with cold sliced meats or chicken. Yields 3 cups.

Approximate nutritional analysis per 1 tbs serving:
Calories 10, Protein 0 g, Carbohydrates 4 g, Fat 0 g,
Cholesterol 0 mg, Sodium 206 mg

DESSERTS

Served at the end of the meal, often at the end of the day, dessert can feel like a great reward. Prepare-ahead desserts solve last-minute timing. To cope with the fats and sugars in many desserts, try reduced-fat versions and smaller portions.

Watermelon Pig

RAINBOW FRUIT SALAD

**6 cups (1.4 L) fresh fruit (grapes, sliced banana,
    pineapple chunks, melon balls, strawberries
    and blueberries)**
¼ cup (60 ml) confectioners sugar
**1 tbs (15 ml) McCORMICK/SCHILLING
    Rum Extract**
sour cream, if desired

Combine all ingredients. Serve chilled with dollop of
sour cream, if desired. Serves 6.

Approximate nutritional analysis per serving:
Calories 96, Protein < 1 g, Carbohydrates 24 g, Fat < 1 g,
Cholesterol 0 mg, Sodium 3 mg

WATERMELON PIG

Using rounded watermelon, cut opening in top of watermelon
leaving section to cut tail. Remove cut-out rind. Cut spiral tail
from tail section by removing small strip. Using cut-out section,
cut a 2-inch circle for snout and 2 triangles for ears. Scoop out
fruit from watermelon leaving just a trace of red showing.
Chill well.

Invert watermelon and drain; place on serving platter.
Decorate outside of watermelon using round wooden picks
to attach reserved circle for snout and triangles for ears. Cut
2 kiwifruit in half crosswise; remove small vertical wedges from
each half to form hoofs. Attach with wooden picks to lower side
of watermelon feet. Use as a container for punch, fruit salads
or desserts.

Courtesy of The National Watermelon Promotion Board.

Nutritional analysis per 2 cup serving watermelon:
Calories 90, Protein 1 g, Carbohydrates 23 g, Fat 0 g,
Cholesterol 0 mg, Sodium 10 mg

STRAWBERRY SAUTÉ

3 tbs (45 ml) butter
¼ cup (60 ml) coarsely chopped walnuts
3 tbs (45 ml) dark brown sugar
2 cups (480 ml) halved or quartered premium
    branded strawberries, such as DRISCOLL'S
3 tbs (45 ml) grated semi-sweet chocolate
¼ cup (60 ml) crumbled cookies

In medium skillet, melt butter until bubbly. Add walnuts; cook and stir briefly, just until nuts begin to color. Add brown sugar and stir for less than 30 seconds. Remove pan from heat. Add strawberries and chocolate. Quickly stir to coat berries and melt chocolate. Spoon over ice cream, custard pie or angel food cake. Sprinkle with crumbled cookies. Serves 4.

Approximate nutritional analysis per serving:
Calories 262, Protein 3 g, Carbohydrates 28 g, Fat 17 g,
Cholesterol 62 mg, Sodium 15 mg

WATERMELON-RASPBERRY DESSERT

⅓ cup (80 ml) raspberry wine vinegar
2 tbs (30 ml) granulated sugar
1 cup (240 ml) fresh raspberries
4 serving-size watermelon wedges with rind,
    chilled
mint sprigs

In small saucepan over medium heat, combine vinegar and sugar; heat to boiling, stirring occasionally until sugar is dissolved. Remove from heat and stir in raspberries. Place watermelon wedges on individual serving plates; spoon raspberry mixture over each wedge. Garnish with mint sprigs. Serves 4.

Approximate nutritional analysis per serving:
Calories 195, Protein 3 g, Carbohydrates 45 g, Fat 2 g,
Cholesterol 0 mg, Sodium 10 mg

Courtesy of the National Watermelon Promotion Board.

QUICK WATERMELON RECIPES

Top seeded watermelon with low-fat fruit-flavored yogurt.
    Thin orange marmalade with lemon or lime juice.
Drizzle over watermelon balls mixed with other fresh fruit.
    Spoon watermelon salsa over low-fat sour cream.
Use as a dip with low-fat corn chips.

Courtesy of the Watermelon Promotion Board.

WATERMELON WITH BLUEBERRY SAUCE

4 cups (960 ml) cubed seeded watermelon
4 tbs (60 ml) lime juice
¼ cup (60 ml) granulated sugar
1 tbs (15 ml) orange juice
2 cups (480 ml) blueberries, fresh or frozen
⅓ cup (80 ml) vanilla or lemon nonfat yogurt

In large bowl, toss watermelon cubes with 3 tbs lime juice; cover and chill. In small saucepan, stir together sugar, orange juice and remaining 1 tbs lime juice. Cook over medium heat, stirring occasionally, for 2 minutes. Add blueberries; continue cooking just until liquid returns to a boil. Cool to room temperature. Divide watermelon between 6 bowls; spoon blueberry sauce over and drizzle with yogurt. Serves 6.

Approximate nutritional analysis per serving:
Calories 104, Protein 2 g, Carbohydrates 25 g, Fat < 1 g,
Cholesterol < 1 mg, Sodium 13 mg

Courtesy of the National Watermelon Promotion Board.

Watermelon with Blueberry Sauce

TANGY ORANGE FRUIT DIP

1 - 8 oz pkg (240 g) **HEALTHY CHOICE Fat Free**
    Pasteurized Process Cream Cheese Product,
    softened
1 cup (240 ml) nonfat plain yogurt
2 tbs (30 ml) orange juice concentrate
1 tbs (15 ml) confectioners sugar

Combine all ingredients; beat well. Chill 2 hours before
serving. Serve with assorted fresh fruit for dipping. Serves 16.

Approximate nutritional analysis per serving:
Calories 28, Protein 4 g, Carbohydrates 3 g, Fat 0 g,
Cholesterol 3 mg, Sodium 112 mg

MANGO SORBET

4 ripe mangos
2 cups (480 ml) crushed ice

Blend and serve. Serves 3.
     Mango Care and Handling Hints: Choose slightly soft
ones for immediate use, firmer ones for use in a few days.
Ripen mangos at room temperature. Whatever the color of a
mango, it is ready to eat when fragrant and soft to the touch.

Courtesy of London Fruit Inc.

CHOCOLATE-DIPPED FRUIT

8 oz (240 g) **GHIRARDELLI Broken Milk Chocolate**
    or any GHIRARDELLI Baking Bar: Bittersweet,
    White, Sweet Dark, Milk or Semi-Sweet
    Chocolate
4-6 cups (960-1440 ml) **fruit of your choice**
    (strawberries, bananas, apples, dried apricots)

Cut fruit into bite size chunks. When dipping strawberries or
apples, rinse with cold water and dry thoroughly. Chop
chocolate into very small pieces. Melt chocolate in top of
double boiler over simmering - not boiling - water, stirring
constantly until smooth. Remove from heat and tilt pan so that
all chocolate comes to the side. Using a tooth pick, pierce fruit
chunk and dip into chocolate about ¼-inch from the top, then
turn up-side-down to catch the drips. When dripping strawberries, hold by the stem or leaves. Place dipped fruit in fluted foil
cupcake liners or aluminum foil. Firm in freezer 10 minutes or
refrigerate ½ hour. Serve the same day. Serves 12.
     Variation: Stir in ½ tsp (3 ml) McCORMICK/
SCHILLING Pure Orange Extract.

Approximate nutritional analysis per serving:
Calories 163, Protein 2 g, Carbohydrates 27 g, Fat 6 g,
Cholesterol 4 mg, Sodium 20 mg

Chocolate-Dipped Fruit

ANGEL HAIR PASTA WITH STRAWBERRY
AND BROWN SUGAR SAUCE

1 cup (240 ml) **thinly sliced premium branded**
    strawberries, such as DRISCOLL'S
⅓ cup (80 ml) **dark brown sugar, divided**
¾ cup (180 ml) **heavy cream**
4 oz (120 g) **angel hair pasta**
2 tbs (30 ml) **chopped, toasted hazelnuts**

In small bowl, toss strawberries and 1 tbs brown sugar.
Cover and set aside. In medium saucepan, combine cream
and remaining brown sugar. Bring to boil, stirring constantly.
Reduce heat and simmer several minutes or until sugar is
dissolved and cream is light brown in color and smooth in
consistency. Remove from heat. Meanwhile, cook pasta
according to package directions, omitting salt. Drain very well.
Return to saucepan to heat, add pasta and toss thoroughly
coated and heated. Place pasta in serving bowl or individual
dishes. Spoon strawberries and juices over pasta. Sprinkle with
chopped nuts. Serve immediately. Serves 4.

Approximate nutritional analysis per serving:
Calories 360, Protein 5 g, Carbohydrates 43 g, Fat 19 g,
Cholesterol 61 mg, Sodium 25 mg

CALIFORNIA SKINNY DIPS

For each recipe, use 2 - pint baskets (960 ml) CALIFORNIA Strawberries. Rinse strawberries and pat dry with paper towels; set aside. For each dip recipe, whisk ingredients to blend thoroughly. Each dip yields ¾ cup dip; enough for 6 servings (about 2 tbs dip per 8 medium strawberries).

HONEY-ALMOND DIP

⅔ cup (160 ml) plain nonfat yogurt
3 tbs (45 ml) toasted, slivered almonds,
    finely chopped
2½ tbs (38 ml) honey

Approximate nutritional analysis per serving:
Calories 100, Protein 3 g, Carbohydrates 18 g, Fat 3 g,
Cholesterol 1 mg, Sodium 50 mg

STRAWBERRY-CREAM DIP

½ cup (120 ml) nonfat light sour cream substitute
¼ cup (60 ml) strawberry fruit spread
    (no sugar added) or strawberry jam

Approximate nutritional analysis per serving:
Calories 70, Protein 2 g, Carbohydrates 15 g, Fat < 1 g,
Cholesterol 0 mg, Sodium 20 mg

FRESH LEMON-POPPY SEED DIP

¾ cup (160 ml) non fat light sour cream substitute
4 tsp (20 ml) honey
1 tbs (15 ml) lemon juice
1 tbs (15 ml) poppy seeds
1 tsp (5 ml) finely grated lemon peel

Approximate nutritional analysis per serving:
Calories 70, Protein 3 g, Carbohydrates 15 g, Fat 1 g,
Cholesterol 1 mg, Sodium 20 mg

CHOCOLATE FUDGE DIP

6 tbs (90 ml) plain nonfat yogurt
6 tbs (90 ml) prepared chocolate fudge sauce
1½ tsp (8 ml) frozen orange juice concentrate,
    thawed

Approximate nutritional analysis per serving:
Calories 120, Protein 3 g, Carbohydrates 19 g, Fat 4 g,
Cholesterol 0 mg, Sodium 55 mg

Courtesy of the California Strawberry Commission.

EASY FRUIT DESSERT

1 medium banana, mashed
1 tbs (15 ml) frozen orange juice concentrate, thawed
1 cup (240 ml) YOPLAIT Fat Free Plain*
    or Vanilla Yogurt
⅛ tsp (.5 ml) ground cinnamon
⅛ tsp (.5 ml) ground nutmeg
1 medium peach or nectarine, cut into 1-inch pieces

* If using plain yogurt add 1 tbs (15 ml) honey.
Mix all ingredients. Cover and refrigerate at least 1 hour. Serve over fruit. Refrigerate any remaining dressing. Yields 1½ cups.

Approximate nutritional analysis per 1 tbs serving:
Calories 12, Protein 1 g, Carbohydrates 3 g, Fat 0 g,
Cholesterol 0 mg, Sodium 10 mg

GELATIN-FILLED PAPAYA

2 papayas
1 - 3 oz pkg (90 g) flavored gelatin
1 cup (240 ml) boiling water
¼ cup (60 ml) cold water
1 tbs (15 ml) lime juice

Cut off stem ends of papayas. With a teaspoon carefully scoop out and discard seeds; set aside. In a small mixing bowl, combine gelatin with boiling water, stirring until dissolved. Add the fresh lime juice and cold water. Refrigerate gelatin until partially set. Spoon gelatin into papayas and chill over-night. To serve, carefully cut papaya into wedges or circles. Serves 4.
    Variations: For variation in color and flavor, lime, lemon, raspberry, strawberry or cherry flavored gelatin may be used. Substitute 2 tbs (30 ml) lemon juice for lime juice and add ½ cup (90 ml) cold water.

Approximate nutritional analysis per serving:
Calories 77, Protein 1 g, Carbohydrates 19 g, Fat < 1 g,
Cholesterol 0 mg, Sodium 16 mg

Opposite: California Skinny Dips

QUICK FRUIT DESSERT

**1 - 21 oz can (630 g) peach, cherry, apple
    or blueberry pie filling
1 tsp (5 ml) lemon juice
2 cups (480 ml) Whole Grain TOTAL Cereal
¼ cup (60 ml) packed brown sugar
2 tbs (30 ml) margarine or butter, softened
1 tsp (5 ml) ground cinnamon**

Heat oven to 350°F (180°C). Grease square pan, 8x8x2 inches. Mix pie filling and lemon juice. Spread in pan. Mix remaining ingredients; sprinkle over pie filling. Bake 15-20 minutes or until filling is hot and bubbly and topping is golden brown. Serve with nonfat frozen yogurt, if desired. Serves 6.

    High altitude: 3500-6500 ft: Heat oven to 375°F (190°C). Bake 20-25 minutes.

Approximate nutritional analysis per serving:
Calories 220, Protein 1 g, Carbohydrates 45 g, Fat 4 g, Cholesterol 0 mg, Sodium 170 mg

CHERRY COBBLER

**1 - 21 oz can (630 g) cherry pie filling
½ tsp (3 ml) McCORMICK/SCHILLING
    Pure Almond Extract
3 tbs (45 ml) butter or margarine
¾ cup (180 ml) flour
1 tbs plus 2 tsp (25 ml) sugar
1 tsp (5 ml) baking powder
dash McCORMICK/SCHILLING Nutmeg
⅛ tsp (.5 ml) salt
1 egg
3 tbs (45 ml) milk**

Mix cherry pie filling with extract. Pour into a 1½-qt casserole. Cut butter into next 5 ingredients. Add egg and milk all at once. Mix until just blended. Spoon over cherry pie filling. Bake in 375°F (190°C) oven 30-35 minutes. Serve warm. Serves 6.

Approximate nutritional analysis per serving:
Calories 324, Protein 4 g, Carbohydrates 62 g, Fat 8 g, Cholesterol 52 mg, Sodium 197 mg

MAPLE-BAKED APPLES WITH RAISINS

**6 medium Macintosh apples
½ cup (120 ml) raisins
6 tbs (90 ml) packed brown sugar
½ cup (120 ml) maple syrup
½ cup (120 ml) orange juice
1 tbs (15 ml) granulated sugar
1 tsp (5 ml) cinnamon**

Core apples from stem ends, leaving bottoms intact. Place in shallow baking dish. Mix raisins and brown sugar; pack into apple cavities. Pour syrup over apples and juice into bottom of dish. Mix granulated sugar and cinnamon; sprinkle over apples. Bake in 350°F (180°C) oven, basting 2-3 times, until apples are tender, 30 minutes to 1 hour. Serve warm or at room temperature, with cream. Serves 6.

Approximate nutritional analysis per serving w/o cream:
Calories 253, Protein < 1 g, Carbohydrates 65 g, Fat < 1 g, Cholesterol 0 mg, Sodium 8 mg

Courtesy of The California Raisin Advisory Board.

SMUCKER'S PEACHY PEAR CRUMBLE

**½ cup (120 ml) SMUCKER'S Peach Preserves
¼ cup (60 ml) lemon juice
¼ tsp (1 ml) ground ginger
6 pears, peeled, cored and sliced
¼ cup (60 ml) flour
¼ cup (60 ml) oatmeal
⅛ tsp (.5 ml) salt
¼ tsp (1 ml) ground cinnamon
1 tbs (15 ml) margarine
1 tbs (15 ml) brown sugar
2 tbs (30 ml) milk
6 tsp (30 ml) low-fat frozen yogurt or nonfat
    sour cream, optional**

Preheat oven to 375°F (190°C). Place SMUCKER'S Peach Preserves, lemon juice and ground ginger in a saucepan, set over medium-high heat. Simmer the ingredients until the preserves are liquefied. Add the pear slices and simmer for 5 minutes.

    While pears are simmering, combine the flour, oatmeal, brown sugar and cinnamon in a small bowl. Blend in the margarine until the mixture resembles a rough meal. Add the milk and loosely combine until just blended.

    Pour the pear mixture into an 8-inch square baking pan. Sprinkle the crumble topping evenly over the surface of the pear mixture. Place the pan in the preheated oven and bake for 25-30 minutes, until the top is lightly browned and bubbling.

    Serve warm plain or with several tbs low-fat frozen yogurt or non-fat sour cream. Serves 6.

    Note: If time is of essence, substitute pear halves packaged in light syrup for the fresh pears in this recipe. Bake for just 15 minutes rather than 25-30 minutes. Top the pear mixture with a few tbs of your favorite granola for a speedy topping.

Approximate nutritional analysis per serving:
Calories 267, Protein 3 g, Carbohydrates 60 g, Fat 3 g, Cholesterol < 1 mg, Sodium 77 mg

Bacardi Peach Cobbler

BACARDI PEACH COBBLER

½ cup (120 ml) BACARDI Light rum
6 cups (1440 ml) peeled and sliced peaches or
    2 (1¼ lb, 675 g each) packages frozen
    peaches, thawed
½ cup (120 ml) brown sugar
3 tbs (45 ml) corn starch
1 tbs 15 ml) lemon juice
2 tsp (30 ml) butter
1 cup (240 ml) chopped walnuts
Streusel Topping (optional)
1 cup (240 ml) biscuit mix
½ cup (120 ml) rolled oats
½ cup (120 ml) brown sugar
4 tbs (60 ml) margerine
½ tsp (2 ml) (cinnamon (ground)

Pre-heat oven to 375°F (190° C). In a large bowl, combine peaches, BACARDI Light rum, brown sugar, corn starch, lemon juice, and walnuts. Place in an oven-proof casserole dish. Dot with margarine. Set aside.

In small bowl, combine all topping ingredients, and working quickly with fingers, mix until it resembles a coarse meal.

Sprinkle over peaches and bake for 45 minutes. Serve warm. Top with vanilla or rum raisin ice cream.

Approximate nutritional analysis per ⅛th recipe with Streusel Topping: Calories 475, Protein 6 g, Carbohydrates 64 g, Fat 20 g, Cholesterol 3 mg, Sodium 87 mg

RUM PEAR CRISP

2 tbs (30 ml) cornstarch
4 firm pears cored and thinly sliced (Bosc or Comice)
2 tbs (30 ml) lemon juice
½ tsp (3 ml) McCORMICK/SCHILLING Cinnamon
½ tsp (3 ml) McCORMICK/SCHILLING
    Ground Ginger
1½ tsp (8 ml) McCORMICK/SCHILLING
    Rum Extract

STREUSEL TOPPING
6 tbs (90 ml) butter, softened
½ cup (120 ml) flour
½ cup (120 ml) light brown sugar, packed
1 tsp (5 ml) McCORMICK/SCHILLING Cinnamon
½ cup (120 ml) old-fashioned rolled oats

Preheat oven to 350°F (180°C). Grease 9-inch glass pie plate or 7x11-inch non-aluminum baking dish. Toss cornstarch with pear slices. Mix lemon juice, spices and extract and toss with pears. Put in prepared dish. Mix Streusel ingredients until crumbly and put on top of pears. Bake 20-25 minutes. Serves 6.

Approximate nutritional analysis per serving:
Calories 324, Protein 3 g, Carbohydrates 53 g, Fat 12 g,
Cholesterol 31 mg, Sodium 8 mg

GINGERED PEACH SNAP

¼ cup (60 ml) packed brown sugar
1 tbs (15 ml) lemon juice
2 tsp (10 ml) McCORMICK/SCHILLING
    Vanilla Extract
1 tsp (5 ml) McCORMICK/SCHILLING
    Ground Cinnamon
¼ tsp (1 ml) McCORMICK/SCHILLING
    Ground Ginger
3 - 16 oz cans (1.4 kg) sliced peaches in juice
½ cup (120 ml) raisins
1 tbs (15 ml) melted margarine
2 tsp (10 ml) packed brown sugar
¾ cup (180 ml) crushed gingersnaps

Combine first 5 ingredients in a large bowl. Add peaches and raisins; toss to coat. Spoon into an 8-inch square baking pan. Combine margarine and brown sugar in small bowl. With a fork, mix in gingersnap crumbs until well blended. Sprinkle over peaches. Bake in 375°F (190°C) oven 35-40 minutes or until bubbly. Serve with lowfat frozen yogurt, if desired. Serves 8.

Approximate nutritional analysis per serving:
Calories 199, Protein 1 g, Carbohydrates 44 g, Fat 3 g,
Cholesterol 0 mg, Sodium 88 mg

CLASSIC PEACHY COBBLER

1 - 29 oz can (870 g) sliced cling peaches
3 tbs (45 ml) lemon juice
1 cup (240 ml) IMPERIAL Light Brown Sugar
1 tsp (5 ml) cinnamon
¾ cup (180 ml) all-purpose flour
½ cup (120 ml) IMPERIAL Granulated Sugar
2 tsp (10 ml) baking powder
¼ tsp (1 ml) salt
¾ cup (180 ml) milk
⅓ cup (80 ml) butter or margarine

Arrange drained, sliced peaches in 9x9-inch baking pan; pour on lemon juice; spread IMPERIAL Light Brown Sugar over peaches. Sprinkle on cinnamon. In mixing bowl combine flour, IMPERIAL Granulated Sugar, baking powder, salt; add milk and beat until smooth. Batter will be very thin. Pour batter over peaches and brown sugar. Drizzle melted butter or margarine over batter. Bake in preheated 350°F (180°C) oven about 35 minutes. Serves 8-10.

Approximate nutritional analysis per serving:
Calories 257, Protein 2 g, Carbohydrates 49 g, Fat 7 g,
Cholesterol 2 mg, Sodium 212 mg

SHORTCAKES

2⅓ cups (560 ml) BISQUICK Original Baking Mix
3 tbs (45 ml) sugar
3 tbs (45 ml) margarine or butter, melted
1½ cups (355 ml) YOPLAIT Fat Free Vanilla Yogurt
2 cups (480 ml) frozen whipped topping, thawed
1 qt (960 ml) sweetened sliced strawberries

Heat oven to 450°F (230°C). Mix baking mix, sugar, margarine and ½ cup of the yogurt until soft dough forms. Gently smooth dough into ball on floured surface. Knead 8-10 times. Roll dough ½-inch thick. Cut with floured 3-inch cutter. Place on ungreased cookie sheet. Bake 8-10 minutes or until golden brown. Fold remaining yogurt into whipped topping. Split shortcakes; spoon strawberries and yogurt mixture between halves and over tops. Serves 6.

    High altitude: 3500-6500 ft: Decrease sugar to 1 tbs (15 ml).

Approximate nutritional analysis per serving:
Calories 370, Protein 7 g, Carbohydrates 55 g, Fat 13 g,
Cholesterol < 5 mg, Sodium 660 mg

Quick Peach Cobbler

QUICK PEACH COBBLER

1 - 21 oz can (630 g) peach pie filling
½ tsp (3 ml) ground cinnamon
1 cup (240 ml) BISQUICK Reduced Fat Baking Mix
1 tbs (15 ml) sugar
⅓ cup (80 ml) water
1 tbs (15 ml) margarine, softened

Heat oven to 400°F (205°C). Mix pie filling and cinnamon in ungreased 1½-qt casserole. Heat in oven 15 minutes or until hot and bubbly; stir.

Mix baking mix, sugar, water and margarine with fork until soft dough forms; beat vigorously 20 strokes. Drop by 6 spoonfuls onto hot peach mixture. Bake 20-25 minutes or until topping is light golden brown. Serve warm. Serves 6.

High altitude: 3500-6500 ft: Heat oven to 425°F (220°C). Omit sugar. Bake cobbler about 20 minutes.

Approximate nutritional analysis per serving:
Calories 200, Protein 2 g, Carbohydrates 42 g, Fat 3 g,
Cholesterol 0 mg, Sodium 260 mg

IDAHO HONEY-BAKED APPLES

6 large ROME Apples
6 tbs (90 ml) IDAHO Honey
¼ cup (60 ml) orange juice
sugar
nutmeg
1 orange

Core apples, being careful not to cut all the way through. Peel about ⅓ of the way down from the stem end. Combine honey and orange juice; pour into centers of apples. Set in baking dish. Pour a little hot water in bottom of pan. Bake at 400°F (205°C) for 50-60 minutes or until apples are tender. Sprinkle tops with a little sugar and nutmeg. Run under broiler to glaze. Quarter orange slices and tuck them in center of apples after glazing. Serves 6.

Approximate nutritional analysis per serving:
Calories 169, Protein < 1 g, Carbohydrates 44 g, Fat < 1 g,
Cholesterol 0 mg, Sodium 1 mg

PEACHY RASPBERRY COBBLER

2 - 16 oz cans (960 g) sliced peaches
1 cup (240 ml) fresh or frozen raspberries
⅓ cup (80 ml) raisins
2 tbs (30 ml) firmly packed light brown sugar
2 tbs (30 ml) lemon juice
½ cup plus 2 tbs (150 ml) Regular, Quick or
    Instant CREAM OF WHEAT Cereal
1 cup (240 ml) all-purpose flour
½ cup (120 ml) sugar
2 tsp (10 ml) baking powder
¼ cup (80 ml) FLEISCHMANN'S Margarine
2 eggs
¼ cup (240 ml) plain or vanilla lowfat yogurt
1 tbs (15 ml) cinnamon-sugar blend
prepared whipped topping, optional

Drain peaches, reserving 1½ cups syrup. Arrange fruit pieces and raisins in greased 8x8x2-inch baking dish; set aside.

In medium saucepan, heat reserved syrup, brown sugar and lemon juice to a boil; slowly sprinkle in 2 tbs cereal. Cook and stir until slightly thickened, about 1-3 minutes; pour over fruit mixture.

In bowl, mix flour, ½ cup cereal, sugar and baking powder; cut in margarine. Blend eggs and yogurt; stir into flour mixture just until moistened. Drop batter by spoonfuls over fruit mixture; sprinkle with cinnamon-sugar blend. Bake at 350°F (180°C) for 35-40 minutes. Serve warm and with whipped topping if desired. Serves 9.

Approximate nutritional analysis per serving:
Calories 288, Protein 4 g, Carbohydrates 51 g, Fat 6 g,
Cholesterol 48 mg, Sodium 177 mg

RHUBARB-STRAWBERRY CLAFOUTI

½ cups (590 ml) sliced ½-inch rhubarb
1½ cups (355 ml) sliced strawberries
⅓ cup (80 ml) sugar
⅛ tsp (.5 ml) nutmeg
1 cup (240 ml) all-purpose flour
½ cup (120 ml) sugar
½ cup (120 ml) LAND O LAKES Butter, softened
¼ cup (60 ml) milk
2 egg yolks
1 egg
¼ tsp (1 ml) salt
¼ tsp (1 ml) cinnamon
cream or ice cream

Heat oven to 400°F (205°C). In medium bowl stir together rhubarb and strawberries. In small bowl stir together ⅓ cup sugar and nutmeg. Sprinkle sugar mixture over rhubarb and strawberry mixture. Place mixture in 9-inch square baking pan. In small mixer bowl combine all remaining ingredients except cream. Beat at low speed, scraping bowl often, until smooth, 1-2 minutes. Spread batter over fruit. Bake 25-35 minutes or until surface is golden and set. Serve with cream or ice cream. Serves 8.

Tip: Frozen rhubarb and strawberries, thawed, well drained, can be used instead of fresh. Increase baking time to 40-50 minutes.

Approximate nutritional analysis per serving w/o cream or ice cream:
Calories 279, Protein 3 g, Carbohydrates 36 g, Fat 14 g,
Cholesterol 110 mg, Sodium 80 mg

FRENCH APPLE DESSERT

STREUSEL
1 cup (240 ml) BISQUICK Reduced Fat Baking Mix
½ cup (120 ml) chopped nuts
⅓ cup (80 ml) packed brown sugar
3 tbs (45 ml) firm margarine

6 cups (1.4 L) thinly sliced pared tart apples
1¼ tsp (6 ml) ground cinnamon
¼ tsp (1 ml) ground nutmeg
¾ cup (180 ml) skim milk
2 tbs (30 ml) margarine, softened
3 egg whites *or*
    ½ cup (120 ml) cholesterol free egg product
1 cup (240 ml) sugar
¾ cup (180 ml) BISQUICK Reduced Fat Baking Mix

Heat oven to 350°F (180°C). Grease rectangular baking dish, 13x9x2 inches. Prepare Streusel; reserve. Spread apples in dish. Beat remaining ingredients in blender on high speed 15 seconds, with hand beater or wire whisk 1 minute or until smooth. Pour over apples. Sprinkle with Streusel. Bake about 55 minutes or until knife inserted in center comes out clean. Cool at least 10 minutes. Serves 12-15.

STREUSEL: Mix baking mix, chopped nuts, brown sugar and margarine until crumbly.

High Altitude: 3500-6500 ft: Heat oven to 375°F (190C). Decrease apples to 5 cups (1.22 L) and baking mix to ½ cup (120 ml).

Approximate nutritional analysis per serving:
Calories 280, Protein 4 g, Carbohydrates 46 g, Fat 9 g,
Cholesterol 0 mg, Sodium 270 mg

FRIED APPLES

4 cooking apples
2 tbs (30 ml) butter, margarine or oil
⅓ cup (80 ml) IMPERIAL Brown Sugar
dash cinnamon

Wash and polish apples; core and cut crosswise into ½-inch thick rings. Heat butter, margarine or oil in heavy skillet; add apple slices. Cover and cook slowly about 10 minutes, or until apples are tender. Remove cover, sprinkle with IMPERIAL Brown Sugar, cinnamon. Cook a few minutes longer to brown apples. Serves 4.

Approximate nutritional analysis per serving:
Calories 213, Protein 0 g, Carbohydrates 39 g, Fat 8 g,
Cholesterol 14 mg, Sodium 76 mg

APPLE DESSERT

1 cup (240 ml) all-purpose flour
1½ cups (355 ml) IMPERIAL Brown Sugar
½ cup (120 ml) butter or margarine
¼ tsp (1 ml) salt
5-6 apples

Mix flour, IMPERIAL Brown Sugar, butter, salt with pastry mixer. Grease oven-proof dish. Alternate layers of thinly sliced apples and crumb mixture, finishing with a layer of crumb mixture. Bake in preheated 300°F (150°C) oven 1 hour, being careful not to burn. Serve with whipped cream. Serves 8.

Approximate nutritional analysis per serving:
Calories 369, Protein 2 g, Carbohydrates 67 g, Fat 12 g,
Cholesterol 0 mg, Sodium 232 mg

APPLE CRUNCH

8 cooking apples, peeled and sliced
1 tsp (5 ml) cinnamon
1 tsp (5 ml) nutmeg
½ cup (120 ml) IMPERIAL Granulated Sugar
½ cup (120 ml) water
½ cup (120 ml) IMPERIAL Brown Sugar
1 cup (240 ml) all-purpose flour
½ cup (120 ml) butter or margarine

Place apples in a greased, 8x8-inch square pan. Sprinkle with cinnamon, nutmeg, IMPERIAL Granulated Sugar. Add water. Combine IMPERIAL Brown Sugar and flour. Cut in butter or margarine very finely. Spread over apples. Bake uncovered in preheated oven at 400°F (205°C) for 20 minutes. Reduce heat to 350°F (180°C) and bake 25 minutes. Cut in squares for serving. Serves 8.

Note: A squeeze of lemon juice enhances apple desserts especially if apples are not tart.

Approximate nutritional analysis per serving:
Calories 339, Protein 2 g, Carbohydrates 59 g, Fat 12 g,
Cholesterol 0 mg, Sodium 158 mg

BAKED APPLE CELESTE

4 large apples, Granny Smith or pippins
3 tbs (45 ml) finely chopped pecans
3 tbs (45 ml) currants
¼ cup (60 ml) cherry preserves
1½ tsp (8 ml) McCORMICK/SCHILLING
　　Cherry Extract
½ tsp (3 ml) McCORMICK/SCHILLING Cinnamon

SOUR CREAM TOPPING
⅔ cup (160 ml) sour cream
2 tbs (30 ml) brown sugar
1 tsp (5 ml) McCORMICK/SCHILLING
　　Cherry Extract

Wash and core apples, keeping bottoms intact. Scoop out half of the center. Mix remaining ingredients and fill apples with this mixture. Bake in 350°F (180°C) oven 45 minutes or until tender. Serve with topping. Serves 4.
　　SOUR CREAM CHERRY TOPPING: Mix together.

Approximate nutritional analysis per serving:
Calories 282, Protein 2 g, Carbohydrates 46 g, Fat 12 g,
Cholesterol 17 mg, Sodium 25 mg

FAVORITE CARAMEL APPLES

½ cup (120 ml) LAND O LAKES Butter
2 cups (480 ml) firmly packed brown sugar
1 cup (240 ml) light corn syrup
dash salt
1 -14 oz can (420 ml) sweetened condensed milk
1 tsp (5 ml) vanilla
12 tart apples, washed, dried
¾ cup (180 ml) chopped salted peanuts

In 2-qt saucepan melt butter. Add brown sugar, corn syrup and salt. Cook over medium heat, stirring occasionally, until mixture comes to a full boil, 10-12 minutes. Stir in sweetened condensed milk. Continue cooking, stirring occasionally, until small amount of mixture dropped in ice water forms a ball or candy thermometer reaches 245°F (118°C), 20-25 minutes. Remove from heat; stir in vanilla. Dip apples in caramel mixture. Place on greased waxed paper. In small bowl place peanuts; dip end of apples in peanuts. Place on greased waxed paper. Yields 12.

Approximate nutritional analysis per serving:
Calories 523, Protein 5 g, Carbohydrates 97 g, Fat 16 g,
Cholesterol 32 mg, Sodium 112 mg

PUMPKIN-RAISIN CUSTARDS

3 eggs, slightly beaten
1 - 16 oz can (480 g) solid pack pumpkin
1 - 13 oz can (390 ml) evaporated milk
½ cup (120 ml) firmly packed brown sugar
2 tsp (10 ml) pumpkin pie spice
½ tsp (3 ml) salt
½ cup (120 ml) raisins

Beat together all ingredients, except raisins, until well blended. Place 6 - 6-9 oz custard cups, individual baking dishes or oven-proof serving dishes in large baking pan. Divide raisins evenly among dishes. Pour pumpkin mixture into dishes. Place baking pan on rack in preheated 350°F (180°C) oven. Pour very hot water into pan to within ½ inch of top of custard. Bake until knife inserted near center comes out clean, about 50-60 minutes. Remove immediately from hot water. Serve warm or chilled. Serves 6.

Approximate nutritional analysis per serving:
Calories 248, Protein 9 g, Carbohydrates 39 g, Fat 7 g,
Cholesterol 124 mg, Sodium 280 mg

Courtesy of the American Egg Board.

Pumpkin-Raisin Custards

COUNTRY APPLE DESSERT

BASE
1 pkg PILLSBURY PLUS Yellow Cake Mix
⅓ cup (80 ml) margarine or butter, softened
1 egg

TOPPING
1 - 21 oz can (630 g) apple fruit pie filling
½ cup (120 ml) firmly packed brown sugar
½ cup (120 ml) chopped walnuts
½ tsp (3 ml) cinnamon
1 cup (240 ml) dairy sour cream
1 egg
1 tsp (5 ml) vanilla

Heat oven to 350°F (180°C). In large bowl, combine cake mix, margarine and 1 egg at low speed until crumbly. Press in ungreased 13x9-inch pan; spread with apple pie filling. Combine brown sugar, walnuts and cinnamon; sprinkle over apple filling. In small bowl, blend sour cream, 1 egg and vanilla; spoon evenly over sugar mixture. Bake for 40-50 minutes or until topping is golden brown. Serve warm or cool. Serves 12.

Approximate nutritional analysis per serving:
Calories 400, Protein 4 g, Carbohydrates 58 g, Fat 18 g,
Cholesterol 45 mg, Sodium 380 mg

FLAN

Classic Caramel Custard

4 whole eggs
3 egg yolks
⅔ cup (160 ml) sugar
5 tbs (75 ml) water
2 cups (480 ml) milk
small piece lemon peel
small piece orange peel
1 oz (30 g) triple sec liqueur
½ cup (120 ml) sugar
1 tsp (5 ml) vanilla extract

In a mixing bowl, beat whole eggs and egg yolks together with a whisk until smooth. Set aside.

In small saucepan, combine ⅔ cup sugar with 5 tbs water and heat over medium heat, stirring constantly, until sugar turns golden. It will become dry; continue to cook until sugar mixture becomes a golden liquid. Pour evenly into 6 heat-proof custard cups. In a medium saucepan, combine milk, lemon peel and orange peel and boil briefly. Remove from heat, discard the peels and add triple sec, additional ½ cup sugar, and vanilla extract. When milk has cooled, stir in eggs with a whisk. Strain mixture, and add evenly into custard cups on top of sugar mixture.

Place cups in a shallow oven proof pan and fill pan with cold water to a level halfway up the cups. Place in a pre-heated 350°F (180°C) oven fro 30-45 minutes - check after ½ hour. Remove from oven when center is tender, but not completely gelled. Cool to room temperature, and chill. Run a knife around the inside surface of cup to separate flan from cup. Invert onto plates to serve. Serves 6.

Approximate nutritional analysis per serving:
Calories 230, Protein 8 g, Carbohydrates 29 g, Fat 9 ,
Cholesterol 258 mg, Sodium 86 mg

Courtesy of Goya Foods.

HEALTHY CHOICE CRÈME CARAMEL

½ cup (120 ml) sugar
2 cup (480 ml) 2% milk
1 - 8 oz carton (240 ml) HEALTHY CHOICE
    Cholesterol Free Egg Product
¼ cup (60 ml) sugar
½ tsp (3 ml) vanilla extract

Place ½ cup sugar in heavy saucepan. Cook over low heat until sugar melts and turns golden brown. Pour immediately into 6 custard cups. Let cool. In medium bowl, combine milk, egg product, ¼ cup sugar and vanilla. Stir until sugar dissolves. Pour into custard cups. Place cups in baking pan; fill with 1 inch of hot water. Bake in 350°F (180°C) oven for 50 minutes or until custard is soft set in the center. Chill in refrigerator.

To serve, run knife around edge of cups and unmold onto serving plate. Serves 6.

Approximate nutritional analysis per serving:
Calories 172, Protein 8 g, Carbohydrates 29 g, Fat 3 g,
Cholesterol 5 mg, Sodium 100 mg

HOLIDAY KIWIFRUIT FROZEN YOGURT WITH RED RASPBERRY SAUCE

2 California kiwifruit, peeled and coarsely chopped
1 tbs (15 ml) honey
1 pt (480 ml) frozen low-fat or nonfat vanilla
    yogurt, softened
1-2 drops green food coloring, optional
1 - 10 oz pkg (300 g) frozen red raspberries
    in syrup, thawed
2 tbs (30 ml) triple sec or other orange liqueur
2 tsp (10 ml) cornstarch
3 California Kiwifruit, ends trimmed
    and sliced lengthwise
fresh mint leaves
fresh or frozen whole raspberries, optional

In food processor or blender, puree chopped kiwifruit; stir in honey. Place in freezer and freeze until slushy, about 45 minutes. In stainless steel bowl, quickly combine softened yogurt, kiwifruit mixture and food coloring; refreeze in bowl. With small ice cream scoop (about 2 tbs) form 12 balls and place on wax paper-lined tray; refreeze.

Meanwhile to make sauce, in food processor or blender puree raspberries. Over saucepan, strain berries through a fine sieve, pressing with back of spoon. Discard seeds. Stir in orange liqueur and cornstarch. Bring to boil, stirring constantly until slightly thickened. Cool; cover and chill. To assemble, spoon about 2 tbs sauce on each of 6 dessert plates or shallow bowls. Arrange kiwifruit slices and yogurt balls on sauce. Garnish with mint leaves and whole raspberries. Serves 6.

Approximate nutritional analysis per serving:
Calories 159, Protein 5 g, Carbohydrates 31 g, Fat 2 g,
Cholesterol 5 mg, Sodium 57 mg

Courtesy of The California Kiwifruit Commission.

Opposite: Holiday Kiwifruit Frozen Yogurt
with Red Raspberry Sauce

RICH EGG BEATERS CUSTARD

2½ cups (590 ml) skim milk, scalded
½ cup (120 ml) sugar
¾ cup (180 ml) EGG BEATERS Real Egg Product
1 tsp (5 ml) vanilla extract

In bowl, blend milk and sugar until sugar dissolves. Slowly stir in egg product and vanilla. Pour mixture into 6 - 6 oz oven proof custard cups. Set cups in pan filled with a 1-inch depth hot water. Bake at 350°F (180°C) for 40-50 minutes or until set. Remove cups from pan; cool to room temperature. Chill until firm, about 2 hours. Serves 6.

Variations: Coffee Custard: Blend 1 tbs instant coffee granules into milk mixture. Proceed as above.

Orange Custard: Stir 1 tsp grated orange peel into milk mixture. Proceed as above.

Approximate nutritional analysis per serving:
Calories 152, Protein 7 g, Carbohydrates 22 g, Fat 7 g,
Cholesterol 139 mg, Sodium 104 mg

PEACH CUSTARD

2 cups (480 ml) slice frozen peaches,
thawed and drained
1 tbs (15 ml) lemon juice
1 tbs (15 ml) powdered sugar
¼ cup (60 ml) margarine, softened
1 cup (240 ml) skim milk
3 egg whites
¾ cup (180 ml) BISQUICK Reduced Fat Baking Mix
1 tbs (15 ml) vanilla

Heat oven to 375°F (190°C). Grease square pan, 8x8x2 inches. Place peaches in pan. Sprinkle lemon juice and powdered sugar over peaches; set aside. Mix in remaining ingredients until well blended. Pour mixture over peaches. Bake 40-45 minutes or until edges are light golden brown and toothpick inserted in center comes out clean. Custard will not look smooth. Serve warm. Serves 6-8.

High Altitude: 3500-6500 ft: Heat oven to 400°F (205°C). Use square pan, 9x9x2 inches.

Approximate nutritional analysis per serving:
Calories 300, Protein 5 g, Carbohydrates 53 g, Fat 8 g,
holesterol 0 mg, Sodium 320 mg

PINEAPPLE STRAWBERRY CRÈME BRULÉE

1 cup (240 ml) milk
¼ cup (60 ml) pineapple juice
⅓ cup (80 ml) cornstarch
1 cup (240 ml) whipping cream, whipped
1 cup (240 ml) fresh pineapple, diced
¾ cup (180 ml) granulated sugar
2 egg yolks
1 pt fresh strawberries
powdered sugar

Combine milk and granulated sugar; bring to a boil. Mix pineapple juice, cornstarch and egg yolks. Add heated milk mixture slowly. Boil until thickened. Chill and add whipped cream and diced pineapple. Ladle into a bowl. Arrange fresh strawberries and sprinkle with powdered sugar. Brown top under a broiler or salamander. Serves 4.

Approximate nutritional analysis per serving:
Calories 506, Protein 5 g, Carbohydrates 64 , Fat 27 g,
Cholesterol 196 mg, Sodium 58 mg

CLASSIC WHITE CRÈME BRULÉE

4 large eggs, at room temperature
⅓ cup (80 ml) sugar
2 cups (480 ml) whipping cream
1 - 4 oz bar (120 g) GHIRARDELLI Classic White
Confection, chopped in small pieces
½ tsp (3 ml) vanilla extract

Preheat oven to 300°F (150°C). In medium bowl, whisk egg yolks with sugar until smooth. In 2-qt saucepan, bring whipping cream to a simmer over medium-high heat. Add white bar to simmering whipping cream. Turn off heat and whisk until white bar is melted. Add white mixture to egg yolk mixture 1 tbs at a time, whisking continuously to prevent eggs from scrambling. Whisk until smooth Add vanilla.

Pour into 4 custard cups. Place cups in 13x9-inch baking pan or broiler. Add enough water so cups sit in 1-1½ inches of water. Bake until set, about 45 minutes. Serve warm, at room temperature, or refrigerate overnight. For a delicious crunchy surface, sprinkle the tops of the créme brulée with 1 tsp sugar and place under broiler until caramelized. Serves 4.

Approximate nutritional analysis per serving:
Calories 695, Protein 11 g, Carbohydrates 37 g, Fat 58 g,
Cholesterol 381 mg, Sodium 135 mg

STRAWBERRY BRULÉE

4 cups (960 ml) fresh strawberries, halved
½ cup (120 ml) soft-style or
whipped cream cheese
½ cup(120 ml) DANNON Vanilla Lowfat Yogurt
3 tbs (45 ml) packed brown sugar, divided

Arrange strawberries evenly in bottom of shallow 8-inch round broiler-proof pan or 2-qt glass ceramic casserole. In small bowl beat cream cheese, yogurt and 1 tbs brown sugar with electric mixer until smooth. Spoon yogurt mixture over fruit. Top with remaining 2 tbs brown sugar. Broil 4-5 inches from heat 2-3 minutes or just until brown sugar melts and starts to darken. Serve immediately. Serves 4.

Approximate nutritional analysis per serving:
Calories 200, Protein 4 g, Carbohydrates 23 g, Fat 11 g,
Cholesterol < 5 mg, Sodium 83 mg

PINK GRAPEFRUIT SORBET

1 large pink grapefruit
1 cup (240 ml) FLORIDA'S NATURAL
Brand Ruby Red Grapefruit Juice
2 cups (480 ml) sparkling apple juice or cold duck
¼ cup (60 ml) sugar
grapefruit rind curls

Grate rind from pink grapefruit and set aside. Carefully peel and section grapefruit, removing white membrane.

Position knife blade in food processor bowl; add grapefruit sections. Process until finely chopped. Add FLORIDA'S NATURAL Brand Ruby Red Grapefruit Juice and grapefruit rind; process until smooth.

Pour grapefruit mixture into freezer can of a 2-qt hand-turned or electric freezer. Add sparkling apple juice or cold duck and sugar; stir well. Freeze according to manufacturer's instructions. Let ripen 1 hour, if desired. Scoop sorbet into individual dessert bowls; garnish with grapefruit rind curls. Serve immediately. Yields 4½ cups.

Approximate nutritional analysis per ½ cup serving:
Calories 66, Protein < 1 g, Carbohydrates 17 g, Fat < 1 g,
Cholesterol 0 mg, Sodium 2 mg

MINT ICE

2 cups (480 ml) water
½ cup (120 ml) sugar
¼ tsp (1 ml) McCORMICK/SCHILLING
Pure Mint Extract
½ cup (120 ml) water

Combine 2 cups water, sugar, Mint Extract, stirring until sugar is dissolved. Pour into ice cube tray and freeze about 5 hours. Put cubes in blender or food processor and puree with ½ cup water. Serve immediately or spoon into dessert dishes or freezer container and refreeze. Yields 3 cups.

Approximate nutritional analysis per ½ cup serving:
Calories 64, Protein 0 g, Carbohydrates 17 g, Fat 0 g,
Cholesterol 0 mg, Sodium < 1 mg

FROZEN ORANGE CREAM

5 tbs (75 ml) orange juice
2 tbs (30 ml) lemon juice
1 cup (240 ml) IMPERIAL Granulated Sugar
⅛ tsp (.5 ml) salt
2 cups (480 ml) heavy cream, unwhipped

Turn temperature control of freezer to coldest setting. Mix juices, IMPERIAL Granulated Sugar, salt and let stand 10 minutes. Stir well, then stir in cream. Pour into refrigerator tray and freeze until firm; then reset temperature control back to normal. No stirring is necessary. Serve in sherbet glasses. Serves 6.

Banana-Orange Cream: Add 4 crushed bananas to the above recipe.

Approximate nutritional analysis per serving:
Calories 407, Protein 2 g, Carbohydrates 37 g, Fat 29 g,
Cholesterol 109 mg, Sodium 75 mg

Frozen Orange Cream

FROZEN CUSTARD ICE CREAM

6 eggs
2 cups (480 ml) milk
¾ cup (180 ml) sugar
2-3 tbs (30-45 ml) honey
¼ tsp (1 ml) salt
2 cups (480 ml) whipping cream
1 tbs (15 ml) vanilla
crushed ice
rock salt

In medium saucepan, beat together eggs, milk, sugar, honey and salt. Cook over low heat, stirring constantly, until mixture is thick enough to coat a metal spoon with a thin film and reaches at least 160°F (71°C). Cool quickly by setting pan in ice or cold water and stirring for a few minutes. Cover and refrigerate until thoroughly chilled, at least 1 hour. When ready to freeze, pour chilled custard, whipping cream and vanilla into 1-gallon ice cream freezer can. Freeze according to manufacturer's directions using 6 parts ice to 1 part rock salt. Transfer to freezer containers and freeze until firm. Yields 1½-2 qts.

VARIATIONS: Banana Nut: Reduce vanilla to 1½ tsp (8 ml). Cook and cool as above. Stir 3 large ripe bananas, mashed and ½ cup (120 ml) chopped toasted pecans into custard mixture. Freeze as above.

Cherry: Reduce vanilla to 1 tsp (5 ml). Add 2 tbs (30 ml) almond extract. Cook and cool as above. Partially freeze. Add 2 lbs (910 g) pitted pureed dark sweet fresh cherries or 1 - 16 oz can (480 g) pitted dark sweet cherries, drained and chopped. Complete freezing.

Chocolate: Add 3 - 1 oz squares (30 g each) unsweetened chocolate to egg mixture. Cook, cool and freeze as above.

Plum: Reduce vanilla to 1 tsp (5 ml). Cook and cool as above. Partially freeze. Add 1½ lbs (685 g) pitted pureed ripe fresh plums. Complete freezing.

Strawberry: Omit vanilla. Cook and cool as above. Partially freeze. Add 2 cups (480 ml) sweetened crushed fresh strawberries. Complete freezing.

Approximate nutritional analysis per serving:
Calories 390, Protein 8 g, Carbohydrates 29 g, Fat 29 g, Cholesterol 249 mg, Sodium 167 mg

NO-CRANK ICE CREAM

2 cups (480 ml) milk
¾ cup (180 ml) IMPERIAL Granulated Sugar
4 tsp (20 ml) flour
¼ tsp (1 ml) salt
3 egg yolks *or* 2 whole eggs
2 cups (480 ml) crushed strawberries
    (or other fresh fruits)
2 tsp (10 ml) pure vanilla extract
2 cups (480 ml) light cream

BUTTERSCOTCH SAUCE

2 cups (480 ml) IMPERIAL Brown Sugar
½ cup (120 ml) butter or margarine
2 tsp (10 ml) cornstarch
1 cup (240 ml) light cream
1 tsp (5 ml) vanilla

Scald the milk in the top of a double boiler. Mix the sugar, flour, salt together and add to the hot milk, stirring. Cook until slightly thickened, about 10 minutes. Beat yolks or eggs. Beat in a little hot mixture. Pour eggs into hot mixture and cook, stirring constantly, until it coats a metal spoon. Chill thoroughly. Add strawberries, vanilla, cream; freeze until mushy. Remove, beat smooth, freeze until firm. Drizzle with Butterscotch Sauce. Yields 1½ qts.

BUTTERSCOTCH SAUCE: Combine all ingredients except vanilla; bring to boil over moderate heat, stirring constantly. Turn heat to low and simmer for 5 minutes. Add vanilla. Serve hot or cold. After standing, sauce may separate into layers; this is corrected by stirring thoroughly. Yields 2 cups.

Approximate nutritional analysis per ½ cup serving Ice Cream:
Calories 215, Protein 3 g, Carbohydrates 18 g, Fat 15 g, Cholesterol 103 mg, Sodium 80 mg

Approximate nutritional analysis per 2 tbs serving Butterscotch Sauce:
Calories 198, Protein 0 g, Carbohydrates 27 g, Fat 10 g, Cholesterol 17 mg, Sodium 90 mg

HOMEMADE VANILLA ICE CREAM

1 qt (960 ml) milk
1¼ cups (295 ml) IMPERIAL Granulated Sugar
dash of salt
2 eggs, beaten
1½ cups (355 ml) heavy cream
2 tsp (10 ml) vanilla

Heat milk until small bubbles begin to appear around the edges of pan; stir in IMPERIAL Granulated Sugar and salt. Stir in some of hot mixture into beaten eggs and mix well. Stir egg mixture back into saucepan and cook over low heat, stirring, for about 2 minutes, being careful not to boil. Stir in cream and let mixture cool; stir in vanilla. Can be frozen in crank-type freezer or in freezing compartment, in which case freeze in refrigerator trays until partially frozen. Scrape ice cream into chilled bowl and beat until smooth. Refreeze in trays until firm. If desired, top with Butterscotch Sauce (previous recipe). Serves 8.

Approximate nutritional analysis per serving w/o sauce:
Calories 367, Protein 7 g, Carbohydrates 38 g, Fat 22 g, Cholesterol 131 mg, Sodium 109 mg

MENGER MANGO ICE CREAM

2 large ripe mangos
½ cup (120 ml) sugar
1 tbs (15 ml) lemon juice
1 cup (240 ml) heavy cream

Scoop out mango flesh and chop roughly, discarding peel and seed. Put chopped mango, sugar and lemon juice in food processor and process until smooth and thick. Pour puree and cream into ice cream canister and freeze according to ice cream freezer instructions. Serves 6.

Approximate nutritional analysis per serving:
Calories 246, Protein 1 g, Carbohydrates 30 g, Fat 15 g,
Cholesterol 54 mg, Sodium 17 mg

SENSIBLY DELICIOUS CHOCOLATE DREAM MOUSSE

1 envelope unflavored gelatin
¼ cup (60 ml) cold water
2 tbs (30 ml) granulated sugar
1 - 12 oz can (360 ml) undiluted CARNATION
    Lite Evaporated Skimmed Milk
1 - 12 oz pkg (360 g) NESTLÉ TOLL HOUSE
Semi-Sweet Chocolate Morsels
1 tbs (15 ml) vanilla extract

In medium saucepan, sprinkle gelatin over water; let stand for 1 minute. Stir over low heat until gelatin is dissolved. Stir in sugar. Add evaporated milk all at once. Continue heating over medium heat, stirring constantly, until milk is steaming hot; do not boil. Pour into blender container; add morsels and vanilla. Cover; blend on low speed until smooth. Pour into small mixer bowl. Chill, stirring occasionally, until mixture mounds. Beat on high speed of electric mixer for 1-2 minutes until thick and light in color. Spoon into serving dishes; chill. Serves 12.

Approximate nutritional analysis per serving:
Calories 195, Protein 4 g, Carbohydrates 22 g, Fat 10 g,
Cholesterol 0 mg, Sodium 40 mg

Sensibly Delicious Chocolate Dream Mousse

MATTUS' LOWFAT ALASKA

Entenmann's No-Fat Pound Cake or another
   prepared or homemade pound cake
1 pt (480 ml) MATTUS' Honey Vanilla
   Lowfat Ice Cream
4 egg whites, room temperature
pinch salt
¼ tsp (1 ml) cream of tartar
½ cup (120 ml) sugar
½ tsp (3 ml) vanilla extract
1-2 tbs (15-30 ml) low fat fudge topping

Remove center of cake, leaving a 1-inch border on sides and
bottom. Fill cake with MATTUS' Honey Vanilla Lowfat Ice
Cream. Freeze until firm, approximately 3 hours.

   Meanwhile, beat the egg whites with an electric mixer at
moderate slow speed until they are foaming throughout, about
2 minutes. Add salt and cream of tartar (stabilizer), increase
speed gradually to high. Slowly add sugar. Once egg whites
form soft peaks, add vanilla. Continue beating egg whites until
shining stiff peaks are formed.

   Preheat oven to 475°F (246°C). Once ice cream-filled
pound cake is frozen firm, top with the meringue forming
peaks. Place into the center of the oven. Cook until peaks are
golden brown, 8-10 minutes. Remove cake from oven and
slowly drizzle low fat fudge topping over top. Flambé with rum
or other liquor if desired. Serve immediately. Serves 8.

Nutritional analysis not available.

HAZELNUT-CHOCOLATE MOUSSE

7 oz (210 g) bittersweet chocolate
2 tbs (30 ml) water
2 tsp (10 ml) vanilla
3 tbs (45 ml) water
1 cup (240 ml) sugar
8 oz (240 g) cream cheese, softened
1 cup (240 ml) Hazelnuts, toasted and chopped
⅓ cup (80 ml) Hazelnut liqueur or Hazelnut extract
1 pt (480 ml) heavy whipping cream
¼ cup (60 ml) sugar
1 tsp (5 ml) vanilla

Melt chocolate and slowly add 2 tbs water until it becomes a
paste. Stir together 2 tsp vanilla, 3 tbs water and 1 cup sugar,
then add chocolate paste and bring to boil over low heat.
Remove from heat and fold in cream cheese, nuts and liqueur,
then set aside to cool. Meanwhile, whip cream, ¼ cup sugar
and 1 tsp vanilla until stiff. Fold chocolate mixture and whip
cream together, being careful not to overmix. Carefully fill a
pie crust or parfait glasses. Top with whipped cream and a
single glazed Hazelnut. Serves 6.

Approximate nutritional analysis per serving:
Calories 912, Protein 8 g, Carbohydrates 73 g, Fat 66 g,
Cholesterol 150 mg, Sodium 150 mg

LIGHT & EASY FRUITED CHOCOLATE MOUSSE

1 - 10 oz pkg (300 g) frozen strawberries
   in syrup, thawed and well drained
1 - 3 oz pkg (90 g) strawberry flavored gelatin
¾ cup (180 ml) boiling water
¼ cup (60 ml) HERSHEY'S European Style
   Cocoa or HERSHEY'S Cocoa
1 cup (240 ml) ice cubes
½ cup (120 ml) frozen light non-dairy
   whipped topping, thawed

In blender container, place gelatin; carefully pour in boiling
water. Cover; blend on low speed until gelatin is completely
dissolved. Add cocoa; continue blending until smooth. Imme
diately add ice cubes, blending until melted. Add reserved
strawberries and light whipped topping; continue blending,
just until combined and smooth. Immediately pour into dessert
dishes; refrigerate until set, about 4 hours. Serves 8.

Approximate nutritional analysis per serving:
Calories 110, Protein 3 g, Carbohydrates 21 g, Fat 2 g,
Cholesterol 0 mg, Sodium 30 mg

CHOCOLATE-ALMOND MOUSSE

¾ cup (180 ml) milk
4 eggs
¼ cup (60 ml) sugar
1 - 6 oz pkg (180 g) semi-sweet chocolate pieces
1 tsp (5 ml) vanilla
½ tsp (3 ml) almond extract
2-3 tbs (30-45 ml) slivered almonds

In medium saucepan, stir together milk, eggs and sugar until
thoroughly blended. Cook over low heat, stirring constantly,
until mixture is thick enough to coat a metal spoon with a thin
film and reaches at least 160°F (71°C). Remove from heat. Stir
in chocolate and flavorings until chocolate is melted. Spoon
into 8 *pot de crème* cups or ¼-cup dessert dishes. Sprinkle with
almonds. Refrigerate several hours of over night. Serves 8.

   Microwave: In small bowl, stir together eggs and sugar
until thoroughly blended. In 1-cup liquid measure, cook milk
on full power until bubbles form at edges, about 2½ minutes.
Stir into egg mixture. Cook on 50% power, stirring every
minute, until mixture is thick enough to coat a metal spoon
with a thin film and reaches at least 160°F (71°C), about 3-4
minutes. Continue as above.

Approximate nutritional analysis per serving:
Calories 201, Protein 5 g, Carbohydrates 20 g, Fat 13 g,
Cholesterol 109 mg, Sodium 46 mg

Bacardi Strawberry Mousse

BACARDI STRAWBERRY MOUSSE

½ cup (120 ml) BACARDI Light rum
1 pkg (10 oz, 280 g) frozen strawberries, thawed
1 cup (240 ml) sugar
2 pkgs unflavored gelatin
2½ cups (600 ml) whipping cream, divided
½ cup (120 ml) water

Soften gelatin in ½ cup water. Heat over low heat until gelatin is dissolved. Cool to room temperature.

   Puree strawberries in food processor or blender. Add sugar and mix well. Add cooled gelatin, and stir well. Place mixture in refrigerator until it starts to set. Whip 1½ cups of the cream. Remove strawberry mixture from refrigerator, add rum and mix well. Fold in whipped cream. Pour in a 2 quart souffle dish or serving bowl. Refigerate. When firm, decorate with remaining cream, whipped (1 cup) and fresh, sliced strawberries. Serves 4-6.

Approximate nutritional analysis per 1 / 6th recipe:
Calories 534, Protein 4g, Carbohydrates 39g, Fat 37g,
Cholesterol 136g, Sodium 40 mg

VANILLA MOUSSE

⅔ cup (160 ml) boiling water
2 envelopes unflavored gelatin
½ cup (120 ml) sugar
1 cup (240 ml) canned evaporated skim milk
1 tsp (5 ml) McCORMICK/SCHILLING
    Pure Vanilla Extract
⅛ tsp (.5 ml) McCORMICK/SCHILLING
    Ground Cinnamon
2 cups (480 ml) ice cubes
fresh berries

Pour water and gelatin into an electric blender. Process on high 30 seconds. Add sugar and process 5 seconds. Add remaining ingredients except fruit and process 1 minute or until mixture is smooth. Pour into dessert dishes and chill 1 hour. Serve topped with fresh berries. Serves 6.

Approximate nutritional analysis per serving:
Calories 128, Protein 5 g, Carbohydrates 21 g, Fat 3 g,
Cholesterol 12 mg, Sodium 47 mg

APRICOT MOUSSE

4 cups (960 ml) DANNON Vanilla Lowfat Yogurt
2 - 16 oz cans (960 g) apricot halves
in heavy syrup, drained
1 tbs (15 ml) sugar
1½ tsp (8 ml) orange-flavored liqueur, optional
1 cup (240 ml) fresh blueberries
4 strawberries
mint leaves, optional

Spoon yogurt into large strainer lined with double thickness of cheesecloth or a coffee filter. Place bowl beneath, but not touching strainer to catch liquid. Cover; chill 24 hours.

Scrape yogurt into a medium bowl. Discard liquid. Place apricots in a food processor or blender. Process until smooth. In a large bowl combine apricot puree, drained yogurt, sugar and liqueur; mix well. Cover; chill at least 30 minutes.

To serve, spoon blueberries into 6 wine glasses or dessert dishes, reserving a few berries for the top. Spoon mousse over berries. Hull strawberries and slice thinly. Top each serving of mousse with a few slices. Sprinkle with remaining blueberries and garnish each with a mint leaf. Serves 6.

Approximate nutritional analysis per serving:
Calories 274, Protein 9 g, Carbohydrates 56 g, Fat 3 g,
Cholesterol 9 mg, Sodium 114 mg

MOLDED BLUEBERRY TAPIOCA CREAM

3 tbs (45 ml) quick-cooking tapioca
3 tbs (45 ml) sugar
⅛ tsp (.5 ml) salt
6 tbs (90 ml) instant nonfat dry milk
1½ cups (355 ml) water
1 egg, separated
2 tbs (30 ml) sugar
1 envelope gelatin
2 tbs (30 ml) water
1 can COMSTOCK Blueberry Pie Filling

TOPPING
¼ cup (60 ml) cold water
2 tsp (10 ml) lemon juice
¼ cup (60 ml) instant nonfat dry milk
1 envelope low-calorie sweetener

In a saucepan mix tapioca, 3 tbs sugar, salt, dry milk, water and egg yolk. Let stand 5 minutes. In a bowl beat egg white until foamy, then slowly beat in the 2 tbs sugar until the egg white stands in soft peaks. Set aside. Soften gelatin in 2 tbs water. Over medium heat cook the tapioca mixture, stirring constantly until it reaches a full boil, about 5-8 minutes.

Add the dissolved gelatin. Pour a little of the hot mixture over the beaten egg whites, blend, then add the rest rapidly, stirring constantly. Stir in the pie filling. Cool about 15 minutes; stir, then pour into lightly oiled 5-cup mold. Chill until firm,
4 hours or more. Serves 6.

TOPPING: Stir the cold water and lemon juice together. Sprinkle dry milk over top and beat at high speed about 5 minutes or until stiff. Blend in 1 envelope low-calorie sweetener. Chill. Yields 1 cup.

Approximate nutritional analysis per serving:
Calories 383, Protein 7 g, Carbohydrates 91 g, Fat 2 g,
Cholesterol 37 mg, Sodium 113 mg

1-2-3 LEMON MOUSSE

1½ cups (355 ml) heavy cream
⅓ cup (80 ml) sugar
¼ cup (60 ml) lemon juice
1 tsp (5 ml) McCORMICK/SCHILLING
Pure Lemon Extract

Beat all ingredients until mixture mounds softly. Spoon into dessert dishes and serve. Serves 6.

Approximate nutritional analysis per serving:
Calories 250, Protein 1 g, Carbohydrates 14 g, Fat 22 g,
Cholesterol 82 mg, Sodium 23 mg

PUMPKIN PUDDING

½ cup (120 ml) sugar
½ cup (120 ml) water
2 envelopes unflavored gelatin
4 eggs, separated
1 - 1 lb can (455 g) cooked pumpkin
6 ice cubes
2-3 tsp (10-15 ml) pumpkin pie spice

In medium saucepan combine sugar, water and gelatin. Let stand 1 minute. Beat in egg yolks using a wire whisk. Cook over medium heat, stirring constantly, until gelatin is dissolved and mixture is thick and foamy, about 3 minutes.

Pour gelatin mixture into 5-cup blender container. Add remaining ingredients. Process at high speed until ice is melted, about 2 minutes. Pour into serving dishes. Chill until set,
1-2 hours. Serves 8.

Approximate nutritional analysis per serving:
Calories 112, Protein 5 g, Carbohydrates 18 g, Fat 3 g,
Cholesterol 106 mg, Sodium 36 mg

Courtesy of the American Egg Board

Opposite: Pumpkin Pudding

SMUCKER'S ENGLISH BERRY PUDDING

1 cup (240 ml) SMUCKER'S Raspberry Preserves
12-16 slices white bread, crusts removed,
    cut into ½ or ¼ triangles
2 cups (480 ml) raspberries, fresh or frozen
2 cups (480 ml) blueberries, fresh or frozen
2 cups (480 ml) sliced strawberries, fresh or frozen

Line a deep 1½-2-qt bowl with plastic wrap. Line the bottom and sides of the bowl with about ½ the triangle bread slices. Completely cover the surface so that there are no gaps between the bread slices.

Heat the SMUCKER'S Raspberry Preserves and 6 cups of mixed berries in a saucepan over high heat. Bring to a boil and simmer the fruit for 5 minutes to release juices. Spoon half the berry mixture into the bread lined bowl. Cover with half of the remaining bread triangles and the remaining berry mixture. Cover the second layer of berries with the remaining bread. Use more bread if needed to completely seal the bowl. Cover the pudding with plastic wrap. Place a plate on top of the bowl to weigh it down slightly. Refrigerate the pudding for 12-24 hours before serving.

To serve, remove the plate and the plastic wrap. Unmold the bowl onto a serving plate. Remove the bowl and carefully peel the plastic wrap from the pudding. Serve the pudding dusted with powdered sugar, whipped cream, frozen yogurt or whipped topping. Serves 8.

Approximate nutritional analysis per serving:
Calories 264, Protein 4 g, Carbohydrates 59 g, Fat 2 g,
Cholesterol 0 mg, Sodium 213 mg

GRAPEFRUIT PARFAIT

4 ruby red grapefruits
½ cup (120 ml) ruby red grapefruit juice
1 envelope unflavored gelatin
½ cup (120 ml) IMPERIAL Brown Sugar
2 cups (480 ml) milk
2 tsp (10 ml) lemon juice
2 tbs (30 ml) IMPERIAL Brown Sugar
1 cup (240 ml) heavy cream, whipped
grapefruit sections for garnish

Cut grapefruit in halves and section; set sections aside and drain. Squeeze sectioned grapefruit halves for juice. Combine juice and gelatin in small saucepan and stir; let stand 1 minute. Warm over low heat just until gelatin is dissolved; add ½ cup IMPERIAL Brown Sugar and stir until sugar dissolves. Stir in milk and lemon juice (it will look curdled) and transfer to medium bowl. Chill just until thickened, stirring occasionally as mixture begins to thicken. Beat 2 tbs IMPERIAL Brown Sugar into stiffly beaten cream. Serve in chilled parfait or wine glasses layered with grapefruit sections. Garnish with more grapefruit sections. Chill until serving time. Serves 8.

Approximate nutritional analysis per serving:
Calories 244, Protein 4 g, Carbohydrates 30 g, Fat 13 g,
Cholesterol 49 mg, Sodium 47 mg

LEMON ANGEL MOLD

1 envelope unflavored gelatin
¼ cup (60 ml) cold water
6 egg yolks
¾ cup (180 ml) IMPERIAL Granulated Sugar
¾ cup (180 ml) lemon juice
grated rind of 2 lemons
¼ tsp (1 ml) salt
6 egg whites
¾ cup (180 ml) IMPERIAL Granulated Sugar
1 angel food cake
2 cups (480 ml) whipping cream
2 tbs (30 ml) IMPERIAL 10X Powdered Sugar
1 tsp (5 ml) vanilla

Combine gelatin and water; set aside. Mix next 5 ingredients and cook in double boiler until slightly thick. Remove and stir in gelatin/water mixture. Refrigerate until partially set. Beat egg whites until stiff, gradually adding ¾ cup IMPERIAL Granulated Sugar. Fold into cooled custard. Shred angel food cake into flakes with a fork. Mix with custard mixture. Pour into lightly buttered angel food cake pan. Chill 8 hours. Unmold and frost with cream which has been whipped with IMPERIAL Powdered Sugar and vanilla. Serves 12.

Approximate nutritional analysis per serving:
Calories 418, Protein 8 g, Carbohydrates 59 g, Fat 17 g,
Cholesterol 160 mg, Sodium 197 mg

CRANBERRY FOOL

1 - 16 oz can (480 g) jellied cranberry sauce
1 tbs (15 ml) grated orange peel
1 tsp (5 ml) almond extract
1 cup (240 ml) heavy cream, whipped
    or 8 oz (240 g) cool whip

Mix together the first 3 ingredients with a whisk or fork. Add whipped cream or cool whip. Fill parfait or dessert dishes. Chill until set. Garnish with whipped cream and orange slice. Serves 6.

May also be used at room temperature as a fruit dip.

Approximate nutritional analysis per serving:
Calories 276, Protein 0 g, Carbohydrates 37 g, Fat 15 g,
Cholesterol 54 mg, Sodium 42 mg

Courtesy of Cape Cod Cranberry Growers' Association.

LEMON CHIFFON PUDDING

1 cup (240 ml) IMPERIAL Granulated Sugar
5 tbs (75 ml) all-purpose flour
3 tbs (45 ml) butter or margarine
3 eggs, separated
1 cup (240 ml) milk
¼ cup (60 ml) lemon juice
½ tsp (3 ml) lemon rind

Mix IMPERIAL Granulated Sugar with flour. Cream with butter. Beat yolks until thick. Add yolks and milk to flour, sugar, butter mixture. Add lemon juice and rind. Beat egg whites until stiff but not dry. Fold into first mixture. Pour into buttered baking dish. Place baking dish in pan with 1-inch hot water. Bake in preheated oven at 350°F (180°C) for 1 hour, 5 minutes or until firm. Serves 6.

Approximate nutritional analysis per serving:
Calories 263, Protein 5 g, Carbohydrates 40 g, Fat 10 g,
Cholesterol 112 mg, Sodium 128 mg

UPSIDE-DOWN CHOCOLATE PUDDING

1 cup (240 ml) all-purpose flour
2 tsp (10 ml) baking powder
½ tsp (3 ml) salt
¾ cup (180 ml) IMPERIAL Granulated Sugar
3 tbs (45 ml) cocoa
1 tsp (5 ml) vanilla
½ cup (120 ml) milk
2 tbs (30 ml) salad oil
½ cup (120 ml) chopped nuts
1¼ cups (295 ml) IMPERIAL Brown Sugar
¼ cup (60 ml) cocoa
2 cups (480 ml) hot water
whipped cream

Combine flour, baking powder, salt, IMPERIAL Granulated Sugar, 3 tbs cocoa into mixing bowl. Add vanilla to milk; then add this with salad oil and nuts to combined dry ingredients. Stir until well blended. Turn into 8x8x2-inch pan. Mix IMPERIAL Brown Sugar and ¼ cup cocoa; sprinkle with batter. Pour hot water over entire surface. Bake at 350°F (180°C) for 40-45 minutes. Spoon out while warm, sauce side up. Top with whipped cream. Serves 8-10.

Approximate nutritional analysis per serving w/o whipped cream:
Calories 282, Protein 3 g, Carbohydrates 54 g, Fat 8 g,
Cholesterol 2 mg, Sodium 207 mg

VANILLA PUDDING

½ cup (120 ml) sugar
2 tbs (30 ml) cornstarch
⅛ tsp (.5 ml) salt
1½ cups (355 ml) plain soymilk
1 tsp (5 ml) vanilla extract

In a saucepan, stir together the sugar, cornstarch and salt. Slowly add the soymilk, stirring to prevent lumps from forming. Bring the mixture to a boil. Lower to simmer, stirring constantly for about 5 minutes, until mixture is creamy and thick. Remove from heat, stir in vanilla and pour into dessert cups. Chill until mixture sets. Serves 4.

Approximate nutritional analysis per serving:
Calories 141, Protein 2 g, Carbohydrates 30 g, Fat 2 g,
Cholesterol 0 mg, Sodium 78 mg

Courtesy of the United Soybean Board.

APPLE-WALNUT BREAD PUDDING

½ loaf French bread, crust trimmed
2 large eggs, beaten
1¼ cups (295 ml) milk
2 tsp (10 ml) McCORMICK/SCHILLING
  Pure Vanilla Extract
1 tsp (5 ml) McCORMICK/SCHILLING
  Black Walnut Extract
½ cup (120 ml) sugar
1 tsp (5 ml) McCORMICK/SCHILLING Cinnamon
½ tsp (3 ml) McCORMICK/SCHILLING Nutmeg
⅓ cup (80 ml) raisins
1 cup (240 ml) diced tart apple
¾ cup (180 ml) toasted, chopped walnuts
2 tbs (30 ml) butter or margarine

Preheat oven to 325°F (165°C). Cut bread into ¾-inch cubes. Butter 7x11-inch baking dish. Combine remaining ingredients except butter. Mix well and add bread cubes. Toss to combine. Spread in pan and dot with butter. Bake 35 minutes or until firm. Serves 6.

Approximate nutritional analysis per serving:
Calories 389, Protein 9 g, Carbohydrates 51 g, Fat 18 g,
Cholesterol 89 mg, Sodium 252 mg

CINNAMON RAISIN BREAD PUDDING

3 cups (720 ml) skim milk
½ cup (120 ml) Regular, Quick or Instant
    CREAM OF WHEAT Cereal
3 eggs, slightly beaten
⅓ cup (80 ml) sugar
1 tsp (5 ml) vanilla extract
⅛ tsp (.5 ml) ground nutmeg
1 - 8¼ oz can (248 g) sliced peaches,
    drained and coarsely chopped
6 slices cinnamon raisin bread, cut into 1-inch cubes
prepared whipped topping, optional

In large saucepan, over medium heat, heat milk to a boil; slowly sprinkle in cereal. Cook and stir until slightly thickened, about 1-3 minutes. Remove from heat; let stand 5 minutes. Stir in eggs, sugar, vanilla and nutmeg. Layer half the cereal mixture, chopped peaches and bread cubes on greased 2-qt round casserole. Repeat layers once. Place casserole in a pan filled with 1-inch depth water. Bake at 325°F (165°C) for 35-40 minutes or until pudding is set in center. Serve warm topped with whipped topping if desired. Serves 8.

Approximate nutritional analysis per serving w/o whipped topping:
Calories 207, Protein 6 g, Carbohydrates 22 g, Fat 3 g,
Cholesterol 82 mg, Sodium 185 mg

FRUIT BREAD PUDDING

4 cups (960 ml) cubed whole wheat bread
½ cup (120 ml) diced dried fruit or raisins
1½ cups (355 ml) skim milk
½ cup (120 ml) HEALTHY CHOICE
    Cholesterol Free Egg Product
¼ cup (60 ml) sugar
1 tsp (5 ml) vanilla
¼ tsp (1 ml) ground nutmeg

In 1½-qt casserole sprayed with vegetable oil spray, combine bread and fruit. In small bowl, combine milk, egg product, sugar, vanilla and nutmeg. Pour milk mixture over bread. Bake in 350°F (180°C) oven for 60 minutes or until knife inserted in center comes out clean. Serves 6.

Approximate nutritional analysis per serving:
Calories 169, Protein 7 g, Carbohydrates 32 g, Fat 2 g,
Cholesterol 2 mg, Sodium 179 mg

SWEET POTATO PUDDING

½ cup (120 ml) molasses
½ cup (120 ml) sugar
⅓ cup (80 ml) melted butter or margarine
1 tsp (5 ml) nutmeg
4 cups (960 ml) grated raw LOUISIANA Yams
1 tsp (5 ml) cinnamon
½ tsp (3 ml) salt
3 eggs, well beaten
1½ cups (355 ml) milk

Combine molasses, sugar, melted butter, spices and salt. Add eggs and milk. Stir in yams, mixing thoroughly. Pour mixture into a well-greased 1-qt casserole and bake in a 350°F (180°C) oven about 1½ hours. Stir twice during baking, turning under the crust which will form on top. Serve warm or cold, with cream. Serves 6.

Approximate nutritional analysis per serving:
Calories 364, Protein 6 g, Carbohydrates 53 g, Fat 15 g,
Cholesterol 142 mg, Sodium 254 mg

Courtesy of Louisiana Sweet Potatoes.

SOUTHERN YAM-DATE PUDDING

1 cup (240 ml) pitted dates, chopped
1 cup (240 ml) seedless raisins
1 cup (240 ml) milk
1½ cups (355 ml) sifted all-purpose flour
1 cup (240 ml) sugar
1 tsp (5 ml) nutmeg
1 tsp (5 ml) cinnamon
¼ tsp (1 ml) salt
3 eggs, well beaten
4 medium LOUISIANA yams, cooked,
    peeled and mashed
1 tbs (15 ml) grated orange rind
½ cup (120 ml) chopped pecans

Combine dates, raisins and milk in saucepan; cook over very low heat 20 minutes, or until dates are tender, stirring occasionally. Sift together flour, sugar, nutmeg, cinnamon and salt. Stir in date mixture. Add eggs and yams; mix well. Stir in orange rind and pecans. Turn into well-greased 2-qt mold or casserole. Cover tightly with waxed paper; secure paper with string. Place on rack in steamer or large saucepan. Add water until mold is half immersed. Cover tightly and steam over medium heat 2 hours. Allow to cool slightly before unmolding. Serves 8.

Approximate nutritional analysis per 1 cup serving:
Calories 446, Protein 8 g, Carbohydrates 89 g, Fat 8 g,
Cholesterol 84 mg, Sodium 118 mg

EASTER BASKET CAKE

1 cup (240 ml) cake flour
1½ cups (355 ml) IMPERIAL Granulated Sugar, divided
½ tsp (3 ml) salt
1 tsp (5 ml) cream of tartar
1½ cups (355 ml) egg whites (10-12 eggs)
1 tsp (5 ml) vanilla extract
1 tsp (5 ml) almond extract

CREAMY BUTTER FROSTING
1 - 1 lb carton (455 g) IMPERIAL 10X Powdered Sugar
3 tbs (45 ml) soft butter or margarine
1 tsp (5 ml) vanilla
¼ cup (60 ml) light cream or milk
few drops yellow food color (to make pale yellow basket color)
shredded coconut
few drops green food color (to make green grass)

All ingredients must be at room temperature. Sift flour with ¾ cup IMPERIAL Granulated Sugar; set aside. Add salt and cream of tartar to egg whites and beat until beginning of soft peak stage. Gradually beat remaining ¾ cup IMPERIAL Granulated Sugar into egg whites, 2 tbs at a time, beating until stiff peaks form. Fold in vanilla and almond extracts. Sprinkle flour and sugar mixture over batter, a few tbs at a time, folding in gently. Transfer batter to ungreased 10-inch tube pan. Bake in preheated 325°F (165°C) oven about 50 minutes, or until top springs back when touched with fingertip. Invert pan immediately and allow cake to cool completely (upside down) before removing from pan. Frost with Creamy Butter Frosting. Serves 12.

CREAMY BUTTER FROSTING: Combine IMPERIAL Powdered Sugar, butter, vanilla, light cream, and yellow food color. If necessary, adjust sugar or cream for proper consistency. After spreading frosting on cake, let dry about 10 minutes before drawing inch-long horizontal and vertical lines in frosting with tines of fork to simulate basket weave.

TO MAKE BASKET: Cut sloping slice from top edge of cake to cake center to form a basket shape, cutting no deeper than ½ inch. Use cut-away cake to fill center hole. Frost top and sides of cake. Cover top of basket with green-tinted coconut made by putting coconut and few drops green food coloring in plastic bag and working with hands until coconut is uniformly tinted. Fill basket with jelly beans or Easter eggs. Complete basket weave texture according to instructions above.

TO MAKE BASKET HANDLE: Stitch two 24-inch lengths of ½-inch wide ribbon or seam binding on both sides to make a tube. Insert a 22-inch length of coat hanger wire through the tube; fold ends of ribbon to cover ends of wire and secure by wrapping with thread. Shape into rounded handle and insert into cake. Decorate handle with bow.

Approximate nutritional analysis per serving Cake and Frosting:
Calories 326, Protein 4 g, Carbohydrates 69 g, Fat 4 g,
Cholesterol 6 mg, Sodium 180 mg

ARROZ CON LECHE
Classic Rice Pudding

5 cups (1.4 L) milk
1 tsp (5 ml) ground cinnamon
1 cinnamon stick
1 orange peel
1 lemon peel
½ cup (120 ml) GOYA Medium-Grain Rice
1 tsp (5 ml) vanilla extract
1 oz (30 ml) light rum
I cup (180 ml) sugar

In a large saucepan, combine milk, cinnamon, cinnamon stick, orange peel and lemon peel. Bring to a boil. Remove from heat for 1 minute, then add rice, vanilla extract and rum. Return to a boil, stir once, reduce heat, and boil gently for 20-25 minutes, or until rice is done. Remove from heat. Discard peel and cinnamon stick and gently stir in sugar. Serves 6.

Approximate nutritional analysis per serving:
Calories 288, Protein 8 g, Carbohydrates 47g, Fat 7 g,
Cholesterol 28 mg, Sodium 100 mg

CARUSO'S GRAND FINALE RICE PUDDING

2¼ cups (540 ml) milk
⅔ cup (160 ml) raisins
½ cup (120 ml) arborio rice
¼ cup (60 ml) sugar
½ tsp (3 ml) salt
3 tbs (45 ml) amaretto liqueur
1 tsp (5 ml) vanilla
1 cup (240 ml) whipping cream

In heavy saucepan bring milk, raisins, rice, sugar and salt just to boil. Immediately reduce heat, cover, and simmer 25-30 minutes until most of the milk has been absorbed. Remove from heat; stir in liqueur and vanilla. Cool to room temperature. Whip cream; fold into rice mixture. Spoon into dessert dishes; chill. Serves 6.

Approximate nutritional analysis per serving:
Calories 359, Protein 5 g, Carbohydrates 43 g, Fat 18 g,
Cholesterol 67 mg, Sodium 63 mg

Courtesy of The California Raisin Advisory Board.

Opposite: Easter Basket Cake

ANGEL FOOD ROYAL

1 cup (240 ml) IMPERIAL Granulated Sugar
½ cup (120 ml) all-purpose flour
4 egg yolks, beaten
⅛ tsp (.5 ml) salt
2 cups (480 ml) milk, scalded
1 tbs (15 ml) unflavored gelatin
2 tbs (30 ml) milk
2 cups (480 ml) whipping cream, whipped
2 tsp (10 ml) vanilla
½ tsp (3 ml) almond extract
1 - 10-inch angel food cake
½ cup (120 ml) chopped pecans

Blend IMPERIAL Granulated Sugar with flour. Add beaten egg yolks and salt. Mix carefully with scalded milk and cook in top of double boiler until thick, stirring constantly. Soak gelatin in 2 tbs milk. Add to hot custard mixture and refrigerate, stirring occasionally, until it begins to set. Fold in whipped cream, vanilla, and almond extract.

With sharp knife, split cake into 2 layers. Spread part of custard mixture on bottom layer; sprinkle with nuts. Place top layer on; cover entire cake with remainder of custard. Refrigerate at least 2 hours before serving. Serves 12.

Approximate nutritional analysis per serving:
Calories 441, Protein 8 g, Carbohydrates 56 g, Fat 21 g,
Cholesterol 131 mg, Sodium 210 mg

Angel Food Royal

SAM HOUSTON WHITE CAKE

¾ cup (180 ml) butter or margarine
1½ cups (355 ml) IMPERIAL Granulated Sugar
3 cups (720 ml) sifted all-purpose flour
1 tbs (15 ml) baking powder
½ tsp (3 ml) salt
1 tsp (5 ml) vanilla
½ tsp (3 ml) almond flavoring
½ cup (120 ml) milk
½ cup (120 ml) water
6 egg whites
½ cup (120 ml) IMPERIAL Granulated Sugar

Cream butter until soft and light. Gradually add 1½ cups IMPERIAL Granulated Sugar and continue creaming several minutes to incorporate as much air as possible. Stir together flour, baking powder, salt. Add vanilla, almond flavoring to milk and water. Add flour alternately with liquid to creamed mixture; beat well after each addition. Beat egg whites until soft peaks form; gradually beat in ½ cup IMPERIAL Granulated Sugar and beat until stiff but not dry; fold into batter, blending well. Pour into 3 greased and floured 9-inch layer pans. Bake in preheated oven at 350°F (180°C) for 25 minutes. Cool 5 minutes, then turn onto cooling racks and remove pans. When cool, fill and frost with chocolate frosting. Serves 12.

Approximate nutritional analysis per serving:
Calories 350, Protein 5 g, Carbohydrates 56 g, Fat 12 g,
Cholesterol 1 mg, Sodium 348 mg

FESTIVE HOLIDAY CAKE

4 egg whites
½ cup (120 ml) IMPERIAL Granulated Sugar
2 cups plus 2 tbs (270 ml) all-purpose flour
1 cup (240 ml) IMPERIAL Granulated Sugar
3½ tsp (18 ml) baking powder
1 tsp (5 ml) salt
½ cup (120 ml) shortening
1 cup (240 ml) milk
⅔ cup (160 ml) flaked coconut
¾ tsp (4 ml) vanilla or almond extract

FILLING
2 egg yolks
⅔ cup (160 ml) dairy sour cream
⅔ cup (160 ml) IMPERIAL Granulated Sugar
1 cup (240 ml) finely chopped pecans
⅔ cup (160 ml) flaked coconut
½ cup (120 ml) finely chopped raisins or whole
currants, plumped, drained thoroughly
½ cup (120 ml) finely chopped candied cherries
or thoroughly drained maraschino cherries

WHITE ICING
1½ cups (355 ml) IMPERIAL Granulated Sugar
½ cup (120 ml) water
2 egg whites, unbeaten
½ tsp (3 ml) cream of tartar
2 tsp (10 ml) vanilla

Heat oven to 350°F (180°C). Grease and flour 2 - 9-inch layer cake pans. Beat egg whites until frothy and soft peaks begin to form. Gradually beat in ½ cup IMPERIAL Granulated Sugar and continue beating until stiff peaks form; reserve. Combine flour, 1 cup IMPERIAL Granulated Sugar, baking powder, salt, shortening in large mixer bowl. Add milk and blend on low speed 30 seconds, then beat 2 minutes on medium speed. Carefully fold in egg whites and coconut with vanilla or almond extract. Pour into pans and bake 30-35 minutes or until done. Cool. Fill between layers and frost top to within 1-inch of edge with filling. Frost entire cake with White Icing.

FILLING: Blend egg yolks and sour cream; stir in IMPE-RIAL Granulated Sugar. Cook over low heat, stirring until mixture begins to simmer. Simmer several minutes until mixture thickens. Remove from heat; stir in remaining ingredients. Cool before adding to cake layers.

WHITE ICING: Combine IMPERIAL Granulated Sugar and water in saucepan; cook over medium heat, stirring to dissolve sugar, until mixture comes to a boil. Pour syrup over remaining ingredients in electric mixer bowl and beat until frosting is stiff and holds well-defined peaks. Spread on cake. Sprinkle with coconut, if desired.

Approximate nutritional analysis per serving Cake w/o frosting or filling:
Calories 297, Protein 4 g, Carbohydrates 46 g, Fat 11 g,
Cholesterol 3 mg, Sodium 305 mg

Approximate nutritional analysis per serving Filling:
Calories 204, Protein 2 g, Carbohydrates 25 g, Fat 12 g,
Cholesterol 41 mg, Sodium 20 mg

Approximate nutritional analysis per serving Icing:
Calories 99, Protein 1 g, Carbohydrates 25 g, Fat 0 g,
Cholesterol 0 mg, Sodium 10 mg

ROCKY ROAD CHOCOLATE CAKE

4 eggs
1½ cups (355 ml) self rising flour*
1 cup (240 ml) butter or margarine, melted, cooled
¼ cup (60 ml) cocoa
1¼ cups (295 ml) IMPERIAL Granulated Sugar
1 cup (240 ml) IMPERIAL Brown Sugar
2 tsp (10 ml) vanilla

ROCKY ROAD FROSTING
1 - 6¼ oz pkg (188 g) miniature marshmallows
4¾ cups (1.1 L) IMPERIAL Powdered Sugar
¼ cup (60 ml) cocoa
6 tbs (90 ml) milk
1 cup (240 ml) toasted, chopped pecans

* All-purpose flour can be used by adding 2¼ tsp (11 ml) baking powder and ¾ tsp (4 ml) salt.

Beat eggs until light. Add remaining ingredients and mix until well blended. Pour into greased and floured 9x13-inch pan. Bake in preheated 350°F (180°C) oven 40-45 minutes or until done. Leave cake in pan and frost with Rocky Road Frosting while cake is hot. Serves 12.

ROCKY ROAD FROSTING: Arrange marshmallows over top of cake. Combine powdered sugar and cocoa; blend in butter or margarine and milk. Stir in toasted nuts. Spread frosting on top of marshmallows. Let cool. Cut into squares. Serves 12.

Note: For a different flavor, add ½ tsp almond flavoring and/or ½ tsp dry instant coffee powder to cocoa and powdered sugar before adding butter and milk.

Approximate nutritional analysis per serving Cake:
Calories 369, Protein 4 g, Carbohydrates 51 g, Fat 17 g,
Cholesterol 71 mg, Sodium 442 mg

Approximate nutritional analysis per serving Frosting:
Calories 339, Protein 2 g, Carbohydrates 62 g, Fat 11 g,
Cholesterol 1 mg, Sodium 74 mg

SNOWMAN CAKE

¾ cup (180 ml) shortening
1 cup (240 ml) IMPERIAL Granulated Sugar
½ cup (120 ml) IMPERIAL Light Brown Sugar
1 tsp (5 ml) vanilla
½ tsp (3 ml) coconut flavoring or almond extract
3 eggs
1½ cups (355 ml) all-purpose flour
1½ tsp (8 ml) baking powder
½ tsp (3 ml) salt
¾ cup (180 ml) milk
1 - 7 oz pkg (210 g) coconut

FROSTING
4 cups (960 ml) IMPERIAL Powdered Sugar
5 tbs (75 ml) shortening
1¼ tsp (6 ml) vanilla
½ tsp (3 ml) salt
½ tsp (3 ml) coconut flavoring or almond extract
5-6 tbs (75-90 ml) milk

Cream first 5 ingredients well. Add eggs; beat well. Combine dry ingredients; add to creamed mixture alternately with milk, ending with milk. Grease one 1½-qt oven proof mixing bowl, two 3-cup oven-proof mixing bowls, one 5-oz oven-proof custard cup. Measure 2 cups batter into large bowl, 1 cup batter into each medium-sized bowl, and fill custard cup ½ full with batter.

Bake in preheated oven at 350°F (180°C) for 50-55 minutes for bowls, 20-25 minutes for custard cup or until done. Cool in bowls 10 minutes; turn out onto wire racks to cool completely.

Place largest cake on serving plate, rounded side up. Spread with frosting. Spread small amount of frosting on flat sides of medium-sized cakes and gently press together to form a ball. Center ball on top of frosted largest cake. Frost all sides. Place smallest cake on top of ball to form head. Secure with toothpicks or drinking straws. Frost. Gently pat coconut over entire snowman. Decorate with gumdrops, licorice ropes, candy canes. Make top hat from black construction paper. Serves 16.

FROSTING: Cream 1 cup IMPERIAL Powdered Sugar with next 4 ingredients. Add milk alternately with remaining powdered sugar. Mix until creamy. Add more sugar or milk, if necessary, to make spreading consistency.

Approximate nutritional analysis per serving:
Calories 435, Protein 3 g, Carbohydrates 65 g, Fat 19 g,
Cholesterol 42 mg, Sodium 215 mg

BURNED SUGAR CAKE

½ cup (120 ml) shortening
1½ cups (355 ml) IMPERIAL Granulated Sugar
2 eggs, beaten
1 tsp (5 ml) vanilla
2½ cups (590 ml) all-purpose flour
2½ tsp (13 ml) baking powder
½ tsp (3 ml) salt
1 cup (240 ml) milk
3 tbs (45 ml) Burned Sugar Syrup (recipe below)
    or dark molasses

POWDERED SUGAR ICING
1 tbs (15 ml) Burned Sugar Syrup
3 tbs (45 ml) milk
2 cups (480 ml) IMPERIAL 10X Powdered Sugar,
    unsifted
chopped nuts

BURNED SUGAR SYRUP
1 cup (240 ml) IMPERIAL Granulated Sugar
1 cup (240 ml) boiling water

Cream shortening and IMPERIAL Granulated Sugar until light and fluffy. Add beaten eggs and beat until thoroughly blended. Add vanilla. Combine dry ingredients and add alternately with milk or water, stirring well after each addition. Stir in burned sugar syrup or dark molasses. Pour batter into 2 - 9-inch layer pans lined on bottom with greased wax paper or use nonstick pans. Bake in preheated 350°F (180°C) oven about 30 minutes, or until done. When cool, fill and frost with Powdered Sugar Icing. Serves 12.

Powdered Sugar Icing: Mix burned sugar syrup and milk with IMPERIAL 10X Powdered Sugar. Sprinkle frosting with chopped nuts.

Burned sugar syrup: Place IMPERIAL Granulated Sugar in large heavy skillet and heat over medium heat, stirring constantly, until sugar melts and browns; it will begin to smoke. Remove from heat and add 1 cup boiling water very carefully; it will foam up. Return to heat, stirring, until sugar is dissolved and makes a thick syrup. This may take 10-15 minutes. Set aside to cool.

Approximate nutritional analysis per serving Frosted Cake:
Calories 373, Protein 4 g, Carbohydrates 69 g, Fat 10 g,
Cholesterol 36 mg, Sodium 170 mg

Bacardi Golden Rum Cake

BACARDI GOLDEN RUM CAKE

½ cup (120 ml) BACARDI Dark Rum
1 cup (240 ml) chopped pecans or walnuts
1 - 18½ oz (555 g) pkg yellow cake mix*
1 - 3¾ oz (112 g) pkg JELL-O Vanilla
    Instant Pudding and Pie Filling
4 eggs
½ cup (120 ml) cold water
½ cup (120 ml) vegetable oil

*If using yellow cake mix with pudding already in the mix,
omit instant pudding, use 3 eggs instead of 4, ⅓ cup oil instead
of ½ CUP.

GLAZE
½ cup (120 ml) BACARDI Dark Rum
¼ lb (225 g) butter
¼ cup (60 ml) water
1 cup (240 ml) granulated sugar

Preheat oven to 325°F (165°C). Grease and flour 10-inch tube
or 12-cup Bundt pan. Sprinkle nuts over bottom of pan. Mix all
cake ingredients together. Pour batter over nuts. Bake 1 hour.
Cool. Invert on serving plate. Prick top. Spoon and brush glaze
evenly over top and sides. Allow cake to absorb glaze. Repeat
until glaze is used up.

    To make glaze, melt butter in saucepan. Stir in water and
sugar. Boil 5 minutes, stirring constantly. Remove from heat.
Stir in rum.

Approximate nutritional analysis per 1/12th recipe:
Calories 545 , Protein 7 g, Carbohydrates 61 g, Fat 27 g,
Cholesterol 102 mg, Sodium 419 mg

EASTER EGG CAKE

1¾ cups (415 ml) all-purpose flour
1 cup (240 ml) IMPERIAL Granulated Sugar
½ tsp (3 ml) salt
1¾ tsp (9 ml) baking powder
½ cup (120 ml) shortening, butter or margarine
2 eggs
½ cup (120 ml) milk

EASY-SPREAD ALMOND
BUTTER CREAM FROSTING
2 cups (480 ml) sifted IMPERIAL 10X
    Powdered Sugar
⅓ cup (80 ml) whipped-type margarine
3 tbs (45 ml) cream
½ tsp (3 ml) almond extract or vanilla extract

Combine flour, IMPERIAL Granulated Sugar, salt, baking powder into bowl. Add other ingredients and beat well with a wire whisk or electric beater for 3 minutes. Pour mixture into 9x13-inch pan generously greased and floured. Bake in preheated oven at 350°F (180°C) for 25-30 minutes, or until cake tests done. Serves 12.

EASY-SPREAD ALMOND-BUTTER CREAM FROSTING: Beat IMPERIAL 10X Powdered Sugar into margarine gradually. Add cream to mixture 1 spoonful at a time. Add almond flavoring. Beat until mixture reaches spreading consistency. Add more IMPERIAL 10X Powdered Sugar, if necessary. Frost top and sides of cake. To achieve a smooth surface, dip spatula frequently into hot water and lightly skim spatula across cake surface.

TO CUT EGG SHAPE: Let cake cool. Cut piece of lightweight cardboard or rigid paper to 9x13-inch size. Then trim to egg-shape oval. Remove cake from baking pan and place on serving patter. Or, place cake on stiff cardboard cut slightly larger than egg-shape oval and covered with colored foil wrapping paper. Set oval on top of cake and trim cake.

TO DECORATE CAKE: Make flower stems from green candy slices; press into frosting in center of cake. Use pink jelly beans for flowers and to decorate sides of cake. Using green food coloring, tint ½ cup shredded coconut for lower portion of cake. Use yellow tinted coconut for top area of cake. Trim with green jelly beans.

Approximate nutritional analysis per serving Cake with Frosting w/o Decorations: Calories 325, Protein 3 g, Carbohydrates 46 g, Fat 15 g, Cholesterol 41 mg, Sodium 206 mg

MUD CAKE

4 eggs
2 cups (480 ml) IMPERIAL Granulated Sugar
1 cup (240 ml) butter or margarine, melted
1½ cups (355 ml) all-purpose flour
⅓ cup (80 ml) cocoa
1 tsp (5 ml) vanilla
1 cup (240 ml) shredded coconut
2 cups (480 ml) walnuts or pecans, copped
1 - 7 oz jar (210 ml) marshmallow cream

FLOODTIDE FROSTING
½ cup (120 ml) butter or margarine, melted
6 tbs (90 ml) milk
⅓ cup (80 ml) cocoa
4 cups (960 ml) unsifted IMPERIAL 10X
    Powdered Sugar
1 tsp (5 ml) vanilla
2 cups (480 ml) walnuts or pecans, chopped

Combine eggs and IMPERIAL Granulated Sugar in mixer and mix at high speed for 5 minutes. Combine melted butter or margarine, flour, cocoa, vanilla, coconut, nuts. Combine the 2 mixtures and mix well. Bake in greased and floured 13x9x2-inch pan in preheated 350°F (180°C) oven 30 minutes, or until cake tests done. For best results, bake on rack in middle of oven. Remove from oven and spread marshmallow cream over top of cake. Wait a few minutes, then frost while cake is still warm. Serves 24.

FLOODTIDE FROSTING: Combine all ingredients and mix well with wire whisk. Spread carefully over marshmallow cream.

Approximate nutritional analysis per serving:
Calories 394, Protein 4 g, Carbohydrates 53 g, Fat 20 g,
Cholesterol 36 mg, Sodium 199 mg

CHOCOLATE PRALINE CAKE

½ cup (120 ml) butter or margarine
¼ cup (60 ml) whipping cream
1 cup (240 ml) firmly packed brown sugar
¾ cup (180 ml) coarsely chopped pecans
1 pkg PILLSBURY PLUS Devil's Food Cake Mix
1¼ cups (295 ml) water
⅓ cup (80 ml) oil
3 eggs

FROSTING
1¾ cups (415 ml) whipping cream
¼ cup (60 ml) powdered sugar
¼ tsp (1 ml) vanilla
pecan halves, if desired
chocolate curls, if desired

Heat oven to 325°F (165°C). In small heavy saucepan, combine butter, ¼ cup whipping cream and brown sugar. Cook over low heat just until butter is melted, stirring occasionally. Pour into 13x9-inch pan; sprinkle evenly with chopped pecans. In large bowl, combine remaining cake ingredients at low speed until moistened; beat 2 minutes at high speed. Carefully spoon about ½ of batter over pecan mixture around edges of pan; spoon remaining batter into center of pan.

Bake for 50-60 minutes or until cake springs back when touched lightly in center. Cool 5 minutes; invert onto serving platter. Cool completely.

TOPPING: In small bowl, beat 1¾ cups whipping cream until soft peaks form. Blend in powdered sugar and vanilla; beat until stiff peaks form. Frost cake with whipped cream. Garnish with pecan halves and chocolate curls, if desired. Store in refrigerator. Serves 15.

High Altitude: 3500-6500 ft: Add ¼ cup (60 ml) flour to dry cake mix. Bake at 350°F (180°C) for 50-60 minutes.

Approximate nutritional analysis per serving:
Calories 480, Protein 4 g, Carbohydrates 48 g, Fat 32 g, Cholesterol 103 mg, Sodium 330 mg

EASY CHOCOLATE CAKE

1 - 4 oz bar (120 g) GHIRARDELLI
** Semi-Sweet Chocolate**
½ cup (120 ml) water
1 cup (240 ml) butter
2 cups (480 ml) sugar
4 large eggs, separated
1 tsp (5 ml) vanilla
2 cups (480 ml) unsifted flour
1 tsp (5 ml) baking soda
1 cup (240 ml) buttermilk or strong cold coffee
½ tsp (3 ml) salt

In heavy saucepan on low heat, melt chocolate with water; set aside. Cream butter with sugar until light and fluffy. Add egg yolks, one at a time, beating after each addition. Mix in melted chocolate and vanilla. Sift flour with soda. Add dry ingredients alternately with buttermilk or coffee to chocolate mixture; mix until smooth. Beat egg whites with salt until very stiff peaks form; fold into batter. Spread into three 8-9-inch round cake pans lined with wax paper. Bake at 350°F (180°C) about 30 minutes. Cool on rack 10 minutes; remove cake. Serves 10.

Approximate nutritional analysis per serving:
Calories 421, Protein 5 g, Carbohydrates 56 g, Fat 21 g, Cholesterol 113 mg, Sodium 204 mg

Easy Chocolate Cake

LIGHT-HEARTED STRAWBERRY SHORTCAKE

2⅔ cups (640 ml) all-purpose flour
2 tsp (10 ml) DAVIS Baking Powder
1¼ cups (295 ml) sugar
½ cup (120 ml) FLEISCHMANN'S Margarine
1 tsp (5 ml) vanilla extract
½ cup (120 ml) EGG BEATERS Real Egg Product
¾ cup (180 ml) skim milk
3 pts (1.4 L) strawberries
1 - 8 oz container (240 g) light prepared
    whipped topping

Combine flour and baking powder; set aside. Reserve
2 tbs sugar. In large bowl, with electric mixer at medium speed,
beat sugar, margarine and vanilla until creamy. Add egg
product; beat 1 minute. Alternately add flour mixture and milk,
blending well after each addition. Divide batter between a
greased 8-inch round cake pan and a greased 8x8x2-inch pan.
Bake at 350°F (180°C) for 20-25 minutes or until toothpick
inserted in center comes out clean. Cool in pans on wire racks
10 minutes. Remove from pans; cool completely on wire racks.

In medium bowl, mash 2 pts hulled strawberries and
reserved 2 tbs sugar; set aside. Hull and halve remaining
strawberries.

Place square cake on large plate. Cut round layer in half
crosswise; place cut edges of each half against 2 adjacent sides
of square cake to form a heart. Slice round and square layers in
half horizontally to make 2 layers. Spread top of bottom layer
with mashed strawberries; replace top layer, cut side down.
Frost top with whipped cream topping; garnish with strawberry
halves. Serves 16.

Approximate nutritional analysis per serving:
Calories 240, Protein 4 g, Carbohydrates 38 g, Fat 6 g,
Cholesterol 0 mg, Sodium 110 mg

ORANGE CAKE

1 cup (240 ml) butter or margarine
2 cups (480 ml) sugar
4 eggs
3 cups (720 ml) flour
½ tsp (3 ml) salt
1 rounded tsp (5 ml) baking soda
1¼ cups (295 ml) buttermilk
grated rind of 1 orange

GLAZE
2 cups (480 ml) sugar
¾ cup (180 ml) FLORIDA'S NATURAL
    Brand Orange Juice
¼ cup (60 ml) rum
grated rind of 1 orange

Cream butter until light. Add sugar, a bit at a time. Add eggs,
one at a time, beating after each. Sift flour with salt. Mix baking
soda in buttermilk. Add flour mixture alternately with milk
mixture, beginning and ending with flour. Add grated orange
rind and vanilla last. Pour into 9-10-inch tube pan lined on
bottom with waxed paper. Bake at 325°F (165°C) for about
1 hour. Serves 16.

GLAZE: While cake is baking, combine all ingredients and
stir occasionally. Do not cook. When the cake is done, leave in
pan and carefully punch a few holes in the top. Pour juice over
cake and let stand until all juice is absorbed and cake is cool.

Approximate nutritional analysis per serving:
Calories 435, Protein 5 g, Carbohydrates 74 g, Fat 2 g,
Cholesterol 53 mg, Sodium 298 mg

CHOLESTEROL-FREE LEMON CHIFFON CAKE

8 egg whites
⅛ tsp (.5 ml) cream of tartar
½ cup plus 3 tbs (165 ml) sugar
2½ cups (590 ml) cake flour
1¼ tsp (6 ml) baking powder
½ cup plus 2 tbs (150 ml) sugar
⅛ tsp (.5 ml) salt
⅛ tsp (.5 ml) vanilla
½ cup plus 2 tbs (150 ml) Egg Beaters, egg substitute
½ cup plus 2 tbs (150 ml) water
⅛ tsp (.5 ml) lemon extract
¼ cup plus 3 tbs (105 ml) POMPEIAN
    Extra Light Olive Oil

Whip egg whites in a very clean mixer at medium speed, about
2 minutes. Slowly add cream of tartar and ½ cup plus 3 tbs
sugar; whip to form soft peaks; set aside. In a separate bowl,
mix cake flour, baking powder, ½ cup plus 2 tbs sugar and salt;
set aside. In a large bowl combine with an electric mixer
vanilla, Egg Beaters, water, lemon extract and POMPEIAN
Extra Light Olive Oil. Add dry ingredients to this mixture.

Fold the reserved whipped egg white mixture into the
above blend of liquid and dry ingredients. Bake in 2 ungreased
layer cake pans for 30 minutes, or until a wooden pick comes
out clean. Remove the cakes from the pans, cool and top each
layer with non-dairy whipped topping. Stack them into a
2-layer cake. Keep chilled until serving. Serves 12.

Approximate nutritional analysis per serving w/o whipped topping:
Calories 271, Protein 7 g, Carbohydrates 42 g, Fat 9 g,
Cholesterol < 1 mg, Sodium 117 mg

Bacardi Double-Chocolate Rum Cake

BACARDI DOUBLE-CHOCOLATE RUM CAKE

1 cup (240 ml) BACARDI Dark rum
1 pkg -18 ½ oz (555 g) chocolate cake mix
1 pkg chocolate instant pudding and pie filling
¾ cups (180 ml) water
½ cup (120 ml) vegetable oil
4 eggs
1 pkg (12 oz, 360 g) semi sweet chocolate
1 cup (240 ml) raspberry preserves
2 tbs (30 ml) shortening
1 oz (30 g) white chocolate

Preheat oven to 350ºF (180ºC). Combine cake mix, pudding, eggs, ½ cup of the rum, water, and oil in large mixing bowl. Using electric mixer, beat at low speed until moistened. Beat at medium speed 2 minutes. Stir in 1 cup of chocolate pieces. Pour batter into prepared greased 12-cup Bundt pan or 10-inch tube pan. Bake 50 to 60 minutes until cake tests done. Cool in pan 15 minutes. Remove from pan, cool on rack.

In small saucepan, heat raspberry preserves and and remaining ½ cup rum. Strain through sieve to remove seeds. Place cake on serving plate. Prick surface of cake with fork. Brush raspberry glaze evenly over cake, allowing cake to absorb glaze. Repeat until all glaze has been absorbed.

In bowl, combine remaining 1 cup chocolate pieces and shortening. Microwave on high 1 minute or until melted. Stir until smooth. Or heat mixture over hot (not boiling) water until chocolate melts and mixture is smooth. Spoon chocolate icing over cake. Let stand 10 minutes. In small bowl, combine white chocolate and 1 tsp water. Microwave on high 30 seconds or until melted. Or melt over hot (not boiling) water. Drizzle on top of chocolate icing.

Approximate nutritional analysis per 1/12th recipe:
Calories 528, Protein 7 g, Carbohydrates 661 g, Fat 27 g, Cholesterol 81 mg, Sodium 422 mg

STRAWBERRY SHORTCAKE

1½ cups (355 ml) IMPERIAL Granulated Sugar
¾ cup (180 ml) shortening
3 beaten egg yolks
2¼ cups (540 ml) all-purpose flour
½ tsp (3 ml) salt
3½ tsp (18 ml) baking powder
¾ cup (180 ml) cold water
¼ cup (60 ml) crushed strawberries
1 tsp (5 ml) almond extract
3 egg whites, stiffly beaten
1 cup (240 ml) whipping cream, sweetened with:
2 tbs (30 ml) IMPERIAL 10X Powdered Sugar
2 pts (960 ml) fresh strawberries sweetened with:
   ½ cup (120 ml) IMPERIAL 10X Powdered Sugar

Cream IMPERIAL Granulated Sugar and shortening; add egg yolks; beat well. Add combined dry ingredients alternately with combined water, crushed strawberries, almond extract (add few drops red food coloring, if desired). Fold in stiffly beaten egg whites.

   Bake batter in 2 waxed-paper-lined 9-inch round cake pans in preheated oven at 350°F (180°C) about 20 minutes, or until cakes test done. Cool and put together with layer sliced, sugared strawberries and cream. Top with more cream and garnish top and sides with whole berries. Serves 12.

Approximate nutritional analysis per serving:
Calories 424, Protein 5 g, Carbohydrates 54 g, Fat 22 g,
Cholesterol 80 mg, Sodium 198 mg

LUSCIOUS LEMON CAKE

CRUST
½ cup (60 ml) butter or margarine
½ cup (120 ml) all-purpose flour
¼ cup 960 ml) chopped pecans

FILLING
4 oz (120 g) cream cheese, softened
½ cup (120 ml) unsifted IMPERIAL 10X
   Powdered Sugar
1 tsp (5 ml) lemon extract
¼ cup (60 ml) cream, whipped or substitute

PUDDING
1 small pkg lemon instant pudding
1½ cups (355 ml) milk
2 tsp (10 ml) lemon juice

Mix crust ingredients and press into 8-inch square baking pan; bake 15 minutes in preheated oven at 300°F (150°C). Whip cream cheese in mixer until fluffy. Add IMPERIAL 10X Powdered Sugar and lemon extract. Blend well. Fold in whipped cream. Spread over cooled crust. Prepare pudding using 1½ cups milk (instead of 2 cups as pkg directs). Spread over cream cheese filling. Top with whipped cream or whipped cream substitute. Chill. Curl piece of lemon rind to garnish, if desired. Serves 9.

Approximate nutritional analysis per serving:
Calories 219, Protein 3 g, Carbohydrates 21 g, Fat 14 g,
Cholesterol 23 mg, Sodium 232 mg

ONE BOWL DEVIL CAKE

2 cups (480 ml) sifted cake flour
1½ cups (355 ml) sugar
2 tsp (10 ml) baking soda
½ tsp (3 ml) cream of tartar
½ tsp (3 ml) salt
1 cup (240 ml) shortening
1½ cups (355 ml) buttermilk
3 eggs
1½ tsp (8 ml) vanilla
1 - 4 oz (120 g) GHIRARDELLI Unsweetened
   Chocolate Bar, melted

Sift cake flour, sugar, soda, cream of tartar, salt into large mixer bowl. Add shortening, half the buttermilk, eggs and vanilla. Beat on medium speed for 2 minutes. Mix in remaining buttermilk and melted chocolate. Beat additional 2 minutes. Spread into 9x13-inch greased cake pan. Bake at 350°F (180°C) for 40-45 minutes. Cool in pan. Serves 14.

Approximate nutritional analysis per serving:
Calories 344, Protein 5 g, Carbohydrates 39 g, Fat 20 g,
Cholesterol 46 mg, Sodium 235 mg

CHOCOLATE-SOUR CREAM FROSTING

½ cup (120 ml) sour cream
3½ cups (840 ml) powdered sugar
1 tsp (5 ml) vanilla
2 oz bar (60 g) GHIRARDELLI Unsweetened
   Chocolate, melted

Beat sour cream with sugar and vanilla until smooth. Mix in melted chocolate. Spread over 9x13-inch cake.

Approximate nutritional analysis per serving:
Calories 134, Protein < 1 g, Carbohydrates 26 g, Fat 4 g,
Cholesterol 4 mg, Sodium 5 mg

CHOCOLATE-WALNUT TORTE

2 - 4 oz bars (240 g) **GHIRARDELLI**
  Bittersweet Chocolate
¾ cup (180 ml) butter
4 eggs, separated
¾ cup (180 ml) sugar, divided
1 tsp (5 ml) vanilla
¼ cup (60 ml) unsifted flour
⅔ cup (160 ml) walnuts, ground
pinch cream of tartar

COCOLATE-RUM GLAZE
1 - 4 oz bar (120 g) **GHIRARDELLI**
  Bittersweet Chocolate
6 tbs (90 ml) butter
1 tbs (15 ml) light corn syrup
1 tbs (15 ml) dark rum, optional

In heavy saucepan on low heat, melt broken chocolate with butter, stirring constantly until smooth; set aside. Beat egg yolks for 1-2 minutes, gradually adding ½ cup sugar and vanilla. Beat in chocolate mixture. Fold in flour and nuts. Beat egg whites with cream of tartar until foamy. Gradually add remaining ¼ cup sugar, beating until stiff peaks form. Blend ¼ of the egg whites into the chocolate mixture; fold in remaining egg whites. Pour into 9-inch spring-form pan lined with parchment paper. Bake at 375°F (190°C) for 30-35 minutes or until sides start to separate from pan but center is still moist. Cool on rack. Remove torte from pan. Frost with Cocolate Rum Glaze. Serves 12.

COCOLATE-RUM GLAZE: In heavy saucepan on low heat, melt broken chocolate with butter, stirring constantly until smooth. Remove from heat. Stir in corn syrup and rum. Place torte upside-down on a rack over tray to catch excess glaze. Spread very thin layer of glaze over top and sides of torte to set surface. Chill 15 minutes to firm glaze. Reheat remaining glaze to thin and pour over top and sides or torte. When glaze is firm, remove cake from rack to large plate. Decorate top and sides with shaved chocolate, if desired. For shiny glaze, store cake at room temperature until serving time. Serves12.

Approximate nutritional analysis per serving
Torte: Calories 320, Protein 5 g,
Carbohydrates 26 g, Fat 24 g,
Cholesterol 102 mg, Sodium 25 mg

Approximate nutritional analysis per serving
Glaze with rum: Calories 105, Protein < 1 g,
Carbohydrates 7 g, Fat 9 g,
Cholesterol 16 mg, Sodium 3 mg

LEMON POUND CAKE

2¾ cups (660 ml) **BISQUICK Reduced Fat Baking Mix**
1 cup (240 ml) sugar
⅛ tsp (.5 ml) ground nutmeg
⅓ cup (80 ml) margarine, softened
6 egg whites *or*
  ¾ cup (180 ml) cholesterol-free egg product
½ cup (120 ml) skim milk
1 tbs (15 ml) grated lemon peel

GLAZE
½ cup (120 ml) powdered sugar
1 tbs (15 ml) lemon juice

Heat oven to 350°F (180°C). Grease and flour loaf pan, 9x5x3 inches. Beat all ingredients except lemon peel and Glaze on low speed 30 seconds, scraping bowl constantly. Beat on medium speed 2 minutes, scraping bowl occasionally. Stir in lemon peel. Pour batter into pan. Bake 40-50 minutes or until toothpick inserted in center comes out clean; cool 10 minutes. Invert onto wire rack; cool completely. Drizzle with Glaze. Serves 12.

GLAZE: Beat ½ cup powdered sugar and 1 tablespoon lemon juice with spoon until smooth.

High Altitude: 3500 to 6500 feet: Decrease sugar to ¾ cup.

Approximate nutritional analysis per serving:
Calories 260, Protein 5 g, Carbohydrates 45 g, Fat 7 g,
Cholesterol 0 mg, Sodium 400 mg

Lemon Pound Cake

VIENNESE HAZELNUT TORTE

4 eggs
¼ cup (60 ml) fine granulated sugar
¾ cup (180 ml) Hazelnuts, finely chopped
¼ cup (60 ml) dry fine bread crumbs
¼ tsp (1 ml) cream of tartar
⅛ tsp (.5 ml) salt
¼ cup (60 ml) fine granulated sugar

TOPPING
1½ cups (355 ml) fresh raspberries
¾ cup (180 ml) red raspberry jelly
½-1 cup (120-240 ml) whipped cream

Separate 3 eggs, put fourth into yolk bowl. Beat until very light, then beat in ¼ cup sugar and continue beating. Folds in hazelnuts and bread crumbs. Beat egg whites until foamy. Add cream of tartar and salt, then continue beating, adding sugar, until stiff peaks form. Fold in yolk mixture. Turn into 2 buttered and floured 10-inch torte pans. Bake at 350°F (180°C) for 30 minutes, or until done.

Top with mixture of raspberries mixed gently with melted red raspberry jelly. Garnish with whipped cream. Serves 10.

Approximate nutritional analysis per serving:
Calories 198, Protein 2 g, Carbohydrates 32 g, Fat 8 g,
Cholesterol 8 mg, Sodium 51 mg

CHOCOLATE-FRUIT TORTE

½ cup (120 ml) margarine or butter
3 tbs (45 ml) unsweetened cocoa
¼ cup (60 ml) water
1 cup (240 ml) all-purpose flour
1 cup (240 ml) sugar
½ tsp (3 ml) baking soda
¼ tsp (1 ml) salt
1 egg, slightly beaten
1 cup (240 ml) DANNON Vanilla or Lemon Yogurt
1 tsp (5 ml) vanilla
½ cup (120 ml) whipping cream
1 - 1 oz can (330 g) mandarin orange sections,
    drained
2 kiwifruit, peeled and sliced
3-4 strawberries, sliced
1 slice carambola (star fruit), optional

Preheat oven to 350°F (180°C). Grease and lightly flour 9-inch round baking pan. In medium saucepan combine margarine, cocoa and water. Bring to boil, stirring constantly. Remove from heat.

In a large bowl combine flour, sugar, baking soda and salt. Stir in egg, ¼ cup yogurt and vanilla. Blend in cocoa mixture. Pour batter into prepared pan. Bake 40 minutes or until set. Cool in pan 10 minutes. Remove from pan; cool on wire rack.

Just before serving, prepare filling. In large bowl beat whipping cream with electric mixer on high speed until soft peaks form. Gently fold in remaining ¾ cup yogurt. Carefully cut cake horizontally into 2 layers. Place bottom layer on serving plate. Spread half of filling on bottom half. Top with remaining cake layer, cut side down. Spread remaining filling on top. Arrange reserved orange sections, kiwi fruit slices, strawberry slices and carambola slice on top. Serves 10.

Approximate nutritional analysis per serving:
Calories 294, Protein 4 g, Carbohydrates 38 g, Fat 15 g,
Cholesterol 39 mg, Sodium 311 mg

APPLE UPSIDE-DOWN CAKE

2 tbs (30 ml) butter or margarine
½ cup (120 ml) IMPERIAL Brown Sugar
½ cup (120 ml) chopped pecans
3 medium cooking apples, pared, sliced
2 tbs (30 ml) lemon juice
½ cup (120 ml) butter or margarine
⅔ cup (160 ml) IMPERIAL Brown Sugar
⅓ cup (80 ml) IMPERIAL Granulated sugar
1 egg
½ tsp (3 ml) vanilla
2 cups (480 ml) all-purpose flour
½ tsp (3 ml) baking soda
1 tsp (5 ml) baking powder
½ tsp (3 ml) cinnamon
½ tsp (3 ml) salt
¼ tsp (1 ml) nutmeg
½ cup (120 ml) buttermilk
whipped cream

In 9x9-inch pan, melt 2 tbs butter or margarine; spread ½ cup IMPERIAL Brown Sugar in bottom of pan. Sprinkle with pecans; arrange apple slices on top; cover with lemon juice and set aside. Cream ½ cup butter or margarine and remaining sugars until fluffy and light. Beat in egg and vanilla thoroughly. Combine remaining dry ingredients; add alternately with buttermilk. Spread batter over apple slices in pan. Bake in preheated oven at 375°F (190°C) for 45 minutes or until done. Place on cooling rack 10 minutes, then turn upside down on plate. Serve warm. Cut into squares and top with whipped cream. Serves 9.

Approximate nutritional analysis per serving w/o whipped cream:
Calories 423, Protein 5 g, Carbohydrates 63 g, Fat 18 g,
Cholesterol 59 mg, Sodium 357 mg

BLACK FOREST TORTE

1¾ cups (415 ml) IMPERIAL Granulated Sugar
1¾ cups (415 ml) all-purpose flour
2 tsp (10 ml) baking soda
1 tsp (5 ml) salt
¼ tsp (1 ml) baking powder
¾ cup (180 ml) cocoa
1 cup (240 ml) softened margarine
1¼ cups (295 ml) buttermilk
1 tsp (5 ml) vanilla
3 eggs

CHOCOLATE FILLING
4 - 1 oz squares (120 g) unsweetened
    baking chocolate, melted
2-2½ cups (480-590 ml) IMPERIAL 10X
    Powdered Sugar
¼ cup (60 ml) hot water
½ cup (120 ml) butter or margarine, melted
½ cup (120 ml) toasted slivered almonds

WHIPPED CREAM
1 cup (240 ml) heavy cream
2 tbs (30 ml) IMPERIAL Granulated Sugar
½ tsp (3 ml) almond extract

Combine all ingredients except eggs in large mixing bowl. Beat at low speed to blend, then beat 2 minutes at medium speed. Add eggs; beat 2 minutes longer. Pour ¼ of batter into each of 4 greased and waxed-paper-lined 8-inch layer cake pans; layers will be thin. Bake in preheated oven at 350°F (180°C) about 15 minutes, or until wooden pick inserted in center comes out clean. Two layers may stand while first 2 bake, if necessary. Cool slightly; remove from pans and continue cooling. Fill and frost layers with Chocolate Filling and Whipped Cream, alternately. Serves 16.

CHOCOLATE FILLING: Combine melted chocolate, IMPERIAL 10X Powdered Sugar, water; mix well. Add melted butter or margarine gradually, beating thoroughly after each addition. Stir in almonds, reserving some for garnish. Filling thickens as it cools. Serves 16.

WHIPPED CREAM: Whip heavy cream with IMPE-RIAL Granulated Sugar and almond extract. Serves 16.

Approximate nutritional analysis per serving Torte w/o Filling or Whipped Cream: Calories 268, Protein 4 g, Carbohydrates 35 g, Fat 13 g, Cholesterol 40 mg, Sodium 455 mg

Approximate nutritional analysis per serving Chocolate Filling: Calories 164, Protein 1 g, Carbohydrates 18 g, Fat 11 g, Cholesterol 0 mg, Sodium 77 mg

Approximate nutritional analysis per serving Whipped Cream: Calories 57, Protein 0 g, Carbohydrates 2 g, Fat 6 g, Cholesterol 20 mg, Sodium 6 mg

BLACK BEAN-CHOCOLATE TORTE

8 oz (240 ml) Black Bean Puree*
4 oz (120 g) semi-sweet chocolate squares,
    melted with: 2 tbs (30 ml) coffee
¼ lb (115 g) butter, unsalted
¾ cup plus 1 tbs (195 ml) sugar
3 eggs, separated
⅓ cup (80 ml) walnuts, ground
1 tbs (15 ml) vanilla extract
confectioner's sugar for garnish

* Bean purees can be made from beans cooked in water until they are soft, with no other flavoring. They are drained and then processed in a food processor until very smooth. That's it. Use either home-cooked beans or canned. The canned varieties must be well rinsed and drained to remove as much of the salt as possible.

Preheat oven to 350°F (180°C) and butter an 8-inch round cake pan. In a small saucepan over lowest possible heat melt the chocolate with coffee. Set aside to cool.

In a large bowl of an electric mixer, cream butter and sugar together until well combined and pale yellow in color. Beat in egg yolks one at a time. Add the cooled chocolate, nuts, vanilla and bean puree to the egg mixture on low speed and mix until just blended.

In a separate bowl beat egg whites until soft peaks form. Add the remaining tbs sugar and continue beating until stiff peaks form. With a rubber spatula folds ⅓ of egg whites into the batter to lighten, incorporating thoroughly. Gently fold in remaining ⅔ of the egg whites until they are completely blended in.

Turn the batter into the cake pan, smoothing the top with the spatula, pushing it to the rim of the pan. Bake the center of oven for 1 hour. The middle of the torte may move slightly when pan is shaken. It is meant to be quite moist. Cool in the pan on a wire rack for 10 minutes. Run a sharp knife around the edge and reverse cake onto rack. Allow to cool completely. Transfer to serving plate. Dust top with confectioner's sugar and serve. Serves 8.

Approximate nutritional analysis per serving: Calories 368, Protein 8 g, Carbohydrates 40 g, Fat 22 g, Cholesterol 110 mg, Sodium 28 mg

Courtesy of the American Dry Bean Board.

SENSIBLY DELICIOUS
CHOCOLATE CHIP SNACKING CAKE

2 cups (480 ml) all-purpose flour
¾ cup (180 ml) granulated sugar
1 tsp (5 ml) baking soda
½ tsp (3 ml) ground cinnamon
¼ tsp (1 ml) salt
¾ cup (180 ml) unsweetened applesauce
⅓ cup (80 ml) nonfat milk
3 tbs (45 ml) margarine, melted
1 egg white
2 tsp (10 ml) vanilla extract
1 - 12 oz. pkg (360 g) NESTLÉ TOLL HOUSE
**   Semi-Sweet Chocolate Morsels, divided**

In large bowl, combine flour, sugar, baking soda, cinnamon
and salt. Stir in applesauce, milk, margarine, egg white and
vanilla just until blended. Stir in 1 cup morsels. Spoon into
greased 9x9-inch baking pan. Sprinkle with remaining morsels.
Bake in preheated 350°F (180°C) oven for 25-35 minutes or
until wooden pick inserted in center comes out clean. Cool in
pan. Cut into 2¼-inch squares. Serves 16.

Approximate nutritional analysis per serving:
Calories 240, Protein 3 g, Carbohydrates 35 g, Fat 10 g,
Cholesterol 0 mg, Sodium 150 mg

LEMON SAUCE WITH ANGEL FOOD CAKE

½ cup (120 ml) sugar
1½ tsp (8 ml) cornstarch
½ cup (120 ml) water
¼ cup (60 ml) HEALTHY CHOICE
**   Cholesterol Free Egg Product**
3 tbs (45 ml) fresh lemon juice
1 - 10 oz pkg (300 g) angel food cake, cut in 8 slices
4 cups (960 ml) assorted fruit (such as sliced
**   kiwifruit, berries, mandarin oranges or grapes)**

In small saucepan, combine sugar and cornstarch. Gradually
stir in water, egg product and lemon juice. Cook over medium
heat stirring constantly until sauce comes to a boil and thickens.
Let cool. Top each cake slice with ½ cup fruit, drizzle with
lemon sauce. Serves 8.

Approximate nutritional analysis per serving:
Calories 308, Protein 7 g, Carbohydrates 70 g, Fat < 1 g,
Cholesterol < 1 mg, Sodium 239 mg

Above: Sensibly Delicious Chocolate Chip Snaking Cake

SWEET AND SPICY FRUITCAKE

3 cups (720 ml) chopped walnuts
2 cups (480 ml) chopped dried figs
1 cup (240 ml) chopped dried apricots
1 cup (240 ml) chocolate chips
1½ cups (355 ml) all-purpose flour
¾ cup (180 ml) granulated sugar
4 large eggs
¼ cup (60 ml) butter or margarine, softened
⅓ cup (80 ml) apple jelly*
2 tbs (30 ml) orange flavor liqueur
1 tbs (15 ml) grated orange peel
1 tbs (15 ml) vanilla extract
2 tsp (10 ml) TABASCO pepper sauce
1 tsp (5 ml) baking powder

* Or, substitute ⅓ cup (80 ml) McILHENNY FARMS Pepper Jelly for apple and omit TABASCO pepper sauce.

Preheat oven to 325°F (165°C). Grease two 3-cup heat-safe bowls. Line bottom and side with foil; grease foil. In large bowl combine walnuts, figs, apricots, chocolate chips, and ¼ cup flour to mix well.

In small bowl with mixer at low speed, beat sugar, eggs and butter until well blended. Add jelly, remaining ingredients and 1¼ cups flour. Beat at low speed until blended. Toss mixture with dried fruit in large bowl. Spoon into prepared bowls. Cover bowls with greased foil. Bake 40 minutes; uncover and bake 40 minutes longer or until toothpick inserted in center comes out clean. Remove to wire racks to cool.

If desired, brush cooled fruitcakes with 1 tbs melted apple jelly and sprinkle each with 2 tbs finely chopped dried apricots. Store in cool place for up to 3 weeks. Yields 2 small fruitcakes, serves 16.

Approximate nutritional analysis per serving:
Calories 340, Protein 7 g, Carbohydrates 39 g, Fat 19 g,
Cholesterol 63 mg, Sodium 124 mg

STRAWBERRY CAKE

1 pkg white cake mix
3 tbs (45 ml) all-purpose flour
3 eggs
¾ cup (180 ml) cooking oil
¾ cup (180 ml) water
1 - 3 oz pkg (90 g) strawberry gelatin
½ cup (120 ml) sliced strawberries, frozen or fresh

FROSTING
2 tbs (30 ml) melted butter or margarine
1½ cups (355 ml) IMPERIAL Powdered Sugar
2 tbs (30 ml) crushed strawberries
whole strawberries for garnish

Combine all ingredients in large mixer bowl and mix well. Bake in greased and floured tube pan in preheated oven at 350°F (180°C) about 40 minutes, or in 2 - 9-inch layer cake pans for 25 minutes, or until done.

FROSTING: Combine melted butter, IMPERIAL Powdered Sugar and crushed strawberries. Drizzle over warm cake. Decorate with choice fresh strawberries with shiny green leaves. Serves 12.

Approximate nutritional analysis per serving glazed:
Calories 434, Protein 4 g, Carbohydrates 57 g, Fat 22 g,
Cholesterol 53 mg, Sodium 223 mg

DEVILED ANGEL CAKE WITH FRUIT TOPPING

1 - 14½ oz pkg (435 g) angel food cake mix
1 - 7¾ oz pkg (233 g) SNACKWELL'S Reduced
    Fat Chocolate Sandwich Cookies, coarsely
    chopped
3½ cups (840 ml) sliced mixed fruit
    (strawberries, kiwifruit, mango and blueberries)

STRAWBERRY SAUCE
1 - 16 oz pkg (480 g) frozen strawberries
    with sugar, thawed
½ cup (120 ml) orange juice
1 tbs (15 ml) cornstarch

Prepare cake mix according to package directions; fold in chopped cookies. Pour into 12-cup tube pan or fluted tube pan. Bake according to package directions. Cool completely.

To serve, cut cake into 14 wedges; top each with ¼ cup sliced fruit and 2 tbs strawberry sauce. Serves 14.

STRAWBERRY SAUCE: In blender or food processor, puree frozen strawberries and orange juice until smooth. Place in a small saucepan. Add cornstarch. Cook, over medium-high heat, until thickened, stirring constantly. Cool completely. Yields 1¾ cups.

Approximate nutritional analysis per serving:
Calories 230, Fat 1 g, Cholesterol 0 mg, Sodium 202 mg

Opposite: Sweet and Spicy Fruitcake

HAZELNUT SNACKING CAKE

1 cup (240 ml) flour
⅔ cup (160 ml) sugar
¼ tsp (1 ml) baking powder
½ tsp (3 ml) baking soda
¼ tsp (1 ml) salt
1 egg
½ cup (120 ml) buttermilk
½ tsp (3 ml) vanilla
⅓ cup (80 ml) butter, melted
¾ cup (180 ml) Hazelnuts, roasted and chopped

GLAZE
½ cup (120 ml) butter
½ cup (120 ml) sugar
¼ cup (60 ml) buttermilk
1 tsp (5 ml) corn syrup
¼ tsp (1 ml) baking soda
½ tsp (3 ml) vanilla or Hazelnut liqueur

Sift together flour, sugar, baking powder, baking soda and salt. Separately combine egg, buttermilk and vanilla. Beat until smooth and add butter. Combine mixtures, add Hazelnuts and mix until smooth. Place in a greased 8x8x2-inch pan. Bake at 375°F (190°C) for 25 minutes or until done. When cake is done, prepare glaze. Serves 8.

GLAZE: Melt butter and stir in sugar, buttermilk, syrup and baking soda. Boil over medium heat for 5 minutes. Remove from heat and stir in flavoring. Poke holes in cake about ½-inch apart. Pour warm glaze mixture over cake. Cool before cutting. Best served at room temperature. Serves 8

Approximate nutritional analysis per serving Cake:
Calories 271, Protein 4 g, Carbohydrates 31 g, Fat 15 g,
Cholesterol 48 mg, Sodium 164 mg

Approximate nutritional analysis per serving Glaze:
Calories 155, Protein < 1 g , Carbohydrates 14 g, Fat 12 g,
Cholesterol 31 mg, Sodium 36 mg

FRONTIER PECAN CAKE

2 cups (480 ml) butter or margarine
4½ cups (1 L) all-purpose flour
¼ tsp (1 ml) salt
1 tsp (5 ml) baking powder
2⅓ cups (560 ml) IMPERIAL Brown Sugar
6 eggs, separated
½ cup (120 ml) milk
1 tsp (5 ml) vanilla
3 tbs (45 ml) instant coffee dissolved in 3 tbs
    (45 ml) hot water, optional
4 cups (960 ml) chopped pecans

Set out butter or margarine to soften. Combine flour, salt, baking powder. Set aside. In large mixing bowl, cream butter and IMPERIAL Brown Sugar. Beat egg yolks until thick and light yellow and add, mixing well. Combine milk, vanilla, dissolved coffee. Add alternately to batter with dry ingredients. Fold in pecans. Beat egg whites until stiff, but not dry, and fold into batter. Pour into greased (bottom only) 10-inch tube pan. Bake in preheated oven at 325°F (165°C) for 1½ hours or until done. Let cool in pan on rack. Remove from pan. Keeps well when tightly wrapped. Serves 16.

Note: Delicious as it is or serve with a dessert sauce of Whipped Cream Imperial (recipe follows).

Approximate nutritional analysis per serving:
Calories 658, Protein 8 g, Carbohydrates 58 g, Fat 45 g,
Cholesterol 81 mg, Sodium 394 mg

BLACKBERRY JAM CAKE

2 cups (480 ml) IMPERIAL Granulated Sugar
1 cup (240 ml) shortening
4 egg yolks, beaten
1 tsp (5 ml) vanilla
3 cups (720 ml) all-purpose flour
1 tsp (5 ml) baking soda
2 tsp (10 ml) cinnamon
1 tsp (5 ml) nutmeg
1 tsp (5 ml) cloves
1 tsp (5 ml) allspice
1 cup (240 ml) buttermilk
1 cup (240 ml) blackberry jam, stirred
4 egg whites, beaten

Cream IMPERIAL Granulated Sugar and shortening until light. Add egg yolks and vanilla. Beat until thoroughly blended. Combine dry ingredients and add alternately with buttermilk. Stir in blackberry jam. Fold in stiffly beaten egg whites. Pour batter into 10-inch tube pan which has been lined on bottom with waxed paper and greased. Bake in preheated oven at 325°F (165°C) for 30 minutes, increase heat to 350°F (180°C) and continue baking about 45 minutes, or until a cake tester or toothpick inserted in center of cake comes out dry and free of batter. Set pan on wire rack and allow cake to cool 20 minutes before moving from pan. Serves 16.

Approximate nutritional analysis per serving:
Calories 492, Protein 6 g, Carbohydrates 76 g, Fat 19 g,
Cholesterol 71 mg, Sodium 116 mg.

ABSOLUTELY OUTSTANDING POUND CAKE

1 cup (240 ml) POMPEIAN Extra Light Olive Oil
6 eggs
1 tsp (5 ml) vanilla
¼ tsp (1 ml) baking soda
2¼ cups (540 ml) sugar
8 oz (240 g) sour cream
3 cups (720 ml) flour
¼ tsp (1 ml) salt

Preheat oven to 350°F (180°C). Generously grease and flour a Bundt or 10-inch tube pan. Sift together the flour, soda and salt; set aside. In the bowl of an electric mixer, cream together the oil and sugar - the mixture will seem granular. Add the eggs, one at a time until each is well blended. Alternate adding the flour mixture and the sour cream to the egg mixture - beginning and ending with the flour mixture. Add the vanilla. Pour the cake batter into the prepared pan. Place in the preheated oven and reduce the temperature to 325°F (165°C). Bake 1 hour and 15 minutes, or until lightly golden and a wooden pick comes out clean. Serves 16.

Approximate nutritional analysis per serving:
Calories 371, Protein 5 g, Carbohydrates 47 g, Fat 19 g,
Cholesterol 86 mg, Sodium 78 mg

DELICATE SPONGE CAKE

6 eggs, room temperature
1 tbs (15 ml) lemon juice
1 tsp (5 ml) grated lemon or orange rind
1 cup (240 ml) IMPERIAL Granulated Sugar
1 cup (240 ml) cake flour
¾ tsp (4 ml) salt

Preheat oven to 325°F (165°C). Lightly grease and flour only the bottom of 10-inch tube pan. Break eggs into large bowl of electric mixer. Add lemon juice and grated rind. Beat at highest speed until soft peaks form, 12-16 minutes. Sift flour and salt while eggs beat. Continue beating eggs at highest speed, adding IMPERIAL Granulated Sugar in fine stream, for about 2 minutes. Change to lowest speed and slowly add flour/salt to mixture. Scrape sides and beat at lowest speed ½ minute. Pour batter into 9-inch tube pan and bake 50 minutes, or until toothpick comes out clean. Invert pan onto rack. Let cool before removing pan. Serve with your favorite topping. Serves 12.

Approximate nutritional analysis per serving:
Calories 131, Protein 4 g, Carbohydrates 23 g, Fat 3 g,
Cholesterol 106 mg, Sodium 165 mg

Above: Absolutely Outstanding Pound Cake

NAMELESS CAKE

1 ½ cups (355 ml) IMPERIAL Granulated Sugar
¾ cup (180 ml) shortening
3 eggs
1 ¾ cups (415 ml) all-purpose flour
½ tsp (3 ml) baking powder
½ tsp (3 ml) baking soda
½ tsp (3 ml) salt
1 tsp (5 ml) cinnamon
2 tsp (10 ml) nutmeg
¾ cup (180 ml) sour milk or buttermilk*
1 tsp (5 ml) vanilla
1 tsp (5 ml) lemon extract
1 cup (240 ml) coarsely chopped nuts, toasted

*To make sour milk, put 1 tbs (15 ml) lemon juice or vinegar in 1-cup measure and add ¾ cup (180 ml) milk.

Cream IMPERIAL Granulated Sugar and shortening until fluffy. Add eggs and beat thoroughly. Combine dry ingredients together and add alternately with sour milk or buttermilk. Add vanilla and lemon extract. Fold in nuts. (To toast nuts, place chopped nuts in a shallow pan and heat in slow oven, 325°F (165°C), about 10 minutes, or until lightly browned. Stir frequently.) Pour batter into an oblong pan 9x13x1½ inches. Bake in preheated oven at 375°F (190°C) about 35 minutes, or until done. Serves 12.

Approximate nutritional analysis per serving:
Calories 298, Protein 5 g, Carbohydrates 24 g, Fat 21 g, Cholesterol 54 mg, Sodium 168 mg

PHILLY 3-STEP LUSCIOUS LEMON CHEESE CAKE

2 - 8 oz pkgs (480 g) PHILADELPHIA BRAND
   Neufchatel Cheese, ⅓ Less Fat than Cream
   Cheese or PHILADELPHIA BRAND
   Cream Cheese, softened
½ cup (120 ml) sugar
1 tbs (15 ml) fresh lemon juice
½ tsp (3 ml) grated lemon peel
½ tsp (3 ml) vanilla
2 eggs
1 - 6 or 9-inch prepared graham cracker crumb crust

Mix Neufchatel cheese, sugar, juice, peel and vanilla with electric mixer on medium speed until well blended. Add eggs; mix until blended. Pour into crust. Bake at 350°F (180°C) for 40 minutes or until center is almost set. Cool. Refrigerate 3 hours or overnight. Garnish with COOL WHIP Whipped Topping and lemon slices. Serves 8.

Approximate nutritional analysis per serving:
Calories 419, Protein 9 g, Carbohydrates 40 g, Fat 25 g, Cholesterol 96 mg, Sodium 480 mg

HEIRLOOM TWEED CAKE

1 ½ cups (355 ml) hot water
1 cup (240 ml) oats, quick or old-fashioned
½ cup (120 ml) butter or margarine
1 ¼ cups (295 ml) packed brown sugar
2 eggs
1 tsp (5 ml) vanilla
1 cup (240 ml) whole wheat flour
½ cup (120 ml) all-purpose flour
1 tsp (5 ml) each: cinnamon, baking powder,
baking soda
½ tsp (3 ml) salt
1 cup (240 ml) raisins
½ cup (120 ml) sunflower seeds
1 cup (240 ml) coconut

Stir together hot water, oats and butter; stir until butter melts. Beat in brown sugar, eggs and vanilla. In another bowl, stir together all dry ingredients. Stir into oat mixture. Stir in raisins and sunflower seeds. Pour batter into greased and floured 9 x13-inch baking pan. Sprinkle coconut evenly over top. Bake at 350°F (180°C) for 35-40 minutes, until pick inserted in center comes out clean. Serves 16.

Alternate baking: Grease Bundt pan. Sprinkle coconut evenly over bottom of pan. Pour batter on top of coconut, and bake 35-45 minutes. Cool in pan 10 minutes; loosen and invert on rack to cool completely.

Approximate nutritional analysis per serving:
Calories 235, Protein 5 g, Carbohydrates 37 g, Fat 11 g, Cholesterol 42 mg, Sodium 155 mg

GOLDEN RAISIN POLENTA CAKE

⅔ cup (160 ml) butter or margarine, softened
2 ⅔ cups (640 ml) sifted powdered sugar
2 eggs
1 tsp (5 ml) vanilla
1 cup (240 ml) flour
⅓ cup (80 ml) yellow cornmeal
⅔ cup (160 ml) golden raisins

In mixer bowl cream butter and sugar until well blended. Beat in eggs and vanilla. Combine flour, cornmeal and raisins: stir into batter until thoroughly blended. Spread batter in well-greased and floured 8½x4¼-inch loaf pan. Bake in 325°F (165°C) oven about 1 hour 25 minutes until crusty on top and pick inserted into center comes out clean. Cool in pan 10 minutes, then invert onto rack to cool completely. Slice to serve. If desired serve with strawberries and whipped cream. Serves 8.

Approximate nutritional analysis per serving: Calories 394, Protein 4 g, Carbohydrates 59 g, Fat 17 g, Cholesterol 94 mg, Sodium 20 mg

Opposite: Philly 3-Step Luscious Lemon Cheese Cake

BANANA WALNUT CAKE

2¼ cups (540 ml) all-purpose flour
2 tsp (10 ml) baking powder
1 tsp (5 ml) baking soda
⅓ cup (80 ml) FLEISCHMANN'S Margarine, softened
1¼ cups (295 ml) sugar
1 - 8 oz carton (240 ml) EGG BEATERS
    Real Egg Product
1¼ cups (295 ml) mashed ripe bananas
⅔ cup (160 ml) plain nonfat yogurt
½ cup (120 ml) PLANTERS Black Walnuts, chopped
confectioners' sugar

Mix flour, baking powder and baking soda; set aside. With mixer, beat margarine and sugar until creamy; blend in egg product and bananas. Add flour mixture alternately with yogurt, blending until smooth. Stir in walnuts.

Spread batter in greased and floured 13x9x2-inch baking pan. Bake at 350°F (180°C) for 45 minutes or until toothpick inserted comes out clean. Cool in pan on wire rack. Dust with confectioners' sugar; cut into squares. Serves 24.

Approximate nutritional analysis per serving:
Calories 141, Protein 3 g, Carbohydrates 22 g, Fat 5 g,
Cholesterol < 1 mg, Sodium 117 mg

HAZELNUT POPPY SEED CAKE

2½ cups (590 ml) sugar
1½ cups (355 ml) butter, softened
5 eggs
1 tsp (5 ml) vanilla
3 cups (720 ml) flour
1 tsp (5 ml) baking powder
¾ cup (180 ml) milk
¼ cup (60 ml) hazelnut liqueur
1½ cups (355 ml) roasted & coarsely chopped
    OREGON hazelnuts
¼ cup (60 ml) poppy seeds
powdered sugar

Preheat oven to 350°F (180°C). Butter and flour a 10-inch tube pan. In a large bowl, with electric mixer at low speed, beat together sugar, butter, eggs and vanilla, just until blended. Increase speed to high. Beat until light and fluffy, about 5 minutes; scrape bowl occasionally.

In separate bowls, combine flour with baking powder, and milk with liqueur. With mixer at low speed, add liquids alternately with flour mixture; beat until well blended. Stir in hazelnuts and poppy seeds. Pour into prepared pan. Bake for about 1 hour 25 minutes. Cool on wire rack for 20 minutes; remove from pan and invert on rack to cool completely. Dust with powdered sugar. Serves 14.

Approximate nutritional analysis per serving:
Calories 552, Protein 8 g, Carbohydrates 62 g, Fat 31 g,
Cholesterol 131 mg, Sodium 57 mg

CHOCO-LIGHT CHEESECAKE

CRUST
10 finely crushed vanilla wafer cookies
1 tbs (15 ml) HERSHEY'S Cocoa or
    Premium European Style Cocoa
1 tbs (15 ml) melted light corn oil spread

1 - 15 oz container (450 g) part-skim ricotta cheese
⅓ cup (80 ml) HERSHEY'S Cocoa or
    Premium European Style Cocoa
¼ cup (60 ml) sugar
1 envelope unflavored gelatin
1 cup (240 ml) cold lowfat 1% milk, divided
1½ tsp (8 ml) vanilla extract, divided
1 envelope dry whipped topping mix

CRUST: Heat oven to 350°F (180°C). Stir together crushed vanilla wafer cookies, cocoa, melted light corn oil spread. Press onto bottom of 8-inch springform pan. Bake 5 minutes or until set; remove from oven. Cool completely. Set aside.

In food processor or blender, blend ricotta cheese until smooth. In small saucepan stir together cocoa, sugar and gelatin; stir in ½ cup milk. Let stand 5 minutes to soften gelatin. Cook over medium heat, stirring constantly, until gelatin dissolves; remove from heat. Pour gelatin mixture and 1 tsp vanilla into ricotta cheese mixture in food processor; blend well. Pour into medium bowl; refrigerate until mixture mounds slightly when dropped from spoon. In cold mixer bowl, beat whipped topping mix, remaining ½ cup cold milk and remaining ½ tsp vanilla until stiff; fold in cocoa mixture. Pour into prepared crust. Refrigerate until firm about 4 hours; remove rim of pan. Cover; refrigerate leftovers. Serves 12.

Approximate nutritional analysis per serving:
Calories 100, Protein 6 g, Carbohydrates 10 g, Fat 4 g,
Cholesterol 15 mg, Sodium 75 mg

Opposite: Choco-Light Cheesecake

BACARDI DAIQUIRI PIE

½ cup (120 ml) BACARDI Light Rum
1 pkg Jello-O Brand Lemon Instant pudding
   and pie filling
1 pkg Jello Lime flavored gelatin
⅓ cup (80 ml) sugar
2 ½ (600 ml) cups water
2 eggs, slightly beaten
2 cups (480 ml) Cool Whip Non-dairy topping, thawed
1 baked 9-inch crumb crust, cooled

Mix pudding, gelatin and sugar in saucepan. Stir in ½ cup water and eggs; blend well. Add remaining water. Stir over medium heat until mixture comes to full boil. Remove from heat; stir in rum. Chill about 1½ hours. To hasten chilling, place bowl of filling mixture in larger bowl of ice and water; stir until mixture is cold.) Blend topping into chilled mixture. Spoon into crust. Chill until firm, about 2 hours. Garnish with additional whipped topping, lime or lemon slices, grated lime or lemon peel, or graham cracker crumbs.

Approximate nutritional anaysis per 1/8th recipe:
Calories 442, Protein 8 g, Carbohydrates 61 g, Fat 17 g,
Cholesterol 68 mg, Sodium 540 mg

APPLESAUCE CAKE

1½ cups (355 ml) all-purpose flour
1 cup (240 ml) soy flour
1¾ cups (415 ml) sugar
¼ tsp (1 ml) baking powder
1½ tsp (8 ml) baking soda
1½ tsp (8 ml) salt
1 tsp (5 ml) cinnamon
½ tsp (3 ml) cloves
½ tsp (3 ml) allspice
½ tsp (3 ml) nutmeg
½ cup (120 ml) soy oil
2 cups (480 ml) applesauce
2 eggs
2 egg whites
1 cup (240 ml) raisins
½ cup (120 ml) walnuts, finely chopped

Preheat oven to 350°F (180°C). Grease a 9x13-inch baking pan. Mix the dry ingredients together thoroughly. Add shortening and applesauce. With an electric mixer, beat for 3 minutes on medium speed. Add the eggs and beat for an additional 2 minutes. Fold the raisins and nuts into the batter. Pour into the baking pan. Bake for 45-50 minutes until cake surface springs back when touched lightly. Serves 12.

Approximate nutritional analysis per serving:
Calories 381, Protein 7 g, Carbohydrates 58 g, Fat 15 g,
Cholesterol 35 mg, Sodium 400 mg

LEMONY CARROT CAKE

1¼ cups (295 ml) all-purpose flour
½ tsp (3 ml) baking powder
½ tsp (3 ml) baking soda
½ tsp (3 ml) salt
⅓ cup (80 ml) margarine or butter
1 cup (240 ml) sugar
1 tsp (5 ml) grated lemon peel
1 tsp (5 ml) vanilla
2 eggs
½ cup (120 ml) DANNON Plain,
   Lemon or Vanilla Lowfat Yogurt
1½ cups (355 ml) shredded carrots

LEMON YOGURT FROSTING
3 tbs (45 ml) margarine or butter
1½ cups (355 ml) sifted confectioner's sugar
½ tsp (3 ml) grated lemon peel
½ tsp (3 ml) vanilla
1-2 tbs (15-30 ml) DANNON Plain,
   Lemon or Vanilla Lowfat Yogurt

Preheat oven to 350°F (180°C). Grease and lightly flour 9x9-inch baking pan. In a small bowl combine flour, baking powder, baking soda and salt. In a large bowl beat margarine with electric mixer 30 seconds. Add sugar, lemon peel and vanilla; beat well. Add eggs, 1 at a time, beating after each addition. Add flour mixture and yogurt alternately to margarine mixture, beating after each addition. Stir in carrots.

Pour batter into prepared pan; spread evenly. Bake 30 minutes or until toothpick inserted into center comes out clean. Cool in pan on wire rack. Spread cake with Lemon Yogurt Frosting. Garnish as desired. Serves 9.

LEMON YOGURT FROSTING: In a small bowl beat margarine until softened. Gradually add confectioner's sugar; beat well. Beat in lemon peel and vanilla. Add enough yogurt to make a spreadable frosting.

Approximate nutritional analysis per serving Cake:
Calories 241, Protein 4 g, Carbohydrates 38 g, Fat 8 g,
Cholesterol 48 mg, Sodium 302 mg

Approximate nutritional analysis per serving Frosting:
Calories 100, Protein < 1 g, Carbohydrates 17 g, Fat 4 g,
Cholesterol < 1 mg, Sodium 53 mg

LEMON POPPYSEED CAKE

1 cup (240 ml) butter or margarine, softened
2 cups (480 ml) sugar
4 eggs
3 cups (720 ml) all-purpose flour
¼ tsp (1 ml) baking soda
1 cup (240 ml) sour cream
2 tbs (30 ml) Poppyseed
2 tsp (10 ml) pure Lemon Extract
1 tsp (5 ml) pure Vanilla Extract
1 tsp (5 ml) grated lemon peel

LEMON GLAZE
1½ cups (355 ml) confectioner's sugar
2 tbs plus 1 tsp (35 ml) water
½ tsp (3 ml) pure Lemon Extract

Preheat oven to 325°F (165°C). In large bowl, cream butter; gradually beat in sugar. Add eggs, one at a time, beating after each addition. In another bowl, combine flour and baking soda; stir ½ mixture into butter mixture. Add sour cream, then remaining flour mixture. Stir in remaining ingredients.

Spoon into a greased 10-inch Bundt pan. Bake 60-65 minutes or until toothpick inserted in center comes out clean. Cool 15 minutes; turn pan out on wire rack and cool completely. Top with Lemon Glaze. Slice and serve with fresh fruit or berries. Serves 16.

LEMON GLAZE: Combine confectioner's sugar, water and pure Lemon Extract. Mix until smooth. Spoon over top of cake, allowing some to run down the sides.

Approximate nutritional analysis per serving:
Calories 375, Protein 59 g, Carbohydrates 43 g, Fat 17 g, Cholesterol 90 mg, Sodium 39 mg

CHOCOLATE FROSTING

3 - 1 oz squares (90 g) unsweetened chocolate
4 ½ cups (1 L) sifted IMPERIAL 10X Powdered Sugar
⅛ tsp (.5 ml) salt
¼ cup (60 ml) hot water
½ cup (120 ml) melted butter or margarine
1 tsp (5 ml) vanilla

In double boiler, melt chocolate over hot water; reserve. Combine remaining ingredients. Add some of the melted chocolate and beat in well. Continue to beat in additional chocolate and IMPERIAL 10X Powdered Sugar until desired chocolate color, flavor and spreading consistency are obtained. Spread between layers and over cake. Fills and frosts three, 9 - inch layers. Serves 16.

Approximate nutritional analysis per serving:
Calories 149, Protein 0 g, Carbohydrates 22 g, Fat 8 g, Cholesterol 16 mg, Sodium 76 mg

7-MINUTE BROWN SUGAR FROSTING

1½ cups (355 ml) IMPERIAL Brown Sugar
⅓ cup (80 ml) cold water
2 egg whites, unbeaten
1 tsp (5 ml) vanilla

Combine IMPERIAL Brown Sugar, water, egg whites in top of double boiler. Place over boiling water (water should not touch upper part of double boiler). Beat with rotary beater or electric mixer 7 minutes. Remove top of double boiler from boiling water. Add vanilla. Continue beating until mixture stands up in stiff peaks when beater is lifted. Spread on cake and sprinkle with toasted coconut, if desired. Makes generous frosting for 2-layer, 8-inch or 9-inch cake. Serves 12.

Approximate nutritional analysis per serving:
Calories 105, Protein 1 g, Carbohydrates 27 g, Fat 0 g, Cholesterol 0 mg, Sodium 18 mg

FLUFFY ORANGE FROSTING

2 egg whites
1½ cups (355 ml) IMPERIAL Granulated Sugar
¼ tsp (1 ml) cream of tartar
⅓ cup (80 ml) orange juice
⅛ tsp (.5 ml) salt
1 tbs (15 ml) grated orange rind
1 tsp (5 ml) rum flavoring

Combine egg whites, IMPERIAL Granulated Sugar, cream of tartar, orange juice, salt in top of double boiler. Cook over gently boiling water, beating constantly with rotary or electric beater until the mixture forms peaks, about 7 minutes. Remove top of double boiler from heat; add orange rind and rum flavoring. Beat until frosting is of spreading consistency. Tint yellow or orange with food coloring, if you wish. Frosts two 9 -inch layers. Serves 12.

Approximate nutritional analysis per serving:
Calories 103, Protein 1 g, Carbohydrates 26 g, Fat 0 g, Cholesterol 0 mg, Sodium 32 mg

MOCHA FROSTING

5 tbs (75 ml) cocoa
5 tbs (75 ml) strong coffee
5 tbs (75 ml) butter or margarine, melted
3 cups (720 ml) IMPERIAL 10X Powdered Sugar
1 tsp (5 ml) vanilla
1 cup (240 ml) coarsely chopped nuts

Combine cocoa and coffee. Cool slightly and add to melted butter or margarine. Gradually add IMPERIAL 10X Powdered Sugar, beating well. Add vanilla and nuts. Frosting may be thinned with cream or thickened with more powdered sugar for desired spreading consistency. Yields 1½ cups. Serves 12.

Approximate nutritional analysis per serving:
Calories 205, Protein 2 g, Carbohydrates 28 g, Fat 1 g,
Cholesterol 18 mg, Sodium 69 mg

READY FROSTING

2 cups (480 ml) IMPERIAL Granulated Sugar
⅔ cup (160 ml) water
6 egg whites
½ cup (120 ml) IMPERIAL 10X Powdered Sugar
2 tsp (10 ml) vanilla
⅔ cup (160 ml) IMPERIAL 10X Powdered Sugar

Put IMPERIAL Granulated Sugar and water over low heat, stirring until sugar dissolves; boil to 240°F (116°C), or until syrup spins a long thread. Meanwhile, mix egg whites and ½ cup IMPERIAL 10X Powdered Sugar; beat until it stands in peaks, as in meringue. Gradually pour boiled syrup over meringue, continuing to beat until thick and creamy. When almost cold, add vanilla and ⅔ cup IMPERIAL 10X Powdered Sugar. Beat until stiff enough to spread. Keep unused portion in refrigerator tightly covered. Keeps for several days. Serves 16.

Approximate nutritional analysis per serving:
Calories 137, Protein 1 g, Carbohydrates 34 g, Fat 0 g,
Cholesterol 0 mg, Sodium 21 mg

GHIRARDELLI CHOCOLATE FROSTING

1 - 4 oz bar (120 g) GHIRARDELLI
**   Semi-Sweet Chocolate**
4 tbs (60 ml) butter
3 cups (720 ml) powdered sugar
⅓ cup (80 ml) hot milk
1 tsp (5 ml) vanilla
⅛ tsp (.5 ml) salt

In heavy saucepan on low heat, melt broken chocolate with butter, stirring constantly. Beat sugar with milk, vanilla and salt until smooth. Add melted chocolate and beat until thick enough to spread on cake.

HOW TO MELT CHOCOLATE: Melt chocolate carefully. Overheating or the addition of moisture may cause chocolate to thicken.

Double Boiler Method: Break chocolate into small pieces and place in top pan of double boiler over hot, but not boiling, water. You may also use a glass or metal mixing bowl on top of saucepan ½ full with water. Allow chocolate to melt, stirring occasionally.

Direct Heat Method: This method may be used if chocolate is to be added to a batter. Do not use for dipping or molding. Use very low, even heat. Stir constantly to avoid scorching. Remove from heat when small lumps remain and stir to complete melting.

Microwave Method: Using microwave safe container, place chocolate in microwave oven at medium power (50%) for 1-1½ minutes. Remove and stir. If not melted, return to microwave and repeat heating step, stirring every 30 seconds, as scorching can occur. When small lumps remain, remove and continue to stir to complete melting.

DATE-PECAN FROSTING

½ cup (120 ml) butter or margarine
1 - 8 oz pkg (240 g) pitted dates, coarsely chopped
¾ cup (160 ml) chopped pecans
1½ cups (355 ml) IMPERIAL Brown Sugar
1 - 5 oz can (150 ml) evaporated milk
½ tsp (3 ml) vanilla
3-3½ cups (720-940 ml) sifted IMPERIAL 10X
**   Powdered Sugar**

Over low heat in heavy saucepan, melt butter or margarine. Add chopped dates and nuts; cook 1 minute. Add IMPERIAL Brown Sugar and cook 2 minutes, stirring constantly. Add evaporated milk and bring to boil. Remove from heat; add vanilla. Gradually add IMPERIAL 10X Powdered Sugar, beating constantly, until of spreading consistency. If frosting is too thick, beat in a few drops of water, a drop at a time. Serves 12

Approximate nutritional analysis per serving:
Calories 392, Protein 2 g, Carbohydrates 70 g, Fat 14 g,
Cholesterol 3 mg, Sodium 124 mg

PERFECT PIE CRUST

1 cup (240 ml) all-purpose flour
½ tsp (3 ml) salt
⅓ cup (80 ml) shortening
3 tbs (45 ml) water

Mix flour and salt; add shortening and cut into flour with fork or pastry blender. Add water and mix gently with fork in stirring motion. Gather pastry into ball and place in pie tin. With tips of fingers, spread pastry along bottom and sides of pie tin, shaping a high, fluted edge. Yields 1 - 9-inch pie shell, serves 8.

Approximate nutritional analysis per serving:
Calories 132, Protein 2 g, Carbohydrates 12 g, Fat 9 g,
Cholesterol 0 mg, Sodium 134 mg

CHOCOLATE SILK PIE

1 envelope unflavored gelatin
¼ cup (60 ml) cold water
1 cup (240 ml) DANNON Plain Nonfat or
**   Lowfat Yogurt**
1 cup (240 ml) skim milk
2 tsp (10 ml) vanilla
1 pkg instant chocolate pudding and pie filling mix
⅓ cup (80 ml) sugar
1 - 6 oz pkg (180 g) graham cracker crumb crust
reduced-calorie whipped topping

In a small saucepan sprinkle gelatin over water; let stand 3 minutes to soften. Stir over low heat until gelatin is completely dissolved. In food processor or blender combine gelatin mixture and remaining ingredients except crust and topping. Process until well blended. Pour into crust. Cover; chill several hours. Top with whipped topping. Serves 8.

Approximate nutritional analysis per serving:
Calories 318, Protein 7 g, Carbohydrates 46 g, Fat 13 g,
Cholesterol 7 mg, Sodium 330 mg

REDUCED-FAT BROWN SUGAR-PUMPKIN PIE

⅓ cup (80 ml) FLEISCHMANN'S Margarine
1¼ cups (295 ml) all-purpose flour
4-5 tbs (60-75 ml) EGG BEATERS
**   Real Egg Product**
1 - 16 oz can (480 g) solid pack pumpkin
½ cup (120 ml) skim milk
½ cup (120 ml) firmly packed dark brown sugar
½ tsp (3 ml) ground allspice
½ tsp (3 ml) ground cinnamon
½ tsp (3 ml) ground ginger

In medium bowl, cut margarine into flour mixture until mixture is crumbly; stir enough water until mixture forms a ball. Set aside ¼ of the dough; roll remaining dough into an 11-inch circle, about ⅛-inch thick. Place in 9-inch pie plate; trim edge evenly with pie plate. Roll out reserved dough and cut into 1-inch leaves; make vein markings in each leaf with back of knife. Attach leaves to edge of crust using 1 tbs egg product. Chill crust until ready to fill.

In medium bowl, blend remaining egg product, pumpkin, skim milk, brown sugar and spices. Pour into prepared crust. Bake at 375°F (190°C) for 45-50 minutes or until set. Cool completely on wire rack. Serves 8.

Approximate nutritional analysis per serving:
Calories 223, Protein 6 g, Carbohydrates 39 g, Fat 8 g,
Cholesterol 0 mg, Sodium 108 mg

APPLE CINNAMON TART

1½ cups (355 ml) quick-cooking oats
1 tbs (15 ml) plus ½ tsp (3 ml) ground
**   cinnamon, divided**
¾ cup (180 ml) frozen apple juice concentrate,
**   thawed and divided**
2 large apples, peeled, if desired and thinly sliced
1 tsp (5 ml) lemon juice
⅓ cup (80 ml) cold water
1 envelope unflavored gelatin
2 cups (480 ml) DANNON Plain Nonfat or
**   Lowfat Yogurt**
¼ cup (60 ml) honey
½ tsp (3 ml) almond extract
fresh mint leaves, optional

Preheat oven to 350°F (180°C). In a small bowl combine oats and 1 tbs cinnamon. Toss with ¼ cup apple juice concentrate. Press onto bottom and side of 9-inch pie plate. Bake 5 minutes or until set. Cool on wire rack.

In medium bowl toss apple slices with lemon juice; arrange on cooled crust in pan and set aside. In a small saucepan combine cold water and remaining ½ cup apple juice concentrate. Sprinkle gelatin over water mixture; let stand 3 minutes to soften. Cook and stir over medium heat until gelatin is completely dissolved; remove from heat. Add yogurt, honey, remaining ½ tsp cinnamon and almond extract; blend well. Pour over apples in crust. Chill several hours or overnight. If desired, garnish with mint leaves. Serves 10.

Approximate nutritional analysis per serving:
Calories 125, Protein 5 g, Carbohydrates 24 g, Fat 2 g,
Cholesterol 3 mg, Sodium 35 mg

Grape-Filled Cookies

GRAPE-FILLED COOKIES

2 cups (480 ml) coarsely chopped seedless
    CALIFORNIA grapes
¼ cup (60 ml) packed brown sugar
½ tsp (3 ml) ground cinnamon
1 tsp (3 ml) lemon juice

SUGAR COOKIE DOUGH
⅓ cup (60 ml) butter or margarine
2 tbs (30 ml) sugar
1 egg
½ tsp (3 ml) vanilla
1 cup (240 ml) flour
¾ tsp (4 ml) baking powder
dash salt

Combine grapes, sugar and cinnamon in saucepan.
Bring to boil; cook and stir over medium heat about 35 minutes
or until thickened. Stir in lemon juice and cool. Roll Sugar
Cookie Dough to ⅛-inch thickness. Cut into 24 - 2½-inch
circles. Place 12 circles on greased cookie sheet. Place a
heaping teaspoonful of grape mixture on each circle leaving an
⅛-inch border around edges. Place remaining circles on filling;
press together with fork. cut 3-5 slits through top circles of
dough. Bake at 400°F (205 °C) 6-8 minutes or until lightly
browned. Cool on wire rack. Yields 12.

SUGAR COOKIE DOUGH: Cream butter or margarine
and sugar until smooth. Beat in egg and vanilla. Combine
flour, baking powder and dash salt; stir in butter mixture.
Wrap and refrigerate at least 1 hour.

Approximate nutritional analysis per cookie:
Calories 124, Protein 2 g, Carbohydrates 18 g, Fat 6 g,
Cholesterol 18 mg, Sodium 112 mg

YOGURT DROP COOKIES

1¼ cups (295 ml) all-purpose flour
½ tsp (3 ml) baking soda
¼ cup (60 ml) shortening
¼ cup (60 ml) margarine or butter
¾ cup (160 ml) sugar
1 egg
½ cup (120 ml) DANNON Vanilla Lowfat Yogurt
1 tsp (5 ml) vanilla

Preheat oven to 350°F (180°C). Grease cookie sheets.
In a medium bowl combine flour, baking soda and orange peel;
set aside. In a large bowl beat shortening and margarine with
electric mixer on medium speed for 30 seconds. Add sugar;
beat on medium speed until fluffy. Beat in egg, yogurt and
vanilla. Stir in flour mixture. Drop teaspoonfuls of dough,
2 inches apart, onto prepared cookie sheets. Bake 8 minutes
or until golden brown. Remove to wire racks to cool.
Yields 36 cookies.

Approximate nutritional analysis per cookie:
Calories 58, Protein < 1 g, Carbohydrates 7 g, Fat 3 g,
Cholesterol 10 mg, Sodium 16 mg

RAISIN NEWTONS

½ cup (120 ml) butter or margarine
½ cup (120 ml) packed brown sugar
½ cup (120 ml) honey
1 egg
2 cups (480 ml) whole wheat flour
1 cup (240 ml) all-purpose flour
1 tsp (5 ml) baking powder
½ tsp (3 ml) baking soda
½ tsp (3 ml) salt

RAISIN FILLING
1 - 15 oz box (450 g) raisins, chopped
1¼ cups (295 ml) orange juice
¼ cup (60 ml) sugar

In large mixing bowl, cream butter and sugar. Beat in honey
and egg. Combine dry ingredients; stir into creamed mixture,
mixing well. Divide dough into halves; wrap each and refrigerate at least 2 hours until firm. Meanwhile, prepare Raisin
Filling.
    Roll one piece of chilled dough to 14x6-inch rectangle.
Spoon half of the filling lengthwise down center in a 2-inch
wide strip to within ½ inch of ends. Fold long sides of dough
over filling, overlapping slightly; press to seal. Place on greased
baking sheet, seam side down (dough may crack a little) .
Repeat with remaining dough and filling. Bake in 400°F
(205°C) oven 12-15 minutes, until golden. Let stand 10
minutes. Remove to cooling rack to cool completely before
cutting into bars. Yields 24.

RAISIN FILLING: In a saucepan combine raisins, orange
juice and sugar. Bring to boil; simmer 10 minutes, stirring
frequently, until liquid evaporates. Cool. Yields 2¼ cups.

OATMEAL COOKIES

½ cup (120 ml) butter or margarine
½ cup (120 ml) IMPERIAL Brown Sugar,
    firmly packed
½ cup (120 ml) IMPERIAL Granulated Sugar
1 egg, beaten
1 tsp (5 ml) vanilla
¾ cup (180 ml) all-purpose flour
½ tsp (3 ml) salt
½ tsp (3 ml) baking soda
1½ cups (355 ml) uncooked quick-cooking oatmeal
¾ cup (180 ml) pecans

Cream butter or margarine with IMPERIAL Brown Sugar and
IMPERIAL Granulated Sugar until light and fluffy. Beat in egg
and vanilla. Combine dry ingredients, oatmeal, pecans and add
to butter-sugar mixture. Form dough into 2 rolls, wrap in foil
and chill or freeze. Preheat oven to 375°F (190°C). Slice
cookies about ¼-inch thick and bake 2 inches apart on greased
cookie sheets about 10 minutes, or until golden brown. Cool
cookies about 2 minutes before transferring to cooling racks.
Yields 36.

Approximate nutritional analysis per cookie:
Calories 86, Protein 1 g, Carbohydrates 10 g, Fat 5 g,
Cholesterol 6 mg, Sodium 78 mg

Sensibly Delicious Oatmeal-Chocolate Chip Cookies

SENSIBLY DELICIOUS OATMEAL-CHOCOLATE CHIP COOKIES

1 ¾ cups (415 ml) cups all-purpose flour
1 tsp (5 ml) baking soda
½ tsp (3 ml) ground cinnamon
½ tsp (3 ml) salt
1 ¼ cups (295 ml) packed dark brown sugar
½ cup (120 ml) granulated sugar
½ cup (120 ml) margarine
½ cup (120 ml) unsweetened applesauce
2 egg whites
1 tbs (15 ml) vanilla extract
2 ½ cups (590 ml) quick or old-fashioned oats,
   uncooked
1 - 12 oz pkg (360 g) NESTLÉ TOLL HOUSE
   Semi-Sweet Chocolate Morsels
½ cup (120 ml) chopped nuts

In small bowl, combine flour, baking soda, cinnamon and salt. In large mixer bowl, beat brown sugar, granulated sugar, margarine and applesauce until sauce. Beat in egg whites and vanilla. Gradually beat in flour mixture. Stir in oats, morsels and nuts. Drop by rounded tbs onto greased baking sheets. Bake in preheated 375°F (190°C) oven for 9-10 minutes for a chewy cookie, or 12-13 minutes for a crisp cookie. Cool for 2 minutes. Remove from baking sheets; cool on wire racks. Yields 48.

Approximate nutritional analysis per cookie:
Calories 120, Protein 1 g, Carbohydrates 19 g, Fat 5 g,
Cholesterol 0 mg, Sodium 65 mg

CLASSIC HOMEMADE CHOCOLATE TRUFFLES

¼ cup (60 ml) whipping cream
2 - 4 oz bars (240 g) GHIRARDELLI Bittersweet
   Chocolate, broken into small pieces
6 tbs (90 ml) unsalted butter, cut into small pieces
⅓ cup (80 ml) GHIRARDELLI Unsweetened Cocoa

In small saucepan bring cream to simmering. Remove from heat; stir in chocolate and butter. Bring ½ inch water to slow simmer in skillet. Stir mixture just until chocolate is completely melted. Remove from heat. Pour chocolate mixture into shallow bowl. Cool, cover and refrigerate until firm, at least 2 hours.

   Pour cocoa into pie plate. Line baking sheet with wax paper. Dip melon baller or small spoon into glass of warm water; shake off excess water and quickly scrape across surface of chilled truffle mixture to form a rough 1-inch ball. Deposit into cocoa. Repeat with remaining truffle mixture.

   Gently shake pie plate to coat truffles evenly; place truffles on wax paper lined container, separating layers with wax paper. Cover tightly and refrigerate up to 2 weeks, or freeze up to 3 months. Yields 30.

Approximate nutritional analysis per serving:
Calories 67, Protein < 1 g, Carbohydrates 5 g, Fat 6 g,
Cholesterol 9 mg, Sodium 8 mg

Classic Homemade Chocolate Truffles

SENSIBLY DELICIOUS CHOCOLATE CHIP COOKIE

3 cups (720 ml) all-purpose flour
1 ½ tsp (8 ml) baking soda
1 tsp (5 ml) salt
1 ¼ cups (295 ml) packed dark brown sugar
½ cup (120 ml) granulated sugar
½ cup (120 ml) margarine, softened
1 tsp (5 ml) vanilla extract
2 egg whites
⅓ cup (80 ml) water
1 - 12 oz pkg (360 g) NESTLÉ TOLL HOUSE
   Semi-Sweet Chocolate Morsels
⅓ cup (80 ml) chopped nuts

In medium bowl, combine flour, baking soda and salt. In large mixer bowl, cream brown sugar, granulated sugar, margarine and vanilla. Beat in egg whites. Gradually beat in dry ingredients alternately with water. Stir in morsels and nuts. Drop by rounded tbs onto lightly greased baking sheets. Bake in preheated 350°F (180°C) oven for 10-12 minutes until centers are just set. Let stand 2 minutes. Remove to wire racks to cool completely. Yields 60.

Approximate nutritional analysis per cookie:
Calories 94, Protein 1 g, Carbohydrates 14 g, Fat 4 g,
Cholesterol 0 mg, Sodium 80 mg

SENSIBLY DELICIOUS CHOCOLATE CRINKLE-TOP COOKIES

1½ cups (355 ml) all-purpose flour
1½ tsp (8 ml) baking powder
¼ tsp (1 ml) salt
1 - 12 oz pkg (360 g) NESTLÉ TOLL HOUSE
 Semi-Sweet Chocolate Morsels, divided
1 cup (240 ml) granulated sugar
2 tbs (30 ml) margarine, softened
1½ tsp (8 ml) vanilla extract
2 egg whites
¼ cup (60 ml) water
½ cup (120 ml) powdered sugar

In small bowl, combine flour, baking powder and salt. In small, heavy saucepan over low heat, melt 1 cup morsels; stir until smooth. In large mixer bowl, beat granulated sugar, margarine and vanilla. Beat in melted chocolate; beat in egg whites. Gradually beat in dry ingredients alternately with water. Stir in remaining morsels. Cover; chill until firm. Shape dough into 1½-inch balls; roll in powdered sugar to coat generously. Place on greased baking sheets. Bake in preheated 350°F (180°C) oven for 10-15 minutes or until sides are set but centers are slightly soft. Cool for 2 minutes. Remove to wire racks to cool completely. Yields 36.

Approximate nutritional analysis per serving:
Calories 100, Protein 1 g, Carbohydrates 16 g, Fat 4 g,
Cholesterol 0 mg, Sodium 45 mg

CHOCOLATE ALMOND BISCOTTI

3 cups (720 ml) all purpose flour
½ cup (120 ml) cocoa
2 tsp (5 ml) baking powder
½ tsp (3 ml) salt
⅔ cup (160 ml) FLEISCHMANN'S Margarine,
 softened
1 cup (240 ml) sugar
¾ cup (180 ml) EGG BEATERS Real Egg Product
1 tsp (5 ml) almond extract
½ cup (120 ml) whole blanched almonds,
 toasted and coarsely chopped
confectioners' sugar glaze

In medium bowl, mix flour, cocoa, baking powder and salt. In large bowl, with electric mixer, beat margarine and sugar for 2 minutes until creamy. Add egg product and almond extract; beat well. Add dry ingredients, beating just until blended; stir in almonds.

On lightly greased baking sheet, form dough into 2 - 12x2½-inch logs. Bake at 350°F (180°C) for 25-30 minutes or until a toothpick inserted in center comes out clean. Let cool on wire rack 15 minutes.

Using serrated knife, slice logs diagonally into 12 - 1-inch thick slices; place cut-side up on baking sheet. Bake at 350°F (180°C) for 12-15 minutes on each side until cookies are crisp and edges are browned. Cool completely on wire rack. Drizzle with glaze if desired. Yields 24.

Approximate nutritional analysis per serving:
Calories 160, Protein 3 g, Carbohydrates 21 g, Fat 7 g,
Cholesterol 0 mg, Sodium 125 mg

OATMEAL-FRUIT BARS

14 oz (420 g) pitted prunes
⅔ cup (160 ml) orange juice
1⅓ cups (320 ml) flour
2 cups (480 ml) rolled oats
¼ tsp (1 ml) salt
1 egg, beaten
3 tbs (45 ml)

In container of electric blender or food processor combine prunes and orange juice. Pulse on and off until pureed; set aside. Preheat oven to 350°F (180°C). In mixer bowl, mix sugar, flour, oats and salt. Add ¼ cup reserved prune mixture, the egg and water. Mix to blend thoroughly. Coat a 9x13-inch baking pan with oil or vegetable cooking spray. Spread half the oat mixture in pan; with the back of a spoon press down into an even layer. Spread the remaining prune mixture evenly over oat layer. Top evenly with remaining oat mixture. Sprinkle lightly with additional oats. Press down firmly. Bake 30-40 minutes until top is golden brown. Cool. Cut into 24 bars.

Approximate nutritional analysis per serving:
Calories 137, Protein 2 g, Carbohydrates 32 g, Fat < 1 g,
Cholesterol 9 mg, Sodium 26 mg

BACARDI RUM BALLS

¼ cup (60 ml) BACARDI Dark rum
1½ cups (360 ml) vanilla wafer crumbs
¼ cup (60 ml) honey
2 cups (480 ml) ground walnuts
confectioners sugar

In medium bowl, combine all ingredients except sugar. Shape into - inch balls. Roll in sugar. Store in tightly covered container. Makes 2½ dozen.

Approximate nutritional analysis per rum ball:
Calories 73, Protein 1 g, Carbohydrates 5 g, Fat 5 g,
Cholesterol 1 mg, Sodium 6 mg

Opposite: Oatmeal-Fruit Bars

CHOCO-LIGHT STRAWBERRY SHORTBREAD BARS

¼ cup (60 ml) light corn oil spread, softened
½ cup (120 ml) sugar
1 egg white
1¼ cups (295 ml) all-purpose flour
¼ cup (60 ml) HERSHEY'S Cocoa
¾ tsp (4 ml) cream of tartar
½ tsp (3 ml) baking soda
dash salt
½ cup (120 ml) strawberry all-fruit spread

VANILLA CHIP DRIZZLE
⅓ cup (80 ml) HERSHEY'S Vanilla Milk Chips
½ tsp (3 ml) shortening

Heat oven to 375°F (190°C). Lightly spray 13x9x2-inch baking pan with vegetable cooking spray. In medium bowl, beat corn oil spread and sugar until well blended. Add egg white; beat until well blended. Stir together flour, cocoa, cream of tartar, baking soda and salt; beat into corn oil spread mixture. Gently press onto bottom of prepared pan. Bake 10-12 minutes or just until set. Cool completely in pan on wire rack. Spread fruit spread evenly over crust. Cut into bars, or other shapes with cookie cutters. Using tines of fork, drizzle VANILLA CHIP DRIZZLE over top; let stand until firm. Yields 26.

VANILLA CHIP DRIZZLE: In small microwave-safe bowl, place vanilla chips and shortening. Microwave at HIGH 30 seconds; stir vigorously. If necessary, microwave at HIGH additional 15 seconds until chips are melted when stirred. Use immediately.

Approximate nutritional analysis per serving:
Calories 50, Protein 1 g, Carbohydrates 10 g, Fat 1 g,
Cholesterol 0 mg, Sodium 45 mg

LUNCHBOX BROWNIES

¼ cup (60 ml) margarine or butter
¾ cup (180 ml) shortening*
¾ cup (180 ml) cocoa*
2 cups (480 ml) IMPERIAL Granulated Sugar
4 eggs, beaten
1 tsp (5 ml) vanilla
1½ cups (355 ml) all-purpose flour
1 tsp (5 ml) baking powder
1 tsp (5 ml) salt
1 cup (240 ml) chopped nuts

FROSTING
¼ cup (60 ml) margarine or butter**
5 tbs (75 ml) cocoa**
¼ cup (60 ml) milk
2 cups (480 ml) IMPERIAL 10X Powdered Sugar
1 tsp (5 ml) vanilla

* 4 squares unsweetened chocolate, melted can be substituted for the cocoa and margarine.
** 1½ squares unsweetened chocolate, melted, can be substituted for the cocoa and 1½ tbs margarine.

Melt margarine or butter and shortening in large saucepan over low heat; stir in cocoa. Remove from heat and add IMPERIAL Granulated Sugar, eggs, vanilla, mixing thoroughly. Combine flour, baking powder, salt; stir into chocolate mixture. Add nuts and mix well. Spread in well-greased 13x9x2-inch pan. Bake in preheated oven at 350°F (180°C) for 30-35 minutes. Spread with frosting while brownies are still warm. Cool; cut into 2-inch squares. Yields 24.

FROSTING: Melt margarine in small saucepan over low heat. Stir in cocoa, milk, IMPERIAL Powdered Sugar; mix well. Remove from heat and stir in vanilla. Spread over warm brownies.

Approximate nutritional analysis per serving:
Calories 278, Protein 3 g, Carbohydrates 36 g, Fat 15 g,
Cholesterol 36 mg, Sodium 192 mg

SENSIBLY DELICIOUS DOUBLE CHOCOLATE CHIP BROWNIES

1 - 12 oz pkg (360 g) NESTLÉ TOLL HOUSE
    Semi-Sweet Chocolate Morsels, divided
1 cup (240 ml) granulated sugar
½ cup (120 ml) unsweetened applesauce
2 tbs (30 ml) margarine
3 egg whites
1¼ cups (295 ml) all-purpose flour
¼ tsp (1 ml) baking soda
¼ tsp (1 ml) salt
1 tsp (5 ml) vanilla extract
⅓ cup (80 ml) chopped nuts

In large, heavy saucepan over low heat, melt 1 cup morsels, sugar, applesauce and margarine, stirring until smooth. Remove from heat. Add egg whites; stir well. Stir in flour, baking soda, salt and vanilla. Stir in remaining morels and nuts. Spread into greased 13x9-inch baking pan. Bake in preheated 350°F (180°C) oven for 16-20 minutes or just until set. Cool completely. Cut into 2-inch squares. Yields 24.

Approximate nutritional analysis per serving with nuts:
Calories 159, Protein 2 g, Carbohydrates 22 g, Fat 7 g,
Cholesterol 0 mg, Sodium 50 mg

Approximate nutritional analysis per serving w/o nuts:
Calories 146, Protein 1 g, Carbohydrates 22 g, Fat 6 g,
Cholesterol 0 mg, Sodium 50 mg

Opposite: Lunchbox Brownies

SENSIBLY DELICIOUS BLONDE BROWNIES

2 ¼ cups (540 ml) all-purpose flour
2 ½ tsp (13 ml) baking powder
½ tsp (3 ml) salt
1 ¾ cups (415 ml) packed brown sugar
6 tbs (90 ml) margarine, softened
2 egg whites
1 ½ tsp (8 ml) vanilla extract
⅓ cup (80 ml) water
1 - 12 oz pkg (360 g) NESTLÉ TOLL HOUSE
    Semi-Sweet Chocolate Morsels

In small bowl, combine flour, baking powder and salt. In large mixer bowl, beat sugar, margarine, egg whites and vanilla until smooth. Gradually beat dry ingredients alternately with water. Stir in morsels. Spread into greased 15x10-inch jelly-roll pan. Bake in preheated 350°F (180°C) oven for 20-25 minutes or until top is golden brown. Cool in pan. Cut into 2-inch squares. Yields 35.

Approximate nutritional analysis per serving:
Calories 140, Protein 1 g, Carbohydrates 22 g, Fat 5 g,
Cholesterol 0 mg, Sodium 95 mg

SLENDERIFIC BROWNIE SNACKING CAKES

½ cup (120 ml) HERSHEY'S European Style
    Cocoa or HERSHEY'S Cocoa
½ cup (120 ml) all-purpose flour
½ tsp (1 ml) baking powder
¼ cup (60 ml) canola vegetable oil
½ cup (120 ml) packed light brown sugar
½ cup (120 ml) granulated sugar
½ cup (120 ml) egg whites, beaten until foamy
2 tsp (10 ml) vanilla extract
powdered sugar, optional

Heat oven to 350°F (180°C). Grease 8-inch square pan. In small bowl, stir together cocoa, flour and baking powder. Set aside. In medium bowl, stir together vegetable oil, brown sugar and granulated sugar; stir in beaten egg whites and vanilla. Gradually stir in cocoa mixture until blended. Pour into prepared pan.

Bake 15-20 minutes or until brownie begins to pull away from side of pan. Cool completely in pan on wire rack. Just before serving, cut into bars or cut with cookie cutters; sprinkle with powdered sugar, if desired. Yields 12.

Approximate nutritional analysis per serving:
Calories 150, Protein 3 g, Carbohydrates 23 g, Fat 5 g,
Cholesterol 0 mg, Sodium 35 mg

Sensibly Delicious Blonde Brownies

INDEX